SEX
AND THE
CONSTITUTION

ALSO BY GEOFFREY R. STONE

Speaking Out!: Reflections of Law, Liberty and Justice

Top Secret: When Our Government Keeps Us in the Dark

War and Liberty: An American Dilemma

Perilous Times: Free Speech in Wartime

Eternally Vigilant: Free Speech in the Modern Era

LIVERIGHT PUBLISHING CORPORATION

A Division of W. W. Norton & Company

Independent Publishers Since 1923

New York • London

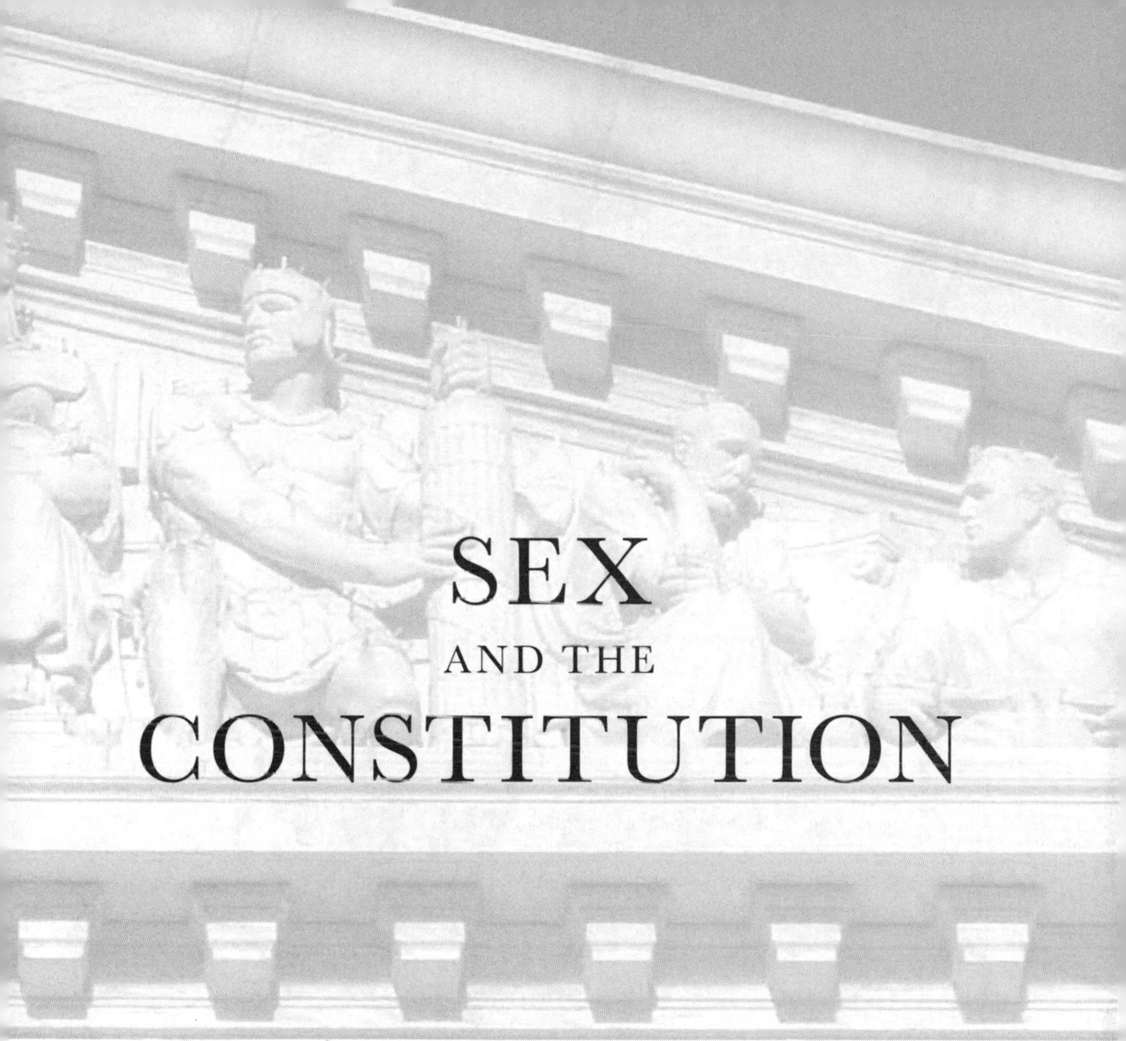

SEX
AND THE
CONSTITUTION

*Sex, Religion, and Law
from America's Origins to the
Twenty-First Century*

GEOFFREY R. STONE

"The Internet Is for Porn" (from *Avenue Q*), words and music by Bobby Lopez and Jeff Marx. Copyright © 2001 by Only for Now, Inc., and Fantasies Come True, Inc. All rights on behalf of Only for Now, Inc. Administered by Seven Summits Music.EX.

For information about permission to reproduce selections from this book, write to Permissions, Liveright Publishing Corporation, a division of W. W. Norton & Company, Inc., 500 Fifth Avenue, New York, NY 10110

For information about special discounts for bulk purchases, please contact W. W. Norton Special Sales at specialsales@wwnorton.com or 800-233-4830

Manufacturing by Quad Graphics, Fairfield, VA
Book design by Abbate Design
Production manager: Anna Oler

Library of Congress Cataloging-in-Publication Data

Names: Stone, Geoffrey R., author.
Title: Sex and the constitution : sex, religion, and law from America's origins to the twenty-first century / Geoffrey R. Stone.
Description: First edition. | New York : Liveright Publishing Corporation, 2017. | Includes bibliographical references and index.
Identifiers: LCCN 2016047264 | ISBN 9780871404695 (hardcover)
Subjects: LCSH: Sex and law—United States—History. | Sexual rights—United States—History. | Sex—Religious aspects—Christianity.
Classification: LCC KF9325 .S76 2017 | DDC 345.7302/53—dc23 LC
record available at https://lccn.loc.gov/2016047264

Liveright Publishing Corporation
500 Fifth Avenue, New York, N.Y. 10110
www.wwnorton.com

W. W. Norton & Company Ltd.
15 Carlisle Street, London W1D 3BS

1 2 3 4 5 6 7 8 9 0

For Julie, Mollie, Madeline,
Jackson, and Amaya

Sex, a great and mysterious motive force in human life, has indisputably been a subject of absorbing interest to mankind through the ages.

—JUSTICE WILLIAM J. BRENNAN JR.
(ROTH V. UNITED STATES 1957)

CONTENTS

LIST OF ILLUSTRATIONS

ACKNOWLEDGMENTS

I WORKED ON *Sex and the Constitution* for more than a decade. Of course, I also did many other things during those years, but *Sex and the Constitution* was always in my mind. It was the first major research project I ever committed myself to without having a clear sense of where it was headed. Particularly in the first half of the book, I started from a clean slate, learning every step of the way. It was a fascinating and often surprising adventure.

During the course of this journey, I had the great good fortune to work with truly extraordinary student research assistants from both the University of Chicago and New York University. They shared my curiosity, my sense of discovery, and my passion for the subject. I am deeply grateful to them for their research, their editing, their writing, their criticism, their diligence, and their good humor. I salute you all: Ariane Andrade, Rhiannon Batchelder, Christina Bell, Ross Fulton, Patrick Garlinger, Kayla Ginsburg, Alexander Glage, Annie Gowen, Devon Hanley, Erica Hauck, Sara Hershman, Jacob Kalow, Chen Kasher, Martha Kinsella, Ajay Kunderia, Jennifer Larson, Brynn Lycrly, Kristin MacDonald, Selina McLaren, Monica Mercado, Jessica Michaels, Rachel Morgan, Josephine Morse, Hillel Nadler, Nicole Naghi, Drew Navikas, Kimberlee Peltser, Elizabeth Porras, Casey Prusher, Kyle Reynolds, Alexander Stone-Tharp, John Sullivan, Charlotte Taylor, Lilit Voskanyan, and Jeremy Weinberg. Thank you!

I have also had the benefit of a steady stream of thoughtful comments, suggestions, counterarguments, and often brutally honest critiques from a host of colleagues, friends, family members, fellow travelers, and naysayers. You have sharpened my thinking, tightened my writing, and supported me in my moments of frustration, weariness, and doubt. For all of your many and varied contributions, I am deeply grateful to Lee Bartell, Andrea Bechert, Mary Behnke, Stephanos Bibas, Stephen Bowen, Corey Brettschneider, Mary Ann Case, Ron Collins, Jane Dailey, Alice Dreger, Elizabeth Emens, Kathleen Fabiny, Harriet Feinberg, Karen Frank, Barbara Fried, Patrick Garlinger, Mary Harvey, Christie Hefner, Gretchen Helfrich, Stephen Holmes, Dennis Hutchinson, Cynthia Jurisson, Karen Kaplowitz, Jennifer Kinsley, Shom Klaff, Brian Leiter, Saul Levmore,

Scott Mendeloff, Richard Michier, Geoffrey Miller, William Nelson, Martha Nussbaum, Gerry Ratner, David Richards, Martha Roth, Michael Schill, Rhonda Sonnenberg, Julie Stone, Mollie Stone, Nancy Stone, David Strauss, Patricia Swanson, Cass Sunstein, Rita Sussman, Patricia Swanson, Lisa Van Alstyne, and Laura Weinrib. I loved hearing your criticisms and even, sometimes, embracing them.

Throughout this process, I had the opportunity to test and refine my thoughts and arguments in a series of workshops, conferences, and lectures. This is an essential part of the academic process, and I was fortunate to be able to explore the implications of this subject in many venues, including the University of Chicago Law School's Work-in-Progress Workshop; the University of Chicago Law School's "Best Ideas" Lecture Series; New York University Law School's Work-in-Progress Workshop; New York University Law School's Legal History Workshop; Columbia University Law School's Philosophy and Law Workshop; the University of Chicago's Ryerson Lecture; the Chicago Humanities Festival; Fordham University Law School's Faculty Workshop; Stanford University Law School's Faculty Workshop; the Melville Nimmer Lecture at the UCLA School of Law; the Aspen Institute; and the Matthews Lecture at the University of Mississippi.

Several excerpts from this work, or at least articles inspired by it, have already been published, including *The History of Obscenity, the British Novel, and the First Amendment*, in *Subversion and Sympathy: Gender, Law, and the British Novel* 65 (Martha C. Nussbaum & Alison L. LaCroix eds., Oxford University Press 2013); *The Second Great Awakening: A Christian Nation?* 26 Ga. St. L. Rev. 1305 (2010); *Same-Sex Marriage and the Establishment Clause* 54 Villanova L. Rev. 617 (2009); *The Perils of Religious Passion* 57 UCLA L. Rev. Discourse 15 (2009); *The World of the Framers: A Christian Nation?* 56 UCLA L. Rev. 1 (2008); *Origins of Obscenity* 31 N.Y.U. J. L. & Soc. Ch. 711 (2007); and *Sex, Violence, and the First Amendment* 74 U. Chi. L. Rev. 1863 (2007).

I want to offer a special word of thanks to both the University of Chicago Law School and the New York University Law School for their generous research support; to Nancy Stone, who was there at the beginning, and whose encouragement was invaluable; to Annie Gowen, my all-time all-star research assistant; to Greg Nimmo, who was tireless in finding me all sorts of obscure sources through the University of Chicago Library system; to Lorrie Ragland and Dawn Hinko, who provided me with extraordinary secretarial and personal support; to Lynn Chu and Glen Hartley, my wonderful literary agents; to Carla Grande, Roberta Kaplan, and Edie Windsor who were very generous with their time; to Will Menaker, Steve Attardo, Marie Pantojan, Bill Rusin, Peter Miller, Cordelia Calvert, and a host of others at Liveright who helped make this publication possible; to Ruth Mandel, who once again was the perfect partner in our quest to find the perfect images; to Patricia Dunn, who was absolutely meticulous in her copyediting; to Bob Weil, the most brilliant editor in the nation; and most of all to Jane Dailey, who supported me, challenged me, advised me, and inspired me through a truly exhausting, yet exhilarating, process.

I am profoundly grateful to all of you. Without you, this book would never have seen the light of day.

PROLOGUE

WE ARE IN the midst of a constitutional revolution. It is a revolution that has tested the most fundamental values of the American people and has shaken constitutional law to its roots. It has bitterly divided citizens, politicians, and judges. It is a battle that has dominated politics, inflamed religious passions, and challenged Americans to rethink and reexamine their positions on issues they once thought settled. It is a story that has never before been told in its full sweep. And, best of all, it is about sex.

In the course of this struggle, American law has called into question the constitutionality of a broad range of government regulations of sexual behavior, including contraception, abortion, obscenity, and sodomy. As a consequence, the United States Supreme Court has found itself confronting fundamental questions about the nature of sexual freedom, the meaning of liberty, equality, and privacy, the legitimacy of government efforts to dictate sexual morality, and the appropriate role of religion in public life. *Sex and the Constitution* explores the remarkable process through which Americans, and especially the justices of our Supreme Court, have navigated these profoundly divisive and important questions.

Not surprisingly, our social mores and our laws governing sexual behavior are deeply bound up with religious beliefs and traditions. A central theme of *Sex and the Constitution* is that American attitudes about sex have been shaped over the centuries by religious beliefs—more particularly, by early Christian beliefs—about sex, sin, and shame. A nettlesome question in constitutional law is how courts should cope with that history in a nation committed to the separation of church and state.

It is a bit of a puzzle that constitutional law has come to play such a central role in shaping our debates over these questions. Nothing in our Constitution expressly guarantees a right to sexual freedom. Supreme Court justices from almost any prior era in American history would be stunned to learn of the role the Supreme Court and our Constitution have come to play in our contemporary disputes—some call them "Culture Wars"—over such issues as obscenity, contraception, abortion, sodomy, and same-sex marriage. The constitutional revolution we are now witnessing is the consequence of a long, complex, and fascinating history. It is a history shaped over the centuries by such diverse and antagonistic voices as Saint Augustine, Thomas Aquinas, Voltaire, Thomas Jefferson, Anthony Comstock, Margaret Sanger, Alfred Kinsey, Harry Blackmun, Jesse Helms, Phyllis Schlafly, and Anthony Kennedy, to name just a few. It is, dare I say, a *great* story.

Sex and the Constitution proceeds in six parts, each of which explores a pivotal era in the historical evolution of sexual mores and of American constitutional law.

PART I, "ANCESTORS," EXPLORES the history of sex, and especially its relation to religion, from the ancient world through the Enlightenment. These chapters lay the foundation for our journey. We can understand the present only if we know how and why we got here and only if we understand that different cultures approach these questions quite differently. It would be a mistake to assume that our own attitudes toward sex, sin, and the law are natural and inevitable.

"Ancestors" begins by exploring what the Greeks, the Romans, and the ancient Hebrews thought about sex. In the pre-Christian world, these societies regarded most forms of sex as natural and properly pleasurable facets of human life. None of these cultures regarded sex as inherently immoral, sinful, or shameful.

Under the powerful influence of Augustine of Hippo at the turn of the fifth century, however, early Christians forged a new understanding of sex and its relation to sin. Over time, the Church came to condemn as "mortal sins" masturbation, fornication, sodomy, and even intercourse in marriage for any purpose other than procreation. Although the Reformation brought with it new religious conceptions of sexuality, especially within marriage, it also led to a successful campaign by Protestant reformers to conscript the authority of the state to enforce their religious precepts about sex, even against those who did not share their faith. The Enlightenment then led to a deep skepticism about Christian doctrine, particularly in the realm of sex. With a new focus on reason rather than faith, a culture of freethinking took hold in some quarters, and by the middle of the eighteenth century London came to be known as a mecca of sexuality. It was against the background of this cultural and social milieu that the American nation was born.

· · ·

PART II, "FOUNDERS," CROSSES the Atlantic and examines the evolution of sexual attitudes in the New World from the crossing of the Mayflower to the framing of our Constitution. It explores the rigid sexual attitudes of the Puritans, who believed that governments were instituted to serve God's commands and to restrain man's sin. Over time, though, the temptations of life's pleasures and the bold new ideas of the Enlightenment gradually eclipsed the world of the Puritans, yielding a set of attitudes about sex in the colonies that was surprisingly tolerant of sexual freedom. This was, after all, a generation deeply committed to "the pursuit of happiness."

What, though, are we to make of contemporary claims that the United States was founded as "a Christian nation"? "Founders" explores this question. Many of the Framers were skeptical of traditional Christianity, and their fascination with deism and their commitment to creating a nation dedicated to the separation of church and state belie the assertion that they intended to establish a Christian nation. To the contrary, the United States was conceived, not in an age of faith, but in an age of reason.

"Founders" next turns to the Constitution itself and to what the Framers thought to be "the fundamental maxims of free government." Here, we dig deeper into the founding generation's understanding of the proper relation between government and religion and explore the critical issue of "unenumerated" rights. If the Constitution does not expressly guarantee a right of sexual freedom, can the Supreme Court legitimately interpret the Constitution to constrain the authority of government to forbid contraception, abortion, sodomy, and same-sex marriage? Almost two centuries later, the challenge of identifying such unenumerated constitutional rights will become a critical pivot point in the judicial battles over constitutional interpretation that have bitterly divided the justices of the Supreme Court.

PART III, "MORALISTS," EXPLORES the resurgence of Protestant religiosity in the United States between the beginning of the nineteenth century and the mid-twentieth century. During this time, various social and religious movements sought once again to enlist the law in a campaign to impose sectarian religious values on society, especially in the realm of sex. This part of the story begins with the explosion of religious zeal during the Second Great Awakening in the early nineteenth century when a powerful evangelical movement sought to capture the authority of the state to command observance of the Sabbath, outlaw blasphemy, and squelch sexual expression and behavior. It was in this era that laws against obscenity appeared for the first time in the United States.

Then, after the Civil War, Anthony Comstock burst upon the scene and initiated a nationwide campaign to root out the "evils" of sexual expression. Comstock's late nineteenth-century crusade left a powerful legacy. Pervasive censorship at every level of government ensured that books, theater, newspapers, magazines, and movies were purged of any hint of sexual content for most of the next century.

The moralists of this era did not limit themselves to issues of sexual expression. Concepts of sin and sexual shame also played a central role in their campaigns to outlaw contraception and abortion, which previously had been legal. As one mid-nineteenth century zealot declared, if women had access to contraception or abortion, what "would keep them chaste?" As a result of such attitudes, laws dealing with contraception and abortion became much more repressive over the course of the nineteenth century than ever before in history.

"Moralists" also explores the history of homosexuality in the United States from the founding through the mid-twentieth century. It was not until the late nineteenth century that persons drawn to same-sex sex came for the first time to be seen as having a distinctive psychological identity. In a society in which the dominant religion deemed homosexuality a heinous sin, the law branded homosexuals as criminals, and the medical profession diagnosed homosexuals as "strange freaks of nature," the vast majority of individuals who harbored same-sex desires did their best to hide their secret shame from family, friends, neighbors, and associates. Even the nation's most committed civil rights organizations in this era turned their backs on homosexuals.

T HE SECOND half of *Sex and the Constitution* turns to the process, beginning in the late 1950s, through which judges, and especially the justices of the Supreme Court, interpreted and applied the Constitution to constrain the ability of religious conservatives to censor sexually-oriented expression, ban contraception and abortion, and persecute homosexuals. It has been a long, sometimes halting, often bitterly divisive process, as the guardians of our Constitution have gradually felt their way forward in an effort to come to grips with complex issues of free speech, equality, religion, individual liberty, and unenumerated rights in the politically charged and often emotionally fraught realm of sexual freedom. The stakes have been high, both for the Court as an institution and for the nation.

PART IV, "JUDGES: SEXUAL EXPRESSION," traces the history of laws regulating sexual expression from the 1950s to the present. Beginning in the mid-1950s, the justices struggled with the vexing challenge of defining "obscenity," and with the question of whether obscenity, however defined, is "speech" within the meaning of the First Amendment. The battle over the regulation of sexually-explicit expression eventually became a central issue in the nation's "Culture Wars," as the newly emergent Christian Right damned such expression as a fundamental threat to the moral decency of the nation.

Despite the concerted efforts of religious leaders, judges, politicians, and presidents to stem the tide of sexually-explicit material, this was not to be. The social changes unleashed in the 1960s, combined with the advent of new communications technologies such as cable television and the Internet, overwhelmed the capacity of the law to constrain sexual expression. But although the Christian Right's campaign to prevent consenting adults from accessing sexual expression failed to win the day, its war on obscenity helped energize a powerful religious and political movement that would vigorously combat the legal recognition of reproductive rights, women's rights, and gay rights. The creation of this powerful movement was an important legacy of the failed crusade to stamp out obscenity.

PART V, "JUDGES: REPRODUCTIVE FREEDOM," addresses the Supreme Court's struggle to grapple with the issues of contraception and abortion. This process ultimately led the Court to recognize a fundamental right of individuals to decide for themselves "whether to bear or beget a child." After first addressing the issue of contraception, the justices then turned to the question of abortion. In *Roe v. Wade*, the Court plunged into the "right to choose"/"right to life" controversy in a way that later divided the nation, energized the Christian Right, reframed the contours of American politics, and profoundly influenced the Supreme Court appointment and confirmation process.

In the years since *Roe*, religious leaders from the Catholic Church and the evangelical community, including such figures as Jerry Falwell, Pat Robertson, and Phyllis Schlafly, have played a critical role in the political and judicial battles over the regulation of abortion. The continuing conflict has seen calls for constitutional amendments to overrule *Roe*, violence directed at abortion providers and clinics, legislative efforts to undermine and circumvent the decision, and partisan efforts to appoint judges and justices at all levels of the federal judiciary who are committed either to supporting or overruling *Roe*. To this day, the future of *Roe* remains uncertain.

P ART VI, "JUDGES: SEXUAL ORIENTATION," returns to the issue of homosexuality, but now in the realm of constitutional law. What, if any, are the constitutional rights of homosexuals? Are they "freaks of nature" and criminal degenerates, or are they a historically oppressed group deserving of constitutional protection? Part VI traces the history of gay rights movements, the fierce pushback from the Christian Right, the ravages of the AIDS epidemic, the gradual evolution of public opinion toward toleration of same-sex love, and the role of the Supreme Court as it has cautiously recognized the fundamental constitutional rights of liberty, dignity, and equality of gays and lesbians.

As an often furiously divided Supreme Court has wrestled with these issues, it has struggled to distinguish between religious conceptions of sin and morality, on the one hand, and constitutionally impermissible animus, on the other. The divide within the Court over these issues has been particularly fierce, as one group of justices tries to give meaning to constitutional concepts like equality and dignity, while the other accuses them of capitulating to political correctness and the "homosexual agenda." On issues ranging from sodomy prosecutions to discrimination against gays and lesbians to same-sex marriage, the Court has once again placed itself at the very center of constitutional controversy.

S EX AND *the Constitution* tells the vital story of our nation's ongoing struggle to reconcile centuries-old religious beliefs with evolving conceptions of individual liberty, personal privacy, and human equality. It illuminates the Supreme Court's quest to find sound answers in the often vague words of our eighteenth-century Constitution to complex and often highly emotional social, political, moral, and legal questions that have been with us from the beginning. And it traces the fundamental way in which our nation evolves with changing circumstances, values, mores, and understandings.

PART I

ANCESTORS

1

THE ANCIENT WORLD

The Triumph of Augustine

Greek Pæderasty

FOR MORE THAN TWO CENTURIES, Americans have fought divisive social, political, and constitutional battles over laws regulating sex, obscenity, contraception, abortion, homosexuality, and same-sex marriage. These conflicts have been divisive in no small part because of the central role religion has played in shaping our laws governing sex. As the Framers of our Constitution anticipated, the incorporation of religious beliefs into the secular law inevitably poses fundamental questions about individual freedom, the separation of church and state, and the meaning of our Constitution.

To understand the roots of these conflicts, it is helpful to have some sense of the ways in which different societies addressed these issues in the past and how our own attitudes toward sex came into being. How did social, cultural, religious, and legal views of sex evolve from the ancient world to the founding of the American republic?

Perhaps surprisingly, the pre-Christian world generally thought of sex as a natural and positive part of human experience. It did not see sex as predominantly bound up with questions of sin, shame, or religion. The emergence of Christianity, however, profoundly changed the then-prevailing understandings of sex. It was in the collapse of the Roman Empire that what later came to be seen as "traditional" American attitudes toward sex first began to take hold. This chapter traces those formative moments in Western culture.

"THE THINGS OF APHRODITE"

FROM THE SIXTH to the fourth century B.C., Greek culture attained its most impressive achievements in literature, philosophy, politics, science, and the arts. The Greeks of this era generally eschewed the legal enforcement of moral or religious notions of "right sexual conduct." Classical Greek morality and law focused not on sexual sin, but on whether an individual's conduct was harmful to others. To the ancient Greeks, *eros* was a primal force which permeated all facets of life.[1]

The Greek gods indulged freely in sexual pleasure. In Greek mythology, Zeus variously became a bull, a swan, and even rain with the goal of seducing mortals. Aphrodite was the goddess of love, beauty, and sexual rapture. Sex was *"ta aphrodísiæ"*—"the things of Aphrodite." It is said that during the festival of Aphrodite her priestesses had sexual intercourse with strangers as a form of worship.[2]

The Greeks approached the human form with no sense that nudity was inherently shameful. To the contrary, the phallus was a potent symbol of fertility, a central theme in Greek religion. A pillar topped by the helmet of Hermes adorned with an erect penis stood at nearly every Athenian's front door. Vases and terra-cottas depicted explicit scenes of vaginal and anal intercourse, masturbation, and fellatio.[3]

Moreover, the Greeks had no concept of "obscenity," a legal notion that would not come into existence in Western culture for another two thousand years. Greek comedy, for example, was often quite bawdy. Aristophanes, a fourth century B.C. playwright, portrayed sexuality in all its many forms. In *The Knights*, he depicted masturbation, fellatio, and male-male anal sex. One character speaks boldly of sucking "cocks in the Prytaneum," while another boasts of selling not only sausages, but occasionally also his "arse." Greek literature playfully described women masturbating, either by hand or with the assistance of a device adapted to the purpose. The Greeks called such devices *baubon* or *olisbos*.[4]

In Herondas's *The Two Friends, or Confidential Talk*, two young women converse excitedly about these *olisboi*. At the end of the conversation, the woman without one hurries off to acquire such a "treasure" for herself. In Aristophanes' *Lysistrata*, the women grieve the loss of the special leather *olisboi* that had been made to perfection by the women of Miletus. Greek vases explicitly depict the use of *olisboi* in every possible manner, position, and combination.[5]

Hetaera *Leaps into Basket Full of Dildos*

Greek men were generally free to pursue premarital and extramarital sexual pleasure, but this freedom did not extend to women—at least not to women of the upper class. A married woman's role was to bear her husband's heirs and to manage his household. A man's sexual pleasure was addressed primarily outside of marriage.*[6] As Xenophon, an early fourth century B.C. Greek historian, observed: "Surely you do not suppose that lust provokes men" to marry "when the streets are full of people who will satisfy the appetites, as are the brothels."[7]

Indeed, prostitution was both common and legal. High-class courtesans, or *hetaerae,* were well educated and highly cultivated.[8] More common prostitutes, male as well as female, were plentiful. In the fourth century B.C., the Greek poet Xenarchus marveled at the number of "very good-looking young things in the whore-houses" of Athens, who were openly "basking in the sun, their breasts uncovered, stripped for action."[9]

Greek men and women employed many means of birth control, including herbal contraceptives, postcoital douching, anal intercourse, and coitus interruptus. Abortion was also common. The fifth-century Hippocratic treatise *Diseases of Women* recommended a number of abortifacients, including herbs and vaginal suppositories. Plato commended such methods as important for ensuring population stability, and Aristotle advocated abortion, as long as it occurred prior to quickening.†[10]

A DISTINCTIVE feature of classical Greek sexual life was the practice of pæderasty. Adult men, both married and single, often had sexual relationships with adolescent boys.‡ The Greek ideal of beauty was embodied most perfectly in the male youth. Solon, the poet and lawgiver, wrote of loving "a lad in the flower of youth, bewitched by thighs and by sweet lips." The mighty gods of Olympus, from Zeus on down, had such relationships, as did Aeschylus, Sophocles, Alcibiades, and Pindar.[11]

---

* The Greeks did not think of women as nonsexual. To the contrary, women were often portrayed in Greek literature as immoderately fond of sex. See Maarit Kaimio, *Erotic Experience in the Conjugal Bed,* in *The Sleep of Reason* 105 (Martha C. Nussbaum & Juha Sihvola eds., Chicago 2002).

† "Quickening" occurs at the moment in pregnancy when a woman first feels fetal movement, usually at four-and-a-half months.

‡ These relationships did not involve children, but post-pubescent adolescents, usually between the ages of fifteen and nineteen. Sex with boys who had not yet reached puberty was punished, sometimes quite harshly.

Greek boys were not taught to see themselves as either heterosexual or homosexual, a distinction that did not exist for another two thousand years. Instead, Greek culture acknowledged that same-sex and opposite-sex sexual desires could naturally coexist in varying degrees in the same individual, just as we today might think of the different desires individuals might have to engage in some sexual acts more than others. To the Greeks, same-sex sex was simply a sexual act. It did not define a type of *person*.[12]

Greek pæderasty assumed relationships based on mutual affection. Plato observed that the adults in these relationships did "everything lovers do" for those "they cherish." They showered them with gifts, verses, attention, and love.[13] Among other things, this was a way for adult men to mentor and socialize their juniors, particularly among the aristocratic class. Xenophon attested that in such relationships the older man took "pains to develop the character of his pupil, his 'beloved,' and pass on everything he knew to the boy."[14]

Many Greeks went beyond mere acceptance of this practice and described it as a particularly admirable form of human relation. Greek poetry and literature associated such relationships with love, integrity, honor, and courage, and many Greeks believed that these relationships embodied the *only* form of eroticism that produced pure, enduring, and spiritual love. In part, this was due to the prevailing view that women were inferior beings who were inappropriate objects of the finer feelings. A man who wanted to love truly had to love another male.[15]

Pæderasty aside, the Greeks were generally ambivalent about other forms of same-sex sexual behavior. Same-sex conduct between adult males was generally frowned upon because it placed an adult man (rather than a youth) in a submissive sexual role. To most Greeks, *that* seemed unnatural. It was the act of being penetrated, rather than the fact of same-sex sex, that troubled the Greeks. Moreover, the Greeks had little tolerance for effeminacy, which they ridiculed as incompatible with a man's role as defender of the state.[16]

Female same-sex sex was less public than male same-sex behavior. But images of sex between women appear on Greek vases and terra-cottas and, according to Plutarch, such relations were especially common in Sparta. The poetry of Sappho, ancient Greece's most brilliant woman poet, has usually been understood as a celebration of lesbian love. It has been said that Greek literature owes to Sappho, who was born in 612 B.C. on the island of Lesbos, the "most memorable cries of love ever uttered by a human voice."[17]

In sum, the ancient Greeks generally regarded sexual pleasure as a natural and healthy part of life that enriched human experience. Although they valued moderation in all things, and understood that unrestrained *eros* could threaten social stability, they neither inherited nor developed a belief that either morality or divine authority commanded the suppression of sexual desire. For the ancient Greeks, the concept of sexual sin simply did not exist.[18]

THE ROMAN WAY

EARLY ROMAN SEXUAL LIFE was quite different from that of the Greeks. Indeed, the early Romans deplored much about the Greeks, whom they regarded as "cunning, effeminate, and degenerate."[19] The early Romans were coarse, hardworking farmers and ruthless warriors. Whereas the Greeks gloried in the human form, the early Romans were uncomfortable with nakedness. As the Roman philosopher and naturalist Pliny the Elder observed, even with respect to statuary, "the Greek habit is to conceal nothing," whereas "the Roman way" is to give all statues "a coat of armor."[20]

Nonetheless, as in Greece, the phallus played a central role in Roman religious life. It represented the divine creative force and was often worn as an amulet by women and as a charm by children. Goblets shaped like phalluses were common, and the god Priapus was portrayed with a giant phallus. Statues of Priapus were often placed in Roman courtyards and gardens.[21]

Prostitution also flourished in Rome. There were as many as thirty-five brothels in Pompeii, for example, for a population of roughly ten thousand, or approximately one brothel for every three hundred inhabitants. As in ancient Greece, high-class courtesans were common. Prostitution was taxed, and prostitutes were required to register with the state. Public bathhouses were common locations for prostitution, and women often appeared on stage to perform sexual acts. Male prostitution was common, and male prostitutes even had their own holiday.[22]

Neither Roman religion nor Roman law paid much attention to same-sex sex.* As in classical Greece, however, there was a strong prejudice

---

* There is even some evidence, though inconclusive, that both male-male and female-female marriages were recognized in Rome. See Craig A. Williams, *Roman Homosexuality* 245–52 (Oxford 1992).

Priapus

against submissive sexual behavior by adult males. The key distinction in Roman sexual culture was between those who penetrated and those who were penetrated, without regard to gender. An adult man who allowed himself to be penetrated endured *muliebria pati*, "a woman's experience," and was no longer considered a real man. The Latin word *mollis* ("soft") was used to ridicule such men. The *mollis* included not only men who allowed themselves to be penetrated, but also those who curled their hair or used depilatories, lavish oils, and perfumes. But while effeminacy opened a man up to scorn, the general understanding was that it was neither unnatural nor inappropriate for a "real" man to penetrate boys and men, as well as girls and women.[23]

. . .

THE END of the second Punic War in 202 B.C. marked a profound change in Roman culture. After almost a century of sustained warfare, Rome finally defeated Carthage. Suddenly, Rome enjoyed unprecedented wealth and power. Millions of slaves flowed into Rome, and the patrician class basked in its newfound opulence. The Roman historian Velleius Paterculus observed that with the fear of Carthage removed, "Rome gave herself up . . . to pleasure."[24]

With changing expectations and opportunities, sex outside of marriage became more common for women as well as men. The Roman historian Livy observed that the new era brought with it "the multiplication of pleasures." By the middle of the second century B.C., the traditional chastity of women had disappeared. The Roman poet Juvenal observed that abortion had become so common that "hardly ever do you find" well-bred women giving birth. This shift in Roman sexual mores was both condemned and celebrated. The historian Sallust complained that "men gave themselves to unnatural vice, and women publicly sold their honour," and the Latin elegiac poet Propertius described Rome as "a sink of lewdness." Others, however, reveled in the new era.[25]

Indeed, any suggestion that the law should interfere with free sexual (as opposed to political) expression would have been met with scorn. Roman poetry and drama in this era were filled with sexual references and eroticism, and Rome's most famous poets spoke quite candidly of sexual matters. They wrote of licit and illicit love and of sexual antics of all kinds. Catullus could be crude ("I will fuck you up the ass and make you go down on me"), and Ovid often wrote playfully about same-sex sex, impotence, ménages à trois, and adultery. His Art of Love has been described as a "sophisticated manual of hedonism" designed to teach "the art of enjoying . . . a woman's body as fully and delightfully as possible."[26]

Writers such as Ovid, Virgil, Horace, Catullus, Tibullus, and Petronius presented male-male and female-female sex in a manner that exemplified later Rome's casual attitude toward such conduct. But unlike ancient Greece, Rome did not idealize such behavior. It was simply another form of sexual pleasure, like oral or anal sex, for those who chose to indulge in it.[27]

Early Christian writers, including Augustine, attributed the fall of Rome in the fifth century A.D. to sexual depravity.[28] In fact, however, Rome's standards of sexuality had little, if anything, to do with its collapse—more than six centuries after the second Punic War. But Augustine's claim reveals the vast gap that existed between the civilizations of Greece and Rome, which regarded sex as a natural part of human life, and the early Christian perspective, which came to view sex as a sinful temptation that must be suppressed.

THE HEBRAIC TRADITION

THE HEBREW BIBLE contains no condemnation of sexual pleasure, "no paeans to celibacy," and no suggestion that the sin of Adam and Eve was sex, rather than disobedience of God. Like the ancient Greeks and Romans, the ancient Hebrews did not prohibit masturbation, premarital sex, oral or anal sex, prostitution, contraception, pornography, lesbianism, or abortion.[29]

As *Song of Songs* and *Proverbs* attest, the ancient Hebrews were not shy about sexual pleasure, particularly within marriage. Indeed, the Hebrew Bible specified the duty of husbands and wives to satisfy each other's sexual needs. The book of *Proverbs*, for example, instructs husbands to find rapture in their wives and to "let her breasts satisfy thee at all times; with her love be thou ravished always." The Hebrew Bible has no strictures against oral sex and it does not forbid sexual relations between unmarried persons.* Although prostitution was socially frowned upon in ancient Israel, the practice was never outlawed. Adultery, on the other hand, could result in the death penalty, but only if committed by a married woman. The prohibition of a wife's adultery addressed the husband's property rights and the need to protect a family's inheritance from illegitimate heirs.[30]

T HERE IS little evidence of the Hebraic attitude toward same-sex sex before the Jewish exile in the eighth century B.C. Thereafter, as the Israelites were dispersed throughout the ancient world, they increasingly sought ways to distinguish themselves from others in order to preserve their distinctive identity. This insistence on maintaining their separateness, and on rejecting the dominant Hellenist and Roman cultures, led post-exilic Jews to promulgate hundreds of rules and rituals in order to keep themselves apart. In addition to the custom of male circumcision, these commands

---

* The Hebrew Bible provides that if a man has intercourse with a virgin he must pay the woman's father fifty shekels and marry the woman. But nothing in the Hebrew Bible prohibits non-marital sex as such, and once a woman is not a virgin, the Hebrew Bible does not condemn non-marital intercourse.

dealt with such diverse matters as beard styles, dietary laws, menstruation, treatment of the dead, incense burning, tattoos, not eating leftovers, mourning, utensils for eating, and latrines.[31]

Included in this multitude of rules was the prescription in *Leviticus* regarding same-sex sex, which provides: "If a man also lie with mankind, as he lieth with a woman, both of them have committed an abomination; they shall surely be put to death."[32] This prohibition, of uncertain date, seems to have originated as part of the effort of the Hebrews to separate themselves from the Gentiles by expressly condemning the then-prevalent Greek practice of pæderasty. Although the passage calls for the death penalty, this shouldn't be taken too seriously. The Hebrew Bible also called for the death penalty for such offenses as witchcraft, prostitution by the daughter of a priest, failure to observe the Sabbath, and cursing one's parent, and there is no evidence that the ancient Hebrews ever seriously or systematically punished same-sex sex under Jewish law.[33]

THE BIBLICAL stories of Onan and Sodom have played central roles in the evolution of Western law and culture, and they therefore deserve a careful look. The story of Onan has been used to teach that both masturbation and contraception are sinful, and the story of Sodom has given us a name for "unnatural" sex. Most scholars agree that both stories have been distorted by later interpretations.

The story of Onan reveals the importance of both procreation and the preservation of patrimony under Hebrew law. Under the ancient Hebraic practice of "levirate" marriage, if a married man died without children, his brother was obligated to cohabit with his widow in order to produce a child. Onan was Judah's son, Er's brother, and Tamar's brother-in-law. After Er died, Judah instructed Onan to fulfill the *levir*'s responsibility. According to *Genesis*, Onan was angry that his and Tamar's descendants "would not be counted as his own; so whenever he had relations with his brother's widow, he wasted his seed on the ground, lest he should give seed to his brother." By taking this action, Onan violated the levirate custom, sentenced Tamar to die as a childless widow, and denied his deceased brother the right to have his name and inheritance preserved. Onan's action "was evil in the sight of the LORD; and He slew him."[34]

The essence of this story, and its core meaning for the ancient Hebrews, focused on Onan's refusal to comply with the demands of levirate marriage. The ancient commentaries understood the episode as teaching fundamental lessons about obedience to the law, complying with God's command to "be fruitful and multiply," and honoring one's family. Later Christian theologians, however, construed the story as a divine condemnation of coitus interruptus, contraception, and masturbation.* In fact, however, the ancient Hebrews, like the ancient Greeks and Romans, prohibited none of these practices.[35]

S ODOM IS first mentioned in *Genesis* in connection with Lot's choosing a place to live. The Hebrew Bible reports that "the men of Sodom were wicked and sinners before the LORD exceedingly." Several chapters later, the Lord tells Abraham that he plans to destroy the city, because the sins committed by its inhabitants were "very great." Abraham pleads with the Lord not to "destroy the righteous with the wicked," and after some haggling the Lord agrees to spare Sodom if it contains ten righteous citizens.

Later, two angels arrive in Sodom and are taken in by Lot. The citizens of Sodom then surround Lot's house and demand that Lot give up the angels so that "we may know them." Lot replies, "I pray you, brethren, do not so wickedly. Behold now, I have two daughters which have not known man, let me, I pray you, bring them out unto you, and do ye to them as is good in your eyes; only unto these men do nothing, for . . . came they under the shadow of my roof."

When the mob attempts to break down the door to Lot's house, the angels curse them with blindness. The following morning, the angels warn Lot to leave the city with his wife and daughters. The Lord then rained "brimstone and fire" upon Sodom and destroyed both Sodom and its sister city, Gomorrah, "and all the inhabitants of the cities, and that which grew upon the ground."[36]

This story has been interpreted in Christian theology as revealing God's condemnation of same-sex sex. But that interpretation strains both the text and other biblical references to the event.[37] In the Jewish tradition, this story has consistently been understood as a moral about the duty of hospitality, having nothing to do with same-sex sex.[38] Although it may seem strange that such significance would be placed on the duty of hospitality, in the desert, hospitality is a necessity of life. Among nomads, hospitality is not only a virtue, but a moral obligation. In the Hebraic culture, "the guest is sacred," and Lot was willing to sacrifice his daughters in order to protect his guests.[39]

---

* It is because of this interpretation that masturbation came to be known as "onanism."

Of course, the story of Sodom can be read as condemning same-sex sex. But there are several subsequent references to Sodom in the Hebrew Bible, none of which suggests a concern about same-sex sex. When the prophet Ezekiel lists the sins of Sodom, for example, he never mentions same-sex sex.[40] Similarly, the New Testament makes several references to Sodom, none of which mentions same-sex sex. Jesus himself apparently believed that Sodom was destroyed for the sin of inhospitality: "Whosoever shall not receive you, nor hear your words, when ye depart out of that house or city, shake off the dust of your feet. Verily I say unto you, it shall be more tolerable for the land of Sodom and Gomorrah in the day of judgment, than for that city."[41]

Moreover, the early Christians understood the story of Sodom as condemning vices unrelated to homosexuality. Origen, for example, one of the preeminent Christian theologians of the third century A.D., explained: "Hear this, you who close your homes to guests! Hear this, you who shun the traveler as an enemy! Lot who lived among the Sodomites . . . escaped the fire on account of one thing only. He opened his home to guests. The angels entered the hospitable household; the flames entered only those homes closed to guests."[42]

Nonetheless, later generations of Christian theologians invoked the story of Sodom as the root justification for Christianity's denunciation of what came to be known as "sodomy."[43]

EARLY CHRISTIANITY

IN THESE ANCIENT CULTURES, sex was regarded as a natural part of life. By the end of the fifth century, however, Christianity came to condemn sexual desire as inherently shameful.[44] This shift took place gradually in a world that was in the process of collapsing.

Jesus himself said little about sex. He criticized adultery (but showed compassion for an adulteress), opposed divorce in the absence of adultery, and warned in the Sermon on the Mount that "whosoever looketh on a woman to lust after her hath committed adultery with her already in his heart." Some Christian theologians later cited this as evidence that Jesus condemned sexual desire, but the text clearly refers to offenses against the marital relation.[45]

On another occasion, the disciples asked Jesus whether it was "not good to marry." Jesus replied that "all men cannot receive" this injunction, adding that "there are some eunuchs, which were so born from their mother's womb; and there are some eunuchs, which were made eunuchs of men; and there be eunuchs, which have made themselves eunuchs for the kingdom of heaven's sake."[46] Some early Christian theologians interpreted this passage as implying that service to God demands abstinence from sex. Others interpreted it more literally, and castrated themselves. Apart from these rather cryptic admonitions, Jesus was silent on the subject of sex.[47]

Paul of Tarsus, on the other hand, who wrote approximately five decades after the death of Jesus, advocated a very constrained view of sex. In his *Epistle to the Romans,* he condemned the "vile affections"[48] of the idolaters: "Even their women did change the natural use into that which is against nature: And likewise also the men, leaving the natural use of the woman, burned in their lust toward one another; men with men working that which is unseemly."[49] Not only did he condemn same-sex sex, but he added that anyone who engaged in fornication would not "inherit the kingdom of God."[50]

Paul's message suggested a radical departure from the prevailing view of the ancient world, for he declared celibacy the ideal, non-marital sex immoral, and same-sex sex unnatural. But Paul's message was mixed. He did not restrict marital sex only to procreation or condemn sexual pleasure as such. Rather, he acknowledged the naturalness of sexual desire and emphasized that husband and wife must not "deprive each other." As for procreation, Paul thought it irrelevant, because the Kingdom of God was imminent. As he put it, "the time is short."[51]

WITH THE passing of the apostolic age, Christian theology evolved in the complex crucible of the Roman Empire, and the early Christians increasingly found themselves in a twilight world of Hellenistic philosophy, pagan mythology, and Gnostic mystery. During this pivotal stage in the development of Christian theology, the church fathers had to contend with several rival philosophical/religious movements, each of which left a mark on Christian doctrine: Stoicism, Neoplatonism, Gnosticism, and Manichænism.[52]

Each of these doctrines emphasized the danger of desire, especially sexual desire. The Manichæns, Gnostics, and Neoplatonists all shared a belief that the material world was fundamentally evil and that sensory indulgence chained man to his bodily desires at the expense of his soul. The Gnostics, for example, preached that the material world, which had come into existence as the result of a catastrophic "fall" in the higher realm, was inherently evil. They taught that man can achieve redemption only by leading a rabidly ascetic life, with rules for the mortification of the flesh and sexual continence. The Gnostics saw castration as a fundamental act of faith.[53]

Similarly, the Stoic philosophers maintained that the only way to achieve true peace was to refuse to indulge one's desires. Musonius Rufus, for example, a first-century Stoic philosopher, condemned sex for any purpose other than procreation, and Titus Lucretius Carus, a Stoic poet, insisted that sexual desire is a sickness that man should avoid entirely.[54]

The defeat of these philosophical and theological rivals was one of the most critical victories in Christian history. But in the process of beating back the forces of Stoicism, Neoplatonism, Gnosticism, and Manichænism, Christian orthodoxy absorbed many of their values. Indeed, by the beginning of the fifth century the Christian attitude toward sex had been more profoundly shaped by the influences of pagan mysticism than by the more earthy views of the classical Greeks, the Romans, or the ancient Hebrews.[55]

SAINT AUGUSTINE AND THE PELAGIAN CONTROVERSY

IT WAS AUGUSTINE who crystallized the early Christian understanding of sex and who, in so doing, ultimately helped shape traditional American views of sexuality more than a millennium later. Born in 354 in Tagaste, now Souk Ahras, in Algeria, the man who became Saint Augustine gave himself up as a young man to lust, an experience that profoundly shaped his later theology. At the age of eighteen, Augustine took up with a woman in Carthage, who bore him an illegitimate son. Under his mother's influence, he abandoned his faithful concubine, sending her back to Africa, and promised to marry an under-age girl. While waiting for her to reach the age of consent, he took up with another mistress. Eventually, he deserted them all. In *Confessions*, Augustine lamented these experiences:

> Love and lust seethed together within me . . . swept me away over the precipice of my body's appetites and plunged me into the whirlpool of sin . . . floundering in the broiling sea of my fornication . . . a frenzy gripped me and I surrendered myself entirely to lust.[56]

The following year, Augustine embraced Manichænism, and for more than a decade he devoted himself passionately to this sect. Manichænism arose out of the teachings of the third century prophet Mani, who lived in southern Babylonia and was crucified in 277 A.D. Mani taught that when man procreates he replicates the forces of evil and chains his soul to the devil. The only path to salvation is to withdraw completely from the temptations of sex and the contaminations of the flesh. Above all, sex is defiling and must be shunned. From the end of the third century, Manichænism swept like a firestorm across Egypt, Greece, Asia Minor, North Africa, and Europe.[57]

To his great frustration, Augustine never moved up the Manichæn hierarchy, in part because of his difficulties with sexual lust. Unable to control his desire, he expressed his ambivalence about sex in his prayer: "Give me chastity, and continency, but do not give it yet."[58] Around 383, Augustine traveled to Rome where he immersed himself in Neoplatonism, which taught that man's ultimate goal must be to free himself from the allure of sensory perceptions. Like the Stoics, the Gnostics, and the Manichæns, the Neoplatonists urged abstinence from all sensual pleasures.[59]

After several more years of struggling unsuccessfully to resist the temptations of the flesh, Augustine was baptized a Christian and committed himself to a life of celibacy. He returned to Tagaste and sought the "perfect" life, selling all his goods and giving the proceeds to the poor. Later, he was ordained a priest.

As Augustine's reputation and influence as a scholar grew, he was appointed Bishop of Hippo in 396, a position he held for the next thirty-four years. Having dedicated himself to continence, Augustine turned his pen against the temptations of sex. Writing as a convert from Manichænism, his fascination with sexuality and evil was influenced by his personal experience and intellectual training. There was nothing, he wrote, that brought the "mind down from the heights" more certainly "than a woman's caresses."[60]

In a critical leap, Augustine linked lust to the expulsion of Adam and Eve from the Garden of Eden.[61] He postulated that while in Paradise, Adam and Eve had never suffered the degradation of sexual desire. As creations of the higher realm, they experienced none of the carnal urges of the animalistic world. After the fall, however, they were afflicted with a crude and animalistic impulse—the insatiable quest for sexual satisfaction.

Augustine was bewildered by "this monstrousness." He regarded the intensity of sexual pleasure as definitive proof that human nature had fallen. As a legacy of Eve's temptation and Adam's fatal failure to resist, man was rendered easy prey to sin. Satan holds him captive and can compel him to do his will. Adam's transgression, he reasoned, had not been one of disobedience, as the ancient Hebrews believed, but one of sex.

Saint Augustine

Thus, every sexual act is born out of evil, and every child born out of evil is born into sin. It is through sex that man passes on sin from one generation to the next.

Man's best hope for redemption therefore lay in repudiating the sexual impulse and, with it, the burden of guilt inherited from Adam. Sex in any form is filthy, defiling, and shameful, so only the celibate can hope to achieve the state of grace that had existed in Eden. Through the brilliance of his intellect, the plague of his personal demons, and the influence of his early Manichæn beliefs, Augustine transformed an ancient Hebrew story about disobedience into a spiritual condemnation of human sexuality. In so doing, he profoundly shaped the future of Western culture and law.[62]

THERE REMAINED the problem of marriage and procreation. In the years immediately after the crucifixion, the Apostles had taught that the Kingdom of God was near, so there was no need for humans to reproduce. But long before Augustine's time it had become clear that the wait would be longer than anticipated. Because both the Hebrew Bible and the New Testament acknowledged the legitimacy of marriage, Augustine reasoned that although celibacy was the ideal, those too weak to be celibate could engage in sexual intercourse in order to beget the next generation of Christians. But sex could *only* be between husband and wife, it could *only* be for the purpose of procreation, and it could *only* be done in the missionary position, which was thought to maximize the chance of procreation.[63]

Moreover, even in these circumstances intercourse must be devoid of any passion or pleasure. A corrupt vessel, the body should be used only for joyless reproduction. Augustine condemned as sinful every other form of sex, including masturbation, oral sex, anal sex, same-sex sex, sex during menstruation, sex during lactation, sex after menopause, and any effort to prevent pregnancy. "The will of God," he maintained, was "not to serve lust" but "to see to the preservation of the race." It was Augustine who, for the first time in the Christian tradition, condemned all sexual desire and pleasure—for the married and unmarried alike.[64]

What did this mean for the vast majority of people who could not resist the lure of sexual pleasure? In Augustine's words, "a cruel necessity of sinning" rests upon the human race, for without God's grace, which is given by God alone and cannot be earned by good deeds, man "cannot by free will overcome the temptations of this life."[65]

IN 411, Pelagius, an austere monk who had become a prominent teacher in Rome, challenged Augustine's view of human nature. Pelagius maintained that God creates each soul independently, unsoiled by any original sin transmitted from Adam. Indeed, he regarded as immoral Augustine's belief that man's nature is so corrupt that he is powerless to obey God's commands. Rather, he insisted that each individual is born with the potential to claim "I have injured no one, I have lived righteously with all," and by choosing to live a just and moral life, earn salvation.[66]

The Pelagians disdained Augustine's condemnation of sex as unadulterated Manichænism. In their view, the sex impulse is perfectly natural, and nothing natural can be evil. They repudiated Augustine's conflation of concupiscence with original sin and charged him with "defaming the good handiwork of the Creator under the influence of a hagridden attitude to sex" resulting from his own adolescent excesses.[67]

The Pelagian challenge led to a series of bitter theological disputes. It was in the resolution of these disputes that the Church finally embraced the Augustinian dogmas of original sin and sexual immorality. Augustine accused Pelagius of mendacity and of spreading heresies. As the tenets of Pelagianism spread, Augustine responded with a series of stunningly effective critiques defending the existence of original sin, the impossibility of a life without sin, and the necessity of grace for redemption.[68]

In an effort to halt the spreading "infection" of Pelagianism, two hundred bishops convened in 418 at the Council of Carthage, which branded Pelagius a heretic. Thereafter, Pope Zosimus issued a papal encyclical categorically condemning Pelagianism. The doctrine of Pelagianism was officially anathematized at the Council of Ephesus in 431, a year after Augustine's death. Augustine's triumph was complete.[69]

N ONE OF this would have mattered had Christianity gone the way of Stoicism, Neoplatonism, Gnosticism, and Manichænism. But, of course, it did not. During the first several centuries of the Christian era, the Romans persecuted the Christians for their heretical and seditious beliefs, but these persecutions were sporadic, ineffective, and counterproductive. By the end of the second century, Christianity had begun to penetrate the higher classes of society, and during the third century, the Roman Empire was so distracted by civil wars and barbarian invasions that it could no longer devote much attention to stopping the spread of Christianity.

The critical moment was the conversion of the Emperor Constantine. The son of a Roman officer, Constantine was proclaimed Caesar by his troops in 306. During the ensuing civil war, Constantine, a pagan, had a vision that he would conquer under the sign of the cross. After winning a stunning military victory, he declared in 313 that the persecution of Christians would no longer be tolerated. Imprisoned Christians were immediately released and received by their brethren with acclamations of joy. Thereafter, Constantine granted the Church one privilege after another.

Ironically, Constantine was not a man of faith. He never understood Christian doctrine and did not get around to being baptized until he was on his deathbed in 337. His decision to endorse Christianity was as much political as religious. But as a political move, it was astute. By the early years of the fourth century, the Roman Empire was reeling from external invasion and internal strife. Rome's military, legal, monetary, economic, transportation, and trading systems had all fallen into disarray. The upper classes were consumed with personal power struggles and paid little attention to responsible rule. Assassinations were commonplace, and one mad, brutal, or incompetent despot followed another.

Alien religious cults, shrouded in mystery, magic, and spiritualism, swept through the Empire. Although paganism was still the religion of choice for the vast majority of Romans, the people had grown disenchanted with what they saw as the stale myths and unedifying superstitions of polytheism. Gradually, they were drawn to the spiritual convictions and moral strictures of monotheism in general, and Christianity in particular.

It was a time of chaos, crisis, alienation, and foreboding. To Constantine, it must have "seemed that Christianity alone—a foreign religion transfigured by almost three centuries of proselytizing within the Empire—held out some hope of unifying the vast and heterogeneous collection of peoples contained within Rome's wide frontiers."[70]

T HE CONVERSION of Constantine meant much more than the end of Christian persecution. From this point onward, the state became involved in the activities of the Church, and the Church became enmeshed in the decisions of the state, a development that eventually would lead the Framers of the American Constitution to adopt the First Amendment. Persecution of those who dissented from Christianity increasingly played a role in imperial legislation. Although Constantine did not establish Christianity as the official religion of the Roman Empire, the Emperor Theodosius formalized this establishment at the end of the fourth century. For all practical purposes, Christianity had conquered Rome.[71]

Then, in 410, the Western world suffered the numbing shock of the sack of Rome by the Visigoths. The invading barbarians carted off the charred remains of great temples and palaces to construct crude villages. Contemporaries described the Roman masses living in hopeless destitution, suffering from alienation, fear, frustration, and lacking any sense of purpose in their lives. Profound questions of divine providence arose in a mood of fear and desperation. Christians proclaimed that the sack of Rome was God's punishment for man's decadence and dissolution and that it was an irrefutable sign that Christianity must now assume responsibility for man's future.[72]

It was at this moment of despair and disillusion that the Church embraced Augustinian doctrine. The unique appeal of Augustinianism lay in its assertion of complete human dependence upon the sovereignty of God. Lacking free will, man had no alternative but to stand in awe of his Maker. With civilization crumbling before his very eyes and darkness drawing down all around him, what else was he to do?

Augustine's triumph was unprecedented in the history of man's attitudes about sex. Before Augustine, most Western societies had condemned adultery (at least by wives); some had denounced same-sex sex; and a few had censured fornication. But no Western culture had ever before condemned *all* human sexuality except marital intercourse for the sole purpose of procreation. Every prior Western culture had regarded most forms of sex as natural and properly pleasurable facets of human existence. By early in the fifth century, however, the dominant strand of Christianity left no doubt of its stance: Sexual desire and its fulfillment, in every manifestation, was sinful and must be suppressed.

From a theological perspective, it was by no means inevitable that the Church would accept Augustine's bleak vision of human nature. Nothing in the Hebrew Bible or the New Testament commands such an understanding, and Augustine's teachings had no noticeable impact on the Eastern Christian Church. But in the West, with the calamitous collapse of the Roman Empire, it was Augustine who captured the dark mood of his time, and whose desolate vision of free will and sexuality set the stage for the Middle Ages, and beyond.[73]

2

THE POWER OF
REVEALED TRUTH

The Devil Prompting Lust

DURING THE OFTEN bleak millennium after the fall of Rome, populations shifted, barbarian rulers came and went, economic, social, and political life became increasingly localized, and secular law largely disappeared. The disintegration of the Roman Empire left the Church as the primary cohesive force in an otherwise uncertain and unstable world. Literacy became almost the exclusive preserve of monasteries. Monks copied what was orthodox and destroyed what was not. Knowledge was largely controlled by the Church. In such circumstances, the writings of the early Christian Fathers took on the power of revealed truth.

Christian dogma, backed by the threat of hellfire and damnation, attained not only religious but social, legal, and political authority. A distinctive concept of sin became church doctrine. This concept was derived, not from the tablets of Moses or the teachings of Jesus, but from the sexual quirks and mystical philosophies of a handful of men who had lived in the twilight years of the Roman Empire. What in 500 A.D. had been a theological exegesis was transformed over the next thousand years into a code of sexual conduct that framed the lives of princes and peasants alike.

This is not to say that church doctrine controlled every facet of day-to-day life. The Middle Ages was a complex era marked by rampant bawdiness as well as extreme asceticism. At different times and in different places, homosexuals flaunted their sexuality, but were also burned at the stake; prostitutes openly prowled the streets, but were also pilloried and tortured; clerics indulged in wanton fornication, but also lived in pristine celibacy. In the chasm between chastity and reality lay sin. More than five hundred years later, we are still grappling with the consequences.[1]

"THE BADGE OF MORAL AUTHORITY"

THE EARLY CHURCH imposed strict demands on the faithful. Those who believed that the rapture was near readily accepted the ideal of celibacy and the renunciation of worldly goods. But as it gradually became apparent that the end was not in sight, it became more difficult both to demand and to exercise such self-restraint. Over time, a double standard emerged. Ordinary Christians, subject to all the temptations of life, would strive to observe the precepts of the Church, even if they could not achieve perfection. Members of the cloth, however, would be held to higher standards.

The most rigorous standards of Christian purity were embodied in the early monastic movement, which began in the second century A.D. As the Christian era unfolded, some of the faithful openly renounced sex, marriage, and all but the minimum of possessions. Their asceticism sometimes took extreme forms. Mortification of the flesh was common. Some wore heavy iron chains, while others adopted the lives of animals, living in the open air and feeding on grass. One gained fame by living atop a column for more than thirty years. Some early Christian ascetics castrated themselves both to demonstrate and to ensure their celibacy.[2]

Many monks were young men who had natural sexual desires. They were supported in their struggle to master their desires by the general ethic of the monasteries, which fervently condemned women as temptresses and as handmaidens of the devil. Most monasteries forbade monks to have any contact with females. But it was a challenge for even the most dedicated monks to suppress all sexual thoughts and desires. A particular sticking point was nocturnal emission. Augustine believed that sexual dreams were the work of "demon-lovers." For the would-be celibate, such dreams, especially those resulting in ejaculation (known as "pollution" in medieval terminology), indicated the distance between aspiration and attainment, providing a gauge for measuring his progress.[3]

Same-sex sex was a particularly serious problem in monasteries. As early as the fourth century, Saint Basil, one of the founders of the monastic movement, warned his disciples to "fly from intimate association with comrades of your own age and run away from them as from fire. . . . When a young brother converses with you or is opposite you in choir, make your response with your head bowed lest per chance by gazing fixedly into his face, the seed of desire be implanted."[4] In 567, the second Council of Tours endorsed the Benedictine rules that monks must never sleep two to a bed and that lamps must be kept burning throughout the night. Same-sex sex was also a problem in convents, and similar rules were enacted for nuns.[5]

UNLIKE MONKS and nuns, who were largely isolated in their monasteries and nunneries, other members of the clergy lived among ordinary people. Could they be expected to be celibate? If marriage was merely a grudging concession to human frailty, shouldn't the priesthood, which served as the community's model for strength and purity, be celibate? Celibacy could be the clergy's "badge of moral authority,"[6] a way to raise clerics above the laity and visibly mark their distinctive service to God. For more than six hundred years after Augustine, the Church wrestled with this issue.

Throughout this era, the Church allowed priests to marry, but clerical marriage was often excoriated by the faithful as a pollution of the priesthood. In the face of such denunciations, the Church gradually began to impose an official policy of celibacy upon the clergy. It was not until the eleventh century, however, that the papacy was sufficiently powerful to insist upon absolute clerical celibacy. Pope Gregory VII's proclamation to this effect triggered furious protests among the clergy, but the Church prevailed.[*][7]

The requirement of clerical celibacy invited a degree of hypocrisy that would come to haunt the Church. In the Middle Ages, many clerics entered the Church, not because of the depth of their faith, but because it was the only way to pursue a meaningful career in law, scholarship, government, or administration. Because such priests could no longer marry, but were unable or unwilling to suppress their sexual desires, many kept concubines or frequented brothels. Monks and itinerant friars were often mocked as "seducers of women," and the popular literature of the time frequently denounced clerical celibacy as a "joke."[†] Womanizing among the clergy was a constant source of embarrassment to the Church, especially when it resulted in bastard children.[8]

---

* The Eastern Christian Church, which had not been much influenced by Augustine, rejected this position.

† The cynicism generated by such conduct was captured in a thirteenth-century poem:

> Priests who lack a girl to cherish
> Won't be mindful lest they perish.
> They will take whom'er they find
> Married, single—never mind!

Brundage, *Pleasures of the Flesh* at 298 (cited in note 7).

Same-sex sex within the clergy was also a concern. In the middle of the sixth century, the emperor Justinian had several prominent bishops tortured, castrated, and exiled for engaging in such conduct. In the twelfth century, Saint Anselm observed that "this sin has been so public" among the clergy "that hardly anyone has blushed for it."[9] After the Church banned clerical marriage, rumors of same-sex sex among the clergy grew ever more rampant, and priests were routinely satirized for their "love of boys."[10]

MEDIEVAL CARNALITY

OUR KNOWLEDGE OF the sex lives of ordinary men and women during the Middle Ages is incomplete. Few people kept diaries or were even literate. Most of our information derives from the writings of clergymen, monks, theologians, and canon lawyers. Certainly, to most people in this era the rudiments of sex were no great mystery. Most people lived off the land and were intimately familiar with the breeding of animals. Moreover, most people lived in small, crowded homes. There was little or no privacy, and it was impractical to think of sex as something done in private.[11]

It was in this setting that the Church implanted in Western culture its judgments about sex and sin. Sexual desire gradually became linked to guilt, humiliation, failure, and shame. This did not happen quickly or uniformly, but as the Church expanded, reached into local communities, and devised ever more potent mechanisms of social control, its success seemed almost inexorable. Not everyone in the Middle Ages accepted the Church's teachings on sex, but few people dared take "no account of it."[12]

Medieval attitudes toward sex reflected an uneasy mix of severe repression and earthy lust. The prevalent view, preached by the Church, was that sex was shameful and defiling. The clergy condemned any "unnatural" sex, which included not only bestiality, anal intercourse, oral sex, same-sex sex, and masturbation, but also any emission of semen outside the vagina and any intercourse even by married couples other than in the missionary position for the sole purpose of procreation. But even in the Middle Ages, noblemen kept mistresses, peasants rolled in the hay, and Geoffrey Chaucer and Giovanni Boccaccio explored human sexuality through poetry and literature.

THE CORE sexual ethic of the Middle Ages, derived from Augustine, was stated unambiguously in 1217 in the Synod of Angers: "Every voluntary emission of semen is a mortal sin in both males and females unless excused by legitimate marriage."[13] Paul of Hungary added that even in marriage, "pollution outside the vessel of nature [i.e., the vagina] however it is done . . . is a vice against nature."[14]

A central challenge to the Church was to instill these beliefs in the people. Preaching the faith was essential, but the Church could not rely on faith alone. Over time, the Church devised a variety of means to enforce compliance with its teachings. The promise of salvation and the threat of damnation certainly encouraged compliance. Salvation could be achieved only through the rituals of the Church, and damnation was no laughing matter. In the hell described by the medieval Church, "the damned hung by their tongues from trees of fire, the impenitent burned in furnaces," and the wicked were "gnawed by demons."[15]

Faced with the choice between salvation and damnation, the faithful had ample incentive to conform their behavior to the teachings of the Church. But, as with any system of punishment, it was essential not to threaten too harshly. If even a single slip would lead to eternal damnation, the sinner, having once slipped, would have no further incentive to restrain his conduct. The Church therefore needed a way to graduate its threats in order to deter sin and induce proper behavior, without undermining its own goals. Over time, the Church developed a complex mix of confession, penance, canon law, and secular civil law to enforce Christian doctrine. Although the Church through these means addressed a variety of sins, including greed, gluttony, sloth, envy, anger, and pride, it focused particularly on lust.

CONFESSION, WHICH WAS integral to the Church's enforcement process, began to emerge as an institution in the sixth century. Seven centuries later, the Fourth Council of the Lateran in 1215 required all Christians, on pain of mortal sin, to confess and undergo penance at least once each year. With compelled confession, enforcement and punishment became more realistic.

But how should each sin be punished? Between the sixth and twelfth centuries, a variety of guides, or "penitentials," were written to instruct priests how to conduct themselves in confession. The sixth century's *Synod of the Grove of Victory*, for example, stated specific penances for such acts as adultery, incest, copulation with animals, masturbation, and other sexual sins. *The Penitential of Cummean*, written by an Irish monk in the seventh century, demanded a year's penance for bestiality, three years for incest with one's mother, four years for oral sex ("those who befoul their lips"), and seven years for *coitus in ano*. Other penitentials addressed nocturnal emission, having intercourse with one's wife "like a dog," seeing one's wife naked, having sex on Sunday, having thoughts about fornication, and having intercourse with one's wife during menstruation. In the eleventh century, Bishop Burchard of Worms's *Decretum* and Saint Peter Damian's *Book of Gomorrah* comprehensively reviewed all prior penitentials and sought to bring order to the previously chaotic and highly localized system by classifying sexual offenses in a carefully ascending order of sinfulness.[16]

The penitentials coached priests how best to induce penitents to confess. They cautioned priests not to inquire about particularly serious sexual matters, such as deviant sexual positions or sodomy, unless justified by the circumstances. Such circumspection was essential to avoid the risk that sinful ideas might unintentionally be "transmitted like a virus from the clergy to the laity."[17] As William Peraldus warned in the thirteenth century in his *Summas on the Vices and Virtues*, these vices must "be spoken of with great caution . . . so that nothing be revealed to men that might give them occasion to sin."[18]

SELF-POLLUTION AND FORNICATION

GIVEN ITS UNDERSTANDING of sex, the Church deemed masturbation a mortal sin. Saint Thomas Aquinas, the influential thirteenth-century philosopher, theologian, and jurist, described masturbation as one of the four "unnatural vices," along with sodomy, unnatural forms of copulation (any position other than the man on top, face-to-face, for the purpose of marital reproduction), and bestiality. The seriousness of masturbation relative to the other unnatural vices was hotly debated. Most theologians concluded that masturbation was a relatively minor sexual offense. The typical penance for masturbation was twenty to thirty days of fasting. One reason for this relative lenity was that people tended to marry late in the Middle Ages, particularly in northern Europe. Although masturbation was a mortal sin, the clergy were inclined to treat it gently because, of all the ways people might cope with their sexual desires, masturbation was the *least* sinful.[19]

Although the penitentials focused on male masturbation, they acknowledged that female masturbation was also a sin. But because it did not involve the waste of semen, it did not fit neatly into the medieval conception of unnatural acts. In dealing with female masturbation, the clergy were particularly concerned about the use of dildos. In the early eleventh century, for example, Bishop Burchard of Worms advised that women should be carefully interrogated to ensure that they had not used a "device in the form of the male sexual organ, the dimensions being calculated to give you pleasure."[20]

The medieval understanding of female masturbation was bound up with the prevailing view of female sexuality. The Church characterized women as temptresses who had inherited Eve's sexually voracious nature. Men were rational and spiritual; women were irrational and carnal. As Saint Jerome, who was known for his influential teachings on Christian moral life, put it in the fourth century, women are sexually "insatiable." Quench their passion, and it immediately "bursts into flame" again.[21] The great thirteenth-century encyclopedist, Vincent of Beauvais, added that women are "not only more lustful than men but more lustful than all female animals with the possible exception of the mare."[22]

Moreover, because women were thought to be inherently inferior, lacking in self-discipline, and deficient in both reasoning and understanding, it was conventional wisdom that they had to be strictly controlled in order to protect them—and men—from their natural carnality. Women's sexuality unnerved medieval men, who feared that women would incite them to impure thoughts, distract them from attaining salvation, and lure them into fornication. Women, in short, were morally dangerous.[23]

NEEDLESS TO say, fornication—broadly defined as any non-marital sexual activity—was prohibited by the Church. Gratian, a twelfth-century monk and Italian jurist who founded the canon law, defined fornication as coitus with any person other than one's spouse. Unlike masturbation, which was not a crime, fornication called forth not only confession and penance, but also prosecution.

As a practical matter, however, fornication was rarely prosecuted. In general, the law intervened only when a man's fornication impinged on the rights of other men to the faithfulness of their wives or the virginity of their daughters. A man who had sex with an unmarried woman who was not a virgin committed only a minor sin.[24] Women were prosecuted for fornication much more often than men, in part because men's sexual transgressions were regarded as less serious than those of women, and in part because the inherent difficulty of proving the offense of consensual fornication was greatly eased when an unmarried woman became pregnant.[25]

HOLY WEDLOCK

ONLY MARRIAGE COULD legitimize sex. As the influential Synod of Angers declared in 1217: "Every voluntary emission of semen is a mortal sin in both males and females unless excused by legitimate marriage. But faith teaches that sexual intercourse between male and female is excused by legitimate marriage as long as the union is in the proper manner."[26] Thus, even within marriage "the proper manner" was critical. The Church taught that sexual passion had no place in Christian marriage and specified in extraordinary detail the permissible time, place, manner, and frequency of marital sex. The Church sternly admonished that a husband and wife should engage in intercourse only rarely, only when they intend to beget a child, only in the missionary position, never orally or anally, and never for the sake of carnal gratification. A confession of oral sex with one's spouse could result in four years of penance and a whipping by the parish priest.

Even in marital intercourse in the proper position and intended for procreation, sexual pleasure was deemed a sin. At the turn of the seventh century, Pope Gregory the Great, the first pope to come from a monastic background, declared that if a married couple derive any pleasure from intercourse, they have "transgressed the law of marriage" and "befouled" their intercourse.[27] The twelfth-century Italian canonist Huguccio proclaimed that marital coitus "can never be without sin, for it always occurs and is exercised with a certain . . . pleasure."[28]

This view of pleasure in marital sex began to change in the thirteenth century. Saint Thomas Aquinas reasoned that because marital coitus is necessary for procreation, God must have imbued sexual intercourse with pleasure in order to induce husbands and wives to reproduce: "To impel man to the act whereby the deficiency of the species is aided, He put delight in copulation."[29] Therefore, it could not be sinful to take moderate pleasure in procreative marital sex. But Aquinas rejected the next step: If God made sex pleasurable even when it is *not* undertaken for procreation, then sex for pleasure must *also* be natural and moral. Without resolving this puzzle, Aquinas insisted that procreation was the *only* legitimate justification for sex.

The penitentials accepted this view, and added a great many more restrictions. They banned married couples from engaging in sex during the wife's menstrual period, during pregnancy, during the daylight hours, while they were naked, in any position other than the missionary position, in church, on Sundays, and on holy days, which covered most of the year.

The sixth century bishop Saint Gregory of Tours warned of divine punishment for those who had sex in any place, time, or manner prohibited by the Church. He told of a woman who had had sex with her husband on a Sunday night and then later gave birth to a severely malformed child who was a "monster." The lesson was clear: "If spouses insist on having sex on Sunday, the children born of this union will have crippled limbs, epilepsy, or leprosy."[30]

B ECAUSE MARITAL SEX was a mortal sin unless intended for procreation, contraception was forbidden. Although early Christians had continued to use contraception, and although early church fathers had not always interpreted the biblical story of Onan* as condemning contraception, by the Middle Ages the Church's position was clear: The use of potions, herbs, coitus interruptus, or any other means of contraception was a mortal sin.

The medieval Church defined contraception as a form of homicide. This seemed reasonable. After all, if a man who spills his seed (that is, who ejaculates anywhere but in a vagina) is to be punished by death—the fate of Onan—then spilling one's seed is self-evidently a grievous offense. It violates the natural order and destroys potential human life. If it is a mortal sin tantamount to homicide for a man to spill his seed, then it must also be a mortal sin for an individual to prevent conception in other ways. As the fifteenth-century Franciscan preacher Bernardine of Siena proclaimed, those who use contraception are "killers of their own children."[31]

Abortion was also condemned by the Church, although abortion within forty days of conception—before the fetus was believed to acquire a human soul—was deemed less sinful than contraception. Although contraception and abortion were both thought to be serious sins, the secular law in the Middle Ages did not treat either as a crime.[32]

CONCUBITUS AD NON DEBITUM SEXUM

THE CHURCH FATHERS regarded same-sex sex as more sinful than fornication, which was at least "natural." In his Epistle to the Romans, Paul denounced those who "leaving the natural use of the woman, burned in their

---

* See chapter 1.

lust one toward another; men with men working that which is unseemly," for they had changed "the natural use into that which is *against nature*."[33] Nonetheless, it was not until 538, in the "new" Rome of Constantinople, that the Emperor Justinian, infusing Roman law with Christian morality, outlawed same-sex sex. Justinian feared that the prevalence of such conduct had caused the Empire to suffer "famines, earthquakes, and pestilences." The law was rarely enforced, however.[34]

Moreover, for the next five centuries few Christian kingdoms had laws expressly forbidding same-sex sex. In part, this was because both the Church and the secular authorities regarded same-sex sex as no different from any other form of "sodomy," which was broadly defined to include any improper release of semen.[35] By the same token, the penitentials of this era rarely focused on same-sex sex as a sin distinct from other types of sodomy. The sixth century *Synod of the Grove of Victory*, for example, stipulated a four-year penance for anal intercourse, a three-year penance for interfemoral intercourse, and a two-year penance for mutual masturbation, but these penalties were applicable without regard to whether the partners were opposite or same sex. It was the *acts* that were sinful, independent of the genders of the participants.[36]

THIS BEGAN to change in the eleventh century. The evolution in thinking about this issue ultimately had a profound impact on American attitudes and laws regarding homosexuality, so it is worth close attention.

It is unclear precisely what triggered the Church's sudden focus on same-sex sex, but the Church was certainly concerned at the time that its new requirement of clerical celibacy might increase same-sex sex among the clergy, who might then turn around and contaminate the laity. In his *Book of Gomorrah*, which attacked the depravity of the clergy in the eleventh century, Saint Peter Damian, a zealous church reformer, produced the first known polemic directed specifically against same-sex sex. Damian classified four "lusts against nature" as part of the "Sodomitical vice": masturbation, mutual masturbation, interfemoral intercourse, and anal intercourse. All of these acts could be opposite-sex as well as same-sex, but Damian focused on same-sex sodomy. He insisted that fornication "in the rear" between two men was morally worse than even bestiality, for "bestiality brings damnation only to oneself, not to another." Damian declared that such conduct merited punishment by death. It was Damian who first coined the term "sodomy."[37]

But the phrases "sodomy" and "sin against nature" remained ambiguous for the next two centuries. They were widely and confusingly used to describe many forbidden sexual activities, opposite-sex and same-sex alike. In the mid-twelfth century, for example, Gratian, a leading scholar of the canon law, continued to use these phrases interchangeably, though he was clear that the worst sexual sin was *coitus in ano*—"a man using a member of his wife not conceded for that purpose." Near the end of the twelfth century, the Third Lateran Council, which was convened by Pope Alexander III, equated the "sin against nature" with the destruction of Sodom, but still left the sin undefined.[38]

In 1220, Paul of Hungary's influential opus, *Summa of Penance*, invoked Augustine and Gratian to conclude that sodomy was a worse sin than incest. Paul explained that this was so because intercourse with one's own mother was "natural," in the sense that it does not involve the wasting of seed, whereas sodomy is, by definition, "unnatural." Paul added that sodomy had become so prevalent that "there come about famine and plagues, and earthquakes." Paul insisted that sodomy must be punished by death, for as the story of Sodom had taught, God will punish not only the sinners for this particular sin, but also those who fail to *prevent* the sin. Thus, the very survival of the community required both the Church and the state to obliterate the scourge of sodomy.[39]

But it was still unclear precisely what acts constituted "sodomy."

T HE MAN most responsible for the hardening of the Church's attitude toward same-sex sex was the renowned theologian Thomas Aquinas, who systematized and expanded upon Augustine's thinking. In 1259, in his mid-thirties, Aquinas left Paris, where he had been a highly regarded teacher of theology, to create a new university in Rome. Over the next fifteen years, he produced his prodigious *Summa Theologica*, which largely rewrote the whole of Christian moral theology. Although Aquinas died before completing the *Summa*, it was unrivaled in its power and scope. Just as Augustine had provided a rationale for the church fathers' antipathy to sex and rendered it acceptable only for marital procreation, so Aquinas offered a rationale for the conviction that same-sex sex was *especially* contemptible in the sight of God.[40]

Aquinas posited that God had instituted the order of nature by which everything was fittingly directed to its proper end; that God had created natural coitus as part of the order of nature for the sole purpose of procreation; that man should not contravene the order of nature; and that man therefore should not engage in any sexual act that is not directed to procreation. Moreover, "right reason" made clear that sexual pleasures, above all others, debauch the mind with lust (*luxuria*). Such pleasures are discordant with the order of nature, even if they are intended for procreation.

Aquinas defined *luxuria* as the sin of excess in sexual pleasure. There is no sin in sexual things as such, he explained, as long as they are undertaken for the proper purpose (reproduction) and in the proper manner (vaginal intercourse in the missionary position). Aquinas divided *luxuria* into six separate acts: simple fornication, adultery, incest, deflowering a virgin (*stuprum*), rape, and vice against nature (*vitium contra naturam*). The first five are mortal sins, but they are not as serious as the vice against nature, because they involve natural coitus (ejaculating into a vagina). Sins against nature are more serious, because they are an affront to God.

Further elaborating his system of classification, Aquinas identified four

Saint Thomas Aquinas

types of *vitium contra naturam*: (1) *luxuria* with oneself (masturbation); (2) *luxuria* with a person of the opposite sex other than in the "natural" manner; (3) *luxuria* with someone of the same sex; and (4) *luxuria* with another species (bestiality). Aquinas ranked these four vices against nature in the order just given in terms of the gravity of the sin.

The critical step taken by Aquinas was the shift in emphasis from sinful acts (mutual masturbation, oral sex, anal sex) without regard to the gender of the participants, to a categorical distinction between opposite-sex and same-sex acts. In his typology, two men who engage in fellatio or anal sex commit a more grievous sin than a man and a woman who engage in the same act.[41]

By the sixteenth century, *Summa Theologica* had become the dominant authority in Christian theology. Aquinas was hailed as the "guarantor" of Christian morality, and questions about which there had once been disagreement were now "crystallized into dogma." The Church gave ultimate authority to Aquinas's speculations at the Council of Trent in 1563, where it enacted them into formal church doctrine.[42]

W HEN DID same-sex sex become not only a sin, but a crime? This is a critical question, because committing a sin is fearful only to the faithful, whereas committing a crime is fearful to everyone. With the initiation of the Inquisition in the thirteenth century, the Church increasingly enlisted secular authorities in its persecution of heretics. This era of repression, triggered in part by anxiety induced by the Crusades, targeted not only Christian heretics, but Muslims, Jews, and homosexuals as well. As the Inquisition progressed, and as the Church sought to impose religious uniformity throughout Europe, it increasingly associated heresy with the "most wicked" sin and began accusing religious dissenters of sodomy. Over time, the "war against religious dissent was fatefully joined with the battle against homosexuality."[43]

There was suddenly a growing panic that same-sex sexual conduct was rampant. A same-sex sex scandal rocked the University of Paris in the late thirteenth century, resulting in the dismissal of many theologians and scholars. Rumors of widespread sodomy raced through Switzerland, Holland, Italy, France, and Spain, and early in the fifteenth century, Saint Bernadine of Siena raged that such behavior had reached epidemic proportions.[44]

Criminal statutes against same-sex sex were suddenly enacted throughout Europe. Typically, these laws called for sodomites to be castrated, dismembered, burned at the stake, drowned, hanged, stoned to death, decapitated, or buried alive. One Castilian edict commanded that anyone found guilty of same-sex conduct shall "be castrated before the whole populace and on the third day after be hung up by the legs until dead, and that their bodies never be taken down."[45] Those accused of same-sex sex became the object of a "program of extermination" that paralleled the attacks on heretics and witches. In this era, same-sex sex passed from being legal—albeit sinful—to being a crime incurring the death penalty throughout most of Europe.[46]

This was the first time that the Church had enacted distinctly Christian sexual morals directly into the secular criminal law. What previously had been a religious sin was now a capital crime. With the Inquisition, the Church transformed the secular law into a tool of Christian doctrine. Many of these laws went so far as to expressly incorporate biblical references into their prohibitions. Although many factors contributed to this change in the Church's attitude toward same-sex sex, it was Aquinas who provided the critical theological rationale that legitimated this shift.[47]

T HE CLERICAL literature in this era largely ignored same-sex conduct between women. In the thousand years of the Middle Ages, there were no more than a dozen scattered references to such behavior in the penitentials, canon and civil law, and popular sermons. The concept of "lesbianism" simply did not exist. To the extent the penitentials addressed such conduct at all, they did so indirectly, and were much more lenient toward sex between women than sex between men.[48]

In part, this was because sex between women, like female masturbation, does not involve the spilling of seed. In that sense, to the medieval Christian, it was completely different from male sodomy. Moreover, canonists had difficulty understanding how women could experience *luxuria* without the aid of a penis, because it was assumed that female sexual satisfaction required penetration. For that reason, the penitentials that did mention sex between women usually focused on the use of penetrative instruments.

Most men viewed female same-sex sex as an amusing, if sinful, effort by women to practice for the challenge of real sex with men. As one (male) commentator observed at the time, "As I have heard many ladies tell, there is nothing like a man; and what they get from other women is nothing but enticements to go and satisfy themselves with men."[49]

Some Church figures, though, sharply condemned women who engaged in same-sex sex. The twelfth-century theologian Peter Abelard, for example, denounced such behavior as "against the order of nature" because God had "created women's genitals for the use of men."[50] Although the criminal law largely ignored female same-sex sex, there were a few prosecutions, and the outcome could be harsh. Two nuns in Spain were burned alive for using "instruments" together, and a woman who had passed herself off as a man in France was burned alive when her artificial phallus was discovered.[51]

Many Christians linked such conduct with witchcraft. This was no laughing matter. In 1298, the Church, citing the biblical injunction in *Exodus* 22:18—"Thou shalt not suffer a witch to live"—launched a vigorous campaign to ferret out and burn witches. The leading handbook for discovering witches, *Malleus Maleficarum* (*The Hammer of Witches*), declared that "all witchcraft comes from carnal lust, which in women is insatiable." Hundreds, perhaps thousands, of women were tortured and burned at the stake because they allegedly had performed "coitus and sodomy with the Devil" and had been "ordered by him to perform sodomy with other humans."[52]

"IN NO WAY SUPERIOR TO THE BEASTS"

DURING THE MIDDLE AGES, life was conceived as a constant struggle against sin, especially lust, and a continual engagement with temptation, confession, penance, and absolution. As the Church expanded its power and influence, sex was transmogrified from a natural part of life into something shameful and filthy, and Augustine's teachings were transformed from abstract theology to religious dogma and secular law. Guilt, humiliation, and sin came to dominate society's understanding of sex and sexual desire, with lasting implications for Western culture and law.

But temptation is not easily conquered. The Church could define moral perfection, but it could not coerce man to attain it. How much did the Church's teachings on sex control the lives of ordinary people? The evidence suggests that many individuals in this era rejected the strict theological dictates against ordinary sexual practices and refused to believe that fornication and other run-of-the-mill sexual offenses would "doom perpetrators to eternal torment in hell."[53]

Moreover, despite the requirements of confession and penance, Church officials tended to be realists. They harangued the faithful about sexual sin and were sometimes vicious in their pursuit of sodomy (to the point of burning at the stake), but for the most part they turned a blind eye to such practices as prostitution, bawdy depictions of sex, early-term abortion, and masturbation.[54]

The medieval Church did not bring man to "perfection" in his sexual behavior, but what the Church did attain was a fundamental shift in the sexual beliefs, values, and practices of Western society. Perhaps the most effective dogma of medieval Christianity was its persistent and pervasive disparagement of sexual desire as something polluted and inherently evil. Ordinary men and women may not have grasped the subtle theological arguments and distinctions of Augustine and Aquinas, but they did come to understand that sex was shameful. As the eminent theological scholar John Colet preached at the end of the fifteenth century, all Christians must "strive after angelic chastity," for in their carnal acts "they show themselves in no way superior to the beasts."[55] The medieval Church's teachings left an indelible mark on Western attitudes and culture, shaping American law into the twenty-first century.

CHALLENGING THE ONE TRUE CHURCH

THE FOURTEENTH-CENTURY Italian poet Petrarch, whose discovery of Cicero's letters is often credited with initiating the Renaissance, insightfully predicted that the thousand years following the fall of Rome was merely a "temporary" age of darkness that would soon draw to a close. He expressed the hope that "this slumber of forgetfulness" would soon end and that man would once again "walk forward in the pure radiance of the past."[56]

In the fifteenth and sixteenth centuries, Europe experienced a new era of rapidly expanding population, burgeoning cities, an influx of wealth from the New World, and the centralization of national authority. Combined, these developments led to the rediscovery of classical science and culture and a rebirth of artistic, scientific, political, and literary creativity. Spurning scholastic theology, Renaissance humanists challenged the medieval Church's conception of man and his place in the universe. Men like Bacon, Descartes, Galileo, Copernicus, and Newton illuminated the sharp distinction between science and theology and opened up new worlds of understanding in mathematics, astronomy, and physics, many of which did not sit well with traditional Christian dogma.

The Reformation, which linked the renewal of human imagination to religious reform, was a natural outgrowth of the Renaissance. Protestant Reformers, led by Martin Luther, exercised the same spirit of questioning that had nurtured the Renaissance. The Reformation brought about significant changes in social, cultural, religious, and legal attitudes toward sex and shattered the authority of the one "true" Church of the Middle Ages.

Luther, a German friar, priest, and professor of theology at the University of Wittenberg, denounced the practices of the Church "in a rising crescendo of protest." Much of Luther's criticism came from deep within the very tradition he challenged. To Luther and his fellow Reformers, the Reformation called for a return to the truths of early Christianity and a rejection of what they deemed the grave distortions that had come to dominate the Church's teachings. Beginning in 1517, the Reformation sought to revive the intimate religious experience of early Christianity and to jettison "the ritualistic and institutional accretions" that the Reformers thought had warped Church dogma and practice over the centuries.[57]

The doctrine of clerical celibacy was a particular target of attack. Once a celibate priest himself, Luther proclaimed that marriage was not merely an uneasy compromise with human frailty, but a divinely inspired institution. He insisted that the doctrine of clerical celibacy "originates with the devil" and called for its abolition.[58]

Luther preached that when undertaken in conformity with the precepts of God, sex could and should be a positive experience: "Just as a gold vessel is ennobled when it is used as a container of a noble wine, and degraded when it is used as a container of excrement and filth, so our body (in this respect) is ordained to an honorable marriage." Sex was ordained by God, "through whose power . . . a natural, ardent desire for women is kindled and kept alive." Luther insisted that continence was unnatural, chastity was "dangerous," and sex was as "necessary to the nature of man as eating and drinking."[59]

T HE KEY for Luther was the connection between sex and marriage. Although sexual desire was natural, it could properly be fulfilled *only* in marriage. Like other Reformers, Luther was uncompromising in his condemnation of non-marital sex. In this sense, the Reformers remained true to the medieval Christian tradition. Within marriage, however, sex was permissible if it arose out of "a desire for children, or to avoid fornication, or to lighten and ease the cares and sadnesses of household affairs, or to endear each other."[60]

But given the availability of marriage, the Reformers insisted that there was no excuse for fornication, adultery, or prostitution. Marriage was "the remedy which God hath appointed" for sexual desire. Luther congratulated the newly married Nicholas Gerbel with these words: "You lucky man, that you have by an honorable marriage conquered that unclean celibacy which is reprehensible because it causes either a constant burning or unclean pollution." He applauded Gerbel for escaping that "most miserable celibacy" that "daily presents such great horrors." Because marriage enables "young men and women" to sate their natural impulses, it is "a paradise."[61]

The Reformers also rejected the medieval Church's view of contraception. Because Protestant theologians acknowledged a broad range of values in marital sex, including not only procreation, but also good health and pleasure, they viewed coitus interruptus and other methods of birth control as both moral and proper.[62]

D ESPITE THEIR doctrinal disagreements, Catholics and Protestants concurred in the vehemence of their condemnation of same-sex sex. This vehemence was presaged by the witch-hunt mentality toward sodomy that had developed during the Renaissance. In Venice, for example, the "sternest city in Italy," sodomites were often burned alive. Venice's extreme condemnation of sodomy, which included both male-male and male-female anal intercourse, was justified by invoking the biblical story of Sodom. As Venice officially proclaimed in 1458, God had "destroyed the whole world for such horrible sins," and it was therefore essential "to liberate our city from such a dangerous divine judgment." In an era in which plagues repeatedly ravaged Renaissance cities, people were terrified by fears of a Sodom-like punishment.[63]

A century later, both Catholics and Protestants invoked the destruction of Sodom to frame "the dominant social image" of anal sex. The sixteenth-century Spanish Catholic Antonio del Corro, who fled Spain to escape the Inquisition, described such behavior as so "filthy" that it could trigger the most "terrible judgments of the sovereign God," and Saint Peter Canisius, a venerated Jesuit Catholic priest, characterized sodomy as a vice so wicked that it "can never be sufficiently detested." Protestants similarly decried sodomy as "a sin so odious" that it "will fright the damned in the darksome Pit." Luther described it as a "heinous" departure "from the natural passion" of man and "altogether contrary to nature." Sodomy was deemed a sin so evil that "it was not God's creation." It was a part of the world of "shadow."[64]

Because both Catholics and Protestants fiercely condemned such behavior, charges of sodomy became a preferred weapon in their polemics against each other. In 1520, for example, Luther wrote Pope Leo X, "I have truly despised your see, the Roman Curia, which . . . neither you nor anyone else

The Execution of the Sodomites

can deny is more corrupt than . . . Sodom ever was." In *Against the Roman Papacy: An Institution of the Devil*, he depicted the governing body of the Catholic Church as an assembly of "catamites." The English Reformed bishop John Bale charged that Catholics "have burnt in their own lusts one to another, . . . that is to say monk with monk, nun with nun, friar with friar, and priest with priest, wrought filthiness." Such accusations were repeated endlessly by the Reformers. In the eyes of Protestants, the Catholic Church was doomed to the same fate as Sodom.[65]

T HE REFORMATION also triggered a pivotal shift in the relationship between religion and government. Before the Reformation, the Church assumed primary responsibility for enforcing compliance with Christian doctrine. Through the use of confession, penance, canon law, and ecclesiastical courts, the medieval Church aggressively ferreted out and punished sexual sin in an effort to coerce individuals to conform their behavior to the demands of Christian doctrine. Those who did not accept Christian beliefs on these matters might be damned, but for the most part they were free to do as they pleased, except for the most serious offenses, such as sodomy.

This changed as a result of the Reformation. Luther believed that faith, not right conduct, was the key to salvation. He insisted that the true Christian must therefore submit *voluntarily* to Christ's precepts. Coercion could not create faith, and right conduct compelled by fear of punishment rather than conscience could not bring redemption. Luther therefore rejected the idea that Reformation churches should attempt to coerce conformity to Christian doctrine. Such compulsion, he argued, was spiritually pointless.

In this respect, Luther emphasized a fundamental distinction between the secular and the spiritual. The state could legitimately punish those who violated the law in order to preserve the peace and good order of society. But the church could not legitimately coerce compliance with its precepts. Although Luther believed that coercion could not enable individuals to gain salvation, he nonetheless encouraged the state to prohibit and punish prostitution, fornication, adultery, and other sexual immoralities, explaining that if the state "wishes to be Christian" it should punish such behavior in order to maintain an orderly society.[66]

Over time, this element of Reformation thought came to play a critical role in legitimating the use of state authority to enforce religious doctrine. If the state "wishes to be Christian," it should enforce Christian values against *all* individuals, whether or not they adhere to the faith, not to ensure their salvation, but to preserve the "good order" of society. What had once been sins punishable by the medieval Church against the faithful were thus transformed by the Reformation into crimes punishable by the state, enforceable even against those who did not share the faith.

This marked a fundamental shift in the history of Western law, and it laid the foundation for many of the complex and often divisive legal and constitutional controversies that have captured the attention of both the American people and the United States Supreme Court over the course of our national history.

3

ENGLAND,
THE ENLIGHTENMENT,
AND "THE AGE OF EROS"

John Cleland's Memoirs of a Woman of Pleasure

AS ENLIGHTENMENT THINKERS in the seventeenth and eighteenth centuries aspired to liberate the pursuit of happiness, they posed fundamental questions about the interrelated concepts of God, reason, nature, and man. They posited that if man could learn to rely upon his reason rather than his faith, he could enter an age of unparalleled social, scientific, intellectual, political, and moral progress.

In this spirit, Enlightenment philosophers like Voltaire, Rousseau, and Diderot challenged traditional Christian beliefs about human sexuality. They maintained that sexual pleasure was not inherently sinful, but was an integral part of man's nature that should be celebrated rather than condemned. Their reasoning would ultimately have a profound impact not only on European culture, but on the American colonies as well, and on the values of those individuals who eventually would design the American Constitution.

The cultural practices, legal concepts, and sexual norms of England in this era had a special impact on the American colonies, and although we might tend to assume that the sexual practices of English society in the decades leading up to the American Revolution were rather staid and stodgy, it turns out that that assumption would be quite wrong.[1]

PURITANS AND LIBERTINES

UNTIL THE SIXTEENTH CENTURY, the Church of England acknowledged the authority of the Pope. But after Pope Clement VII refused in 1527 to annul the marriage of Henry VIII to Catherine of Aragon, Henry repudiated the authority of the Catholic Church. This split triggered a profound change in English life. Miracle-working relics and images were destroyed, priests were dispersed, confession was forbidden, and the power of priests to remit sins was "declared a pious fraud."[2]

Like other Protestant denominations, the Anglican Church rejected the Augustinian ideal of marital chastity. As "conjugal affection" became the ethical norm, English theologians explained that the purpose of marriage was not only procreation, but also to provide "mutual society, help and comfort," including sexual pleasure. Although sex outside of marriage was still deemed sinful, the realities of English life and law in the sixteenth, seventeenth, and eighteenth centuries were generally quite tolerant of such "sin."[3]

Indeed, the English common law took a rather relaxed approach to sex. Although the influential seventeenth century barrister and judge Sir Matthew Hale could confidently proclaim that Christianity was "parcel of the laws of England," most forms of sinful sex—including masturbation, mutual masturbation, oral sex, fornication, adultery, prostitution, and incest—were deemed beyond the purview of the common law courts. For the most part, the common law concerned itself with sexual activity only when it was undertaken in public, involved children or the use of force, or constituted "buggery" (anal intercourse) or bestiality.

Premarital sex was common in England throughout this era. Such behavior was often premised on a promise by the man to marry the woman, especially if she became pregnant. With such an understanding, sexual relations were generally regarded as "within" marriage and therefore not a violation of community norms. The typical promise was expressed by a dung-carrier to his lover, who "kissed his hand and clapt [it] into her hand and swore by his faith that if he got her with child he would marry her." As a consequence of this custom, half of all brides were pregnant upon marriage.[4]

T HE PURITANS were not pleased. A distinct group within the Church of England, the Puritans in the sixteenth and seventeenth centuries insisted that the Reformation had not gone far enough. The Puritans regarded themselves as "the godly." They sought to restore Christianity to the simplicity it had known in the days of the Apostles, demanded greater personal piety, and declared that the Church of England must be purified of any liturgy, ceremony, or practices not found in Scripture.

Among their many grievances, the Puritans criticized the common law courts for their lenient approach to sex. They proclaimed that the enforcement of sexual morals was a necessary and proper responsibility of the civil authorities. William Lambarde, a Puritan member of Parliament in the sixteenth century, insisted that the secular courts should take action against sexual miscreants, asserting that if people were "in adulterie, or fornication together," then the law should "carie them to prison." But this was not the law.[5]

This state of affairs changed for a brief period after the Puritan Revolution of 1650, when the Puritans, under Oliver Cromwell, took control of the British government and imposed severe "anti-pleasure principles" on the nation. They suppressed horse racing, stage plays, alehouses, and brothels, and the Rump Parliament passed an "Act for Suppressing the Detestable Sins of Incest, Adultery, and Fornication." This legislation authorized the death penalty for such sins. But the Puritan Revolution was short-lived, the law was rarely enforced, and it was repealed after only a few years with the Restoration of the monarchy.[6]

Almost from the moment of his return from exile in 1660, King Charles II, in direct defiance of the Puritans, set the tone of his court in terms of personal pleasure. The open pursuit of sexual liberty was now condoned in ways previously unknown. Charles himself had numerous mistresses, many of whom visited him by boats that conveniently docked just below the king's bedchamber. Bisexuality flourished in the Restoration court, abetted by the popular fads of cross-dressing, masquerade, and transvestism. Restoration eroticism celebrated pornography, which was used not only to arouse sexual desire, but also to shock the more staid elements of English society.

Sexual promiscuity became "a hallmark of fashion at court and in high political circles." It was expected that men of stature would keep a mistress, and in some instances they were advised to do so lest they be "ill looked down upon for want of doing so." Even wives openly committed adultery, which came to be "rather esteemed a fashionable vice than a crime."[7]

Restoration sexuality was daring, cynical, and naughty. A familiar symbol of the Restoration court was the "rake," a carefree, witty, sexually irrepressible aristocrat who combined libertinism with serious intellectual pursuits and patronage of the arts. The rake was typically depicted with an elegant, devil-may-care attitude, a twinkle in his eye, and a young woman on each arm.

John Wilmot, the second Earl of Rochester, was the "exemplar of the libertinism of the 1670s." Rochester composed satirical and bawdy poetry, for which he became the toast of the court. His infamous poem *Signior Dildo*, for example, told of how an Italian bride reluctantly surrendered "the vigor and discretion" of her dildo in order to wed the Duke of York. Rochester achieved renown not only for his naughty poetry, but also for his many mistresses and his casual "contempt for everything that others respect." In 1680, he described the twin maxims by which he lived his sexual life: "Do nothing to the hurt of any other" and pleasure ought "to be indulged as the gratification of our natural appetites." Rochester believed it "unreasonable to imagine" that these appetites had been "put into man only to be restrained," and he disdained as unnatural the traditional Christian value of sexual asceticism.*[8]

WITH INCREASED urbanization, prostitution in England became more common and more visible. By the late seventeenth century, prostitutes were openly plying their trade on the streets of London and in the many bawdy houses that had grown up around the city. It is estimated that one of every twenty women between the ages of fifteen and twenty-two was a prostitute, and men from all levels of society frequented prostitutes at least occasionally. Although Christian doctrine condemned such conduct, many people "came to believe that since nature, and presumably nature's God, had implanted sexual desire in human beings, it could not be that the pursuit of those desires was evil."[9]

In response to such openly sinful behavior, the Societies for the Reformation of Manners came into existence in London in the 1690s. Drawn primarily from the emerging middle class, these associations were dedicated to policing a city that seemed to have lost all sense of self-control. By 1740, however, the Societies collapsed for want of support, and London came to be known as "the Mecca of sexuality."[10]

Catalogues of the more fashionable prostitutes were now openly sold and circulated. Among the most successful was *Harris's List of Covent Garden Ladies.* Each entry in *Harris's* directory described the woman's age, height, eyes, hair color, complexion, legs, breasts, and social skills. Some entries described the woman's sexual preferences, whether she encouraged her clients to have multiple orgasms, and the size, appearance, and effects of her clitoris and vagina. All this was presented in the language of "romantic sensuality." Miss Lister's vagina, for example, was an "Elysian font in the centre of a black bewitching grove." Referring to her skill at fellatio, Miss Noble was said to have a tongue with "a double charm, both when speaking and when silent; for the tip of it, *properly applied,* can talk eloquently to the heart."[11]

---

* There were female as well as male libertines. Perhaps the most famous was Teresia Constantia Phillips. One of the most beautiful women of her generation, she was famous for her sexual liaisons with prominent men, her bigamy, and her autobiographical exposés.

. . .

THIS ERA of sexual permissiveness stimulated an increased demand for contraception. Exploiting this demand, a number of self-proclaimed experts, many of whom were quacks and charlatans, produced widely read publications on the subject. The most common method of contraception was coitus interruptus. Others included magic (for example, the woman spits in the mouth of a dead frog three times before intercourse), herbal potions (made, for example, from hemlock or poplar tree bark), pessaries, douches of rue and castor oil, sexual positions thought to prevent conception, exposing the womb to cold air after intercourse, sneezing heartily after intercourse (the woman), and abstinence at certain periods during the woman's menstrual cycle (an early form of the "rhythm" method). Some of these methods worked better than others.

The condom gradually came into use during this era. Gabriele Falloppio, the Italian anatomist and physician, first experimented with a linen condom in the mid-sixteenth century as a protection against syphilis. In the early eighteenth century, condoms began to be marketed and used specifically to prevent conception. By this time, most condoms were made either from sheep gut or fish skin. They were sold in brothels and by specialist wholesalers. Casanova raved that condoms could "put the fair sex under shelter from all fear."[12]

It is impossible to know how common abortion was in England in this era. Records suggest that abortion was particularly common among single and widowed women who sought to avoid the stigma and consequences of illegitimate births. But married women also used abortion to end unwanted pregnancies. As Lady Caroline Fox wrote her husband in the 1740s upon learning that she was pregnant for the third time in as many years, "I'm certainly breeding. I took a great deal of physic yesterday in hopes to send it away." Soon thereafter she wrote her husband that she had been successful, noting "is not that clever?"[13]

Women used a variety of means to achieve abortion, including bleedings, strenuous exercise, tight lacing, pessaries, and, as in Lady Caroline's case, herbal abortifacients. By the mid-eighteenth century, "female pills" were readily available in shops for the purpose of inducing abortion. The most popular of these, Dr. John Hooper's Female Pills, contained a high dose of iron in the form of ferrous sulphate. The leading competitors included Widow Welch's Female Pills, Fuller's Female Benedictine Pills, and Mr. Sherrat's Female Pills. At least some of these pills were effective, either by directly affecting the uterus or by mildly poisoning the pregnant woman.

Public attitudes toward abortion turned on the circumstances. The time of abortion was critical. Abortions before quickening—the moment in pregnancy when a woman first feels fetal movement, usually at around four-and-a-half months—were generally not regarded as immoral. The prevailing view was that the fetus was not "ensouled" until the fourth month. English medical texts reflected this view, and most people believed that abortion prior to quickening was not a sin. Women who used abortifacients before quickening usually described themselves as trying to bring on menstruation, rather than trying to abort. The common law regarded abortion as a crime, if at all, only after quickening.[14]

MOLLIES AND TRIBADES

SODOMY WAS NOT a crime in England until 1533, when Parliament first declared such conduct unlawful. The statute was enacted as part of Henry VIII's effort to assert royal prerogative against the papacy. Because sodomy had long been considered a clerical vice, the law gave Henry's agents a legal tool with which to harass the monasteries. Thus, largely for political reasons, what had previously been only a religious sin in England now became a crime against the state. The new prohibition was expressly defined in religious terms, though. The standard indictment accused the defendant of "being seduced by the Instigation of the Devil" and with committing "a Detestable and Abominable Sodomitical Sin" to "the great Displeasure of Almighty God." The offense was officially described as a crime "not to be named among Christians."[15]

The new law was not directed at same-sex sex. Rather, "sodomy" was understood to include buggery, whether between two men or between a man and a woman, and bestiality. As Sir Edward Coke, the greatest jurist of his time, explained early in the seventeenth century, the crime of sodomy required "penetration . . . either with mankind, or with beast." It did not forbid mutual masturbation or oral sex between men, nor did it prohibit any sex between women.[16]

Consensual anal intercourse was almost impossible to prove, because there were no offspring to explain, the act was almost invariably done in private, both participants could be punished by hanging, and neither was therefore likely to confess. As a consequence, prosecutions under the act were rare.[17]

• • •

IT WAS generally thought at this time that most individuals experienced sexual desire in varying degrees for people of both the same and the opposite sex. There was no sense of a distinctive "homosexual" identity. Indeed, the literary and theatrical image of the seventeenth-century sodomite was typically of "a young man-about-town, with his mistress on one arm and his 'catamite' on the other." Those who engaged in same-sex sex were assumed to be yielding to a temptation experienced in varying degrees by most people—like the temptation to masturbate or to engage in oral sex.[18]

This began to change in the final years of the seventeenth century. With the growth of the great cities of Europe, homosexual subcultures began to emerge that differed in both scale and behavior from those that had existed earlier. Homosexuals had always met surreptitiously, but now they met publicly "in the parks and the latrines, the public arcades and taverns" of Paris, Amsterdam, and London. Sir Simonds D'Ewes observed in his private diary that sodomy seemed so "frequent" in London that only a special divine dispensation could avert a Sodom-like retribution.[19]

The growing concern about sodomy was triggered in part by the establishment of dozens of "molly houses" in London in the late seventeenth century. Scattered along the area north of the Thames, the molly houses served as gathering places for men interested in same-sex sex. Some were in private homes, others in private rooms in public taverns. Those who frequented molly houses included men from all walks of life. The world of the molly house developed its own jargon, manners, and gestures, often of an effeminate nature, which became signals by which mollies could identify one another in other settings. Some mollies wore feminine clothes, used makeup, and adopted feminine nicknames. By 1700, as many as several thousand men in London thought of themselves as "mollies" (out of a population of approximately half-a-million). The openness and overt effeminacy of the mollies was something new.[20]

Journalists who reported on these activities scandalized the public with descriptions of extravagant effeminacy and transvestism. In May 1726, the London Journal reported, "We hear that 20 Houses have been discovered which entertained Sodomitical Clubs" at which "great numbers of these monsters . . . make their execrable bargains, and then withdraw into some dark corners to perpetrate their odious wickedness." These reports alarmed God-fearing, middle-class citizens, who viewed such behavior as threatening to the very foundations of civilization. Partly in response to "renewed warnings of imminent divine judgment on a sinful nation," the Societies for the Reformation of Manners declared the mollies a "blot upon . . . the new English supremacy in the world." The Reverend Thomas Bray, a leader of the Societies, characterized the molly houses as "an evil force invading our land."[21]

The Societies launched a vigorous campaign against the molly houses, resulting in the first mass arrests of homosexuals in English history. Conviction resulted in stiff fines, imprisonment, and sometimes "fatal manglings of the pillory." Soon thereafter, though, the raids on the molly houses ceased. This was apparently due at least in part to the realization that, like brothels, the mollie houses actually played a useful social function. By drawing the mollies off the streets, they shielded respectable society from their presence. Thus, as long as the mollies remained discreet, the better part of wisdom was to look the other way.[22]

Sexual relationships between women were also well known in this era. The word most often used to describe a female who sought sexual pleasure with other females was "tribade." Although not as pejorative as "sodomite," the term had negative connotations. But female same-sex sex was viewed much more leniently than sex between men. Indeed, in England in this era women were never prosecuted for same-sex relations. Rather, sex between women usually was "met with gossip and giggles rather than gallows and gibbets."[23] The idea of sex between women did not much concern the men who constructed religious and legal doctrine, because sex between females did not seem to them to be sex at all. The very concept of sex was deeply bound up with phallic penetration, so without a penis there was simply no "sex" to be had.[24]

SEXUAL LITERATURE: "PUNISHABLE ONLY IN THE SPIRITUAL COURT"

FROM THE EARLY NINETEENTH CENTURY to the present, moral and religious concerns over sexually-oriented expression have played a central role in legal and constitutional debates about freedom of speech in the United States. In ancient times, though, sexual explicitness in drama, poetry, art, and sculpture was not considered offensive, shameful, or harmful. Although Greece and Rome punished seditious, blasphemous, and heretical expression, they did not punish expression because it was "obscene."

After the rise of Christianity, censorship on religious grounds became more prevalent, but for more than a thousand years neither the Church nor the state censored sexual expression because it was thought to be obscene.

Indeed, the English language did not even have a definitive word for offensive sexual expression until the sixteenth century, and even then the word—"bawdy"—did not have a negative connotation. Bawdy ballads, poems, and plays might have offended some people, but they were not thought to present a problem appropriate for official intervention.[25]

In the Middle Ages, a wide range of sexually-explicit fables, or fabliaux, were shared with great joy in taverns, around campfires, and in castles. The fabliaux were short tales, usually in verse, frequently dealing with sex. Most often, they involved a man and a woman, not married to one another, and the woman's husband, who was cuckolded, and "usually deserved to be." The unmarried man was often a lusty priest or a member of the lower classes. The woman was typically portrayed as an unscrupulous, querulous, and shameless deceiver. The purpose of the fabliaux was to entertain, and the more ludicrous the sex, the greater the humor. The fabliaux freely employed profanity, pornography and scatology.[26]

Marie de France's late twelfth-century fabliau, *Another Story of a Woman and Her Paramour*, is a good illustration. A peasant "saw his wife going toward the woods with her lover." When she came home, he "upbraided" her. His wife, feigning astonishment, cried out, "I am dead! I shall die tomorrow, or perhaps today! It happened thus to my grandmother and to my mother." She then tearfully told her husband that in both of their cases, "a little before their deaths," a "young man was seen leading them, when no one was actually with them." Terrified, the gullible peasant swears that he had never seen a man with his wife and would "never speak a word . . . about it again." The moral of the fable is that women "have one more trick than the devil."

MORE SERIOUS works, such as Giovanni Boccaccio's *The Decameron* and Geoffrey Chaucer's *The Canterbury Tales*, both of which were published in the late fourteenth century, included a broad range of sexual stories. Boccaccio wrote *The Decameron* as the Black Death decimated Europe, killing a third of the population between 1348 and 1351. It opens with a bone-chilling description of the plague in Florence, which lost almost 80 percent of its inhabitants. Ignorance of the cause (a disease transmitted by fleas carried by rats) deepened the public's sense of horror. To most people, the only possible explanation was divine wrath and, as with the Flood, it seemed that God once again intended the virtual extermination of mankind.

Against this backdrop, Boccaccio presents a merry group of seven ladies and three young men who gather at an elegant villa outside Naples to idly pass the time while the plague (hopefully) passes. Every day for ten days each of the companions tells a story, so that *The Decameron* comprises a total of one hundred witty, tragic, heroic, and often licentious tales of the human condition. Roughly a third of the stories are bawdy, dealing with adultery, incest, *ménages à trois*, sodomy, mistaken identity, same-sex sex, masturbation and, as was common in this era, the sexual misadventures of priests and nuns.[27]

In "Ninth Day, Second Story," for example, a beautiful young nun, Isabetta, falls in love with a young man and they arrange to meet secretly in her cell "to their mutual delight." The other nuns in the convent who see the young lover sneaking out of Isabetta's cell knock loudly at the Abbess's door so she can catch Isabetta in the act. Unbeknownst to the nuns, the Abbess has in her room a priest "whom she often had brought to her bedroom in a chest."

Flustered by the racket, the Abbess dresses hurriedly and puts on her head not her nun's veil, but the priest's pants. The nuns and the Abbess rush off to Isabetta's cell in such a fluster that no one notices the Abbess's headgear. After the Abbess finds Isabetta and her lover "in each other's arms," she accuses Isabetta of jeopardizing the good name of the convent and threatens her with terrible punishments.

Isabetta, however, notices what the Abbess has "on her head, with suspenders dangling on either side." After she politely calls attention to the sight, the Abbess changes her tone, declaring that "everyone there should enjoy herself whenever possible, provided that it be done . . . discreetly." And thus "the Abbess went back to sleep with her priest, and Isabetta with her lover; and . . . the other nuns, without lovers, sought their solace secretly in the best way they knew how."[28]

In *The Canterbury Tales*, Chaucer turned both the French fabliaux and *The Decameron* to his own ends. One of the epic works of world literature, *The Canterbury Tales* tells of thirty pilgrims who journey from London to Canterbury to visit the shrine of Saint Thomas Becket. To pass the time, the pilgrims, from all levels of society, tell stories that are full of humor, shrewdness, and insight. They reveal much about human nature, and they are often wickedly bawdy.

In "The Merchant's Tale," for example, two lovers have intercourse in a pear tree, while the wife's jealous and blind husband stands below, waiting for her to drop pears from the tree. In "The Reeve's Tale," two Cambridge students end up "swiving" a mother and daughter in the same room. In "The Miller's Tale," which is generally regarded as one of the finest examples of bawdy comedy ever written, Nicholas, a clever young scholar, tricks John, a "wealthy lout," into enabling him to make love to his wife.[29]

TWO CENTURIES later, the Renaissance produced its own share of sexually-explicit literature. The most influential author of erotic writings during this era was Pietro Aretino, an Italian poet and satirist who was one of the most versatile writers of the sixteenth century. Aretino's *Ragionamenti*, written in about 1535 in Venice, is a serious work of comedy that mocked the pretensions of Renaissance society.[30]

In *The School of Whoredom*, a part of *Ragionamenti*, Nanna, an experienced whore, passes on to her eager young daughter, Pippa, the tricks of the trade. Like any mother, Nanna wants the best for her daughter. She teaches Pippa that their chosen profession is an art whose skills must be mastered. In one scene, Nanna explains to Pippa how her patron "will begin fondling your tits, shoving his entire face in as if to drink from them, and then he'll slide his hands down your body, little by little, to reach your little cunt. After a few little pats, he'll start feeling your thighs, and since your buttocks act like a magnet, they'll soon draw his hand." The ultimate lesson was that for the pleasure of anal sex, the patron would eagerly pay a substantial premium.[31]

BY THE sixteenth century, the English Crown came to be increasingly concerned about the dangers of unrestrained publication, which had been made possible by Johannes Gutenberg's invention of the printing press. In 1557, the Crown incorporated the Stationers' Company "for the protection of . . . readers of books." The royal charter declared it unlawful for any person to set up a printing press without a license and empowered the Stationers' Company to seize and burn any book published without a license and to order the imprisonment of any person who published a book without its imprimatur. But the state at this time still had no interest in obscenity. It authorized the denial of licenses only for books that were seditious, blasphemous, or heretical.[32]

This indifference to sexually-explicit expression reflected then-prevailing standards. The Elizabethans delighted in "coarse and robust humor."[33] In the latter part of Elizabeth's reign, however, the Puritans began demanding a stricter set of sexual standards. In 1580, the Puritan leader William Lambarde drafted a bill to restrain "licentious" publications. Lambarde's bill would have prohibited the publication of "books, pamphlets, songs and other works" intended to promote the "art of making lascivious ungodly

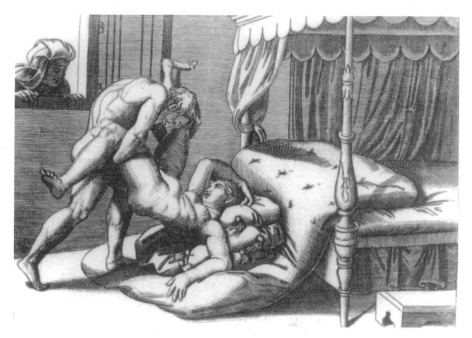

Pietro Aretino's Ragionamenti *(1535)*

love." Lambarde argued that such publications triggered "the high displeasure of God" and encouraged the "corruption of common life and manners." The bill reflected the growing discomfort of moralists with the rapid spread of erotic material. But Lambarde's proposal was rejected by the Elizabethan parliament.[34]

I T WAS not until 1708 that England experienced its first obscenity prosecution. James Read, a printer, was charged with publishing *The Fifteen Plagues of a Maiden-Head*, a lengthy poem that related the frustration of a maiden who was desperate to lose her virginity:

O! stroke my Breasts, those Mountains of Delight,
Your very Touch would fire an Anchorite;*
Next let your Palm a little stray,

---

* Anchorites were mystics in medieval Europe who chose to leave society to live completely isolated and ascetic lives.

And dip thy Fingers in the milky way:
Then having raiz'd me, let me gently fall,
Love's Trumpets found, so Mortal have at all. . . .
Poor Pris'ners may, I see, have Mercy shewn,
And Shipwreck'd Men may sometimes have the Luck
To see their dismal Tempests overblown,
But I poor Virgin never shall be *Focked*. . . .[35]

The Queen's Bench Court found that this publication created "no offense at common law." As the court explained, "This is for printing bawdy stuff. . . . It is stuff not fit to be mentioned publicly. . . . [But there] is no law to punish it. . . . It indeed tends to the corruption of good manners, but that is not sufficient for us to punish." The court dismissed the indictment, holding that "writing an obscene book . . . is not indictable, but punishable only in the Spiritual Court."[36]

MEMOIRS OF A WOMAN OF PLEASURE

ENGLISH LAW FIRST punished an obscene publication in 1727 in the case of *Rex v. Curll*.[37] The dispute involved Edmund Curll, one of the most notorious rascals of his day. In the rumble-tumble world of eighteenth-century publishing, in which piracy and plagiarism were the order of the day, Curll was "conspicuous as a beast of prey."[38]

In 1724, Curll published *Venus in the Cloister: or, the Nun in her Smock*, an English translation of a French anti-Catholic tract. The story begins with a scene of voyeurism, as the nun Angelica spies through a keyhole as Sister Agnes masturbates. Later, Angelica watches as her own lover, a monk, has sex with another nun. More than fifty sex aids are used in the convent by everyone from the Abbess to the youngest nun. Most of the story is in the form of a dialogue among the nuns:

ANGELIQUE: Oh! Let me look at you uncovered. . . . Kneel down on the couch. . . .
AGNES: Well, have you gazed enough at the outrage of this innocent? Oh God! How you handle it! . . . What, you kiss it? . . .
AGNES: (spanking Angelique): Do you know that this portion of you is growing ever more lovely? A certain fire animates it. . . . I will never tire of looking at it. I see everything I desire right up to your

naturehood. Why do you hide that part with your hand?
ANGELIQUE: Oh, dear, you can examine it as well as the result. . . .[39]

Several months after he published *Venus in the Cloister*, Curll was indicted. His counsel argued that the *Read* decision had definitively established that the publication of a pornographic work was not punishable under the common law. The three justices were divided. Justice Fortescue voted to reaffirm *Read*, concluding that although the publication of *Venus in the Cloister* "is a great offense" to public morals, there is no "law by which we can punish it." Justice Reynolds disagreed. He conceded that "there may be many instances where acts of immorality are of spiritual cognizance only," but argued that this is not one of them. Justice Probyn, who cast the deciding vote, opined that Curll's publication was "punishable at common law, as an offense against the peace, in tending to weaken the bonds of civil society, virtue, and morality." As punishment, the court imposed a modest fine.[40]

DESPITE A rapidly growing proliferation of sexually-explicit writings and the precedent of Curll's case, obscenity prosecutions remained extremely rare in eighteenth-century England. *The Toast*, a satirical work attributed to William King, published in 1736, has been described as one of the most pornographic "works ever printed." Although it contained detailed descriptions of the sexual adventures of a hermaphrodite, it was not prosecuted.[41]

English readers in the eighteenth century had ready access not only to pornographic works of fiction, but also to a constant stream of sexually-explicit poems, whore catalogues, prints, and anti-Catholic and antigovernment tracts. Although pornography initially served primarily as a form of entertainment and sexual stimulation, during the Enlightenment it gradually became a "vehicle of protest against the authority of Church and State, and finally against middle-class morality."[42]

Spurred by a growing interest in previously unexplored issues of human sexuality, as well as the opportunity to make a fast buck, English writers produced a slew of "sex guides." The most successful of these, *Aristotle's Masterpiece*, which purported to be written by Aristotle, went through some thirty editions between 1684 and 1790. Another influential quasi–medical book, *Rare Verities: The Cabinet of Venus Unlocked*, by Giovanni Benedetto Sinibaldi, offered its "amorous readers" engrossing descriptions of lustful maids and addressed such issues as sex-change, how to enlarge one's pudenda, and how to lengthen or shorten one's "Yard."

Other popular subjects in eighteenth-century "non-fiction" sexual literature included techniques of masturbation, dildos, and flagellation. Among the more famous examples of such titillating works were *Historia flagellantilum*, which purported to be a historical survey of flagellation in nunneries and monasteries; *Monsieur Thing's Origin*, which traced the amorous adventures of a dildo; and, most famously, *Onania; or, The Heinous Sin of Self-Pollution, and All its Frightful Consequences, in Both Sexes, Considered*, which popularized the misleading use of the word "onanism" as a synonym for masturbation.[43]

As illustrated by *Venus in the Cloister*, many pornographic works in this era were barely disguised anti-Catholic tracts. Typically set in monasteries or convents, these writings depicted the real or imagined sexual adventures of monks and nuns.[44] Gervaise de Latouche's *History of Dom Bougre*, published in English in 1743, described the hero's nocturnal orgies with monks and nuns:

> Sometimes I was put on a bench, completely naked; one Sister placed herself astride my throat in such a way that my chin was hidden in her pubic hair, another one put herself on my belly, a third one, who was on my thighs, tried to introduce my prick into her cunt; two others again were placed at my sides so that I could hold a cunt in each hand; and finally another one, who possessed the nicest breast, was at my head, and bending forward, she pushed my face between her bubbies; all of them were naked, all rubbed themselves, all discharged; my thighs, my belly, my chest, my prick, everything was wet, I floated while fucking.[45]

Pornography was also used to pillory the nobility. In 1771, for example, Charles Théveneau de Morande, a French expatriate living in London, published *Le Gazetier cuirassé*, which skewered Louis XV and his mistress, Madame du Barry. Morande chronicled in exquisite detail du Barry's alleged lesbian relations with her maids, her career as a prostitute, and her seduction by a monk. Marie Antoinette suffered similar treatment. *L'orgie royale*, published in London in 1789, depicts Louis XVI asleep on a sofa while Marie Antoinette has sex beside him with the Comte d'Artois and the Duchesse de Poignac. Scandalmongers and popular pornographers filled the pages of such eighteenth-century English periodicals as *The Bon Ton*,

The Covent Garden, and *The Rambler* with licentious tales about foreign dignitaries and the English aristocracy.[46]

O NE OF the most important literary developments of the mid-eighteenth century was the appearance of the novel. Early novels, such as Daniel Defoe's *Moll Flanders,* Samuel Richardson's *Clarissa,* Tobias Smollett's *The Adventures of Roderick Random,* Henry Fielding's *Tom Jones,* and Laurence Sterne's *Tristram Shandy,* all dealt playfully with such themes as seduction, adultery, voyeurism, incest, and fornication. The illustrations for these novels often emphasized the erotic facets of the work. By the mid-eighteenth century, one critic could complain that this new literary form was marked by "extreme indecency" and undue emphasis on "fornication and adultery." The increasing popularity of sexuality in the novel coincided with a growing demand for realism and the Enlightenment's challenge to traditional Christian beliefs about sex.[47]

The foremost example of mid-eighteenth-century pornography was John Cleland's *Memoirs of a Woman of Pleasure,* which came to be known by the name of its heroine, Fanny Hill. First published in England in 1748, *Memoirs* employs the familiar plot of the innocent country girl who comes to London and enjoys a series of amorous adventures, which in Fanny's case involved masturbation, lesbianism, fetishism, group sex, sadomasochism, and flagellation. Literary historians speculate that Cleland made a bet with friends that he could "write the 'dirtiest' book in the English language without using a single 'dirty' word."[48]

Cleland was arraigned before the Privy Council for writing an obscene book. He pleaded poverty as an excuse. Reflecting the prevailing attitude of the time, the President of the Council, the Earl of Granville, resolved the prosecution by awarding Cleland a pension of £100 a year on condition that he not repeat the offense. *Memoirs* went on to become the most successful pornographic work of the eighteenth century. Unfortunately for Cleland, he had sold the copyright to a publisher for a mere £20.[49]

As Cleland's case illustrates, through the late eighteenth century English law yielded nothing conclusive about the concept of literary obscenity. There was no agreed-upon definition of the term, no rationale for its regulation, and only sporadic skirmishes over the issue. Throughout this era, neither influential citizens nor government officials made any concerted effort to curb the proliferation of erotica. By the 1780s, when the United States was contemplating its Constitution, London was awash in all sorts of sexually-explicit material. At this critical moment in American history, English law was largely silent on the issue of obscenity.[50]

"THE AGE OF EROS"

SEX FIGURED PROMINENTLY in eighteenth-century culture. Societies dedicated to the celebration of libertinism sprang up in England throughout the century. In the 1750s, for example, Sir Francis Dashwood founded a libertine club at Medmenham Abbey. Its members—including such prominent persons as the Prince of Wales, the Earl of Queensberry, John Wilkes, and the son of the Archbishop of Canterbury—dressed as monks and participated in secret rituals. Accompanied by their mistresses and prostitutes, the members of the Medmenham Society entered the abbey under the Society's motto, inscribed over the entrance—*Fay ce que voudras*—"Do as you wish."[51]

Sexual flagellation was a particular libertine fascination, especially among the upper class. Most scholars believe that the interest in flagellation derived from the use of flogging in schools as a form of discipline—a practice that apparently had unexpectedly erotic connotations. Eighteenth-century pornography glorified spanking and whipping, and there were even brothels that specialized in flagellation. Mrs. Theresa Berkley ran a house where patrons could be whipped, beaten, stuck with pins, and mounted on the "Berkley Horse"—a special rack for whipping. Business was so brisk that she was able to retire after only eight years.[52]

Libertinism reached its apogee in the writings of the Marquis de Sade, who explored fetishism, bestiality, buggery, analingus, necrophilia, masochism, and, of course, what came to be known as sadism. Sade's works brought together "reason, eroticism, libertine pleasure, and a disdain of emotional passion." In unleashing pain and even bodily mutilation as means of producing "an ecstasy of sexual pleasure," Sade's "narrativization of sexual fantasies knew no bounds."[53]

At the core of libertinism was an emphatic repudiation of Christian doctrine. The libertines rejected the view that the denial of pleasure is natural and actively pursued their beliefs not only in their sexual behavior, but also in more serious pursuits. The Dilettanti Society, for example, was founded in 1732 by libertines who were particularly interested in the sexual values and practices of the ancient world. The Society helped fund several archaeological expeditions, and Sir William Harcourt's discovery of ancient amulets in the shape of male genitals gave proof to the belief

Flagellation

that classical cultures had radically different conceptions of sex than those preached by Christianity. Based in part on these findings, Richard Payne Knight published *Discourse on the Worship of Priapus*, which revealed that the religions of the classical world had been distorted over the centuries by Christian scholars. Knight correctly observed that such amulets and other archaeological discoveries reflected a world that was "intensely sexual" and that "worshipped the powers of generation and creation."[54]

THE SEXUAL freedom advocated by the libertines reflected and reinforced important changes in eighteenth-century society. Those changes were the product of many factors, including dramatic advances during the Enlightenment in the fields of history, anthropology, philosophy, and biology; the emergence of secularism; the growth of a literate middle class with an interest in rationalism and scientific inquiry; and the impact of eye-opening discoveries about the very non-Christian attitudes toward sex that were prevalent in such places as India, Tahiti, and China.[55]

Gradually, these influences led to a new vision of sexuality. Enlightenment *philosophes* redefined sex not as sinful, but as an "agent of progress, order and happiness."[56] Rejecting the extreme views of both the Puritans and the libertines, the *philosophes* attempted to articulate a new understanding of sex rooted in rationality and in the belief that man has a natural and inalienable right to the pursuit of happiness.

A loose coalition of political theorists, cultural critics, and religious skeptics in Europe and colonial America, the *philosophes* pursued an ambitious program of "secularism, humanity, cosmopolitanism, and freedom, above all, freedom in its many forms—freedom from arbitrary power, freedom of speech, freedom of trade, freedom to realize one's talents, freedom of aesthetic response, freedom, in a word, of moral man to make his own way in the world." In 1784, near the end of this era, Immanuel Kant opined that the central theme of the Enlightenment was "*Sapere aude*—'Dare to know.'"[57]

Such thinkers as Locke, Hume, Voltaire, Bentham, Diderot, and Kant critically scrutinized what they regarded as deeply ingrained spheres of "ignorance and 'prejudice.'" Dedicated to the power of reason, they challenged the dictates of traditional Christianity. Voltaire dismissed Christianity "as miserable, vicious, and backward." The *philosophes* saw the classical Greeks as the exemplars of human civilization and credited them with creating a robust "spirit of inquiry." With the triumph of Christianity, however, that spirit had died. In Condorcet's words, Christianity feared the "spirit of investigation," and under the authority of the Church, curiosity became heresy. The *philosophes* charged that Christianity's "central myth was incredible" and that its sacred book was "an incoherent collection of primitive tales." They dismissed Christianity as nothing more than the irrational "product of men's fears," and Rousseau declared that a "revolution was necessary to bring men back to common sense."[58]

A MONG THEIR many challenges to Christianity, the *philosophes* contested Christian sexual doctrines as arbitrary restrictions "imposed upon man in his ignorance." They insisted that sexual pleasure was presumptively good, rather than sinful, and advocated a positive appreciation of sensuality. Diderot wrote that Christianity had "attached the labels 'vice' and 'virtue' to actions that are completely independent of morality." Invoking reason to challenge "morality based on religious dogma," Voltaire asserted that it is natural to seek pleasure and that passion is "good in itself." Baron d'Holbach, a French-German philosopher who was prominent in the French Enlightenment, added that "most of the precepts" that Christianity prescribes are "ridiculous," and that to "prohibit men their passions is to forbid them to be men." The *philosophes* sought to reassert the naturalness of sexuality and to "celebrate it as an integral and praiseworthy part of man's nature."[59]

"Free love" was much debated during the Enlightenment, and the frank discussion of sex was seen as a healthy part of interpersonal relations. Mary Wollstonecraft, an English writer, philosopher, and advocate of women's rights, encouraged the "unreserved discussion" of sexuality and urged individuals to "speak of the organs of generation as freely as we mention our eyes or our hands." During the Enlightenment, "freedom was as much a project as an idea," and the practice of sexual liberty was one of constant reinvention.[60]

But the *philosophes*, unlike the libertines, did not advocate unrestrained "sexual liberty." Although Diderot mocked the Christian view of sex and insisted that the sexual impulse was natural, he did not define "natural" as "without boundaries." Rather, he suggested that "to know what is good and evil" individuals must judge the effects of their conduct on their "personal welfare and the public good." The *philosophes* therefore attempted to redefine acceptable sexual conduct by seeking "rational rules to guide it."[61]

T HE WIDESPREAD writing about sex in this era led to "a sort of downward osmosis" through which an upper-class philosophy was gradually absorbed by the larger culture.[62] As the English historian Peter Wagner has observed, the "age of Enlightenment" might properly be termed "the age of Eros." With the collapse of the Puritan ethic and the gradual secularization of society, a new ethic emerged—an ethic that included the embrace of sexual pleasure.[63]

By the 1770s, sexually titillating novels, following the example of *Memoirs of a Woman of Pleasure*, had become increasingly popular, newspapers openly advertised sexual services, and sexually-explicit prints and sex manuals were readily available in London shops. Dildos and other sex aids were routinely imported from abroad, and men of sufficient means could even order life-size dolls for their sexual enjoyment.

Sex therapy also became popular. Its most famous exponent was James Graham, who lectured to large and often "fashionable crowds about the invigorating properties of happy sexuality" and provided guidance as to how sex could be made more exciting and more enjoyable. Among the techniques he advocated was the use of pornography to arouse the passions. Graham's famous "celestial bed," which he guaranteed would intensify sexual pleasure, attracted a steady stream of couples willing to pay £50 for a night between its sheets.*[64] Though moralists worried that the loosening of sexual standards might undermine the moral fiber of the nation, the authorities made no serious effort to curb this newfound sexual freedom.[65]

E NLIGHTENMENT SEXUALITY had clearly defined limits, however. Enlightenment attitudes toward female sexuality, for example, were clearly ambivalent. On the one hand, the *philosophes* rejected the traditional Christian belief that women were carnal temptresses. On the other hand, Enlightenment-era men generally did not treat women, or their sexuality, with equal respect. A wife was expected to be a virgin on her wedding night and faithful thereafter; a husband was expected to have gained sexual experience before marriage, and his wife was expected to overlook his infidelities. Women who were openly sexual, such as Harriette Wilson, who had relations with the Prince of Wales and four future prime ministers, and Con Phillips, who wrote scandalous memoirs that detailed her many affairs, tended to be denigrated as "wantons and whores." Although in theory the Enlightenment accepted women as "intelligent and rational creatures," misogyny was deeply ingrained in Western culture and many men still saw women "as men's playthings."[66]

Enlightenment tolerance also did not extend to same-sex sex. Even during the Enlightenment, most people continued to regard sodomy as repugnant, although prosecutions were rare and punishments generally mild.[67] The *philosophes* themselves were divided on the regulation of same-sex sex. Although they universally rejected the burning of homosexuals as barbaric, most regarded same-sex sex as unnatural. Some Enlightenment thinkers, however, had qualms about prohibiting same-sex sex. Montesquieu, for example, noted with some concern the similarities between laws against sodomy and laws against witchcraft. But only Condorcet, the

---

* Twelve feet long and nine feet wide, the celestial bed was "supported by forty pillars of brilliant glass" and covered by a "super-celestial dome" on which "brilliant plates of looking-glass" reflected "the happy couple" in the bed below. According to Graham, "The intenseness of the pleasure that is enjoyed in performing the venereal act, under the full influences of the combined electrical fire in my celestial bed!" is so great that "the entranced pair," no "longer inhabitants of this world, . . . are launched upon oceans of extacy!" Peter Otto, *James Graham as Spiritual Libertine*, in *Libertine Enlightenment* 204, 209–13 (Peter Cryle & Lisa O'Connell eds., Palgrave 2003).

eighteenth-century French philosopher and political scientist, went so far as to suggest that consensual sodomy "cannot be part of the criminal law" because it "does not violate the rights of anyone."[68]

Lesbians fared much better during the Enlightenment than male homosexuals.* The difference in attitudes toward male and female same-sex sex was evident in the reception of John Cleland's *Memoirs of a Woman of Pleasure*. The work's depictions of same-sex sex between women caused hardly a ripple, but Fanny's description of buggery triggered Cleland's prosecution and was expurgated from virtually all subsequent editions for almost two centuries.[69]

P ERHAPS SURPRISINGLY, it was during the Enlightenment that masturbation first became a source of serious public anxiety. Until the eighteenth century, the public attached little significance to masturbation. Even the medieval Church treated it leniently. But the anonymous publication in 1708 of *Onania; or, The Heinous Sin of Self Pollution*, changed all that. A best-selling work throughout the eighteenth century, *Onania* warned that male masturbation caused "*Stranguaries, priapisms* . . . fainting fits and epilepsies . . . consumptions . . . excessive seminal emissions, a weakness in the *penis*, and a loss of erection."[70]

In 1758, S. A. D. Tissot published an influential monograph that explained that masturbation affects females in much the way it affects males, but in addition causes fits of hysteria, incurable jaundice, violent cramps, pains in the nose, and uterine tremors that deprive women of decency and reason. Other experts maintained that female masturbation causes nymphomania. It was thus in this era that "the dread figure of the nymphomaniac began to loom large" in the public imagination and the "age of masturbatory" anxiety first burst upon the Western world.[71]

Despite these anomalies, though, most people, especially those of the upper class, embraced the sexual openness of the Enlightenment as a major step forward from the days when sex was abomination and self-denial was the path to salvation. This profound change in attitude would eventually make itself felt in the American colonies and would shape the views of those who wrote and ratified the United States Constitution.

But before we get too far ahead of ourselves, we must turn back the clock and cross the Atlantic—as did the Puritans.

---

* The word "lesbian" first appeared in 1736 in William King's *The Toast*, a satirical attack on the Duchess of Newburgh.

PART II

FOUNDERS

4

FROM PURITANISM TO THE PURSUIT OF HAPPINESS

Puritans

THOSE WHO MIGRATED to the New World had many reasons for doing so. Almost all of the early colonists came to improve their economic conditions, but those who settled in New England had strong religious reasons as well. The Puritans, in particular, sought to create close-knit religious communities, centered on the family and the church, which would serve as models of moral order. By contrast, those drawn to the Chesapeake colonies of Virginia and Maryland had more varied backgrounds and brought no overriding religious or moral mission.[1]

The Puritans "had a fearsome interest in controlling social deviancy." Their penal systems emphasized retribution, humiliation, and shame. Because they did not have long-term prisons, incarceration was a temporary measure, intended to detain an individual for only a short period. As an alternative, the Puritans lopped off ears and sentenced offenders to "wear letters, suffer branding, be whipped, and be subjected to the stocks."[2] Execution was the prescribed penalty for serious offenses, including blasphemy, sodomy, murder, adultery, and witchcraft.

Religion played a central role in the promulgation of the Puritan legal codes. As the Reverend John Davenport observed in 1669, "The Law of Nature is God's law, written as with a pen of iron and the point of a diamond." The Puritans injected a fierce religious fervor into the English common law tradition. To the Puritans, the only proper laws were "divine ordinances, revealed in the pages of Holy Writ and administered according to the Word of God."[3]

In 1636, "Moses, His Judicials," prepared by John Cotton and Nathaniel Ward, provided that any person "shall be put to death" who "shall have or worship any other God, but the Lord God," or if he or she "be a Witch," or "shall blaspheme the Name of God," or "committeth adultery." These laws were drawn from specific biblical passages, which were expressly cited in the judicials as the source of secular authority.[4] The Puritans, in a stark departure from English common law traditions, declared it the duty of secular courts to enforce religious principles. The 1656 "Lawes of Government" of New Haven, for example, charged the colony's court with ensuring "the purity of Religion" and expressly declared that "the Supreme power of making Lawes . . . belongs to God only" and that "Civill . . . Courts . . . are the Ministers of God. . . ."[5]

Over time, and under the influence of the Enlightenment, the idea of higher law in the American colonies became more secular, and this view gradually led both to a more permissive sexual culture and to the principles of the emerging conception of American constitutional law.[6]

But we begin with the Puritans, who injected a deeply religious element into American law that continues to shape our constitutional battles even now, in the twenty-first century.

THE PURITAN WAY

THE VOYAGE OF the *Mayflower* in 1620 took sixty-five perilous days. The 102 Pilgrims suffered through storms, seasickness, disease, and miserable living conditions in order to reach the New World. Unlike the noblemen, craftsmen, and adventurers who had founded Jamestown in Virginia fifteen years earlier, the Pilgrims traveled as intact families. They knew that more than 80 percent of those who had settled Jamestown had died of disease, starvation, or Indian attack, often "in the most bloody manner."[7] The Pilgrims were willing to endure all this in order to escape the dictates of England's state church and what they saw as the evil corruptions of England's increasingly sexualized culture.

Like all Puritans, those on the *Mayflower* believed that the Church of England had to be purged of its failings. But the Pilgrims were Puritans "with a vengeance." Rather than attempting to change the Church of England from within, they fled to Holland in 1608, and then set out from there to the New World in "the conviction that God" wanted them to go.[8]

John Winthrop, the first governor of Massachusetts Bay Colony, made clear to those who undertook this journey that they had entered into a new covenant with God. He explained that under this covenant, if they succeeded in establishing "a due forme of Government," they would be rewarded, but if they failed, if they embraced "this present world and prosecute[d] our carnall intencions," God would "surely breake out in wrathe against us." Winthrop had no doubt about what he meant by a "due forme of Government." It would be dedicated to suppressing sin and saving "men from their own depravity."[9]

The mission of those Puritans who ventured across the Atlantic was not merely to escape persecution, but to establish "a Citty upon a Hill," so that "the eies of all people are uppon us." The goal was to become "a story and a by-word through the world," so all the world would want to follow their example.[10]

T HE PURITANS who arrived in America were certain they could find the rule for any situation in the Scriptures. They "regarded the Bible as a complete guide to Christian living," and in their efforts to shape the world to those strictures they could be "positively ferocious." For the Puritans, it was not enough not to be sinful. As the Puritan leader Thomas Hooker explained in 1654, the true believer must actively seek to destroy all sources of temptation: "What ever sins come within his reach, he labors the removal of them." In short, "a zealous enforcement of morality on others" was essential.[11]

This insistence on imposing moral behavior on others was necessary to ensure that God would bestow prosperity on the community and not destroy it, as he had Sodom and Gomorrah. Puritanism was therefore ruthless in inflicting its will upon "dissenters and those whom it judged sinners." To the Puritans, intolerance of contrary beliefs was not only justified, but mandatory.[12]

T HE PURITANS, at least early on, lived simple and austere lives based on the principle that excessive leisure was a sin. On the other hand, the Puritans could be quite earthy in their sexual relations within marriage. Puritan ministers rejected the idea that sex was "inherently dangerous or evil" and scorned "the 'popish' advocacy of a . . . celibate life." "Conjugal love," wrote the pastor Samuel Willard, should be expressed through "conjugal union," through which husband and wife "become one flesh."[13]

Although the Puritans accepted sexual desire within marriage, they condemned it in any other context as "unclean." They carefully policed sexual behavior in order to channel it into its only "proper setting and purpose—as a duty and a joy within marriage." This was central to the Puritan code. If there was one sin the Puritans had in mind when "they proclaimed that

Whipping Sinners

man was inherently depraved and tainted by original sin," it was the sin of sex outside of marriage. Anyone who challenged this norm could expect severe, often public punishment. As the legal historian William Nelson has observed, the Puritans "equated crime with sin and thought of the state as the arm of God on earth."[14]

The Massachusetts Code of 1648 authorized judges to do what English judges of the time would not do: punish fornication by fine, corporal punishment, or an order to marry, according to what was "most agreeable to the word of God." Adultery, sodomy, and bestiality were capital offenses. Intercourse between a married man and a single woman was defined as mere fornication, whereas intercourse between a married woman and a man (single or married) was deemed the much more serious offense of adultery. The image of strict Puritan judges humiliating those who transgressed the community's religious definitions of crime, popularized by such works as Nathaniel Hawthorne's *The Scarlet Letter*, was well-grounded in fact.[15]

. . .

ALTHOUGH PURITAN ministers preached that all forms of non-marital sex "endangered the souls of the perpetrators," they reserved their strongest condemnations for sodomy. Cotton Mather, the leading Puritan minister in Massachusetts at the turn of the eighteenth century, declared that sodomitical acts were "vile . . . abominations" that must be punished "with death, without mercy." Other Puritan leaders decried sodomy as "unnatural filthiness."[16] In his sermon, "The Cry of Sodom," published in 1674, the Reverend Samuel Danforth condemned the "crying sin" of Sodom and warned that "God executeth dreadful Vengeance" for such "grievous Wickedness" and that the "Land cannot be cleansed, until it hath spued out this Unclean Beast."[17]

As in England at the time, the Puritan prohibition of "sodomy" did not focus on same-sex sex. Rather, it banned anal penetration (of either a man or a woman) or penetrative bestiality (involving either a man or a woman). The prohibition did not cover non-penetrative same-sex sex or sex between women. So defined, prosecutions for sodomy were rare, and there was only one execution for sodomy (not involving bestiality) in Puritan New England.[18]

Because the early colonies were rural, bestiality was a particular concern. Samuel Danforth, the minister at Roxbury, Massachusetts, characterized bestiality as an "abominable confusion in the sight of God" that "pollute[d] the very beast," making it "unworthy to live among beasts."[19] Indeed, the Puritans believed that the mating of humans and animals could produce monstrous offspring. They therefore punished not only the human, but the beast as well. In one instance, New Haven judges convicted George Spencer to death for bestiality on the basis of evidence that he had a deformed eye that resembled that of a piglet born with "butt one eye in the middle of his face."[20]

FROM THE outset, the Puritans were confident that in their own insular communities, far removed from the corruptions of the Old World, they could enforce their strict moral laws, even though others before them had failed. As it turned out, though, despite severe penalties and aggressive efforts to ferret out sexual transgressions, the Puritans could not stamp out sexual sin. As early as 1642, William Bradford, the governor of Plymouth Plantation, bemoaned the colony's failure to "suppress the breaking out of sundrie notorious sins." In 1662, the Puritan minister Michael Wigglesworth complained that the Creator would be appalled to learn what had happened to the Puritans: "If these be they, how is it that I find instead of holiness Carnality?"[21]

When the Puritans first journeyed to the New World, they expected other godly people to follow. What they did not anticipate was that future waves of emigration would bring to New England a flood of "lusty Elizabethan Englishmen." As William Bradford complained, the influx of these "wicked persons and profane people" radically changed the culture for those who had come "for religion's sake." By 1640, "the number of unregenerate" who had crossed the ocean to settle in New England outnumbered the Puritans.[22]

As the children and grandchildren of the early Puritans were exposed to the later arrivals, they tended to gravitate toward the company of the sinners. By the 1660s, clerical jeremiads routinely castigated the people for defaulting on the Puritan covenant with God. Their failures ran the gamut, from heresy, Sabbath-breaking, and lying (especially in commercial dealings), to sexual transgression. The clergy accused women of throwing "temptation in the way of befuddled men," complained that the "bastardy rate was rising," and bewailed the fact that prostitution—already rampant in London and much of continental Europe—had established a foothold even in staid Boston.[23]

By this time, New England's rapidly growing towns and seaports had become breeding grounds for "all manner of dissipation." Sailors waiting for their "next voyage were eager to pleasure themselves, and the wives of absent seamen were often happy to oblige." The small port of Charlestown, Massachusetts, had several "disorderly" houses for all sorts of "wanton practices." In 1672, after Alice Thomas was convicted of "giving frequent, secret and unreasonable Entertainment in her house to Lewd Lascivious and Notorious persons of both Sexes," and "giving them opportunity to commit carnall wickedness," the Massachusetts General Court lamented that "the sin of Whoredom and Uncleanness grows amongst us."[24]

Although the Puritans aggressively punished every breach of the laws of God, often quite brutally, in the end it was a losing battle. By the late seventeenth century, the hopes of the Puritan colonists had been shattered. As the process of declension set in, and as succeeding generations proved they could not live up to the high moral standards set by the original colonists, the lamentations of the authorities intensified. In 1684, Increase Mather, a prominent Puritan minister who served as President of Harvard College, observed that "things look at this day with a dark and dismal face." The Puritans had originally declared adultery a capital offense, but the punishment proved too severe for the crime and the crime too common for the punishment. A sense of resignation settled over the Puritan communities, and the quest for moral purity gradually dissipated.[25]

By the late seventeenth century even such publications as *Venus in the Cloister*; *Scoggin's Jests*, which emphasized vulgar and scatological humor; *The London Jilt*, which featured bawdy tales of London prostitutes; and the pornographic poems of the Earl of Rochester had made their way from Europe into the bookshops of Boston. The availability of such works both reflected and affected cultural values. By bringing sexuality into the open and exciting the sexual imagination, such publications helped to transform and, in the eyes of the Puritans, erode moral standards.[26]

For all practical purposes, the Salem witch trials of 1692 marked the end of the Puritan experiment in the New World. As the historian Kai Erikson has observed, by that time the Puritans were "no longer participants in a great adventure, no longer residents of a 'city upon a hill,' no longer members of that special . . . elite who were destined to bend the course of history according to God's own word. They were only themselves, living alone in a remote corner of the world, and this seemed a modest end for a crusade which had begun with such high expectations."[27]

"LIFE'S PLEASURES" IN EIGHTEENTH-CENTURY NEW ENGLAND

THE TWENTIETH-CENTURY HISTORIAN Crane Brinton once quipped that in the sexual realm we now permit "much that the nineteenth century forbade," but whether we have yet returned "to eighteenth-century standards is a nice point for critical discussion." Indeed, by the eighteenth century, most colonists held increasingly permissive views about many of "life's pleasures." They tended to view those who deviated from traditional moral standards "with a mixture of tolerance, amusement, and titillation." For most eighteenth-century Americans, sexual freedom was not the offense it was to either their seventeenth-century forebears or their nineteenth-century descendants.[28]

By the beginning of the eighteenth century, profound changes had transformed New England from a remote Puritan outpost into an economically and socially sophisticated part of the British Empire. This transformation had important implications for the definition of sexual mores and for the regulation of sexual behavior. As the Puritans were assimilated into the increasingly diverse New England community, their rigid views of sexual morality began to fade, and as the commercial interests of the region became more central to everyday life, the legal system shifted its focus away from the preservation of morals and toward what came to be seen as more pressing commercial and economic concerns. Moreover, the growing influence of Enlightenment ideas about religion, morality, and reason deepened the already ongoing secularization of New England society. As the colonists embraced a spirit of independence and revolutionary change and were emboldened by Enlightenment rhetoric about "the pursuit of happiness," they felt freer than ever to assert their personal liberty.[29]

T HIS IS not to say that eighteenth-century New Englanders embraced a libertine attitude toward sex. As in England, the ideal of marriage remained central to both religious and community norms, and as the legal system withdrew from the enforcement of strict Puritan sexual morals, new social mechanisms arose to moderate the impact of change.[30] This was particularly true during the Great Awakening of the 1730s and 1740s, when evangelical ministers traveled from town to town in an effort to reawaken spirituality. These preachers attacked what they saw as the licentious elements in society. Jonathan Edwards, for example, a leading voice in the Great Awakening, preached against "lewd practices" and the "breakings out of gross sins; fornication in particular."[31]

Edwards and his fellow evangelicals preached that salvation occurred through the outpouring of God's grace in what they termed a spiritual "New Birth." They urged "born again" men and women, called "New Lights," to challenge state authority in matters of faith and sin. But although the Great Awakening was a "transforming event in the religious history of colonial America," it soon burned itself out, and as the eighteenth century progressed even the evangelical congregations abandoned their fervent condemnation of sexual lapses.[32]

By the time of the American Revolution, New Englanders had stopped using the criminal law to prosecute most forms of consensual sex. Although sodomy remained on the books as a capital crime in New England throughout the eighteenth century, and although New England newspapers routinely characterized such conduct as "detestable," "abominable," and "atrocious," there were no convictions for consensual adult sodomy in New England in the entire eighteenth century. Neither the people nor the authorities thought that same-sex sex between consenting adults, however troubling morally, was an appropriate matter for legal intervention.[33]

Indeed, the image of the "fop" was familiar to eighteenth-century New Englanders. Several of the most popular novels of the era included descriptions of men engaged in sodomitical pursuits. Tobias Smollett's *The Adventures of Roderick Random*, for example, included a character, Earl Strutwell, who was "notorious for a passion for his own sex." Thus, although such conduct was certainly not condoned, it tended to be viewed as a mere "social" offense.[34]

SEX IN THE CAROLINAS, THE CHESAPEAKE, AND THE MID-ATLANTIC COLONIES

OF COURSE, THE American colonies were not limited to New England. The Carolinas, for example, presented a radically different picture from Puritan New England. In 1711, the Anglican minister John Urmston described the settlers of North and South Carolina as "loose, dissolute, and scandalous," and Charles Woodmason, another Anglican minister, characterized the Carolinas as a den of "debauchery" in which polygamy was "common," "concubinage general," and "bastardy no disrepute." He charged that the residents of the Carolinas lived "in Concubinage" freely "swopping their wives." They had no shame, "for Nakedness is not censurable or indecent here, and they expose themselves often quite Naked." Woodmason decried the region's "licentiousness," "lasciviousness," and "lewdness."[35]

Religion had little influence over the "wild, sparsely settled and ill-governed expanses of early Carolinas." Many of the Southern clergy were adventurers who had obtained their ordination under doubtful circumstances. In the backcountry, where even such questionable ministers were in short supply, men and women tended to pass from one cohabiting relationship to another with no regard for the formalities or constraints of marriage. It was not so much that these settlers were rampantly promiscuous, but that they practiced a rather high level of informality in defining their sexual and personal relations, which tended to be serially monogamous. They neither married nor divorced in any conventional sense, and when a couple did formally wed, the bride was usually "visibly pregnant."[36]

Southern ministers, legislators, and magistrates occasionally tried to impose traditional marital and sexual standards upon these communities, but usually to no avail. The ministers were too few and the law too weak to have much effect. In 1790, a bill was introduced in the North Carolina assembly to prohibit the sins of adultery, incest, and polygamy, but the law that was enacted prohibited only polygamy. That was all the moralists could push through the state legislature.[37]

Between New England and the backcountry of the Carolinas were the

Mid-Atlantic and Chesapeake colonies. These colonies had laws prohibiting fornication, adultery, and sodomy, but they were quite lax in their prosecution of private sexual transgressions. From the beginning of the eighteenth century, New York, New Jersey, and Pennsylvania almost never punished consensual sexual offenses, and although Maryland and Virginia sometimes punished adulterers in the early 1700s, their use of the criminal law for that purpose soon waned. There were occasional complaints in the Chesapeake colonies that the laws against sexual immorality were too rarely enforced, but they fell on deaf ears.[38]

"AN AMAZING VARIETY OF EROTICA"

AS IN ENGLAND at this time, colonial bookstores in the eighteenth century contained an "amazing variety of erotica." Although they could not quite replicate the breadth or depth of the stock of their London counterparts, Americans could find pretty much whatever they wanted. Cultural and political leaders like Thomas Jefferson and Benjamin Franklin collected many of these works. Jefferson counted among his library Boccaccio's *The Decameron*, several bawdy Restoration plays, and Charles Johnstone's *Chrysal*, which portrayed vivid scenes of sexuality, lust, and sexual scandal. When Robert Skipwith asked Jefferson for advice about a future library, Jefferson recommended 379 volumes, including a number of erotic works by Vanbrugh, Le Sage, Smollett, Fielding, and Sterne.[39]

In a less literary vein, a broad range of bawdy humor was sold by hawkers throughout the colonies, and sexually-explicit anti-papist tracts were especially popular. Purported medical books on procreation, midwifery, venereal disease, and masturbation served as a widely available form of pornography, as did several versions of *Aristotle's Masterpiece*. Other works available in colonial bookshops included such erotic fiction as *Venus in the Cloister*, *The London Jilt; or, The Politick Whore*, and *Letters of an Italian Nun and an English Gentleman*. In short, eighteenth-century Americans had access to "all the erotica their European contemporaries were reading."[40]

There were no prosecutions for obscenity during the entire colonial era. All of the colonies had laws against blasphemy and heresy, but "sexual materials not having an antireligious aspect" were left alone. The first true obscenity prosecution in the United States did not occur until well into the nineteenth century. Throughout the colonial era, the distribution, exhibition, and possession of pornographic material was not thought to be any of the state's business.[41]

THE CITY OF BROTHERLY LOVE

ONE OF THE MOST exciting ventures in the middle colonies was William Penn's effort to establish a community in which respect for religious
freedom would serve as an example of "enlightened government for the
world." Penn pledged that all who agreed "to live peaceably and justly
in civil society" would "in no ways, be molested or prejudiced . . . in
matters of faith and worship." Although the colony suffered occasionally
from sectarian squabbling, Penn's experiment ultimately proved a success, as Philadelphia grew to become a central crossroads of the American colonies.[42]

By the time of the American Revolution, Philadelphia was North America's most cosmopolitan and most ethnically and religiously diverse city. A
robust and intellectually vibrant community, Philadelphia boasted some of
the continent's first libraries, medical schools, and philosophical societies. It
embodied the spirit of the Enlightenment and became the cultural, social,
political, economic, and intellectual center of eighteenth-century American
thought.

The sexual culture of eighteenth-century Philadelphia was renowned
"for its lack of restraint." Premarital sex, adulterous affairs, and casual sex
were commonplace. The city swarmed with young men and women who
flocked to Philadelphia in search of work, opportunity, and excitement.
The new arrivals were eager to experience the personal freedom made
possible by urban life in a community dedicated to the pursuit of individual liberty.[43]

As in London, the anonymity of urban life made sexual transgression
easy, and both premarital and extramarital sex became more common.
Between 1767 and 1776, approximately one-third of all brides were pregnant at marriage and, as one commentator observed, husbands and wives
who were "inclined to cheat on their spouses found ample opportunity to
do so." Visitors to Philadelphia described the city as sexually open. Moreau
de Saint-Méry, an aristocratic Frenchman who spent several years in Philadelphia, observed that Philadelphians had embraced a culture of unbridled
sexuality, and Gottlieb Mittelberger, a German schoolteacher, reported
that premarital sex was routine and that fornication was no longer of any
interest to the authorities.[44]

The prevalence of casual sexual relations in the late eighteenth century reflected a new culture of individual freedom. As Philadelphians cast
off the bonds of traditional morality, the "pursuit of happiness" became

central to everyday life. As in London at the time, prostitution was commonplace. One visitor observed that the "prostitutes in Philadelphia are so many that they flood the streets at night." In 1784, *The Philadelphiad* described a Philadelphia house of prostitution "as a central and recognized institution of the city."[45]

Tales of prostitutes were common in pamphlets, plays, songs, almanacs, and broadsides, which presented prostitution as a pervasive and accepted part of life. This is not to say that prostitution raised no hackles among Philadelphia's moralists. As the most visible aspect of the city's sexual culture, prostitution provoked frequent objections on the grounds that it created disorder, threatened the institution of marriage, undermined the community's moral fiber, and exploited fallen women. The latter concern was particularly potent. One visitor observed that it was usually women "without sure means of subsistence" who turned to prostitution, particularly "the wives of seafaring men," married women whose husbands had abandoned them, women whose husbands had died in the Revolution, and single women who lacked other means of support. For many of these women, the turn to prostitution led to a "descent into infirmity."[46]

The more staid members of Philadelphia's governing elite lamented these developments. The minister of Philadelphia's oldest church derided the "licentious manners" of his fellow Philadelphians and condemned as "pernicious" their approach to "matrimonial affairs." But there was never any organized effort to shut down Philadelphia's open sexual culture. As the historian Clare Lyons has observed, social, cultural, and political changes in Philadelphia in the 1760s and 1770s legitimated the "pursuit of happiness" as an essential facet of individual freedom.[47]

Like fornication, adultery, and prostitution, sodomy was unlawful but never prosecuted. In the "live and let live" atmosphere of late eighteenth-century Philadelphia, the authorities never raided taverns that openly welcomed same-sex intimacy or policed sodomy in any way. This was not because Philadelphians were unaware of same-sex sex. To the contrary, by midcentury, Philadelphia booksellers were offering for sale a broad range of works dealing with same-sex sex, including sex between women.[48]

Philadelphia maintained its cultural ties with Europe in part through the importation of books, including those of an erotic nature. Philadelphia booksellers hawked such popular European works as *Venus in the Cloister, The English Rogue, The London-Bawd,* and *The Illustrious French Lovers.* After midcentury, the subject of sex was an increasingly frequent topic of locally produced poems, songs, pamphlets, and plays. Almanacs printed in Phila-

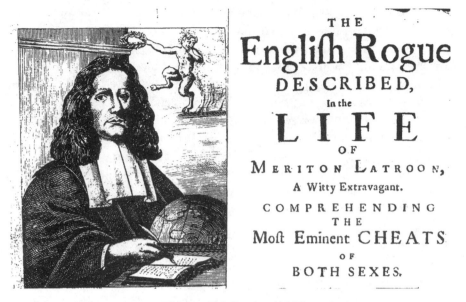

The English Rogue *(1666)*

delphia between 1750 and 1775 regularly included items addressing seduction, premarital sex, adultery, and prostitution. *Father Abraham's Almanack* was in the vanguard in publishing tales of sexual intrigue. Such pieces as "Written to a Friend after a Debauch" and "Of the Pleasures of Libertines" depicted a permissive and freewheeling attitude toward sex and introduced readers to the new "urban pleasure culture."[49]

The significant shifts in sexual attitudes and openness in Philadelphia were in part a reflection of the larger effort to put Enlightenment ideas about the pursuit of happiness into action. In the struggle to redefine the traditional relationships of individuals to one another and to the state and to give meaning to the Enlightenment ideals of liberty and equality, issues of sexual freedom took on new political meaning. In a profound shift away from early colonial thought, the Declaration of Independence, reflecting the values and norms of the Enlightenment, boldly proclaimed in 1776 that the proper end of government is not the restraint of sin, but "the pursuit of happiness."

NONE OF this is to suggest that by the time of the American Revolution the colonists had embraced a form of rampant libertinism. To the contrary, few if any of the American colonists lived their lives according to the precepts of the Earl of Rochester. At the same time, though, the colonists had clearly and emphatically rejected the values of the Puritans. Their attitude toward sex was thus neither libertine nor Puritan. They regarded sex as a natural part of human life and as an essential element of individual freedom, and they therefore abandoned the use of the criminal law to enforce moral and religious sexual norms. But the vast majority of the colonists still lived their sexual lives in a restrained manner without a wholesale abandonment of traditional moral values.

A good example of the colonists' approach to sex was the practice of "bundling." The easing of sexual standards in the eighteenth century posed a challenge to parents who wanted to protect their unwed daughters from the consequences of pregnancy. Even in a society with increasing sexual freedom, most parents remained committed to protecting their daughters "from the personal tragedy of seduction and abandonment." This concern was heightened by the advent of a new form of "seduction literature," which emphasized the perils of premarital sex. Most of these cautionary tales featured "ruined" maidens who had been seduced by charming young men and then abandoned to face their plight alone. In the usual scenario, the young woman wound up pregnant, homeless, destitute, and degraded. Often, she had to resort to prostitution to support herself and her child.[50]

In a highly pragmatic response to this concern, the parents of daughters often allowed young unmarried couples to sleep together in their homes. In this way, the girl's parents would be in a much better position to monitor the relationship and to hold the young man accountable should their daughter get pregnant. This practice, known as "bundling," assumed that the courting couple would either remain clothed or separated in bed by a "bundling board." The high rate of premarital pregnancy in this era, however, suggests that these safeguards were often evaded.[51]

WE MUST GUARD AGAINST "OUR OWN . . . LICENTIOUSNESS"

THE EIGHT LONG YEARS of the Revolutionary War had a profound impact on the new nation. During the war, social disruption, personal mobility, economic and military hardship, the presence of an occupying army, and long absences between loved ones affected most aspects of society. The stresses and dislocations of wartime, combined with the challenges to traditional authority embodied in both Enlightenment thought and Revolutionary republican philosophy, deepened the quest for personal autonomy and loosened still further the conventional bounds of sexual behavior. All of the trends in sexual attitudes and conduct that had begun before the Revolution were accelerated as the realities of the war set in.[52]

The late eighteenth-century trend toward greater sexual freedom was reinforced by the Revolution-era belief that in a free society, individuals had a right to personal autonomy, even in their sexual lives. Although this belief was consistent with the ideals of personal freedom embodied in the American Revolution, it was also in tension with those ideals. Republican philosophy held that "a virtuous people would be guided by rational thought and concern for the common good." In a free and self-governing society, citizens have to restrain their personal desires and act with an abiding sense of reason. Greater sexual freedom was thus seen as both an expression of American Revolutionary values and a threat to those values.

The political elite of Revolutionary America were confident that they could balance individual freedom with individual responsibility, but some of the nation's leaders feared that the common man, who was uneducated and had "less fully developed mental capacities," would not be able to handle this degree of personal liberty. Benjamin Rush—a social reformer, educator, and physician in Philadelphia—worried, for example, that if freedom and the responsibility of self-governance were thrust too quickly onto the people, the experiment in American self-government was destined to fail.[53]

After the nation had won its independence, Rush warned that the American people must still learn "to guard against the effects of our own ignorance and licentiousness." He cautioned that sexual excess, especially among the lower classes, would have "a pernicious influence upon morals, and thereby prepare our country for misery." He urged Americans to "awaken at last to check the vice which taints the atmosphere" of our nation in order to prevent sexual license from undermining "the rest of society." "The American war is over," Rush declared, "but this is far from being the case with the American Revolution."[54]

5

THE WORLD OF THE FRAMERS

A Christian Nation?

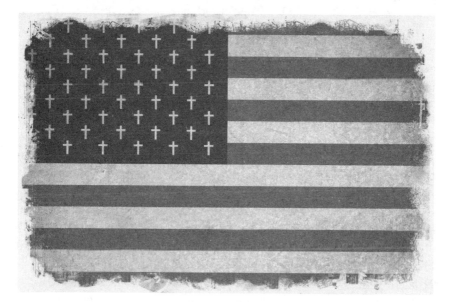

ODERN-DAY EVANGELICAL CHRISTIANS often assert that
the United States was founded as a "Christian nation," but
that in recent decades out-of-control secularists have broken
faith with our religious traditions.[1] This claim has played an
important role in contemporary debates about both the appropriate role of
religion in the formation of public policy and the proper understanding and
interpretation of the Constitution—especially with respect to such controversial issues as contraception, obscenity, abortion, sodomy, and same-sex
marriage.

To what extent is this claim true? What did the Framers of our Constitution think about religion, in general, and Christianity, in particular?
Presumably, their views about such matters should help inform our understanding of the proper meaning and interpretation of the Constitution, perhaps especially on issues relating to the regulation of sex.

In the generations leading up to the American Revolution, traditional
sources of religious authority were increasingly called into question. A new
and exciting sense of freedom was in the air. Under the influence of Enlightenment ideals, the American colonists created a bold new conception of
freedom, a conception that involved new understandings of religion, man,
rights, and the state. With the Declaration of Independence, these new
understandings became the foundation of the American political tradition,
a tradition that "was born in the full illumination of the Enlightenment."[2]

Thomas Paine reminded Americans that they had boldly thrown off
the prejudices of the Old Order and had embraced a new, enlightened, and
more rational conception of man: "We see with other eyes; we hear with
other ears; and think with other thoughts, than those we formerly used."
The ignorance and superstition of the Old World, he declared, had finally
been expelled, and the "mind once enlightened cannot again become dark."[3]

Against this background, was the United States in fact founded as a "Christian nation"?

"NOT IN AN AGE OF FAITH, BUT IN AN AGE OF REASON"

THE PURITANS ESTABLISHED rigidly theocratic societies. Their churches defined the word of God, and citizenship was tied directly to religious faith. The Puritans "meant for only godly Christians to rule." They surely meant to establish a "Christian state." But their vision of the New World shattered, and the Revolutionary era was a period of serious decline not only for the Puritans, but for traditional Christianity more generally. By the time the Framers began drafting the United States Constitution in Philadelphia in 1787, formal church membership had declined to the point where only between 10 and 20 percent of all Americans were affiliated with a church. Evangelicalism, as defined and understood by its modern exponents, played at most a "negligible role in the founding era."[4]

In an enlightened age, even the authority of God "was not immune to challenge." In an era that emphasized nature and reason more than faith and revelation, Americans no longer accepted the strict Puritan emphasis on "the absolutism of the Old Testament's Jehovah," and many of the nation's founders went far beyond that in questioning the continuing relevance of traditional Christianity.[5]

The United States was conceived "not in an Age of Faith . . . but in an Age of Reason." The Framers were highly critical of what they saw as Christianity's excesses and superstitions. They believed that people should be free to seek truth through the use of "reason and the dictates of their consciences," and they concluded that a secular state, "supporting no religion, but protecting all, best served that end."[6]

It is no accident that, unlike the Fundamental Orders of Connecticut, the United States Constitution cited as its ultimate source of authority not "the word of God," but "We the People." The goal of the Framers, in short, was not to create a "Christian nation." To the contrary, the Constitution expressly prohibited the use of any religious test for holding office, and the First Amendment made clear that there "would be no Church of the United States" and that the United States would not "represent itself to the world" as a Christian nation. Indeed, from the Declaration of Independence through the adoption of the Bill of Rights, no one of any consequence referred to the United States as "a Christian nation."[7]

. . .

UNLIKE THE later French Revolution, though, the American Revolution was not a revolution *against* Christianity. The most influential thinkers in pre-Revolutionary France, including Voltaire, Montesquieu, Diderot, and d'Holbach, sharply repudiated Christianity. In the words of Voltaire, "Every sensible man . . . must hold the Christian sect in horror."[8] Most of the Founding Fathers in the United States, however, attended church at least occasionally and identified at least to some degree with one or another of the Christian denominations. But as men of the Enlightenment, few of the founders put much stock in traditional Christianity. Indeed, many of the leaders of the Revolutionary generation were not Christians in any conventional sense. They were broad-minded skeptics who viewed religious passion as divisive and irrational, and who consistently challenged, both publicly and privately, traditional Christian dogma.[9]

The most important religious trend of the mid-eighteenth century— the belief in deism, or rational religion—had a profound influence on the founding generation. Deism has its roots in ancient Greek philosophy, but its influence on Revolution-era Americans is usually traced to a series of British writers in the late seventeenth and early eighteenth centuries. The rationalist philosopher John Toland, for example, argued that in order to be credible, a religion must be logical and it must be consistent with the laws of nature. Thomas Woolston, a theologian trained in the Anglican church, challenged the doctrine of miracles, concluding that the New Testament's account of Jesus' miracles was "broken, elliptical and absurd." And the essayist Matthew Tindal charged in 1730 that revealed theology was nothing more than wishful thinking and irrational superstition.[10]

The deists were not necessarily atheists. Although they challenged the beliefs of Christianity (and of other religions) that they could not reconcile with reason, most accepted the idea of a Supreme Being. But the deists' God was not the Judeo-Christian Deity, who intervenes in human affairs and listens to personal prayers, but a more distant, impersonal force of nature whom the deists referred to as the "Creator," the "First Cause," the "Grand Architect," and "Nature's God."[11]

The deists believed that the Supreme Being who created the universe, including the laws of nature, was a benign God, that the Creator had revealed both its existence and its nature in the laws of nature, and that it had given man the capacity to understand those laws through the exercise of reason. Most deists did not accept the divinity of Jesus, the truth of miracles or revelation, or the doctrines of original sin or predestination. They rejected these concepts as "antithetical to the dictates of reason" and argued that such doctrines had "not only kept mankind in the shackles of superstition and ignorance," but also "insulted the majesty and dignity of God." Most deists believed that people had no need to read the Bible, pray, be baptized or circumcised, attend church, or conform to any of what they regarded as the irrational beliefs and practices of Christianity—or any religion.[12]

Of course, there were more radical and less radical versions of deism. Some deists flatly rejected Christianity; others regarded themselves as Enlightened Christians. The more radical deists maintained that Christianity had wielded a dangerous moral influence on humanity by convincing people that they were tainted by original sin, a belief that often fostered self-loathing at the expense of self-improvement. Because they saw Christianity as historically intolerant and repressive, they viewed it as a fundamental impediment to human progress.

More moderate deists shared an abiding confidence in man's inherent goodness, believed in the potential for progress through reason, rejected miracles and revelation as tall tales, mistrusted the sacraments and the clergy, believed in man's obligation to live a moral life (as defined by reason rather than by Scripture), and believed in a benevolent but impersonal Creator who ruled from the distant past through the immutable laws of nature.[13]

Deism had a powerful effect on the colonists. Many of our Founding Fathers, including Thomas Paine, Thomas Jefferson, Benjamin Franklin, Ethan Allen, and Gouverneur Morris, were deists, and many others, including John Adams, James Madison, Alexander Hamilton, James Monroe, and George Washington, were at least partial deists who accepted most elements of the deist critique of Christianity.[14]

As the historian Frank Lambert has noted, the significance of deism for the creation of the United States "can hardly be overstated." From roughly 1725 to 1810, deistic beliefs played a central role in the framing of the American republic. The founding generation viewed religion, and particularly religion's relation to government, through an Enlightenment lens that was deeply skeptical of orthodox Christianity.[15]

Of course, not all of the Founding Fathers were deists. Many, like Patrick Henry, Samuel Adams, John Jay, and Elias Boudinot, were traditional Christians. But it is instructive to consider some of those who were, in varying degrees, influenced by deism, including Benjamin Franklin, Thomas Jefferson, John Adams, George Washington, and Thomas Paine, because they played a central role in defining the values, aspirations, and understandings of the American republic.[16]

FRANKLIN: A "THOROUGH DEIST"

BENJAMIN FRANKLIN WAS the embodiment of the American Enlightenment. He had "a deep dislike of religious enthusiasm," and as he made clear in his *Autobiography*, he was a "thorough Deist." Franklin dismissed much of Christian doctrine as simply "unintelligible," and he was quite critical of how Christianity had affected mankind:

> If we look back into history for the character of the present sects in Christianity, we shall find few that have not in their turns been persecutors, and complainers of persecution. The primitive Christians thought persecution extremely wrong in the Pagans, but practiced it on one another. The first Protestants of the Church of England blamed persecution in the Romanish church, but practiced it against the Puritans. These found it wrong in the Bishops, but fell into the same practice themselves."[17]

Only days before his death in 1790, in response to an inquiry about his religious beliefs, Franklin replied: "Here is my Creed. I believe in one God, the Creator of the Universe: That he governs the World by his Providence. That he ought to be worshiped. That the most acceptable Service we can render to him, is doing good to his other Children." These, he added, are "the fundamental Principles of all sound Religion."[18]

With respect to Jesus, Franklin observed, "I think the System of morals & his religion, as he left them to us, the best the World ever saw, or is likely to see; but I apprehend it has received various corrupting changes." Turning to the question of Jesus' divinity, Franklin wryly concluded near the end of his life: "I have . . . some Doubts as to his Divinity: tho' it is a Question I do not dogmatize upon, having never studied it, & think it needless to busy myself with it now, when I expect soon an Opportunity of knowing the Truth with less Trouble."[19]

Like most deists who rejected the doctrines of original sin and predestination, Franklin believed in a deity who "delights" in man's pursuit of virtuous behavior, which Franklin defined as "the Knowledge of our *true Interest*; that is, of what is best to be done in all the Circumstances of Humane Life, in order to arrive at our main End in View, HAPPINESS." In Franklin's opinion, man achieves happiness by satisfying his own needs and by promoting the well-being of his fellow men. He believed that for man to pursue his own happiness pleases the Creator, because a truly benevolent deity "delights in the Happiness of those he has created."

Franklin believed that people serve God best not when they obey dogmas and profess belief in miracles, but when they perform good works on behalf of humanity. He faulted Christianity for not being "more productive of good works than I have generally seen it: I mean real good works, works of kindness, charity, mercy, and public spirit; not holiday-keeping, sermon-reading or hearing, performing church ceremonies, or making long prayers filled with flatteries and compliments."[20]

Franklin regarded all religions as more or less interchangeable in their most fundamental tenets, which he believed required men to pursue their own happiness and to treat others with kindness and respect. He regarded Jesus as a wise moral philosopher, but not necessarily as a divine or divinely inspired figure, and he had no particular use for Christian doctrine insofar as it departed from the core teachings of Jesus. A longtime friend despaired "that a man of Franklin's "general good character and great influence" was such "an unbeliever in Christianity."[21]

JEFFERSON: A "DELIRIA OF CRAZY IMAGINATIONS"

NO MEMBER OF the founding generation "embodied America's democratic ideals . . . more than Thomas Jefferson." "The principles of Jefferson," said Abraham Lincoln, "are the definitions and axioms of free society." Like Franklin, Jefferson was a true Enlightenment *philosophe*. A thoroughgoing skeptic, Jefferson "subjected every religious tradition, including his own, to scientific scrutiny." He had little patience for talk of miracles, revelation, or resurrection. Jefferson saw his age as a unique opportunity for man to push back the forces of darkness and to unleash man's reason in order to comprehend the true order of the universe.[22]

Jefferson, who spent five years in Paris in the 1780s, shared the confidence of Diderot, Voltaire, and the other French *philosophes* that the universe was comprehensible and that in the long run the application of reason would reveal its mysteries. On the subject of religion, Jefferson cautioned his nephew, Peter Carr, to "shake off all the fears & servile prejudices under which weak minds are servilely crouched." He urged Carr to "question with

Thomas Jefferson

boldness even the existence of a god; because, if there be one, he must more approve of the homage of reason, than that of blindfolded fear."[23]

Like Franklin, Jefferson admired Jesus as a moral philosopher. He wrote John Adams that the moral beliefs espoused by Jesus reflected "the most sublime and benevolent code of morals which has ever been offered to man," and on another occasion he described Jesus' character as "the most innocent" and "the most eloquent . . . that has ever been exhibited to man."[24] Although Jefferson denied Jesus' divinity, he ascribed to Jesus "every *human* excellence" and maintained that Jesus himself "never claimed any other."[25]

But Jefferson insisted that Jesus' teachings had been distorted out of all recognition by a succession of "corruptions." He described such doctrines as predestination, the inefficacy of good works, and original sin as "demoralizing dogmas," "dross," "distortions," "abracadabra," "insanity," a "hocus-pocus phantasm," and a "deliria of crazy imaginations."[26]

In a letter to John Davis, a Massachusetts Unitarian, Jefferson disdained the "metaphysical abstractions," "maniac ravings," and "foggy dreams" of Jesus' followers, who, he said, had so burdened Christianity "with absurdities and incomprehensibilities, as to drive into infidelity men who had not the time, patience, or opportunity to strip it of its meretricious trappings." He concluded that "ridicule" was the only sensible response to Christianity's many "unintelligible propositions." The clergy, he wrote, were "false shepherds" and "usurpers of the Christian name," who were like "scuttle fish," which shroud themselves in "darkness" to make themselves "impenetrable to the eye of a pursuing enemy."[27]

Jefferson was not, however, a godless man. Though committed to the separation of church and state and fiercely anticlerical, he was also a man of "deeply felt private religious conviction" who believed intensely in a benign Creator whose "only revelation to man is made through Nature and Reason."[28]

At least publicly, Jefferson described himself as a Christian, but only on his *own* terms. Three years after his election as President, he wrote Benjamin Rush, his close friend and fellow signatory of the Declaration of Independence, "I am a Christian, in the only sense in which [Jesus] wished anyone to be; sincerely attached to his doctrines, in preference to all others."[29]

Jefferson thought it important to "hold fast to those moral precepts which are of the essence of Christianity, and of all other religions," but emphatically rejected adherence to what he regarded as arbitrary and irrational dogmas concerning such matters as "vestments, ceremonies, physical opinions, and metaphysical speculations, totally unconnected with morality, and unimportant to the legitimate objects of society," over which "oceans of human blood have been spilt, and whole regions of the earth have been desolated by wars and persecutions, in which human ingenuity has been exhausted in inventing new tortures for their brethren." Jefferson expressed his hope to John Adams "that the human mind will someday get back to the freedom it enjoyed 2000 years ago," before what he decried as the perversions of true Christianity.*[30]

Like other deists, Jefferson believed that the Creator had endowed man with a moral compass—an "innate" and natural "sense of right and wrong." Man's "moral sense, or conscience," Jefferson reasoned, "is as much a part of man as his leg or arm." All people, he wrote, have "implanted in our breasts" a "moral instinct" and a "love of others," which "prompts us irresistibly to feel and to succor their distresses." Jefferson praised this moral instinct as "the brightest gem with which the human character is studded," and he believed that it was this natural moral disposition that made democracy possible.[31]

To Jefferson, then, the nature of virtue was neither dependent upon nor "to be comprehended" through "Christian revelation," but was "clearly evident in nature and discernible through the exercise of reason." The "dogmas of religion," he wrote, are quite distinct from "moral principles," and Jefferson had no difficulty with the proposition, often disputed at the time, that even atheists could be moral.[32] For Jefferson, the fundamental precepts of morality, which are held in common "in all religions," were captured by Jesus' maxims, "Treat others as you would have them treat you," and "Love they neighbor as thyself." As Jefferson never tired of saying, "The essence of virtue is in doing good to others."[33]

Jefferson strongly opposed any effort to equate Christian doctrine with secular law or to incorporate Christian doctrine into the law. Jefferson was, of course, the primary drafter of the Declaration of Independence. In the light of his views as a naturalistic deist, and in the light of the similar views of many of the other signers, it is important to note the precise language of the Declaration. It does not invoke "Jesus," or "Christ," or "the Father," or "the Lord," or any of the other traditional characterizations of the Christian deity. Rather, it invokes "Nature's God," "the Creator," "the Supreme Judge," and "Divine Providence."

The Declaration of Independence was a document of the Enlightenment. It was not a Puritan, Calvinist, Methodist, Baptist, Episcopalian, Catholic, or Evangelical Christian statement. It was, rather, a statement

---

* In an effort to reconcile Christianity with the Enlightenment and to separate the essence of Jesus' teachings from the corruptions of superstition and irrational dogma that he felt were added later, Jefferson produced his own "scissors-and-paste" version of the New Testament that offered what he thought to be a useful guide to social harmony in a republican society. See Thomas Jefferson, *The Jefferson Bible: The Life and Morals of Jesus of Nazareth* (Henry Holt 1995).

that deeply and *intentionally* invoked the language of American deism. It is a document of its own time, and it speaks eloquently to what Americans of that time believed.[34]

ADAMS: "BE JUST AND GOOD"

JOHN ADAMS SAW the world as a hostile place, both "to himself and to the American cause, which was the great passion of his life." None of the founders was more well read or more thoughtful than Adams about the aspirations and possibilities of the Enlightenment.[35]

Like Jefferson, Adams believed that the original teachings of Jesus were sound, but that they had been tainted by the corruptions that were later "grafted onto them." As Adams grew older, he became increasingly suspicious of religious dogma. As he wrote to Benjamin Rush, "There is a germ of religion in human nature so strong that whenever an order of men can persuade the people by flattery or terror that they have salvation at their disposal, there can be no end to fraud, violence, or usurpation."[36]

Religion and churchgoing were important to Adams throughout his life, and to a greater extent than either Franklin or Jefferson he believed in a personal God. But like other deists, he rejected the rigid dogmas he had inherited from his Puritan forebears in favor of a simpler, less obscure version of Christianity. His reading and reflection led him to reject such doctrines as predestination and original sin. The Creator, he declared, "has given us Reason, to find out the Truth, and the real Design and true End of our Existence." For Adams, Christianity was preeminently the religion of "reason, equity, and love," and he jettisoned all religious doctrines "that could not be verified independently by human reason." Adams never endorsed the more radical ideas of the French *philosophes*, but he was "a thoroughgoing deist."[37]

Reflecting his deistic principles, Adams wrote privately to Jefferson that his religion could be "contained in four short Words, *'Be just and good.'*" On another occasion, Adams wrote in his diary that the greatest testament to Christianity was the principle central to all great religions and ethical codes: "Love your Neighbour as yourself, and do to others as you would that others should do to you."[38]

Adams was acutely aware of the need to separate religion from politics. "Nothing" he wrote, "is more dreaded than the national government meddling with religion." As Adams wrote to Benjamin Rush, "I mix religion with politics as little as possible." His *Dissertation on the Canon and Feudal Law*, written in 1774, was a sharp attack against the civil and ecclesiastical tyranny of earlier Catholic and Protestant establishments, and he devoted several chapters of his *A Defence of the Constitutions of Government of the United States of America*, which he wrote in 1788, to condemning "the horrors of religious wars, crusades, inquisitions, and pogroms." Adams warned that given the opportunity, Christian "evangelicals would whip and crop, and pillory and roast" in America just as they had in Europe.[39]

One of the delegates to the Second Continental Congress was a clergyman who wanted Congress to focus upon America's "Christian identity." Adams wrote his wife Abigail that "as he is the first gentleman of the cloth who has appeared in Congress, I cannot but wish he may be the last. Mixing the sacred character with that of the statesman . . . is not attended with any good effects." As president, Adams signed the 1797 Treaty of Tripoli, which was unanimously approved by the Senate, and in which the United States, in resolving disputes with the Barbary pirates, emphatically affirmed that "the Government of the United States . . . is not in any sense founded on the Christian religion."[40]

I N 1817, nine years before the end of his life, Adams wrote to Jefferson, "Twenty times, in the course of my late Reading, have I been upon the point of breaking out, 'This would be the best of all possible Worlds, if there were no Religion in it.'" But he then added that "without Religion this World would be Something not fit to be mentioned in polite Company, I mean Hell."[41]

This ambivalence reflected Adams's lifelong belief that man is driven by a passion for wealth, power, and prestige, and that all of history proved that the People, unrestrained, tend to be "unjust, tyrannical, brutal, barbarous, and cruel." This view of man posed a serious problem for Adams as a political theorist, for like the other founders he knew that self-governance ultimately depends on the character of the People. No republican government can last, he observed, unless there is "a positive Passion for the public good." Given his skepticism about man's tendency to misbehave, Adams doubted whether the People had the integrity necessary to make the republican experiment succeed.[42]

He therefore warned that unless a public-spirited virtue could "be inspired into our People," they "will not obtain a lasting Liberty." It was here that Adams, like many of the founders, believed that religion could play a role in helping to shape both the "people's moral conduct" and their "ideas about justice, decency, duty, and responsibility." Religion, he believed, could be a critical source of republican virtue.[43]

But when they invoked "religion" as the foundation of sound republican government, neither Adams nor most of the other founders meant traditional Christianity, with all of its many dogmas and tenets. Rather, as Adams wrote to Jefferson, the essence of his religious beliefs was captured in the phrase, "Be just and good." And, as Jefferson replied, "What all agree in, is probably right."[44]

The vast majority of the founders believed that the principle "be just and good" could play a critical role in nurturing the sort of public-spiritedness that they deemed essential to self-governance, and they believed that some version of what Rousseau called "civil religion," and what Jefferson referred to as "Nature's God," would be salutary in fostering the spirit of American republicanism. But this was a far cry from endorsing the sanctity of Christian doctrine.[45]

WASHINGTON: "A ROMAN STOIC RATHER THAN A CHRISTIAN SAINT"

COMPARED WITH FRANKLIN, Jefferson, and Adams, George Washington was not a learned man. He was a man of affairs, rather than a man of ideas. His greatness lay in his character, which left an indelible mark on the nation. Two of his greatest acts of moral integrity were his resignation as commander-in-chief of the Continental Army after the Revolution and his decision not to run for a third term as President in 1796. In these, and many other acts, Washington's conduct epitomized the sort of public-spirited and disinterested republican integrity that the new nation desperately needed.

Washington was, in his own words, "no bigot myself to any mode of worship." He believed that an unseen but benevolent power guided both the universe and human affairs, and he variously referred to this force as "Providence," the "Almighty Ruler of the Universe," the "Great Architect of the Universe," and the "Great Disposer of Events."[46]

Washington was quite reticent about his own religious beliefs. He paid little attention to religion in his personal life and was not an avid churchgoer. He was "neither religiously fervent nor theologically learned." He described his own religious tenets as "few and simple." One of his biographers, Joseph Ellis, observed that, at his death, "Washington did not think much about heaven or angels; the only place he knew his body was going was into the ground, and as for his soul, its ultimate location was unknowable. He died as a Roman stoic rather than a Christian saint."[47]

It is not even clear that Washington considered himself a Christian. Although he maintained a connection with the Anglican Church, this was prudent behavior for a cautious political leader, whether or not he was a true believer. Perhaps more revealingly, Washington's personal papers offer no evidence that he believed in biblical revelation, eternal life, or Jesus' divinity. In several thousand letters, he never once mentioned Jesus, and the name of Jesus was conspicuously absent from his will. All in all, Washington's commitment to Christianity has aptly been characterized as "limited and superficial."[48]

Although, unlike Jefferson, Washington was not openly contemptuous of Christianity, clergymen who knew him bemoaned his skeptical approach to Christianity. The Reverend Dr. Bird Wilson sadly acknowledged, for example, that Washington "was not a professing Christian," and Bishop William White admitted that no "degree of recollection will bring to my mind any fact which would prove General Washington to have been a believer in the Christian revelation." Washington has variously and accurately been described as a "cool deist," a "warm deist," a "theistic rationalist," a "Stoic," and a "Christian Deist."[49]

In fact, Washington is probably better understood as a man of honor than a man of religion. Washington strived to be just "because justice was right and because lack of it would cost him some of his self-respect." As the historian Peter Henriques has concluded, the "key for Washington was to act in concert with [his] conscience, which had more power for him than revealed religion." Washington "was confident he knew what was 'just' and 'right,' and he did not rely on some kind of revealed religion or Holy Book to tell him so."[50]

As president, Washington was acutely sensitive to different religious traditions and was careful not to invoke Christianity. His official speeches, orders, and other public communications scrupulously reflected the perspective of a deist. His references to religion omitted such phrases as "Jesus," "Christ," "Lord," "Father," "Redeemer," and "Savior," and he invariably edited such terms out of his official documents whenever his subordinates tried to insert them. Instead, he used such deistic phrases as "Providence," the "Supreme Being," and the "Deity."[51]

Like Adams, however, Washington believed that some form of ethical belief was indispensable both to public morality and republican government, and he had no qualms about acknowledging the role religion could play in nurturing the nation's well-being. In his Farewell Address, for example, he warned that "reason and experience both forbid us to expect that national morality can prevail in the exclusion of religious principle."[52]

PAINE: "A VILLAIN AND AN INFIDEL"

THOMAS PAINE ARRIVED in Philadelphia from England in 1774. Two years later, he published *Common Sense*, which helped catalyze the colonies and inspire the Declaration of Independence. After the Revolution, Paine returned to England and published *The Rights of Man*, a forceful defense of republicanism based upon the theory of natural rights. Paine soon followed up with *The Age of Reason*, which sharply criticized Christian doctrine and declared that "reason, not supernaturalist creeds or dogma," must be man's sole guide in moral and religious matters.[53]

In his seminal work, *The Age of Reason*, published in 1794, Paine announced, "I believe in one God, and no more, and I hope for happiness beyond this life. I believe in the equality of man; and I believe that religious duties consist in doing justice, loving mercy, and endeavoring to make our fellow-creatures happy. . . . I do not believe in the creed professed by the Jewish Church, by the Roman Church, by the Greek Church, by the Turkish Church, by the Protestant Church, nor by any church that I know of. My own mind is my own church."[54]

Paine maintained that "the religion of Deism is superior to the Christian Religion," because it "is free from those invented and torturing articles that shock our reason." Deism's creed, he wrote, "is pure and sublimely simple. It believes in God, and there it rests. It honours Reason as the choicest gift of God to man, and . . . it avoids all presumptuous beliefs, and rejects, as the fabulous inventions of men, all books pretending to revelation."[55]

Paine was merciless in his attack on Christian doctrine. He denied "that the Almighty ever did communicate anything to man, by any mode of speech, in any language, or by any kind of vision." He characterized Christianity as a "fable, which, for absurdity and extravagance, is not exceeded by anything that is to be found in the mythology of the ancients." He castigated the Bible as a forgery, pointed out its internal contradictions, contrasted its teachings with the findings of science, and harangued it for its immorality. "It is," he charged, "a book of lies, wickedness and blasphemy;

Thomas Paine

for what can be greater blasphemy than to ascribe the wickedness of man to the orders of the Almighty?"[56]

Paine maintained that by demanding unquestioning belief in miraculous intervention and revelation, insisting that believers accept superstition as truth, and denying believers the right to criticize religious dogma, Christianity had fundamentally undermined the freedom of conscience and incited intolerance and persecution. In Paine's words, "The most detestable wickedness, the most horrid cruelties, and the greatest miseries, that have afflicted the human race, have had their origin in this thing called revelation, or revealed religion."[57]

Indeed, he added, the Christian religion has "served to corrupt and brutalize mankind" by demanding blind adherence to Church dogma rather than the pursuit of knowledge and happiness. "Of all the systems of religion that ever were invented," he concluded, "there is none more derogatory to the Almighty, more unedifying to man, more repugnant to reason, and more contradictory in itself than this thing called Christianity."[58]

As a deist, Paine was not an atheist. But, in his view, to understand God, man must use reason and scientific investigation to study God's handiwork. That, he insisted, "is the true theology." His works—*Common Sense*, *The Rights of Man*, and *The Age of Reason*—were the most widely read political tracts of the eighteenth century. Paine was "the greatest spokesman of popular deism," and to traditional Christians he was "a villain and an infidel."[59]

THROUGHOUT THE second half of the eighteenth century, observant Christians worried deeply about the impact of deism. The Revolutionary era was a period of decline for American Christianity, and the rise of deism was seen as a continuing threat. Members of the educated class, from which men like Adams, Washington, Jefferson, Monroe, and Madison hailed, frequently expressed deist opinions in their conversations and letters, and by the latter years of the eighteenth century, colleges like Yale, William & Mary, and Princeton had become hotbeds of deism. Even staid, Puritan Harvard had become embroiled in free thought. Although the interest in deism began among the educated class, it gradually spread among the general populace through newspapers, journals, broadsides, and books. By the final decades of the century, deism was no longer confined to the elite, but had grown to encompass the masses.[60]

The Christian establishment responded with a vengeance. As early as 1759, the Congregational minister Ezra Stiles warned that "Deism has got such Head in this Age of Licentious Liberty" that it is necessary to "conquer and demolish it," and Jonathan Edwards, the foremost theologian of the Great Awakening, charged that deists were "infidels."

In 1784, Ethan Allen, the leader of the "Green Mountain Boys" and the hero of the Battle of Ticonderoga, published a book-length argument for deism. His *Reason: The Only Oracle of Man* was furiously condemned by the clergy. Timothy Dwight, the president of Yale, accused Allen of championing "Satan's cause," Ezra Stiles charged that Allen was "profane and impious," the Reverend Uzal Ogden castigated him as "an ignorant and profane deist . . . with a mind replete with horror," and the Reverend Nathan Perkins called him "one of the wickedest men that ever walked this guilty globe." A few years later, in 1788, Dwight published a biting anti-deist work, *The Triumph of Infidelity*.[61]

"THE CIVIL MORALITY NECESSARY
TO DEMOCRACY"

DID THE FRAMERS intend the United States to be "a Christian nation"? Clearly, they did not. The Declaration of Independence marked a fundamental shift. Before 1776, public expressions of faith in the colonies were often overtly Christian. In declaring themselves independent of Britain, however, the American founders invoked the language and spirit of the Enlightenment. The Declaration was signed by men of widely diverse religious beliefs, ranging from traditional Christians to committed deists. What was most critical at that moment in our nation's history, however, was what united, rather than what divided, the signers. Although the Declaration expressly acknowledged "Nature's God," the "Creator," and "Divine Providence," it carefully and quite consciously eschewed any invocation of Christianity or the Christian religion.[62]

This did not mark the founders as irreligious, but it did mark them as open-minded about differences of religious opinion. Among the founders of our nation were men like Jefferson, Paine, Franklin, Washington, and Adams, who embraced Enlightenment values rather than traditional Christian doctrine in setting the United States on its path to independence. At the same time, though, the Framers were acutely aware that, in James Madison's words, the republican form of government "presupposes" certain qualities of civic virtue among the people. Although Enlightenment thought reconceived the concept of virtue "as public and civic rather than as private and devotional," many members of the founding generation still believed that there was a direct link between religion and civic virtue.[63]

This was certainly true of those who held traditional religious beliefs. Phillips Payson, for example, an influential Congregationalist minister, maintained that religion is "of the highest importance to . . . civil society . . . as it keeps alive the best sense of moral obligation." John Witherspoon, a Presbyterian clergyman and president of the College of New Jersey (later Princeton), warned that even a "good form of government" cannot protect the people against their natural "profligacy and corruption of manners" unless religion informs their values. And Benjamin Rush wrote to the famous lexicographer Noah Webster that although "Reason produces great and popular truths," it "affords *motives* too feeble to induce mankind to act agreeably to them." Religion, he insisted, "unfolds the same truths and accompanies them with *motives*, agreeable, powerful, and irresistible."[64]

Even those founders who challenged traditional Christian beliefs generally agreed that religion could help foster republican virtue. In a letter to Rush, for example, John Adams opined that "Religion and Virtue" are the necessary "Foundations . . . of Republicanism and of all free Government." Similarly, Alexander Hamilton reasoned that liberty depends upon morality and that "morality *must* fall with religion," because religion can help "confine" man "within the bounds of social duty."[65]

Even Benjamin Franklin thought religion had a role to play in sustaining the morals of ordinary citizens. In a letter admonishing a young writer who had made a particularly strident attack on religion, Franklin cautioned:

> You yourself may find it easy to live a virtuous Life without the Assistance afforded by Religion; you . . . possessing a Strength of Resolution sufficient to enable you to resist common Temptations. But think how great a Proportion of Mankind consists of weak and ignorant Men and Women . . . who have need of the Motives of Religion to restrain them from Vice, to support their Virtue, and retain them in the Practice of it till it becomes *habitual*. . . . If Men are so wicked as we now see them *with Religion* what would they be if *without it?*"[66]

Thus, even the deists among the Framers recognized that religion could and should play a useful role in helping "to preserve the civil morality necessary to democracy." But the Framers drew a sharp distinction in their understanding of the specific precepts of religion that are necessary to promote a self-governing society. For most of them, the central teaching of religion should be the obligation of each individual to treat others with kindness and respect, rather than the particular details of Christian doctrine.[67]

The Framers were also quite wary about the proper relation between religion and law in a free society. They valued religion, but given their knowledge of the religious strife that had plagued man's history and their appreciation of the importance to individual liberty of both freedom of and freedom from religion, "they saw the wisdom of distinguishing between private and public religion." Each individual must be free to pursue his own faith in his own way, but in the "public business of the nation," it was essential for the government to speak of religion "in a way that was unifying, not divisive."[68]

It is with this understanding that the Framers turned to the challenge of creating the American Constitution.

6

"THE FUNDAMENTAL MAXIMS OF FREE GOVERNMENT"

Signing of the Constitution

I N THEIR INTENSE deliberations over the American Constitution and the Bill of Rights, the regulation of sex was far from the minds of the Framers. But in their debates and decisions about the freedom of speech, the freedom of religion, judicial review, and unenumerated rights, the Framers confronted a series of fundamental issues that have defined and structured the complex interaction between sex, religion, and constitutional law ever since.

A central issue facing the Framers at the Constitutional Convention in 1787 concerned the appropriate role of religion in the new national government. From fourth-century Rome on, it had been commonplace for Christian societies to have an established religion and to prohibit practices deemed heretical or sinful by that religion.

By the time of the Revolution, however, Americans had grown deeply divided over the appropriate role of religion in their new state governments, and this issue soon spilled over into their debates over a national Constitution. In 1776, nine of the thirteen colonies still had established churches. Even in those colonies, though, the eighteenth century had wrought substantial change. Increasing secularism, a growing commitment to individual liberty, and a dramatic increase in religious diversity had combined to foster a new spirit of toleration. The established state churches were still supported with public funds, and the right to hold public office was often still limited to members of the established church, but none of the colonies any longer prohibited the practice of dissenting religions. Baptists, Methodists, Catholics, Jews, and Lutherans were free to practice their faith, even in Congregationalist Massachusetts and Anglican Virginia. But the byword in most of the colonies was religious toleration, not religious equality. This was about to change, with profound implications for the future of American law.

"THE CARE OF EACH MAN'S SALVATION BELONGS ONLY TO HIMSELF"

FOR THE GENERATION of the Framers, John Locke was the most influential Enlightenment philosopher on the issue of church-state relations. It was Locke who delineated the fundamental principles that Jefferson, Madison, and the other founders would later embrace and expand upon. In his 1689 *Letter Concerning Toleration,* Locke wrote that the state is "a society of men constituted only for the procuring, preserving, and advancing their own civil interests." Because "the care of each man's salvation belongs only to himself," the legitimate jurisdiction of the state ought not "in any manner . . . be extended to the salvation of souls." Thus, "[i]f a Roman Catholic believe that to be really the body of Christ, which another man calls bread, he does no injury thereby to his neighbor. If a Jew does not believe the New Testament to be the word of God, he does not thereby alter anything in men's civil rights. If a heathen doubt of both Testaments, he is not therefore to be punished as a pernicious citizen."[1]

In the debates over the new state constitutions that began in the mid-1770s, two primary positions emerged on the issue of church-state relations. The more conservative position defended the status quo in those states that had an established church. Advocates of this position insisted that an established state religion is essential to a peaceful, well-ordered society and that the absence of an official church would produce divisiveness and chaos. Thus, although dissenters were free to worship according to the dictates of their own consciences, they could still be compelled to support the established church.[2]

The competing position rejected mere toleration in favor of religious equality. The advocates of this view maintained that religion was a matter for individual conscience and rejected as tyrannical the idea that government should establish or even prefer one religion over any other. The most dramatic clash over this view occurred in Virginia, where a lengthy struggle culminated in the enactment of Thomas Jefferson's Virginia Statute for Religious Freedom.

Jefferson first proposed this statute in 1779. The preamble condemned those "legislators and rulers" who have "assumed dominion over the faith of others, setting up their own opinions and modes of thinking as . . . true and infallible." Jefferson reasoned that "[i]f any man err from the right way, it is his own misfortune, no injury to thee, nor therefore art thou to punish him in the things of this life because thou supposest he will be miserable in that which is to come."

Jefferson insisted that "the legitimate powers of government extend to such acts only as are injurious to others. But it does me no injury for my neighbor to say there are twenty gods, or no God. It neither picks my pocket nor breaks my leg." Thus, under Jefferson's Virginia Statute for Religious Freedom, Anglicans, Congregationalists, Baptists, Methodists, and Presbyterians would have to stand on an equal footing with "the Jew and the Gentile, the . . . Mahometan, the Hindoo, and infidel of every denomination."[3]

The struggle to enact Jefferson's law came to a head in 1785. Because Jefferson was in Paris at the time as Minister to France, it fell to James Madison to lead the charge. In his "Memorial and Remonstrance against Religious Assessments," Madison, building upon the arguments of Locke and Jefferson, denied both that "the Civil Magistrate is a competent Judge of Religious Truth" and that "the Civil Magistrate . . . may employ Religion as an engine of Civil policy." Noting that "the legal establishment of Christianity" had been tried for "almost fifteen centuries," Madison maintained that the result, "more or less in all places," had been "superstition, bigotry and persecution."[4]

The enactment of the Virginia Statute for Religious Freedom, a momentous victory in the American quest for religious liberty, set the stage for what was to happen two years later at the Constitutional Convention in Philadelphia.[5]

ONE OF THE "GLORIES OF THE NEW CONSTITUTION"

THE MEN WHO GATHERED in Philadelphia in 1787 faced profound questions about church-state relations in the new national government. Most of them had participated in the state constitutional conventions in the preceding fifteen years, so they were well aware of the various arrangements that had been adopted by the different states. They were also acutely aware of both the religious diversity that had arisen in America during the eighteenth century and the lessons of history. The Framers viewed religion not "as an integrative force," but as a potentially "divisive" factor that threatened to undermine "their desire to form a 'more perfect union.'"[6] As James Madison, the chief architect of the Constitution, observed, religious zeal has throughout history "inflamed [men] with mutual animosity, and rendered them much more disposed to vex and oppress each other, than to co-operate for their common good."[7]

Not only did the Framers decide not to establish a particular religion in the new national Constitution, but they *expressly* provided that "no religious Test shall ever be required as a Qualification to any Office or public Trust under the United States."[8]

This judgment triggered a sharp response from some quarters during the ratification debates. William Williams of Connecticut, for example, a delegate to the Continental Congress, complained that the Constitution should contain "an explicit acknowledgment of the being of a God, his perfections and his providence." Major Thomas Lusk of Massachusetts, a delegate to the Massachusetts ratification convention, shuddered "at the idea that Roman Catholics, Papists, and Pagans might be introduced into office," and a delegate to the North Carolina ratification convention cautioned with some alarm that even "Papists . . . and Mahometans" could become President of the United States.[9]

But the proponents of the "no religious test" clause were resolute. In *Federalist* Nos. 51 and 56, Madison cited the clause as one of the "glories of the new Constitution," and future Supreme Court Justice James Iredell lauded it as a fundamental "principle of religious freedom." Many clerical leaders also supported the clause, including the Virginia Baptist leader John Leland, the Reverend Samuel Langdon of New Hampshire, and the Reverend Daniel Shute of Massachusetts. In the end, after "one of the most important public debates ever held in America over the place of religion in politics," the states ratified the Constitution, in part because it contained no reference to God or Christianity and because it expressly forbade the use of any religious test for public office.[10]

"TO PURSUE THE COMMON GOOD"

THOSE WHO DRAFTED the Constitution faced innumerable challenges. One of those challenges, directly relevant to any inquiry into the relationship between sexual freedom and the Constitution, focused on the nature of rights and how the new Constitution would recognize and protect them. This was an issue that deeply vexed and divided the Framers.

Traditional republican theory held that liberty could be achieved in a self-governing society only if citizens were willing to surrender their private interests for the greater good. Without such disinterestedness and self-sacrifice, self-governance was impossible.[11] This posed a dilemma, because most leaders of the Revolutionary generation doubted the capacity of ordinary individuals to rise above self-interest to act in furtherance of the common good. John Adams worried, for example, that the people lacked the necessary "passion for the public good" for self-governance to succeed.[12]

The initial solution, embraced by Jefferson, Franklin, Washington, Adams, Hamilton, and other advocates of republicanism, was the assumption that men like *them* would govern the nation. They believed that the responsibility to lead should and would be vested in men who were reasonable, honest, tolerant, educated, disinterested, and committed to the public good, men who stood "on elevated ground" and who therefore had a broad "view of human affairs," men who were "free of the prejudices, parochialism, and religious enthusiasm" of the common people.[13]

But what if the People did not elect the "right" leaders? This was a source of some concern. Indeed, after the Revolution, as the new state governments were gradually democratized, men of modest origin and little education were consistently elected to public office. As new opportunities for wealth and power emerged, self-governance seemed to foster competitiveness and acquisitiveness rather than a spirit of selflessness. Political horse-trading, pork-barrelling, and parochialism ran rampant, and a rash of self-interested debtor-relief laws threatened to undermine economic stability.

It quickly became evident to men like James Madison that "the aggregate interests of the Community" were being swamped by the "pursuit of self-interest." Madison observed that such conduct called "into question the fundamental principle of republican Government, that the majority who rule in such Governments, are the safest Guardians both of public Good and private rights."[14]

S UCH WAS the mood of the nation when the Framers of the Constitution met in Philadelphia in the summer of 1787. As they observed the political shenanigans of selfish merchants, price-gouging farmers, and factious legislators in the state assemblies, they were reluctantly compelled to reconsider the republican ideals of the Revolution. The challenge was to figure out how to curb the dangers of rampant democracy while at the same time preserving core republican principles.[15]

Compounding this challenge was the Framers' recognition that the weak central government they had created in the Articles of Confederation could not meet the needs of a growing, vital, and economically robust nation. In part, the American Revolution had been a revolt against the very idea of a powerful central government. The national government established in the Articles of Confederation was therefore designed to ensure that it would never be able to impose undue taxes, undermine individual liberties, or impose military authority on the states. But with the evident failure of that structure to meet the needs of the nation, it was clear that a stronger national government was essential.

In light of the dismal experience of the state governments, however, there was more reason than ever to fear the possible excesses of a more powerful national government. Concerns about a strong national government came from several directions. Jefferson worried that elected officials, corrupted by power and by the influence of special interests, would run roughshod over the interests of those who had elected them. Madison was concerned that elected officials would be too responsive to the demands of their constituents and would sweep aside the rights of minorities. Jefferson, in other words, "worried about the rights of the majority; Madison worried about the rights of the minority." It was in their struggle to adjust these competing goals and dangers that the Framers devised the multilayered jigsaw of bargains, balances, checks, and cross-checks that comprise the American Constitution.[16]

The radically new governmental structure proposed in the Constitution of 1787 attempted both to empower the new national government to meet the needs of the nation and to divide and separate power in multiple layers in order to limit its capacity to do harm. To achieve these goals and both to constrain and to balance the potential power of the new national government, the Constitution expressly specified the limited powers of the national government; separated the legislative branch into two distinct houses; established an independent judiciary, with justices guaranteed life tenure in order to insulate them from majoritarian pressures; and created an executive, selected by an electoral college rather than by direct popular election, who could veto acts of Congress but whose vetoes could, in turn, be overridden by supermajorities of both houses.

"THE PEOPLE THEMSELVES": THE BILL OF RIGHTS AND THE ORIGINS OF JUDICIAL REVIEW

THE CONSTITUTION THAT was proposed for ratification in 1787 did not contain a bill of rights. In part for this reason, the Anti-Federalists opposed ratification. They charged, among other things, that the proposed new national government was designed to "raise the fortunes of the well-born few" at the expense of the common people. The Anti-Federalists rejected the claim that there existed a disinterested class of elite gentlemen who would or could feel "sympathetically the wants of the people" and speak for their "feelings, circumstances, and interests." That elite, they cautioned, had their own interests to promote, and however well educated and cultured they might be, they would use their political power to further those interests at the expense of other members of the community.[17]

The Anti-Federalists were especially disturbed by the absence of a bill of rights that would protect the People against this more powerful national government. If a central purpose of the Constitution was to secure the rights of the People, they asked, why was there no bill of rights? They were certain that the proposed central government would inevitably infringe on individual freedoms if those freedoms were not specified in the Constitution in the most definite and precise manner.

The brilliant orator and Anti-Federalist champion Patrick Henry recalled that in "Britain the people and the Crown had struggled for over a century over the uncertainties of *implied* rights until the matter had finally been settled in the acceptance of an *explicit* Bill of Rights." Richard Henry Lee of Virginia, who had served as president of the Continental Congress under the Articles of Confederation, maintained that "universal experience" had taught that "the most express declarations and reservations are necessary to protect the just rights and liberties of mankind from the silent, powerful and ever active conspiracy of those who govern."[18]

The drafters of the proposed Constitution offered several arguments in defense of their decision not to include a bill of rights. First, because the new national government had only specified and limited powers, it had no constitutional authority to invade areas of individual liberty.

Second, any enumeration of rights in the Constitution would necessarily be incomplete and would therefore create a dangerous inference that rights that were not expressly enumerated were not protected by the Constitution. Thus, a bill of rights could well be counterproductive in the long run.

Third, a bill of rights would serve little, if any, practical purpose, for in a self-governing society the majority could simply disregard whatever rights were "guaranteed" in the Constitution. The protection of individual freedom, they argued, must therefore be found in the self-discipline and mutual respect of the People and in the checks and balances and separation of powers that were built into the new government, rather than in a list of "rights" that could have no real restraining effect on the majority. If rights were to be honored, they argued, it would have to be because the structure of government had been well designed to achieve that end and because of the wisdom, tolerance, and virtue of the nation's people and leaders.[19]

These were plausible arguments, but they did little to temper public skepticism about the proposed Constitution. The Anti-Federalists continued to insist that the proposed new federal government would dangerously empower the political elite to run roughshod over the rights and interests of ordinary Americans.

T O GET a fuller sense of this debate, which proved critical to American constitutional history, it is necessary to delve a bit more deeply into the history of rights. As the legal historian Jack Rakove has observed, the earliest declarations of rights in England, like Magna Carta of 1215 and the 1689 Declaration of Rights, were quite different from the bills of rights enacted by the American people after 1776. Those earlier declarations were *compacts* negotiated between a monarch and his subjects. But now that Americans had banished monarchy and would govern themselves, why would they need to negotiate such a compact with *themselves*? The very idea seemed incoherent. Americans would, of course, protect their *own* rights, so a formal bill of rights was wholly unnecessary.

Moreover, the earlier declarations of rights were never understood as the ultimate source of the rights that they protected. Rather, they were regarded as mere "confirmations" of preexisting natural rights. Thus, the rights that the Constitution existed to protect were seen as "inalienable, indefeasible rights inherent in all people by virtue of their humanity."[20] As the Philadelphia statesman John Dickinson wrote in 1766, these rights "are born with us; exist with us; and cannot be taken from us by any human power. . . . In short, they are founded on the immutable maxims of reason and justice." Alexander Hamilton added in 1775 that the "rights of mankind are not to be rummaged for, among old parchments, or musty records," but are "written, as with a sunbeam, in the whole *volume* of human nature." These rights were thought to exist independent of whether they were codified in a statute, constitution, or bill of rights. Thus, any formal listing of these rights was simply superfluous.[21]

Despite these arguments, by the time of the Revolution, Americans had begun to worry that their rights might not be secure if they were not explicitly incorporated into the texts of their new state constitutions. They feared that rights "left unmentioned might lose their authority—literally be lost and forgotten, and thus cease to be rights." Thus, during the Revolution, eleven of the thirteen states, all but Connecticut and Rhode Island, enacted new constitutions, and eight of them included a bill of rights.[22]

It remained a puzzle, though, how these bills of rights were to be integrated into the new conception of a constitution. Were these declarations of rights mere statements of aspiration, or were they meant to be enforceable and, if so, by what means? And what about those states that did not adopt a bill of rights? Did their citizens have no rights?[23]

I T WAS against this backdrop that the Framers considered the question of a national bill of rights. Madison, the most influential of the Framers, understood early on that the protection of rights in a republican government posed a novel question. Whereas traditional theory had focused on rights as necessary to protect the People against an unelected monarch, Madison recognized that in a republic, rights were necessary to protect segments of the community against the self-interested and unrestrained desires of the majority.

As Madison observed the actions of the state legislatures between 1775 and 1787, he realized that they often acted unjustly because legislators were *too responsive* to the demands of their constituents. The real source of the problem, he concluded, "lies among the people themselves," because they too often saw politics as a means to enforce their private interests over and against both the public good and the rights of their fellow citizens. This led Madison to pose the following question: "In republican Government the majority . . . ultimately give the law. Whenever therefore an apparent interest or common passion unites a majority what is to restrain them from unjust violations of the rights and interests of the minority?"[24]

To solve this problem, Madison suggested several strategies, including a complex system of checks and balances within the government itself. But Madison was skeptical about the value of a written bill of rights. He was confident that a written guarantee of rights would not restrain the self-interest of a passionate majority, and following his lead the Constitutional Convention rejected the notion of a national bill of rights.[25]

In the face of strenuous objections by the Anti-Federalists during the ratification debates, however, it became necessary to reconsider the issue. On December 20, 1787, Thomas Jefferson wrote Madison from Paris that after reviewing the proposed Constitution, he regretted "the omission of a bill of rights." He insisted that "a bill of rights is what the people are entitled to against every government on earth . . . & what no just government should refuse or rest on inference."[26]

In response, Madison reiterated his doubt that a bill of rights would provide minority interests with any meaningful protection, noting that "experience proves the inefficacy of a bill of rights on those occasions when its controul is most needed," for "repeated violations of these parchment barriers have been committed by overbearing majorities in every State." In

James Madison

light of that experience, he asked, "What use . . . can a bill of rights serve in popular Governments?"

Answering his own question, Madison observed that although a bill of rights might not check the passions of self-interested majorities, it might nonetheless prove at least modestly useful, because "the political truths declared in that solemn manner" might over time take on "the character of fundamental maxims of free Government," and thus come to be so valued throughout society as to "counteract the impulses of interest and passion."[27]

Jefferson replied that Madison's skepticism about the possible effectiveness of a bill of rights failed to address one potentially important consideration "which has great weight with me, the legal check which it puts into the hands of the judiciary." A national court, he observed, "if rendered independent" of the legislature, could serve as a powerful "legal check" on majoritarian abuse.[28]

THIS EXCHANGE apparently carried some weight with Madison, as did the fact that several states, including Massachusetts and Virginia, had made clear that they would not vote to ratify the proposed Constitution in the absence of an assurance that there would be a national bill of rights. On June 8, 1789, Madison proposed a bill of rights to the House of Representatives. At the outset, he reminded his colleagues that "the greatest danger" to liberty was "not found in either the executive or legislative departments of government, but in the body of the people, operating by the majority against the minority."[29]

In defense of his proposal of a bill of rights, Madison first reaffirmed his own observation about the educational value of a bill of rights: "It may be thought all paper barriers against the power of the community are too weak to be worthy of attention. . . . [Y]et, as they have a tendency to impress some degree of respect for them, to establish the public opinion in their favor, and rouse the attention of the whole community, it may be one means to controul the majority from those acts to which they might be otherwise inclined."[30]

Madison then turned to the objection that "it is unnecessary to load the constitution" with a bill of rights, because declarations of rights have not been "found effectual in the constitution of the particular states." Although acknowledging that "there are a few particular states" in which some of the rights guaranteed in the state constitutions have "at one time or other, been violated," he maintained that it does not necessarily follow that the express guarantee of such rights cannot "have, to a certain degree, a salutary effect against the abuse of power."[31]

Then, echoing Jefferson's letter to him, he stated the case for judicial review, contending that if these rights are "incorporated into the constitution, independent tribunals of justice will consider themselves . . . the guardians of those rights; they will be an impenetrable bulwark against every assumption of power in the legislative or executive; they will be naturally led to resist every encroachment upon rights expressly stipulated for in the constitution by the declaration of rights."[32]

It was understood, though, that for judges to be able to undertake this function effectively they had to be independent of the other branches of government and must hold their positions by a permanent tenure. John Adams explained that without that independence, it would be unrealistic to

John Adams

expect judges to act with the necessary "impartiality." The critical shift in the American constitutional system was the recognition that judges needed independence not only from the executive, but, in Madison's words, from "the people themselves."[33]

Future Supreme Court Justice James Iredell penned an eloquent statement in support of judicial review in a newspaper essay in 1786. Iredell explained that "an act of Assembly, inconsistent with the constitution, is *void*, and cannot be obeyed, without disobeying the superior law" to which we are "irrevocably bound." Judges must therefore refuse to enforce any law that is not "warranted by the constitution." Iredell emphasized that "this is not a usurped or a discretionary power, but one inevitably resulting from the constitution of their office, they being judges *for the benefit of the whole people, not mere servants of the Assembly.*"[34]

During the ratification debates, Alexander Hamilton strongly endorsed judicial review as "obvious and uncontroversial" in *Federalist* No. 78.[35] Hamilton argued that constitutional limits could "be preserved in practice no other way than through the medium of the courts of justice." The "independence of the judges," he reasoned, is "requisite to guard the constitution and the rights of individuals from the effects of those ill humours which the arts of designing men . . . sometimes disseminate among the people." Judges, he insisted, have a duty to resist invasions of constitutional rights even if they are "instigated by the major voice of the community."[36]

In short, although the idea of judicial review was novel, it was "a fundamental element of the original intention of the Constitution." This innovation would come to play a central role in the controversies that would arise two centuries later about whether laws dealing with such issues as obscenity, contraception, abortion, homosexuality, and same-sex marriage could be reconciled with the "fundamental maxims of justice" embodied in the national Constitution.[37]

UNENUMERATED RIGHTS: THE "IMMUTABLE MAXIMS OF REASON AND JUSTICE"

ONE OF THE ARGUMENTS against enacting a national bill of rights was the concern that an enumeration of some rights might be taken to imply that other rights, not expressly included in the enumeration, were not protected by the Constitution. The Framers clearly rejected the idea that there was a closed set of well-defined and well-established "inalienable and indefeasible" rights. To the contrary, they fully understood that, like all facets of knowledge, the identification and recognition of individual rights was an ongoing work in progress.

Because they conceived of rights as inherent in nature and "founded on the immutable maxims of reason and justice," they understood them much as they understood the laws of science. That is, just as they knew that they did not know all there was to know about biology and physics, so too did they know that they did not know all there was to know about their rights. Just as reason, observation, and experience would enable man to gain more insight into philosophy, science, and human nature, so too would they enable him to learn more over time about the nature and substance of his inalienable rights, which would have to be distilled "from reason and justice."[38]

But this still left the underlying problem. One solution was not to enumerate any rights. As James Iredell argued to the North Carolina ratifying convention, a bill of rights would be "dangerous" because no one "could enumerate all the individual rights." He posited the following scenario:

Suppose . . . an enumeration of a great many [rights], but an omission of some, and that long after all traces of our present disputes were at an end, any of the omitted rights should be invaded, and the invasion complained of; what would be the plausible answer of the government to such a complaint? Would they not naturally say, . . . "So long as the rights enumerated in the bill of rights remain unviolated, you have no reason to complain. . . ." Thus a bill of rights might operate as a snare, rather than a protection.[39]

Jefferson found this argument unpersuasive. As he suggested to Madison, "Half a loaf is better than no bread. If we cannot secure all our rights, let us secure what we can." Madison came to the same conclusion, but went even further, proposing a specific constitutional provision to solve the problem. As part of the proposed bill of rights he presented to Congress, he suggested an amendment declaring that the recognition in the Constitution "of particular rights, shall not be so construed as to diminish the just importance of other rights retained by the people." With some tinkering, this proposal was eventually adopted as the Ninth Amendment: "The enumeration in the Constitution, of certain rights, shall not be construed to deny or disparage others retained by the people."[40]

The adoption of this amendment left interesting and challenging questions for the future: What were the other rights "retained by the people"? By what process would those rights be identified? Was the interpretation and enforcement of the Ninth Amendment, like the interpretation and enforcement of the other provisions of the Bill of Rights, to be left to the judiciary—the "impenetrable bulwark" against unwarranted legislative or executive assumption of power? Might these "unenumerated" rights even come to include liberties relating to such issues as sexual freedom? The right to use contraceptives? The right to abortion? The right to same-sex marriage?[41]

"A WALL OF SEPARATION"

THE SHIFTING CONCEPTION of the proper role of religion in public life in the late eighteenth century shaped how the newly independent states reconceived their legal systems. The spirit of Republicanism brought about a more "enlightened" approach to the law. Not only did state legislatures moderate the harsh penal codes of the colonial era, abolishing such brutal punishments as whipping, the pillory, branding, and mutilation, but the Revolution also led to a profound change in the common understanding of the very *purpose* of the law. The early colonists conceived of the state as the arm of God on earth. Crime was "looked upon as sin." After the Revolution, Americans sought to establish legal systems shaped not so much by the principles of Christianity, but by the "principles of Republicanism."[42]

This shift was evident even in staid Massachusetts. In the pre-Revolutionary era, the law focused on the prosecution of "religious" crimes. Between 1760 and 1774, for example, the majority of all criminal prosecutions in Massachusetts fell within what the English legal scholar William Blackstone categorized as "Offences against God and Religion," and almost 40 percent of all criminal prosecutions were for sexual crimes, such as fornication, adultery, cohabitation, lewdness, and prostitution.[43]

After the Revolution, prosecutions in Massachusetts for religion-based offenses ceased almost entirely, the number of prosecutions for fornication dropped more than 90 percent, and prosecutions for "Offenses against God and Religion" dropped by almost 60 percent. The political and cultural changes wrought by the Revolution cast doubt upon efforts to use the law to enforce religious precepts against conduct that did not directly threaten the public order. As a result, the law in this era became increasingly "secularized." Its primary goal came to be viewed, not as the enforcement of Christian dogma, but as the promotion of social order. It was no longer deemed "proper for government . . . to impose" religious values "on individuals . . . who did not voluntarily share them."[44]

WHAT, THOUGH, if anything, would the Bill of Rights say about religion? Because those who drafted the Constitution determined that the new national government, which was granted only limited powers, would have no authority over religion, many of them maintained that there was no need for a specific provision prohibiting the government from intruding on religious freedom. Such a provision, they argued, would be superfluous.

Nonetheless, during the ratification debates the Anti-Federalists demanded a bill of rights that would protect not only the freedom of speech, the freedom of the press, the freedom from unreasonable searches and seizures, and the freedom from cruel and unusual punishments, but also the freedom of religion. In the end, the demand for an express constitutional guarantee of religious freedom carried the day. On September 25, 1790, Congress approved what would become the First Amendment's guarantee of religious liberty: "Congress shall make no law respecting an establishment of religion, or prohibiting the free exercise thereof."

The precise meaning of the prohibition against any law "respecting an establishment of religion" was uncertain. As the historian Leonard Levy has observed, "It is astonishing to discover that the debate on a bill of rights occurred on a level of abstraction so vague as to convey the impression that Americans . . . had only the most nebulous conception of the meanings of the particular rights they sought to ensure." Indeed, even the most articulate advocates of "the freedom of speech," "the freedom of the press," "the free exercise" of religion, and the prohibition of any law "respecting an establishment of religion" offered no "analysis of what these rights meant, how far they extended, and in what circumstances they might be limited."[45]

This should not be surprising, for in drafting the Bill of Rights, the Framers were "not trying to resolve concrete disputes," but to affirm broad principles. The enactment of the First Amendment therefore constituted a vague declaration, and a challenge, for the future.[46]

Moreover, the very concept of an "establishment of religion" was nebulous. What constituted an "establishment" had varied greatly over the centuries in both Europe and the United States. Even in 1790, the contours of the concept differed significantly, even among the states that still had an established religion. Although "establishment" clearly denoted some form of legal union of government and religion, the precise nature of that union was ill-defined and open-ended.

Historically, for example, some establishments required attendance at the officially approved church, some prohibited anyone to advocate dissenting doctrine, some authorized only the established clergy to perform official functions, some reserved the right to hold political office only to members of the established church, some used public funds to support the established church and its clergy, some enforced laws designed to compel compliance with the beliefs of the established religion (such as laws against blasphemy and Sabbath-breaking), and so on. Against this background, there was no clear understanding of what constituted an "establishment of religion."

Adding to this uncertainty, the Framers of the Establishment Clause prohibited not only the "establishment of religion," but any law "*respecting* an establishment of religion." This was clearly an effort to ensure that the Establishment Clause would be construed broadly, rather than narrowly. Given the concerns of the Framers, and especially of the Anti-Federalists, this made perfect sense. The prospect of a strong national government generated considerable anxiety. Because the United States, even in the 1780s, contained a religiously diverse and heterogeneous population, each religious group was anxious that some other sect or coalition of sects might seize the power of the national government and establish a nationwide religious norm that would disadvantage it. The safest course was to enact a broad guarantee that protected all religious groups against this danger.

THE FRAMERS certainly understood the importance, if not all the implications, of what they had done. George Washington, for example, celebrated the Religion Clauses of the First Amendment as a major national achievement, and James Madison characterized the Establishment Clause as a beacon of liberty. "We are teaching the world the great truth," Madison wrote, that "Religion flourishes in greater purity, without than with the aid of Govt." Although admitting "that it may not be easy, in every possible case, to trace the line of separation, between the rights of Religion & the Civil authority," Madison nonetheless insisted that the "tendency to a usurpation on one side, or the other, or to a corrupting coalition or alliance between them, will be best guarded against by an entire abstinence of the Government from interference, in any way whatever, beyond the necessity of preserving public order, & protecting each sect against trespasses on its legal rights by others."[47]

It was Thomas Jefferson, however, who first crystallized the central meaning of the Establishment Clause. A decade after the First Amendment was enacted, President Jefferson wrote the Baptists of Danbury, Connecticut, assuring them that "I contemplate with sovereign reverence that act of the whole American people which declared that their legislature should 'make no law respecting an establishment of religion, or prohibiting the free exercise thereof,' thus building a *wall of separation* between church and State."[48] Although the overarching spirit of the Establishment Clause was clear, the precise contours of the "wall of separation" have remained a continuing source of controversy ever since.

THE END OF THE ENLIGHTENMENT

THE FOUNDERS ENVISIONED the United States as "an Enlightenment ideal." Their dream was that America would be a beacon of hope for the future—a new kind of "City on a Hill." With the French Revolution of 1789 following hard on the heels of the American Revolution, it seemed that the world was on the cusp of a new era of individual liberty, dignity, and equality based on a new commitment to human reason.

At the time when Americans adopted their Constitution, a time when they fervently believed in "the pursuit of happiness," there were no laws in the United States against obscenity, there were no laws restricting the use of contraceptives, there were no laws forbidding the dissemination of information about contraception, and, following the English common law, there were no laws restricting abortion pre-quickening. Moreover, although there were still laws on the books against consensual sodomy, those laws had not been enforced anywhere in the United States for almost a century. That was the world of the Framers.

But as the violence of the French Revolution spun into a fearsome Reign of Terror in 1793, Americans were shocked to see self-styled "rationalists" transformed into a new "type of tyrant"—"ideological rather than religious" in nature. As the guillotine became the public image of the French Revolution, the horrors of Paris came "to be linked in popular opinion with the . . . political radicalism and religious skepticism of the French *philosophes.*"

Doubt and reaction soon set in, and the "Enlightenment project" began to be viewed with increasing suspicion and alarm. The backlash in both

Europe and America pushed the rationalism of the eighteenth century off center stage, and at the turn of the nineteenth century the Second Great Awakening burst upon the United States, as a "new wave of . . . religiosity" swept the nation.[49]

By the end of his life in 1826, Thomas Jefferson could look back with a sense of despair, noting that American society was "going backward." The ordinary people, in whom Jefferson had placed such confidence, now "seemed more sectarian and less rational than they had been at the time of the Revolution." Instead of becoming "more enlightened," they now clung ever more tightly to the "superstition" of the past.[50]

It is to this era that we now turn.

PART III

MORALISTS

7

THE SECOND
GREAT AWAKENING

"A Spasm Among the Populace," Cane Ridge, Kentucky,
August 6, 1801

I N THE DECADES following independence, the Second Great Awakening, which lasted from roughly the 1790s to the 1840s, marked a
reemergence of religious zeal as millions of Americans were "born
again" in emotionally charged revival meetings.* Although mainstream Protestants tended to dismiss these spectacles as mass hysteria
dressed up as religion, they were stunningly effective in their influence on
American culture. The Second Great Awakening triggered a nationwide
campaign to transform American law and politics through the lens of evangelical Christianity. Indeed, it was in this era that the claim that the United
States is a "Christian nation" first took root.

The Second Great Awakening posed fundamental questions about the
appropriate role of religion in American politics. Both the Framers of our
Constitution and the nineteenth-century evangelicals believed that public
morality was necessary for self-governance, but they differed sharply in
their understanding of the proper relationship between Christianity and
public morality. The Framers believed that the principles of public morality should be discovered through the exercise of reason, whereas the evangelicals insisted that they must be grounded in Christian revelation; the
Framers maintained that the principles of public morality must be rooted
in the obligation to "do good to one's fellow man," whereas the evangeli-

---

* The First Great Awakening was an international movement that began in the 1730s. It was
grounded in a rejection of Enlightenment values and was spread by powerful preaching that gave
listeners a sense of deep personal revelation of their need of salvation by Jesus Christ. The leading
figure in the United States, Jonathan Edwards, emphasized the importance of immediate, personal religious experience and decried the very notion of scientific inquiry and progress. The First
Great Awakening largely burned itself out by 1743.

cals declared that those principles must be found in the obligation to obey God. In short, the early nineteenth-century evangelicals preached that only Christianity could save America from sin and desolation.[1]

The events of the Second Great Awakening are important not only in their own right, and not only because they so directly challenged the values and aspirations of the Framers, but also because they foreshadowed many of the issues that have arisen in contemporary disputes over the appropriate role of religion in efforts to use the secular law to forbid obscenity, contraception, abortion, homosexuality, and same-sex marriage. Indeed, the similarities are quite striking.

"A SPASM AMONG THE POPULACE"

THE EMERGENCE OF the Second Great Awakening was due in large part to the sense of rootlessness caused by the secularization, urbanization, and industrialization of society in the late eighteenth century, the terrifying violence of the French Revolution, and the often bitter social and political divisions that erupted in the United States in the 1790s. In 1798, for example, an anxious Benjamin Rush, a signer of the Declaration of Independence who faithfully attended Christ Church in Philadelphia, predicted "nothing but suffering to the human race" as long as the world continued to embrace "paganism, deism, and atheism." Two years later, with the bitterly contested election of Thomas Jefferson—an outspoken critic of traditional Christianity—as President of the United States, conservative religious leaders warned that the nation faced "a spiritual deterioration hardly to be equaled in the darkest chapters of Christian history."[2]

By appealing to the anxieties of the common man, the charismatic preachers of the early nineteenth century excited a wave of mass religious fervor. The most cataclysmic explosions of this religious passion took place in what was then viewed as the West. The meeting that dominated the American vision of evangelical revivalism took place at Cane Ridge, Kentucky, on August 6, 1801. At an event organized by eighteen Presbyterian ministers, a huge crowd estimated at between ten and twenty-five thousand attended the gathering, as scores of preachers held forth simultaneously in all corners of the site.[3]

Cane Ridge created "a spasm among the populace," a violent outburst of emotions. In the flickering light of campfires, those seeking salvation "fell in droves" as they shrieked, laughed, barked, yelped incantations, and ran in circles. According to Barton Warren Stone, who attended the Cane Ridge revival, people "affected with the jerks" would utter "a piercing scream" and suddenly "fall like a log on the floor, earth, or mud, and appear as dead." With Cane Ridge, the claim that only Christianity could save America became a war cry and the revival meeting became the central mode of evangelical salvation.[4]

The evangelicals preached that the United States was God's new "spiritual Israel" and that Americans therefore had a fundamental duty to spread the gospel. An essential goal of the Second Great Awakening was "to make America the world's greatest example" of a Christian nation. Over the next forty years, the Second Great Awakening affected politics, culture, education, relations between the sexes, attitudes about sex, and perhaps most fundamentally, social and political norms about the proper relation between religion and government in a free and democratic society—questions that divide our nation to this day.[5]

"MORAL MILITIA"

IF THERE WAS a single moment that marked the intellectual beginning of the Second Great Awakening, it was the appointment in 1795 of Timothy Dwight as the president of Yale. A distinguished theologian, Dwight believed that a conspiracy of infidels and deists threatened the very existence of the American nation. Yale students like Asahel Nettleton, Nathaniel William Taylor, and Lyman Beecher, who would later become leaders of the evangelical movement, were moved by Dwight's "fusion of belief in a powerful Calvinistic God" with his own more modern conception of sin and free will. Dwight taught that human beings are "moral agents" and that Christianity should foster not only faith, but "benevolent action."[6]

No one better exemplifies the spirit of the moral campaign launched by the early nineteenth-century evangelicals than Dwight's protégé, Lyman Beecher, a Presbyterian preacher from New Haven. Building on Dwight's teachings, Beecher became his generation's most powerful advocate of moral reform. He "decried the moral decay of society and warned that if reformation did not occur, the nation's doom was assured." Beecher cautioned that if left unchecked, sin would "sunder the ties of society." He took as his mission not only the winning of individual souls, but the wholesale "transformation of society."[7]

In 1803, Beecher preached a sermon before the Moral Society of East Hampton, Long Island, titled "The Practicality of Suppressing Vice by Means of Societies Instituted for That Purpose," in which he argued that God-fearing Christians must "act in concert against evil." He called for the creation of moral societies committed to bringing "public opinion" into line with the sacred order. He exhorted these societies to stigmatize what he deemed "moral crimes," explaining that it was morally unacceptable that "the name of God is blasphemed; the bible is denounced; the Sabbath is profaned; the public worship of God is neglected." Beecher preached that Christianity was the essential "corner stone" of American government. "Remove it," he warned, "and the building falls."[8]

By 1812, Beecher came to the conclusion that the signs of "national desolation" were everywhere. He therefore renewed his call for the creation of a multitude of reform societies that would act as a sort of "moral militia." He called for the vigorous enforcement of laws against "immorality" and advocated an aggressive campaign "to devise ways and means of suppressing vice and guarding the public morals." The principles of the Gospel, Beecher declared, must be "the governing rule of all mankind."[9]

B Y THE late 1820s, western New York was the area in which the evangelical revivals had achieved their greatest intensity. The dominant figure was Charles Grandison Finney. The son of farmers, Finney was the youngest of his parents' fifteen children. Born again in 1821, Finney preached that the "conversion experience, accompanied by a once-and-for-all decision for Christ, was the central event in the spiritual life of Christians." Finney saw himself as restoring Christianity from the "corruptions that had been foisted upon it."[10]

Finney journeyed from town to town, holding revival meetings that typically lasted several days. A man of boundless energy, Finney preached nearly every day, and often several times a day. Upon arriving in a new town, he would identify promising candidates for conversion. He would seat them visibly at the front of the church, in what he called "the anxious bench." The idea was that as they experienced conversion, their experience would in turn influence others. He preached that God had made man "a moral free agent," that evil was the result of choice, that sin and disorder would melt away when people "chose good over evil and convinced others to do the same," and that if Christians worked together and "dedicated their lives to the task, they could convert the world."[11]

Finney was masterful in the pulpit. A former lawyer, his preaching style demonstrated formidable courtroom skills. His prayer meetings were carefully orchestrated, he always made sure that every seat was filled, and he actively discouraged participation by "scoffers, cranks, and the merely curious." Individual conversions, during which sinners often broke into tears, became grand public spectacles.

Charles Grandison Finney

Finney carried his message across the towns and cities of the northeast, making "new hearts in hundreds of thousands of middle class men and women," setting them off on an emotional "crusade to remake society in God's name." News of Finney's success in New York triggered a wave of religious enthusiasm, and large-scale revivals quickly spread across Ohio, Michigan, and New England. The ultimate goal of these revivals was, in short, "the Christianization of the world."[12]

SUNDAY MAIL: "TO RESTORE GODLY ORDER"

FROM 1800 THROUGH the 1840s, evangelical Christians converged on American politics *en masse*. Evangelical ministers politicked for Sunday closing laws, blasphemy prosecutions, temperance legislation, and a host of other morals-based laws. As Beecher's call for the creation of voluntary reform associations took hold, cooperation among evangelicals flourished. Baptists, Presbyterians, Methodists, and Episcopalians joined forces in the campaign for moral reform. The interlocking network of evangelical organizations became known as "the Benevolent Empire." Its goal was to "create the functional equivalent of an established church."[13]

The central premise of the evangelical political movement was that morality is necessary for republican government and that Christianity is necessary for morality. The evangelicals believed that only the Bible could show Americans "how to live their lives." In the words of the historian John West, the evangelicals "edged perilously close" to declaring that only Christians could be "good citizens." Beecher maintained, for example, that Christians should vote only for candidates who accept "the doctrines and institutions of the Gospel."[14]

Reflecting the growing concerns of many Americans, Georgia Congressman Wilson Lumpkin denounced what he characterized as the "Christian party in politics." Fearful that the evangelicals were attempting to "sacrilize the world," critics attacked their campaign as "dangerous to free government."[15]

Frances Wright, one of the most outspoken opponents of the evangelical movement, warned packed houses that the evangelicals were promoting "a system of error" that would fill the nation with "discord." An upper-class Scottish woman who had been raised in part by a granduncle who was a professor of moral philosophy at the University of Glasgow, Fanny Wright was a determined and deeply humanist reformer who came to America in 1824 to promote her liberal ideals. She denounced revivalism as an "odious experiment" and characterized women converts as its special "victims" because the demands of evangelical Christianity subordinated the freedom and dignity of women.[16]

Wright cut a unique figure as an unmarried woman discussing political philosophy on a public stage. As such, she often faced the evangelicals' most vehement scorn. They decried her as "intolerably offensive and disgusting" and as "the Red Harlot" for flouting their vision of properly demure womanhood by taking the stage as a public advocate in her own voice. Wright, in turn, mocked the idea that evangelical theology was necessary for public morality. She charged that rather than fostering true morality, the evangelicals more often "subverted the principles of freedom."[17]

FOR LYMAN BEECHER and his followers, the sins that most directly threatened the nation were "public violations of the sacred—breaking the Sabbath, taking the Lord's name in vain, neglecting worship." The

United States would be destroyed, he warned, if Americans failed to preserve "a Godly order." This view led the evangelicals to demand that government honor the Sabbath.[18]

Although Sabbath observance had traditionally not played a central role in Christian theology, the Puritans had elevated it to an essential part of God's covenant and declared Sabbath-breaking a crime, punishable by a fine, a whipping, or a turn in the stocks. As American society became more tolerant and pluralistic, the enforcement of laws against Sabbath-breaking waned. Although the laws remained on the books, by the mid-eighteenth century Americans had come to view such legislation as incompatible with the nation's commitment to religious diversity and the separation of church and state.

But during the Second Great Awakening, the evangelicals reignited this issue in what became a bitter dispute over Sunday mail delivery. In the first decades of the nation's history, the United States Post Office delivered mail seven days a week, including the Sabbath. As late as 1810, Congress expressly ratified this practice by enacting legislation specifically requiring local postmasters to deliver the mail "on every day of the week."[19]

In 1827, however, Lyman Beecher declared that if Sabbath-breaking was not forbidden, irreligion would "prevail" and the nation would be infected with "immorality" that would undermine "republican institutions." The following year, a group of evangelicals founded the General Union for Promoting the Observance of the Christian Sabbath, with the express goal of reestablishing "Godly order to a fallen community." The evangelicals filed hundreds of petitions with Congress demanding the abolition of Sunday mail delivery. Their most direct argument was straightforwardly religious: The Sabbath had "been instituted by God; therefore, it must be respected." Many petitions warned that "any nation that disregards the Sabbath will bring on itself divine retribution."*[20]

The opponents of ending Sunday mail delivery emphasized both the economic interests of the nation and the concern that if Congress acceded to the evangelicals' petitions it would effectively be enacting a law "respecting the establishment of religion" and "injecting itself into a religious con-

---

* The petitions also invoked the right of conscience, maintaining that for the government to require postal employees to work on the Sabbath violated the right of religious liberty under the Free Exercise Clause of the First Amendment, which provides that "Congress shall make no law . . . prohibiting the free exercise" of religion. U.S. Const. Amend. I.

troversy over what day constitutes the Sabbath." They characterized the evangelical position as the "first step" in a nationwide campaign to inject "religion into politics" and to "subvert republican government." One opponent described the evangelical proposal as "an entering wedge—the first step to priestly despotism." After all, the critics asked, if Sabbath-breaking could be outlawed because it is inconsistent with Christian dogma, then what would be next?[21]

The most vigorous opponent of ending Sunday mail service was Congressman Richard Johnson of Kentucky, who would later serve as Martin Van Buren's vice president. Johnson wrote two influential congressional committee reports on the controversy. Noting that "religious combinations to effect a political object are . . . dangerous," he reasoned that a law forbidding Sunday mail delivery would threaten "the spirit of the Constitution" and "the religious rights of citizens."[22]

Johnson insisted that the very fact that those demanding an end to Sunday mail delivery argued that Sabbath-breaking violated "divine law" was itself a sufficient constitutional ground to reject their position, and he cautioned that if the evangelicals had their way, they would eventually seek legislation forbidding "people from writing letters on the Sabbath" and compelling their "attendance at public worship." Johnson's reports were widely distributed and read throughout the nation.[23]

For several years, the evangelical campaign to end Sunday mail service "engulfed the nation" in controversy. Many Americans feared that the campaign presented a serious threat "by evangelicals to impose their religious beliefs" on the nation. At public meetings throughout the United States, speakers denounced the leaders of the evangelical movement as "religious zealots" who were attempting "to undermine America's republican government."[24]

In the end, Congressman Johnson's position carried the day, in part because of support from traditional Protestants who were skeptical of the revival movement and were concerned that "a state-supported Sabbath . . . would 'cleave asunder'" the liberating effects of religious disestablishment. The evangelicals' demand that the government cease Sunday mail service went down to defeat.*[25]

---

* In 1912, an alliance of ministers and postal clerks finally convinced Congress to close the post offices on Sundays.

BLASPHEMY: "A GROSS VIOLATION OF DECENCY"

BECAUSE EVANGELICALS IN this era insisted that the United States was "a Christian nation" and that Christian piety was "the highest expression of morality," they called upon the government to prosecute blasphemy. Blasphemy consists of speaking ill of "sacred matters." Defenders of blasphemy prosecutions argue that they are necessary to avert divine wrath, enforce conformity with dominant religious beliefs, insulate those beliefs from the contagion of doubt, protect the sensibilities of believers, and avoid retaliation by believers against those who deride their beliefs.[26]

Punishment for blasphemy—and for heresy, which is the spreading of "false" religious doctrine—became the norm in Christian societies after Constantine embraced Christianity in the fourth century. Augustine advocated the persecution of those who defamed Christian doctrine on the theory that a society that fails to punish blasphemers and heretics is doomed to suffer the worst calamities that could befall mankind.[27]

From the fifth century through the Reformation, persecution for blasphemy and heresy was commonplace. During the Middle Ages, the penalty for blasphemy included death, cutting off the lips, and burning or tearing out the tongue. In the thirteenth century, Thomas Aquinas reasoned that blasphemy was a worse sin than murder, for blasphemy "is a sin committed directly against God," whereas murder is merely "a sin against one's neighbor." Even Luther endorsed the penalty of death for blasphemy, which he defined as any denial of the true Christian faith. During the sixteenth and seventeenth centuries, executions and other brutal punishments for blasphemy and heresy were inflicted throughout Europe.[28]

In the American colonies, though, blasphemy prosecutions were relatively rare, especially in the Southern and Mid-Atlantic colonies. In New England, however, the Puritans took blasphemy quite seriously. Invoking *Leviticus,** the early Puritan codes declared blasphemy a capital offense. From the 1660s through the 1680s, the Puritans initiated approximately twenty blasphemy prosecutions. In one case, the defendant was prosecuted for calling God a bastard; in another, for stating that the devil was as merciful as God. Although the Puritans never executed anyone for blasphemy, they whipped, pilloried, and mutilated those found guilty of the offense.

---

* "He that blasphemeth the name of the Lord, he shall surely be put to death." *Leviticus* 24:16 (King James Version).

By the late seventeenth century, the penalties for blasphemy grew more lenient, even in New England, and by the eighteenth century, blasphemy prosecutions disappeared almost entirely. Although blasphemy laws remained on the books, by the time of the American Revolution the idea that the government could legitimately punish an individual for disparaging Christianity had fallen into disrepute. The very concept was seen as incompatible with the core aspirations of a society committed to religious toleration, the disestablishment of religion, and the principle of free expression. By 1776, the law of blasphemy had come to be regarded as a "relic of a dead age."[29]

WITH THE Second Great Awakening, however, prosecutions for blasphemy suddenly reemerged. In 1811, for example, New York prosecuted one Ruggles for the common law offense of blasphemy for stating in a tavern that "Jesus Christ was a bastard, and his mother must be a whore." Ruggles was convicted and sentenced to three months in prison.

Speaking for the New York court, Chancellor James Kent, a conservative jurist who viewed religion as the bulwark of the social order, declared that Christianity was an integral part of the law of the land and that blasphemy that "insulted and defamed" Christianity was therefore "a gross violation of decency and good order." Kent explained that other religions were not protected against such derision, because "we are a Christian people, and the morality of the country is deeply ingrafted upon Christianity, and not upon the doctrines" of Judaism, Islam, or Hinduism. Kent dismissed these other faiths as mere "imposters" and "superstitions." The evangelicals of this era fervently invoked the *Ruggles* decision as the "supreme proof" that the United States was, after all, a Christian nation.[30]

In 1824, Pennsylvania prosecuted one Abner Updegraph for deriding the Bible as "a mere fable" during a public debate over the fallibility of the Bible. Although the Pennsylvania Supreme Court reversed the conviction on a technicality, it upheld the doctrine that blasphemy was a crime. The court explained that Updegraph's language was so "insulting" when "spoken in a Christian land" that it must be punished as "directly tending to a breach of the peace." The court added that because "Christianity is part of the common law of this state," the law does not protect "the malicious reviler of Christianity."[31]

As Perry Miller, a historian of Puritan New England, has observed, those "who wrote the Constitution would have been astounded could they have been brought back to hear lawyers saying that in the Common Law were reflected 'the principles of Divine Law, as promulgated by Moses, and as expounded by Christ." Indeed, around the time of *Updegraph*, both John Adams and Thomas Jefferson vigorously condemned such prosecutions. Adams wrote Jefferson that laws against blasphemy were "a great embarrassment" and he called for the repeal of all such laws. Jefferson wrote a celebrated attack on the claim that Christianity was incorporated into the law of the land, concluding that this claim was a sheer fabrication.[32]

The union of Christianity and the law was asserted most forcefully in this era by Chief Justice Lemuel Shaw of the Supreme Judicial Court of Massachusetts, in the nineteenth century's most memorable blasphemy prosecution. The case involved Abner Kneeland, a cantankerous, outspoken, former minister who was widely known for his radical views on politics, religion, slavery (he was an abolitionist), and birth control. A prolific author, editor, and lecturer, Kneeland was prosecuted for publishing an article in 1833 in which he declared that "the whole story concerning" Christ was "as much a fable and fiction as that of the god Prometheus" and that the miracles of the Bible were nothing more than "trick and imposture."

Kneeland was dragged through a succession of trials (most of which ended in hung juries), until the authorities finally secured a conviction on their fifth try. Kneeland was sentenced to sixty days in jail. In an opinion by Chief Justice Shaw, the Supreme Judicial Court of Massachusetts upheld Kneeland's conviction. Shaw reasoned that blasphemy consists of "speaking evil of the Deity" with the "impious purpose" of alienating "the minds of others from the love and reverence of God." Shaw held that Kneeland's conviction was consistent with the Massachusetts Declaration of Rights, because the guarantees of freedom of speech and religious liberty do not protect individuals who "disparage the Supreme Being."[33]

These prosecutions clearly reflected the values of the Second Great Awakening, for they both reinforced and reaffirmed the growing conception of America as a Christian nation.[*]

---

[*] As the force of the Second Great Awakening waned, the demand for blasphemy prosecutions dissipated. Since 1838, there have been only a smattering of blasphemy prosecutions in the United States, and a broad consensus has emerged that Jefferson and Adams had it right. In 1952, the Supreme Court of the United States finally put the matter to rest, holding in a unanimous decision that "it is not the business of government in our nation to suppress real or imagined attacks upon a particular religious doctrine" or to protect "any or all religions from views which are distasteful to them." The First Amendment, the Court declared, renders any such government action unconstitutional. *Burstyn v. Wilson*, 343 U.S. 495, 505 (1952).

THE TEMPERANCE MOVEMENT

IN THE EARLY NINETEENTH CENTURY, Americans consumed alcohol with little sense that their behavior might be deemed immoral. The Puritans had never been abstemious, and traditional Christianity had never discouraged drinking. Most early nineteenth-century Americans regarded alcohol as an ordinary part of everyday life. Indeed, most people considered alcohol to be safer and more healthful than the drinking water that was then commonly available.[34]

In 1812, however, Timothy Dwight castigated drinking as a sin, and Lyman Beecher later embraced the cause. In his *Six Sermons* on the subject, first published in 1826, Beecher described intemperance as "the sin of our land" and warned that the evils of intemperance would destroy the nation. He insisted that the only solution was "the banishment of ardent spirits from the list of lawful articles of commerce."[35]

Later that year, evangelicals in Boston established the American Society for the Promotion of Temperance. This issue caught the public's imagination, and by 1828 more than four hundred temperance societies had sprung up across the nation. Within a decade, these societies had established more than five thousand chapters. The early temperance organizations pressured retailers to forego the sale of alcoholic beverages and encouraged their members to take a "pledge" to abstain. Although more than a million Americans took the pledge, it soon became clear that voluntary abstention could not save the nation. The temperance societies then demanded the enactment of laws prohibiting the sale of alcohol.[36]

In 1836, the American Temperance Movement was formed on the platform of total prohibition. The evangelical vision of the temperance issue closely tracked its larger understanding of America. Along with Sabbath-breaking and blasphemy, drink "became an important symbol of sin." The evangelicals preached that many of the evils that had befallen mankind could be traced to the "intemperate use of spirituous liquors." Maine passed the first statewide alcohol ban in 1846, followed by Vermont, Rhode Island, Michigan, and eight other states over the course of the next decade. Although mainstream Protestants maintained that the demand for prohibition was not rooted in either moral or religious principles and that it unreasonably limited individual freedom, the evangelical advocates of temperance insisted that any use of alcohol was immoral and must therefore be banned.[37]

SLAVERY: "THE BLOOD OF SOULS"

THE ISSUE OF SLAVERY sharply divided nineteenth-century evangelicals. During the Revolutionary era, Presbyterian and Methodist churches tended to condemn slavery, but once the idealism of the Revolution had played itself out, the nation turned its attention to economic and commercial expansion. By the early years of the nineteenth century, slavery had become so central to the Southern economy that all but its staunchest opponents came to regard it as a necessary, if regrettable, part of the economic life of the nation. Churches that had once called for abolition now settled for "condemning slavery in theory," but treating its continued existence as a "political matter separate from the sphere of the church." They called not for abolition, "but for the Christian treatment of slaves and for their conversion to Christianity."[38]

Those concerned with the immorality of slavery focused primarily on colonization. In 1817, the American Society for Colonizing the Free People of Color of the United States was formed with the goal of creating a colony in Africa for freed slaves. Colonizationists believed that because of differences in color, ability, culture, and circumstance, blacks could never achieve equality in the United States. Complete geographical separation was therefore the best solution.[39]

William Lloyd Garrison, the nation's most eloquent proponent of abolition, had initially been inspired by Lyman Beecher's vision of evangelical reform. Garrison began his career within that tradition, editing a newspaper dedicated to the cause of temperance, but his advocacy of emancipation soon alienated him from Beecher and from most evangelicals. Invoking the evangelical belief that America stood "on a great precipice, ready to plunge into darkness," Garrison accused his fellow citizens, and especially the evangelicals, of neglecting their moral responsibilities by ignoring the plight of a "multitude of miserable human beings." Garrison declared slavery "the bell weather of America's fidelity to its covenant with God" and charged that the "blood of souls" is upon Christianity.[40]

By the early 1830s, Garrison's religious conviction had been deeply shaken by the evangelicals' rejection of his position. Ironically, although Garrison's call for abolition was greeted with hostility by most evangelicals, it won the enthusiastic support of many of those whose religious views he himself had "once condemned as irreligious," including the Quakers, Unitarians, and freethinkers. On one occasion, Garrison searched in vain for a church or hall in Boston in which to speak. Lyman Beecher refused to assist him, dismissing Garrison's call for abolition as "misguided." It was Abner Kneeland, soon to be charged with blasphemy, who came to Garrison's aid and who sponsored his speech under the auspices of the Society of Free Enquirers. In his address, Garrison excoriated the Christian churches who had rebuffed his appeal.[41]

Invocations of the Bible played a central role in the debate over slavery. Abolitionists, such as Theodore Dwight Weld, who published *The Bible Against Slavery* in 1837, invoked St. Paul's speech in Athens, in which he pronounced that God "hath made of one blood all nations of men for to dwell on all the face of the earth." But the defenders of slavery also invoked the Bible, quoting, for example, Noah's declaration in *Genesis* 9:25: "Cursed be Canaan; a servant of servants shall he be unto his brethren." Indeed, some of the most ardent supporters of slavery, such as the Baptist clergyman Thornton Stringfellow, enthusiastically cited biblical passages to prove that "God's Chosen People practiced chattel slavery and that God, far from issuing a blanket condemnation of the institution, prescribed legal rules for it." By the 1830s, Southern clergymen and politicians were frequently invoking the Bible in defense of slavery. Each side insisted that it had "the better of the argument."[*42]

"AROUSED LUST"

THE SECOND GREAT AWAKENING had a profound impact on social and legal attitudes toward sex. As noted earlier, by the late eighteenth century most Americans had embraced a relatively relaxed approach to sex, and the states had pretty much ceased enforcing their criminal laws against consensual adult sex. Revolution-era Americans simply did not consider such conduct worthy of serious legal concern. The Framers were not libertines, but they were men of their age, and their age—the age of Henry Fielding's *Tom Jones* and John Cleland's *Memoirs of a Woman of Pleasure*—was not shy about sexual pleasure.

Before the Second Great Awakening, there had never been any legal effort to censor sexual expression in either the colonies or the states. To

---

* During the twentieth-century civil rights struggle, segregationists as well as integrationists invoked biblical authority. Indeed, Christian theology was "deeply interwoven" into "the segregationist ideology that supported the discriminatory world of Jim Crow." Jane Dailey, *Sex, Segregation, and the Sacred after Brown*, 91 J. Am. Hist. 119, 121–22 (2004).

the contrary, eighteenth-century Americans enjoyed a freewheeling market in erotic literature. This attitude changed during the Second Great Awakening, though, as a new "ethic of sexual restraint took hold." Evangelical Christians, whose religious moralism condemned sexual expression as sinful, declared war against the "sins of the flesh."[43]

In 1815, at the height of the Second Great Awakening, Philadelphia tavern owner Jesse Sharpless suffered the first-ever American obscenity prosecution. In what had once been considered America's most freewheeling city, he was charged with exhibiting for a fee an image of "a man in an obscene, impudent, and indecent posture with a woman." Sharpless's counsel argued that his client's action warranted no greater punishment than "the frowns of society," but the Pennsylvania Supreme Court disagreed. Invoking the old English precedent of *Rex v. Curll*,[*][44] Chief Justice William Tilghman found that by displaying the image, Sharpless had incited "inordinate and lustful desires," which he held to be a violation of public decency. Tilghman added that because exposure to such "lascivious" images could corrupt the morals of young people by "inflaming their passions," it set an "evil example" and was therefore fit for criminal prosecution.[45]

Several years later, the Supreme Judicial Court of Massachusetts held that one Peter Holmes could be convicted for publishing "a lewd and obscene" book—John Cleland's infamous *Memoirs of a Woman of Pleasure*.[46] *Sharpless* and *Holmes* were prosecutions under the common law. The nation's first statutes prohibiting the distribution of obscene literature were enacted in the 1820s, at the height of the Second Great Awakening, in Vermont, Connecticut, and Massachusetts.

THROUGHOUT THE Second Great Awakening, the evangelicals aggressively promoted strict sexual standards and condemned sexual desire as "sinful lust." This condemnation applied not only to sexually-explicit expression, but also to information about birth control, which they deemed particularly dangerous because birth control "removed the fear of pregnancy." They maintained that this fear was "necessary for the protection of female virginity." The aroused female, they preached, could not be trusted, for following the example of Eve, she would naturally be driven "to satisfy her lusts."[47]

In 1831, Charles Knowlton, a Massachusetts physician, published *Fruits*

---

* See chapter 3.

of Philosophy; or, The Private Companion of Young Married People, a pathbreaking work that "attempted to apply science to sexual relations." Knowlton argued that people's understanding of sex and sexuality must move into the realm of medicine. He recommended a specific method of female douching, involving a reusable syringe and common chemicals, listing its many advantages: "It requires no sacrifice of pleasure; it is in the hands of the female; it is to be used after, instead of before connexion, a weighty consideration in its favor." In defense of birth control, Knowlton cited the need for sensible family planning, invoked Thomas Malthus's arguments for population control, and rejected celibacy as an impractical check on the sex drive.[48]

Knowlton's book was not the first to counsel birth control—Richard Carlile's *Every Woman's Book; or, What is Love?* (1826) and Robert Dale Owen's *Moral Physiology* (1830) preceded *Fruits of Philosophy* by a few years, but Knowlton was the first medical adviser to be prosecuted for his advice. Knowlton was sentenced to hard labor by a Massachusetts court, which took the evangelical line and officially declared all books discussing contraception, even those written by physicians in a medical manner, morally unacceptable.[49]

T HE GROWING concern with sexual expression was closely bound up with anxiety about masturbation. Critics of erotic literature warned that such material incited youths to practice what at the time was euphemistically called the "secret vice." In the 1830s, Sylvester Graham, the son and grandson of Connecticut clergymen, was the most prominent champion of this view. Graham insisted that "by abusing his organs, and depraving his instinctive appetites," man becomes "a living volcano of unclean propensities and passions." Graham taught that self-pollution endangered the entire body, because the "convulsive paroxysms attending" sexual activity "cause the most powerful agitation to the whole system that it is ever subject to."

According to Graham, the "body should undergo such excitement only a few times in its lifetime." Graham expressly condemned erotic literature, because it stimulated "lascivious thoughts," which promote the secret vice, resulting in debility, insanity, and even death. Graham deemed masturbation the worst form of sexual indulgence, because it has no justification in reproduction and is therefore "wholly unnatural." He developed a new whole-grain food, marketed today as the Graham cracker, which he touted as the most effective means for dampening the sexual passions.

Those who feared the effects of masturbation "saw danger lurking everywhere." Luther Bell, the superintendent of an asylum in Boston, lamented that "every library, . . . every printshop, has something, prose, poetry, or picture, which can be perverted . . . to the base use of exciting the passions, and which is impressed into the service of pollution." Opponents of masturbation warned that those who fell victim to the practice would be "reduced to a state of utter degradation." Parents were cautioned to be on the lookout for early signs of self-abuse in their children. If they were not attentive, their sons would face lives of failure, debility, violence, and confinement in an asylum, and their daughters would suffer terrible illness, rampant fornication, and ultimately a life of prostitution. In this era, a broad range of devices, employing padlocks, live wires, and physical restraints were devised and widely sold to parents to prevent masturbation.[50]

It was these fears, fed by the evangelical view of sex during the Second Great Awakening, that led to the first federal legislation prohibiting the importation of "indecent and obscene" materials in the Tariff Act of 1842, and then to the explosion of state and federal anti-obscenity laws after the Civil War during the age of Anthony Comstock, laws that remain on the books to this day.*[51]

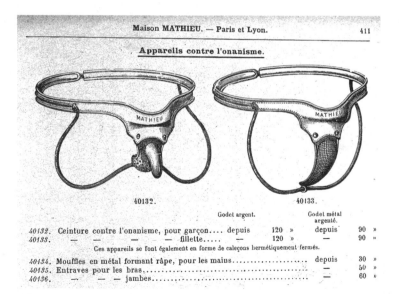

Anti-Masturbation Devices

---

* See chapter 8.

FREETHINKERS AND FREE LOVE

THE STEADY ENCROACHMENT of religious zeal into the nation's legal and political discourse during the Second Great Awakening ignited an aggressive defense of Enlightenment principles. Progressive reformers, known variously as freethinkers, free enquirers, sex radicals, and rationalists, vigorously condemned what they saw as a dangerous evangelical campaign to appropriate the meaning of American morality. The freethinkers invoked the Founding Fathers, rather than the Bible, to lay claim to what they saw as the nation's core ideals. Dedicated to the pursuit of rationality, they rooted their arguments in the emerging sciences of economics and physiology.

Several dozen freethought newspapers appeared between 1825 and 1850, with such names as *The Anti-Superstitionist* and *The Herald of Reason and Common Sense*. They pledged to enhance "the condition of man by disseminating the knowledge of that which is true, and thereby better enabling him to judge of what is probably false." The most prominent freethinkers lectured extensively, often to packed houses.[52]

The unlikely star of the freethinking lecture circuit was Fanny Wright, who exploded into the freethought lecture circuit in 1828 with a series of lectures to overflow audiences in halls from Cincinnati to Philadelphia to New Orleans. Among other things, Wright and her fellow freethinkers demanded what they deemed a rational reassessment of the institution of marriage. Wright challenged the social and legal disabilities that effectively deprived wives of personhood and property. She argued that in marriage "female dignity" was undermined by a legal state of "helplessness"; that in marriage "the guardianship of a woman's virtue" was "transferred from herself to others"; and that this intolerable surrender of women's self-determination constituted a "mass of absurdity, injustice, and cruelty."[53]

In the 1830s, Abner Kneeland, who had earlier been convicted of blasphemy, published a "Marriage Catechism," in which he argued that the subjugation of women in marriage "is so arbitrary, so tyrannical, so cruel, and so unjust that I am astonished it should be so long suffered in a free country." Some freethinkers went so far as to compare marriage to the "curse" of "African slavery."[54]

WHEREAS THE evangelicals aggressively promoted strict sexual standards, the freethinkers countered that sex was a natural and vital part of life. Fanny Wright boldly described sexual desire as "the noblest of

Frances Wright

the human passions" and as a natural "source of human happiness." Robert Owen, a Welsh social reformer who came to the United States in 1824, taught that sexual desire gives "social intercourse much of its charm and zest." Owen emphatically rejected the evangelicals' claim that any effort to interfere with conception was unnatural, arguing that "nature, giving sexual passion to humankind, gives also the power to control its effects."[55]

The evangelical preachers condemned Wright and her fellow freethinkers as agents of "the Antichrist." In 1830, Lyman Beecher described their teachings as "poisonous" and accused them of attempting to supplant Christian morals with "the rage of lust." The freethinkers were undaunted. They continued to contest the prevailing social understandings of sex and marriage. Their commitment to female autonomy and to nontraditional marriage coincided with a burgeoning "free love" movement, which insisted that men and women were joined by love, not paperwork, and that the legal status of marriage transformed a spiritual connection into "chattel slavery."[56]

Building upon the freethought critique of marriage, several free love communities, such as Modern Times in Brentwood, New York, and the Free Love Network in Berlin Heights, Ohio, came into being. In these and similar communities, men and women lived openly with one another without the bonds of marriage. These communities were harshly condemned and often subjected to physical attack because they promoted what the evangelicals deemed immoral fornication. Because of the continuous harassment these communities suffered, most shuttered within a few years.[57]

THE END OF THE SECOND GREAT AWAKENING

THE SECOND GREAT AWAKENING put religious practice in the United States on a long-term upward path. By the middle of the nineteenth century, as many as one-third of all Americans were affiliated with a Christian church, a substantial increase from the Revolutionary era. And it was in this era that the campaign to downplay the "deistic propensities" of the Framers and to claim that the United States had been founded as "a Christian nation" first took hold.[58]

By the mid-1830s, however, the Second Great Awakening began to wane. The more extreme elements of the evangelical movement contributed to this outcome. Their rabid anti-Catholicism and vehement political nativism scared off many moderates, and their demands that Christians vote only for Christians, that public education be infused with Christian values, and that the Constitution be amended "to recognize the authority of Christ" all served to undermine the movement's credibility with mainstream Protestants.[59]

In 1836, Calvin Colton, a former revival preacher, astutely warned that the "fanaticism" of the evangelicals would generate "disrespect and disgust." He was right. By the end of the decade, political contests at both the local and national levels increasingly found radical evangelicals "on one side and nearly everyone else on the other." By 1840, the impulse for aggressive evangelical reform had ground to a halt.[60] But this was only temporary.

8

"TENDING TO CORRUPT THE PUBLIC MORALS"

The Meaning of Obscenity

Anthony Comstock

IN THE ERA before 1815, government efforts to censor speech were directed at religious heresy and seditious libel, rather than sexual expression. Despite the availability of a broad range of sexual literature, erotic speech received scant legal attention. It was the religious agitation of the Second Great Awakening that first triggered efforts to suppress sexual expression.

By the 1840s, however, there was once again an upsurge in the availability of pornography. As industrialization and urbanization transformed the nature of cities, New York came to be known as the "carnal showcase of the Western world." In the increasingly close quarters of urban life, prostitution flourished and sexual expression filled New York's newsstands. Daguerreotypes (an early form of photographs first introduced in the 1830s) of women in various stages of undress could be purchased from stationery stores and from the ever-present pushcart vendors who plied the city's streets.[1]

With the rise of the "sporting" press, weekly newspapers like the *Flash*, the *Rake*, the *Libertine*, and the *Whip* trumpeted a sense of ribald manhood, celebrating such pursuits as gambling, boxing, prostitution, and sex. The central theme was that "man is endowed by nature with passions that must be gratified." The sporting press declared brothels to be "as essential to the well-being of society as churches" and openly advertised their offerings, often featuring interviews, profiles, and reviews of favored courtesans. Madams achieved celebrity status.[2]

In an effort to rein in these publications in the early 1840s, New York district attorney James R. Whiting charged the *Sunday Flash* with unlawfully publishing "obscene" material. The charge stemmed from a rather typical sporting-press tale detailing the "seduced-and-abandoned" story of Amanda Green, a prostitute at a West Broadway brothel. Her descent began at the hands of an older man, who seduced her with wine; the next morning, at "the crowing of the cock, she was no more a maid." After the cad proved unfaithful, Amanda turned to another lover and then another and soon thereafter to prostitution.[3]

Given the relative dearth of American precedent on the law of obscenity and the absence of any New York statute addressing the question, Whiting turned to the English common law and to a handful of English jurists for guidance. A leading English authority, Francis Ludlow Holt's treatise on *The Law of Libel*, maintained that because society must uphold morality, the law has a duty to punish "obscene" writings, the "tendency of which is . . . to poison the springs and principles of manners."[4]

Although the *Flash*'s editors were acquitted by the jury, the relentless prosecutors pressed on. They eventually succeeded in convicting the editors of the *Flash* in subsequent prosecutions involving an article describing streetwalkers cruising the Battery and a cartoon depicting a maid leading a gentleman to bed with a warming pan positioned suggestively between his legs. William Snelling, one of the *Flash*'s editors, defended his publication on the ground that the supposed "dirt of the *Flash* is all in your own imaginations."[5]

Despite these occasional prosecutions, the selling power of sex did not escape the notice of the burgeoning American publishing industry. Sex became a standard subject for a species of "racy" short novels and pam-

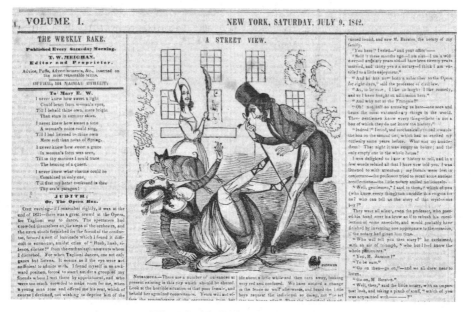

The Weekly Rake, *July 8, 1842*

phlets that went so far as to depict bondage, homosexuality, and even inter-racial sex. The prosecution of the printer Henry R. Robinson in 1842 offers an unusually clear sense of the era's erotica market. In the interest of maintaining a sanitized public record, courts in this era typically provided few details about the content of allegedly obscene works. But, for whatever reason, Robinson's indictment expressly identified several of the objectionable works, including an anal sex scene from *Memoirs of a Woman of Pleasure*, a *ménage à trois* scene from Giovanni Benedetto Sinibaldi's *The Cabinet of Venus Unlocked*, and a rich diversity of erotic engravings. Despite Robinson's copious collection of sexually-explicit material, the case against him was dismissed because it was not yet a crime merely to *possess* obscenity, and there was insufficient evidence to prove that Robinson had ever sold or displayed any of these works to others.[6]

During the next twenty years, with the nation's preoccupation with slavery and Civil War, sexual expression was not high on the list of the nation's concerns. With the end of hostilities in 1865, however, and with an almost frenetic return to "normalcy," the male sporting culture entered the highest rungs of society as America was propelled into the Gilded Age. In New York, the commercial sex trade now penetrated even into Broadway theaters, where special balconies were reserved for flirty call girls who offered postshow "entertainment." The English actress Lydia Thompson took Broadway by storm with a chorus line of burlesque dancers, and a new breed of "concert saloons" began presenting live, semi-clothed entertainment, combining the services of the bar, the theater, and the brothel. These new entertainments placed sex into the forefront of American society as never before.[7]

Not everyone was cheering.

"THERE OUGHT TO BE A LAW"

IN THE 1840S, a group of ministers and righteous businessmen established the Young Men's Christian Association (YMCA) to give God-fearing young men a place for proper leisure activities outside the "moral Maelstrom" of the cities. During the Civil War, the YMCA formed a network of army chaplains and Protestant prayer groups, dubbed the "Christian Commission," to maintain the moral standards of the troops. The Commission distributed religious literature to the soldiers and set up troop libraries stocked with such moralistic works as Sylvester Graham's *Lectures on Chastity*. When the Commission became aware of a robust market among the troops in rather less wholesome reading materials, the YMCA decided to take action. Its first step was to alert Congress to the problem, but Congress, tied up with more pressing concerns, was uninterested.[8]

In the era immediately after the war, the YMCA launched a comprehensive study to document the state of vice in New York City. The study detailed the existence of sexual materials so lurid that some members of the YMCA executive board literally could not believe they existed. When an independent investigator produced tangible proof of their existence, the YMCA board decided that if there was not already a law prohibiting such materials, there surely ought to be.[9]

Because New York still had no statute forbidding the distribution of obscenity, earlier prosecutions had been brought under vague common law principles. Under the influence of the Second Great Awakening, however, some twenty states had enacted criminal obscenity statutes, with the oldest, Vermont's, dating to 1821.

Against that background, the YMCA board drew up proposed legislation to address the issue in New York. In 1868, after an aggressive lobbying campaign, the YMCA finally got its bill through the New York legislature. The new law made it a crime for any person to sell or give away any "obscene and indecent" book, pamphlet, drawing, painting, or photograph, or any article for "indecent or immoral use," or any article or medicine "for the prevention of conception" or the "procuring of an abortion." Over time, the New York law became a model for other states and for the federal government.[10]

Having secured the enactment of this legislation, though, the YMCA board feared that law enforcement officials, who had more pressing priorities, would not devote sufficient resources to suppress the burgeoning market for indecent materials. The board therefore decided that extralegal methods were necessary to achieve the organization's goals. The board thus established its own private task force to ensure the vigorous implementation of its hard-won statute. The YMCA's chief inspector in this campaign, Anthony Comstock, would dominate the national debate over obscenity for the next four decades.[11]

ENTER COMSTOCK

ANTHONY COMSTOCK WAS born in 1844 in New Canaan, Connecticut. His father was a prosperous farmer, and his mother was a devout Congregationalist. She died when Comstock was only ten years old, but her religious fervor remained alive in her son. Based on an unwavering conviction that the devil's temptations were omnipresent, Comstock believed to his very core that abstinence from all impure thoughts and behaviors was the only faithful path to righteousness.

In 1864, Comstock enlisted in the Union Army. He had expected to find a sense of moral camaraderie among the troops, but instead he looked on with disgust while the members of his company consumed "the worst species of yellow-covered literature." In his journal, which he kept scrupulously throughout his life, Comstock complained bitterly of his fellow soldiers' "sin and wickedness."[12]

After the war, Comstock moved to New York City, where he launched a personal campaign against immorality. He was a 24-year-old sales clerk in a dry goods shop when one of his close friends was "led astray, corrupted and diseased," and eventually died from a mysterious ailment, probably a venereal infection. Believing erotica to have been the cause of his friend's corruption and demise, Comstock tracked down the erotica dealer whom he thought responsible for feeding his friend's lust, purchased erotic material from him, and promptly turned it over to the police, thereby instigating his first-ever arrest for vice. Comstock was furious when the bookseller was sentenced to only a modest fine.[13]

Although still working full time as a sales clerk, Comstock began researching the city's extensive erotica market. After leading police on an ambitious sweep of erotic booksellers, resulting in seven arrests in a single day, Comstock felt ready to take on the market's biggest names. In 1872, he learned that a trio of prominent publishers were responsible for the vast majority of the city's sexual material. He resolved to shut them down. Working systematically, Comstock sought out and questioned the publishers' underlings and then persuaded the police to join him on a series of successful raids. The leaders of the YMCA were so impressed with Comstock's energy, enthusiasm, and effectiveness that they offered him a full-time job.[14]

He stepped easily into his new role. After organizing his squad, which he named the "Committee for the Suppression of Vice," Comstock returned to the hunt. He led several successful raids on local publishers but soon realized that to make a truly major impact he needed national legislation. With the enthusiastic backing of the YMCA, Comstock journeyed to Washington to lobby for a federal law. Comstock recruited Supreme Court Justice William Strong, who had once campaigned unsuccessfully to insert "God" into the Constitution, to draft a federal statute. Comstock warned Congress that obscenity was a "hydra-headed monster" that required a potent legislative weapon.[15]

On March 3, 1873, President Ulysses Grant signed into law the "Act for the Suppression of Trade in, and Circulation of, Obscene Literatures and Articles of Immoral Use." The new legislation, which was adopted by Congress with little attention, established a broad ban on all items that could be deemed "obscene, lewd, lascivious, or filthy," but it did not define those terms. The act established six categories of obscenity: print and pictorial erotica, contraceptives, abortifacients, information about contraception or abortion, sexual implements and toys, and advertisements for any of the above. The law authorized severe penalties, including hard labor, and it empowered the Post Office to censor and to confiscate any objectionable material. Comstock was appointed a special postal agent and, fittingly, the law came to be known as the Comstock Act.[16]

In less than a year in his new role, Comstock made fifty-five arrests, won twenty convictions, and confiscated and destroyed thousands of "indecent" books, magazines, pictures, playing cards, and sex "objects." His modus operandi was to scan newspapers for suspicious ads and then to solicit the material through the mail by sending decoy letters.[17]

In his writings and public lectures, Comstock passionately affirmed the sacredness of his mission. On the day that President Grant signed the new federal law, Comstock wrote in his private diary: "Oh how can I express the joy of my Soul or speak the mercy of God!" In his 1880 book *Frauds Exposed*, Comstock described erotica as "a canker worm" and asserted that "lust defiles the body, debauches the imagination, corrupts the mind, deadens the will, destroys the memory, sears the conscience, hardens the heart, and damns the soul."[18]

Comstock never wavered in his belief in the corrupting power of sexual expression. Writing in his 1883 book *Traps for the Young*, Comstock insisted that "one cannot get away from a book that has once been read." Sinful books, he maintained, were traps laid by Satan "to capture our youth and secure the ruin of immortal souls." Comstock analogized obscenity to "a contagious disease" and characterized it as "a worse evil than yellow fever or small-pox." There was, he wrote, "no more active agent employed by Satan . . . to ruin the human family and subject the nations to himself than EVIL READING."[19]

Comstock led the national campaign to suppress obscenity from 1873 until just before his death from pneumonia in 1915. For four decades, he was the most visible symbol of the movement to rid the United States of the "poisons, debauches and curses" of obscenity. His grave at Evergreens Cemetery in Brooklyn is marked by a line from *Hebrews* 12: "Lay aside every weight—looking unto Jesus—despising the shame."[20]

IN DEFENSE OF THE "CANKER WORM"

COMSTOCK'S FAME AND POWER made him the archenemy of those who opposed his Victorian-era prudery. The liberal press mocked his dedication as obsession and condemned his methods as duplicitous. Civil liberties lawyer Morris Ernst derided Comstock as a "psychotic masturbator-with-guilt." He was hardly alone in that analysis. Arthur Garfield Hays, another prominent free speech advocate and cofounder of the American Civil Liberties Union, noted that Comstock "was surrounded in his home by three women—a repressed wife, years older than himself, a bed-ridden sister-in-law, and an adopted girl child who was weak-minded. . . . No wonder he thought that any modest woman would undress only in the dark." The purity of Comstock's devotion was ridiculed in light of allegations that he sometimes sat through entire sex shows before arresting the performers, and even a judge once characterized Comstock's motivations as "wanton."[21]

The late nineteenth-century freethinkers, who condemned the rigidity of traditional marriage and the injustice of stereotypical sex roles, also took up the issue of obscenity. Although a small and diffuse group, these "sex radicals" were a vocal brigade of authors, editors, and lecturers who questioned the mores of late nineteenth-century Victorian sexuality. Figures like public health advocate Dr. Edward Bliss Foote, anarchist Ezra Heywood, freethinker D. M. Bennett, and civil libertarian Moses Harman all challenged Comstock's regime on the ground that both the store of public knowledge and the integrity of the individual benefitted from the free circulation of information and ideas about sex. They insisted that sex was a legitimate and important subject for free expression and that it should not be silenced because some people were fearful, ignorant, prudish, and intolerant.[22]

The sex radicals in the post–Civil War era faced repeated prosecution. In 1876, Dr. Foote attracted the first major prosecution under the federal Comstock Act. Foote's popular home guide, *Plain Home Talk About the Human System*, served a large and eager medical-advice market by providing clear and practical information about sex and contraception. Foote taught that the body's "sexual appetite is just as natural as the appetite for food." At Comstock's initiation, Foote was prosecuted and convicted for distributing information about contraception. The presiding judge ruled that medical advice was not exempt from the statutory prohibition.[23]

Ezra Heywood faced obscenity charges the following year. Born in 1829, Heywood was caught up in the great religious ferment of the Second Great

Awakening. As a young man, he entered Brown University planning to study for the ministry. He grew increasingly disillusioned with the church's failure to condemn slavery, however, and gradually came to view organized religion as littered with self-righteous abstractions that ignored the suffering of slaves, poor people, wage laborers, and women. He never became a minister. Instead, by the early 1860s, he had become an anarchist.

As a social philosopher who advocated free love, free speech, women's rights, and sex education, Heywood believed in the sovereignty of the individual and viewed marriage as the forced surrender of a wife's personhood. In 1876, he penned *Cupid's Yokes: or, the Binding Forces of Conjugal Life*, a pamphlet that presented his critique of marriage. The tone of *Cupid's Yokes* was scholarly, but it was unfailingly direct.

Heywood asserted that adults should understand the physiology of sexual relations, and he encouraged people to give "serious attention to the momentous issues of Sexual Science." He asked, "If government cannot justly determine what ticket we shall vote, what church we shall attend, or what books we shall read, by what authority does it watch at key-holes and burst open bed-chamber doors to drag lovers from sacred seclusion?" Heywood attacked Comstock as a "religious mono-maniac" fueled by "the spirit that lighted the fires of the inquisition."[24]

To Comstock, *Cupid's Yokes* advanced a "vile creed." He pursued the prosecution of Heywood's "most obscene and loathsome book" with tireless zeal, staging a dramatic public arrest at a Boston free love convention where Heywood was speaking. Comstock's *Traps for the Young* presents a characteristically dramatic account of the arrest, describing a massive crowd with "lust in every face." Comstock knew, however, that "God was there to help me," and in the end he got his man. Heywood was convicted and sentenced to two years in prison.[25]

A CENTRAL question in the application of the Comstock Act, and in the application of the various state obscenity statutes as well, was the meaning of "obscenity." Because there was so little American law on the issue, most courts relied heavily on the English precedents, and especially on the landmark decision in *Regina v. Hicklin*, an 1868 English case concerning the distribution of an anti-Catholic pamphlet, *The Confessional Unmasked*, which described the sexually inappropriate questions that priests supposedly asked women during confession about sexual intercourse and oral and anal sex.

Chief Justice Alexander Cockburn, who wrote the opinion in *Hicklin*, hung the question of obscenity on "whether the tendency of the matter . . . is to deprave and corrupt those whose minds are open to immoral influences." Cockburn held that *The Confessional Unmasked* was obscene because it "would suggest to the minds of the young of either sex, or even to persons of more advanced years, thoughts of a most impure and libidinous character." This British doctrine would come to dominate American law for almost a century.[26]

In 1879, for example, D. M. Bennett, the founder and publisher of *Truth Seeker*, a radical freethought periodical, sold Ezra Heywood's *Cupid's Yokes* through the mail in direct defiance of Comstock. Bennett was promptly arrested, prosecuted, and convicted. In upholding Bennett's conviction under the Comstock Act, federal judge Samuel Blatchford, who was subsequently appointed to the Supreme Court of the United States by President Chester Arthur, explored the meaning of "obscenity." Following the lead of *Hicklin*, Blatchford held that a book is obscene under American law if it is "offensive to decency." It "need not be obscene throughout the whole of its contents," but if the book is "obscene, lewd, or lascivious or indecent even in part, it is an obscene book, within the meaning of the law." *Cupid's Yokes*, Judge Blatchford concluded, was certainly "obscene."[27]

T HE TRIALS of the sex radicals in these early cases demonstrated the difficulties of presenting a defense to an obscenity charge under the *Hicklin* standard. There were several problems:

> First, neither the Comstock Act nor the judicial doctrine defined what was meant by "obscenity." They instead provided a string of synonyms—"lewd," "lascivious," "indecent"—none of which was defined. The courts simply assumed that juries would understand these words according to their "ordinary acceptation and use."[28]

> Second, the *Hicklin* standard allowed a work to be judged on the basis of isolated passages rather than in the context of its larger meaning. A single phrase, passage, or image was sufficient to warrant a criminal conviction—even if the work as a whole was unobjectionable.[29]

> Third, in the interest of minimizing exposure to "obscene" material, courts typically refused to describe offending works or images in official court documents. Such judicial modesty, which remained a fea-

ture of obscenity prosecutions until well into the twentieth century, prevented anyone from knowing what was and was not obscene.[30]

Finally, material could be deemed obscene if it had the capacity to corrupt the *most susceptible* members of society. Juries were therefore instructed to hold material obscene for adults if they found that it could corrupt an impressionable adolescent. This standard effectively limited adults to only those materials that were deemed appropriate for children.[31]

T HE SEX radicals and their supporters challenged the constitutionality of the Comstock Act, but without success. Francis E. Abbot, a philosopher who sought to redefine religious principles in accord with scientific inquiry, and Colonel Robert Ingersoll, a freethought orator who was nicknamed "The Great Agnostic," founded the National Liberal League in 1876 "to roll back the wave of intolerance, bigotry and ignorance which threatens to submerge our cherished liberties."[32]

In 1878, on behalf of the National Liberal League, Ingersoll brought a petition with more than fifty thousand signatures to Congress calling for repeal of the Comstock Act as "unconstitutional," "ill-advised," and "contrary to the spirit and progress of our age." But Comstock beat down the petition by appearing personally before Congress with exhibits of erotica in tow in order to demonstrate that the Act was necessary to the nation's moral well-being.[33]

Just how far enforcement of the Comstock Act reached is illustrated by the prosecution of Moses Harman, who argued that sexual expression could serve society in valuable ways. In 1886, Harman promised his readers that his journal *Lucifer* would be an uncensored forum, and shortly thereafter he published a letter to the editor from a subscriber, W. G. Markland. The letter related the true story of a wife who, after undergoing a difficult birth, had not yet healed sufficiently to resume intercourse. Her husband forced himself on her anyway, causing her death. Markland queried: "Can there be legal rape? Did this man rape his wife? Would it have been rape had he not been married to her? . . . If a man stabs his wife to death with a knife, does not the law hold him for murder? If he murders her with his penis, what does the law do?"[34]

For publishing this letter, Harman was prosecuted and convicted of violating the Comstock Act. The federal court refused even to describe the letter in its opinion, noting that it was "so filthy" that its mere recitation would shock "the common sense of decency and modesty." The court explained that from the day that "Adam and Eve ate of the fruit of the tree of knowledge," man has "carried with him the sense of shame—the feeling that there are some things on which the eye—the mind—should not look." When "men and women become so depraved" that "they will not veil" their own eyes from such indecent thoughts and images, then the government must "perform that office for them." As Harman's conviction powerfully illustrates, in the late nineteenth century *any* reference to sex, sexuality, or sexual organs could be deemed "obscene."[35]

The Comstock Act would remain in effect for several more decades, but its opponents continued to agitate against it. Ezra Heywood was imprisoned again in 1890 for publishing the word "fuck," and Moses Harman was prosecuted again in 1905 for publishing an article advising women to avoid sex during pregnancy. Meanwhile, the free speech advocates continued to mock Comstock. Dr. Edward Bliss Foote published a children's tale that depicted Comstock as a venomous spider, and Heywood advertised and distributed a douching syringe bitingly dubbed "the Comstock."[36]

After the New York Public Library excluded the Nobel Prize–winning playwright George Bernard Shaw's *Man and Superman*, Shaw observed: "Nobody outside America is likely to be the least surprised. Comstockery is the world's standing joke at the expense of the United States." Such incidents, he added, confirm "the deep-seated conviction of the Old World that America is a provincial place, a second-rate country-town civilization."[37]

As the nineteenth century yielded to the twentieth, free speech increasingly became an issue of national importance, especially as more extreme ideologies took on political significance. The Free Speech League was organized in 1901 by Edward Bond Foote, the son of Edward Bliss Foote, and Edwin Walker, Moses Harman's son-in-law. The League had one simple goal: "to make it possible for anybody to say anything anywhere." At the dawn of the Progressive Era, the League's early membership consisted of a small, disparate, and far-flung group of dedicated free speech advocates, including civil liberties lawyers like Gilbert Roe and Theodore Schroeder and prominent journalists like Lincoln Steffens, an early muckraker who exposed widespread government corruption, and Leonard Abbott, a leading figure in the Social Democratic Party.[38]

At a time when most free speech advocates were more concerned with political speech than with sexual expression, Schroeder, the leader of the Free Speech League, firmly included within his opposition to speech restrictions a dedicated concern with what he deemed arbitrary and repressive social judgments about the boundaries of sexual propriety. The Free Speech League thus fervently supported obscenity defendants like Ida C. Craddock, a Chicago woman who was prosecuted for distributing *The Wedding Night*, an instructional pamphlet on human sexuality for married couples; Margaret Sanger, a national leader in the cause of women's reproductive freedom, who was prosecuted under the Comstock Act for advocating birth control; and members of Washington State's Home Colony, who were prosecuted for promoting nude bathing. H. L. Mencken, one of the most influential American writers of the first half of the twentieth century, lauded Schroeder as having "done more for free expression in America than any other."[39]

SERIOUS LITERATURE AND
THE STANDARDS OF THE DAY

FOR THE MOST PART, the literary elite of this era escaped Comstock's attention because they willingly conformed to Victorian social norms. "Serious" authors, editors, publishers, booksellers, and critics embraced a stern sense of decency that twentieth-century critic Malcolm Cowley compared to "that of a rather strict girls' boarding school." Prudish editors routinely excised even relatively tame sexual references. To cite just one example of the prudish editorial policy at the time, Herman Melville's first book, *Typee: A Peep at Polynesian Life*, a somewhat autobiographical account of his time as a captive on an island in the South Pacific, was bowdlerized to remove his description of the welcome given to the arriving sailors by semi-nude native girls. In a similar vein, in a speech entitled "The Librarian as a Censor," Arthur Bostwick, president of the American Library Association, advocated the elimination from library lists of any book with an "immoral tendency."[40]

While there was therefore little need for Comstock to concern himself with most serious late nineteenth-century literature, one species of serious fiction did attract his attention. Uncensored versions of such classics as Boccaccio's *The Decameron*, Chaucer's *Canterbury Tales*, and *The Arabian Nights* continued to circulate throughout the United States, even though federal law banned their further importation. Comstock was not in the least impressed by the classic status of such works, sniffing that "[g]arbage smells none the less rank and offensive because deposited in a marble fount or a gold or silver urn."[41]

Near the turn of the twentieth century, a new school of serious literature began to emerge. As literary naturalism gradually displaced the gentility of the Victorian era, American authors began to address the grittiness of lower-class urban life. Authors such as Stephen Crane in *Maggie: A Girl of the Streets*, published in 1893, and Theodore Dreiser in *Sister Carrie*, published in 1900, increasingly touched upon controversial social problems, including poverty, alcoholism, sexual promiscuity, and—most notably for obscenity scolds—prostitution. To naturalist writers, prostitution represented the apex of dejection and loneliness and therefore presented an irresistible subject for literary exploration. But censors regarded the very subject as unpalatable. George Bernard Shaw's *Mrs. Warren's Profession* was banned in New Haven in 1905, for example, even though it neither explicitly mentioned nor endorsed prostitution.[42]

Another work about prostitution in this era led to the first significant judicial opinion to acknowledge changing social mores. Daniel Carson Goodman's *Hagar Revelly* charted the decline of a poor working girl who fell into several amorous misadventures resulting in a loveless marriage and the prospect of a dreary future. The young woman was presented as impulsive, fond of pleasure, and sensuous. In several passages, the work was certainly racy. In 1913, in *United States v. Kennerley*,[43] the government prosecuted the publisher of the work for violating the Comstock Act.

In ruling on the application of the statute to this work, Judge Learned Hand, one of the most distinguished federal judges of his generation and, during World War I, a hero in his defense of free speech, reexamined the legal definition of "obscenity." In *Kennerley*, Judge Hand conceded that the *Hicklin* test had been universally "accepted by the lower federal courts" and that under that test several passages of the book "might be found obscene, because they certainly might tend to corrupt the morals of those into whose hands it might come and whose minds were open to such immoral influence." But he rejected the *Hicklin* standard, noting that however "consonant" that standard might "be with mid-Victorian morals," it "does not seem to me to answer to the understanding and morality of the present time."

Hand reasoned that few would be "content to reduce our treatment of sex to the standard of a child's library." He therefore concluded that the word "obscene" should be defined in terms of "the present critical point in the compromise between candor and shame at which the community may have arrived here and now." By substituting the "community standard" of contemporary adult norms for a standard focusing on "whether the tendency" of the material is to "corrupt those whose minds" are especially "open to immoral influences," Hand refocused the concept of obscenity in a wholly new direction. This was the first critical step in a lengthy judicial struggle to make sense of the legal definition of "obscenity" in an evolving society.[44]

BANNED IN BOSTON

NOT ALL COMMUNITIES have the same moral standards, and Boston in this era was famous for having the strictest censorship in the nation. This was due, at least in part, to the city's distinctive Catholic identity. Although the "Boston Brahmin" elites were largely Protestant, Boston was at heart a Catholic town with a large Irish and Italian immigrant population, and the Catholic Church's vigorous condemnation of sexual expression generated a powerful engine for censorship. The Catholic-run Legion of Decency lobbied aggressively for aggressive censorship of sexual material, and the National Organization for Decent Literature, which was run by priests, developed lists of what it considered "obscene" publications, put pressure on local booksellers not to sell such works, and even developed its own obscenity code.[45]

It was the New England Watch and Ward Society, however, originally founded with Anthony Comstock's encouragement in 1878 as the New England Society for the Suppression of Vice, that really ran the show in Boston. Led by a succession of prominent local figures, the Society wielded enormous influence among Boston city officials and instituted a definitive process for screening books, plays, and films for "inappropriate" content.

The Society created the Boston Booksellers Committee to review all new publications and to dispatch warning letters to local booksellers whenever it deemed particular works indecent. Although the Committee had no legal authority, booksellers heeded its "advice" in order to avoid prosecution, particularly because the district attorney's office worked closely with the Committee. Even book reviewers for the Boston newspapers refused to review books that had been "listed" by the Committee.[46]

As literature grew both more realistic and more daring in the early years of the twentieth century, vice societies throughout the nation became ever more aggressive in their efforts to pressure publishers. Works that had even the potential to excite moralist condemnation were routinely denied publication by publishers who wanted no part of either public censure or an obscenity prosecution. In 1917, H. L. Mencken, then the editor of the literary magazine *The Smart Set,* ruefully conceded that the power of the censors' condemnation was so great that it affected even his own editorial evaluations.[47]

AFTER COMSTOCK

AFTER ANTHONY COMSTOCK'S death in 1915, the power of the nineteenth-century anti-obscenity societies began to wane. Comstock's successor at the Society for the Suppression of Vice, John S. Sumner, suffered a series of embarrassing defeats in the early 1920s. In one of his first major efforts, Sumner orchestrated the arrest of the New York bookseller Raymond Halsey in 1922 for selling a Romantic-era French novel, Théophile Gautier's *Mademoiselle de Maupin: A Romance of Love and Passion.* Written in 1835, *Mademoiselle de Maupin* is a sensuous depiction of its two main characters' search for a sublime sexual experience. Although the work is certainly erotic, its intent was to depict and to celebrate sex as an act of great beauty.

To Sumner's dismay, Halsey was acquitted on the criminal charge of selling obscenity. Halsey then audaciously turned around and sued Sumner and the Society for the Suppression of Vice for malicious prosecution. In a stunning victory, Halsey won a jury award of $2,500. In upholding this verdict, the state appeals court changed New York's definition of obscenity by requiring both an evaluation of the "whole book" and consideration of its literary merit. As the court explained, although "many paragraphs, . . . taken by themselves, are undoubtedly vulgar and indecent," the "author's felicitous style," the "passages of purity and beauty," Gautier's literary reputation, and the work's status in the French literary canon justified the jury's conclusion that it was unreasonable to accuse Halsey of selling an obscene book. The literati cheered.[48]

THE CHANGING social and cultural norms of the Roaring Twenties reflected a sharp departure from Anthony Comstock's world of Victorian prudery. With the end of World War I, a sense of personal freedom, including sexual freedom, was once again in the air. This was an era of flappers, sexy masquerade balls, and daring sexual innuendo. A new generation of postwar publishers began taking greater risks, and the judiciary handed Sumner another defeat in 1922 by vindicating three sexually-oriented works published by Thomas Seltzer: D. H. Lawrence's *Women in Love* (1920), Arthur Schnitzler's *Casanova's Homecoming* (1920), and the anonymous *A Young Girl's Diary* (1919). Seltzer took the courtroom drama public, attracting newspaper coverage and endorsements of the three works from literary critics and psychologists. Sigmund Freud, for example, endorsed *A Young Girl's Diary* as "a gem." The charges were dismissed. In reaching this result, the New York court again emphasized the literary value of the works, deeming them "a distinct contribution to the literature of the present day," despite their sexual content.[49]

Sumner then struck out yet again in 1922 in his pursuit of brash young publisher Horace Liveright's new English translation of *Satyricon*, a classic first-century Roman work that, despite surviving only in fragments, features explicit descriptions of homosexual love. The New York court dismissed the obscenity charge on grounds of literary merit, noting that "[t]he works of art and literature of an ancient age cannot be judged by modern standards. The good of possessing those literary and cultural records of the past that constitute the very spiritual continuity of civilization cannot be outweighed by any imaginary evil."[50]

Down but not out, Sumner decided that the vice societies needed new allies. Although public support for literary censorship dwindled during the 1920s, one demographic remained vehemently opposed to the increasingly liberal tendencies of the publishing industry. The religious press railed against the new wave of sensuous literature and its editorial pages were filled with demands for censorship. Under Sumner's leadership, an array of religious and culturally conservative organizations—including the Protestant Episcopal Diocese, the Catholic Club, the Boy Scouts, and the Knights of Columbus—banded together in 1923 to establish the Clean Books League, with the goal of enacting new laws in New York that would overturn the recent spate of judicial decisions, abolish the "whole book" standard, and forbid the admission of expert testimony on literary merit.[51]

The book world was cautious. Few publishers wanted to come out openly in favor of "dirty" books. But Horace Liveright, the most high-profile of the more adventurous publishers, spearheaded an aggressive response to the League's proposed legislation. A charismatic and

Horace Liveright

controversial figure, Liveright married into a wealthy family, enabling him to launch his own publishing house. A man whose personal life was often as ribald and scandalous as the books he published, Liveright's taste for risk led him both to publish many of the works that incensed the Clean Books League and to sign many of the era's finest authors at the very beginning of their careers, including T. S. Eliot, Eugene O'Neill, E. E. Cummings, William Faulkner, Ernest Hemingway, Dorothy Parker, and Sherwood Anderson.[52]

Liveright publicly defended his provocative publishing practices in an essay denouncing censorship as "stupid, ignorant, and impudent, and . . . against the fundamental social principles of all intelligent Americans." He recruited Theodore Dreiser, Edgar Lee Masters, Gertrude Atherton, and other prominent writers to journey to Albany to oppose the Clean Books League's proposed new obscenity legislation. Perhaps his greatest coup, though, was to get Democratic minority leader and future New York City mayor Jimmy Walker to lead the charge against the bill. Walker opposed the bill on the floor of the state assembly with a sharp, succinct, and persuasive rebuke: "No woman was ever ruined by a book." The League's bill failed to pass.[53]

THEATER AND FILM

BROADWAY DURING THE 1920S was awash in sexual themes. There were dramas about a Chinese brothel (*The Shanghai Gesture*), unrepentant prostitutes (*Lulu Belle*), and marital infidelity (*The Constant Wife*). The subject that generated the greatest controversy, though, was homosexuality. French playwright Edouard Bourdet's 1926 play *The Captive*, which starred Basil Rathbone of Sherlock Holmes fame, presented a nuanced portrayal of a woman's awakening to her homosexuality.

Although there was no explicit depiction of sex, and although the play was commended by much of the New York press (the proudly liberal *New York Evening Post* assured readers that it did "no violence even to the most sensitive"), it was nonetheless raided by the police and shuttered. The critic George Jean Nathan, writing in the *American Mercury*, captured the reaction of authorities in New York when he condemned *The Captive* as "the most . . . evil-fraught play ever shown in the American theater." The actors were released from custody only after they swore never again to perform the play.[54]

The daring actress Mae West was undaunted, however. She took one look at the crowds lining up for *The Captive* and decided to produce her own homosexual stage drama. *The Drag* was a bawdy comedy that openly depicted the culture and characters in New York's gay underground. It boldly featured male characters named "Kate" and "The Duchess" and culminated in a grand drag ball with men in floor-length gowns. The Society for the Suppression of Vice threatened prosecution if the play opened, and *The Drag* therefore never made it to the stage in New York. The New York legislature, outraged by the prospect of a theatrical production about homosexuality, responded to *The Drag* by amending the state's obscenity law to expressly ban any work "depicting or dealing with the subject of sex degeneracy or sex perversion."[55]

Mae West

The play that eventually got West brought up on obscenity charges was a 1927 burlesque revue that was boldly titled *SEX*. West's performance, which depicted the misadventures of the sassy Montreal prostitute Margy LaMont, was infused with sexual innuendo. The *New York Daily Mirror* trashed *SEX* as a "Monstrosity Plucked from a Garbage Can" and *Variety* termed it "a nasty red-light district show." Answering the call of the critics, the police raided the play, and West wound up spending ten days in the Women's Workhouse on Welfare Island on an obscenity conviction. Undeterred, her subsequent plays—and movies—continued to focus on sex. West insisted that "audiences *wanted* 'dirt'"—and, she added emphatically, 'I'll give it to them!'"[56]

THE BURGEONING film industry, still silent throughout most of the 1920s, faced even more serious challenges than the theater. Organizations like the New York Society for the Suppression of Vice heatedly warned that movies allow "the young [to] see things they never should be allowed even to hear or think about," and that in a world with movies "the downfall of young girls is not remote." Between 1909 and 1921, eight states and more than thirty cities instituted official censorship boards that screened films in advance to determine whether they were obscene, and state courts routinely upheld the authority of government to deny licenses to "immoral" movies.[57]

In response to the maddeningly diverse decency standards imposed on movie producers by different communities across the nation, the film industry retained former Postmaster General William Hays, who had managed Warren Harding's successful run for the presidency in 1920, to preside over the new Motion Picture Association of America (MPAA). Hays was charged with drafting a voluntary code for the entire film industry. In 1930, under the prodding of several Catholic organizations, which insisted that the widespread popularity of movies imposed a "special Moral Responsibility" to protect traditional family values, the MPAA promulgated what came to be known as the Hays Code, which governed the movie industry through the 1950s.[58]

The drafters of the Hays Code explained that it was designed to insure that "no picture should lower the moral standards of those who see it." It prohibited any scenes of "excessive and lustful kissing" or of "lustful embraces" and provided that "passion should be treated in such a manner as not to stimulate the lower and baser emotions." It banned any depiction of "dances suggesting or representing sexual actions or indecent passion," any scenes of "miscegenation (sex relationship between the white and black race)," and any use of "profanity (this includes God, Lord, Jesus Christ—unless used reverentially—Hell, S.O.B., damn Gawd), or other profane or vulgar expressions, however used." In short, the Hays Code prohibited the depiction of anything that might be taken as in any way implying the existence of sex, including even scenes of married couples sleeping in the same bed.[59]

Still not satisfied, a committee of Catholic bishops established the national Legion of Decency in 1934 to ensure that "motion pictures conform to the accepted and traditional morality upon which the home and civilisation are founded." When the Legion and similar organizations, such as the Federal Council of Churches of Christ in America, threatened a national film boycott unless Hays allowed the Legion's representatives to enforce the Hays Code, the MPAA capitulated.[60]

Hays thereafter appointed Legion of Decency representative Joseph Breen to head the MPAA's Production Code Administration, which had the authority to interpret and apply the Hays Code. Under this new structure, every movie script had to be submitted in advance to Breen for approval. Any producer who failed to comply risked a $25,000 fine. In the Legion of Decency's heyday, producers were effectively compelled to make cuts from their scripts in order to avoid a rating of "Condemned," which would trigger a nationwide Catholic-led boycott. Movies like *A Streetcar Named Desire* (1951), *Duel in the Sun* (1946), and *Lolita* (1962) were all heavily censored by the Legion of Decency before they could be publicly released. This pervasive system of censorship effectively purged Hollywood of all sex—and all sexual controversy—until the mid-1950s.[61]

"DIRT FOR DIRT'S SAKE"

IN THE MEANTIME, courts continued to struggle in their effort to give some clear, consistent and coherent meaning to the legal concept of "obscenity." One state court opinion in 1947 summed up the various tests that were then being used by courts in different jurisdictions: whether the work tends to "excite lustful and lecherous desire," whether it tends "to have the effect of stimulating sexual impulses," whether it is "calculated to excite in a spectator impure imaginations," whether it is intended to be lewd for mercenary purposes, whether it tends "to lower the standards of right and wrong specifically as to the sexual relation," and whether it contains "dirt for dirt's sake."[62] These various formulations all attempted in one way or another to implement the *Hicklin* standard's emphasis on "tendency to deprave and corrupt."

Typical of the judicial decisions in this era was *Commonwealth v. Friede*, a 1930 decision of the Supreme Judicial Court of Massachusetts, which upheld an obscenity conviction for selling to an undercover police agent a copy of Theodore Dreiser's *An American Tragedy*, which had been published by Horace Liveright. At his trial, Donald Friede, the defendant bookseller, was represented by Arthur Garfield Hays and Clarence Darrow, but to no avail. The prosecutor read selected passages of the work to the jury. Those passages included a scene in which the main character visits a house of prostitution and another in which the main character and his pregnant girlfriend attempt to secure an abortion. The prosecutor characterized the book as containing "the most disgusting, the most filthy, the most vicious, the most devilish" material that "a human being could think of." Although *An American Tragedy* has been acclaimed as a masterpiece of American fiction, the jury convicted.

In upholding Friede's conviction, the Supreme Judicial Court of Massachusetts concluded that "even assuming great literary excellence, artistic worth and an impelling moral lesson in the story, there is nothing essential to the history of the life of its principal character that would be lost" if the passages the jury found to be obscene were omitted from the text. Thus, *An American Tragedy* was obscene.[63]

ALTHOUGH *FRIEDE* reflected the prevailing approach in this era, judges were beginning to move ever so haltingly away from the *Hicklin* standard and toward a more nuanced definition of obscenity. A few illustrative decisions suggest the nature of the progression.

In 1918, Mary Ware Dennett, a women's rights activist who cofounded the Voluntary Parenthood League and was a fierce advocate of women's suffrage, decided to educate her two adolescent boys about sex and romance. To her dismay, she found that the existing literature gave "very misleading and harmful impressions." She concluded that such presentations had "done children much harm in giving them the impression that there is an essential baseness in the sex relation."[64]

Dennett took matters into her own hands and wrote *The Sex Side of Life*, a pamphlet for adolescents that argued that sex, in a healthy, monogamous relationship, is an integral part of healthy adulthood. The pamphlet became popular throughout the 1920s, but its frankness shocked one Virginia mother, who flagged the attention of the postal censors, who promptly declared *The Sex Side of Life* obscene.[65]

At her trial in 1928, Dennett's defense counsel, Morris Ernst, who would later gain even greater renown for his defense of James Joyce's *Ulysses*, was prevented by the judge from defending the pamphlet in terms of either the author's good intentions or the work's endorsement by several respectable organizations. The trial judge declared such matters legally irrelevant. Instead, the judge enlisted a triad of clergy—a rabbi, a minister, and a priest—to "aid the conscience of the court." After hearing their opinions, the judge held the work obscene. Dennett was fined $3,000, but she refused to pay and announced that she would rather go to prison.[66]

In 1930, the United States Court of Appeals reversed her conviction. Writing for the court, Judge Augustus Hand (Judge Learned Hand's cousin) conceded that any writing that explains "the functions of the sex organs is capable in some circumstances of arousing lust." But, he reasoned, "it can hardly be said that, because of the risk of arousing sex impulses, there should be no instruction of the young in sex matters," or that "the risk of imparting instruction" necessarily "outweighs the disadvantages of leaving them to grope about in mystery and morbid curiosity and of requiring them to secure such information, as they may be able to obtain, from ill-informed and often foul-minded . . . playmates."

Judge Hand therefore held that "an accurate exposition of the relevant facts of the sex side of life in decent language and in a manifestly serious and disinterested spirit cannot ordinarily be regarded as obscene." The *Dennett* decision was hailed as an important victory for free speech, a resounding defeat for the *Hicklin* standard, and "a landmark in the history of America's attitude toward sex."[67]

PERHAPS THE most pivotal case in this era in the gradual whittling away of the *Hicklin* test involved James Joyce's *Ulysses*, an intricate, stream-of-consciousness depiction of an ordinary day in the life of Dubliner Leopold Bloom. One of the twentieth century's most revered novels, *Ulysses* was lambasted by moralists for its shocking use of foul language and explicit sexual imagery. Written over a seven-year period, *Ulysses* was first published in its entirety in 1922 in Paris, where it caused a literary sensation. In 1933, the publisher Random House and lawyer Morris Ernst arranged to import the French edition and to have a copy seized by federal authorities when the ship was unloaded, setting up the legal challenge.[68]

The case came before federal district court Judge John M. Woolsey, a former admiralty lawyer who taught occasionally at Columbia Law School before being appointed to the bench by President Calvin Coolidge. Judge Woolsey's opinion in *United States v. One Book Called "Ulysses"* proposed a new standard for judging obscenity. Woolsey acknowledged *Ulysses'* vulgarity and sexual explicitness but, building on Morris Ernst's argument, concluded that Joyce's decision to use such language and imagery had been in service of the book's literary expression. Woolsey defended Joyce's use of four-letter profanities on the grounds that they were "old Saxon words known to almost all men and, I venture, to many women," and explained that they had been used by Joyce precisely because they "are such words as would be naturally and habitually used . . . by the types of folk whose life, physical and mental, Joyce is seeking to describe." Woolsey found *Ulysses* to be "a sincere and honest book" and concluded that none of the explicit sexual material constituted "dirt for dirt's sake."[69]

The United States Court of Appeals affirmed in 1934 in another influential opinion by Judge Augustus Hand. Hand agreed with Woolsey that obscenity could not be determined by the mere presence of sexual images or phrases, but had to be judged in terms of a work's "dominant effect."

Hand's opinion in the *Ulysses* case represented the first time that a federal court of appeals had embraced the "whole book" standard. Hand observed that while "numerous long passages in *Ulysses* contain matter [that] is obscene under any fair definition of the word," they "give meaning to the whole, rather than . . . promote lust or portray filth for its own sake."

Moreover, Judge Hand noted that *Ulysses* "is rated as a book of considerable power by persons whose opinions are entitled to weight." Indeed, Joyce's work has become "a contemporary classic." Thus, taken as a whole, *Ulysses* did not "tend to promote lust" and was not "dirt for dirt's sake." Judge Hand concluded that *Ulysses* was not "obscene" within the meaning of the Comstock Act, "even though it justly may offend many."*[70]

THE "EVIL STENCH" OF OBSCENITY

ALTHOUGH A HANDFUL of courts in these years were gradually moving away from the *Hicklin* definition of obscenity in favor of an approach requiring that the work "be considered as a whole" and judged in terms of its effect, not upon those who are most susceptible to moral corruption, "but upon all those whom it is likely to reach,"[71] this remained an issue of continuing dispute.

Perhaps the most controversial of the obscenity convictions in the post–World War II era involved the American novelist Henry Miller. Born to German Lutheran parents in New York City in 1891, Miller as a young man became active in the Socialist Party, wrote several unpublished books in the 1920s, including *Crazy Cock* and *Lovely Lesbians*, and then moved to Paris where he informed a friend, "I start tomorrow on the Paris book: First person, uncensored, formless—fuck everything!"

Miller's *Tropic of Cancer* (1934) and *Tropic of Capricorn* (1939) were autobiographical novels about a struggling writer, his Parisian social circle, and his many sexual encounters. They were clearly written with every intention of shocking audiences. In the opening scene of *Tropic of Cancer*, Miller described his protagonist as "cunt-struck," and his sexual descriptions and imaginings throughout the work respected no boundaries of conventional morality or taste.[72]

Nonetheless, Miller gained respect among the literati both in England

---

* For another influential opinion on obscenity in this era, see *Commonwealth v. Gordon*, 66 Pa. D. & C. 101 (Phila. 1949).

and in the United States. George Orwell, for example, described Miller in 1940 as "the only imaginative prose-writer of the slightest value who has appeared among the English-speaking races for some years past." Others were less complimentary. George Bernard Shaw conceded that "[t]his fellow can write," but nonetheless complained that Miller "has totally failed to give any artistic value to his verbatim reports of bad language."[73]

A decade later, in 1951, the *Tropics* came before the federal courts, which declared them obscene. A federal district court judge expressed horror at the books' "evil stench," noting as examples several descriptions of female genitalia that employed "such detailed vulgar language as to create nausea in the reader. If this be important literature, then the dignity of the human person and the stability of the family unit . . . are lost to us." The judge rejected the literary merit defense as "mere sophistry" and refused to consider the "filthy scatological portions" of the works as part of the literary whole. In the judge's view, Miller aimed to shock, and his work was therefore properly deemed dirt rather than art.[74]

F ROM *COMMONWEALTH V. SHARPLESS* in 1815 through the battles over Henry Miller's *Tropics* in the early 1950s, the primary concern of courts was whether any particular work was "obscene" within the meaning of the common law, the Comstock Act, or a state statute. Throughout this period, which spanned almost two centuries, it was universally assumed that whatever obscenity was, it was not protected by the First Amendment. Indeed, the Supreme Court of the United States in these years simply took it for granted that "obscenity" was not within the "freedom of speech, or of the press" guaranteed by the Constitution. In 1931, for example, the Court observed in passing that society's interest in promoting decency "may be enforced against obscene publications,"[75] and a decade later the Court casually included "the lewd and the obscene" among the "limited classes of speech . . . the prevention and punishment of which have never been thought to raise any Constitutional problem."[76]

But the issue remained unresolved until 1957, when the Supreme Court finally addressed the question head on.*[77]

---

* We return to this question in chapter 12.

9

CONTRACEPTION AND ABORTION

From the Founding to the 1950s

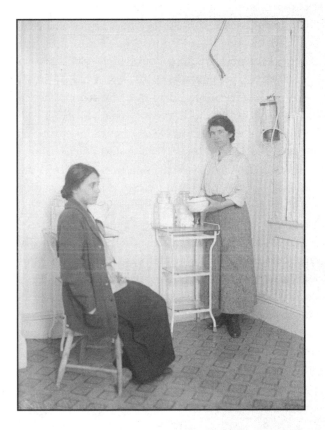

Margaret Sanger, Brownsville Clinic, October 1916

I N THE EIGHTEENTH and early nineteenth centuries, there were no
laws prohibiting either contraception or abortion before quickening.*
Although we do not know the precise extent to which people used
contraception or abortion in this era, we do know that over the course
of the nineteenth century there was a marked increase in the use of birth
control because the birth rate fell dramatically from 1800 to 1900. In the
colonial era, the average family had nine children. By 1900, that number
was only three. In the agrarian world of the eighteenth century, children
were an important economic asset; by the end of the nineteenth century,
with greater urbanization and industrialization, children were increasingly
seen as a financial burden that could cause a family's economic ruin. For
most families, then, birth control of one sort or another came to be seen as
essential to family well-being.[1]

Moreover, and at the same time, the writings of the early nineteenth-century British economist Thomas Robert Malthus generated a
growing concern about the dangers of overpopulation. Malthus predicted
that continued population growth would lead to poverty and social decline.
Many of Malthus's followers saw birth control as a solution to the loom-
ing challenge of overpopulation. Birth control would thus promote both the
individual's and the society's welfare.[2]

These changes brought about a dramatic shift in attitudes toward birth
control. During the Second Great Awakening, abortion was still perceived
primarily as the business of prostitutes and as a "recourse for the desper-

---

* "Quickening" is the moment in pregnancy when a woman first feels fetal movement, usually
at four-and-a-half months.

ate." In the years after 1840, however, the social character of the practice began to change. Abortion rates soared, and a high proportion of those having abortions, particularly in growing urban areas, were for the first time married women of middle- or upper-class status.[3]

By the 1850s, contraception and abortion were increasingly recognized as legitimate and morally acceptable practices to maintain and improve a family's economic welfare, and advertisements for birth control products and services were commonplace. By the 1870s, approximately 20 percent of all pregnancies were purposefully terminated. But then the moralists moved in.[4]

WHAT WOULD KEEP THEM CHASTE?

AMONG THE VARIOUS behaviors targeted during the Second Great Awakening, reproductive control presented a particular paradox. For many people, any form of birth control was seen as a challenge to God's will. For others, though, some form of "designed maternity" was seen as essential to the preservation of well-functioning families, a goal that also had strong moral and religious significance. In the 1840s, for example, Henry Clarke Wright, a pastor of the Congregational Church and fervent abolitionist, preached about the pitfalls of the "unwelcome child." He taught that for couples who wanted "healthy, intelligent children and happy marriages, only 'designed maternity' would do."[5]

Moreover, the Victorian attitudes about women in this era were self-contradictory. As the historian Linda Gordon has observed, women in the Victorian era were viewed as both lacking any sex drive and as potentially "depraved, lustful monsters." This contradiction stemmed from a lack of confidence in "the reality of the sexless woman," which was a construct laid uneasily, and uncertainly, on top of the earlier conception of women as "highly sexed" temptresses in the spirit of Eve.[6]

This ambivalence brought to the surface the unnerving question: "If women and men need no longer fear pregnancy as an outcome of sexual intercourse, what would keep wives faithful and daughters chaste?" As women gained control over their own reproductive destinies, the seemingly pernicious thought began to creep into the public consciousness that even for women, sex could be separated from reproduction and that freedom from pregnancy could unleash women's biblical lasciviousness. Such unbridled female sexuality would surely destabilize families, undermine social relations, and corrupt the nation's morality.[7]

. . .

O VER THE course of the nineteenth century, the law struggled with the religious and moral paradox of reproductive control. In the 1830s, Americans began to learn through publications and public lectures about ways to control or prevent pregnancy. Matters that previously had been passed on in private from woman to woman now came into the light, and the increasingly public nature of these discussions further legitimized the idea of birth control.

In 1831, Robert Dale Owen wrote the first important American tract on birth control. *Moral Physiology; or, A Brief and Plain Treatise on the Population Question* went through nine editions in its first five years. The work was part of Owen's larger effort "to banish religious superstition." He maintained that "reproductive control" was an essential part of a woman's "duty as an efficient and well-organized wife and mother." But he added that even unmarried women should have access to birth control, because "men who seduced women went unpunished by society, while women and their illegitimate offspring had to endure scorn and abuse."[8]

Shortly after Owen's book appeared, the Massachusetts physician Charles Knowlton published *Fruits of Philosophy; or, The Private Companion of Young Married People*, which expressly advocated contraception. Birth control, he argued, would prevent overpopulation, reduce prostitution, reduce the occurrence of abortion and infanticide, and protect the health and well-being of women and their families.

Unlike Owen, who argued that coitus interruptus was the best means of birth control, Knowlton favored postcoital spermicidal douching. He objected to coitus interruptus because, in his view, a fundamental purpose of sex was pleasure. He maintained that coitus interruptus interfered with the pleasure of both the man and the woman, whereas his preferred birth control method preserved sexual pleasure, was "sure, cheap, convenient, and harmless," and placed both the right and the responsibility for birth control in the woman's hands. Knowlton also supported the right of women to have abortions.[9]

H OW WOULD the law respond to these disparate publications and to the growing desire of Americans to learn how to control their reproductive destinies? As we have seen, the Commonwealth of Massachusetts, invoking the still-nascent doctrine of obscenity, repeatedly prosecuted Knowlton for *The Fruits of Philosophy*, even though the text was clearly intended to convey health information about birth control in a responsible and thoughtful manner.*[10]

The Knowlton prosecutions were an important turning point in the history of the regulation of information about birth control, because they marked the first step in what would come to be an important judicial expansion of the concept of obscenity to include information about the prevention of pregnancy. Although this argument was still only implicit in the pre–Civil War era, it would come to dominate in the decades to come.[11]

But despite the attention paid by the legal authorities in Massachusetts to Knowlton's work, prosecutions of those who disseminated information about reproductive control in this era were rare. For the most part, such material was still thought to be none of the law's business.

THE TOLERATION of information about birth control in these years extended even to information about abortion. Throughout this era, abortifacients were widely available from mail-order firms and pharmacists. Daily newspapers regularly ran ads for products that promised to "cure" pregnancy—a euphemism for terminating a pregnancy. Ads for "Cherokee Pills," for example, promised that if used during the first three months of pregnancy, "the unfailing nature of their action would infallibly prevent pregnance." At this time, the line between contraception and abortion was fuzzy. Many advertisements and informational materials discussed methods for inducing menstruation (even after insemination). Although these publications were clearly intended to help women terminate unwanted pregnancies, they were not treated any differently than publications dealing with contraception.[12]

In the 1840s, the flamboyant Ann Lohman Restell, popularly known as "Madame Restell," was the most famous abortionist in New York City. Born in England, Restell emigrated to America in 1831, where she was forced to make a living as a seamstress. She gradually developed an interest in women's health, and began selling birth control products such as "preventative pills." She then turned to abortion and served a genteel, middle- and upper-middle class clientele. She charged between $50 and $100 per abortion. Her abortion business on Greenwich Street proved highly profit-

* See chapter 8.

able, yielding a considerable fortune and a lush mansion on Fifth Avenue. Madame Restell touted her "celebrated powers for married ladies," and advertised extensively in the penny press of the day. For example:

> To married women: Is it but too well known that the families of the married often increase beyond what the happiness of those who give them birth would dictate? In how many instances does the hard-working father, and more especially the mother, of a poor family remain slaves throughout their lives, urging at the oar of incessant labor, toiling to live, living but to toil. . . . Is it desirable, then, . . . for parents to increase their families, regardless of consequences to themselves, or the well-being of their offspring, when a simple, easy, healthy, and certain remedy is within our control?[13]

Ads of this sort were common at the time, and the abortion trade competed openly, each boasting of its greater effectiveness, safety, and confidentiality. There were, of course, critics. Indeed, Madame Restell was often the subject of hostile press attention. The *New York Tribune* attacked her repeatedly in a series of editorial tirades against abortion, and the conservative editor of the *New York Sunday Morning News* described her practice as a "monstrous and destructive" service that "strikes at the root of all social order." Not one to shy away from a fight, Restell wrote editorials in her defense, insisting that her practice was perfectly moral and proper because she was providing women with the ability to lead effective and fulfilling lives.[14]

"THE EVIL OF THE AGE"

IN THE EIGHTEENTH and early nineteenth centuries, the prevailing view was that there was no human life until quickening. Blackstone's *Commentaries* (1765), for example, stated that life "begins in contemplation of law as soon as an infant is able to stir in the mother's womb," and James Wilson, one of the Framers of the American Constitution, observed that "in the contemplation of law, life begins when the infant is first able to stir in the womb." American courts followed the traditional English common law in holding that abortion before quickening was lawful, as long as the mother gave her consent.[15]

Several generally available works, including William Buchan's *Domestic Medicine* (1782), Samuel K. Jennings's *The Married Lady's Companion* (1808), and Dr. Thomas Ewell's *Letter to Ladies* (1817), offered instruction about how to "restore menstrual flow" by such methods as bloodletting, drinking a concoction of iron and quinine, drinking tincture of black hellebore (a powerful purgative), violent exercise, douching with very hot brandy, and strong blows to the stomach. Physicians, who knew that dilation of the cervix, irritation of the uterus, and rupturing the amniotic sac could bring on contractions, used these and similar techniques to terminate unwanted pregnancies.[16]

D URING THE Second Great Awakening, several states enacted laws dealing with abortion. Connecticut passed a statute in 1821, for example, declaring it unlawful for any apothecary to sell any poisonous substance for the purpose of causing or procuring "the miscarriage of any woman, then being quick with child." The Connecticut law also made it a misdemeanor for anyone to attempt to induce a post-quickening abortion and a felony if the woman died "in consequence thereof."[17]

By 1841, ten of the twenty-six states had enacted similar laws. But these laws merely codified the traditional common law understanding of abortion. As under the common law, these statutes applied only to post-quickening abortions, and even in that situation they did not punish the woman. These laws were premised on the twin judgments of the common law that human life did not begin until quickening and that women who sought abortions even post-quickening were not themselves criminals, but "victims of their own moral weaknesses who needed state protection."*

The codification of the common law of abortion in these years reflected no "popular outcry" against abortion and no "public disapproval of the nation's traditional" approach. Neither the popular press nor the religious community called for any change in the traditional view that abortion before quickening was not a matter for state concern.[18]

This was about to change.

I N 1845, New York enacted a novel anti-abortion statute that declared it unlawful for any person to administer, prescribe, advise, procure, or use any "medicine, drug, or substance or thing whatever," or to perform or submit to "any operation, or other means whatever, with intent" to cause

---

* Beginning in 1828, several states, including New York, New Jersey, Indiana, Ohio and Missouri, legalized abortion even after quickening when "necessary to preserve the life of the mother."

"a miscarriage." The New York law applied without regard to whether the abortion was pre- or post-quickening and it applied even to the woman herself. This was a radical departure from the common law. Over time, the New York approach would become a model for the nation.[19]

Madame Restell was one of the first targets of the new law. She was arrested and charged with illegally procuring a pre-quickening abortion for one Maria Bodine. The trial generated daily headlines and Madame Restell was convicted and sentenced to a year in prison on Blackwell's Island.[20]

SEVERAL FACTORS contributed to this change in the law. First, the number of abortions had increased dramatically in the first half of the nineteenth century, to the point where abortion opponents came to refer to it as "The Evil of the Age." Beginning in the 1840s, abortion became a business "openly traded in the free market." Abortion-related advertising appeared regularly "in urban dailies and rural weeklies, in specialty publications, in popular magazines, in broadsides, on private cards, and even in religious journals," and abortion rates soared from approximately 4 percent of pregnancies in the early years of the nineteenth century to approximately 20 percent by the 1850s.[21]

Second, religious perspectives on abortion shifted during the Second Great Awakening. The traditional Protestant conception of the fetus had assumed that it was not alive until quickening. The new evangelical doctrine of "instantaneity," however, undermined that assumption. To early nineteenth-century evangelicals, the conversion experience, which involved "a sudden, quick transformation" resulting in "rebirth," demonstrated that "one could experience the turning point in an instant." If religious rebirth could occur in an instant, then it followed that human life could be created at the very moment of conception. Abandoning the conventional view that "human life was dormant like an unsprouted seed, until the mother could first sense foetal stirrings," evangelicals of the Second Great Awakening preached that a separate, distinct, and precious life came into being at the instant of conception.[22]

Third, some medical professionals came to the view, based partly on religion and partly on science, that life begins at conception. In 1839, for example, Hugh Lenox Hodge, a professor at the University of Pennsylvania Medical School, published a pamphlet in which he confidently asserted that embryos could think and could perceive right and wrong.[23]

THE AMERICAN MEDICAL ASSOCIATION

PERHAPS THE MOST important cause of the dramatic late nineteenth-century shift in the legal approach to abortion was the aggressive stance taken by the fledgling American Medical Association. This was at a time before doctors were licensed and when they were struggling to gain professional credibility and to assert their dominance over the nation's health care. In the era before the Civil War, doctors were few and far between, there was no standardized training or licensing of physicians, and most health care issues were routinely addressed with home remedies within the family. The newly founded AMA sought to wrest control over health care from the non-professionals, and especially from midwives, who had traditionally been the primary health care providers for pregnant women.[24]

In 1857, the Boston gynecologist Horatio Storer initiated a "Physicians Crusade Against Abortion" and persuaded the AMA to create a Committee on Criminal Abortion. The Committee, chaired by Storer, presented its report at the AMA's 1859 meeting in Louisville. The report decried the growing frequency of the "heinous" act of abortion "among all classes of society, rich and poor, single and married," and maintained that the primary cause of this "general demoralization" of women was the "widespread popular ignorance of the true character" of abortion and the belief "that the foetus is not alive till after the period of quickening."

The report declared that this belief was based "upon mistaken and exploded medical dogmas" that had distorted public conceptions of both morality and the law. It explained that "the frightful extent" of abortion was due in part to "grave defects of our laws," which failed to recognize "the independent and actual existence of the child before birth, as a living being," from the very moment of conception. Proclaiming that physicians must be the "guardians" of human "offspring in utero," the report called upon the AMA to "publicly express its abhorrence of the unnatural and now rapidly increasing crime of abortion," and to publicly recommend "a careful examination and revision" of the law as it "relates to this crime."

Specifically, the report called upon the AMA to condemn "the act of producing abortion, at every stage of gestation, except as necessary for preserving the life of the mother," and announced that only doctors should be permitted to determine whether such necessity existed. Cynics pointed out that this was essentially a power grab from midwives, who previously had dominated women's gynecological and obstetrical care. After some deliberation, the AMA endorsed the Committee's recommendations.[25]

SIX YEARS later, Storer received an award from the AMA for his essay, *Why Not? A Book for Every Woman* (1865), which condemned abortion in no uncertain terms. *Why Not?* was widely read and was frequently distributed by physicians to patients who were considering an abortion.[26] In this essay, Storer made essentially two arguments against abortion. First, because physicians had determined "that the foetus in utero is alive from the very moment of conception," for a woman "to extinguish the first spark of life is a crime of the same nature, both against our Maker and society, as to destroy an infant, a child, or a man."

Second, Storer argued that abortion is "a thousand times more dangerous" to the woman than childbirth, in terms of both immediate risk of death and long-term disease and debility. He maintained that many women who have an abortion "become confirmed invalids, perhaps for life," and develop "serious and often fatal organic disease," such as cancer. Some die, either immediately or later, as a result of "moral shock from the thought of the crime," whereas others are driven to insanity. He added that children born to a woman after she has had an abortion tend to be "unhealthy, deformed, or diseased," and that they too will therefore bear the price of their mother's "heinous" act.

Storer emphatically rejected the proposition that the woman should be able to decide this question for herself, noting that if she were given this responsibility "her decision . . . would be . . . warped by personal considerations," particularly because, during pregnancy, "woman's mind is prone to depression, and, indeed, to temporary actual derangement, under the stimulus of uterine excitement." Moreover, he added, women were born to bear children. "This . . . is the end for which they are physiologically constituted and for which they are destined by nature." It therefore followed that for a woman "intentionally to prevent the occurrence of pregnancy, otherwise than by total abstinence from coition," or "intentionally to bring it, when begun, to a premature close, are alike disastrous to a woman's mental, moral, and physical well-being."[27]

As evident in Storer's reasoning, many of the doctors who most aggressively championed the AMA's position viewed abortion as a moral—as well as a strictly medical—issue. Indeed, the doctors who most fervently championed the anti-abortion cause tended to associate abortion with lewdness, unrestrained sex, obscenity, and rebellious and insatiable women, and they agitated for a broad range of anti-vice initiatives, including laws regulating such sins as gambling, drinking, and prostitution.[28]

Over the next several decades, the AMA launched an aggressive campaign to rid the nation of abortion. The success of this campaign was facilitated by the late nineteenth-century "social purity" movement, which sought to impose conservative religious and moral "values on the whole society" and to give "the state greater power over areas of life once considered private." The desire of women to control their own bodies and lives was thus castigated by doctors and religious leaders alike as the product of a deformed and insatiable appetite for sex and a selfish desire for economic well-being. As the leading voice of the anti-abortion movement, Horatio Storer insisted that women must remain within their "God-given sphere." The purpose of "American women," he declared, was to produce children, not to "butcher" them.[29]

With increasing leverage, the AMA was able to effect a complete transformation in public perceptions and understandings of pre-quickening abortion. By the end of the century, every state had enacted legislation absolutely prohibiting abortion—pre- or post-quickening—unless a doctor certified that it was necessary to save the life of the woman. Women who sought abortions were now themselves subject to prosecution, and government for the first time aggressively sought to suppress all information about abortion.[30]

But despite the threat of criminal sanctions, the medical profession's warnings about the dangers of abortion, and the preaching of religious moralists, women continued to seek abortions in record numbers. By the turn of the twentieth century, as many as two million abortions were being performed in the United States annually, and almost a third of all pregnancies ended in abortion. As a result of the late nineteenth-century abortion laws, these abortions now had to be performed illegally, in less safe circumstances, and by less reliable practitioners than in the past.[31]

ENTER COMSTOCK (AGAIN)

UNTIL THE 1870s, contraception and information about contraception were generally unregulated in the United States. With advances in the vulcanization of rubber by Charles Goodyear in 1839, condoms, which had previously been made from animal intestines, became commonplace. By the 1860s, rubber condoms, pessaries, diaphragms, IUDs, and syringes for douching were being widely advertised and sold by pharmacists and mail-order businesses. In 1868, Barham Zincke, an English clergyman who toured the United States, was struck by the prevalence of small families. He noted that "there is no secret as to the various means resorted to" for achieving this result, for "they are advertised in every newspaper . . . in every city."[32]

This began to change in 1873 when Congress enacted the Comstock Act, which made it a crime, among other things, for any person to send through the mail "any drug or medicine, or any article whatever, for the prevention of conception" or any advertisement for such articles or any information about "when, where, how, or of whom, or by what means, any of the articles in this section . . . can be purchased or obtained."[33]

The Comstock Act represented a triumph of the moralists' assault on sin, sex, and reproductive control. It reflected the belief, vigorously advanced by Anthony Comstock, that information about contraception is "obscene" because it deals with sex and encourages immoral thoughts and behavior. Comstock insisted that "religion and morality are the only safe foundations for a nation's future posterity," and that birth control must therefore be outlawed. This was so, Comstock explained, because the availability of contraceptives reduces the risk that individuals who engage in premarital sex, extramarital sex, or prostitution will suffer the consequences of venereal disease or unwanted pregnancy. Thus, he reasoned, the availability of contraceptives is immoral, because it facilitates immoral conduct.[34]

In the twenty years after Congress enacted the Comstock Act, most states enacted "little Comstock acts" of their own, many of which went even further than the federal law. Some made it a crime not only to sell information about contraception, but also to give such information away, to possess it, or even to share it with others orally. Connecticut declared it unlawful for any person to purchase, possess, or even *use* contraceptives.[35]

W ITH THE Comstock Act in place, a triumphant Anthony Comstock rolled up his sleeves and aggressively enforced the law. Never one to shun publicity, in 1878 he orchestrated the arrest of Madame Restell. Comstock personally rang the bell of Madame Restell's basement office on East 52nd Street, claiming to be a married man whose wife had already given him too many children. He said he was worried about her health and hoped Restell might be able to help. She sold him some pills. Comstock returned the following day with a police officer and had her arrested. Rather than suffer the indignity of another prosecution and imprisonment, the despondent sixty-seven-year-old Restell committed suicide by slitting her own

The Arrest of Madame Restell, February 1878

throat in the bathtub. Comstock later boasted that Restell was the fifteenth target of his investigations to commit suicide. Closing his file on Restell, he penned a final comment: "A bloody ending to a bloody life."

Several years later, Comstock went after Ida Craddock, a marriage advice writer who authored conservative sex manuals with such titles as *The Wedding Night* and *Right Marital Living*, which included references to contraception. Despite being represented by such eminent figures as Clarence Darrow, Craddock was repeatedly prosecuted and convicted. Exhausted by the endless prosecutions and grueling prison sentences in the city workhouse, where she had endured inhumane conditions and harsh treatment, Craddock finally committed suicide in 1902 by slashing her wrists and inhaling natural gas on the morning she was once again to be sentenced to the city workhouse.

Craddock left a letter to the public in which she wrote: "Perhaps it may be that in my death more than in my life, the American people may be shocked into investigating the dreadful state of affairs which permits that unctuous sexual hypocrite, Anthony Comstock, to wax fat and arrogant, and to trample upon the liberties of the people."[36]

Following Comstock's example, vice societies dedicated to the suppression of birth control sprang up in cities across the nation. Most of the men who led these organizations had been raised in deeply religious families, and they marched ardently in Comstock's footsteps. British playwright George Bernard Shaw later coined the phrase "Comstockery" to refer to "America's fit of extreme moralizing" in this era.[37]

T HE EFFECT of the Comstock laws on information about birth control did not go unopposed. In 1878, for example, the National Liberal League, which resisted the injection of religion into government policy, sent Congress a petition with seventy thousand signatures protesting the ban on information about contraception. Many physicians in the late nineteenth century insisted that family limitation was a sound and reasonable choice and that the morality of such choices was not a proper subject for government intervention. Some commentators pointed out the irony that laws banning contraceptives had led to a sharp increase in the number of abortions. Jurors, who were often skeptical about the wisdom of these laws, frequently refused to indict or convict those who promoted or sold contraceptives.

Although the Comstock acts made it unlawful for individuals to sell or distribute information about contraception, enterprising entrepreneurs often found ways to circumvent the law. In an effort to mask the true purpose of their products, advertisers employed a broad array of creative euphemisms to describe them as means for preventing disease and promoting good health. Condoms were advertised for their value in preventing the transmission of venereal disease; IUDs were sold to correct prolapsed uteri; antiseptics used for contraceptive douching were marketed for the treatment of burns, whooping cough, and morning sickness. Buyers, though, knew the real purpose of the products. Thus, despite the fervent efforts of those who enforced the federal and state Comstock laws, contraceptives often slipped through the cracks.[38]

WHAT DID late nineteenth-century feminists think of all this? Perhaps surprisingly to us today, they had complex and shifting positions about abortion and contraception. Critics of feminism in this era consistently attributed to feminists an insistence on the right to abortion and birth control. This served both to trivialize the feminists' larger demands for political and social equality and to reinforce the claim that feminists were "radicals," because what they demanded was essentially a corruption of the "natural" order.

In fact, however, reproductive rights were not among the central demands of most women's rights advocates at this time. They were more focused on the right to vote and on reform of the laws governing marriage and divorce. Some women's rights advocates went so far as to actively oppose abortion. Elizabeth Cady Stanton, for example, a leading figure in the early women's rights movement who served as president of the National Woman Suffrage Association from 1869 until her death in 1902, condemned abortion as "the degradation of woman."[39]

Some feminists went even further and opposed even legal contraception, because they believed that unrestrained male lust was an important cause of women's oppression. They sought to put women in control of their own lives not by enabling them to prevent unwanted pregnancies, but by empowering them to say "no" to unwanted sex. In their view, the availability of contraception made it more difficult for women to resist overbearing male sexuality. Contraception was therefore not a source of women's liberation, but a cause of their subordination.[40]

Thus, women's rights advocates in this era had mixed views on the issue of reproductive freedom. Some feminists were sincerely opposed to abortion and or/contraception for moral, religious, or feminist reasons. Most of the others, including many who personally supported reproductive rights, sought to avoid the issue as part of a strategic decision designed to establish the credibility of the feminist movement and to prioritize its goals.

MARGARET SANGER AND THE BIRTH OF
THE BIRTH CONTROL MOVEMENT

WITH THE ENACTMENT of the federal and state Comstock laws, it became difficult for American women, especially poor women, to obtain information about contraception. Although manufacturers continued to market their products, they could no longer explain, or even mention, their purpose. Other sources of information dried up almost completely.

In the spring of 1914, Margaret Sanger, who was born in upstate New York in 1879, rallied a small group of radical friends in her New York City apartment to launch *The Woman Rebel*, "a militant-feminist monthly" that addressed a range of issues of interest to women, including marriage inequities, women in the labor market, and, most especially, "a woman's need to control her own fertility." A dynamic, titian-haired woman of Irish ancestry, Sanger was endowed with unfailing charm, fierce determination, and persuasive wit.

In direct defiance of the federal Comstock Act, Sanger announced in the very first issue of *The Woman Rebel* that she would "advocate the prevention of conception" and that she would "impart such knowledge in the

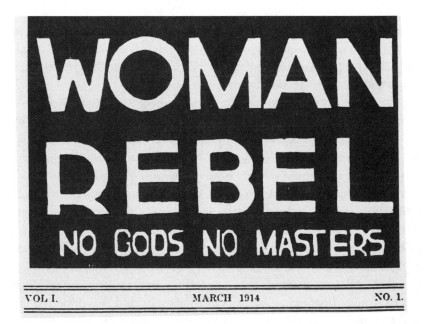

The Inaugural Issue of Margaret Sanger's The Woman Rebel

columns of this paper." It was at this time that Sanger and her group first coined the term "birth control." The campaign Sanger initiated that spring would grow into "one of the most far-reaching social reform movements in American history."[41]

SANGER'S FATHER, a freethinking socialist and soapbox orator, had inspired her from a very early age to think for herself and to defy conformity. Her Irish Catholic mother, who bore eleven children, died of tuberculosis in 1899 at the age of 50. Sanger later said that her mother died so young because "she had too many children and had worked herself to death" taking care of them. After training to be a nurse, Sanger married William Sanger, a quixotic artist who shared his wife's progressive views.

The couple moved to New York City in 1911, joined the Socialist Party, and soon became part of the radical culture of Greenwich Village. Margaret Sanger tended obstetrical patients in the tenement districts on the Lower East Side, an experience that exposed her for the first time to the squalor and suffering caused by the combination of poverty and unwanted pregnancy. Sanger later wrote about how pregnant women, desperate to avoid childbirth, brought "themselves around" by drinking "drops of turpentine on sugar, steaming over a chamber of boiling coffee or of turpentine water, rolling down stairs, and finally inserting slippery-elm sticks, or knitting needles, or shoe hooks into the uterus." These poor, immigrant women beseeched Sanger to reveal to them the "tricks" that well-to-do women used to keep their families small.

After treating several patients for septicemia, an infectious disease associated with the use of unsterilized abortion tools, and then watching them die, Sanger determined to learn more about reproductive control. She later wrote that as a result of this experience, "I resolved that women should have knowledge of contraception. They have every right to know about their own bodies. I would strike out—I would scream from the housetops. I would tell the world what was going on in the lives of these poor women. I *would* be heard."[42]

SANGER SAW contraception as a ticket to personal freedom for women. Unwanted pregnancies and limitless childbearing were not only dangerous to women's health, but they prevented women from developing their skills and capacities as individuals and limited their potential as productive members of society. She believed fiercely that if women could achieve the "basic freedom" of voluntary motherhood, they would then be able to help "remake" the world.[43]

Like others in the politically vibrant culture of Greenwich Village in the pre–World War I era, Sanger was influenced by the radical anarchist Emma Goldman. A Russian Jew who arrived in the United States in 1885, Goldman soon became the nation's most notorious advocate for free speech and the rights of labor. In the 1890s, the fiery Goldman took up obstetric nursing and midwifery and, like Sanger a decade later, dealt with poor, immigrant women who "lived in continual dread of conception." Goldman noted that these women frequently resorted to desperate methods to end their pregnancies, often "with great injury" to themselves. "It was harrowing," she wrote, "but it was understandable."[44]

Goldman, who traveled often to Europe, introduced her fellow Greenwich Village intellectuals to the works of Sigmund Freud, the English sexologist Havelock Ellis, and the English socialist Edward Carpenter, who wrote about sexual liberation for women and homosexuals. Ellis's writing especially inspired Sanger. Ellis wrote that "sex lies at the root of life, and we can never learn" reverence for life "until we know how to understand sex."[45]

I N 1911, Sanger began writing a series of articles for *The Call*, a socialist daily, about how women were being exploited in the workplace. In early 1913, she turned her attention to sex, first in a series designed to help mothers teach their children about sex, and then in a series titled "What Every Girl Should Know," which dealt more daringly with topics like venereal disease and masturbation. When Anthony Comstock caught wind of Sanger's final piece in the series, which focused on the "Consequences of Ignorance and Silence," he ordered the essay suppressed because it used "obscene" words like "syphilis" and "gonorrhea." In its next issue, in the space usually dedicated to Sanger's essays, *The Call* printed in large block letters: "WHAT EVERY GIRL SHOULD KNOW—NOTHING! BY ORDER OF THE POST-OFFICE DEPARTMENT." Comstock's action triggered strong protest from free speech advocates, and he eventually had to relent. The essay was thereafter published in *The Call* and then later as a stand-alone book.[46]

Because of the widespread suppression of information about birth control, Sanger found it almost impossible to learn herself what methods of contraception worked well and in what circumstances. At the suggestion of Big Bill Haywood, the leader of the International Workers of the World (the "Wobblies"), Sanger journeyed in the summer of 1913 to France, where such information was more readily available. She returned to New York more certain than ever "that family limitation must play a central role in lifting up working people, especially women, to overcome the inequalities of the capitalist system."[47]

The following year, Sanger began publishing *The Woman Rebel*, in which she urged her readers "to speak and act in defiance of convention." Sanger's first issue on birth control focused on class differences. She contrasted the women of the upper class, who have "all available knowledge and implements to prevent conception," with the women of the lower class, who are "left in ignorance of this information." She attacked the "blood-sucking men with M.D. after their names" who hypocritically performed secret abortions for rich women that poor and working class women could not afford.[48]

Sanger wrote that it was a woman's duty "to look the whole world in the face with a go-to-hell look in the eyes, to have an ideal; to speak and to act in defiance of convention." A few days later, the postmaster of New York informed Sanger that that issue of *The Woman Rebel* could not be distributed through the United States mail and that it would be confiscated under the authority of the Comstock Act.[49]

In August of 1914, federal officials indicted Sanger for violating the Comstock Act. Sanger insisted that her articles did not violate the law, because although they discussed birth control, they did not offer any specific contraceptive advice. On the eve of trial, Sanger fled the country for Britain, but only after distributing 100,000 copies of *Family Limitation*, a 16-page pamphlet that offered detailed information that she had gathered about the most effective and available means of contraception. The pamphlets were distributed with a letter asking that they be passed on to "poor working men and women who are overburdened with large families." As she wrote to her friend Upton Sinclair, Comstock now will have something "to really indict me on."[50]

WHILE SANGER was still in exile, Anthony Comstock had her husband William arrested for selling a copy of *Family Limitation* to an undercover vice officer. The publicity surrounding William's arrest in 1915 excited widespread public discussion of birth control. The newly founded *New Republic* endorsed birth control, arguing that the "relief which it would bring to the poor is literally incalculable." The *New York Tribune* observed that "at last birth control—that matter about which men, and especially women, have thought so much and have dared talk so little and then furtively—is to be brought out into the open." Even the Biloxi, Mississippi, *Daily Herald* complained that "William Sanger and Mrs. Sanger, his wife . . . are being hounded, prosecuted and doubtless, persecuted by Comstock."[51]

In March 1915, after attending a defense meeting for William Sanger, the suffragist Mary Ware Dennett, Free Speech League vice president Lincoln Steffens, and several other prominent liberals founded the National Birth Control League. Two months later, an overflow crowd of more than two thousand attended a meeting on birth control at the New York Academy of Medicine at which several doctors called for a change in the nation's policies. Dr. Abraham Jacobi rallied the audience by predicting that in the future "people will wonder how they could have been so stupid and callous. What is now a crime will be considered a beneficial measure."[52]

Comstock's dudgeon saw no bounds. He raged in response: "Can't poor people learn self-control? Can't everybody, whether rich or poor, learn to control themselves? . . . Are we to have homes or brothels?" A prominent anti–birth control doctor echoed this view, insisting that wives who wanted to have sex without the risk of pregnancy were no better than prostitutes, and a leading opponent of women's suffrage maintained that the fear of pregnancy was "the last barrier against immorality" and that instead of making contraception available "to the poorer classes, . . . it should be taken away from the well-to-do." Father John A. Ryan, an outspoken Catholic priest and a professor at Catholic University, wrote to the National Birth Control League that "the practice which your organization desires to promote" is "immoral, degrading, and stupid" because it involves "the perversion of a human faculty."[53]

Despite these reactions, it was clear that attitudes were beginning to change. Emma Goldman launched a nationwide lecture tour, including speeches on birth control, in New York, Pittsburgh, Cleveland, Detroit, Chicago, Minneapolis, Denver, Portland, and Los Angeles. Copies of Sanger's *Family Limitation* were distributed throughout the tour. As Dr. Ben Reitman, the flamboyant anarchist from Chicago, wrote in a tribute to "O brave Margaret Sanger" in *Mother Earth* in the fall of 1915, even "Anthony Comstock, though aided by all the powers of government or hell, cannot stop this stupendous movement." At the end of one of Goldman's lectures, the police arrested her and Reitman for "circulating literature of an illegal character." The judge dismissed the charges, explaining that "ignorance and prudery are millstones about the neck of progress."[54]

Shortly thereafter, William Sanger came to trial in 1915. The courtroom was filled with prominent supporters of birth control, including the anarchist Alexander Berkman, the socialite Gertrude Minturn Pinchot, and the feminist leader Elizabeth Gurley Flynn. Sanger admitted that he had broken the law, but maintained that it was the "law" itself that was on trial. The case drew national headlines, and Anthony Comstock himself bombastically testified for the prosecution. The judge, a devout Catholic, called William Sanger "a menace to society" whose crimes violated "not only the laws of the state, but the laws of God." He then sentenced him to thirty days in prison. In protest, the crowd burst into "a medley of shouts and cries."[55]

Ten days later, Anthony Comstock, who over the decades had become America's most feared moralist, died of pneumonia. By the time of his death he had become in the eyes of many Americans a tiresome "relic of a bygone era" and a "target of ridicule." *The Masses*, a popular left-wing journal that featured such writers as Max Eastman, Carl Sandburg, Bertrand Russell, and Sherwood Anderson, ran a political cartoon that depicted "a rotund Comstock before a judge, clutching a young mother, saying 'Your Honor, this woman gave birth to a naked child!' "[56]

The Masses, September 1915

By the end of 1915, "the public silence over birth control had been broken" and birth control leagues had been established in cities across the nation. There was now growing public support for amending the Comstock laws, and *Family Limitation* continued to be widely distributed. Several months later, the charges against Margaret Sanger, which had led her into exile, were dismissed, because the prosecuting attorney did not want to make her into any more of "a martyr" than she already was.[57]

On July 1, 1916, Alexander Berkman, the longtime lover of Emma Goldman, predicted what he saw as the outcome of the struggle for birth control: "The end is not hard to foresee. . . . The law will be ignored and defied with increasing frequency till general sentiment will compel its repeal. What is a crime today will be an accepted and approved fact tomorrow."[58]

"GOD MUST HAVE SENT YOU TO US"

AFTER HER RETURN from exile in early 1916, the dismissal of the charges against her, and a triumphal national tour, Margaret Sanger made up her mind to open the nation's first birth control clinic in a working-class neighborhood of Brooklyn. Although she wanted to recruit a doctor to run the clinic, even sympathetic doctors were unwilling to challenge the establishment in so direct a manner. Sanger therefore signed up her sister, Ethel Byrne, a registered nurse, for the position. On October 16, 1916, Sanger, Byrne, and their staff opened the nation's first birth control clinic at 46 Amboy Street in the Brownsville neighborhood in Brooklyn.

From her studies in Europe, Sanger had concluded that the diaphragm was, on balance, the best contraceptive option for women. Diaphragms were difficult to obtain, however, so her clinic also offered advice on how to use condoms, pessaries, cervical caps, suppositories, and douching syringes. For a ten-cent registration fee, women could get instruction on how to use each of these contraceptive devices and information about how to obtain them. This was all in clear violation of New York's Comstock Act, which made it a crime for anyone to sell or exhibit contraceptives or to impart information about how to use them.

Sanger and her staff distributed leaflets announcing the opening of the clinic, and more than a hundred women came on the first day. The women who visited the clinic came from a broad range of ethnic backgrounds, including Russian, Italian, Hungarian, and Polish. Most were working mothers—chambermaids, scrubwomen, and sweatshop workers. One woman had had fifteen children by the age of thirty-six; another had seven surviving children out of eleven and had self-aborted more than a dozen times. A Russian woman told Sanger, "God must have sent you to us. We are too poor to pay a doctor to tell us what you have told us. If the police fight you, they must fight us too."[59]

STILL, THE GHOST of Comstock, who had met his Maker the year before, lived on. Four days after the clinic opened, a woman undercover agent made her appearance. Sanger and her staff immediately recognized her for what she was, but boldly served her nonetheless. Several days later, the police returned to the clinic to arrest Sanger. She refused to go quietly, shouting at the undercover police woman, "You're not a woman! You're a dog!" Two weeks later, after she was released on bail, Sanger defiantly reopened the clinic, but she was immediately arrested again. The authorities then ordered the building owner to evict the clinic, and it closed for good.

The state decided to try Ethel Byrne, who had also been arrested, before Sanger. Byrne's attorney argued that women have a fundamental right to control their own fertility and that the New York law prohibiting women from obtaining information about contraception was therefore unconstitutional. He maintained that the law infringed a woman's "free exercise of conscience and pursuit of happiness," because it denied her the right to enjoy the pleasure of sexual intercourse without fear of pregnancy.

The judge ridiculed this assertion and added that fear of pregnancy is an essential deterrent to fornication. Byrne was convicted and sentenced to thirty days in Blackwell's Island prison in the middle of New York's East River. As bold as her sister, Byrne immediately announced that she would provide birth control counseling to the women in the prison and that she would go on a hunger strike. Her hunger strike and deteriorating health during her incarceration drew national attention, as prison officials had to force-feed her just to keep her alive.

When Sanger's trial began a week later, the courtroom was packed with supporters. A memorable tableau of "huddled masses" and elegant dowagers, the audience included both "shawled and tired-faced slum mothers" and smartly-dressed socialites who made up the Committee of One Hundred, a group of well-heeled women who were dedicated to Margaret Sanger and the cause of birth control. The involvement of these women helped reframe the movement from one identified with radical socialists and anarchists to one endorsed by the elite of modern society.

Nonetheless, Sanger, like her sister, was convicted and sentenced to thirty days in prison. The judge offered her clemency if she promised to obey the law against contraception, but she refused, stating defiantly: "I cannot respect the law as it stands to-day." Sanger was then sent to the Queens County Penitentiary to serve her time.[60]

Observers could not help but notice that the authorities were playing into Sanger's hands. As a Lexington, Kentucky, newspaper editorial noted, "The folly of making a martyr of Mrs. Sanger . . . by imprisonment and persecution is bearing fruit throughout the country. Instead of squelching the doctrine preached by her, public sentiment is being strongly aroused in its favor."[61]

CONTRACEPTION: A MORTAL SIN?

IN THE NINETEENTH CENTURY, the Catholic Church did not play a dominant role in the effort to prevent women from exercising control over reproduction. This changed in the early twentieth century, however, as the Church began to take a more active stance in the debate over contraception.

In Europe, the Catholic clergy had made birth control an issue in response to growing evidence that Catholics, especially in France, were limiting the size of their families. The Church focused initially on coitus interruptus, the most common form of birth control, which the clergy decried as the crime for which God had put Onan to death. The clergy then attacked contraception more generally on the premise that it "plainly wars with the primary end of marriage [procreation] and tends per se to the extinction of society."[62]

In the United States, the growing strength of the birth control movement caught the attention of Catholic leaders. In 1916, Father John Ryan published an article in which he condemned contraception as a "mortal sin." Three years later, the American Archbishops and Bishops of the Catholic Church published a "Pastoral Letter" declaring that reproduction is a marital duty, condemning the notion that economic and domestic happiness is a legitimate ground for avoiding reproduction, and proclaiming that such "selfishness . . . is, in God's sight, a 'detestable thing.' "[63]

Priests began speaking out openly against birth control and several Catholic organizations condemned the "unnatural and utterly anti-Christian propaganda" of those who sought to promote contraception. In March 1917, Pope Benedict XV responded directly to the agitation over birth control in the United States, and several Catholic publications excoriated Margaret Sanger personally. Nonetheless, most American Catholic leaders still refrained from mounting a concerted attack on the birth control movement, largely because they were not yet comfortable addressing so delicate a subject in public discourse.[64]

AFTER MARGARET SANGER returned from a tour of war-torn Germany in 1920, she made almost fifty speeches on birth control in venues across the country. In a new book, *Woman and the New Race*, she wrote that "the most far-reaching social development of modern times is the revolt of woman against sex servitude." She added that "no woman can call herself free until she can choose consciously whether she will or will not be a mother." In early 1921, she addressed the National Woman's Party (NWP), the nation's leading women's rights organization, and attempted to persuade the NWP to endorse birth control as an essential part of its post–Nineteenth Amendment agenda.* The NWP declined the invitation, explaining that it had to keep its focus on enacting laws guaranteeing equal rights for women. Sanger no doubt thought that in neglecting birth control, the NWP was missing the forest for the trees.[65]

Later that year, Sanger undertook her most ambitious program to date. She organized the "First American Birth Control Conference" at the richly ornamented Plaza Hotel in New York City. The three-day event, from November 11 to November 13, 1921, brought together a broad array of internationally-respected speakers, including economists, eugenicists, gynecologists, biologists, and social scientists. More than three hundred invited guests participated in the conference, including more than one hundred from the American Public Health Association. In a closed-door session, the participants discussed and debated the competing merits of a broad range of contraceptive methods.

On the final night of the conference, which was dedicated to a discussion of the morality of birth control, the New York police raided the event. Sanger was lifted onto the stage by supporters to the chant of "Defy them! Defy them!" She responded: "This meeting is not suspended. It is a legal meeting. . . . We have a right to hold it under the Constitution. . . . Let them club us if they want to." The police dragged Sanger off the stage and carted her off to the police station, with hundreds of protestors marching behind them singing "My Country 'Tis of Thee."[66]

The following day, the press learned that Catholic Archbishop Patrick

---

* The Nineteenth Amendment, which was ratified in 1920, granted women the right to vote.

J. Hayes had pressured the police to shut down the meeting. Two days later, Archbishop Hayes issued a statement in which he challenged the morality of the birth control movement, declaring that the "law of God and man, public policy, human experience, are all condemnatory of birth control as preached by a few irresponsible individuals."

Sanger responded by questioning the morality of Catholic doctrine. A furious Archbishop Hayes answered with a vehement condemnation of birth control in a pastoral letter to the Archdiocese: "Children troop down from heaven because God wills it. . . . Woe to those who degrade, pervert, or do violence to the law of nature as fixed by the eternal decree of God Himself!" He damned birth control as "satanic" and as an "unclean abomination." Sanger shot back that she had "no objection to the Catholic Church inculcating its doctrines to its own people," but declared its effort to "enforce its opinions and code of morals upon" those who do not share its teachings "an interference with the principles of this democracy."[67]

As the historian Peter Engelman has observed, this "episode marked a shift in birth control opposition." In the past, the government had been the "chief antagonist," but in this incident, as the government gradually receded "into the background," Sanger managed to "pull back the curtain on the new enemy." As Sanger later wrote, "It was now a battle . . . against the machinations of the hierarchy of the Roman Catholic Church."[68]

BIRTH CONTROL IN THE TWENTIES

DESPITE THE NOW fervent opposition of the Catholic Church, the birth control movement gained steam in the 1920s. Indeed, by 1923, Annie Porritt, a suffragist and birth control activist, could claim that the "whole of the United States has . . . become equilibrated to the idea of Birth Control."[69] In that same year, *Life* magazine published a satirical poem, "Birth Control of the Seas," that included the following verse:

> The Turbot told it at the Crab's
> She had it from the Sole—
> The very latest thing in thought
> To-day, is birth control.[70]

During this pivotal decade, in which the nation often seemed to be at war with itself over moral issues, Americans clearly were becoming more comfortable with the idea of sexual pleasure, and a desire for sexual fulfillment was increasingly shaping "the normative behavior of many Americans." Sex suddenly flourished in the popular culture, and to this day we "link the era with carnal images of flappers, dance halls, and the back seats of Fords."

The "new woman" was seen as daring and flirtatious in a way that would have been impossible in the Victorian era. Middle- and upper-class women in particular sought ready access to contraception and casually "skirted government prohibitions." As the journalist Ruth Millard recalled, "Methods of birth control were discussed over tea cups" and the Comstock laws "were violated hourly, but no charges were pressed." The birth rate fell by 30 percent from 1895 to 1925, no doubt due in part to the increased use of birth control.[71]

I N RESPONSE, the Catholic Church rallied its troops and strengthened its opposition to birth control. In 1924, on the eve of the New York State Birth Control Conference in Syracuse, local Catholics pressured the city council to enact a law forbidding the public discussion of birth control. (The mayor vetoed the measure.) The mayor of Albany surrendered to pressure from local Catholics and prohibited Margaret Sanger from speaking, and throughout the mid-1920s the Catholic mayor of Boston, James Michael Curley, banned Sanger from speaking in public halls within the city.

More fundamentally, the Catholic Church was extremely effective at blocking legislation that would have repealed the state and federal Comstock acts (insofar as they deal with contraception). Although most state and federal legislators used birth control themselves, they were unwilling publicly to take on the Church, which aggressively maintained that the use of contraception was an "unnatural, harmful, indecent, and selfish act that debased marriage and ran counter to the tenets of Christianity." One Catholic assemblyman in New York called those who sought to legalize birth control "blasphemers" who should be "swept from the face of the earth."

On December 31, 1930, Pope Pius XI issued *Casti Connubii: On Christian Marriage*, which condemned birth control on the ground that "Evil is not to be done that good may come of it." The *Casti Connubii* ushered in a new era of Catholic clerical attacks on birth control. In such circumstances, the issue of contraception was simply "too politically hazardous" for most legislators to address, despite the continuing efforts of Sanger, Mary Ware Dennett, and other feminist leaders to change the laws.[72]

"MANY PEOPLE HAVE CHANGED THEIR MINDS"

AT ALMOST THE same time that the Pope was issuing his encyclical, Walter Lippmann, the renowned columnist, was writing in 1929 in *A Preface to Morals* that religion had lost control of "family issues" because there was "no longer any compulsion to regard the sexual life as within the jurisdiction of the commissions of the Lord." This was an increasingly popular view. As another commentator observed in the *Birth Control Review,* "If religion does not assist man to use his reason to adapt to his environment, but rather tends to make it more difficult for human beings to coordinate their activities and to develop healthy and aspiring views of life, it becomes one of the chief forces that blocks progress, and increases human suffering and misery."[73]

Even within the religious community, voices began to be heard in support of birth control. The Protestant pastor Harry Emerson Fosdick wrote that "our present laws are thoroughly unwise. . . . [P]hysicians ought to be trusted with authority to give contraceptive information to those to whom they think it ought to go." In 1930, the Lambeth Conference of Bishops of the Anglican Church announced its support for contraception. The following year, a committee of the Federal Council of the Churches of Christ in America endorsed birth control, and the Episcopal Bishop Wilson R. Stearly described birth control clinics as "a godsend and blessing to many harassed and troubled souls."[74]

NONETHELESS, BIRTH CONTROL advocates could not get the law changed. Even in the twenty-eight states that had no laws prohibiting birth control, the existence of the federal Comstock Act made doctors wary about prescribing or even discussing contraceptives with their patients. It was clear to Sanger and others that continued progress would be slow, at best, unless the Comstock Act could be amended. Members of the National Committee on Federal Legislation for Birth Control, which Sanger founded in 1929, repeatedly drafted bills in Congress to amend the Comstock Act, but their efforts were repeatedly beaten back. Connecticut congressman William Citron, a Jew, refused to support the proposed legislation, for example, explaining that "the Catholics would crucify me if I voted for this bill." Representative Henry Ellenbogen, a Pennsylvania Democrat, also declined to support the bill, noting that "The R.C. [Roman Catholics] have been busy getting all their people to write letters, and even friendly Congressmen are afraid."[75]

In a series of highly publicized hearings in 1934 on proposed birth control legislation, Father Charles Coughlin, the famously demagogic and anti-Semitic radio priest, testified before the House Judiciary Committee. Focusing his glare on Margaret Sanger, who was seated just a few feet away, Coughlin reminded the congressmen of "God's fundamental command, 'Increase and multiply,' not 'Control and destroy,'" and condemned non-procreative marital sex as "legalized prostitution."

Although Sanger characterized Coughlin's performance as a "half-hour of grossness," and reporters recorded "scornful laughter" and groans from both the members of Congress and the audience, the bill did not make it out of committee. Hazel Moore, the principal lobbyist for the National Federation for Constitutional Liberties, who had led the charge in Congress for birth control legislation, finally exclaimed in frustration, "Senators are Cowards."[76]

THE ECONOMIC woes of the Depression triggered a further drop in birth rates. From 1930 to 1940, only 58 percent of women in their prime childbearing years had more than one child, a sharp decline from prior generations. Women achieved this primarily through the widespread use of birth control. Despite the legal obstacles, the contraceptive business boomed. A 1932 survey of western Florida found condoms for sale in 376 retail outlets, including pool rooms, cigar stores, soda fountains, shoeshine parlors, and grocery stores. In some parts of the country, saleswomen went door-to-door peddling IUDs, diaphragms, and contraceptive jellies. By 1938, annual sales of birth control products were estimated at a quarter-of-a-billion dollars.[77]

Although Congress refused to change the law, judges began to reflect the change in public opinion. In 1930, for example, in a case involving a trademark dispute between two condom manufacturers, a federal court of appeals ruled for the first time that condom manufacturing was a lawful enterprise (because condoms could lawfully be used to prevent the spread of venereal disease) and that condom manufacturers were therefore entitled to trademark protection. Three years later, a federal court of appeals ruled that the interstate transportation of a contraceptive device could not be deemed illegal unless the government could prove an intent to use the product for illegal (that is, contraceptive) purposes.[78]

In a groundbreaking decision in 1936, the United States Court of Appeals for the Second Circuit continued this trend by narrowly construing a federal statute that had been modeled on the Comstock Act of 1873. The case began several years earlier when Margaret Sanger ordered a package of "Koyama Suction" pessaries from a Japanese doctor in order to test their effectiveness. The pessaries were delivered to Dr. Hannah Stone, a gynecologist in New York. Section 305(a) of the federal Tariff Act made it a crime for any person to import "into the United States from any foreign country . . . any article whatever for the prevention of conception." Customs officials confiscated the pessaries because they were commonly used to prevent conception.[79]

In *United States v. One Package of Japanese Pessaries*,[80] the Court of Appeals, in an opinion by Judge Augustus Hand, who had previously written several critically important opinions on the issue of obscenity,* held that the statute did not prohibit the importation of contraceptives for *lawful* purposes. As an example, the court explained that a doctor could lawfully provide a patient with condoms to prevent infection or with a diaphragm to prevent a pregnancy that might endanger the patient's health. Although acknowledging the moral motivations of those who drafted the Comstock Act, the court pushed those motivations aside insofar as the use of contraceptives served what it deemed to be legitimate medical purposes. This was revolutionary.

This change in statutory interpretation clearly reflected the historic shift in public opinion since 1873, when the Comstock Act had been enacted. As Judge Learned Hand, Augustus's cousin and one of the most distinguished jurists of the twentieth century, observed in his concurring opinion in *One Package*, "Many people have changed their minds about such matters in sixty years."[81] By the 1930s, nationwide polls indicated that as many as 70 percent of Americans supported the dissemination of birth control information, and in 1937 the American Medical Association finally came around and expressly endorsed the dissemination and teaching of birth control methods.[82] Nonetheless, the state and federal laws against the sale, distribution, and advertisement of products for the *purpose* of birth control remained on the books.

D ESPITE THE changes in public and legal attitudes toward contraception, there was no doubt about the illegality of abortion. Every state continued to make abortion a crime, except in the rare case in which doctors might certify that abortion was necessary to save the life of the woman. In the first half of the twentieth century, between 10 and 25 percent of all

---

* See chapter 8.

married women had at least one illegal abortion and, not surprisingly in light of the prevailing societal attitudes toward unwed mothers, almost 90 percent of all premarital pregnancies ended in an illegal abortion. By the 1950s, approximately one million women had an illegal abortion each year, representing roughly 20 percent of all pregnancies.[83]

Prosecutions for abortion were rare, convictions were even rarer, and sentences (when there was a conviction) were generally lenient. When the law was enforced, it was generally only against those who actually performed the abortion. Although technically in violation of the law, the women, their husbands, and their lovers were almost never prosecuted. Even those who performed abortions were rarely prosecuted, unless the woman died.[84] Those who performed illegal abortions in this era included licensed physicians; individuals with some medical training, such as nurses, dentists, chiropractors, and physiotherapists; midwives; a broad range of barbers, prostitutes, salesmen, elevator operators, and doormen; and, of course, the women themselves, who often self-induced an abortion. Doctors who performed illegal abortions almost always said that they did so because it was the "right" thing to do, given the plight of the women they served. The law, though, said otherwise. Eventually, the Supreme Court would decide the question.[85]

10

"STRANGE FREAKS
OF NATURE"

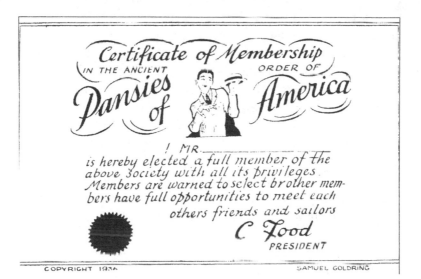

Certificate of Membership
IN THE ANCIENT · ORDER OF
Pansies of America

! MR._____
is hereby elected a full member of the
above Society with all its privileges.
Members are warned to select brother members have full opportunities to meet each
others friends and sailors

C Food
PRESIDENT

COPYRIGHT 1936   SAMUEL GOLDRING

ALTHOUGH THE CONCEPT of the "homosexual" as a distinct type of person did not exist until the late nineteenth century, same-sex sex has been present from the very dawn of civilization. But because such conduct was condemned as immoral, sinful, and unlawful for the better part of two millennia, individuals who engaged in such behavior generally did their best to keep their actions and their desires secret. As a consequence, we have only limited knowledge of the day-to-day lives of homosexuals who lived in centuries past.

In recent decades, though, scholars have increasingly managed to piece together the history of homosexuality in the United States. Drawing on that scholarship, this chapter explores the history of homosexuality in the United States from the nation's founding to the Second World War, a narrative that would not have been possible a generation ago.

LOOKING THE OTHER WAY

AT THE TIME of the American Revolution, all thirteen colonies deemed sodomy a capital offense. Although the precise definition of the "crime against nature" was obscure, most courts followed the English precedents and limited the crime of sodomy to anal intercourse and bestiality. The crime was defined without regard to whether the act was committed by individuals of the same sex or the opposite sex. Neither oral sex nor mutual masturbation constituted sodomy, even if done by two persons of the same sex. Moreover, as applied to anal intercourse, sodomy laws in the late eighteenth century generally were enforced only in cases involving either a child or the use of force. Consensual anal intercourse between two adults was unlawful but in practical effect was almost never the subject of prosecution.[1]

In the nineteenth century, state legislatures repealed the death penalty for sodomy. Prosecutors and courts continued to construe the crime narrowly, and criminal convictions for same-sex sex between consenting adults were extremely rare. Although people were definitely aware of same-sex sex, they tended to look the other way.*[2]

Popular literature of the mid-to-late nineteenth century suggests that the existence of same-sex relationships was an acknowledged part of the culture. Theodore Winthrop's *John Brent* (1862), for example, described the relationship between Richard Wade and John Brent in great detail, including Wade's wish to be "a squaw to be made love to" by Brent. Wade's desire for same-sex sex apparently did not put off readers—the book went through twenty-eight editions.

Bayard Taylor's novel *Joseph and His Friend: A Story of Pennsylvania* (1870) praised love between men as "as tender and true as the love of women." Walt Whitman, an "iconic figure" in the movement "for gay self-definition and gay rights," wrote of his own homosexuality with an almost shocking frankness: "I share the midnight orgies of young men." Whitman's Calamus poems, first published in 1860 in *Leaves of Grass*, celebrated "manly intimacy and love." In general, however, and despite these examples, same-sex sex was not a frequent, much less polite, subject of discussion in the nineteenth century.[3]

As the century progressed, however, and as America became more urbanized, an active homosexual subculture began to develop in some cities. In an 1896 article on "Sex and Art," for example, the author noted the existence of a "secret organization," known as "The Fairies of New York," in which men who were "fond of the actor's life" dressed "in female attire" and sang "in imitation of the female voice." Soon thereafter, a New York State special legislative committee began exploring the apparently widespread presence of male prostitutes in New York City.[4]

O F COURSE, same-sex sexual relationships in this era were not limited to men. The mid-nineteenth-century actress Charlotte Cushman, for example, openly maintained a series of serious, long-term relationships with

---

* There were 105 recorded sodomy prosecutions in the United States in the nineteenth century, approximately one per year, falling into roughly three equal categories: bestiality, anal sex between an adult man and a boy, and sexual assault by a man of a woman or by a man of a man involving attempted or actual anal penetration.

women. But such a complete and open renunciation of heterosexual attraction by a woman was rare. In a society in which women had little independence and were pressured to marry and have children, most homosexual women had few life options. They generally had to submerge themselves in the roles of wife and mother, while perhaps pursuing close "friendships" with other women. Even when those friendships had sexual elements, they were almost always secret and largely ignored by the law. Indeed, as late as 1839, there was still no popular name for sex between women. The general view was that women were interested in sex only to procreate, to satisfy a husband, or to earn money. This conception of women's sexuality allowed women to show each other a level of affection that would have raised eyebrows if exhibited by men.[5]

Matters began to change toward the end of the nineteenth century. As the nation's economic structure was transformed, even women began finding opportunities for personal independence and social mobility. As jobs for women became more available, women who had previously been reliant on husbands to provide the basic necessities of life were now better able to forego marriage without fear of deprivation. Many independent women found long-lasting companionship with other women who had also chosen work over traditional family roles. These long-term relationships between unmarried women came to be known as "Boston marriages," a phrase derived from Henry James's 1885 novel, *The Bostonians*, a bittersweet tragicomedy centered on an odd triangle of characters who vie for one another's affections. Although we do not know how many of these relationships were sexual in nature, the suspicion of sex was certainly in the air.[6]

"STRANGE FREAKS OF NATURE"

NEAR THE END of the nineteenth century, same-sex sex came under closer scrutiny and persons drawn to such behavior began to be seen not just as individuals who chose to have sex with a person of the same sex, but as persons possessed of a distinctive psychological identity. It was in this era that the concept of the "homosexual" first came into being.

Two leading studies of homosexuality near the end of the nineteenth century, *Psychopathia Sexualis* (1886) by the Austro-German psychiatrist Richard von Krafft-Ebing, and *Studies in the Psychology of Sex: Sexual Inversion* (1897) by the British physician and psychologist Havelock Ellis, suggested links between homosexuality and insanity and posited that homosexuality was a congenital pathology.

In an 1888 article on "Perversion of the Sexual Instinct," Krafft-Ebing observed that an individual afflicted with "sexual predilections . . . for those of his or her own sex, with an aversion for sexual intimacy with those of the opposite sex," was a "strange freak of nature." In his view, persons with such predilections suffered from a sexual pathology "that reflected a broader mental or physical 'degeneration,' or reversion to a prior evolutionary status."[7]

These works marked the beginning of a profound shift in thinking about same-sex sex from a purely moral/religious perspective to a medical/scientific perspective, and a corresponding shift from a focus on the sinfulness of certain behavior to an emphasis on the inherent makeup of certain individuals. For the first time, articles in medical journals began to debate the nature and dynamics of same-sex sexual attraction.

Among the questions most often discussed were whether homosexuality was congenital or acquired, whether it was curable or incurable, and whether it should be accepted as an unavoidable condition or actively resisted and suppressed. The medical community used several terms to classify people who exhibited what were thought to be deviant sexual inclinations. The most common were "invert" and "pervert." An individual who engaged in same-sex sex could fall into either category.[*]

S OMEONE WHO sought same-sex sex merely for reasons of lust was deemed a "pervert." The concept of sexual perversion extended beyond same-sex sex and included a broad range of "unnatural" sexual desires and actions. In 1881, the American psychologist Dr. E. C. Spitzka described sexual perversion as encompassing (1) an absence of sexual desire; (2) an excess of sexual desire; (3) sexual desire at an "abnormal time of life"; and (4) sexual desire that "is not of such a character as to lead to the preservation and increase of the species."[8] Although the concept of sexual perversion was couched in medical terminology, the underlying logic was clearly grounded in religious and Victorian understandings of sexual propriety. Sexual desires, relationships, and conduct that fell outside of

---

[*] Homosexuality was not removed from the official list of psychological abnormalities by the American Psychological Association until 1973.

the strict boundaries of those understandings were presumptively deemed "perverted."[9]

By contrast, an "invert," or a "pure" homosexual, was "a person whose general mental state is that of the opposite sex." Such persons sought out same-sex sex not out of a sense of unrestrained lust, but because of their peculiar personal inclinations. Such persons were described as being "improperly reversed" because they were thought to possess the mind of a person of the opposite sex.

As the American social psychologist Dr. William Lee Howard reasoned in 1904, because the brain rather than the body is "the primary factor" in determining a person's sex, and because male inverts were actually women (who naturally desired men) even though they appeared to be men (for whom such a desire would have been perverted), the sexual desire of male inverts "for their—apparent—own sex" is "really a normal sexual feeling." On this view, inverts were not men or women, but an "intermediate" or "third sex." They were "mental hermaphrodites."[10]

But how did this happen? A prevalent belief in the late nineteenth century was that the human embryo contained both male and female sex organs, but shed one of them during the process of development. One theory of homosexuality was that the male homosexual shed the female sex organ in utero when he should have shed the male sex organ. He was thus a female inadvertently trapped in a male's body. The matter was simply reversed for female homosexuals.

Experts who believed sexual inversion was congenital pointed to what they saw as early warning signs of inversion in childhood. Adolescent symptoms of female sexual inversion were thought to include being a careless child; enjoying boys' games; playing mostly with boys; and menstruating early. For male inverts, the early symptoms were thought to include playing with dolls; having a sweet, female disposition; being artistic, poetical, and imaginative; and having "a tendency to rather weak philosophizing."[11]

By the turn of the century, this new concept of homosexuality began to take hold, although the terms "homosexual" and "heterosexual" did not enter the popular lexicon for several more decades.[12]

WOMEN WERE particularly intriguing. In attempting to make sense of a seeming increase in female homosexuality at the turn of the century, experts concluded that the women's emancipation movement, combined with the growing economic independence of women, had unleashed inborn homosexual tendencies in women, especially those engaged in the suffrage movement. Dr. James Weir argued in 1895 that "every woman who has been at all prominent in advancing the cause of equal rights [for women has] either given evidences of masculo-femininity, or has shown, conclusively, that she was the victim of psycho-sexual aberrancy."[13]

The female invert came to be seen as especially dangerous. As Havelock Ellis posited, the invert was powerless to change her biological makeup. If her homosexual instincts were directed only at other female inverts, "society would have no grounds for alarm." But because "many women, though not genetically inverted, possessed a genetic predisposition, a weakness, for the advances of other women," homosexual behavior could become an acquired trait. Thus, in an "unwholesome environment," such as a women's boarding school, college, boardinghouse, or political organization, these women "could succumb to the blandishments of the 'congenital invert.'" Ellis and his followers therefore "depicted the female invert not as a genetic anomaly and a helpless victim," but as a sexual predator who threatened the natural standing and dominance of men.[14]

PHYSICIANS IN this era, like those who followed them for much of the next century, hotly debated whether homosexuality was curable. In 1884, Dr. James Kiernan, a prominent professor of legal psychiatry in Chicago, concluded that "to remove this condition is out of the question." He believed, however, that individuals could learn not to act on the condition, and to that end he advised cold sitz baths, a course of intellectual training to enhance the patient's will to resist, and confinement in an asylum. In his pioneering 1908 work *The Intersexes: A History of Similisexualism as a Problem in Social Life*, Dr. Edward I. Prime-Stevenson, writing under the pseudonym Xavier Mayne, argued that homosexuality "cannot be 'cured'" and that the "shame of a gross blunder falls to the physchiater who promises a 'cure' for what is not a disease."[15]

At around the same time, Havelock Ellis maintained that the best course of action for congenital homosexuals was complete "sexual abstinence," because this would prevent them from "harming" other members of society. Other physicians proposed a broad range of remedies for homosexuality, including sedatives, continual association with people of the opposite sex, hypnosis, sex with prostitutes, the severe study of abstract subjects, rectal massage, burning the neck and lower back with hot irons or chemicals, hor-

Havelock Ellis

mone treatment, electric stimulation, psychoanalysis, sterilization, and even intense bicycle riding. Many physicians advocated castration, clitoridectomy, or removal of the ovaries, even though the evidence suggested that such measures did not in fact eliminate homosexual inclination.[16]

Some doctors favored the sterilization of homosexuals in order to prevent the condition from being passed on to the next generation. Those holding this view generally believed not only that homosexuality was a genetic defect, but that it was a symptom of degeneration—a condition that would get worse with each succeeding generation. Sterilization was therefore justified in order to preserve "the interest of civilization." The sterilization of homosexuals became increasingly common over the next several decades. By 1938, thirty-two states had enacted sterilization laws that could be invoked to "fix" homosexuals and to prevent them, and other misfits such as imbeciles and epileptics, from passing their degeneracy on to the next generation.[17]

A DEBATE flared within the medical and legal communities over whether sexual inversion merited legal punishment. Some doctors distinguished between "congenital" and "acquired" homosexual tendencies, arguing that "inborn inversion" was a disease that the victim could not prevent. Such individuals, they argued, could not be held legally or morally responsible for having a disease. The proper response to their plight was therefore medical treatment rather than legal punishment.

Havelock Ellis, for example, strongly opposed laws that punished private, consensual same-sex sex, arguing that "more damage was done by trying to cure inverts than by leaving them alone." Similarly, Dr. Kiernan argued that homosexuality impaired the will to such an extent that there could be no legitimate legal responsibility for actions caused by the disease. Echoing this sentiment, Dr. C. H. Hughes, a St. Louis psychologist who founded the journal *The Alienist and Neurologist* in 1880, argued that the criminal law, which "protects society by punishing the criminal," was inappropriate for congenital homosexuals and that medicine was preferable because it "would mercifully protect both society and the maimed victim of a sexually and mentally degenerate organism." Hughes added, however, that because "acquired sexual vice" could be prevented, criminal sanctions for non-congenital homosexual conduct were deserved.[18]

T HE ADVENT of Sigmund Freud's psychoanalytic theory overwhelmed much of the speculation of the late nineteenth- and early twentieth-century "sexologists." Freud rejected the concept of a degenerate third sex and argued instead that homosexuality was the consequence of stunted, or "arrested," sexual development. He believed that humans were born with an undifferentiated sex drive, and that one's sexual orientation formed later. But he observed that while most people develop a heterosexual orientation, it was not uncommon for them to experience a homosexual phase along the way.

Freud theorized that those few individuals for whom homosexuality was not a phase but a final orientation must have experienced some trauma at an early stage of life that prevented them from developing "normal" sexual feelings toward members of the opposite sex. He was never quite sure what caused this arrested development, but at different times he posited that it might variously be due to obsession with one's own genitals or "to a family constellation of seductive mother and weak father" in males and to penis envy in females.[19]

Despite the negative connotations that might be associated with "arrested development," Freud argued that no moral or social opprobrium should attach to homosexuality. He was dubious that homosexuality could be cured, and he even speculated that in other areas of life, homosexuals were generally well adjusted and characterized by "especially high intellectual development." He emphatically rejected the notion that homosexuality was a sign of degeneracy. In a 1935 letter to the gay son of one of his patients, Freud wrote that homosexuality "is nothing to be ashamed of, no vice, no degradation; it cannot be classified as an illness." He added that it "is a great injustice to persecute homosexuality as a crime, and cruelty too."[20]

Most of Freud's successors failed to embrace his compassionate view of the matter. For the most part, they latched onto the idea of arrested development as a defect that, through treatment, could be fixed. Dr. Wilhelm Stekel of Vienna, for example, insisted in 1930 that the "disease" of homosexuality "is not a congenital condition but a psychic state which can be handled by treatment correctly applied."[21]

FAIRIES, QUEERS, AND TRADE

IN A SOCIETY in which the dominant religion excoriated homosexuality as "a heinous sin, the law branded it a serious crime, and the medical profession diagnosed homosexuals and lesbians as diseased," the vast majority of individuals who suspected themselves of harboring homosexual desires naturally felt themselves to be "inferior—less moral, less respectable, and less healthy than their fellows." Such people did their best to suppress their "filthy" desires and to hide their secret shame from family, friends, neighbors, and associates. Exposure, after all, promised only humiliation, rejection, scorn, blackmail, and economic ruin. As a patient seeking a cure for his homosexuality wrote, "The knowledge that I am so unlike others makes me very miserable. I form no acquaintances outside of business, keep mostly to myself, and . . . do not indulge my sexual feelings." The terrible fear of discovery kept the secret lives of most homosexuals invisible, even to one another.[22]

. . .

T HE DAWN of the twentieth century, though, saw the emergence of a more visible homosexual subculture, particularly in some of the nation's rapidly growing cities. The anonymity of these large urban centers made it possible for at least some homosexuals to begin to construct their own identities based in part on their attraction to people of their own sex. By 1910, cities like New York, Boston, Washington, Chicago, St. Louis, San Francisco, and Philadelphia had significant homosexual communities. Venues catering to those seeking the company of their own sex included clubs, baths, cafés, restaurants, bars, and music halls. As the historian George Chauncey has observed, those "who participated in that world" began to forge "a distinctive culture with its own language and customs, its own traditions and folk histories, its own heroes and heroines."[23]

The participants in this gay subculture had not yet begun to use the term "gay," but instead differentiated among several different types of homosexually active men. "Fairies" were overtly effeminate homosexuals, akin to the English "fops." The primary distinguishing characteristic of fairies was their assumption of the female gender role. Fairies were easily associated with "the third sex," or inverts, of the medical literature, on the theory that they were women trapped in men's bodies. They usually adopted female mannerisms, such as standing with hands on hips, a limp wrist or swishy walk, and tended to use a feminine vocal inflection or timbre. Many adopted a female persona, going by such names as Princess Salome, Lady Violet, and the Duchess of Marlboro. Fairies often plucked their eyebrows, bleached their hair, and donned flamboyant clothing, including tight-cuffed trousers, flowered bathing trunks, flashy hatband feathers, and bright red neckties.[24]

Not surprisingly, Anthony Comstock and his band of epigones were horrified by the very existence of such characters. "Those inverts," he declaimed, "are not fit to live with the rest of mankind." Invoking a Hester Prynne–like trope from Nathaniel Hawthorne's *The Scarlet Letter*, he added that "they ought to have branded in their foreheads the word 'Unclean,' and as the lepers of old, they ought to cry 'Unclean! Unclean!' as they go about." Their punishment, he roared, "ought to be imprisonment for life."[25]

A NOTHER CATEGORY of homosexual was the "queer." Queers desired sex with other men, but they did not identify with the female gender characteristics adopted by fairies. To the contrary, they generally looked and acted like other men. They recognized that they were homosexual, but maintained that their homosexuality "revealed nothing abnormal in their gender persona." Many queers considered the terms "fairy" or "faggot" derogatory, and reserved them exclusively for those homosexuals who openly carried themselves in an unmanly manner.[26]

Queers tended to look down on the fairies' effeminacy. They blamed the more visible and flamboyant fairies for the negative public perception of homosexuality and feared being associated with them. As one "queer" put it in the early twentieth century, "I don't object to being known as homosexual, but I detest the obvious, blatant, made-up boys whose public appearance and behavior provoke onerous criticism." He added that with the fairy seen by the public as the representative homosexual, "I don't begrudge normal people their feelings against homosexuals."[27]

On the other hand, the fairies' greater visibility provided cover under which queers could more easily pass as straight in the larger society. This was important, because anyone unmasked as gay was at the very least "threatened with loss of livelihood and loss of social respect." In effect, queers were better able to escape detection because those looking for homosexuals tended to think only of fairies.

Outside the realm of the gay subculture, queers, whose sexual inclinations generally were not apparent to heterosexuals, had to develop a variety of complex social codes and subtle cues to identify themselves to one another, without alerting the heterosexuals among whom they lived and worked. Fairies, of course, had an even more difficult time, for if they were to pass as straight they had to conceal their "real" personae entirely by constructing a more masculine charade.[28]

Among the most sought-after sexual partners for both fairies and queers in this era were known as "trade." Trade were usually masculine men, such as sailors and soldiers, who regarded themselves as sexually "normal," but who would on occasion consent to a same-sex sexual encounter either for pleasure or money. Some were even virulently homophobic. But as long as trade maintained the masculine role (most often as the penetrator or the recipient of oral sex), they did not consider themselves to be homosexual.[29]

T HIS SUBCULTURE of early twentieth-century fairies, queers, and trade, although suppressed from the nation's collective memory for decades, is now well documented, especially in San Francisco and New York City. The Bowery, a large thoroughfare on Manhattan's Lower East Side, became notorious as a working-class red-light district. Several establishments served as prime gathering places for homosexuals, and many places hired fairies, sometimes dressed in drag, to sing, dance, and entertain the crowds. Similar establishments flourished in Harlem and in San Francisco's Barbary Coast district. Some lesbians also entered this sexual underworld, where they attended balls wearing tuxedos and waltzed with other more feminine-looking women. These were perhaps the first public appearances of what would later come to be known as "butches" and "femmes." [30]

These bars, jazz clubs, and restaurants were not designed exclusively for homosexuals, but attracted a mixed crowd. In some of these clubs, both mixed-sex and same-sex couples used back rooms for private sexual encounters. The nature of these clubs appears at the time to have been known by people from all walks of life. Indeed, the existence of the gay subculture was hardly a secret. Ordinary people read about fairies and queers in magazines and newspapers, saw them portrayed on stage in both vaudeville and burlesque, and encountered them in shops, restaurants, and bars.

As one New Yorker declared in 1918, "Our streets and beaches are overrun by . . . fairies." "Slumming" on the Bowery, which was popular among upper- and middle-class men and women in the early years of the twentieth century, typically included a tour with stops at several hot spots where shocked men and women could enjoy drinks, dancing, music, "scandalous shows," and, "for a price, access to women and fairies of the lower classes."[31]

For the most part, this subculture was ignored—if not protected—by the New York City police, who were usually quite happy to accept bribes to leave well enough alone. Not surprisingly, this did not sit well with some elements of society. Anthony Comstock's Society for the Suppression of Vice, the nation's most powerful anti-homosexual organization, was especially active in attempting to cleanse the city of moral decay. The society raided bathhouses and theaters and sometimes prevailed upon the police to make mass arrests. These raids could sometimes be quite violent, resulting in serious physical injury to those arrested. Egged on by the society and similar reform groups, urban police departments ramped up their efforts to suppress homosexuality in the years leading up to World War I.[32]

WORLD WAR I, PROHIBITION, AND THE TWENTIES

THE ENTRY OF the United States into World War I had a significant impact on gay life. The war pulled many young men away from their small towns of origin and the protective oversight of their families and landed them in the intensely single-sex environment of the military, often in New York City, a primary port of embarkation to the theater of war in Europe. With its already developed gay subculture, New York introduced tens of thousands of small-town soldiers to the novelty of gay culture. To the moral crusaders, this situation presented a potential "crisis of alarming proportions."[33]

As the war progressed, the anti-vice societies became ever more concerned that the war itself might have triggered an increase in "perversion." This led the moral reform societies, the police, and military authorities to focus for the first time on homosexuality as a major social problem. During Comstock's reign, the Society for the Suppression of Vice had orchestrated police raids on bookshops with gay literature and clubs with gay performers, but it was not until World War I, after Comstock's death in 1915, that his successor—John Sumner—went after homosexuals with a vengeance. His agents organized police raids on theaters, restaurants, clubs, and bathhouses where gays tended to congregate, resulting in the arrests of some two hundred men on charges of "disorderly" conduct. Other anti-vice organizations soon followed suit, placing suspected gay meeting places under intense surveillance. Arrests of gays on charges of disorderly conduct skyrocketed from 92 in 1916 to more than 750 in 1920.

The crime of disorderly conduct was a vaguely constructed catchall designed to empower the police to impose a certain conception of proper behavior in public places. For the most part, it was used to restrain conduct that might upset upstanding citizens. Although there was no law declaring it a crime for gays or lesbians to associate with one another in a cafeteria or public park, to dance with someone of the same sex, or to wear clothing usually associated with the other gender, all of these behaviors were now swept up under the omnibus charge of disorderly conduct.

Such convictions were no small matter. They often carried significant fines and sentences of up to ten days in the workhouse. Moreover, the arrests themselves, even without a conviction, could have devastating extralegal consequences due to the disclosure of an individual's homosexuality to family, friends, employers, and landlords. To add insult to injury, in response to these stepped-up police efforts, many restaurants, bars, and clubs with a gay clientele began to exclude any customers or conduct that might mark them as gay-friendly.[34]

TRANSFORMED BY the horrors of World War I, many young Americans, especially those living in cities, were determined to upset the order of things. Many came to believe that the values of their parents' generation had led the world into a pointless and brutal war. They had learned that life is transitory and fragile and that it is meant to be lived. This generation's insistence on challenging the staid cultural norms of the Victorian era, reflected in their attitudes toward obscenity and birth control,* also led them to explore unconventional art and literature, to indulge new fashions such as short skirts and bobbed hair, and to question the received wisdom about sex.

In the cultural entrepôt of postwar New York, men's boardinghouses, dormitories, and hotels became centers of gay activity. The YMCA, which was intended to provide a morally upright haven for pure young men in a city filled with sin, became a center of gay society. Male couples lived together, single men brought male sexual partners to their rooms, and new transplants to the city were often introduced for the first time to the city's homosexual subculture in the "Y." In the gay community, the Y came to be celebrated as the place "for never ending sex" where "there is always some-

NIGHT NO. 10
in FAIRY-LAND

Our Tireless Picket Tracks the Restless Androgyne to
CHILDS on Fifth Avenue and to LOUIS' on
49th Street.

* See chapters 8 and 9.

one waiting to have an affair." Gay men joked that the letters Y-M-C-A stood for "Why I'm So Gay."[35]

As the transgressive behavior that marked the decade of the 1920s exploded across the nation, the gay communities in New York, Chicago, New Orleans, Baltimore, San Francisco, and other cities held enormous drag balls patterned on the debutante and masquerade balls of the mainstream culture. These events grew to be giant spectacles, attracting hundreds and even thousands of spectators.

Langston Hughes, one of the earliest innovators of the then-new literary art form called jazz poetry, recalled the famous Hamilton Club Lodge Ball in Harlem, at which it was fashionable for the city's social leaders to occupy boxes "and look down from above at the queerly assorted throng on the dancing floor, males in flowing gowns and feathered headdresses and females in tuxedoes and box-back suits." What became known as a "pansy craze" engulfed New York City, as pansies (another term for "fairies") became the subject of novels, Broadway plays, movies, and newspaper and magazine cover stories. In nightclubs, pansy acts involving female impersonators were the most popular in the city.[36]

T HE 1920S was also the era of "lesbian chic" in which female bisexual experimentation came to be seen as "in." Close relationships between women were now "assumed to be sexual (perhaps even in cases when they were not)." Lesbian speakeasies opened in New York, Buffalo, Chicago, San Francisco, and other cities. One sociologist described lesbian parties in Chicago where "some of [the women] would put on men's evening clothes, make love to the others, and eventually carry them off in their arms into the bedrooms."[37]

Popular novels by such authors as Ernest Hemingway (*The Sun Also Rises* and *A Farewell to Arms*) and Sherwood Anderson (*Poor White* and *Dark Laughter*) openly explored lesbian and female bisexual relationships. In one memorable and revealing exchange at a Greenwich Village party, a psychoanalyst attempting to diagnose Edna St. Vincent Millay's persistent headaches inquired whether it had ever occurred to her that she "might perhaps, although you are hardly conscious of it, have an occasional impulse toward a person of your own sex?" Millay responded "with the nonchalance requisite for a true bohemian, 'Oh, you mean I'm homosexual! Of course I am, and heterosexual too, but what's that got to do with my headache?' "[38]

1920s Drag Ball

DESPITE THE lighter side of this transformational decade, the plight of most homosexuals in the United States remained bleak. Some gays and lesbians chose to be single, but most, especially those in positions of prominence, took a spouse of the opposite sex, hoping desperately to submerge or at least to hide their true nature.* In 1926, Dr. Joseph Collins published *The Doctor Looks at Love and Life*, one of the first popular books about sex to receive serious attention in the mass media. His discussion of homosexuality was widely read. Collins predicted that "[i]t will probably be difficult to convince the generation succeeding ours that, when this country was at the zenith of her commercial prosperity, it was improper to utter the word homosexuality, prurient to admit its existence and pornographic to discuss the subject."

Collins bemoaned the fact that "[w]e are shorter of tolerance in this

---

* In some instances, two lesbians managed to wed and to live openly as a married couple, with one of them assuming the identity of a man.

country than of any other virtue," and observed that "a more enlightened viewpoint" would come only through "understanding." He called upon readers to understand that homosexuals, through no fault of their own, "live in a state of constant fear; fear that their secret will be guessed; fear that they will become the prey of blackmailers; fear that they will fall into the clutches of the law." "Small wonder," he added, that some of them, "intolerant of their endowment and ever conscious of the conflict that it imposes, take their own lives."[39]

In 1928, Radclyffe Hall, a highly acclaimed English author, published *The Well of Loneliness*, "the most influential lesbian novel of the twentieth century." The main character is Stephen Gordon, a young woman of landed birth. The novel explores Stephen's coming of age as a lesbian and her relationship with Mary, the great love of her life. In the end, "in a supreme gesture of self-sacrifice," a brokenhearted Stephen cedes Mary to a man so Mary can live a "normal" life.[40]

In one scene, Hall described Stephen's visit to a gay bar in Paris:

> As long as she lived Stephen never forgot her first impressions of the bar known as Alec's—that meeting place of the most miserable of all those who comprised the miserable army. That merciless . . . haunt to which flocked the battered remnants of men whom their fellow men had at last stamped under; who, despised of the world, must despise themselves, beyond all hope, it seemed, of salvation. There they sat closely herded together at the tables. . . . Stephen never forgot their eyes, those haunted, tormented eyes of the invert.[41]

The book ends with the heroine's plaintive cry, "God, . . . rise up and defend us. Acknowledge us, oh God, before the whole world. Give us also the right to our existence!"[42]

DEPRESSION

THE ECONOMIC MISERY caused by the Depression led to a general societal withdrawal from the cultural openness and experimentation of the 1920s. The era of flappers, pansies, speakeasies, and female impersonators drew to a close in the grim atmosphere of the mid-1930s. As the Depression dashed the confidence of the American people, gay men and lesbians began to seem less amusing and more threatening to the nation's core beliefs and values. Within a few years, the vibrant pre-Depression homosexual subculture of queers, fairies, cross-dressers, and pansies was so completely obliterated and then blotted out of the nation's consciousness that later generations of Americans—gay as well as straight—"were all but unaware of their existence."[43]

With the end of Prohibition in 1933, the sale of alcohol was once again legal, but it was now subject to extensive new forms of government regulation. State liquor boards were granted broad authority over establishments that sought to sell liquor. The goal was to ensure that the return of alcohol to the public sphere did not lead to the sorts of evils that Prohibition was meant to prevent. It was necessary, in other words, to ensure that restaurants, bars, and other establishments that were licensed to serve liquor did so in a respectable manner. Any licensee who did not take steps to prevent disorderly conduct was subject to license revocation.

In this setting, most state liquor boards ruled that the presence of any "undesirables" was sufficient justification to yank a tavern's license. This came to include homosexuals, even if they conducted themselves in an orderly manner. The mere presence of homosexuals could now cost a tavern or restaurant its liquor license. With the stakes so high, bar and restaurant owners became increasingly vigilant for signs of homosexuality among their patrons. Homosexuals were no longer welcome. This drove much of gay society even deeper underground and gave rise to the exclusively gay bars that would come to serve as a nexus of gay society in the decades to come.[44]

The effort to blot from public view the very existence of gays and lesbians soon extended from bars and nightclubs to other venues. Pansy clubs, female impersonators, drag balls, and fairies in public places, which had once seemed charming, were no longer considered appropriate or acceptable. Moral crusaders attacked female impersonation acts as a celebration of sexual deviancy. Between 1935 and 1937, female impersonation was banned from the stage in cities throughout the nation. The vaudeville circuit, which had once openly featured gay characters and humor, banned even the use of the words "fairy" and "pansy" in vaudeville routines anywhere in the nation.[45]

In response to a boycott organized by the Catholic-led Legion of Decency, the Hollywood censorship code was amended in 1934 to forbid any movie to make any reference to "sexual perversion." This led to the elimination of *any* reference to gays and lesbians in the movies. In a similar vein, the National Organization for Decent Literature of the Catholic Church, founded in the 1930s, undertook a concerted attack on written works dealing with homosexuality. To avoid the blacklist, newspaper editors and book publishers steered clear of any such material, thus driving almost any sympathetic depiction of homosexuality out of print.[46]

. . .

T HE "LESBIAN CHIC" of the 1920s also went deep into the closet. In the minds of the public, lesbians were no longer considered harmless. Rather, they came to be perceived as dangerous, and were often portrayed as vampires eager to prey on unsuspecting and vulnerable women and girls. In Sheila Donisthorpe's popular novel *Loveliest of Friends* (1931), for example, she described lesbians as

> crooked, twisted freaks of nature who stagnate in dark and muddy waters and are so cloaked with . . . viciousness and selfish lust that, drained of all pity, they regard their victims as mere stepping stones to their further pleasures. [They leave] their prey gibbering, writhing, sex sodden shadows of their former selves, conscious of only one desire in mind and body, which, ever festering, ever destroying, slowly saps their health and sanity.[47]

To live openly as a lesbian in the 1930s "was not a choice for the faint-hearted." Women who a decade earlier might have happily been "out" now retreated to the security of the marriage relation. To friends and family, "and perhaps even to their husbands, they appeared to be simply heterosexual married women."[48]

The image of the gay man also took on an increasingly sinister cast. Beginning in the 1930s, a growing public anxiety over sex crimes recast the dominant image of homosexuals not as amusingly effeminate fairies but as potentially dangerous psychopaths capable of committing the most unspeakable crimes. As one national magazine put the point, "Once a man assumes the role of homosexual, he often throws off all moral restraints. . . . Some male sex deviants . . . descend through perversions to other forms of depravity, such as drug addiction, burglary, sadism, and even murder." In time, "the terms *child molester, homosexual, sex offender, sex psychopath, sex degenerate,* [and] *sex deviate* . . . became interchangeable in the minds of the public." Demonized not only as perverts, but now as child molesters as well, "homosexuals became the new enemy of the people," and arrests for sodomy increased dramatically.[49]

As gays and lesbians disappeared deeper and deeper into the closet, fewer heterosexuals came to know homosexuals as individuals, giving special power to the negative public depictions. As the historian George Chauncey has observed, the "state built a closet in the 1930s and forced gay people to hide in it."[50]

11

COMING OUT

Frank Kameny, July 4, 1965

ONE OF THE EARLIEST voices in defense of the rights of homosexuals was Emma Goldman, the passionate anarchist who was also one of Margaret Sanger's most committed supporters. An avid proponent of sexual fulfillment and free love, Goldman declared in 1915 that the "social ostracism" of homosexuals was nothing short of "dreadful." It was, she observed, "a tragedy that people of a differing sexual orientation" are so humiliated and so proscribed in a world that "displays such gross indifference" to their plight.

To Goldman's dismay, even her anarchist comrades tried to silence her on this issue, arguing that most Americans already denounced anarchism as "depraved" and that it would therefore be "inadvisable" for them to stir up even more opposition to their cause by taking up the defense of what most Americans regarded as "perverted sex-forms." Goldman was undeterred, but she could rally few to her cause before she was deported to Russia in 1919 because of her outspoken opposition to the draft during World War I.[1]

Five years later, Henry Gerber, a World War I veteran, established the Chicago Society for Human Rights—the first homosexual rights organization in the United States. Gerber immediately confronted a problem—the most natural supporters of the organization, gay men and women, were unwilling publicly to support the Society for fear of exposure. The Society managed to publish just two issues of its magazine, *Friendship and Freedom*, before the authorities shut it down. The precipitating event was a late-night raid of Gerber's home, during which one of the arresting officers declared that Gerber would get a heavy prison sentence "for infecting God's own country."*[2]

---

* Gerber's lawyers managed to get the charges dismissed because the police had failed to obtain a search warrant, but Gerber was suspended from his post office job for "conduct unbecom-

As Gerber discovered, the capacity of gay men and women to join together to advance their common interests was undermined by their ability to hide who they were. Unlike African Americans and women, whose identities were unmistakable, homosexuals could and did mask their true selves. This was both an advantage and a burden. On the one hand, they could avoid much of the overt hatred and discrimination that would befall them if their homosexual inclinations were known; on the other hand, they could not effectively organize to advocate for their own cause if they remained in the shadows.

For most gays and lesbians, the act of "coming out"—of acknowledging one's same-sex desires and behavior to others—"was a lonely, difficult, and sometimes excruciatingly painful experience." The sexual impulses experienced by gay men and women left them with a profound "sense of difference from family, community, and society." Despite the brief openness of some facets of gay and lesbian culture in a few major cities during the 1920s, the pervasive religious condemnation of the homosexual's "sinful" desires, compounded by a steady stream of stories in the media and in popular literature depicting homosexuals as sexual psychopaths, degenerates, and social misfits, shaped homosexuals' own understanding of who they were, as well as what others thought of them. Society inflicted upon homosexuals "a burden of self-hate" that led them to interpret their sexuality as a psychological and moral failing. In such circumstances, most gay men and women spent their lives in isolation from even their own kind.[3]

THE GOOD WAR

THROUGHOUT WORLD WAR II, the Code of Military Justice prohibited any member of the armed forces to engage in "sodomy," that is, to engage "in unnatural carnal copulation with another person of the same or opposite sex."[4] Like the traditional concept of sodomy, this prohibition was not directed only at homosexuality. Rather, it prohibited certain sexual conduct, whether engaged in by homosexuals or heterosexuals.

In prior wars, prospective soldiers were not asked about their sexual orientation and the military made no effort to prevent homosexuals from enter-

---

ing a postal worker." Even after dissolving the Chicago Society for Human Rights, Gerber was unable to find new employment because of his support of gay rights. He spent the rest of his life in poverty.

ing the service. Although military officials in World War I were well aware of the presence of homosexuals in the ranks, they almost never court-martialed members of the military for consensual sodomy. Given the nation's need for soldiers and sailors, even known homosexuals were permitted to serve their country as long as they were discreet.[5]

In the lead-up to World War II, however, the Selective Service for the first time instituted a policy intended to prevent homosexuals from entering the military. In its initial formulation, the policy was not directed specifically at homosexuals. Rather, it was designed to avoid some of the psychological problems that had plagued American soldiers during World War I, when there had been no prescreening of the emotional makeup of prospective soldiers. To avoid a recurrence of the many cases of shell shock and severe emotional trauma that afflicted soldiers in the Great War, the military, in conjunction with a team of psychiatrists, instituted a new psychological screening program to weed out men who were psychologically unsuited to military service.

At first, the program paid no particular attention to an individual's sexual practices or inclinations, but as the screening process evolved, the Army's surgeon general determined that homosexuality should itself be a disqualifying characteristic. This created an almost impossible task for those charged with carrying out the screening. How were they to determine who was a homosexual? The military assigned this responsibility to draft boards and military doctors. At induction physicals, millions of men were routinely asked whether they had ever had homosexual urges or experiences. The exercise was largely pointless, because gay men who were determined to serve their country, and in any event did not want to be "outed," simply lied about their sexual proclivities—something they had of necessity learned to do quite well in their civilian lives.

Apart from asking individuals directly about their sexual inclinations and activities, those doing the screening focused on such indicia as "feminine bodily characteristics," "effeminacy in dress or manner," or a "patulous [expanded] rectum." Needless to say, these were not definitive measures of homosexuality, and during all of World War II fewer than four thousand men were excluded from joining the military because of their sexual orientation. It is, of course, impossible to know precisely how many homosexuals did join the military in those years, but the best estimates suggest that more than half-a-million gay men and lesbians managed to serve their nation in the armed forces during World War II.[6]

In truth, the military was more interested in recruiting soldiers than in excluding homosexuals, and gay men and lesbians eager to defend their country found little to prevent them from doing so. Robert Fleischer, for example, sought to volunteer in 1943. He was anxious about being rejected: "My God, . . . couldn't he see my curly platinum blond hair that was partly bleached, the walk, maybe the sissy *S* in my voice—all the things that I thought would give me away?" The only question the recruiter asked Fleischer about his sexuality was "Do you like girls?" to which he honestly answered "yes." And that was the end of the inquiry.[7]

EVEN WITHIN the armed services, the military took a relatively tolerant approach toward suspected homosexuals—as long as they kept their sexual conduct private. Identifiably gay soldiers were often channeled into "stereotypically homosexual jobs," serving as "clerks, medics, hospital corpsmen, chaplains' assistants, and female impersonators in musical revues." In that way, the nation could still benefit from their service in wartime. The Women's Army Corps (WAC), an all-volunteer unit, adopted

Soldiers in Drag

a similar view, discouraging any overt homosexual conduct, but warning against "indulging in witch hunting or speculation" about lesbian activities. As the historian Lillian Faderman has observed, the "firm public impression during the war years that a women's corps was 'the ideal breeding ground for lesbians' had considerable basis in fact."*8

Reflecting the army's silent acceptance of gay and lesbian soldiers during the war, in 1943 the federally funded National Research Council and the *Infantry Journal* jointly published *Psychology for the Fighting Man*, which calmly observed that if homosexual soldiers "are content with quietly seeking the satisfaction of their sexual needs with others of their own kind, their perversion may continue to go unnoticed and they may even become excellent soldiers."9

Although the military did not actively seek to purge homosexuals from the ranks, it took a very different position if a soldier was caught in a compromising act. In 1941, Secretary of War Henry Stimson ordered that all persons found to have committed sodomy must be court-martialed and, if found guilty, sentenced to five years of hard labor. The military brigs were notorious for guards who relished the opportunity to beat gay prisoners. If thrown in the brig, a gay man "found himself in a no man's land, where even his gay friends avoided him to protect themselves."10

The use of courts-martial proved too burdensome and too costly, however, so in 1942 Stimson authorized Section 8 discharges for "sodomists." A Section 8 discharge, or a "blue" discharge (because of the color of the paper), was neither a dishonorable nor an honorable discharge, but it precluded former service members from receiving any government benefits, including health care, college tuition, occupational training, or loans to start new businesses. Even more devastating, a Section 8 discharge often meant that the former soldier would not be able to get a job in civilian life or get into a college or university. As one congressman noted at the time, it was almost impossible for a former soldier to become a productive citizen "if he is walking around with a blue discharge."11

---

* On one occasion, General Eisenhower asked a WAC sergeant to remove the lesbians in her battalion. The sergeant responded: "Yessir. If the General pleases I will be happy to do this investigation. . . . But, sir, it would be unfair of me not to tell you, my name is going to head the list. . . . You should also be aware that you're going to have to replace all the file clerks, the section heads, most of the commanders, and the motor pool." To which Eisenhower replied: "Forget the order."

. . .

BY THE time the war ended in 1945, most Americans were weary of dealing with death, disruption, and chaos. They were ready to settle back into a normal life again. But "normal" meant different things to different people. The relative tolerance gay men and lesbians had experienced in the military was no part of "normal." Having fought to keep their nation free, gay and lesbian soldiers quickly saw their wartime freedoms disappear. As the nation sought to restore its prewar sense of order, churches, politicians, the media, schools, and government agencies launched a campaign to reconstruct the nuclear family, push women back into their traditional roles, and promote a more conservative sexual morality. Homosexuals, many of whom were unable or unwilling to conform to the traditional family ideal, once again stood out as sexual perverts whose very existence threatened the postwar American family.[12]

As the war drew to a close, and as gay and lesbian soldiers suddenly became dispensable to the military, the witch hunts began. Suspected lesbian and gay soldiers were now called in and cross-examined about their sexual feelings and practices and compelled to disclose the names of their sexual partners. It was not unusual for them to be physically abused, subjected to public humiliation, and committed to hospital psychiatric units. At the end of the war, Marvin Liebman, who was stationed abroad, wrote a letter to a friend that revealed his sexual orientation. When his commanders learned of the letter, they ordered him, in a move that was hardly unusual, confined in a psychiatric ward surrounded by barbed wire. After confessing his homosexuality, he was forced to march in front of his entire squadron while his commanding officer bellowed, "I would like you men to see how a New York Jew faggot drills." Liebman recalled that he "became a pariah, bitterly lonely and desperately unhappy. I was shunned by everyone." Eventually, Liebman was given a Section 8 discharge and shipped home. This incident was repeated over and over again.[13]

The military had a particularly difficult time identifying lesbians, who tended to be more discreet than gay men about their sexual relations. But once the call went out to round up the "sickos," the military investigators were tireless in searching the women's barracks and their private possessions for incriminating letters and photographs. They employed wiretaps, informants, and polygraphs. They kept records of which women gave each other gifts, traveled together, and ate together. They awakened women suspected of lesbian tendencies in the middle of the night for questioning. One

WAC recalled that when her interrogation was finally over she "left that base feeling like a real piece of shit." Fired repeatedly after she left the military when employers learned of her blue discharge, she "had no ego left, no self-image, no confidence." For years, she "never told a soul about it."[14]

In Tokyo, some five hundred women soldiers were issued blue discharges because of accusations of homosexuality or of harboring homosexual tendencies. In one particularly tragic incident, recalled by a member of the WACs, the military authorities "called up one of our kids—Helen. They got her up on the stand and told her that if she didn't give names of her friends they would tell her parents she was gay. She went up to her room on the sixth floor and jumped out and killed herself. She was twenty."[15]

In the waning days of the war, such injustices were enacted in American military bases across the globe. More than nine thousand gay men and lesbian soldiers and sailors were drummed out of the army and navy with blue discharges. Faced with such inquisitions, homosexual soldiers had nowhere to turn. Organizations to support the rights of homosexuals did not yet exist, and even civil liberties organizations were afraid to get involved, even when these soldiers "pleaded with them for support."[16]

THE LAVENDER SCARE

THE FALL OF the Iron Curtain, the Soviet detonation of an atomic bomb, the Berlin blockade, the fall of China, and the Korean War left the nation in a state of shock and fear. Faced with a new "Cold War," national leaders demonized current and former members of the Communist Party, and a host of political opportunists fed—and fed upon—the fear that America was infested with insidious, malignant, and dangerous enemies. Fearful of domestic subversion and terrified of nuclear annihilation, Americans turned against one another in what would prove to be one of the most repressive periods in American history.

On February 9, 1950, Joseph R. McCarthy, a little-known senator from Wisconsin, delivered a Lincoln Day address at a dinner sponsored by the Republican Women's Club in Wheeling, West Virginia. In the course of that speech, McCarthy infamously pulled out a piece of paper and proclaimed that "I have here in my hand a list of 205—a list of names that were made known to the Secretary of State as being members of the Communist Party and who nevertheless are still working on and shaping policy in the State Department." This statement was a complete fabrication, but it initiated a firestorm that raged for more than a decade.[17]

Three weeks later, John E. Peurifoy, head of the State Department's security program, testified before a Senate committee investigating the loyalty of government workers. In response to a question about the number of State Department employees who had resigned while under investigation for being possible security risks since 1947, he volunteered that ninety-one of those employees were in the "shady category." When pressed, he clarified that he meant that they "were homosexuals."[18]

McCarthy immediately followed up, telling a Senate subcommittee that a "flagrantly homosexual" State Department employee, dismissed as a security risk, had been restored to his position of trust because of pressure from an official in the Truman administration. From that point on, it did not take long for the growing panic over national security to evolve into a witch hunt directed not only at suspected Communists, but at suspected gays and lesbians as well.[19]

In the following months, Democratic Representative John J. Rooney of New York accused the Commerce Department of "laxity in weeding out homosexuals"; Republican Senator Kenneth Wherry of Nebraska, the Republican floor leader, asked his colleagues whether they could "think of a person who could be more dangerous to the United States of America than a pervert?"; and Guy George Gabrielson, the chairman of the Republican National Committee, warned in a letter to the party faithful that "perhaps as dangerous as the actual Communists are the sexual perverts who have infiltrated our Government in recent years."[20]

On May 20, 1950, a Senate Appropriations Committee subcommittee unanimously called for a full Senate investigation "of alleged homosexuals in the Executive Branch of the Government." Three months later, Senator Wherry explained in an interview in the *New York Post* that "You can't hardly separate homosexuals from subversives." Asked whether "he would be content to get the homosexuals out of the 'sensitive posts,' leaving alone those who have nothing to do with military security," Wherry replied, "There should be no people of that type working in any position in the government."[21]

The conflation of "Communists and queers" led the American public to view them as indistinguishable threats. The association was quite natural, for at the height of the Cold War, Americans viewed Communism as atheistic, un-Christian, immoral, and degenerate. As one congressman asserted in 1950, "The Russians are strong believers in homosexuality." Tabloid journalist Arthur Guy Mathews went even further, warning that "Communists are now converting American youth to homosexuality to defeat us from within."

By the summer of 1950, White House aide David Lloyd warned that the issue of homosexuals in government posed "a political problem of considerable magnitude." Indeed, three of President Truman's top advisers cautioned him that "the country is really much more disturbed over the picture which has been presented so far of the Government being loaded with homosexuals than it is over the clamor about Communists being in Government."[22]

THE "LAVENDER SCARE," as it came to be called (to distinguish it from the "Red Scare"), was now well underway. Republicans fumed that the State Department was as riddled with sex perverts as it was with Communists, and a *New York Daily News* commentator wrote that "the foreign policy of the U.S." is "dominated by an all-powerful, super-secret inner circle of highly educated, socially highly placed sexual misfits" who are "susceptible to blandishments by homosexuals in foreign nations."[23]

In December 1950, a Senate Committee issued a report that officially declared "sexual perverts" to be dangerous to the nation and demanded "strict and careful screening to keep them off the Government payroll." Noting the "lack of emotional stability which is found in most sex perverts, and the weakness of their moral fiber," the report accused federal agencies of failing to take "adequate steps to get these people out of Government."[24]

In response to these concerns, government agencies began using lie detectors to determine whether their employees were homosexuals; the U.S. Postal Service began monitoring the recipients of publications of special interest to homosexuals; and government agents began subscribing to gay pen pal clubs in an effort to "catch" government employees who might be secret homosexuals. At the same time, the FBI began compiling lists of gay bars and other gay gathering places around the country and gathering information from local vice-squad officers about suspected homosexuals. On April 1, 1951, J. Edgar Hoover announced that the FBI had identified 406 "sex deviates in government service."[25]

Hoover's own obsession with homosexuality was evident years earlier when he published a widely circulated article in 1937 in the *New York Herald Tribune*, titled "War on the Sex Criminal." In that piece, Hoover, who was himself suspected of being a homosexual, warned that "the present apathy of the public toward perverts, generally regarded as 'harmless,' should be changed to one of suspicious scrutiny." Such persons, he cautioned, though seemingly harmless, can become "the loathsome mutilator and murderer of tomorrow."[26]

At the height of the Lavender Scare, Hearst reporters Jack Lait and Lee Mortimer published their best-selling book *Washington Confidential*. In a chapter entitled "Garden of Pansies," the authors captured the mood in the nation's capital, noting that the "good people shook their heads in disbelief with the revelation that more than 90 twisted twerps in trousers had been swished out of the State Department." They reported that they had discovered "at least 6,000 known homosexuals on the government payroll, . . . and these comprise only a fraction of the total."[27]

THE FEAR of homosexuals in government captured the public's imagination. The shift in public attitudes from the 1920s was dramatic. According to a newspaper report, 75 percent of Joseph McCarthy's mail in 1950 focused on "sex depravity" rather than Communist infiltration, and some members of Congress encouraged McCarthy to "refocus" his attention away from Communists to homosexuals. The investigations of the McCarthy era "ultimately expended more resources in its anti-homosexual witch hunts than in its anti-Communist ones (though most Americans saw them as the same campaign)." Upon assuming office, President Dwight Eisenhower issued an executive order declaring "sexual perversion" a serious security risk.[28]

A reign of terror came to define the lives of gay and lesbian public servants. From 1950 to 1955, the number of individuals driven out of government service each year because of their sexual orientation increased dramatically. Gay men and women employed in any capacity by the government worried "every time the phone rang" that this might be "the call that would lead to accusations of homosexual behavior and a grueling interrogation about their sex life."

The pressure in such interrogations to "name names" was extraordinary, thus intensifying the fear. Indeed, "having seen it happen to others, they knew it could happen to them." For those who lost their jobs, the consequences could be severe. One government employee with a master's degree, for example, wound up digging ditches after he was dismissed for his sexual orientation. During the Lavender Scare, some five thousand gays and lesbians lost their federal jobs as a result of the government's witch hunt—and this does not include the many more individuals who did not dare apply for government employment for fear of public exposure and humiliation.[29]

THE HUNT for homosexuals in government contributed to, and reflected, a nationwide atmosphere of "persecution and purge." In 1952, for example, the McCarran-Walter Immigration and Nationality Act for the first time prohibited aliens alleged to be homosexual from entering or remaining in the United States. Throughout the nation, the authorities stepped up their efforts to drive gays and lesbians out of public view. States and cities enacted new laws that put out of business any bar or other establishment that catered to "sex perverts," and massive raids and street arrests received widespread coverage in the press.*[30]

In Washington, D.C., aggressive measures taken by the Metropolitan Police Department, the FBI, the U.S. Park Service, and the Civil Service Commission left the gay community "permeated with fear." In Philadelphia, arrests of gays and lesbians in public places climbed to more than 1,200 per year. In Baltimore, the police arrested 162 gay men on a single day. In New Orleans, the police arrested 64 lesbians in a raid on a lesbian bar. The chief of police in San Francisco launched an aggressive campaign to "clean the homosexuals from the streets" and from all "spots where the homosexuals congregate."[31]

In Miami, local politicians ordered beach sweeps for homosexuals, and the former head of the Miami vice squad, a Baptist deacon, citing *Leviticus* 18:22 and 1 *Corinthians* 6:9, proclaimed that the only way to "love a homosexual" is to "put him in prison." A Florida legislative investigating committee began ferreting out homosexuals in higher education. As a result, many professors and teachers suspected of homosexuality lost their jobs, and hundreds of students suspected of homosexuality were either expelled or dropped out of college.[32]

I N LIGHT of the intensity of the anti-homosexual fever that now gripped the nation, gays and lesbians found themselves increasingly isolated. As the historian Barry Adam has noted, the terror of the McCarthy era "exacted an immense toll from ordinary lesbians and gay men, with thousands being thrown out of work and imprisoned in jails and mental hospitals." As one lesbian recalled, "At work you completely avoided people. If you did make friends, you had to be sure never to bring them into your home. Never to tell them who and what you really were. We were all terrified."[33]

---

* "Queer-baiting" became so prevalent in these years that it came to be used not only by McCarthyites, but by their opponents as well. There were widespread accusations that Joseph McCarthy, who remained unmarried for almost all of his life, was himself a homosexual, and it was in part a concern about the possibly homosexual relationship between Roy Cohn, who was definitely gay, and his assistant, G. David Schine, that led to the Army-McCarthy hearings that ultimately led to McCarthy's political demise.

The media contributed to the purge of homosexuals from government positions through a steady stream of lurid and fearmongering articles and editorials; medical researchers enthusiastically investigated the use of castration, lobotomies, and electroshock to "cure" homosexuality; psychiatrists propagated the view that homosexuality was an illness that must be eradicated; churches endorsed the persecution of gays and lesbians; and Hollywood aggressively revised the realities of history by casting historical figures who were in fact homosexual (such as Michelangelo, Rudolph Valentino, and Hans Christian Andersen) as heterosexuals. Any reference to homosexuality in the media had to be excoriating. In 1954, when the magazine *ONE* published a short story about a lesbian, the postmaster general of Los Angeles yanked it from the mails. A federal district court held the story to be obscene because its sympathetic treatment of homosexuality was "indecent" to "the great majority" of Americans.[34]

Once again, civil rights groups, refusing to follow the lead of Emma Goldman, turned their backs on gays and lesbians. In 1957, the national board of the American Civil Liberties Union adopted a policy statement declaring that "it is not within the province of the [ACLU] to evaluate the social validity of the laws aimed at the suppression or elimination of homosexuals." Although homosexuals had traditionally been loathe to organize to protect themselves against oppression, it was now apparent that "something *had* to be done."[35]

"A PARTICULARLY VICIOUS CIRCLE"

THE VERY THOUGHT of initiating a homosexual emancipation movement in the 1950s was beyond daunting. The prevailing view in society that homosexuals were sick, perverted, and disloyal criminals and sinners naturally deterred most gay men and women from openly revealing their homosexual tendencies. This made any effort to organize virtually impossible. Moreover, most gay men and lesbians still thought of their "affliction" as a personal flaw, rather than as a cause for political or legal action. The idea of organizing to promote something called "gay rights" was unthinkable to the overwhelming majority of homosexuals.

Writing under the pseudonym Donald Webster Cory, the sociologist Edward Sagarin observed in 1951, in his groundbreaking work *The Homosexual in America*, that the ability of homosexuals to mask their identities trapped them "in a particularly vicious circle." The disdain, rejection, and shame that came with openly acknowledging one's homosexuality, he explained, were so great that pretense is almost universal; on the other hand, only a leadership that would acknowledge [their homosexuality] would be able to break down the barriers. . . . Until the world is able to accept us on an equal basis as human beings entitled to the full rights of life, we are unlikely to have any great numbers willing to become martyrs. . . . But until we are willing to speak out openly and frankly in defense of [ourselves] . . . we are unlikely to find the attitudes of the world undergoing any significant change.[36]

DESPITE THESE obstacles, a small group of male homosexuals founded the Mattachine Society in Los Angeles in 1951.* The Society's central mission was to inspire "socially conscious homosexuals" to "provide leadership" and to assist "our people who are victimized daily as a result of our oppression." Mattachine broke new ground in conceiving of homosexuals as an "oppressed minority," analogous to African Americans and Jews.[37]

Mattachine maintained that the essential "first task of a homosexual emancipation movement" was to challenge the internalization by homosexuals of society's extremely negative and hostile conceptions of who they were and to instill in them a sense of self-worth and personal value. The leaders of the organization therefore sought to develop in its members a "strong group consciousness free of the negative attitude that gay men and women typically internalized" about themselves.

Although conceding that gays and lesbians were different from heterosexuals, Mattachine "projected a vision of homosexual culture with its own positive values, and attempted to transform the shame of being gay into a pride in belonging to a minority with its own contribution to the human community." At the same time, though, the leaders of the Society understood that it was still necessary to develop "a secret, cell-like structure" for the organization in order to protect its members from the dangers of exposure.[38]

At the outset, participants in Mattachine's small-group meetings were

---

* As explained by one of the founders of the Society, the name *Mattachine* was taken from the *Société Mattachine*, a Renaissance-era secret fraternity of men who performed dances and rituals throughout the countryside. They never performed unmasked, in part because their performances were often "protests against oppression." The founders of the Mattachine Society took the name because "we 1950s Gays were also a masked people, unknown and anonymous, who might become engaged in morale building and helping ourselves and others, through struggle, to move toward . . . change."

"petrified that the government might get a list" of their names. They feared that at any moment "the cops would come barging in and arrest everybody." Many of the early members by necessity used false identities. After a while, though, members began to relax and be themselves. As one member recalled, it was an experience "we didn't know before." Men and women whose experiences as homosexuals had previously been limited to secret sexual encounters and relationships now found themselves meeting with dozens of other gay men and women who were openly discussing their homosexuality. It was, for most of them, extraordinary.[39]

By mid-1953, Mattachine had roughly a hundred ongoing discussion groups in California, though the number of participants remained vanishingly small. That same year, several members of the organization launched a magazine, *ONE*, which was designed to serve as a forum in which gays and lesbians could present their views both to the general public and to one another.[40]

The Mattachine Society and *ONE* were dominated by gay men. In 1955, Del Martin and Phyllis Lyon launched the Daughters of Bilitis,* the nation's first lesbian political organization. In time, the leaders of Bilitis discovered the Mattachine Society and *ONE* and began working together in what they termed the "homophile" movement. The following year, Daughters of Bilitis published the first issue of the *Ladder*, a publication dedicated to discussing issues of interest to lesbians. Its goal was to encourage gay women "to take an ever-increasing part in the . . . fight for understanding of the homophile minority." The circulation of these journals was never large, though, rarely exceeding a thousand. In the 1950s, it took considerable courage not only to publish such magazines, but even to subscribe to or read them.[†41]

By 1960, almost a decade after the founding of the Mattachine Society, these organizations were still barely limping along. Although they had chapters in cities across the nation, the total number of active members of

---

* Daughters of Bilitis took its name from *Songs of Bilitis*, a book of erotic poems by Pierre Louÿs, first published in Paris in 1894.

† The collaboration between these organizations did not always go smoothly. Gay men and women had very different experiences in society and they did not always share the same perspectives. For example, the members of Daughters "found gay male promiscuity and the police harassment that accompanied it an encumbrance that seemed to make lesbians guilty by association in the eyes of society." Moreover, attitudes of male superiority and condescension often infuriated the members of Daughters. Members of Mattachine often treated Daughters as if it were a mere "ladies auxiliary," which on one occasion led one leader of Daughters to respond, quite simply, "Up yours!"

Mattachine and Daughters of Bilitis combined was less than four hundred. The dangers of exposure were simply too great for most gays and lesbians to risk participation.* By the early 1960s, it was clear that this initial emancipation movement had failed either to mobilize a broad homosexual constituency or to generate any serious dialogue with straight society about the rights of gays and lesbians. The leaders of the movement found themselves frustrated, divided, and exasperated.[42]

ALFRED KINSEY, EVELYN HOOKER, AND THE AMERICAN LAW INSTITUTE

WHILE ALL THIS was going on, though, the scientific and legal communities began to take a fresh look at the issue. In 1948, Dr. Alfred Kinsey, a previously obscure professor at Indiana University, published a groundbreaking work—*Sexual Behavior in the Human Male*.[43] The most shocking of Kinsey's many surprising findings about male sexual behavior concerned homosexuality. Based on interviews with more than 10,000 subjects, Kinsey reported that 50 percent of adult men had had erotic responses to their own sex, 37 percent had had at least one homosexual experience post-adolescence, 10 percent had been "more or less homosexual for at least three years between the ages of 16 and 55," and 4 percent had been exclusively homosexual throughout their lives. These data were completely unexpected.

Almost everyone, including Kinsey, had previously believed that homosexuality was limited to a small number of idiosyncratic and diseased individuals. In light of the data, though, Kinsey concluded that "it is difficult to maintain the view that psychosexual reactions between individuals of the same sex are rare and therefore abnormal or unnatural." Equally surprising, Kinsey concluded that "[m]ales do not represent two discrete populations, heterosexual and homosexual," but exist on a continuum of variable sexual orientation. Kinsey was confident that Americans would abandon their "superstitions" about homosexuality "once they considered the scientific evidence he had assembled."[44]

---

* A case in point was Newton Arvin, one of Truman Capote's first lovers, who was a distinguished literary critic and professor of English literature at Smith College for thirty-eight years. He was dismissed by Smith College in 1960 after his sexual proclivities came to light when he was found in possession of same-sex sexual material showing semi-nude men.

In the repressive era of the late 1940s, *Sexuality in the Human Male* had a huge national impact. It remained on the *New York Times* bestseller list for twenty-six weeks, sold more than a quarter-of-a-million copies, and quickly generated more than two hundred major symposia among professionals in the field. For gay men and women, its publication was "a watershed moment." As a gay man from Chicago observed at the time, "It simply blasted this damn country wide open." After it hit the stands, people began to "look at the straightest guy in the street" and wonder, "are you gay?"[45]

There were sharp (but largely unpersuasive) attacks on Kinsey's methodology. His findings were vilified by members of the clergy and by conservative journalists and politicians, who feared that if the figures were accurate it would stigmatize the nation in the eyes of the world. One conservative psychiatrist warned that if Kinsey's figures were "only approximately correct, then 'the homosexual outlet' is *the predominant national disease,*" and the head of Union Theological Seminary characterized Kinsey's data as evidence of a "degradation in American morality approximating the worst decadence of the Roman era."[46]

In 1953, Kinsey followed up with *Sexual Behavior in the Human Female.*[47] He found that 28 percent of women had experienced erotic attraction to other women and that 13 percent of adult women had had homosexual experiences to orgasm (compared to 37 percent of men). The news that women could achieve orgasm with other women (and thus without the aid of a penis) was in itself stunning to most Americans. *Sexual Behavior in the Human Female* proved even more polarizing than its predecessor.[48]

In an essay entitled "Sex and Religion in the Kinsey Report," the theologian Reinhold Niebuhr criticized Kinsey's work as an example of "moral anarchism," and in "The Bible and Dr. Kinsey" the conservative evangelist Billy Graham warned that "it is impossible to estimate the damage this book will do to the already deteriorating morals of America." Democratic New York Congressman Louis Heller charged Kinsey with "hurling the insult of the century against our mothers, wives, daughters and sisters," and J. Edgar Hoover, in a response reminiscent of the actions of Anthony Comstock, launched an investigation and campaign of harassment against Kinsey's Institute for Sex Research. In 1954, House Republicans initiated a congressional inquiry into the private foundations that supported Kinsey's research. Under sustained pressure, the Rockefeller Foundation thereafter announced that it would no longer fund his research.[49]

. . .

WHILE KINSEY's research on homosexuality focused on accumulating and analyzing quantitative data, Evelyn Hooker's work was more qualitative in nature. Hooker's interest in this research was spurred by her interactions with several of her psychology students at U.C.L.A., who revealed to her that they were gay. One of them suggested that it was her duty to learn more about "people like us." Accepting that challenge, Hooker received a grant from the National Institute of Mental Health in 1953 to conduct a study designed to determine whether homosexuality was, as generally assumed, psychologically pathological.

Over the course of two years, she administered a battery of detailed psychological tests to men, half of whom were exclusively homosexual and half of whom were exclusively heterosexual. She then submitted the results to a blind panel of independent experts, who rated each individual's psychological and social adjustment on a scale from superior to maladjusted. The ratings, published in 1957, showed no association between maladjustment or psychopathology and homosexuality. Although many clinical psychologists were certain they would be able to identify the homosexuals from the results of the tests, they were unable to do so.

Like Kinsey's revelations, Hooker's were startling to most Americans. The research of scientists like Kinsey and Hooker deeply disturbed and angered those who despised and feared homosexuality, but it also led others to question the conventional understanding of homosexuality.[50]

THE AMERICAN LAW INSTITUTE (ALI), a highly respected association of the nation's most eminent lawyers, judges, and law professors, is dedicated to the scholarly study of the law and to developing comprehensive "model" legal codes that reflect the best of contemporary legal thought. Building upon England's Wolfenden Committee Report—which had called for the decriminalization of consensual sodomy in England in 1957—the ALI, after a decade of work, published its influential Model Penal Code in 1961. The ALI's new Model Penal Code called for the elimination of all criminal prohibitions against consensual sodomy. Because every state still prohibited consensual sodomy, the ALI's proposal was highly controversial.[51]

The written comments to the Model Penal Code explained the drafters' reasoning:

We deem it inappropriate for the government to attempt to control behavior that has no substantial significance except as to the morality of the actor. Such matters are best left to religious, educational and other social influences. Apart from the question of constitutionality which might be raised against legislation avowedly commanding adherence to a particular religious or moral tenet, it must be recognized, as a practical matter, that in a heterogeneous community such as ours, different individuals and groups have widely divergent views of the seriousness of various moral derelictions.[52]

Those who condemned the ALI position and who defended the need for laws prohibiting consensual sodomy insisted that it was perfectly appropriate for the state to forbid immoral conduct simply because it was immoral. As an analogy, they pointed to laws prohibiting cannibalism.

University of Pennsylvania law professor Louis B. Schwartz, one of the lead drafters of the 1962 Model Penal Code, responded to these arguments. Although conceding that the cannibalism example posed an interesting line-drawing problem, Schwartz affirmed the ALI's conclusion that no sufficient "harm to the secular interests of the community is involved in atypical sex practice in private between consenting adult partners," particularly in light of the "protection to which every individual is entitled against state interference in his personal affairs when he is not hurting others."[53]

While this debate raged, Illinois in 1961 became the first state in the nation to decriminalize consensual homosexual sodomy. In addition to the justifications put forth by the drafters of the Model Penal Code, the supporters of decriminalization in Illinois expressed concern that "the police in Chicago were harassing homosexuals outrageously."[54]

It is revealing that in both the ALI discussions and the deliberations in Illinois, homosexuals—the individuals most directly affected by these debates—were not in any way present in the process. As one homosexual writer observed (under a pseudonym), "The homosexual is, unfortunately, in a position before the law where he cannot effectively fight back."[55]

This was clearly evident in 1964 when the New York legislature debated whether to follow Illinois's lead, adopt the ALI position, and repeal the state's sodomy laws. The proposal went down to defeat when an outraged Roman Catholic hierarchy—led by Cardinal Francis Spellman of New York, who was himself suspected of being a homosexual—mounted an all-out lobbying campaign against the bill. No other state repealed its law against consensual sodomy until Connecticut adopted the Model Penal Code approach in 1969.

Nonetheless, over the course of the 1960s, momentum gradually grew for a change in the law. Coming on top of Kinsey's and Hooker's research, the ALI's Model Penal Code spurred serious discussion of the issue. As a practical matter, though, the issue of gay rights was largely drowned out in the 1960s by the turmoil over the civil rights movement, the controversy over Vietnam, and the women's liberation movement.[56]

COMING OUT

FRANKLIN KAMENY, an astronomer with the United States Army Map Service, was dismissed from the federal civil service in 1957 for being a homosexual. A slight man with a booming voice and a rapid-fire speaking style, Kameny challenged his firing in court, losing twice before petitioning the Supreme Court for review. After the Supreme Court declined to consider his appeal in 1961, he urged the chapters of the Mattachine Society in both Washington, D.C., and New York City to adopt a more aggressive approach and to call for the acceptance of homosexuals "as full equals" in society, with "basic rights and equality as citizens," and for recognition of "our human dignity," our "right to the pursuit of happiness," and our "right to love whom we wish."

Analogizing his demand for equal rights for gays to the similar demands of African Americans and Jews and rejecting the notion that homosexuals should become like heterosexuals, he noted that "I do not see the NAACP" looking into "the possibility of bleaching the Negro," and "I do not see any great interest on the part of the B'nai B'rith . . . in the possibility of solving problems of anti-semitism by converting Jews to Christians." What we "are interested in," he explained, is "obtaining rights for our respective minorities AS Negroes, AS Jews, and AS HOMOSEXUALS."

Kameny publicly declared, "I take the stand that not only is homosexuality . . . not immoral, but that homosexual acts engaged in by consenting adults are moral, in a positive and real sense, and are right, good, and desirable, both for the individual participants and for the society in which they live." These were words rarely before spoken in public.[57]

Kameny, who otherwise was described as "the most conventional of men," spearheaded a new militancy in the movement for gay rights. He insisted that "all the problems of the homosexual are . . . questions of prejudice and discrimination" and urged homosexuals and their organizations to stop "talking about homosexuality to other homosexuals" and to adopt a direct-action strategy similar to that of the black civil rights movement. Kameny maintained that it was "absolutely necessary" for gay men and women not to be "timid" in presenting their views. He called for *action*, declaring that homosexuals must be "impatient with . . . their traditional role as . . . a mere passive, silent" minority against whom those in power inflict their "prejudices." On April 17, 1965, Kameny led a small band of homosexuals to the front of the White House carrying signs declaring "Fifteen Million U.S. Homosexuals Protest Federal Treatment" and "Homosexuals are American Citizens, Too." Kameny even managed to bring a reluctant ACLU around to championing the rights of homosexuals.[58]

OTHER ACTIVISTS soon followed Kameny's lead. In 1967, a Los Angeles police campaign against gay bars sparked a rally of several hundred homosexuals on Sunset Boulevard. That same year, Rita Mae Brown, who would later go on to be a distinguished writer and feminist, and Robert A. Martin, an openly gay student who had been admitted to Columbia University only "on condition that he undergo psychotherapy and not attempt to seduce other students," founded Student Homophile Leagues at New York University and Columbia.

The following year, the Columbia students picketed a psychiatric seminar on homosexuality, demanding that it was "time that talk stopped being *about* us and started being *with* us." Soon thereafter, the North American Conference of Homophile Organizations resolved that "homosexuality is in no way inferior to heterosexuality as a valid way of life" and adopted Kameny's "Gay is Good" credo, a position that would have been unthinkable a decade earlier.[59]

By the late 1960s, at the height of the "sexual revolution" and the civil rights movement, some fifty activist homophile organizations had sprung up across the nation, eclipsing the more tentative organizations of the prior decade. These groups were increasingly militant, particularly in their protests against police harassment. In early 1969, Carl Wittman, a gay SDS leader living in San Francisco, penned *The Gay Manifesto*, a five-thousand-word document, in which he declared:

We have pretended everything is OK, because we haven't been able to see how to change it—we've been afraid. In the past year there

has been an awakening of gay liberation ideas and energy. How it
began we don't know; maybe we were inspired by black people and
their freedom movement. . . .

[O]ur first job is to free ourselves; that means clearing our heads
of the garbage that's been poured into them. . . . Liberation for gay
people is defining for ourselves how and with whom we live. . . . If
we are liberated we are open with our sexuality. Closet queenery
must end. *Come out.* . . . We've been playing an act for a long time,
so we're consummate actors. Now we can begin to be [who we are],
and it'll be a good show![60]

This was the first time anyone had used the term "coming out" in this manner, and a powerful social and political term was thus born. For gay libera-
tionists, the act of "coming out" was not merely an act of self-identification,
but a "radical, public act that would impact every aspect of a person's life."[61]

Despite the greater militancy of the gay rights rhetoric in the 1960s, gay
activists were still speaking mostly to themselves. Part of the problem was
that the vast majority of gays and lesbians were still closeted. The fear of
coming out, which could lead to profound humiliation and dire personal
consequences, kept most homosexuals in the shadows. Indeed, at this time
the total membership of all gay rights organizations combined was still
barely five thousand, and "of these only a few hundred could be said to have
come out of the closet by publicly identifying themselves as homosexuals."
Thus, although the gay rights movement achieved isolated victories in the
late '60s, its shift in tone, ambition, and direction still "passed largely unnoticed" in the larger society.[62]

STONEWALLED

AT AROUND 1:00 A.M. on Saturday morning, June 28, 1969, the New
York police raided the Stonewall Inn, a dingy, Mafia-owned gay bar on
Christopher Street in Greenwich Village. It was the only bar for gay men in
New York City where dancing was allowed. The interior was painted black,
with pulsing black lights. If police were spotted, regular white lights were
turned on, signaling that everyone should stop dancing or touching.

Police raids on gay bars were frequent. Five other New York bars had
been raided in the previous three weeks, but on this night at the Stonewall
the drag queens, bar boys, and lesbians who had been either in the bar or
in the gathering crowd of onlookers outside resisted the usual police harass-

ment. As one historian described the scene, "The authorities took on men in wigs in a bar and all hell broke loose."[63]

When the police entered the bar and began dragging the gays and transvestites out into the waiting paddy wagon, patrons and bystanders began sassing the police and throwing coins and bottles. When a police officer slugged a drag queen, she hit him with her purse and he then clubbed her. She cried out to the growing crowd to "do something." As the paddy wagon drove off, the crowd became more unruly and the remaining eight policemen barricaded themselves in the bar. The crowd then surged at the Stonewall, throwing rocks through the windows, setting bonfires, and using a parking meter as a battering ram to try to break down the door. Sylvia Rivera, a street queen who had been in the Stonewall during the raid, recalled thinking: "You've been treating us like shit all these years? Uh-uh. Now it's our turn! . . . It was one of the greatest moments in my life."

After the riot squad arrived to rescue the barricaded police officers, they lined up in a phalanx formation to clear the street. In response, the queens lined up opposite them in Rockette fashion, performing high kicks and

Stonewall, June 28, 1969

mockingly singing: "We are the Stonewall girls, we wear our hair in curls, we wear no underwear, we show our pubic hair." The riot police "went nuts" and began clubbing any "faggot or queen they could run down."

The next night, thousands of gay men and women from all over the region gathered on Christopher Street, leading to yet another confrontation with the police. The *New York Mattachine Newsletter* reported that "the police were scared shitless and the massive crowds of angry protestors chased them for blocks screaming 'Catch them! Fuck them.'" The humiliation of the police by a group of "fags" was now complete.[64]

T HE EVENTS at Stonewall have come to occupy a symbolic place in history as the moment when gay identity crystallized and the gay rights movement kicked into high gear. As the poet Allen Ginsberg remarked shortly after the riots, "You know the guys there were so beautiful—they've lost that wounded look that fags all had ten years ago."[65]

On June 29, 1969, the day after Stonewall, the Mattachine Action Committee issued a flier calling for organized resistance. The following month, Martha Shelley, a lesbian firebrand, organized a rally of more than five hundred gay and lesbian activists in Washington Square Park, three blocks from the Stonewall. Shelley and others "fired up the crowd with a new defiant tone of 'Gay Power.'" A month later, she and other gay and lesbian activists formed the Gay Liberation Front, which was mirrored by dozens of similarly militant organizations that now sprang up in cities across the nation. As Shelley explained, "We didn't want to be accepted into America the way it was. We wanted America to change." This was a new tone for the gay rights movement. It was "angry, confrontational, and destabilizing."[66]

In the ensuing months, the Gay Liberation Front picketed the *Village Voice* for refusing to print the word "gay,"* *Time* magazine and the *San Francisco Examiner* for their demeaning coverage of gays and lesbians, and Western and Delta airlines for their discriminatory employment practices. Gay Liberation Front members burst into medical conventions in San Francisco, Los Angeles, and Chicago to protest sessions on the "correction" of homosexuality, decrying such practices as "barbarism" and demanding equal time to speak.

---

* The *New York Times* refused to use the word "gay" until 1987. Until then it insisted on using the word "homosexual."

On June 28, 1970, some five thousand people commemorated the one-year anniversary of Stonewall by marching from Greenwich Village to Central Park, and thousands more marked the occasion in similar marches in Chicago and Los Angeles. These were the nation's first Gay Pride parades. After witnessing the parade in Central Park, Frank Kameny wrote that he was "awestruck by the vast throngs of confident humanity wending their way into a promised land of freedom-to-be."[67]

At a time of general social upheaval during which previously oppressed groups increasingly challenged traditional social, religious, and cultural norms, the burgeoning gay rights movement began to form links with other minority causes. In 1970, the North American Conference of Homophile Organizations resolved to support both women's liberation and the movement for black equality. Black Panther leader Huey Newton, who with Bobby Seale had founded the Black Panther Party in 1966 to resist police violence against African Americans, reciprocated, describing homosexuals as possibly "the most oppressed people in the society." [68]

The gay rights movement's relationship with the women's movement was complicated. In 1970, Rita Mae Brown, who by this time was newsletter editor of the New York chapter of the National Organization for Women, attempted to call attention to lesbianism in the women's movement. Betty Friedan, a Smith graduate who had published the seminal *The Feminine Mystique* in 1963 and was now NOW's national president, responded by denouncing the "lavender menace" that threatened the credibility of feminism, fearing that the public association of the women's movement with lesbians would damage the cause. Brown and other suspected lesbians were purged from NOW. A year later, after internal deliberations, NOW "acknowledge[d] the oppression of lesbians as a legitimate concern of feminism." In 1973, NOW created a National Task Force on Sexuality and Lesbianism.[69]

THE DECADE after Stonewall saw gradual progress in the cause of gay rights. Just a few months after Stonewall, the National Institute of Mental Health Task Force on Homosexuality, chaired by Evelyn Hooker, called for a national reassessment of employment practices that discriminated against gays and lesbians. Shortly thereafter, the American Sociological Association passed a resolution against discrimination on the basis of homosexuality. In 1972, a lesbian was allowed to retain custody of her children in a contested divorce for the first time in American history. In 1973, in a stunning development, the American Psychiatric Association's Council voted to delete homosexuality from the *Diagnostic and Statistical Manual of Mental Disorders*, the chief diagnostic and reference tool of mental health professionals. As the *New York Times* headline put the point, "Doctors Rule Homosexuality Not Abnormal."

In 1975, the federal government dropped its long-standing ban on the U.S. Civil Service employing homosexuals, and voters in Massachusetts elected Elaine Noble to the state's House of Representatives, making her the first openly homosexual candidate elected to public office in the history of the United States. Shortly thereafter, President Jimmy Carter for the first time invited gay and lesbian activists to meet with him at the White House.

By the end of the 1970s, twenty-nine cities had enacted laws prohibiting employment discrimination on the basis of sexual orientation, twenty-two states had repealed their laws prohibiting consensual sodomy, and more than 80 percent of Americans lived in states that had wholly or substantially decriminalized consensual same-sex sodomy.[70]

BACKLASH

THE MYTH OF STONEWALL has always suggested that things improved overnight for gays and lesbians, but despite the progress in the 1970s, a welter of disappointment, discrimination, and oppression continued. For example, a bill introduced in Congress in 1974 by Democratic Representatives Bella Abzug and Ed Koch of New York to amend the Civil Rights Act of 1964 to prohibit employment discrimination on the basis of sexual orientation died in committee. Beyond that, though, the gay rights movement sparked a vitriolic backlash.[71]

The most dramatic example arose during the debate over a proposed ordinance in Dade County, Florida. On January 18, 1977, the county commission passed, by a five-to-three vote, an ordinance that made it unlawful for any person to discriminate on the basis of sexual orientation in employment, housing, or public services. Local religious groups demanded an immediate repeal of the ordinance. Prominent among those calling for repeal was Save Our Children, a newly formed Christian group founded by Anita Bryant, a nationally known entertainer and former Miss America beauty queen.

A born-again Baptist, Bryant insisted that the anti-discrimination ordinance not only violated God's biblical commandments, but also infringed her "children's right to grow up in a healthy decent community." At a press conference in early February, Bryant, surrounded by clergy representing all of Miami's major churches, declared that she had proof that gays were "trying to recruit our children to homosexuality."[72]

Bryant was supported in her campaign by the National Association of Evangelicals, which had more than three million members. The Association raised large amounts of money through its television programs like the "PTL Club," the "700 Club," and "The Old Time Gospel Hour." The pastor Jerry Falwell campaigned vigorously in favor of repealing the Miami ordinance, and other leaders of the Christian Right, including Pat Robertson and Jim and Tammy Bakker, supported Bryant's campaign. Miami's archbishop submitted a letter calling on local congregations to vote for repeal, and in a dramatic special referendum on June 7, 1977, Dade County's voters repealed the ordinance by an overwhelming vote of 202,319 to 83,319.[73]

Anita Bryant

The victory in Dade County generated momentum for a new, religion-based, anti-gay movement. Bryant vowed to "carry our fight against similar laws throughout the nation that attempt to legitimate a lifestyle that is . . . perverse and dangerous to the sanctity of the family, dangerous to our children," and "dangerous to our survival as one nation, under God." The campaign took on an ugly tone as bumper stickers appeared throughout the land with such messages as "Kill a Queer for Christ." Within two years, laws that had been enacted to protect gays from discrimination were repealed in cities across the nation.[74]

The campaigns to repeal these laws charged that they promoted "child molesting," "gay recruiting," and "boy prostitution." These charges were repeated in a widely circulated letter by the Rev. Jerry Falwell: "Please remember, homosexuals do not reproduce! They recruit! And, many of them are out after my children and your children." Echoing the tone of evangelicals during the Second Great Awakening, a fundraising letter from another conservative Christian organization took a more ferociously religious tack, calling on Americans of faith to unite to prevent "militant gays" from pressuring government "into passing Satan's agenda instead of God's." As the historian Michael Bronski has observed, "Bryant and her supporters made no secret that they saw this fight as a religious battle for the Christian soul of America." Shortly after the referendum in Dade County, Florida became the first state in the nation to enact a law expressly prohibiting gay couples from adopting children.[75]

T HE ANITA BRYANT phenomenon was only one manifestation of a much larger religious backlash against the social and cultural changes of the 1960s and 1970s. Just as the Second Great Awakening was in part a response to the secularism of the Enlightenment and the American Revolution, the advent of the Moral Majority was triggered by a fear that traditional moral and religious values were being overwhelmed by the counterculture, the pill, abortion-on-demand, women's liberation, sexual permissiveness, ever more explicit pornography, and rampant homosexuality. In the words of the legal scholar William Eskridge, this late twentieth-century explosion of Christian fundamentalism "revived Anthony Comstock's moralizing politics."[76]

For the first time since the mid-nineteenth century, fundamentalist Christians came together politically to defend America against what they saw as a cancerous trend toward sexual immorality. The sexual revolution had a profound impact on American religion. Most mainstream Protestants and Jews found ways to adapt their religious beliefs to changing sexual mores. They endorsed family planning, accepted the realities of abortion, and cautiously welcomed gays and lesbians into their congregations. Most white evangelicals, mainstream Catholics, and African-American Baptists, on the other hand, united in the face of the upsurge in "moral hedonism," put aside their long-standing differences, and formed a new political alliance in defense of "traditional family values." Protestant fundamentalists, in particular, entered the political fray in a manner that transformed American politics.

White evangelicals, who represented almost a quarter of the population, vigorously opposed the Equal Rights Amendment (ERA), sexual expression, reproductive freedom, and homosexuality. Preachers like Jerry Falwell and Tim LaHaye castigated homosexuals as "haters of God." Phyllis Schlafly, who founded the Eagle Forum in 1972 to defend "traditional family values," claimed that the ERA would promote homosexuality and legalize homosexual marriage. The Southern Baptist Convention declared homosexuality an "abomination in the eyes of God." It was an all-out, no holds barred, religious counterattack against the call for gay rights.[77]

As THE battle over gay rights began to rage, and as homosexuals in the 1960s and 1970s began for the first time to demand a voice in America's public life, acquired immunodeficiency syndrome (AIDS) struck the gay male community with a vengeance. The disease quickly became associated in the public mind with homosexuality. It was, in some quarters, deemed God's punishment for homosexual sodomy. Jerry Falwell roared that "AIDS is not just God's punishment for homosexuals, it is God's punishment for the society that tolerates homosexuals," and Patrick Buchanan, the conservative commentator who served as a senior adviser to Ronald Reagan, declared that "AIDS is nature's retribution for violating the laws of nature." Communities across the nation enacted new laws discriminating against people with AIDS in insurance, housing, and the workplace.

During the 1980 presidential campaign, the Republican nominee, Ronald Reagan, actively courted Catholics and the Moral Majority. To secure their support, he rejected any thought of devoting "government time or money" to an illness that "threatened only gay men." Rather than invest federal funds in medical research or launch a public health campaign to address the AIDS epidemic, the Reagan White House turned its back on the problem and allowed the tragedy "to spread unchecked." Over the course of the next decade, AIDS, which was sneeringly referred to as "the gay cancer," would ravage the gay community, killing more than a quarter-of-a-million gay men and leaving hundreds of thousands more to wonder if they might be next.[78]

PART IV

JUDGES

*Sexual Expression
and the
Constitution*

12

OBSCENITY AND
THE FIRST AMENDMENT

"A Corrupting and Debasing" Influence

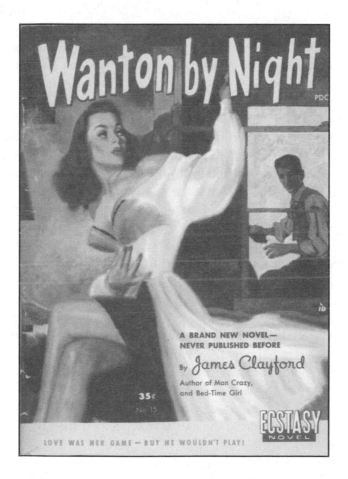

"Without Redeeming Social Value," Roth v. United States
(1957)

U NTIL THE 1950S, the Supreme Court had little to say about the possible relevance of the Constitution to laws dealing with such issues as obscenity, contraception, abortion, and homosexuality. Until then, the general assumption was that government could legitimately—and constitutionally—forbid behavior that the majority deemed immoral. This assumption came to be questioned, though, as social attitudes began to change and as the Supreme Court, especially in the era of the Warren Court, began to look more closely at the constitutionality of such regulations.

The issue that first opened up this line of judicial inquiry was the continuing legacy of Anthony Comstock. Put simply, could laws that forbade the production, sale, distribution, exhibition, or possession of obscenity be squared with the First Amendment? It was in its efforts to address this question that the Court first directly embraced the challenge of addressing the relationship between sex and the Constitution.*

Through most of history, whether in ancient Greece and Rome, the Middle Ages, the Renaissance, the Enlightenment, or the American colonies, society made no serious effort to interfere with the dissemination of sexual expression, however bawdy, erotic, or pornographic it might be. This changed in the United States, though, during the Second Great Awakening and even more dramatically during the Victorian era and the reign of Anthony Comstock. By the late nineteenth century American obscenity law commanded the suppression of virtually *all* sexually-oriented expression. Indeed, every jurisdiction in the nation now banned the sale, distribution,

---

* Earlier decisions that dealt with issues relating to sex focused on the question of compelled sterilization. See *Skinner v. Oklahoma*, 316 U.S. 535 (1942); and *Buck v. Bell*, 274 U.S. 200 (1927).

or possession of indecent expression, and American courts held that a work could be deemed "obscene" if even an isolated passage had a tendency to "deprave or corrupt" even the most susceptible members of society.

As we have seen, a few American judges in the early and mid-twentieth century began to question that approach and argued that, as a matter of statutory interpretation, for a work to be judged "obscene" it should be evaluated "as a whole" and in terms of its impact on the average rather than the most vulnerable individual. But organizations like the New York Society for the Suppression of Vice, the Legion of Decency, and the National Organization for Decent Literature worked feverishly—and generally successfully—to suppress books, magazines, plays, and movies that *they* deemed immoral.*[1]

The argument for suppression was clear. Censors of sexual expression insisted that the exposure of individuals to descriptions and images of sexually "immoral" behavior would both harm the individual and trigger a dangerous erosion in society's "moral standards." But that raised the question: Were those concerns sufficient to justify the suppression of free expression in light of the First Amendment's guarantee that government "shall make no law . . . abridging the freedom of speech, or of the press"? Beginning in the late 1950s, that constitutional question finally came to the fore.

THE NEW PURITY CRUSADE

AS A RESULT of World War II, which triggered a boom in the market for sexy new paperbacks and girlie magazines, American culture underwent a tectonic shift. Soldiers in Europe discovered and smuggled back in duffel bags French nudie magazines that were far more explicit than anything then available in the United States. Hugh Hefner first published *Playboy* in 1953 with an initial capital investment of $10,000. By 1956, the magazine had grossed $3.5 million, and *Playboy* was only one of a wave of racy new publications.

The explosion in paperback book sales, a market that did not much exist until the late 1930s, also had a dramatic impact. It was now possible to buy cheap and often quite erotic paperbacks at newsstands, dime stores, and local drugstores. Grace Metalious's 1956 blockbuster novel *Peyton Place*, for example—which vividly detailed the sex lives of three women in a small,

---

* See chapters 7 and 8.

gossipy New England town, and which tantalizingly explored such previously suppressed themes as lust, incest, adultery, and abortion—sold 3.5 million copies in its first months on the market and remained on the *New York Times* bestseller list for an astonishing fifty-nine weeks. Sex, in short, was in the air.[2]

Civic and religious groups organized from one end of the nation to the other in a fierce effort to squelch sexualized material that offended their sensibilities. They called for new and more aggressive laws against "obscene" publications, more rigorous enforcement of existing laws, more restrictive licensing requirements for movies with sexual themes, and aggressive boycotts of publishers, filmmakers, movie distributors, and booksellers who refused to comply with their demands.[3]

In the mid-1950s, at the height of the McCarthy era, the House of Representatives appointed a special select committee on "Pornographic Materials" to determine whether existing laws were adequate to stem the tide of publications containing "immoral, offensive, and other undesirable matter," and a Senate committee concluded that sexually-oriented materials were undermining American values and corrupting the nation's youth.[4] The Catholic Church played a central role in this new purity crusade, rousing citizens to inundate publishers with severe letters of protest. Among the books targeted were such classics as Erskine Caldwell's *God's Little Acre*, Norman Mailer's *The Naked and the Dead*, Vladimir Nabokov's *Lolita*, and even James Michener's Pulitzer Prize–winning novel *Tales of the South Pacific* because they dared to mention sex, even in ways that were breathtakingly tame by both historical and contemporary standards.[5]

Other media were affected as well. Joseph Breen, the Legion of Decency's representative on the board of the association of Motion Picture Producers and Distributors of America (the MPPDA), ran the MPPDA's censorship office with an iron fist. The Catholic Church actively lobbied the MPPDA to deny its seal of approval even to such artistically admired movies as Otto Preminger's *The Moon is Blue* because it contained words like "virgin," "seduce" and "pregnant," and Vittorio de Sica's *The Bicycle Thief* because it showed a young boy urinating—with his back to the camera.

In 1956, when Elvis Presley appeared on the Ed Sullivan Show, the cameramen were directed to shoot only from the waist up because Elvis's pelvic gyrations were considered too sexually suggestive for television. Even comic books came under the censor's glare as outraged moralists demanded, and got, aggressive congressional investigations into the comic book industry. This led to the adoption in 1954 of the Comics Code Authority, which transformed the world of comic books from an art form that could be edgy, scary, violent, and sexy into a genre limited only to children's cartoons.[6]

Through all of this, there was still no accepted understanding of the legal meaning of "obscenity." Although state legislatures tried to clarify their statutory prohibitions by adding to their definitions such words as "indecent," "disgusting," "lewd," "filthy," "improper," "immoral," "lascivious," "impure," "licentious," and "vulgar," the addition of these words was hardly clarifying. When it came to deciding which works were and were not obscene, the substance of the law remained a mystery.[7]

"MORE SPEECH, NOT ENFORCED SILENCE"

UNTIL 1957, THE Supreme Court studiously avoided ruling on whether the First Amendment protects obscene expression. Its reluctance was understandable. Unless it was prepared to hold that obscenity, like most other speech, was protected by the First Amendment, it would have to undertake the unenviable task of trying to figure out just what made a work "obscene" for purposes of the Constitution. As Justice Robert Jackson presciently warned in 1948, shortly after returning from his service as chief U.S. prosecutor at the Nuremburg Trials, such an undertaking risked turning the Court into the nation's "High Court of Obscenity."[8]

A central question, even more basic than the constitutional *definition* of "obscenity," was whether laws forbidding the sale, exhibition, and possession of something called "obscenity" could be reconciled with the Constitution. Given that the First Amendment expressly provides that government "shall make no law . . . abridging the freedom of speech, or of the press," how can laws banning "obscene" books, pamphlets, magazines, and movies be constitutional? Doesn't "no law" mean "*no* law"?

Justice Oliver Wendell Holmes had already confronted this conundrum in his 1919 opinion for the Court in *Schenck v. United States*, which dealt with the prosecution of individuals who criticized the war and the draft during World War I. Holmes offered his famous hypothetical of the "false cry of fire in a crowded theater" to demonstrate that it would be absurd to treat the First Amendment as an absolute. Common sense, he insisted, dictates that "no law" cannot logically mean "*no* law."[9]

From that moment on, the Court has acknowledged that although the government may not constitutionally "abridge" the "freedom of speech," it was necessary for the Court to define *the* "freedom of speech" that the government may not abridge in order to make sense of the First Amendment.

That freedom, in other words, is not self-defining. In the early years of the twentieth century, the prevailing view was that government could constitutionally forbid speech whenever "the natural and probable tendency and effect of the words" was to bring about harmful consequences.[10] Under that standard, the government could clearly suppress obscene expression, for as the moralistic opponents of obscenity had long argued, exposure to such material has at least the potential to corrupt moral standards and to tempt otherwise right-thinking individuals into engaging in sexually degrading and inappropriate behavior.

Over time, however, this "bad tendency" understanding of the First Amendment fell into disrepute as judges came to understand that it offered no meaningful protection to free speech. With this insight, the Supreme Court eventually embraced the "clear and present danger" test for restrictions of speech thought to be "dangerous" to the public welfare. Under that standard, which was first fully articulated by Justices Oliver Wendell Holmes and Louis Brandeis, even provocative, controversial, immoral, and offensive expression is presumptively protected by the First Amendment unless it "so imminently threaten[s] immediate interference with the lawful and pressing purposes of the law that an immediate check" is necessary to prevent grave harm.[11]

As Justice Brandeis explained in a brilliant opinion in 1927, this must be the test for the suppression of speech under the First Amendment because in a free society, except in a genuine emergency, the proper response to expression that advances ideas or arguments or morals that one rejects is "not enforced silence," but counter-speech that attempts to persuade one's fellow citizens of the "rightness" of one's views.[12] This understanding of the First Amendment, which came to be settled doctrine in the Supreme Court by the 1940s, posed a serious challenge to the constitutionality of laws outlawing obscene expression.[13]

Indeed, by the 1950s the Court was applying the clear and present danger principle even to expression that was thought to encourage immoral sexual conduct. In 1959, for example, in *Kingsley International Pictures Corp. v. Regents of the University of the State of New York*,[14] the Supreme Court unanimously held unconstitutional a New York statute that prohibited the exhibition of any motion picture that portrayed acts of "sexual immorality" as "desirable, acceptable, or proper." New York, one of the nation's most tolerant states, had applied that law to forbid the exhibition of the film *Lady Chatterley's Lover* because it depicted adultery in a manner that could be taken to suggest that such behavior might in some circumstances be morally acceptable.

The state argued that its law was justified because the movie attractively portrayed conduct that was both immoral and contrary to the "legal code of its citizenry." The Court, in an opinion by Justice Potter Stewart—an Eisenhower appointee who was generally quite deferential to government authority, except on issues of free speech*—responded that this justification "struck at the heart of constitutionally protected liberty," because the First Amendment "protects advocacy of the opinion that adultery may sometimes be proper." Applying the clear and present danger test, Stewart concluded that the New York law was clearly unconstitutional.[15]

Although this was a groundbreaking decision, the statute at issue in *Kingsley Pictures* was not directed at "obscenity." Rather, it was directed at speech, whether obscene or not, that depicted immoral sexual behavior in a favorable light. Would the outcome in *Kingsley Pictures* have been any different if the film had been found to be "obscene"?

In prior decisions, the Court had suggested in passing that "obscene" speech might not be entitled to the same constitutional protection as other speech and that restrictions on such expression might therefore not have to be tested by the clear and present danger standard. But it had never directly addressed that question, and it had never explained why that might be so. At some point, the Court would have to tackle those issues.[16]

"PAPA KNOWS BEST"

SAMUEL ROTH WAS a character. Born in 1893 in the Carpathian Mountains in Eastern Europe, Roth emigrated to America as a child and grew up in the tenements on the Lower East Side of New York. He soon discovered a natural talent for writing, editing, and publishing. As a young man, he started a poetry magazine called *The Lyric*, in which he published not only his own work, but also poems by such then-unknown authors as Archibald MacLeish and D. H. Lawrence. He established a bookstore in Greenwich Village that became famous as the Poetry Bookshop. During a trip to England, when he was in his early twenties, Roth was intrigued by a German sex manual that he picked up from one of the pornography stalls in London. When he returned to New York, he translated, advertised, and

---

* Justice Stewart's special solicitude for the freedom of speech and of the press was often explained as a consequence of his experience as a student as chairman of both the *Yale Daily News* and the *Yale Law Journal*.

distributed the pamphlet, but he was promptly ordered by the postal inspectors to stop sending it through the mails.

Several years later, in 1927, Roth began circulating advertisements for his impending publication of *The Perfumed Garden*, a pornographic fifteenth-century Arabian classic. An offended recipient of Roth's circular tipped off John Sumner, Anthony Comstock's faithful successor at the New York Society for the Suppression of Vice, and Sumner promptly had Roth arrested. Roth was fined $5,000 for sending an obscene circular through the mails, given a suspended two-year prison sentence, and "sternly warned to stop publishing Arab literature." The following year, Sumner struck against Roth again, ordering him arrested for having several obscene photographs and books in his possession at a book auction.

Samuel Roth

This time, the judge sentenced Roth to three months in the workhouse on Welfare Island.

After his release, an undaunted Roth published an unauthorized version of D. H. Lawrence's *Lady Chatterley's Lover*, describing it as "No. 1 of the modern amatory classics." At this time, Roth was busy in his Broadway loft supervising the writing and publication of a growing list of pornographic titles, such as *Venus in Furs, Celestine: The Diary of a Chambermaid*, and *The Intimate Journal of Rudolph Valentino*. Over the next several decades, Roth continued to generate and distribute his racy publications, landing in jail several more times for publishing obscene materials.

By the early 1950s, despite unrelenting harassment by postal authorities, Roth and his fifteen-man staff were keeping the mails inundated with books, magazines, and circulars that skirted the borderline of the legal. His list included such titles as *Her Candle Burns Hot, Beautiful Sinners of New York*, and an unexpurgated version of *Lady Chatterley's Lover*, a bit of literary piracy that infuriated D. H. Lawrence's widow.

In 1955, Roth, now in his early sixties, was indicted once again on twenty-six counts of mailing allegedly obscene pictures, magazines, and books. At his trial for violating the federal Comstock Act, his lawyers offered psychological testimony to prove that sexually-explicit literature was harmless, even healthy, but the jury, after nine days of testimony, found Roth guilty on four counts—principally for distributing Aubrey Beardsley's *The Story of Venus and Tannhäuser*, which portrays sex and sexuality in an erotic but light-hearted manner, several issues of his magazine *Good Times*, which contained several "nudie" pictures of the shaved pubic-hair variety, and several more sexually-explicit works like *Wild Passion* and *Wanton by Night*. The court sentenced Roth to five years in prison and a $5,000 fine. Roth appealed, asserting that the Comstock Act violated the First Amendment.[17]

I N UPHOLDING Roth's conviction, the judges of the United States Court of Appeals concluded that because Roth had been convicted for selling "obscenity," there was no serious First Amendment issue. It therefore rejected Roth's attack on the constitutionality of the Comstock Act.[18] In a remarkable concurring opinion, however, Judge Jerome Frank, one of the nation's most influential legal philosophers and one of the most distinguished jurists of his generation, questioned the very notion that obscenity could be punished consistent with the First Amendment.

Judge Frank warned that any effort of government to censor writings merely because they might stimulate in the reader sexual thoughts that the legislature deems "undesirable" poses serious dangers to the freedom of speech, because it is an "easy path" from there "to governmental control of adults' political and religious reading." Indeed, Frank warned, "any paternalistic guardianship by government of the thoughts of grown-up citizens" leaves them "all too ready to adopt towards government officers the attitude that, in general, 'Papa knows best,'" an attitude he regarded as incompatible with the most fundamental assumptions of a free society.

Moreover, Frank made clear that the Framers of the First Amendment did not share the "Victorian" view of sex that was said to justify the federal obscenity statute. To the contrary, he explained, the "prudish" moral code of the mid-nineteenth century, which accepted as dogma that any acknowledgment of sexuality would inexorably lead to sexual misbehavior, was most definitely "not the moral code of those who framed the First Amendment." And on the central question of constitutional interpretation, Frank declared that courts must interpret and apply the First Amendment according to the views of the Framers, rather than "according to the later 'Victorian' code."

In the end, though, Judge Frank reluctantly voted to affirm Samuel Roth's conviction, because the Supreme Court had occasionally referred to the Comstock Act as "valid," and it was not appropriate for an "inferior court" to hold otherwise. And so, Frank kicked the ball up to the Supreme Court to see what it would do.[19]

"A GREAT AND MYSTERIOUS MOTIVE FORCE"

IN 1957, SAMUEL ROTH finally made it to the Supreme Court of the United States. For the first time in American history, the Court, in *Roth v. United States*, would directly address the issue of obscenity and the First Amendment.[20] Chief Justice Earl Warren assigned the daunting task of writing the Court's opinion to Justice William J. Brennan Jr., who had been on the Court for only a few months. One might have thought that Warren, the former governor of California and the 1948 Republican vice presidential candidate, would have seized the opportunity to write the Court's first-ever decision on the question of obscenity for himself, but the man known as a great liberal found the whole issue of obscenity "distasteful." Indeed, according to Brennan, "Warren was a terrible prude." In obscenity cases, he "would not read any of the books or watch the movies." At a personal level, Warren was revolted by such material and wanted to steer clear of the issue.[21]

Brennan, an Irish-Catholic Democrat from New Jersey, was an interesting choice to write the opinion. A decade earlier, when he was a justice on the New Jersey Supreme Court, Brennan came to the attention of Attorney General Herbert Brownell Jr., President Eisenhower's chief legal affairs adviser, when he gave a speech that seemed to Brownell to suggest a markedly conservative bent. For this reason, and also because Eisenhower was looking to appoint a Catholic justice as he approached the 1956 election, he nominated Brennan to the Court. Ironically, in light of Brennan's eventual role as a leading liberal on the Warren Court and as one of the most progressive justices ever to serve on the Supreme Court, the National Liberal League opposed his confirmation because they feared he would be unduly influenced by his religious beliefs. When all the dust settled, though, only one member of Congress voted against Brennan's confirmation—Senator Joseph McCarthy (R-Wisconsin), who accurately anticipated Brennan's liberal inclinations.

I N A landmark decision that has shaped the law of obscenity ever since, the Supreme Court upheld Samuel Roth's conviction for violating the federal Comstock Act. Justice Brennan saw the issue clearly: "The dispositive question is whether obscenity is utterance within the area of protected speech and press."[22]

In addressing this question, Brennan began with the history, noting that the guarantees of free expression in effect in most of the states that ratified the Constitution did not provide absolute protection to free speech. All but one of those states, for example, authorized the prosecution of libel. More to the point, Brennan maintained that there was "sufficiently contemporaneous evidence to show that obscenity, too, was outside the protection intended for speech and press."[23]

Brennan was surely right that there are some types of speech that do not receive the full protection of the First Amendment. This was precisely the point Justice Holmes had made thirty-eight years earlier with his famous false cry of fire hypothetical. But Brennan's contention that there was "sufficiently contemporaneous evidence to show that obscenity, too, was outside the protection intended for speech and press" was simply wrong. Every law and every judicial decision he cited to support this assertion either involved mockery of religion, which was quite a different matter, or took place during the Second Great Awakening, well *after* the adoption of the First Amendment. In fact, there is no credible evidence that the "original understanding" of the First Amendment affirmatively excluded obscenity from the scope of its protection.

Brennan did not rely entirely on history, though. Turning to the central purpose of the First Amendment, Brennan declared that "all ideas having even the slightest redeeming social importance—unorthodox ideas, controversial ideas, even ideas hateful to the prevailing climate of opinion—have the full protection" of the First Amendment. But obscenity, Brennan maintained, is not within that protection, because it is, by definition, "utterly without redeeming social importance." This judgment was evident, he explained, in the fact that all forty-eight states had laws forbidding obscenity and that over the past century Congress had enacted twenty different laws prohibiting the importation and interstate distribution of obscenity.

In short, Brennan reasoned, the punishment of obscenity has "never been thought to raise any Constitutional problem," because such speech is "no essential part of any exposition of ideas" and is of "such slight social value as a step to truth that any benefit that may be derived from [it] is clearly outweighed by the social interest in order and morality." Hence, Brennan concluded, "obscenity is not within the area of constitutionally protected speech or press."[24]

This was the critical step in the Court's analysis. Obscenity is not protected by the First Amendment because it is "utterly without redeeming social importance." But why is sexual expression of any less "social importance" than any other form of speech? Why is it of less "social importance" than speech that is violent, or sexist, or racist, or socialist, or moralizing in nature? The Court in *Roth* just assumed away the question, no doubt because the very idea that the First Amendment would protect such "immoral" and "offensive" sexual expression was beyond the capacity of most of the justices even to contemplate. Anthony Comstock, dead for four decades, had won the day.

T HAT DID NOT end the matter, though, for Brennan next turned to the vexing question: What is obscenity? Brennan began by emphasizing that not all expression about sex is "obscene." To the contrary, he explained, "sex, a great and mysterious motive force in human life, has indisputably been a subject of absorbing interest to mankind through the ages; it is one of the vital problems of human interest and public concern." Thus, "sex and obscenity are not synonymous," and the mere portrayal of sex in art, literature, and scientific works does not automatically remove the speech from the protection of the First Amendment.

But what, then, makes some portrayals of sex obscene? Obscenity, Brennan reasoned, is material which deals with sex in a manner "appealing to prurient interest." In a footnote, he explained that what this means is that speech dealing with sex is obscene if it has "a tendency to excite lustful thoughts" and create "lascivious longings." In common parlance, material which deals with sex in a manner appealing to prurient interest is material that makes the reader or viewer horny.[25]

This definition of "obscenity" immediately raised two further questions: First, who is the relevant audience in determining whether the material appeals to prurient interest? Second, what if only a single passage of a work appeals to prurient interest? Is the whole work then to be deemed obscene?

Turning to the first question, Brennan rejected the *Hicklin* standard—the traditional English test for obscenity, which had been adopted early on by most American courts and which allowed material to be judged by the effect of even an isolated excerpt or image on the most susceptible person. Concluding that the *Hicklin* standard was insufficiently protective of free speech, Brennan instead endorsed the approach that had been adopted by several recent lower court decisions: "whether, to the average person, applying contemporary community standards, the dominant theme of the material" appeals to the prurient interest.[26]

Turning to the second question, Brennan embraced the approach of the trial judge in *Roth*, who had instructed the jury that books, images, and movies must be judged "as a whole," and not on the basis of "detached or separate portions" or scenes.[27]

Finally, Brennan addressed the issue of vagueness. The vagueness issue has two components. First, it is unfair to criminally punish individuals who cannot reasonably ascertain whether their conduct is unlawful. Second, if a law regulating speech is vague, that ambiguity will deter individuals who would otherwise engage in constitutionally protected expression because of a fear that their speech might later be deemed unlawful. This "chilling effect" has long been recognized as a central First Amendment concern.

The problem of ambiguity had, of course, long plagued the law of obscenity, and Brennan admitted that the Comstock Act, which prohibited the mailing of any publication that is "obscene, lewd, lascivious, or filthy," was far from clear. He nonetheless concluded, however, that when applied according to the "proper standard for judging obscenity" these words "give adequate warning of the conduct proscribed."[28] Although Brennan would later come to regret this judgment, he upheld the conviction of Samuel Roth.

JUSTICES HUGO BLACK and William Douglas dissented. Black and Douglas had long established themselves as fervent supporters of free speech, especially during the excesses of the McCarthy era. In his dissent-

Justice William J. Brennan Jr.

ing opinion in *Roth*, Justice Black, joined by Douglas, brought that perspective to bear on the issue of obscenity.

A Democratic senator from Alabama with awkward ties to the Ku Klux Klan, Hugo Black had been appointed to the Court in 1937 by Franklin Roosevelt. Throughout his career, Black embraced a rigidly textualist approach to constitutional interpretation. With respect to the First Amendment, Black insisted that the phrase "Congress shall make no law . . . abridging the freedom of speech" meant what it said. The language, he argued, is "absolute." This, he insisted, was the judgment of the Framers, and "courts have neither the right nor the power to make a different" evaluation.*[29]

Thus, in his dissenting opinion in *Roth*, Black acknowledged that he could "understand (and at times even sympathize) with programs of civic groups and church groups to protect and defend the existing moral standards of the community," and could even "understand the motives of the Anthony Comstocks who would impose Victorian standards on the community," but he nonetheless concluded that "when speech alone is involved," the government cannot, consistent with the First Amendment, "become the sponsor of any of these movements."[30]

In short, then, Black and Douglas, like Judge Frank in the United States Court of Appeals, flat-out rejected the argument that there is anything constitutionally distinctive about obscenity. In their view, the real reason for treating such expression differently under the First Amendment is that it offends the moral standards of the majority, a reason they found fundamentally incompatible with the Constitution.†

T HE SUPREME COURT handed down its decision in *Roth* on June 24, 1957. The reactions of the press and the legal academy tended to be negative. Newspapers observed pointedly that this was the first time in American history that the Supreme Court had ever upheld the authority of government to ban obscene expression.[31] The distinguished legal scholar Louis Henkin published a sharp and influential critique of *Roth* in the *Columbia Law Review*. Henkin argued that the judgment that obscenity is not

---

* The counterargument is that even taking a textualist approach and even if we accept that the government cannot constitutionally make any law "abridging the freedom of speech," it is still necessary to define the "freedom of speech" that may not be "abridged."

† Justice John Marshall Harlan also dissented.

a "valuable" form of expression was rooted in "aspirations to holiness" and was directly related "to laws against sacrilege and blasphemy." As Henkin put the point, "Obscenity, at bottom, is not crime. Obscenity is sin." Laws prohibiting obscenity, he therefore maintained, are an unconstitutional "relic . . . of our religious heritage."[32]

Roth left the substance of obscenity law obscure. As Justice Brennan later conceded, the justices were "hopelessly divided" over the definition of obscenity, leaving legislators, prosecutors, lower court judges, police officers, jurors, publishers, and movie distributors in a state of confusion.[33] Seven years after the decision in *Roth*, the Court in *Jacobellis v. Ohio*[34] overturned the obscenity conviction of a movie theater manager who had exhibited the internationally acclaimed French film *The Lovers*. Directed by Louis Malle, *The Lovers* tells the story of a bored middle-aged wife who has an adulterous affair with a young man. Although six justices voted to reverse the conviction, they offered five different explanations for the result. In exasperation, Justice Potter Stewart famously declared: "I shall not today attempt further to define the kinds of material I understand to be embraced within [the concept of obscenity]; and perhaps I could never succeed in intelligently doing so. But I know it when I see it, and the motion picture involved in this case is not that."[35]

MEMOIRS OF A WOMAN OF PLEASURE REVISITED

IN THE DECADE after *Roth*, attitudes in the United States toward sex and sexual expression began to change dramatically. The Victorian prudery of the 1950s was increasingly pushed aside by the dawning of the sexual revolution in the 1960s. With the advent of the pill, women's liberation, and the publication of such works as Helen Gurley Brown's *Sex and the Single Girl* and Dr. David Reuben's *Everything You Always Wanted to Know About Sex* (*But Were Afraid to Ask)*, sexual freedom and sexual explicitness began to reshape American culture.

In 1965, the award-winning film *The Pawnbroker*, which addressed the Holocaust from the perspective of a survivor, won the MPPDA's seal of approval even though it included several scenes showing bare female breasts. Three years later, the old Hays Code was finally replaced by a more liberal industry rating system. In 1969, full-frontal male and female nudity appeared in the movie *Medium Cool*, which told the story of a television news reporter who found himself caught up in the violence during the 1968 Democratic National Convention.

That same year, the X-rated *Midnight Cowboy*, which starred Dustin Hoffman and Jon Voight and featured both nudity and strong sexual content, won the Oscar for best picture. The much more explicit Swedish import *I Am Curious (Yellow)*—which included several graphic scenes of nudity and sexual intercourse, including a scene in which a young woman kissed her lover's flaccid penis—played to packed houses in cities across the nation. On Broadway, hit plays like *Hair* and *Che!* featured nude actors and actresses, and in *Hair* the song "Sodomy" went so far as to joyously proclaim that "masturbation can be fun." Even mainstream magazines like *Newsweek* and *Time* for the first time included images of full-frontal nudity.[36]

I N 1966, in the hope of clarifying the law of obscenity, the Supreme Court decided a trio of cases: *Memoirs v. Massachusetts*,[37] *Mishkin v. New York*,[38] and *Ginzburg v. United States*.[39] *Memoirs* involved John Cleland's infamous novel *Memoirs of a Woman of Pleasure* (aka *Fanny Hill*), which was first published in London in 1748. Banned repeatedly over the centuries, Cleland's work included scenes of lesbianism, group sex, masturbation, flagellation, fetishism, and sadomasochism.* Predictably, it was banned in Massachusetts. In a stunning six-to-three decision, reflecting the changing values of the time, the Supreme Court held that *Memoirs of a Woman of Pleasure* was not obscene.

Justice Brennan again wrote the lead opinion, although this time he was joined only by Chief Justice Warren and Justice Abe Fortas, who had recently been appointed to the Court by President Lyndon Johnson. Brennan began by insisting that "three elements must coalesce" in order for material to be deemed obscene: "the dominant theme of the material taken as a whole" must appeal to a prurient interest in sex; the material's depiction of sex must be "patently offensive" to contemporary community standards; and the material must be "utterly without redeeming social value."[40]

At trial, a coterie of English professors had testified that *Memoirs of a Woman of Pleasure* had literary merit, displayed a skill in characterization and a gift for comedy, and contained "a moral, namely, that sex with love is superior to sex in a brothel." Nonetheless, the Supreme Judicial Court of Massachusetts found Cleland's work to be obscene. It explained that although the book had "minimal literary value," it did not have sufficient "social importance," in light of its graphic sexual content, to merit constitutional protection.[41]

---

* Cleland's *Memoirs of a Woman of Pleasure* is discussed in chapter 3.

Justice Brennan emphatically rejected this understanding of the First Amendment. He explained that even if a work appeals to the prurient interest and is patently offensive in its depiction of sex, it is nonetheless protected by the First Amendment unless it is also "utterly without redeeming social value." Thus, even if, as the Massachusetts court had held, the work possessed "only a modicum of social value," that was sufficient for constitutional protection. John Cleland's *Memoirs of a Woman of Pleasure*, Brennan concluded, was not obscene within the meaning of the First Amendment.[42]

Although the Supreme Court's decision in *Memoirs* held that the First Amendment protected a work that had been suppressed and censored for two centuries,[43] it left the law of obscenity in a shambles. The justices were all over the lot: Justices Hugo Black and William Douglas reiterated their view that sexually-explicit expression is fully protected by the First Amendment; Justice Potter Stewart maintained that only something he called "hard-core" pornography could be prohibited; Justices Tom Clark and Byron White insisted in dissent that sexually-explicit speech is obscene, even if it has social value, if it appeals primarily to the prurient interest and depicts sex in a patently offensive manner; and Justice John Marshall Harlan dissented on the ground that although the federal government could prohibit only "hard-core" pornography, the states had greater freedom to restrict sexual expression.

As Justice Harlan, a notably thoughtful justice, warned in his dissenting opinion in *Memoirs*, given this utterly chaotic state of affairs he did not see how the Court in the future could "escape the task" of reviewing the constitutionality of every single obscenity conviction in the United States "on a case-by-case basis." This was clearly not, in Harlan's view, a happy prospect.[44]

"DIRTY BOOKS DAY"

ADDING TO THE doctrinal chaos created by *Memoirs* were the Court's 1966 decisions in *Mishkin* and *Ginzburg*, which were handed down on the same day as *Memoirs*. In *Mishkin*, the defendant was convicted of violating New York's obscenity statute for his role in the production and distribution of a wide array of cheaply prepared "paperbound pulps." According to Justice Brennan, who again delivered the opinion of the Court, the fifty books involved in *Mishkin* portrayed "sexuality in many guises," including fetishism, homosexuality, and sadomasochism. Many had covers with drawings of "scantily clad women being whipped, beaten, tortured, or abused."

Among the titles were *Mistress of Leather, Bound in Rubber, The Whipping Chorus Girls, I'll Try Anything Twice,* and *Swish Bottom.*[45]

Mishkin contended that books depicting such "deviant" sexual practices could not be obscene because they did not appeal to the prurient interest of the "average person." Faced with this rather ingenious claim, the Court adjusted the prurient appeal requirement of *Roth* to include materials that appeal to the prurient interest of only a "deviant sexual group."[46]

In *Ginzburg,* the third case in the trilogy, the defendant, Ralph Ginzburg, was indicted by United States Attorney General Robert F. Kennedy and then convicted in federal court of violating the federal Comstock Act for mailing several publications and advertisements for publications dealing with sex. The publications included an issue of Ginzburg's own quarterly publication *EROS* and his volume *The Housewife's Handbook on Selective Promiscuity.*

Although the works at issue in *Ginzburg* were only modestly erotic, the Court, in another opinion by Justice Brennan, took note of the fact that Ginzburg had engaged in the "sordid business of pandering" to the erotic interests of his customers. For example, he had sought mailing privileges from the postmasters of Intercourse and Blue Ball, Pennsylvania, and Middlesex, New Jersey, for the obvious purpose of marketing his materials "on the basis of salacious appeal." The Court held that the commercial exploitation of the sexual nature of the materials was relevant in determining the "ultimate question of obscenity," because it suggested that Ginzburg was exploiting their prurient appeal.*[47]

NOT LONG after the Court handed down its decisions in *Memoirs, Mishkin,* and *Ginzburg* on what came to be known as "dirty books day,"[48] the Court complicated obscenity law still further. Sam Ginsberg and his wife operated "Sam's Stationery and Luncheonette" in Bellmore, Long Island. Among other things, they sold magazines, including some "girlie" magazines that featured partially nude photos of women showing their buttocks and nipples. Although the magazines were not "obscene" under the Court's previously announced standards, Ginsberg was nonetheless prosecuted and convicted for violating a New York statute that prohibited the sale to any person under seventeen years of age of any material found to be "obscene for minors," whether or not it would be obscene for adults. The New York law defined as "obscene for minors" any image showing

---

*Justices Black, Douglas, Harlan, and Stewart dissented in four separate opinions.

human nudity that appeals to the prurient interest of minors, is patently offensive under prevailing standards of what is suitable for minors, and is utterly without redeeming social value for minors.[49]

In *Ginsberg v. New York*,[50] decided in 1968, the Court, in another opinion by Justice Brennan, upheld Ginsberg's conviction. The central question was whether New York could constitutionally expand the definition of obscenity in this manner in order to protect minors. Although noting that the evidence failed to prove that exposure to such material significantly impaired the moral development of youth, Brennan nonetheless held that because obscenity is outside the protection of the First Amendment, the challenged law was constitutional because the legislature could rationally find that exposure to such material might be harmful to minors.*[51]

With each new decision, and each new wrinkle, the concept of "obscenity" was growing ever more confusing.

"PRIVATE THOUGHTS"

AND THEN IT got worse. Suspecting that Robert Eli Stanley was engaged in illegal bookmaking, the police searched his home in Atlanta, Georgia, in an effort to seize betting paraphernalia. They found none, but instead discovered three reels of 8 mm pornographic film in a desk drawer in an upstairs bedroom. Stanley was arrested, charged, and convicted for violating a Georgia law prohibiting the knowing possession of obscene material.

In a unanimous decision in 1969 in *Stanley v. Georgia*,[52] the Supreme Court held that the private possession of obscene material could not constitutionally be made a crime. Justice Thurgood Marshall, who as chief counsel to the NAACP Legal Defense and Education Fund had argued *Brown v. Board of Education* to the Court fifteen years earlier, and who had recently been appointed to the Court by President Lyndon Johnson, authored the Court's opinion.

Marshall recognized, as the Court had held ever since *Roth*, that obscenity is not protected by the First Amendment. But this case, Marshall noted, involved not the sale, distribution, or exhibition of obscene material to the public, but the right "to be free, except in very limited circumstances, from unwanted governmental intrusions into one's privacy." Quoting Justice Louis Brandeis, Marshall observed that the "makers of our Constitution

---

* Justices Douglas, Black, and Fortas dissented.

'conferred, as against the government, the right to be let alone—the most comprehensive of rights and the right most valued by civilized man.'"[53]

Marshall declared that if the First Amendment means anything, it "means that the State has no business telling a man, sitting alone in his own house, what books he may read or what films he may watch." Our whole constitutional heritage, Marshall added, "rebels at the thought of giving government the power to control men's minds" in this way. This being so, the Court held that the First Amendment prohibits the government from "making mere private possession of obscene material a crime."[54]

For those seeking a way out of the mess the Court had created, *Stanley* seemed a promising development. Defense lawyers in obscenity cases immediately sought to extend the logic of *Stanley*. After all, if there is a constitutional right to read or view obscene material in one's home, then there must logically be a right to buy it; if there is a right to buy it, there must be a right to sell it; if there is a right to sell it, there must be a right to distribute it; and if there is a right to distribute it, there must be a right to produce it. Or so the argument went.[55]

REDRUP

IN THE MEANTIME, though, the Court continued to struggle—unhappily—with the definition of obscenity. Eventually, the Court gave up. In *Redrup v. New York*,[56] the Court overturned obscenity convictions in three cases arising out of the sale of sexually-explicit paperback books and magazines carrying such names as *Lust Pool*, *Shame Agent*, *High Heels*, and *Swank*. In a brief, unsigned opinion, the Court wearily announced that with each justice applying his own definition of obscenity, a majority of the justices had concluded, after toting up the votes, that the materials were not obscene.

The Court's inability to articulate a definition of obscenity that could command a majority of the justices led to an era of unmitigated chaos. Beginning with *Redrup*, the Court initiated the practice of *per curiam* (unsigned) reversals or affirmances of convictions for the sale or exhibition of materials that at least five members of the Court, applying their own separate and distinct standards, deemed to be or not to be obscene. Over the course of six years, some thirty-one cases were disposed of in this fashion. The full opinion in the Court's 1970 decision in *Walker v. Ohio* is typical: "The judgment of the Supreme Court of Ohio is reversed. *Redrup*."[57]

With *Redrup*, the Court gave up the struggle to adopt a coherent, consistent, predictable definition of obscenity. Justice John Marshall Harlan complained to a friend just before he died of spinal cancer in 1971 that the "obscenity problem [is] almost intractable," and Justice Brennan later observed that the *Redrup* approach resolves cases as between the parties, but offers only the "most obscure guidance" to lower courts, legislators, publishers, and the police. "It comes as no surprise," he added, that attempts to follow our lead "have often ended in hopeless confusion."[58]

Even worse, the justices felt the responsibility to review every obscenity conviction in the nation in order to determine for themselves whether the work at issue was or was not obscene. After all, in the absence of a single, coherent standard, who else could decide the question? As Justice Robert Jackson had warned twenty-five years earlier, the Court had turned itself into the nation's "High Court of Obscenity."[59] And the justices hated it.

Each year, the justices and their clerks had to gather in one of the Court's conference rooms to watch the movies that were at issue in pending obscenity cases. Justices Douglas and Black never went, because in their view there was no such thing as obscenity. Black quipped, "If I want to go see [a dirty] film, I should pay my money." In his final years on the Court, when Justice Harlan was losing his eyesight, his law clerks or a fellow justice had to describe to him the action on the screen. This was, to say the least, awkward. There were moments of levity, however, mixed in with the misery of having to spend hours at this task. The law clerks, for example, frequently mocked Justice Stewart's definition of obscenity, shouting out raucously in the darkened room: "That's it, that's it, I know it when I see it."[60]

This state of affairs continued until 1973, when the Burger Court took charge.

"A MAGNA CARTA FOR PORNOGRAPHERS"

BEFORE THAT COULD happen, though, Congress, concerned about the growing proliferation of sexually-explicit material, authorized President Lyndon Johnson to appoint a special blue-ribbon Commission on Obscenity and Pornography to determine whether exposure to sexually-explicit material caused "antisocial behavior" and to recommend appropriate means to address the increasing availability of such material. The Commission's eighteen members included psychologists, sociologists, constitutional experts, and religious leaders from across the ideological spectrum. After two years of comprehensive research and study, the Commission issued its report on September 30, 1970.

The Commission found that in recent years, movies, books and magazines had become significantly more explicit in their presentation of sex. What the Commission called "general release films" now dealt candidly with such issues as "adultery, promiscuity, abortion, perversion, spouse-swapping, orgies, male and female homosexuality, etc.," and what it called "skin flicks," which could be seen by patrons in a limited range of adults-only theaters and left almost nothing to the imagination. There was also now a wide range of adults-only magazines devoted principally to photographs of female and male nudity "with emphasis on the genitalia" and with "a considerable amount of implied sexual activity." The Commission found that 85 percent of adult men and 70 percent of adult women had seen such explicit sexual material and that more than 70 percent of minors had been exposed to such images by the time they had reached age eighteen.[61]

The Commission also evaluated research on the effects of exposure to sexually-explicit materials. It found that most people reported that their exposure to such material affected them more positively than negatively. Moreover, surveys of psychiatrists, psychologists, social workers, and other experts disclosed that in their judgment, exposure to sexually-explicit material did not have harmful effects on either adults or adolescents. This was a radical departure from the prevailing wisdom of the Victorian era, the age of Anthony Comstock, and even the 1950s.[62]

In light of these findings, the Commission concluded that there was not sufficient justification to forbid "the consensual distribution of sexual materials to adults."[63]

A T THE same time, though, the Commission recommended the enactment of laws making it a crime for any person knowingly to provide or exhibit sexually-explicit material to minors without the permission of their parents, or knowingly to place sexually-explicit material upon public display. With respect to the protection of minors, the Commission noted that although there was no evidence demonstrating that exposure of children to such material causes "delinquency, sexual or nonsexual deviancy, or severe emotional disturbances," there was also no definitive evidence that such exposure might not be harmful in at least some instances. The Commission therefore reasoned that parents should be able to decide for themselves whether such material was appropriate for their children and that it was therefore sensible for legislation to assist parents in controlling the access of their children to such material "during their formative years."

With respect to the prohibition of public displays of obscenity, the Commission noted that unwanted exposure to explicit sexual materials can cause "considerable offense" to many Americans. Because such unwanted intrusions upon "individual sensibilities" could be avoided without significantly interfering with consensual communication among adults, the Commission concluded that it was reasonable for government to restrict public displays of sexually-explicit material on billboards, display racks, newsstands, theater marquees, and unsolicited advertisements sent to an individual's home.[64]

T HE COMMISSION's report triggered a firestorm of criticism. One of the five dissenting members, Charles H. Keating Jr., head of Citizens for Decent Literature, characterized the Commission's recommendations as "shocking and anarchistic" and as advocating "a libertine philosophy!" Keating declared that "for those who believe in God, in His absolute supremacy as the Creator and Lawgiver of life, in the dignity and destiny which He has conferred upon the human person, in the moral code that governs sexual activity—for those who believe in these 'things,' no argument against pornography should be necessary."[65]

Two other dissenting members, Father Morton A. Hill, a founding member of Morality in Media, and Winfrey C. Link, who served as chairman of the Tennessee Commission on Youth's Guidance Subcommittee on Pornography and Obscene Literature, castigated the report as "a Magna Carta for the pornographer" and characterized the Commission's conclusions as "insupportable" and "preposterous."[66]

By the time the Commission completed its report, Richard Nixon had succeeded Lyndon Johnson in the White House. A great many Americans, especially those in the so-called "Silent Majority" to whom Richard Nixon had appealed during the 1968 presidential campaign, were appalled by what they saw as the rampant immorality and social degradations of the "sexual revolution" of the 1960s. Not surprisingly, then, upon seeing the report, Vice President Spiro Agnew, who would become famous for his invective language and his attacks on those he decried as "nattering nabobs of negativism," declared that "as long as Richard Nixon is President, Main Street is not going to turn into smut alley."[67]

President Nixon, who had run for president on a platform calling for a return to civic virtue and public morals, emphatically repudiated what he described as the report's "morally bankrupt conclusions." Calling pornography a "pollution of our civilization," Nixon proclaimed that pornography "should be outlawed in every state in the union." Indeed, he promised: "So long as I am in the White House, there will be no relaxation of the national effort to control and eliminate smut from our national life."[68]

MILLER AND PARIS ADULT THEATRE

DURING HIS 1968 CAMPAIGN for the White House, Richard Nixon sharply criticized what he decried as the "liberal activism" of the Warren Court and promised to transform the Court as an institution. Nixon pledged to appoint justices "who would follow a properly conservative course of judging" and who would see themselves as "servants of the people" rather than as "superlegislators" who acted as if they had a free hand to impose their own ideological viewpoints "upon the American People."

Nixon's opportunity to reshape the Court presented itself more quickly than anyone could have imagined. For a combination of reasons involving age, health, and politics, four of the Warren Court justices—Earl Warren, Hugo Black, John Marshall Harlan, and Abe Fortas—left the Court in the first two years of Nixon's presidency, and he was therefore quickly able to remake the Court in his own image. Nixon appointed four "conservative" justices who, he confirmed, were committed to a philosophy of judicial restraint and strict construction of the Constitution. Across a broad spectrum of issues, including criminal justice, privacy, freedom of religion, freedom of speech, voting rights, equal protection, and sexual expression, the American people now expected, with a mixture of enthusiasm and dismay, a constitutional revolution.

And, indeed, with the arrival of Chief Justice Warren Burger and Justices Harry Blackmun, Lewis Powell, and William Rehnquist, the Supreme Court by the spring of 1972 was a very different institution than the one that had decided *Roth*, *Memoirs*, and *Stanley*. Although the Warren Court had been hesitant, conflicted, and inconsistent in its extension of First Amendment protection to sexually-explicit expression, by the time *Stanley* was decided in 1969 the direction at least seemed clear. Indeed, there is every reason to believe that had there been no change in the makeup of the Court between 1969 and 1973, a substantial majority of the Warren Court justices would have embraced an approach to obscenity that built on the implications of *Stanley*. But that was not to be. With Burger, Blackmun, Powell, and Rehnquist replacing Warren, Black, Harlan, and Fortas, everything was up for grabs.[69]

WARREN BURGER first came to national prominence at the 1952 Republican Party Convention when he successfully delivered the Minnesota delegation to Dwight Eisenhower. A grateful Eisenhower appointed Burger assistant attorney general. Then, in 1956, Eisenhower appointed Burger to the United States Court of Appeals for the District of Columbia Circuit. In that role, Burger clashed often with his more liberal brethren and began giving speeches and writing articles that were sharply—sometimes harshly—critical of the Warren Court.

In his private correspondence with his boyhood friend Harry Blackmun, he wrote contemptuously of the Warren Court in 1967, stating that "if I were to stand still for some of the idiocy that is put forth as legal and constitutional profundity I would, I am sure, want to shoot myself in later years." Referring to the justices then on the Supreme Court, Burger continued, "These guys just *can't* be right." In another letter to Blackmun two years later, Burger was again severely critical of the Warren Court, adding that Nixon "can only straighten that place out if he gets four appointments." Soon thereafter, Nixon nominated Warren Burger to succeed Earl Warren as Chief Justice of the United States.*70

Even more than his predecessor, Warren Burger loathed pornography. He despised "smut peddlers" and was determined that "something had to be done to suppress them." In Burger's view, obscenity was "vulgar" and "citizens had a right to be protected from it." At one point, he argued behind the scenes that obscenity is "like filth in the streets that should be cleaned up and deposited in dumps." The new chief justice could hardly wait for the newly-constituted Burger Court to get its hands on the obscenity issue. Burger considered it fortunate that the justices of the Warren Court had never managed to get five votes to agree on a definition, because that would have settled the law. Their failure to agree on a single approach left the door open for him to reshape a critically important area of the law on which the Court, in his view, had been "stumbling" since 1957. He eagerly welcomed the challenge.71

O N JUNE 21, 1973, the Supreme Court handed down its decisions in two landmark obscenity cases: *Miller v. California*,72 and *Paris Adult Theatre v. Slaton*.73 In *Miller*, the defendant, Marvin Miller, operated one of the West Coast's largest mail-order dealers in sexually-explicit material.

---

* In June 1968, Earl Warren, fearing that Nixon would be elected president, worked out an arrangement with President Lyndon Johnson whereby Warren would step down as chief justice and Johnson would appoint Justice Abe Fortas as his successor. The plan was foiled, though, when the Senate refused to confirm Fortas as chief justice.

Chief Justice Warren E. Burger

In the events leading up to his prosecution, Miller mailed advertising brochures for several sexually-explicit books to a broad range of individuals. The brochures advertised works with such titles as *Intercourse, An Illustrated History of Pornography,* and *Sex Orgies Illustrated*. They consisted primarily of photographs and drawings explicitly depicting men and women in groups of two or more engaging in a variety of sexual activities, with genitals often prominently displayed. Miller was convicted of violating California's anti-obscenity statute.

Paris Adult Theatre involved two Atlanta, Georgia, movie theaters and their owners and managers. The prosecution was triggered by the exhibition of two movies, *Magic Mirror* and *It All Comes Out in the End*, which depicted scenes of simulated fellatio, cunnilingus, and group-sex intercourse and left "little to the imagination." At the entrance to the theaters was a sign, prominently displayed, stating clearly that the theaters exhibited "Atlanta's Finest Mature Feature Films," and warning that in order to enter, patrons "must be 21 and able to prove it" and that "if viewing the nude body offends you, Please Do Not Enter." The question presented was whether, in such circumstances, the theater owners and operators could be criminally punished for exhibiting obscene movies.[74]

The justices wrestled behind the scenes to work out a new alignment. It was soon apparent that Chief Justice Burger and Justices Rehnquist and White were on one side, and that Justices Brennan, Douglas, Stewart, and Marshall were on the other. For more than a year, Burger and Brennan struggled to win over Justices Blackmun and Powell.

When Lewis Powell arrived at the Court, he was inclined to join the Warren Court holdovers in extending the logic of *Stanley* and recognizing a First Amendment right of consenting adults to purchase, possess, read, and view obscene materials. But Powell, a Southern gentleman from Virginia who had practiced corporate law for most of his career and served a stint as president of the American Bar Association, had never in his life seen pornography, or anything remotely like it. His first exposure was when the justices viewed the movie *Vixen*, a soft-core feature film with nudity but no explicit sexual intercourse. Although the film was tame by obscenity standards, Powell was mortified. As he told his laws clerks, he had "had no idea such movies were even made." He was "shocked and disgusted" and "did not wish to discuss it further."

Justice Harry Blackmun, Burger's longtime friend from Minnesota, dithered even longer than Powell, but he too eventually relented. Like Burger, he had a deep personal distaste for such vulgar fare and he expressed doubt in a memo to his brethren that "commercial exploiters of pornography" had a constitutional right to "rot an unwilling community." In the end, the four Nixon appointees, joined by Justice Byron White, who had consistently been one of the most conservative members of the Warren Court on this issue, made up the new majority.[75]

I N TWO five-to-four decisions, the Court held that the materials at issue in *Miller* and *Paris Adult Theatre* could be banned. With evident relish, Chief Justice Burger delivered the opinion of the Court in both cases, with Justices Douglas, Brennan, Stewart, and Marshall dissenting.

In *Miller*, the Court focused on the definition of "obscenity." Burger began by noting that since *Roth*, "no majority of the Court has at any given time been able to agree on a standard to determine what constitutes" obscenity. Burger described this as an "intractable" problem, but one he was determined to solve. Abandoning all prior efforts to define obscenity, Burger offered a new definition: To find that any particular work is "obscene," a court must conclude that the average person, applying contemporary community standards, would find that the work, taken as a whole, appeals to the prurient interest; that the work depicts or describes sexual conduct in a patently offensive manner; and that the work, taken as a whole, lacks "serious literary, artistic, political, or scientific value."

The third prong of Burger's test was critical, because the new definition of obscenity expressly jettisoned the "utterly without redeeming social value" test of *Memoirs*. From now on, a sexually-explicit work that satisfied the first two prongs of the standard would be deemed obscene unless it had *serious* social value.*[76]

In dissent, Justice Douglas reiterated his long-standing objection to the view that obscenity is outside the protection of the First Amendment. Indeed, he declared it nothing short of "astounding" that the Court would permit punishment for ideas merely because they are "offensive." Such an

---

* Burger also held that in determining whether a work was obscene under contemporary community standards, trial courts should apply local rather than national standards. Under this new approach, a book or movie might be obscene in Iowa City but not in Chicago. By placing reliance on local standards, the Court in *Miller* made it much more difficult for the Supreme Court to determine in the future whether any particular work was obscene.

approach, he roared, "cuts the very vitals out of the First Amendment," because the Constitution "was not fashioned as a vehicle for dispensing tranquilizers" to the most thin-skinned among us.[77]

Justice Brennan, joined by Justices Stewart and Marshall, expressed alarm at Burger's abandonment of the "utterly without redeeming social value" element of the test. That element, he explained, was indispensable to the Court's conclusion in *Roth* that obscenity was unprotected by the First Amendment. He therefore charged that the newly-constituted Burger Court's revised definition was wholly incompatible with "fundamental First Amendment premises" and constituted an open "invitation to widespread suppression of sexually-oriented speech."[78]

H AVING REDEFINED "obscenity" in *Miller*, Burger turned next to *Paris Adult Theatre*, which posed the question whether the government could constitutionally censor obscene materials that are sold or exhibited only to consenting adults. Ever since *Stanley*, this question had lurked in the background, and it had been brought front and center by the recommendations of the 1970 report. In *Paris Adult Theatre*, the Burger Court held that the state's legitimate interests in banning obscenity are not limited only to protecting children and unconsenting adults. Rather, the state could constitutionally ban obscenity even for consenting adults in order to preserve "a decent society."[79]

In his dissenting opinion in *Paris Adult Theatre*, Justice Brennan explained that in the light of experience, he had come to the conclusion that the approach he had initiated sixteen years earlier in *Roth* should now be abandoned. Given the serious problems caused by the inherent ambiguity of the very concept of obscenity, Brennan now argued that government should be permitted to restrict such expression only if it can demonstrate a "very substantial interest" in doing so.

Brennan then maintained that the state's interests in protecting children and unconsenting adults were sufficiently substantial to meet this standard, but that its interests in denying consenting adults the freedom to read or view such material were simply too speculative to justify the suppression of free speech, even if it is obscene. Invoking Justice Louis Brandeis, Brennan concluded that if government is concerned that exposure to sexually-explicit materials might sometimes lead to antisocial conduct by adults, then it should abide by the general wisdom that "among free men, the deterrents ordinarily to be applied to prevent" antisocial conduct and crime are not the suppression of free expression, but "education and punishment for violations of the law."[80]

As an analogy, Brennan invoked *Roe v. Wade*,[*][81] which the Court had decided only a few months earlier. Interestingly, the Court's 1973 decision in *Roe* had been joined not only by the four dissenters in *Miller* and *Paris Adult Theatre*, but also by Chief Justice Burger and Justices Blackmun and Powell. With that fact clearly in mind, Brennan noted that the prohibition of obscenity for consenting adults, like the prohibition of abortion, was predicated on unprovable assumptions about "morality, sex, and religion." But the "existence of these assumptions," he declared, cannot validate a statute that substantially undermines the guarantees of the First Amendment, any more than they can validate a law that denies the "constitutionally protected privacy interests of a pregnant woman."[82]

In the wake of these decisions, University of Chicago law professor Harry Kalven, one of the nation's leading First Amendment scholars at the time, observed with "disappointment" that the Court's gradual movement toward greater First Amendment protection for obscenity in the late 1960s had been abruptly halted by the "changes in personnel" on the Court. Kalven chastised the Burger Court for narrowing the scope of First Amendment protection for sexual expression and broadening the "scope of permissible regulation." The question left hanging was whether, with Richard Nixon in the White House and the newly-constituted Burger Court now firmly entrenched, America was headed into a new Victorian era with respect to sexual expression.[83]

---

* *Roe v. Wade* is discussed in chapter 16.

13

THE END OF OBSCENITY?

Ronald Reagan and Edwin Meese, the Oval Office

I T WAS WARREN BURGER'S hope that his 1973 opinions in *Miller* and *Paris Adult Theatre* would stem the tide of sexually-explicit material in the United States. But despite his expansion of the definition of obscenity, this was not to be. The social changes unleashed in the 1960s and 1970s, shifting cultural values, and the advent of new technologies—including VHS, DVD, cable television, and the Internet—simply overwhelmed the capacity of the law to constrain sexual expression. As the flood of sexual material outpaced the capacity of prosecutors to respond, community standards soon became more tolerant of what would once have been regarded as "patently offensive" depictions of sex, and the real-world definition of obscenity shrank down to a small fraction of what had once been thought to be obscene.

In a sense, the proliferation of sexual expression had precisely the effect the moralists feared—it "eroded" the standards of the community to the point where depictions once deemed shocking were now seen as unexceptional. And as the category of sexual expression that could satisfy even the new *Miller* standard narrowed, so that only the very hardest of what had once been thought to be hard-core pornography could warrant conviction, it became less sensible for government officials to expend scarce prosecutorial resources on what increasingly came to be seen as essentially futile efforts to suppress the market for such expression.

By the early years of the twenty-first century, one could plausibly wonder, given the pervasiveness of sexually-explicit pornography on the Internet and elsewhere in society, whether we had reached the end of obscenity. How did this come to pass?[1]

THE MEESE COMMISSION

WITH THE ELECTION of Ronald Reagan in 1980, the United States entered a new era in the realm of morality politics. The vigorous reassertion of moral values as a central theme in national political discourse was triggered by growing controversy over such issues as abortion, women's liberation, the proposed Equal Rights Amendment, the rise of the gay rights movement, and the increasing proliferation of pornography. What would come to be known as the Christian Right had largely coalesced by the end of the 1970s, but the presidential race of 1980 thrust it even deeper into the national spotlight.

In April 1980, a huge crowd of some 200,000 people rallied in the nation's capital in a "Washington for Jesus" celebration, and during the 1980 presidential campaign, Ronald Reagan actively courted the evangelical vote. In a famous campaign speech, Reagan, speaking to a meeting of evangelical ministers, declared that "I know you can't endorse me, but . . . I want you to know that I endorse *you*." After his election, Reagan inaugurated what the scholars David Domke and Kevin Coe have aptly described as the "God Strategy" in American politics.[2]

It was inevitable that Reagan would turn his attention to obscenity. Frustrated by the rapidly growing availability of sexually-explicit materials in the years after *Miller* and *Paris Adult Theatre*, Reagan's attorney general, Edwin Meese, who served as Reagan's liaison to the evangelical community, announced the formation of a new eleven-member commission in 1985 to recommend "more effective ways" to contain "the spread of pornography." From the outset, critics objected that the Meese Commission had been stacked with members who were pre-committed to the conclusion that such material must be suppressed.[3]

The Meese Commission's report, issued in July of 1986, began by observing that in the years since the 1970 Report of the Commission on Obscenity and Pornography, the world had seen extraordinary technological changes, including the advent of cable, VCRs, DVDs, and the Internet, that had vastly expanded the opportunities—and dangers—of modern communications. Moreover, the Meese Commission noted with some dismay that despite the efforts of the Burger Court, in most parts of the nation prosecutions for obscenity were virtually nonexistent because public officials no longer perceived obscenity as a serious crime. As a consequence, the nation was now "pervaded by sexual explicitness."[4]

The Commission argued that there were several ways in which sexually-explicit expression could harm either individuals or society. These ranged from corrupting the moral tone of society to inflicting psychological harm on children to causing violence against women.[5] The Commission emphatically rejected the view that obscenity laws should be repealed with respect to consenting adults. In terms of enforcement priorities, though, it urged that special attention should be paid to the prosecution of obscene materials that "portray sexual violence."[6]

Because it reaffirmed the notion that consenting adults should be denied access to sexually-explicit material, the Meese Commission Report was controversial. Social scientists, including several the report cited, criticized the Commission's analysis of cause and effect; free speech advocates charged that the Commission gave too little weight to the value of free expression; and even William F. Buckley Jr.'s conservative *National Review* complained that the Commission simply "found the conclusion it was looking for." Perhaps ironically, many religious bookstores refused to carry the report because it included detailed quotations from and descriptions of pornographic books and films.

CEOS

ADOPTING ONE OF THE central recommendations of the Meese Commission Report, in 1986 Attorney General Edwin Meese established a new "strike force" in the Criminal Division of the Department of Justice—the Child Exploitation and Obscenity Section (CEOS). The creation of CEOS was meant to signify a new and more energetic federal effort to stamp out obscenity, even for consenting adults. Declaring that obscenity had become "more and more frequently associated with violence and depravity," Meese charged this new unit with the responsibility of prosecuting purveyors of obscenity. Between 1986 and 1992, during the administrations of Ronald Reagan and George H. W. Bush, CEOS targeted some of the nation's largest producers and distributors of pornography.

Its greatest catch was Reuben Sturman, who had been identified by the Meese Commission as the nation's leading purveyor of pornography.[7] Born in 1924 on Cleveland's East Side, Sturman started his own business after World War II selling comic books out of the trunk of his car. By the late 1950s, his business had grown into a successful magazine distribution company with warehouses in eight cities. At the suggestion of an employee, Sturman began to sell sex magazines. An astute businessman, he soon discovered that sex magazines generated twenty times more revenue than

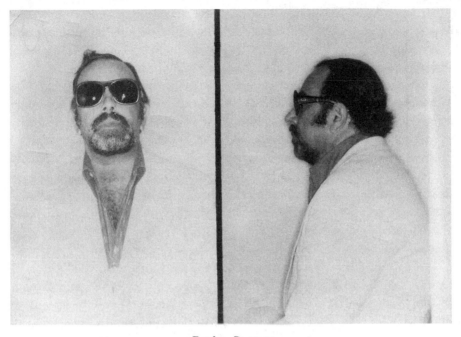

Reuben Sturman

comic books. By the late 1960s, Sturman was the largest distributor of "dirty" magazines in the nation.

Sturman is credited with inventing a hugely successful device: the peep booth. By enclosing coin-operated projectors in a small booth with a screen and a door that could be locked, Sturman gave his customers the opportunity to view sex films in private. The invention was an immediate success and Sturman put his peep booths in adult bookstores and sex shops in virtually every city in the nation. By some estimates, Sturman's peep booths grossed as much as $2 billion during the 1970s. Over time, the six-to-eight-minute films that were shown over and over again in the peep booths evolved from women wearing bikinis, to women wearing pasties, to completely nude women, to graphic sexual activity. Needless to say, the peep booths were thoughtfully stocked with a generous supply of paper tissues.*

---

* Peep booths go back at least to the sixteenth century, but until Sturman they required live women, thus limiting their availability. Sturman's innovation was the use of short films, which vastly expanded the capacity of peep shows to meet the demand in the years before cable, home video, and the Internet.

In 1974, Sturman was one of the first entrepreneurs in the nation to recognize that the future of the sex business lay in videotapes, because customers could collect them and watch them at home. He put his films on video, opened retail video stores, and began distributing hard-core videos throughout the nation. Independent producers of adult material had to deal with Sturman if they hoped to gain widespread distribution, and independent adult bookstore owners relied on him for access to all the newest products.

Sturman was repeatedly indicted on federal obscenity charges, but in each instance he avoided conviction. At one point, he even had the audacity to sue FBI Director J. Edgar Hoover for allegedly violating his civil liberties. Throughout these legal battles, Sturman insisted that people should have the freedom to read or watch whatever they want, and that he should have the freedom to sell it.

Unable to convict Sturman on obscenity charges, the Department of Justice switched tactics in the late 1980s and focused on his financial records instead of his videotapes. After a fierce legal battle, and using a strategy reminiscent of the one it had used to bring down Chicago mobster Al Capone in 1932, the Department of Justice finally succeeded in convicting Sturman of tax evasion in 1989. He was sentenced to ten years in prison and ordered to pay more than $2 million in fines. Sturman died in prison in 1997 at the age of seventy-three. Ironically, with Sturman behind bars, the porn industry became more competitive and thus more robust than ever. This, no doubt, was not the outcome the government had hoped for.[8]

ANOTHER CEOS victory involved Minnesota adult bookstore and theater owner Ferris Alexander, who, according to former CEOS Chief Patrick Trueman, had "monopolized the illegal pornography industry in Minnesota for decades."[9] From the 1960s to the early 1990s, anti-porn crusaders in Minnesota cast Alexander as "Public Enemy Number One—a dirty old man whose unseemly wares corrupted neighborhoods from Rochester to Minneapolis to Duluth."[10]

Alexander was finally arrested in 1990 and charged with racketeering, tax fraud, and transporting obscene materials in interstate commerce. After a four-month trial, the jury, applying the *Miller* standard, found that four of his videos and three of his magazines were obscene. Alexander was sentenced to six years in prison and all of his properties, including thirteen theaters and bookstores and $9 million in inventory, were seized by the federal government in a highly controversial civil forfeiture action.[11]

Writing about Alexander after his death in 2003, a journalist in Minneapolis observed that although "the government crushed the man, his cause triumphed," because the "materials that constituted the basis for Alexander's obscenity conviction . . . are now common fare." As the lawyer who represented Alexander observed, "Today, you can go almost anywhere in this country and see this sort of stuff." Indeed, he noted, the materials distributed by Sturman and Alexander now seem "quaint."[12]

SHIFTING REALITIES

THE ADVENT OF the Internet had a profound impact on the availability of sexually-explicit expression, on the evolution of community standards, and on the priorities of law enforcement. Suddenly, and for the first time in human history, it was possible for individuals to access such material instantly in the privacy of their homes without ever venturing out into an adult theater, a video store, or a bookstore, and (in most instances) without spending a dime. Suddenly, millions of ever more sexually-explicit websites could be accessed with the mere click of a mouse.

Moreover, many of these websites exist outside the boundaries of the United States and thus, as a practical matter, outside the reach of American law enforcement. Even if the government could shut down a website based in California or Florida, a person searching for "extreme sex" could instantly find thousands of erotic websites based in Sweden, Denmark, Brazil, Vietnam, or Japan. With such material so readily available on the Internet, what was the point of devoting limited prosecutorial resources to prosecuting adult bookstores or theaters, which were tame by comparison?

And, of course, as more and more people were exposed to ever more explicit sexual material on the Internet, the meaning of "patently offensive to contemporary community standards" shifted as well. Even more confusing, when dealing with the Internet, it is unclear precisely what "community standards" should govern in deciding whether any particular work—which is accessible simultaneously everywhere—is obscene. Should it be the "community standards" of the community where the trial takes place? Of the community where the material was put on the Internet? Of the national community? Of the community of Internet users? Prosecutors grappling with these questions faced a steep uphill battle.

Thus, by the time Bill Clinton assumed the presidency in 1993, the practical realities of combatting obscenity had changed radically. In short, the strategy of criminal prosecution seemed increasingly like a dead end. Moreover, unlike Ronald Reagan, Bill Clinton was hardly a champion of the Christian Right. But because of his own alleged sexual adventures, Clinton was vulnerable politically on the issue of sexual morality. Thus, when the subject of obscenity arose during the 1992 campaign, he promised that "aggressive enforcement" of the federal obscenity laws would be "a priority of the Clinton/Gore administration." After he assumed office, however, the Department of Justice, under the direction of Attorney General Janet Reno, reassessed the Department's priorities and decided to shift its energies away from the seemingly futile prosecution of adult obscenity and to focus instead on enforcing the laws against child pornography.[13]

The critical feature of child pornography is that it depicts *real* children engaged in *actual* sexual conduct. The problem of child pornography entered the public consciousness in the late 1970s when the market for such material first grew to a noticeable size. Before then, it was difficult for pedophiles who were interested in such material to find one another and it was difficult for anyone to distribute child pornography anonymously on a large scale. The market for child pornography exploded beginning in the late 1970s, however, with the advent of digital technology and then the Internet. The Internet, in particular, enables individuals to create, access, and share such material worldwide at the click of a button and it facilitates the creation of online communities of individuals who seek access to child pornography.[14]

There were no laws in the United States directed specifically at child pornography until 1977, when a flurry of states first enacted legislation making it a crime not only to cause minors to engage in sexual conduct (which was traditionally prohibited as child sexual abuse), but also to produce, sell, exhibit, distribute, or possess any sexually-explicit material that shows a real child engaged in actual sexual conduct (typically defined as including "sexual intercourse, deviate sexual intercourse, sexual bestiality, masturbation, sadomasochistic abuse, or lewd exhibition of the genitals"). By 1993, the federal government and almost every state had such a law.[15]

In the past, such material would simply have been deemed obscene, but with the sharp narrowing of the definition of obscenity, legislators came to the conclusion that laws directed specifically at child pornography were necessary in order to protect children, whether or not the material was legally obscene. Even though the act of causing a child to engage in actual sexual conduct for the purpose of creating sexually-explicit images or movies could independently be prosecuted as child sexual abuse, these laws were deemed necessary both to reduce the financial incentive individuals might have to produce and distribute such materials and to protect individuals from the psychological harm of knowing that such images of them were continuing to circulate in society.

The federal government first enacted child pornography legislation in the Protection of Children Against Sexual Exploitation Act of 1977.[16] The Meese Commission declared in 1986 that the production and sharing of such material caused serious harm to children and urged the federal government to strictly enforce the prohibition on child pornography. In response to that recommendation, Congress enacted new legislation that increased the penalties for producing, distributing, and possessing such material.[17]

It was these developments that led the Clinton administration to refocus its energies away from prosecutions of traditional adult obscenity and toward child pornography. Thus, from 1993 through 2000, the Clinton administration initiated an average of only twenty criminal prosecutions per year against the sale or distribution of adult obscenity. This represented a significant decrease from the preceding six years. The decision to reduce the number of adult obscenity prosecutions was sharply criticized by some religious groups. Concerned Women for America, for example, an organization dedicated to bringing "Biblical principles into all levels of public policy," condemned Clinton for loosing "a dangerous predator on our communities," and the Baptist Press charged that the government's shift in priorities reflected Clinton's own "moral fabric."[18]

On the other hand, the number of federal prosecutions for child pornography increased every year during the Clinton administration, rising steadily from 79 in 1993 to 563 in 2000. Over the course of eight years, the Clinton administration initiated a total of 2,326 child pornography prosecutions, resulting in 1,765 convictions. The shift in emphasis was dramatic.[19]

"TO ADVANCE THE CAUSE OF JUSTICE"

WHEN GEORGE W. BUSH assumed the presidency in 2001 after a bitterly disputed election, many people expected a resurgence of old-fashioned adult obscenity prosecutions. Bush stood, after all, for a return to traditional American values. Living up to that promise, Attorney General John Ashcroft—who had been raised in a deeply religious evangelical family and who as an elected official had earned perfect marks from the Christian Coalition—proudly declared in 2002 that "the Department of Justice is committed unequivocally to the task of prosecuting obscenity." Obscenity was once again proclaimed to be a "priority," and Ashcroft promised Congress a new crackdown on sexually-explicit material generally.[20]

Thus, by the end of 2003, a born again president and his even more devout attorney general could boast that they had initiated "the largest expansion of federal obscenity prosecutions in years," and they declared a nationwide "crusade against online pornography." This was somewhat misleading, however, because their focus was not on what earlier generations had deemed "obscene," but on new and more extreme forms of obscenity that emphasized brutality, bestiality, and defecation. The plain and simple fact was that in light of the extraordinary proliferation of sexually-explicit material on the Internet, those who now prosecuted obscenity had to focus on material that was deemed so extreme that it could be legally prohibited even in the twenty-first century. And that was what the Bush administration went after.[21]

In April 2003, for example, the FBI raided the offices of Extreme Associates in western Pennsylvania. According to Mary Beth Buchanan, the United States attorney who oversaw the prosecution, Extreme Associates' videos were among "the most vile, offensive and degrading material" on the Internet. As an illustration, she cited *Forced Entry*, a sexually-explicit video that "depicts several rape scenes, where women are beaten, slapped, spit upon and degraded in every way possible" and then "ultimately killed." This prosecution was the first major test of the Bush administration's campaign against obscenity, and it turned out to be representative of the prosecutions to come.*[22]

But despite the early assurances of Attorney General Ashcroft that the Bush administration would reenergize the government's attack on adult obscenity, the Department of Justice under Ashcroft's direction actually filed fewer than ten adult obscenity prosecutions between 2001 and 2005—even less than the Clinton administration—all of which were directed at the most extreme forms of pornography. The Bush administration's tepid approach to adult obscenity infuriated the religious right. Patrick Trueman, the former head of CEOS—who by this time was senior legal counsel for the Family Research Council, an organization dedicated to defending "faith, family and freedom from a Christian world view"—condemned the Bush administration in 2005 for focusing on only "the hardest material," such as "bestiality or rape films." In response to the explanation that the government needed to focus its resources primarily on child pornography, Trueman complained that this was nothing more than "an excuse for doing nothing on obscenity."[23]

---

* After six years of litigation, the defendants in the Extreme Associates case finally pleaded guilty in 2009. The defendants were sentenced to one year and one day in prison.

When Alberto Gonzales, the son of migrant workers who had risen to serve as a justice on the Texas Supreme Court, succeeded John Ashcroft as attorney general in February 2005, he reaffirmed the Department's commitment to "the aggressive prosecution of purveyors of obscene materials." Soon thereafter, under intense pressure from conservative Christian groups to "crack down on smut," Gonzales, with much fanfare, announced the creation of a new Obscenity Prosecution Task Force within the Department of Justice. The goal of the new task force was to pressure state and local prosecutors to target the most offensive forms of obscenity. Although the result was another short-term uptick in cases brought against producers of extreme sexual material involving "violence or degradation," there were no prosecutions of the mainstream, multibillion-dollar porn industry whose materials twenty-five years earlier would clearly have been deemed obscene.[24]

Alberto Gonzales

Some members of Congress chastised the Bush administration for not being more aggressive in its pursuit of pornography, but most prosecutors had little appetite for prosecuting the purveyors of such material. As a lawyer who represented obscenity defendants observed at the time, "If you talk to prosecutors on the front lines, they've got fraud, gang activity, organized crime, and drug cartels to contend with. Nobody wants resources redirected to dirty movies." Indeed, he added, "Whoever gets that assignment is the laughingstock of the department."[25]

In 2005, Congressman Frank Wolf (R-Virginia) sponsored a grant to the conservative organization Morality in Media to set up the website obscenitycrimes.org to enable citizens to report what they thought to be "obscene" websites and materials. Although the site generated tens of thousands of tips and complaints, Gonzales's Obscenity Prosecution Task Force did not follow up on a single one. The former chief of CEOS, Patrick Trueman, complained that "Gonzales talked a good game, but there's been no follow through." Indeed, between 2005 and the end of the Bush administration, the government brought an average of only five prosecutions annually against adult obscenity.[26]

Conservative religious organizations were outraged by what they saw as the hypocrisy of the Bush administration. Phil Burress, president of Citizens for Community Values, which "exists to promote Judeo-Christian moral values," criticized the Bush administration for failing to take seriously "a cancer that is eating away at the souls of our children . . . and is devastating families," and Robert Peters of Morality in Media insisted that the failure of the Bush administration to enforce obscenity laws had led to an "explosion of obscenity" that "undermined the right of all Americans to live in a decent society."[27]

I LLUSTRATIVE OF the adult obscenity cases that were actually brought during the Bush administration were the prosecutions of Garry Ragsdale and Paul Little. Ragsdale, a police officer, and his wife Tamara were tried and convicted in 2003 in a federal district court in Texas for selling several obscene videos on their Internet website. One of the videos, an hourlong Japanese-language film entitled *Brutally Raped 5*, was touted by the Ragsdales as depicting "the actual rape of a young woman." As described by the United States Court of Appeals, "In the first half of the video, the woman seems to consensually engage in various sexual activities with as many as three different males." The second half of the video depicts in graphic detail, among other things, the woman "being hoisted up by her ankles upside down with chains and then being sodomized with various objects and seemingly tortured with hot wax. She is also flogged with a whip by a female dominatrix and subsequently sodomized with a baseball bat, which is secured in place with a heavy rope." The Court of Appeals affirmed the jury's finding that under the *Miller* standard, the film was obscene. Garry and Tamara Ragsdale were sentenced to 33 and 30 months in prison, respectively.[28]

Paul Little, known professionally as Max Hardcore, was a pornographic actor, director, and producer who rose to prominence in 1992 with his film series *The Anal Adventures of Max Hardcore*. His films, which received numerous awards from the porn industry, typically involved scenes in which he urinates on women, fists them, inserts specula into their vaginas or anuses to widen them to an extreme degree, forces them to vomit on themselves, and appears to inflict pain and humiliation on them.

In 2007, Little was charged by CEOS with transmitting obscene material over the Internet and through the U.S. mails. The jury in Tampa, Florida, was initially divided over whether the films were obscene under the *Miller* standard,* but after fourteen hours of deliberation the jurors finally returned a verdict of guilty and Little was sentenced to forty-six months in prison. After his release from prison in 2012, Little announced that he wanted "to do good in the world," and thus went back into the porn industry.[29]

In July of 2008, just one month after Paul Little's conviction, Attorney General Michael Mukasey, who had succeeded Alberto Gonzales a year earlier, testified before a Senate Judiciary Committee oversight hearing. Senator Orrin Hatch (R-Utah), a longtime foe of obscenity, expressed what he described as the "concern of many that in enforcing the obscenity laws, the Justice Department is targeting too narrow a range of obscene material. The most extreme material may make a conviction more likely, but that conviction has little impact on the overall obscenity industry." Hatch criticized that strategy as "misguided." Attorney General Mukasey responded that "what we try to do is to bring those cases that we can win."[30]

This was a telling exchange. The Department of Justice in the Bush administration made what at least appeared to be a serious effort to combat extreme adult obscenity,[31] but because it focused on only a handful of the most extreme purveyors of the most outrageous material, the government's effort had, in Hatch's words, "little impact." By going only after videos in

---

* Three of the jurors were of the view that in light of what else was available on the Internet, these films were "really no big deal."

which men urinate in a woman's mouth, women eat their own excrement, women have sex with horses, men engage in bukkake,* and women and men engage in violent sadomasochistic behavior, the government enabled 99.99 percent of the pornography market to flourish.

But if the government was going to bring cases it could actually win, it had no choice but to go after the most extreme fare. In a world of limited prosecutorial resources, at the state as well as the federal level, priorities had to be set, and as much as people like Orrin Hatch may have wanted to turn back the clock to the "good old days" when *Lady Chatterley's Lover*, *Playboy*, and *Deep Throat* were thought to be obscene, those days were long gone. Technology had changed, society had changed, cultural values had changed and, as a result, the law had changed.

Over the course of a century, what constituted "obscenity" had dramatically evolved from modest textual references, to sex education and contraception, to classic novels like *Memoirs of a Woman of Pleasure* and *Ulysses*, to nudie magazines, to adult movies showing an erect penis,† to films that showed graphic images of oral and anal sex, to turn-of-the-twenty-first-century pornography that emphasized fisting, bukkake, and women eating feces. Except for the moral satisfaction—and political benefit—of punishing a Garry Ragsdale or a Paul Little because what they portrayed was deeply disgusting and offensive to most people, little was actually accomplished by such sporadic, costly, and ultimately ineffective prosecutions.

By 2009, the American legal system had, for all practical purposes, reached the same conclusion as the 1970 Commission on Obscenity and Pornography: The private consumption of pornography by consenting adults is "just not harmful enough to merit public enforcement."[32] Robert Peters, the president of Morality in Media, an organization established in 1962 to combat pornography, reluctantly conceded, "The war is over and we have lost."[33]

"THE WAR IS OVER AND WE HAVE LOST"

AFTER PRESIDENT BARACK OBAMA assumed office in 2009, the Department of Justice decided not to initiate any new prosecutions against adult obscenity. Instead, Attorney General Eric Holder focused the department's

---

* Bukkake is a form of group sex in which men take turns ejaculating on a woman's face.

† This was Justice Byron White's test of what was "patently offensive" in the 1960s and 1970s.

resources exclusively on child pornography. Not surprisingly, this decision triggered some sharply critical responses. Members of the Republican-controlled House Appropriations Committee, for example, warned that this approach threatened "the welfare of families and children."[34]

Some members of the Senate were unhappy as well. Forty-four senators sent a letter to Holder, drafted by Orrin Hatch, urging the department "vigorously to enforce federal obscenity laws" in order "to combat the growing scourge of obscenity in America." The letter invoked a congressional briefing at which several handpicked witnesses, at Hatch's invitation, presented testimony to the effect that exposure to obscene material could cause sexual harassment, sexual violence, and pornography addiction. The letter concluded by declaring it essential for the Department of Justice to recognize the magnitude of the "crisis" and to initiate a comprehensive program to investigate and prosecute "all major producers and distributors of adult obscenity."[35]

Similar objections were voiced in the private sector. The World, a "Christian views" website, charged that the Obama administration's non-prosecution policy had caused adult pornography to "saturate" the nation. Patrick Trueman, who had moved on to become the president and CEO of Morality in Media, the nation's largest anti-pornography organization, named Holder the nation's "leading facilitator of pornography" and urged his organization's members to "flood the DOJ switchboard" to demand stricter enforcement of the nation's obscenity laws.[36]

In response to the House Appropriations Committee and the letter from the senators, Assistant Attorney General Ronald Weich explained that the Department of Justice was focusing its limited resources on the most egregious cases, especially those that "facilitate child exploitation."[37] Even former Attorney General Alberto Gonzales, who had created the Obscenity Prosecution Task Force in the first place, defended the Obama administration's policy. Gonzales said that he had "always considered child pornography a bigger priority than adult pornography," and that it was therefore reasonable for prosecutors to give adult obscenity cases "a back seat" when faced with competing prosecutorial priorities.[38]

At the behest of the Christian Right, the Republican Party included a statement in its platform at the 2012 Republican Convention declaring that "current laws on all forms of pornography and obscenity need to be vigorously enforced." Although Republican presidential candidate Mitt Romney gave lip service to this commitment, the issue did not make a dent in the 2012 presidential campaign. Indeed, this would have been a rather awkward position for Romney to have advanced with any conviction, because during the years he served on the board of directors of Marriott hotels, from 1993 to 2002 and again from 2009 to 2011, the hotel chain routinely sold pay-per-view pornography to its guests.

T HE PRACTICAL reality is that essentially unrestrained adult obscenity is here to stay. Today, with the mere click of a button, search engines will instantaneously find virtually limitless websites that offer access, usually free of charge, to graphically explicit videos of masturbation, anal sex, lesbian sex, oral sex, bondage, sadomasochism, and literally anything else the mind can imagine. Whether this is good, bad, or indifferent is at this point largely irrelevant. The law has simply been overwhelmed by technology and by changing social mores.

State and local obscenity prosecutions have also been few and far between in recent years and, when they occur, they too focus almost exclusively on the most extreme forms of sexual expression. Unlike federal prosecutions, state and local prosecutions are directed primarily at local store owners, rather than Internet distributors. Most of these prosecutions have been pursued in only a handful of states, including Alabama, Kansas, Louisiana, Missouri, and Texas. In most of these cases, the primary concern of prosecutors is either the sale of child pornography or the sale of sexual material to minors.[39]

The challenge for the future is no longer how to *ban* such adult obscenity, but how to deal with its existence. Approximately 36 percent of all Internet users visit at least one adult website every month. Of those who visit such websites, the average user does so 7.7 times per month, or almost 100 times each year. The average length of each visit is 11.6 minutes. More than a third of all persons who visit adult websites are women.

Perhaps surprisingly, residents of states whose citizens have the most conservative positions on religion are the most likely to visit adults-only websites. Indeed, the state whose residents spend the most time on pornographic websites is Utah. Moreover, according to Baylor University, 40 percent of all evangelical Protestant clergymen admit to struggling with pornography and 53 percent of the men who belong to Promise Keepers, a "Christ-centered organization dedicated to motivating men to influence their world through a relationship with Jesus Christ," visit "pornography sites every week."[40]

As the puppets in the Broadway musical *Avenue Q* joyously sang:

The Internet is really really great . . . FOR PORN!
I've got a fast connection so I don't have to wait . . . FOR PORN!
But, there's always some new site . . . FOR PORN!
I browse all day and night . . . FOR PORN!

It's like I'm surfing at the speed of light . . . FOR PORN! . . .
The Internet is for porn! . . .
Why you think the net was born?
Porn! Porn! PORN![41]

PORN AND THE BIRTH OF THE CHRISTIAN RIGHT

ALTHOUGH THE "WAR" to prevent consenting adults from accessing sexually-explicit books, magazines, movies, and websites was effectively "lost" by the turn of the twenty-first century, the struggle had profoundly important consequences for the nation. The failed campaign to suppress sexual expression laid the foundation for a critical shift in American politics, a shift that has framed our political discourse to this day. The "Culture Wars," which bore a striking resemblance to the Second Great Awakening, began with porn.

The New York Society for the Suppression of Vice, which was founded by Anthony Comstock in 1873 to preserve public decency, was dissolved in 1951 because by midcentury the suppression of pornography was no longer considered a pressing public problem. But with the rise of new and ever more extreme forms of sexual expression in the 1960s, new organizations entered the fray. Citizens for Decent Literature (CDL), for example, which was founded by Charles H. Keating, a former navy pilot with "a deeply held loathing for smut," rose to prominence in the 1960s and reshaped the discourse of anti-porn activism. Building on the work of organizations like CDL, the restoration of "morality" increasingly became a central theme in the rhetoric of the New Right.[42]

After the President's Commission on Obscenity and Pornography issued its report in 1970 calling for an end to legal sanctions against the distribution of sexually-explicit materials to consenting adults, the New Right had a field day. Not only did Vice President Spiro Agnew lash out against "these radical-liberals" who were indifferent to a "child's constant exposure to a flood of hard-core pornography," but Senator Robert Dole (R-Kansas) called for an investigation of the members of the Commission, and President Richard Nixon "categorically rejected" the report's "morally bankrupt conclusions."[43]

As the nation entered the 1970s, the leaders of the New Right put pornography, and a more general call for a return to "traditional" moral values, at the forefront of their political agenda. Despite all the bombast about pornography, however, for the most part, politics rather than policy was the goal. As Nixon adviser John Dean observed at the time, the 1970 Commission Report provided "an excellent opportunity" for the president "to be very vocally placed on the right side of this issue." In short, the pornography issue gave conservative politicians an opportunity to cultivate and exploit moral "outrage."[44]

I N THE late 1970s, as a new era of evangelical fervor burst onto the scene, America entered what might be termed the "Third Great Awakening." The pivotal event was Anita Bryant's campaign to repeal the gay rights ordinance in Miami in the late 1970s.* Among the religious leaders who flocked to Florida to support Bryant's campaign was the Reverend Jerry Falwell, who founded the Moral Majority in 1979. A strident segregationist in the early 1960s, Falwell rose to national prominence in the 1970s as a televangelist on his *Old Time Gospel Hour*. The Moral Majority, with its explicit links to the Born Again Movement, soon established chapters in every state in the nation, published a newsletter with three million readers, and broadcast a daily radio program on more than three hundred stations. In his 1980 book *Listen, America!*, Falwell condemned the spread of pornography for generating a national "atmosphere of sexual license."[45]

In the 1980 presidential election, Ronald Reagan aggressively cultivated and ultimately obtained the active support of the Christian Right. Once in office, however, Reagan generally paid only lip service to the evangelical cause. But Reagan knew how to protect his base, so he spoke frequently on issues of morality. In a 1983 address to the National Association of Evangelicals, for example, he invoked the dangers of pornography, noting that America was "in the midst of a spiritual awakening and a moral renewal." Ultimately, however, Reagan recognized that words alone would not be enough to satisfy the evangelicals, so in 1985 he appointed the Meese Commission, the clear purpose of which was to endorse conservative Christian perspectives on issues of sex and pornography. As intended, the Meese Commission Report was lauded by the Christian Right.[46]

Although the evangelical community's campaign to suppress sexual expression collapsed by the turn of the twenty-first century, their losing war on pornography nonetheless helped energize a powerful religious, moral, and political movement that continues to this day to play a central role in our debates about reproductive rights, women's rights, and gay rights. That was, indeed, the most lasting legacy of the evangelicals' failed crusade to stamp out obscenity in America.

------

* See chapter 11.

14

SEX AND SPEECH IN THE TWENTY-FIRST CENTURY

George Carlin

A S THE LEGAL CONCEPT of "obscenity" evaporated in the early years of the twenty-first century, more focused issues involving the regulation of more specific types of sexually-oriented expression came to the fore. The central question might be stated as follows: Although the government can no longer constitutionally, or at least realistically, prohibit consenting adults from reading or viewing most of what once was thought to be obscenity in order to avoid the moral and other harms historically associated with such material, to what extent can it still regulate more *narrowly defined* types of sexually-oriented expression in order to further other, more *narrowly defined* interests?

There are several situations in which the Supreme Court has held that the government can still constitutionally regulate certain types of sexual expression even though the speech at issue might no longer be deemed "obscene." These include, for example, laws designed to shield children and unconsenting adults from exposure to sexual expression; laws regulating live sexual performances; laws regulating child pornography; and laws excluding sexual expression from government-funded schools, libraries, theaters, and arts programs. Each of these issues poses a distinct challenge in the Court's continuing effort to reconcile the First Amendment with competing moral, social, and religious concerns.

"BURN THE HOUSE TO ROAST THE PIG"

IN ITS 1966 DECISION in *Ginsberg v. New York*,[1] the Supreme Court held that the government can constitutionally protect children from exposure to material that is "obscene for minors" even if it is not obscene for adults. This principle works reasonably well when it is possible to separate children from adults. For example, although the state cannot constitutionally prohibit movie theaters from showing sexually-explicit but non-obscene movies to adults, it can constitutionally forbid them to admit children to the theater if the movie is obscene for minors. The same principle applies in bookstores. The state cannot constitutionally prohibit bookstores from selling books or magazines to adults that are obscene for minors, but it can prohibit bookstores from selling such materials to children. In the movie theater and bookstore situations, it is relatively easy to separate the adults from the children. Problems arise, however, when the separation is more difficult.

The Supreme Court first confronted this dilemma in 1957 in *Butler v. Michigan*.[2] Alfred Butler was convicted of violating a state law prohibiting any person to sell a non-obscene but sexually-explicit book that might have a corrupting influence on the morals of youth. The Court unanimously overturned Butler's conviction. In the words of Justice Felix Frankfurter, this was a misguided effort "to burn the house to roast the pig," for the state cannot constitutionally "reduce the adult population . . . to reading only what is fit for children."[3]

Are there no situations, then, in which the state can restrict the access of adults to constitutionally protected sexual expression in order to shield children from being exposed to such material? The Court considered a variation of this question in its 1971 decision in *Cohen v. California*.[4]

PAUL ROBERT COHEN was arrested in 1968 for wearing a jacket bearing the words "Fuck the Draft" in a corridor of the Los Angeles county courthouse. Cohen was convicted of violating a California law prohibiting any person to disturb the peace. Cohen insisted that his message was protected by the First Amendment, even though children were present.

The case presented a memorably awkward moment. No one had ever in history used the word "fuck" in an oral argument to the Supreme Court. Chief Justice Burger, who most definitely did not want that state of affairs altered on his watch, began the argument by informing Cohen's counsel, Melville Nimmer, that "the Court is thoroughly familiar" with the facts of the case so you need not "dwell on" them. Nimmer, understanding that it was important to his case not to concede even implicitly that the word should be deemed unspeakable, responded: "I certainly will keep very brief the statement of facts. What this young man did was to wear a jacket on which were inscribed the words 'Fuck the Draft.'" Burger's irritation was evident.[5]

The Court held that Cohen's use of the word "fuck" in this context was protected by the First Amendment. Justice John Marshall Harlan, who authored the Court's opinion, explained that this was not an obscenity case, because "whatever else may be necessary to give rise to the States' broader power to prohibit obscene expression, such expression must be, in some significant way, erotic." No one could plausibly maintain that Cohen's message would sexually stimulate its audience.

The state argued, however, that even if the speech was not obscene, it could nonetheless regulate it in order to protect children and unconsenting adults from being exposed to such offensive language. Justice Harlan acknowledged that some viewers would surely be offended by Cohen's expression and that some parents might be upset. But "outside the sanctuary of the home," he observed, we are often subject to "objectionable speech." Because the use of the word "fuck" has expressive power, Harlan concluded that, absent a more "compelling reason for its actions," the state could not constitutionally make the public display of the word "fuck" a criminal offense.

Is there a limit to this principle? Suppose above the words "fuck the draft" on his jacket Cohen had drawn an image of a naked man with an erect penis "fucking" the director of the local draft board? Suppose he placed that image on a billboard?

In its 1975 decision in *Erznoznik v. City of Jacksonville*,[6] the Court considered the constitutionality of a Jacksonville, Florida, ordinance that made it unlawful for any drive-in movie theater to exhibit any motion picture showing nudity if the screen was visible from any public street or place. The city argued that the ordinance was justified as a means to protect the sensibilities of both unconsenting adults and minors.

The Court, in an opinion by Justice Lewis Powell, who had cast the critical fifth vote two years earlier in *Miller* and *Paris Adult Theatre* to adopt Chief Justice Burger's conservative reformulation of obscenity doctrine, rejected both arguments. Invoking *Cohen,* Powell held that the limited privacy interests of individuals on the public streets cannot justify the censorship of otherwise constitutionally protected expression merely because the images might offend some viewers. Moreover, he reasoned, the ordinance could not be justified on the ground that it protected children from exposure to images of nudity, because not all nudity can "be deemed obscene even as to minors."[7]

Cohen and *Erznoznik* thus made clear that except perhaps in exceptional circumstances, the government cannot constitutionally ban non-obscene sexual images or words in public in order to protect the sensibilities of either adults or children, at least if the speech is not "obscene for minors." The Court had come a long way from the days of Anthony Comstock. What the Court did *not* decide in *Erznoznik,* however, was whether the city could constitutionally prohibit drive-in movie screens or billboards from exhibiting images that *are* obscene for minors.

"FILTHY WORDS"

THREE YEARS LATER, the Court confronted an interesting twist on *Cohen* and *Erznoznik* in *FCC v. Pacifica Foundation,*[8] which involved a radio broadcast. When radio first came into existence in 1920, there were no regulations governing who could use which frequencies. This led to a period of chaos in which different broadcasters constantly tripped over each other's programming. At the urging of station owners, Congress enacted the Radio Act of 1927. This law created the Federal Radio Commission, which was given authority to regulate the use of the nation's radio frequencies by issuing licenses to radio stations. On the theory that the airwaves were government property, and that the government could therefore regulate their use, the law empowered the Commission to impose conditions on the licenses to ensure that licensed stations would operate in the "public convenience, interest, or necessity." To that end, a specific provision of the act forbade any person to broadcast any "indecent" material in a radio communication.

Several years later, Congress enacted the Communications Act of 1934, which created the Federal Communications Commission (FCC) and brought the new technology of television, as well as radio, within its jurisdiction. For the next forty years, the FCC struggled to define the meaning of "indecent," but because broadcasters were highly risk-averse and did not want to air anything that might offend, few issues arose.* This began to change in the late 1960s, however, as the culture evolved and as sexually-explicit language and images became more common.[9]

FCC v. Pacifica Foundation involved the infamous recording "Filthy Words" by the comedian George Carlin. One of the greatest comedians of his generation, Carlin was born in 1937 in Manhattan. Although raised

---

* In 1931, Robert Gordon Duncan became the first person convicted of violating the Radio Act of 1927 for referring to an individual as "damned" and using the expression "By God" in an irreverent manner. In 1937, a mildly risqué radio skit called "Adam and Eve," featuring Mae West as Eve, resulted in an FCC reprimand of NBC.

in a Catholic family, he emphatically rejected religion. After a brief stint in the Air Force, where he was court-martialed repeatedly for inappropriate behavior, Carlin began his professional comic career in the late 1950s. In 1962, Carlin was in the audience at the Gate of Horn in Chicago when one of his heroes, Lenny Bruce, was arrested on obscenity charges for using the word "schmuck," the Yiddish word for penis, during his onstage comic routine. Bruce was an important influence on Carlin's comedy, especially as a role model who persistently challenged the limits of propriety. During the 1960s, Carlin became famous for portraying a range of comic characters, such as the Hippy-Dippy Weatherman, on late night talk shows. After his death in 2008, Carlin was described as the "dean of counterculture comedians" and was awarded the Mark Twain Prize for American Humor.

In his twelve-minute monologue "Filthy Words," Carlin discussed "the words you couldn't say on the public, ah, airwaves, um, the ones you definitely wouldn't say, ever." He proceeded to list those words ("shit, piss, fuck, cunt, cocksucker, motherfucker, and tits"), which he described as the "ones that will curve your spine [and] grow hair on your hands," and then repeated them in a variety of colloquialisms. The recording includes frequent laughter from the audience.

On October 30, 1973, a New York radio station, owned by Pacifica Foundation, broadcast the monologue. Pacifica had a long history of daring radio broadcasts. In 1955, for example, it brought the controversial beat generation poets Allen Ginsberg and Lawrence Ferlinghetti to the airwaves, to the consternation of the FCC, which complained that their poetry was "vulgar," and in the early 1960s Pacifica was investigated by the House Un-American Activities Committee on suspicion of being "subversive."

A few weeks after the New York station broadcast "Filthy Words" a man who had heard the broadcast while driving with his young son wrote a letter complaining to the Federal Communications Commission. Not coincidentally, the man who filed the complaint was a member of the national planning board of the faith-based pro-censorship watchdog group Morality in Media. Pacifica responded to the complaint by explaining that the monologue had been played during a program about contemporary society's attitude toward language, and that immediately before its broadcast it had advised listeners that the program included "sensitive language which might be regarded as offensive to some." Pacifica characterized Carlin as "a significant social satirist" who used "words to satirize as harmless and essentially silly our attitudes towards those words." There were no other complaints about the broadcast. The FCC sustained the complaint, ruling that broadcasters may not air language that describes sexual activities or organs in terms that are patently offensive as measured by contemporary community standards at times of the day when children are likely to be in the audience.

In light of its decision in *Cohen v. California*, one might have expected the Supreme Court to overturn the FCC's ruling, but it did not. Justice John Paul Stevens authored the plurality opinion in *Pacifica*.* Stevens had grown up in a wealthy family in Hyde Park, Illinois, attended the University of Chicago, served a stint in the military, and then graduated from Northwestern University Law School with the highest grade point average of any student in the history of the school. After serving as a law clerk to Supreme Court Justice Wiley Rutledge, Stevens returned to Chicago where he was a highly respected member of the bar. Known as a moderate conservative, he was appointed by President Richard Nixon to the federal Court of Appeals in Chicago in 1970 and then to the Supreme Court of the United States in 1975 by President Gerald Ford. Stevens succeeded Justice William Douglas, thus moving the Court to the right. Although his views on the First Amendment evolved over the course of his thirty-five-year tenure as a justice, Stevens tended to be quite conservative on free speech issues in his early years on the Court. In short, he was no William Douglas.

Stevens's opinion in *Pacifica* reflected his early conservatism about the freedom of speech. At the outset, Stevens declared that Carlin's use of these words was "vulgar," "offensive," and "shocking." Although acknowledging that the Court had held in *Cohen* that such words could not constitutionally be forbidden in public discourse, Stevens nonetheless argued that different rules must apply to different mediums of expression. Broadcasting, he insisted, is different from a message on a jacket, in a book, in a movie, or in a newspaper.

This was so, he explained, for three reasons. First, the airwaves are owned by the government, and the government has greater authority to control speech on its own property than might otherwise be the case. Second, indecent material presented over the airwaves confronts individuals not only in public, but also in the privacy of their homes, where the "right to be left alone plainly outweighs the First Amendment rights of an intruder." Third, broadcasting is "uniquely accessible to children." Stevens therefore held that the government's interest in supporting the authority of

---

* There was no majority opinion. Justice Stevens's opinion was joined only by Chief Justice Burger and Justice Rehnquist. Justice Powell filed a concurring opinion that was joined by Justice Blackmun.

parents to protect the "wellbeing" of their children in their own homes was sufficiently weighty to justify a restriction on indecent expression over the airwaves.[10]

In dissent, Justice Brennan, joined by Justice Thurgood Marshall, rejected the proposition that the government can censor non-obscene, constitutionally protected expression merely because it might enter the home or upset children and their parents. Although conceding that the privacy interests of individuals in the home are "deserving of significant protection," Brennan maintained that Stevens had both overstated the importance of the privacy interests at issue when an individual "voluntarily chooses to admit radio communications into his home" and ignored the magnitude of the impact of the challenged restriction on the First Amendment rights of both those who wish to transmit and those who wish to receive such communications over the airwaves.[11]

I N THE years since *Pacifica,* the FCC has continued to wrestle with its prohibition of "indecent" expression on radio and television. Despite its victory in *Pacifica,* the FCC exercised considerable restraint over the next decade. It held that prohibitable "indecency" consisted only of the repeated use of Carlin's "seven dirty words" between the hours of 6:00 A.M. and 10:00 P.M., when children are most likely to be in the audience. Applying that standard, the Commission brought no indecency enforcement actions between 1978 and 1987.

Beginning in 1986, however, Morality in Media, a faith-based organization dedicated to upholding Christian standards, and the National Federation for Decency (later renamed the American Family Association), led by the Methodist minister Donald Wildmon and committed to promoting a biblical ethic of decency in laws dealing with such issues as pornography, homosexuality, and abortion, joined forces with other Christian Right organizations and the Reagan administration to pressure the FCC to expand its prohibition of "indecent" expression.

Yielding to the demands of the Christian Right, the FCC, which by this time had been stacked by Reagan appointees, announced in 1987 that in the future it would enforce a more aggressive definition of "indecency," no longer limited only to the repeated use of Carlin's seven dirty words.[12] Despite its new understanding of what could constitute "indecent" expression, though, the FCC continued to exercise restraint for the next fourteen years. Then, in 2001, newly elected President George W. Bush appointed

Michael Powell to chair the commission. Powell initiated an aggressive indecency enforcement effort, and Powell's successor, Kevin Martin, who served through the end of Bush's presidency, declared the elimination of "indecency" on radio and television between 6:00 A.M. and 10:00 P.M. "a key component of his FCC policy."[13]

During the Bush administration, the FCC sought to punish broadcasters in several highly publicized incidents in order to make an example of them. These included U2 singer Bono's exclamation, in accepting a Golden Globe Award, that "this is really, really fucking brilliant," and Cher's statement, when accepting her 2002 Billboard Music Award, that "people have been telling me I'm on the way out every year, right? So fuck 'em." Several other cases involved instances of fleeting nudity. For example, there was a scene in an episode of ABC's television show *NYPD Blue* in which the nude buttocks of an adult female character were visible for approximately seven seconds and the side of her breast was visible for an instant.[14]

In the past, the FCC had taken the position that when "sexual" references or images were made in only a "fleeting" manner, they would not support a finding of indecency. In 2004, however, the Commission declared for the first time that it would treat the airing of inappropriate words and images as "indecent" even if they appeared only briefly and in passing. Applying its new rule, the Commission held that the Bono, Cher, and *NYPD Blue* broadcasts violated the prohibition on "indecency." Insisting that its new formulation of the rule was necessary to "safeguard the well-being of the nation's children," the FCC in these years assessed penalties against broadcasters totaling almost $8 million.[15]

The networks challenged the FCC's new formulation of the prohibition against indecent expression on two distinct grounds: that it had been adopted in an improper manner, and that it violated the First Amendment. In *FCC v. Fox Television Stations*,[16] decided in 2009, the Supreme Court, in a five-to-four decision, held that the new rule had been properly enacted, but did not address the constitutional issue.

Perhaps the most striking feature of Justice Scalia's opinion in the case was that he repeatedly wrote f*** and s***, rather than spelling out the words at issue. By contrast, in 1971, when the Court decided *Cohen*, Justice Harlan wrote in so many words that Paul Cohen had used the word "fuck," and in 1978, when the Court decided *Pacifica*, Justice Stevens quoted in full George Carlin's monologue, including the words "shit, piss, fuck, cunt, cocksucker, motherfucker, and tits." Justice Scalia, on the other hand, insisted on using ***s to avoid writing the words that were at the very heart of the case. This was, to say the least, odd. A judge should not let his own squeamishness distort his presentation of the facts of a case.

Three years later, the case came back to the Supreme Court to consider the constitutional question. In a unanimous decision, the Court held that the FCC's new definition of indecency was unconstitutional, but it did so without addressing the First Amendment. Rather, the Court held that the interpretation of the statute that was in place when these broadcasts took place gave no notice that "a fleeting expletive or a brief shot of nudity" would be deemed "indecent." Because the FCC, in an excess of enthusiasm, had applied its new rule retroactively, it failed to give fair notice of what was forbidden, thereby denying those who were fined due process of law.

The Court added that, in light of its resolution of the case, it was unnecessary for it to consider whether *Pacifica* should be overruled because its reasoning had "been overtaken by technological change." The Court thus left for another day the question whether *Pacifica* and its approach to indecency on television and radio was an obsolete relic of a bygone era. Nonetheless, as anyone who watches over-the-airwaves television or listens to the radio knows, at least in those media, the central principle of *Pacifica* is still intact.[17]

PUTTING THE BURDEN WHERE IT BELONGS

WHAT, THOUGH, OF other media? To what extent can the government constitutionally regulate other means of communication—such as cable television and the Internet—in order to prevent minors from being exposed to "indecent" expression? In 1996, Congress enacted a law requiring cable operators who provide channels "primarily dedicated to sexually-oriented programming" to limit their transmission to between the hours of 10:00 P.M. and 6:00 A.M.[18] Invoking *Pacifica*, the government argued that this was a constitutionally permissible way to prevent minors from seeing "indecent" images.

In 2000, in *United States v. Playboy Entertainment Group, Inc.*,[19] the Supreme Court, in a five-to-four decision, held the law unconstitutional. Justice Anthony Kennedy authored the Court's opinion. A Reagan appointee who was expected to be a solid conservative, Kennedy over time would come to play a decisive role in shaping the Court's decisions on such divisive issues as indecent expression, abortion, homosexuality, and same-sex marriage— almost always to the bitter disappointment of the Christian Right and those who had appointed him.

In *Playboy Entertainment Group*, Justice Kennedy, citing the Court's earlier decisions in *Cohen* and *Erznoznik*, held that the constitutionally permissible "solution" in this setting was not for the government to interfere with the transmission of constitutionally protected material, but for homeowners who did not want images of sexually-explicit conduct to enter their homes to use blocking devices (including various kinds of filters) that would make these programs or channels inaccessible. This approach, Kennedy concluded, would put the burden where it belongs—on those who want to shield themselves and their children from such material, while leaving consenting adults free to watch such programs whenever they wanted. The Court distinguished *Pacifica*, and explained that cable was different from over-the-air broadcasting because the government does not own the cable network and because there is no long-standing tradition of government regulation or licensing of cable. The First Amendment must therefore apply with full force in the environment of cable.[20]

A ND THEN there is the Internet. In 1996, Congress enacted the Communications Decency Act (CDA) in an effort to protect minors from exposure to "indecent" material on the Internet.[21] The next year, in *Reno v. American Civil Liberties Union*,[22] the Supreme Court unanimously held the CDA unconstitutional. Although the government argued that the case should be controlled by *Pacifica*, the Court, in an opinion by Justice Stevens—the author of *Pacifica*—distinguished that decision on two primary grounds. First, unlike the airwaves, and like cable, the government does not own the Internet and there is no long-standing tradition of government regulation of the Internet. Second, unlike the situation in *Pacifica*, where the FCC allowed indecent programming during hours when children were unlikely to be in the audience, no similar safe haven was technologically possible on the Internet.

Stevens explained that in order to deny minors access to potentially harmful speech, the CDA burdens "a large amount of speech that adults have a constitutional right to receive and to send to one another." The decision was a narrow one, however, and the Court left open the question whether some more narrowly drawn restriction might be permissible, particularly if it was limited only to expression that is "obscene for minors."[23]

In response to the decision in *Reno*, Congress almost immediately enacted the Child Online Protection Act (COPA), which was designed to address the constitutional deficiencies the Court had identified in the CDA. COPA declared it a crime for any person knowingly to disseminate on the Internet any material that is obscene for minors, as defined by *Ginsberg.** COPA recognized an affirmative defense, however, for those who made such material available on the Internet if they attempted in good faith to prevent minors from accessing the material. This could be accomplished by requiring users to provide a credit card, debit card, adult access code, adult personal identification number, or any other reasonable measure that would enable persons seeking access to demonstrate that they are at least eighteen years old.[24]

In effect, what Congress attempted to do in COPA was to treat the Internet in more or less the same way that we treat movie theaters. That is, the government can constitutionally prohibit movie theaters from admitting minors to movies that are obscene for minors as long as it does not interfere with the First Amendment right of adults to see those movies. COPA tried to do the same thing for the Internet.

Nonetheless, in a five-to-four decision in 2004, the Supreme Court, in *Ashcroft v. American Civil Liberties Union*,[25] held COPA unconstitutional. Justice Anthony Kennedy again authored the opinion of the Court. Even though COPA restricted only material that was obscene for children, Kennedy held that the legislation unconstitutionally limited the First Amendment rights of adults. This was so, he reasoned, because a better solution was for parents to use filtering software to block inappropriate material on their computers in a way that would preserve access for adults to constitutionally protected material "without having to identify themselves or provide their credit card information." Kennedy was especially concerned that by creating a potentially permanent record of who visits adult websites, the age verification requirement would have a significant chilling effect on the willingness of adults to exercise their First Amendment right to visit these sites.[26]

In this sense, the Internet is different from the movie theater, because even though adults must demonstrate (either visually or by showing identification) that they are over 18 in order to enter the theater, there is no permanent record of their decision to do so. But given the realities of the Internet, the age verification requirement might discourage many adults from viewing constitutionally protected expression, and Kennedy concluded that this

---

* This was defined in COPA to include any material that "(A) the average person, applying contemporary community standards, would find, taking the material as a whole and with respect to minors, is designed to appeal to, or is designed to pander to, the prurient interest; (B) depicts, describes, or represents, in a manner patently offensive with respect to minors, an actual or simulated sexual act, or a lewd exhibition of the genitals or post-pubescent female breast; and (C) taken as a whole lacks serious literary, artistic, political, or scientific value for minors." 47 U.S.C. § 231(e)(6).

was simply too high a price to pay, especially in light of the availability of the alternative ways to protect children.*

What is clear from these decisions is that by 2004 the Supreme Court had grown extremely reluctant to trade off the First Amendment rights of adults in order to shield minors from inappropriate sexual material, including even material that is "obscene for minors." This no doubt reflects both the Court's growing wariness of government efforts to regulate the freedom of sexual expression and its skepticism about the seriousness of the harm caused to children by exposure to such material. In this sense, the Court continues vigorously to enforce Justice Felix Frankfurter's fundamental insight that the government cannot constitutionally "reduce the adult population . . . to reading only what is fit for children."[27] If anything, this precept has taken on even greater vitality with the passage of time.

"PEOPLE SHOULD NOT EXPOSE THEIR PRIVATE PARTS INDISCRIMINATELY"

WHAT ABOUT LIVE sex shows? If people perform on a stage what they have a constitutional right to show on a movie screen or on the Internet, are they protected by the First Amendment? At first blush, one might think that as long as the live performance can be viewed only by consenting adults, the answer must be "yes." After all, why should it matter whether the viewer sees a video of people having sex on a computer, a movie of people having sex on a screen, or a live performance of people having sex on a stage? Interestingly, it is not that simple.

As a general proposition, the Supreme Court has held that the government can constitutionally punish individuals for engaging in otherwise unlawful conduct even if they engage in that conduct for expressive reasons. Under this doctrine, a law prohibiting speeding can constitutionally be applied to an individual who speeds in order to film a scene of someone speeding for a movie, and a law prohibiting wiretapping can constitutionally be applied to a journalist who wiretaps a phone call in order to gather

---

* Justice Breyer, joined by Chief Justice Rehnquist and Justice O'Connor, dissented on the ground that the availability of filtering software was insufficient to offset the legitimate need for age-verification. Justice Scalia also dissented. He argued that because COPA was directed at entities engaged in "the sordid business of pandering" by "deliberately emphasiz[ing] the sexually provocative aspects" of their content, it raised "no constitutional concern." 542 U.S. at 676.

information for a story. This is a well-established doctrine. It is based on the premise that in these circumstances, the government is not *attempting* to restrict speech. Rather, in these situations a law directed at non-expressive conduct merely has an *incidental effect* on speech. Such laws are presumptively constitutional, even as applied to expressive activity.[28]

Now consider laws against public nudity. Such laws, like laws against speeding and wiretapping, are not directed at speech. They are designed to protect individuals from the offense of seeing naked people in public. Thus, for purposes of a law prohibiting public nudity, it makes no difference whether an individual sunbathes in the nude on a public beach, goes shopping downtown in the nude, dances naked on a public street, or gives a speech in the nude in a public park. The law prohibits public nudity without regard to whether the individual is engaging in speech. The "incidental effects" doctrine therefore effectively disposes of the argument that a law banning public nudity violates the First Amendment—even when it has the incidental effect of punishing an individual for dancing naked on a public street. He is being punished for being naked in public, not for dancing.

But suppose the individual wants to dance naked, not on a public street, but in a privately owned bar or theater for the entertainment of consenting adults. If a city passes a law *expressly* prohibiting nude dance performances in such circumstances, the law would be directed specifically at speech and therefore would not fall within the incidental effects doctrine. Such a law would be analogous to a law expressly prohibiting nude dancing in movies, and would thus be unconstitutional.

But what if the government does not pass a law expressly prohibiting nude dance performances in privately owned bars and theaters? Suppose instead the government argues that a nude dance performance in a bar or a theater violates its *general* law against public nudity. That is, the government maintains that its anti-public nudity law prohibits nudity in public without regard to whether the nudity takes place on a public beach, on a public street, or in a privately owned bar or theater that is open to the public. The city insists that its concern is not with the speech, but with the public nudity, and that applying its prohibition to a nude performance in a theater or a bar is no different than applying it to a nude performance on a public street. What result?

THE SUPREME COURT addressed this question in 1991 in *Barnes v. Glen Theatre, Inc.*[29] The case involved the constitutionality of Indiana's public indecency statute, as applied to the Kitty Kat Lounge, which presented nude dancing as a form of entertainment for its patrons. The Indiana law made it a crime for any person to appear "in a state of nudity" in any "public place." The state courts of Indiana interpreted the statute as requiring nude dancers in establishments like the Kitty Kat Lounge to wear pasties and a G-string. Needless to say, a law imposing such a requirement on movies would clearly be unconstitutional.

Public performances of erotic dances have a long and rich history. Erotic dancing as a form of performance art dates back to the ancient world. In the ancient Sumerian myth of the goddess Inanna, for example, the goddess removed an article of clothing at each of the seven gates to the Underworld. In ancient Greece, the auletrides were female dancers, acrobats, and musicians who performed naked in an alluring manner before audiences of men. In ancient Rome, nude dancing was similarly common and played a central role, for example, in the celebrations honoring Flora, the goddess of blossoming flowers.

Beginning in the seventh century, however, the Christian Church began to forbid such behavior, and by the Middle Ages any form of nude dancing as a form of public entertainment in Europe pretty much disappeared from view. During the English Restoration, though, striptease again became popular. *The Rover*, for example, which was written by Aphra Behn in 1677, included a sensuous—and comical—male striptease. Striptease became a regular form of entertainment in the brothels of eighteenth-century London, where "posture girls" would strip naked on tables to entertain the guests. By the 1880s and 1890s, Parisian shows such as the Moulin Rouge and Folies Bergère featured scantily-clad women dancing in public, and a famous act in the 1890s featured a woman who slowly removed her clothes in a vain search for a flea that was supposedly crawling on her body. In the 1920s and 1930s the famous Josephine Baker danced topless in the *danse sauvage* at the Folies Bergère. The shows in these venues were notable for their sophisticated choreography and for their costumes, which typically included glitzy sequins and feathers.

In the United States, the seductive Middle Eastern "belly dance" became popular after its introduction by the dancer Little Egypt on the Midway at the 1893 World's Fair in Chicago, and in 1896 the famous vaudeville trapeze artist Charmion performed a "disrobing" act during her acrobatic performances. In the 1920s and 1930s, striptease became especially popular in traveling carnivals and burlesque theaters, with such famous strippers as Gypsy Rose Lee, Blaze Starr, and Sally Rand gracing the stage in Florenz Ziegfield's revues and in venues like the infamous Minsky's on New York's 42nd Street. Throughout this period, perform-

Sally Rand

ers and producers battled with the police over whether such performances were obscene.

The 1960s saw an explosion of striptease, particularly in the form of topless go-go dancing. Carol Doda of the Condor Night Club in San Francisco is credited with being the first topless go-go dancer. The club went "bottomless" in 1969 and thus began the trend toward full nudity in American striptease dancing. In 1981, the Supreme Court made clear that nude performance dancing, like other forms of performance dancing, is expression protected by the First Amendment.[30]

A decade later, though, in *Barnes*, the Court, in a five-to-four decision, held that the application of Indiana's anti-public nudity law to the nude dancers in the Kitty Kat Lounge did not violate the First Amendment. In a plurality opinion, Chief Justice Rehnquist reaffirmed that "nude dancing of the kind sought to be performed here is expressive conduct" within the meaning of the First Amendment. He emphasized, however, that the Indiana law did not ban nude dancing "as such," but rather proscribed public nudity in general. Noting that laws banning public nudity "are of ancient origin" and reflect "moral disapproval of people appearing in the nude among strangers in public places," Rehnquist concluded that the law served substantial government interests that were "unrelated to suppression of free expression." This was so, he reasoned, because the "evil that Indiana seeks to address is not erotic dancing, but public nudity." Thus, the law could constitutionally be applied to the nude dancers in the Kitty Kat Lounge.[31]

Justice Byron White, joined by Justices Thurgood Marshall, Harry Blackmun, and John Paul Stevens, dissented. Justice White was usually quite conservative on these sorts of issues—recall that he was the only Warren Court holdover to join the four Nixon appointees in the Court's 1973 obscenity decisions in *Miller* and *Paris Adult Theatre*. White reasoned in *Barnes*, though, that although laws forbidding public nudity serve the legitimate purpose of protecting children and unconsenting adults from possible offense, that purpose could not possibly justify a prohibition of nude dancing in theaters and bars where the "viewers are exclusively consenting adults." He therefore argued that *Barnes* could not credibly be characterized as an incidental effects case, because the *reason* for the general law against public nudity—protecting children and unconsenting viewers from possible offense—was wholly irrelevant to nude dancing at the Kitty Kat Lounge.

White maintained that the application of the anti-public nudity law to the dancers in the Kitty Kat Lounge could be explained only by the state's constitutionally impermissible interest in preventing consenting adults from viewing what the state regarded as "harmful" speech. In the view of the four dissenting justices, then, there was no First Amendment distinction between a law prohibiting nude dancing in a movie and a law prohibiting nude dancing in a bar, as long as the audience in both cases consisted entirely of consenting adults. The Indiana law, White concluded, was plainly unconstitutional as applied to the nude dancers in the Kitty Kat Lounge.[32]

In a separate opinion, Justice Antonin Scalia responded to White's argument. Scalia had been appointed to the Court in 1986 by President Reagan, at the height of Reagan's effort to satisfy the Christian Right by moving the Court still further to the right, especially on such issues as sexual expression and abortion. An only child born to Sicilian immigrants living in New Jersey, Scalia was raised in a "deeply religious" Roman Catholic family. He graduated first in his class from Jesuit Xavier High School in Manhattan, where he was seen as both "brilliant" and as an "archconservative Catholic" who, in the words of a classmate, "could have been a member of the Curia."

Scalia then went on to graduate *summa cum laude* from Georgetown University and *magna cum laude* from Harvard Law School. After practicing law for several years in Cleveland and then teaching law at the University of Virginia, he served from 1971 to 1977 in the executive branch in both the Nixon and Ford administrations. Scalia then joined the faculty of the University of Chicago Law School, where he established himself as a serious scholar in the fields of both constitutional and administrative law. In 1982, Scalia, along with Robert Bork and Edwin Meese, helped found the conservative Federalist Society, which is dedicated to "reordering priorities within the legal system to place a premium" on "traditional values."

That same year, President Reagan appointed Scalia to the United States Court of Appeals for the District of Columbia and then, in 1986, at the recommendation of Attorney General Edwin Meese, to the Supreme Court of the United States. The first Italian American justice, Scalia was confirmed by a vote of 98–0. Once on the Court, Scalia became the most forceful—and at times the most intemperate—advocate in the defense of "traditional values" in a series of often bitter controversies over such issues as sexual expression, abortion, homosexuality, and same-sex marriage.[33]

In his concurring opinion in *Barnes*, which neatly anticipated what would become his trademark approach to issues relating to sex and the Constitution, Scalia emphatically rejected White's contention that the only reason for restricting nudity in public places is to protect children and unconsenting adults from offense. In Scalia's view, the purpose of Indiana's anti–public nudity statute was not to prevent offense, but "to enforce the traditional moral belief that people should not expose their private parts indiscriminately." Indeed, he insisted, the Indiana nudity law would be violated "if 60,000 fully consenting adults crowded into the Hoosierdome to display their genitals to one another, even if there were not an offended innocent in the crowd."

Thus, in Scalia's view, the application of the anti–public nudity law to the Kitty Kat Lounge was not directed at expression and was not about protecting people from offense. Rather, it was about prohibiting *immoral conduct*—exposing oneself in a public place to strangers. With that understanding of the statute, Scalia concluded that the Indiana anti–public nudity law had only an incidental effect on the performances in the Kitty Kat Lounge and therefore could constitutionally be applied to such conduct.[34]

. . .

WHAT ARE we to make of this disagreement? It seems clear that as long as no constitutional right is at issue, the government ordinarily can regulate conduct because it deems the conduct immoral. This has always been an awkward justification for government action, however, because "moral" justifications for laws are often closely bound up with religious beliefs. Because of our constitutional commitment to the separation of church and state, it is unconstitutional for the government to enact laws for the express purpose of enforcing religious beliefs. As the Supreme Court noted in 1961 in a case involving Sunday closing laws, if a law's purpose "is to use the State's coercive power to aid religion," it violates the Establishment Clause of the First Amendment.[35] Is it "immoral," apart from certain religious precepts, for people to appear naked before other consenting adults in a public place? If so, why? What makes it "immoral"? How are we to separate the moral from the religious?

The question posed by the White-Scalia debate in *Barnes* is whether a bare moral justification for prohibiting consenting adults from appearing nude in the presence of other consenting adults is sufficient to sustain an "incidental" restriction on speech. Because of the clear religious overtones implicit in such "moral" justifications, this argument should not be deemed sufficient to empower the government to restrict what otherwise would be a constitutional right. Justice White had the better of the argument in *Barnes*. Not surprisingly, this issue, which played a central role during the Second Great Awakening, recurs across a broad array of constitutional controversies involving government restrictions not only on sexual expression, but also on contraception, abortion, homosexuality, and same-sex marriage.

In *Barnes*, though, the Court, by a five-to-four vote, effectively settled the nude dancing/live sex show question, unless and until some future set of justices decides to revisit the question. Under the holding in *Barnes*, as long as the government bans all public nudity and all sex in public places, it can constitutionally apply that prohibition to nude dancing and live sex shows, even if the audience consists entirely of consenting adults, and even if movies of precisely the same behavior would be protected by the First Amendment.

Barnes does leave several interesting and important questions unanswered, however. For example, if the state can constitutionally ban nude dancing in the Kitty Kat Lounge, can it also ban nudity in a "legitimate" theater production, even if the nudity is important to the theme of the play, and even if the play has serious artistic, literary, and theatrical value? As in *Barnes*, the answer should be "no." But this remains an open question.

CHILD PORNOGRAPHY

THE PROBLEM OF CHILD pornography came increasingly to dominate the attention of state and federal law enforcement in the last third of the twentieth century when, with advances in communications technology, the market for such material first grew to a noticeable size. By the turn of the twenty-first century, almost all of the prosecutorial resources that had once been devoted to chasing down the purveyors of obscenity had been redirected to the pursuit of child pornography.

The Supreme Court first considered the constitutionality of laws prohibiting child pornography in its 1982 decision in *New York v. Ferber*.[36] In 1977, New York enacted a law, similar to the laws in nineteen other states at the time, that made it a crime for any person knowingly to produce, exhibit, or sell any material containing a "sexual performance" by a child under the age of sixteen. The statute defined "sexual performance" as any depiction of a child engaged in "sexual intercourse, deviate sexual intercourse, sexual bestiality, masturbation, sado-masochistic abuse, or lewd exhibition of the genitals."[37]

Paul Ira Ferber, the proprietor of a Manhattan bookstore specializing in sexually-oriented products, was prosecuted under this law for selling two films to an undercover police officer. The films were devoted almost entirely to showing young boys masturbating. A jury held that the films were not obscene within the meaning of *Miller*, but convicted Ferber of violating New York's child pornography statute. The New York Court of Appeals held that Ferber's conviction violated the First Amendment because the films were not obscene and were therefore entitled to constitutional protection.[38] The Supreme Court, in a unanimous decision, reversed and upheld Ferber's conviction.

Justice Byron White wrote the opinion of the Court. At the outset, White conceded that the judgment of the New York Court of Appeals "was not unreasonable in light of our decisions." This case was different, however, because it involved works that are not only sexually-explicit, but show actual sexual acts by children. The question, then, was whether the government could constitutionally proscribe such works, even if they are not obscene.[39]

It is worth noting that at almost any time in American history before the 1970s, the material at issue in *Ferber* would unquestionably have been deemed obscene. By 1982, however, the obscenity doctrine no longer reached such material. The puzzle for the Court was whether some new doctrine should permit its prohibition.

Justice White acknowledged that laws prohibiting the dissemination of child pornography might have the effect of suppressing some valuable expression, but he nonetheless concluded that the government must be permitted to suppress pornographic depictions of actual children engaged in such conduct. This was so, White maintained, for at least four interrelated reasons. First, the government's interest in taking away the incentive for individuals to commit child sexual abuse in order to create such material is of "surpassing importance."[40] Second, because it is often difficult for government to track down the individuals who produce child pornography, it is imperative for the government to "dry up the market" by punishing those who sell, distribute, or possess such material. Third, because the continuing public circulation of this material can cause ongoing psychological and other harm to the victim, the government has a compelling interest in halting its distribution. And fourth, even if such images are a necessary part of a literary, scientific, or educational work, it should be possible for the person producing the work to do so either by using an adult actor who can pass as a minor or by using some other form of "simulation."[41]

In light of these considerations, White concluded that images of actual children engaging in actual sexual conduct can be restricted, even if they are not obscene, because of the state's overriding interest in preventing harm to the children who are unlawfully sexually abused in the production of child pornography.*

The decision in *Ferber* poses an interesting First Amendment puzzle. Suppose someone steals a camera in order to make a movie. Surely, the government can punish him for the theft. But can it also suppress the movie in order to take away the incentive to steal the camera? Or, if a journalist commits a burglary in order to steal documents that will enable her to write a story, can the government not only punish the reporter for burglary, but also forbid the publication of the article? Or if someone films an illegal dogfight, can the government punish not only those who held the unlawful dogfight, but also those who distribute or possess the video?† In other

---

* In *Ashcroft v. Free Speech Coalition*, 535 U.S. 234 (2002), the Court held that government could not constitutionally forbid as child pornography non-obscene sexually-explicit images that merely *appeared* to depict minors engaging in sexual conduct, but which were in fact produced without using real children.

† In *United States v. Stevens*, 559 U.S. 460 (2010), the Supreme Court held that the child pornography precedent does not extend to the dogfighting situation.

words, does *Ferber* state a general principle that applies across-the-board, or is it a one-off rule designed to deal with the special challenge of child pornography?

D ESPITE THE considerable efforts of state and federal authorities to suppress child pornography, the Department of Justice reported in 2012 that the past decade had "seen a sharp increase in the severity and depravity of child pornography offenses, fueled in large part by swiftly advancing technological changes. These changes made it possible for offenders to easily store large numbers of images of child sexual abuse, to create safe havens online where they could communicate and bond with other individuals who encourage and promote the sexual exploitation of children, and to utilize sophisticated methods to evade detection by law enforcement."

To address this challenge, the number of defendants prosecuted by federal authorities for producing or distributing child pornography has continued to increase every year. In fiscal year 2011, federal prosecutors indicted 2,929 defendants for such offenses. This represented a 42 percent increase over 2006. The Department noted that many of its child pornography investigations "are global in scope." Indeed, for the most part, the American adult sex entertainment industry has stayed away from the production of child pornography. As a consequence, most child pornography available in the United States is created either by foreign producers, particularly in Russia, Eastern Europe, and Asia, or by amateurs—increasingly by minors themselves.[42]

PUBLIC MUSEUMS, LIBRARIES, SCHOOLS, AND ARTS PROGRAMS

ALTHOUGH THE GOVERNMENT cannot constitutionally prohibit consenting adults from reading, viewing, or disseminating to other consenting adults non-obscene sexually-explicit expression, to what extent must it affirmatively *support* the production, exhibition, or dissemination of such material or make it available in public schools, libraries, theaters, and museums? It might seem that the answer is "never," but it is not that simple.

Suppose, for example, a city creates a public art museum that will not exhibit any painting or photograph that depicts a naked person. Or, suppose a city establishes an arts funding program in which it makes grants to promising local artists, but stipulates that no grants shall be made to any artist whose work depicts naked people engaged in sexual acts? Do such policies violate the First Amendment?

The city in these hypotheticals would no doubt argue that because it has no constitutional obligation to create *any* art museum or *any* grant program, it should be free to decide which art and which artists it will and will not support. The Supreme Court has long held, however, that even in circumstances in which the government need not support or permit *any* speech, the First Amendment limits the government's discretion to favor some messages or speakers over others.

This is, in essence, an *equality* principle. No individual has a constitutional right to a tax deduction for child-care expenses, but if the government decides to create such a deduction it cannot constitutionally provide it only to whites, or only to Christians, or only to people who vote Democratic. Similarly, although a city has no constitutional obligation to provide grants to local artists, it cannot constitutionally exclude artists whose work conveys a pro-life message or criticizes the mayor.

In short, the First Amendment requires the government to be even handed when it creates and administers such programs. This principle applies not only to government grants, but to any situation in which the government chooses voluntarily to permit speech that it is not constitutionally required to allow. For example, a city is under no First Amendment obligation to allow individuals to hand out leaflets inside its public buses, but if it decides to allow this means of expression it cannot constitutionally exclude pro-Republican or antiwar messages.

How does this doctrine apply to non-obscene but sexually-explicit expression? Note that in all the above examples, the government expressly discriminated on the basis of the *point of view* of the speaker. The Supreme Court has long held that such "viewpoint-based" restrictions are almost always forbidden by the First Amendment.* Such restrictions are thought to be especially threatening to First Amendment values because they are likely both to distort public debate and to be motivated by government hostility to particular points of view. For that reason, viewpoint-based restrictions are

---

* One exception to this principle is the "government speech" doctrine. That is, when the government itself conveys a specific message of its own, it is not constitutionally required to convey the opposite message.

essentially *per se* prohibited in the context of government museums, libraries, theaters, grant programs, public buses, and the like.[43]

The Court has tended to be more tolerant, however, of content-based restrictions that are not based on viewpoint. For example, suppose a city creates a public library, but decides that because of limited resources, it will collect only books dealing with history or only works of fiction. Or suppose a city creates a grant program that will support only artists whose work addresses issues of race. Or suppose a city-run theater presents a series of plays on the subject of war. The Supreme Court has held that such limitations are permissible, even though they are based on the content of the speech, because they are justified by the reality of limited resources and because they do not discriminate on the basis of viewpoint.[44]

H OW DO government programs that exclude sexually-oriented expression fit into this picture? The Supreme Court confronted this question in the school library context in its 1982 decision in *Board of Education v. Pico*.[45] Acting on the recommendations of a politically conservative organization, members of a local board of education on Long Island removed nine books from the school library because they were thought to be "anti-American," "anti-Christian," "anti-Semitic," and "just plain filthy." The list included such works as Kurt Vonnegut's *Slaughterhouse-Five*, Bernard Malamud's *The Fixer*, Desmond Morris's *The Naked Ape*, Beatrice Sparks's *Go Ask Alice*, and *The Best Short Stories by Negro Writers*, which was edited by Langston Hughes.

The Court, in an opinion by Justice William Brennan, held that the members of the school board "possess significant discretion to determine the content" of the school library, but that the First Amendment does not permit them to exclude or remove books if their motivation for doing so is to exclude specific *viewpoints* with which they disagree.

What about books that are explicitly sexual in nature? The Court explained in *Pico* that the members of the school board would not violate the First Amendment if they removed books from the library because they were "vulgar," because such a motivation "would not carry the danger of an official suppression of ideas." Sexual explicitness, in other words, is not itself a point of view. Thus, the removal or exclusion from a school library of publications deemed educationally "unsuitable" for children because of their sexual content, such as *Memoirs of a Woman of Pleasure*, *Lady Chatterley's Lover*, or *Playboy*, would not violate the First Amendment.[46]

• • •

C ONGRESS AND President Lyndon Baines Johnson created the National Endowment for the Arts (NEA) in 1965, at the height of The Great Society, "to nurture American creativity, to elevate the nation's culture, and to sustain and preserve the country's many artistic traditions." From the outset, Congress recognized the risks in creating such a program, acknowledging that "the best art is often controversial, even confrontational." Thus, in creating the NEA, Congress expressed a profound commitment to shielding public arts funding from the dangers of political, moral, religious, and ideological censorship. Twenty-five years later, a series of controversies erupted that tested the limits of that commitment.[47]

It all started in 1990 with the artist Andres Serrano's photograph, *Piss Christ*, which depicted a plastic Christ on a wooden cross submerged in the artist's own urine. Serrano, a New York artist who had for years been exploring the meanings of sacred symbols, had received an NEA grant through the Southeastern Center for Contemporary Art. *Piss Christ* created a storm of protest from the Christian Right. Outraged that taxpayer dollars had been used to fund such "anti-Christian bigotry," a broad coalition of Christian Right activists initiated a crusade against the NEA. In response, the NEA explained that it fully supported the creation of artistically innovative works—whether or not they might be "offensive to some individuals."[48]

At approximately the same time as the controversy over *Piss Christ*, the Corcoran Gallery of Art in Washington, D.C., used funds from an NEA grant to support an exhibition of works by the artist Robert Mapplethorpe, who had died of AIDS in 1989. A highly regarded photographer, Mapplethorpe was famous for his homoerotic portraits depicting New York's gay male sadomasochistic culture in the 1970s. The photographs in the exhibition were often shocking in content, but remarkable for their technical and artistic mastery. One of the more disturbing photographs was "a self-portrait of the artist, bare ass in the foreground, face turned toward the camera with an expression that was at once both sad and mischievous, and a bullwhip inserted firmly in his anus."[49]

The use of NEA funds to support Mapplethorpe's exhibition triggered another furious outcry. Senator Alfonse D'Amato (R-New York), for example, fumed that such works should not be supported "with the use of the taxpayer's money," and the Rev. Donald Wildmon of the American Family Association urged Americans to contact their senators to demand that the government end its "anti-Christian" support for such "pornography."[50]

Senator Jesse Helms (R-North Carolina), one of the most stridently conservative senators of his generation, fought tooth-and-nail throughout his career against what he deemed the immoral "liberal" agenda of civil rights, obscenity, feminism, gay rights, and abortion. Faced with the Mapplethorpe controversy, Helms declared that federal funding for such "art" was "an insult to taxpayers," who "have a right not to be denigrated, offended, or mocked with their own tax dollars." He therefore proposed legislation to forbid the use of any NEA funds "to promote, disseminate, or produce materials" that depict "homoeroticism . . . or individuals engaged in sex acts." Helms explained that "I do not propose that Congress 'censor' artists. I do propose that Congress put an end to the use of federal funds to support outrageous 'art' that is clearly designed to poison our culture."[51]

Congress appointed an independent commission to make recommendations about possible "content restrictions" governing future funding decisions of the NEA. The commission concluded that the government may not choose those artists "to be funded—and, often more important, those *not* to be funded—in a manner which punishes what Congress views as 'dangerous content.'" The commission therefore recommended "against legislative changes to impose specific restrictions on the content of works of art supported by the Endowment."[52]

In the face of these recommendations, the Helms proposal went down to defeat, but in its stead Congress enacted legislation directing the NEA, in establishing procedures to judge the artistic merit of grant applications, to "tak[e] into consideration general standards of decency and respect for the diverse beliefs and values of the American public."[53]

SOON THEREAFTER, NEA Chairman John Frohnmayer, who had been appointed by President George H. W. Bush, blocked a series of grants that had been recommended by an NEA advisory panel to support the work of four performance artists, including Karen Finley. Finley was well known in the late 1980s for her use of food, nudity, music, and discourse on stage to address such issues as incest, rape, domination, the sexualization of women, violence, and AIDS. One commentator described Finley's performances as "mainly centered around the oppression of women and resultant feelings of rage and self-loathing, but also addressed sexual repression, domestic abuse, homosexuality, and other taboo subjects." Finley's performances were "confrontational, provocative, often scatological, and left no room for neutrality."[54] Finley and the three other performance

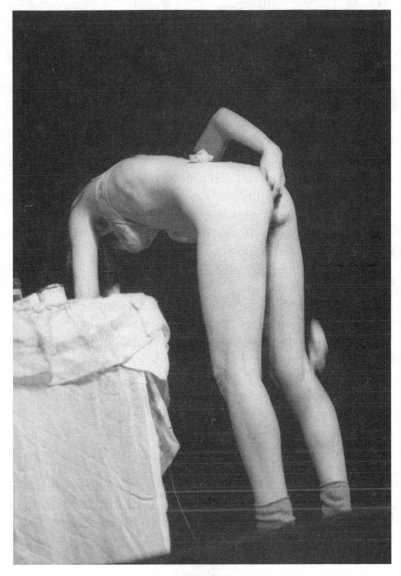

Karen Finley

artists who had also been denied NEA funding, John Fleck, Holly Hughes, and Tim Miller, all of whose work also dealt with issues of sexuality and homophobia, challenged the denial of their grants on the ground that the new "general standards of decency" provision, on which the decision was based, violated the First Amendment.[55]

. . .

IN 1998, in *National Endowment for the Arts v. Finley*,[56] the Supreme Court rejected the claim that the new provision was unconstitutional. Justice Sandra Day O'Connor, the first woman to serve on the Court and a generally cautious and moderate justice, authored the opinion of the Court. The artists maintained that for the NEA even to consider "general standards of decency" in making grants was a classic example of impermissible viewpoint discrimination. Justice O'Connor, however, accepted the NEA's characterization that the challenged provision was "merely hortatory" and did not preclude awards to projects that might be thought to be "indecent." O'Connor therefore concluded that the mere consideration of "general standards of decency" as one factor among many did not mandate or authorize anything like "invidious viewpoint discrimination."[57]

By writing a very narrow opinion in *Finley*, O'Connor left many questions unanswered. Most obviously, suppose Congress had enacted Jesse Helms's proposal and had forbidden the NEA to fund any artist whose work depicts "homoeroticism." Would such a restriction be a permissible restriction, analogous to a program that authorized a government funding agency to support only works of art dealing with science or history, or would it more properly be understood as an impermissible viewpoint-based restriction? That issue remains unresolved to this day.

WHAT HAVE WE WROUGHT?

SO, WHERE DOES this leave us? Compared to the 1950s, when any depiction of sex in books, movies, or magazines was tightly constrained, we are now inundated with all sorts of sexually-explicit material. We have gone from a world in which an airbrushed photograph of a partially naked woman was forbidden even to consenting adults, to one in which consenting adults can see pretty much anything and everything they can possibly imagine on the Internet. From the standpoint of free speech, we have seen a revolution in the realm of sexual expression. Even the Framers, who were much more open to sexuality than their descendants who lived under the thumb of Anthony Comstock, would be stunned.

The restrictions that now exist are quite specific and limited. First, there remains a strong presumption in favor of protecting unconsenting adults and children when they are out in public. Despite the decisions in *Cohen* and *Erznoznik*, which limited the authority of government to shield unconsenting adults and children from sexually-explicit expression in public, it remains the case that when we are out in public we are largely free from unwanted exposure to anything but relatively modest sexual expression.

Second, the government can constitutionally prohibit the sale or exhibition to children of material that is obscene for minors, but only if it can do so without significantly interfering with the First Amendment rights of adults.

Third, sexual expression on radio and on broadcast television (CBS, NBC, ABC, PBS, and many local stations) is sharply constrained by the combination of FCC regulation and *Pacifica*. Although cable television and the Internet provide virtually unlimited access to sexual expression, the traditional broadcast media remain a relatively safe harbor for those who prefer not to encounter such expression. The question for the future is whether the Court will continue to adhere to *Pacifica*, or whether it will at some point hold that there is no longer any principled justification for treating the broadcast media differently from all other forms of communication.

Fourth, the government can constitutionally prohibit the production, distribution, and possession of child pornography. Simulated child pornography, however, is protected by the First Amendment.

Finally, the government itself can generally decline to subsidize sexually-explicit expression in its schools, libraries, museums, and arts programs, as long as it makes reasonable, viewpoint-neutral judgments, based on limited resources, about what speech it wants to promote. This is most evident, for example, when the government decides which books to purchase for a public library, which films or plays to present in a public theater, and which types of art to support in a public arts funding program.

A LTHOUGH WE have not embraced the constitutional position advanced by Justices Hugo Black and William Douglas in *Roth*, which would have accorded sexual expression precisely the same First Amendment protection as other speech, much of the sexual material available to consenting adults today is far more explicit than anything that they ever imagined. But has this triumph of free speech—and the consequent rejection of Comstockery—been good for the nation? That is a more complex question. On the one hand, a fundamental precept of American constitutional law is that, all things considered, the freedom of speech is a positive good. As a matter of first principles, the Constitution denies government the authority to decide for the American people what speech—what ideas, what values, what facts, what opinions, what images—they will be allowed to express or consider or hear or view.

Those who would suppress sexual expression, however, have always insisted that such speech is different. The Framers of the First Amendment, they argue, never imagined—or intended—that the Constitution would protect a three-minute video of three naked people engaging in fellatio, cunnilingus, and anal sex. How, the critics ask, does such speech promote the values of the First Amendment and how does its availability make this a better society?

On the positive side, many Americans believe that it is a good thing that we now have a remarkably "robust, uninhibited and wide-open" freedom of sexual expression. Like Justices Black and Douglas, they would argue that there was *never* a legitimate constitutional justification for treating sexual expression as less "valuable" than other forms of expression. The very notion that sexual expression is entitled to less constitutional protection than other types of speech, they would argue, was bogus from the beginning.

Neither Anthony Comstock, nor William Brennan, nor Jesse Helms, they would argue, has ever offered a *principled* justification for according sexual expression less than full constitutional protection. In the end, they would argue, the rationale for that notion rests on nothing more than the view that such speech makes some people squeamish, that it is "immoral," that it leads people to have "wrong" values, to accept "bad" ideas, and to engage in "impure" and "sinful" behavior. Fundamentally, they would argue, the rationale for forbidding obscenity is rooted in particular religious beliefs. That sort of rationale for suppressing free speech, they would argue, is *precisely* what the First Amendment was designed to prevent.

B UT WHAT of the consequences of greater freedom of sexual expression? Are they good or bad? On one side of this question there is, of course, the principle of freedom of speech. In some sense, in terms of individual liberty, the more freedom of expression, the better. But freedom of expression is not merely a principle. It has consequences, some of which presumably are positive.

The greater availability of sexual expression, for example, enhances the ability of individuals to understand and to satisfy their own sexual needs and desires; gives them a much richer exposure to unconventional forms of artistic excellence; entertains, amuses, enlightens, and excites; enables individuals to learn more about sex and its many varied possibilities, opening up their imaginations to new and different and rewarding experiences; deepens their understanding of the health and safety aspects of various forms of sexual behavior; enables people to understand better what many will find to be the surprising (and perhaps shocking) nature of other people's sexual inclinations, needs, desires, and behaviors, perhaps changing their own views of their fellow citizens; enables them to improve their own sexual "performance" in ways that add new spark to flagging marriages; and so on. All of this, in varying degrees and for different individuals, captures at least some of the potential individual and social benefits of a much broader freedom of sexual expression.

What, though, of the other side of the question? What are the *negative* consequences of greater freedom of sexual expression? As the two presidential commissions on obscenity clearly demonstrated, it is difficult, if not impossible, to ascertain with any certainty the precise costs of sexual expression. Those who oppose and are appalled by the current freedom of sexual expression insist that this state of affairs harms adults, children, families, and society in general. These harms, they insist, go well beyond the bare proposition that sexual explicitness is immoral.

Some researchers suggest that the increasing availability of ever more hard-core forms of sexual expression has negative as well as positive consequences. Although the findings are tentative, and although exposure to such expression "does not affect all individuals in the same way," several significant harms are said to be associated with the current availability of sexual expression.* There is evidence, for example, that continued exposure to sexual imagery can cause in some users compulsive and obsessive behaviors that at least some clinical and psychological researchers analogize to behavioral addiction. As with gambling, there is some evidence that obsessive pornography viewing can have "negative consequences to a person's functioning in his or her work or relationships."[58]

Other researchers assert that the proliferation of certain kinds of sexual messages and imagery "can cause particular harm to women, be they girlfriends or wives of consumers, or consumers themselves," by shaping "cultural expectations about female sexual behavior" in ways that enshrine "relationships based on disrespect, detachment, promiscuity, and, often, abuse."[59] By changing people's understanding of what is "normal," "acceptable," and "ordinary" sexual behavior, exposure to such expression can change their sexual expectations. To the extent this merely opens up new horizons, it can be quite positive. But to the extent it creates expectations

---

* It is important to note that there is no consensus within the scientific community about the actual consequences of even sustained exposure to sexually-explicit material. Researchers are divided on the question.

that people should engage in sexual behavior that is abusive, degrading, violent, or dangerous, it can lead to dysfunctional and harmful consequences.

There is also evidence of a correlation between continued exposure to sexually-explicit expression and marital discord. Surveys suggest that husbands or wives* who spend significant amounts of time viewing sexually-explicit material on the Internet are more likely to have extramarital affairs and more likely to divorce than those who do not engage in that behavior. Whether it is the exposure to sexual material that causes the infidelity and divorce, or the unhappiness of the marriage that causes individuals to turn to sexually-explicit material on the Internet, remains an open question. But the evidence suggests that there is at least to some degree a relationship between sustained exposure to sexual imagery and marital dysfunction.[60]

Finally, there is the alleged harm to children caused by their exposure to sexual expression. There is no doubt that minors are far more likely to encounter sexually-explicit images today than ever before in American history.† Studies have found, for example, that 45 percent of teenagers report having friends who regularly view sexually-explicit material on the Internet and that as many as 70 percent of teenagers have accidentally stumbled across such material.

Whether such exposure is actually "harmful" to minors, however, is another question. One study found that 23 percent of minors who inadvertently came across such material on the Internet were "extremely" or "very upset" by the incident. Some minors, like some adults, no doubt become obsessed with viewing such material, and others no doubt mimic their sexual expectations and behaviors on what they see on the Internet.

It has been reported, for example, that female adolescents are now more likely to tolerate "emotional, physical, and sexual abuse in dating relationships" because they increasingly see such conduct both normalized and "eroticized in pornography." Research also suggests that there is a correlation between teenagers viewing sexual imagery online and engaging in oral and anal sex, and that both adolescent boys and girls who regularly view such material online are more inclined to view women as sexual objects.

---

* Studies suggest that women now represent as much as 30 percent of all Internet consumption of sexual expression, and that 31 percent of college-age women and 87 percent of college-age men now view such material.

† We should not exaggerate this point, though. Historically, most children grew up in homes with little privacy for their parents' sexual behavior and on farms where they were routinely exposed to the reproductive activities of horses, cows, pigs, and chickens. In that environment, sex was not nearly as invisible as it is in most homes today.

This might in turn have triggered some of the apparent increase in recent years in sexual harassment and sexual assault on college campuses.[61]

W HAT ARE we to make of these concerns? The first and perhaps most important point is that free speech *always* comes at a cost. Speech that questions the wisdom of fighting a war may cause soldiers to desert, incite agitators to blow up troop trains, demoralize citizens, and embolden the enemy. Speech that defends the morality of abortion may encourage women to engage in what others regard as immoral "baby-killing." Religious condemnation of homosexuality as a sin can incite prejudice, discrimination, and violence against gays and lesbians, and can inflict serious emotional harm on minors who have discovered themselves to be homosexual. News reports, movies, and television shows depicting real or imagined murders, rapes, bombings, school shootings, terrorist attacks, genocide, earthquakes, floods, and alien invasions can strike terror into the hearts of children. Advocacy that women should be sexually "pure and innocent" and that "a woman's place is in the home" can reinforce attitudes that limit women's freedom and cause them to be treated as weak, frail, and inferior. And on and on and on.

The central insight of the First Amendment is that speech cannot constitutionally be censored or suppressed merely because it has harmful consequences. Except in unusual circumstances,* the general rule embraced by the Supreme Court is that government cannot constitutionally prohibit speech because its message might cause harm unless it can convincingly demonstrate that the speech creates a clear and present danger of grave harm to the nation.[62]

As Louis Brandeis, one of the most insightful and eloquent justices ever to serve on the Supreme Court, explained in 1927 in his brilliant concurring opinion in *Whitney v. California,* "Those who won our independence believed that the final end of the State was to make men free to develop their faculties." They "valued liberty both as an end and as a means," and they "believed liberty to be the secret of happiness and courage to be the secret of liberty." Although they "recognized the risks to which all human institutions are subject," they "knew that order cannot be secured" through suppression and that "the path of safety lies in the opportunity to discuss

---

* One such circumstance, as we have seen, is when a particular category of expression, such as obscenity, is deemed to have only "low" First Amendment value.

freely" those ideas and values about which we may disagree. The "fitting remedy for evil counsels," he observed, is not suppression, but "good ones."

Thus, Brandeis reasoned, "fear of serious injury cannot alone justify suppression of free speech. . . . Men feared witches and burnt women. It is the function of free speech to free men from the bondage of irrational fears." So long as "there be time to expose through discussion the falsehood and fallacies" of the speech we loathe, and so long as there be time "to avert the evil by the processes of education, the remedy to be applied is more speech, not enforced silence." If freedom is to be preserved, Brandeis insisted, "only an emergency can justify repression."[63]

THIS DOES not mean that we cannot mitigate what we perceive to be the negative consequences of sexually-explicit expression. But as Brandeis explained, the primary remedy for potentially harmful speech is not suppression, but counter-speech that informs and educates people about the perceived dangers. To the extent that critics see sexually-explicit speech as akin to cigarettes, alcohol, and gambling in its capacity to overwhelm the individual's will, the proper response is to warn people about the dangers of abuse and to help those who succumb to temptation. To the extent that they fear that such expression can warp people's values, the proper response is to educate them about the "right" values and expectations. Of course, there is no guarantee that such efforts will carry the day. In the end, some of us will simply disagree with what others believe to be the "right" values to live by. In a free society, that is our right.

THE ISSUE is more complicated with respect to children because they do not have the same capacity to make responsible judgments for themselves about right and wrong. In part for that reason, the Court has continued to adhere to the doctrine that some sexually-explicit material is obscene for children, even though it is constitutionally protected for adults. In practical effect, though, it is difficult, if not impossible, to shield children in today's world from exposure to sexually-explicit expression.

The primary remedy therefore rests largely in the hands of parents. By using filters on home computers, by speaking with their children about the possibility that they might encounter sexually-explicit expression, by talking with them after they do encounter such material, by guiding them in what they believe to be "best" ways to think about intimacy and sex, and by educating themselves about the best ways to manage their parental responsibilities, parents can create a reasonably safe environment for their children.

In truth, this is no different from the trust we place in parents more generally. In almost all ways, we rely upon parents to educate their children about possible dangers. In everything from crossing streets to playing near the water to choosing friends to walking alone at night to eating right to smoking and drinking and drugs, we rely upon parents to protect their children from harm. The same is true today in terms of protecting children from the harm caused by exposure to sexually-explicit expression. Of course, not all parents are good at meeting this responsibility, and the challenge might be even greater today than in the past, now that both parents often work. But when all is said and done, in no area of life do we prohibit adults from doing something in order to prevent children from doing it. The same principle now applies to sexual expression.

Perhaps ironically, we are where we are today not only because citizens voted to make some of this material legal, not only because judges held that the Constitution protects some of this material, but also because technology overwhelmed the capacity of the law to constrain our freedom. The challenge for the future is to make the best of it.

PART V

JUDGES

*Reproductive Freedom
and the
Constitution*

15

THE CONSTITUTION
AND CONTRACEPTION

*Estelle Griswold, "A Right of Privacy Older Than the Bill of
Rights,"* Griswold v. Connecticut *(1965)*

B Y THE LATE 1930S, a substantial majority of Americans had come to support the legalization of contraceptives. But because of strong religious opposition, it was next to impossible to repeal the Comstock-era laws prohibiting their sale or distribution. During and after World War II, as young women increasingly entered both college and the workforce, family planning came to be seen as ever more essential to the changing nature of the family and to women's lives. Although Americans often found ways to obtain various forms of birth control, the nineteenth-century statutes remained on the books, the more reliable methods of contraception were therefore often inaccessible, and access to these methods was especially difficult for poor and unmarried women.*[1]

Throughout the 1950s and '60s, the public became ever more supportive of legalizing birth control, and most states, especially those without large Catholic populations, finally either repealed or at least modified their Comstock-era prohibitions. A significant impetus for this change in public opinion was the rising concern about overpopulation. The fear was that with a rapidly growing population, there would not be sufficient resources to maintain the nation's and the world's standard

---

* At this time, the most common methods of birth control were condoms, diaphragms, spermicidal suppositories, vaginal sponges, cervical caps, intrauterine devices, coitus interruptus, the rhythm method, and abortion. In 1951, Gregory Goodwin Pincus, an American biologist, urged G. D. Searle, a pharmaceutical manufacturer, to explore the possibility of developing an oral contraceptive using the progesterone hormone. Nine years later, the federal Food and Drug Administration approved the use of "the pill," if prescribed by a physician and legal under state law.

of living. In his widely read bestseller, *The Population Bomb*, the Stanford biologist Paul Ehrlich warned that uncontrolled population growth threatened "to create an explosion as disruptive and dangerous as the explosion of the atom and with as much influence on prospects for progress or disaster, war or peace."[2]

Increasingly, biologists, economists, and other experts cautioned that overpopulation could be "a precipitating factor in war, famine, resource exhaustion, pollution, and many of the world's ills."[3] In 1957, Margaret Sanger, still a major force at the age of seventy-seven, and no longer being jailed for her views, organized a population control conference in Washington, D.C., to support the International Planned Parenthood Federation, which directly linked the growing concern with overpopulation to the right to use contraceptives. Controlling the size of one's family thus became not only a matter of personal self-interest, but an ethical imperative.[4]

Many Protestant denominations for the first time announced their support for birth control. At the Methodist Church's 1956 General Conference, for example, the Church unanimously approved birth control, and the Council for Christian Social Action of the United Church of Christ declared in 1960 that "responsible family planning is today a clear moral duty" and that "public law and public institutions should sanction the distribution through authorized channels of reliable information and contraceptive devices."[5]

The Catholic Church, however, was of a different mind. In 1930, Pope Pius XI had issued an encyclical denouncing those who would separate sex from reproduction and declaring that "any use whatsoever of matrimony exercised in such a way that the act is deliberately frustrated in its natural power to generate life is an offense against the law of God and of nature, and those who indulge in such are branded with the guilt of a grave sin."[6]

Three decades later, a pontifical study commission, appointed to consider the question of contraception, acknowledged that "the regulation of conception appears necessary for many couples who wish to achieve a responsible, open and reasonable parenthood" and recommended that contraception should be deemed permissible in aid of "responsible parenthood." But in 1968, Pope Paul VI, who deeply admired Pius XI and shared his conservative views on reproduction, rejected this recommendation, reaffirming in no uncertain terms that "any action which either before, at the moment of, or after sexual intercourse, is specifically intended to prevent procreation" is "absolutely excluded." The Pope appealed to the leaders of all nations to oppose any action "which would introduce into the family those practices which are opposed to the natural law of God."*[7]

Not surprisingly, in those states with large Catholic populations legislators refused to amend their nineteenth-century laws. With the laws in those states effectively frozen in place, it seemed increasingly likely that some sort of constitutional challenge was on the horizon.[8]

B UT WHAT would be the constitutional basis for such a challenge? The Constitution guarantees the freedom of speech, the freedom of religion, the freedom from unreasonable searches and seizures, the freedom from cruel and unusual punishment, and the right to equal protection of the laws, but nowhere does it say anything about the right to use contraceptives. How, then, could there be such a right?

The question was not without precedent. In fact, the Court had on several occasions recognized the existence of other "unenumerated" rights. These were rights that, although not expressly guaranteed in the text, were nonetheless held to be *implicitly* protected by the Constitution. There are several possible textual sources for the recognition of such rights. The Ninth Amendment, for example, provides that "the enumeration in the Constitution, of certain rights, shall not be construed to deny or disparage others retained by the people." This certainly implied the existence of unenumerated rights.[†]

In addition, the Due Process Clauses of the Fifth and Fourteenth Amendments provide that no person shall be deprived "of life, liberty, or property without due process of law." Although this language might seem at first blush to guarantee only "procedural" rights, the Court had long held that these clauses guarantee "substantive" rights as well. As the Supreme Court explained in 1923 in *Meyer v. Nebraska*, the "liberty" guaranteed by the Due Process Clause "denotes not merely freedom from bodily restraint but also the right of the individual . . . to marry, establish a home and bring up children, . . . and generally to enjoy those privileges

---

* This position was not particularly popular with American Catholics. By this time, a majority of Catholics in the United States supported the use of contraception, and the day after the release of the Pope's encyclical some six hundred Catholic theologians issued a statement expressing a dissenting position. "Married couples," they maintained, "may responsibly decide according to their own conscience that artificial contraception in some circumstances is permissible and indeed necessary to preserve and foster the value and sacredness of marriage."

† The adoption of the Ninth Amendment is discussed in chapter 6.

long recognized . . . as essential to the orderly pursuit of happiness by free men."*[9]

In light of that principle, suppose a state enacts a law making it a crime for any person to have more than two children. Is such a law constitutional because no provision of the Constitution expressly guarantees the right to have more than two children? Or, suppose a state enacts a law making it a crime for any person, including married couples, to have sex more than once a month. Is such a law constitutional because no provision of the Constitution expressly guarantees such a right? Or suppose a state adopts a law forbidding divorced people to remarry? Is such a law constitutional because no provision of the Constitution expressly guarantees the right to marry?

Are some rights so obvious and so fundamental that they are protected by the Constitution even though the Framers did not expressly include them in the Bill of Rights? If such unenumerated rights exist, how are judges to know what they are? And if such rights exist, is the right to use contraceptives in order to prevent unwanted pregnancies one of them? That was the question.

GETTING TO GRISWOLD

CONNECTICUT'S COMSTOCK ACT, which had been enacted at the height of the late nineteenth century's moralistic crusade, made it a crime for any person to use "any drug, medicinal article or instrument for the purpose of preventing conception," or to assist, counsel, or aid any person in the use of "any drug, medicinal article or instrument for the purpose of preventing contraception."[10] The law went so far as to forbid doctors to give medically-necessary contraceptive advice to married couples.

Between 1923 and 1962, twenty-nine bills were introduced in the Connecticut legislature in a futile effort to repeal or at least to amend the statute. In every instance, the bill went down to defeat at the hands of the Democratic majority, which was heavily Catholic. As one commentator observed, the Connecticut anti-contraceptive law "was protected from repeal by the local power of the Catholic Church, to the detriment of those who did not share

---

* In the first quarter of the twentieth century the Court invoked substantive due process to protect a wide variety of unenumerated rights. See, e.g., *Lochner v. New York*, 198 U.S. 45 (1905) (liberty of contract); *Meyer v. Nebraska*, 262 U.S. 390 (1923) (right to learn a foreign language); *Pierce v. Society of Sisters*, 268 U.S. 510 (1925) (right to send children to private school).

the Church's views on the issue. As such, it was special interest legislation, with a nagging establishment of religion undertone."[11]

On November 1, 1961, in direct defiance of the Connecticut law, Estelle Griswold, the executive director of the Planned Parenthood League of Connecticut, and Charles Lee Buxton, a physician and professor at the Yale University Medical School, defiantly opened a birth control clinic in New Haven with the goal of providing unlawful birth control advice and contraceptives to married women. Griswold and Buxton were promptly arrested, tried, and convicted for violating the Connecticut law. They maintained that the statute was unconstitutional. The state courts rejected the argument out of hand, concluding that nothing in the Constitution guarantees a right to distribute or to use contraceptives.[12]

In a groundbreaking decision, the Supreme Court of the United States held in *Griswold v. Connecticut*[13] that the Connecticut statute violated the United States Constitution.

T HE SUPREME COURT had addressed related issues in the past. In *Buck v. Bell*,[14] for example, the Court confronted the question of compelled sterilization. Carrie Buck, "a feeble-minded white woman," was committed to the Virginia State Colony for Epileptics and Feebleminded. Buck was the daughter of a feebleminded mother in the same institution, and the mother of an illegitimate feebleminded child. In 1924, when she was eighteen years old, she was ordered to be sterilized under the authority of a Virginia statute authorizing the sterilization of "defective" individuals with "hereditary" mental conditions who could "safely" be discharged from confinement only if they were incapable of having offspring.*

The question presented to the Supreme Court was whether such compelled sterilization violated the Constitution. In an opinion by Justice Oliver Wendell Holmes, the Court rejected Buck's claim that her compulsory sterilization violated her right not to be deprived of "liberty . . . without due process of law." In light of the state's findings that Buck was "the probable potential parent of socially inadequate offspring, likewise afflicted," that she could "be sexually sterilized without detriment to her general health," and that "her welfare and that of society" would be "promoted by her steriliza-

---

* Many scholars believe that Buck was not "feebleminded" but, like many women at the time, was deemed such because she was guilty of promiscuity for having a child out of wedlock.

tion," the Court held that there could be no constitutional objection to the procedure.

In dismissing Carrie Buck's argument, Holmes analogized compulsory sterilization to compulsory vaccination, the constitutionality of which the Court had upheld twenty years earlier in *Jacobson v. Massachusetts*.[15] Holmes reasoned that if the state can compel an individual to be vaccinated in order to prevent the spread of smallpox, then it can also compel an individual to be sterilized to prevent the spread of "imbeciles." "Three generations of imbeciles," Holmes concluded, "are enough."*[16]

T HE SUPREME COURT next confronted the issue of compelled sterilization in its 1942 decision in *Skinner v. Oklahoma*.[17] By this time, in light of events in Nazi Germany, government-compelled sterilization was viewed with greater concern. *Skinner* involved the constitutionality of Oklahoma's Habitual Criminal Sterilization Act, which defined as a "habitual criminal" any person who was convicted three or more times of felonies "involving moral turpitude." The Act, which was a eugenics measure designed to weed habitual criminals out of the gene pool, provided that such persons could be sterilized upon a jury finding that they could "be rendered sexually sterile without detriment" to their general health. The Act specified that certain felonies, such as embezzlement and "political offenses," were not to be considered crimes of moral turpitude.[18]

Jack T. Skinner, a resident of one of the most impoverished Dust Bowl states in the nation, was convicted in 1926 for stealing chickens, and then in 1929 and 1934 for robbery with firearms. The Oklahoma attorney general instituted proceedings to have Skinner sterilized. Skinner maintained that such compulsory sterilization violated his rights under the Constitution. The Supreme Court unanimously agreed.

Justice William O. Douglas authored the opinion of the Court. A brilliant, but often idiosyncratic, jurist, and a committed civil libertarian, Douglas had been appointed to the Court by President Franklin Roosevelt three years earlier at the age of forty, making him one of the youngest justices in American history. Throughout his career, Douglas was a power-

---

* Before *Buck* reached the Supreme Court, most lower courts had found such laws unconstitutional. In time, Holmes's opinion in *Buck* would come to be regarded as one of his greatest failures as a justice.

ful voice for individual freedom, as illustrated by his stance on the issue of obscenity.

Douglas began his opinion in *Skinner* by noting that "this case touches a sensitive and important area of human rights" because Oklahoma deprives certain individuals of a right which is "basic to the perpetuation of a race— the right to have offspring." Douglas reasoned that the Oklahoma statute violated the Equal Protection Clause of the Fourteenth Amendment* because its classification of crimes as either manifesting or not manifesting "moral turpitude" made little sense. As Douglas observed, a person who

Justice William O. Douglas

---

* "No State shall . . . deny to any person . . . the equal protection of the laws."

stole chickens three times could be sterilized under the law, but a person who embezzled three times or who accepted political bribes three times could not be sterilized. Although conceding that states generally have broad latitude to treat different crimes differently in terms of sentencing, Douglas insisted that this case was different because compulsory sterilization infringes on "one of the basic civil rights of man." Marriage and procreation, he observed, "are fundamental to the very existence and survival of the race," and if the state exercises the power to sterilize "there is no redemption for the individual whom the law touches." Such an individual has suffered an "irreparable" injury and "is forever deprived of a basic liberty."[19]

Douglas explained that because the law created an inequality among individuals that affected this fundamental liberty, the distinctions embedded in the statute could not be upheld merely because they might be "rational." Although this was the usual standard under the Equal Protection Clause for reviewing the constitutionality of laws treating some criminal offenses differently than others, Douglas concluded that in this case the challenged law must be subjected to "strict scrutiny" because the specific penalty imposed touched upon a fundamental right.[20] Thus, in *Skinner*, the Court held for the first time that laws that infringe the implied fundamental right to procreate are especially problematic under the Constitution.

NINETEEN YEARS later, in *Poe v. Ullman*,[21] which was decided in 1961, several plaintiffs brought a test case to challenge the constitutionality of the same Connecticut statute that would later confront the Court in *Griswold*. Pauline Poe, a married woman with no children, had had three consecutive pregnancies ending in infants with multiple congenital abnormalities from which each had died shortly after birth. A well-regarded physician in Connecticut advised Mr. and Mrs. Poe that the cause of the infants' abnormalities was genetic and that any further pregnancies would likely end the same way. The physician advised them to use contraception, but because of the Connecticut law he could not recommend or prescribe any contraceptive device or medication. Mr. and Mrs. Poe and their physician sued the Connecticut attorney general to challenge the constitutionality of the law.[22]

When the case reached the Supreme Court, the Court decided not to decide the case. In the view of Justice Felix Frankfurter, who wrote the lead opinion, because none of the individuals involved had actually been prosecuted for violating the Connecticut statute, there was no dispute to be resolved. The Court therefore dismissed the case without reaching the merits of the claim.

What is memorable about *Poe* is not the Court's disposition of the case, but the fact that all three justices who reached the merits of the issue concluded that the Comstock-era law could not be squared with the Constitution. In reaching this conclusion, Justice John Marshall Harlan, an always thoughtful and moderately conservative justice appointed by President Dwight Eisenhower, began by observing that a statute making it a criminal offense for married couples to use contraceptives is "an intolerable and unjustifiable invasion of privacy in the conduct of the most intimate concerns of an individual's personal life." The Constitution, he reasoned, protects not only those rights that are expressly specified in the Constitution, but all "rights 'which are . . . *fundamental;* which belong . . . to the citizens of all free governments.'"[23]

Harlan then maintained that because the Connecticut statute deprived individuals of "a substantial measure of liberty in carrying on the most intimate of all personal relationships," the state could not constitutionally defend the law on the mere ground that it promoted "the moral welfare of its citizenry." Rather, invoking *Skinner*, Harlan insisted that when a law intrudes so deeply into "a most fundamental aspect of 'liberty,'" it must be deemed unconstitutional unless the state can demonstrate that the law is necessary to further a compelling state interest. Under that standard, Harlan concluded that the Connecticut statute was clearly invalid.[*][24]

THE RIGHT TO "MARITAL PRIVACY"

THIS, THEN, WAS the background to *Griswold*. It was to avoid the outcome in *Poe* that Estelle Griswold openly established the Planned Parenthood clinic, arranged for contraceptives to be publicly dispensed to married couples, and intentionally invited her arrest, prosecution, and conviction. Because the Supreme Court now had an actual conviction before it, it could not evade the constitutional issue.[25] In a landmark seven-to-two decision, the justices held the Connecticut anti-contraception law unconstitutional as applied to married couples.

Justice Douglas, who had authored the decision in *Skinner* more than two decades earlier, and who had once explained his judicial philosophy by

---

* Justices William Douglas and Potter Stewart also dissented.

asserting that the Constitution "was designed to take the government off the backs of the people," wrote the opinion of the Court. Douglas began by conceding that the Supreme Court does "not sit as a super-legislature to determine the wisdom, need, and propriety of laws." But this case, he maintained, was different, because the Connecticut law "operates directly on an intimate relation of husband and wife."

Douglas observed that over the years, the Court had often protected constitutional rights that were not expressly mentioned in the Constitution, including the right of association, the right to educate a child in a school of the parents' choice, the right to study a foreign language, the right to read, and the freedom of thought.[26] Douglas reasoned that, as those decisions implied, the "specific guarantees in the Bill of Rights have penumbras, formed by emanations from those guarantees that help give them life and substance." Moreover, he added, many of those guarantees are designed to safeguard the most fundamental "privacies of life." This understanding of the Constitution, he argued, was "evident in the text of the Ninth Amendment."

Douglas therefore concluded that the Connecticut law, by invading the most private intimacies of the marriage relationship, infringed "a right of privacy older than the Bill of Rights." Without deciding whether the state could constitutionally regulate the manufacture or sale of contraceptives generally, or could prohibit their use by unmarried persons, Douglas held that a law forbidding *married* couples to use contraceptives could not be squared with the constitutional right of marital privacy.[27]

I N AN influential concurring opinion, Justice Arthur Goldberg, joined by Chief Justice Earl Warren and Justice William Brennan, emphasized the importance of the Ninth Amendment. Goldberg explained that the Ninth Amendment was designed to quiet "fears" that a list of specifically enumerated rights might later be interpreted as implying that other rights were not protected by the Constitution. It was therefore adopted in order to make clear that "the Framers did not intend" that the list of specifically enumerated rights should "be construed to exhaust the basic and fundamental rights which the Constitution guaranteed to the people."

Goldberg added that "in determining which rights are fundamental" for purposes of the Ninth Amendment, judges "must look to the 'traditions and [collective] conscience of our people.'" The proper inquiry, he explained, is whether the right involved "is of such a character that it cannot be denied without violating those 'fundamental principles of liberty and justice which lie at the base of all our civil and political institutions.'" Applying this test, Goldberg concluded that "the entire fabric of the Constitution and the purposes that clearly underlie its specific guarantees demonstrate that the rights to marital privacy and to marry and raise a family are of similar order and magnitude as the fundamental rights" that are expressly enumerated in the Constitution.[28]

Justice Hugo Black, joined by Justice Potter Stewart, dissented. On a range of constitutional issues, especially those dealing with the freedom of speech, Black was regarded as a rock-ribbed liberal. But he rooted his liberalism in a strongly literalist interpretation of the Constitution. Thus, he could not agree that "the evil qualities" of the Connecticut law were sufficient to render it unconstitutional. Black chastised the Court for talking "about a constitutional 'right of privacy' as though there is some constitutional provision . . . forbidding any law ever to be passed which might abridge the 'privacy' of individuals," when "there is not." In short, in Black's view, nothing in the text of the Constitution expressly addressed this issue, and that was the end of the matter.[29]

G RISWOLD WAS a daring decision. The Court dismissed the traditional view that a state's moral judgments about sex must override personal interests in marital intimacy. The public response to *Griswold* was quite positive. Even the Catholic leadership was muted in its reaction. The nation's foremost Catholic theologian, John Courtney Murray, wrote a widely read memo to Boston's Richard Cardinal Cushing in which he argued against the Church's position on contraception, and the liberal Catholic magazine *Commonweal* went so far as to praise the *Griswold* decision as "long overdue."[30] According to a Gallup poll taken shortly after the decision, more than 80 percent of all Americans, and 78 percent of all Catholics, now supported the wider availability of birth control.

At the same time, the "sexual revolution" of the 1960s reinforced the argument that access to contraception was an essential component of the "right" to sexual freedom, and the rise of the women's movement made the availability of contraceptives more than ever an issue of women's rights. In increasing numbers, women now claimed reproductive control as a fundamental right, as they vigorously entered the public discourse to share their stories, condemn what they saw as their sexual oppression, and demand social and legal change.[31]

Growing public support for the legalization of contraceptives emboldened legislators in several states to reconsider their Comstock-era laws. New York, Ohio, Minnesota, and Missouri, for example, repealed their laws prohibiting the sale or distribution of contraceptives. Efforts to overturn the federal Comstock law repeatedly failed in Congress, however, until Republican Senator George H. W. Bush introduced a bill in 1969, twenty years before he became president, to remove contraceptives and information about contraceptives from the 1873 law. The federal repeal bill was finally signed into law by President Richard Nixon on January 8, 1971.[32]

A central question posed by some of these liberalizing laws was whether contraceptives should be legal not only for married couples, but for *unmarried* persons as well. Opponents of extending access to contraceptives to unmarried persons insisted that such a policy would encourage premarital sex, extramarital sex, and other forms of immoral behavior. From a constitutional perspective, this posed an interesting dilemma. The constitutional right that the Supreme Court had recognized in *Griswold* was grounded in the privacy of the marriage relation. By definition, that right did not extend to unmarried individuals. How the Supreme Court would resolve that issue was an open—and potentially perplexing—question.[33]

WHETHER "TO BEAR OR BEGET A CHILD"

IN 1879, MASSACHUSETTS enacted its version of the Comstock Act, making it a crime for any person to sell, distribute, or give away any drug, medicine, instrument, or device "for the prevention of conception."[34] For decades, birth control supporters attempted to persuade the Massachusetts legislature to repeal or at least amend this law, but their efforts were always in vain. Massachusetts was a heavily Catholic state, and elected officials were not about to buck the Church.

After the Supreme Court's decision in *Griswold*, however, and after a prolonged legislative and political battle, Massachusetts finally repealed its Comstock-era law and enacted a new "reform" statute that allowed married persons to obtain contraceptives. The new law still made it a felony, however, punishable by up to five years in prison, for any person, including a licensed physician or pharmacist, to sell, prescribe, give away, or distribute "any drug, medicine, instrument or article whatever for the prevention of conception" to any *unmarried* person.[35]

The new law was a hard-bought compromise that was grudgingly accepted by the state's Catholic leaders only because it forbade any distribution of contraceptives to unmarried persons. But that compromise was not good enough for those who believed that the right to use contraceptives should be extended to unmarried as well as married persons.[36]

BILL BAIRD was a pioneer in the battle for reproductive rights. He was jailed eight times in five states in the 1960s for lecturing on birth control. His advocacy on behalf of reproductive rights began in 1963 when, as a medical student, he witnessed the tragic and bloody death of an unmarried African American mother of nine children who died of a self-inflicted coat hanger abortion while staggering into Harlem Hospital for help. When he spoke on the subject of reproductive freedom, he usually gave away birth control samples to his listeners. He was arrested for these activities in Massachusetts, New York, New Jersey, Virginia, and Wisconsin. In 1967, students at Boston University petitioned Baird to challenge Massachusetts's new law, because it made it a crime for unmarried persons to obtain contraceptives.

Bill Baird

On April 6, 1967, Baird, who had dropped out of medical school because he couldn't afford to stay in school while supporting his three children, gave an hour-long speech at Boston University on the subjects of birth control, abortion, and overpopulation. At the end of the lecture, he gave a woman student a condom and a package of contraceptive foam. Seven Boston police officers who had been assigned to attend the meeting promptly came to the stage and arrested him. Baird was convicted and sentenced to three months in Boston's Charles Street Jail. He maintained that the Massachusetts law was unconstitutional. He persisted in a five-year legal struggle to win his point.[37]

In 1972, in *Eisenstadt v. Baird*,[38] the Supreme Court, in an opinion by Justice William Brennan, the Court's only Catholic justice, reversed Baird's conviction and held the Massachusetts anti-contraception statute unconstitutional. The central question in the case was whether the state could constitutionally treat married and unmarried persons differently in this respect.

The state sought to justify its distinction between married and unmarried persons by arguing that it had a legitimate moral justification for attempting to deter single individuals from engaging in premarital sex. Brennan responded that this purpose was insufficient to justify the statute, because it "would be plainly unreasonable" for Massachusetts to prescribe "pregnancy and the birth of an unwanted child as punishment for fornication."[39]

Brennan acknowledged that the right of privacy the Court had emphasized in *Griswold* was focused on "the marital relationship," but citing both *Stanley v. Georgia** and *Skinner v. Oklahoma*, he declared that "if the right of privacy means anything, it is the right of the individual, married or single, to be free from unwarranted governmental intrusion into matters so fundamentally affecting a person as the decision whether to bear or beget a child." That, the Court held, was the core right at issue in these cases. By treating married and unmarried persons differently with respect to the exercise of that fundamental right, the Massachusetts law violated the Equal Protection Clause. The lone dissenter in *Eisenstadt* was a very frustrated Warren Burger.[40]

---

* The Court held in *Stanley* that the state cannot constitutionally prohibit the private possession of obscene materials in the home, noting that such an intrusion violated the individual's "fundamental . . . right to be free, except in very limited circumstances, from unwanted governmental intrusions into one's privacy." *Stanley v. Georgia*, 394 U.S. 557, 564 (1969). See chapter 12.

. . .

ALTHOUGH *EISENSTADT* was cast as a narrow decision about whether the state could constitutionally discriminate between married and unmarried persons in the distribution and use of contraceptives, what it did in fact was to proclaim the existence of a new fundamental right, hinted at in both *Skinner* and *Griswold*, but brought to life for the first time in *Eisenstadt*: "the right of the individual . . . to be free from unwarranted governmental intrusion into matters so fundamentally affecting a person as the decision whether to bear or beget a child." *Skinner* had dealt with the right *to* bear or beget a child; *Griswold* and *Eisenstadt* dealt with the right *not* to bear or beget a child.

This sentence in *Eisenstadt* was particularly telling, because at the very time Justice Brennan was writing this opinion, the issue of abortion was waiting in the wings. This passage therefore not only crystallized the doctrine arising out of *Skinner*, *Griswold*, and *Eisenstadt*, but also—quite consciously—laid the foundation for the Court's later decision in *Roe v. Wade*,[41] which was argued to the Court on the very morning that Brennan first circulated to the other justices his opinion in *Eisenstadt*.*[42]

SANGER'S TRIUMPH

WHERE DO THESE decisions leave us? Unlike the world of the 1890s, the 1920s, or the 1940s, when it was a crime under state and federal law to sell, distribute, or advertise contraceptive products, today there is a *constitutional right* to purchase, sell, distribute, use, discuss, and advertise contraceptives. This right derives from what the Supreme Court has defined as the fundamental freedom of individuals to decide for themselves, free from undue government interference, "whether to bear or beget a child." This right extends, not only to married couples, but also to unmarried persons and even to minors.

The central question today is no longer whether the adherents of certain

---

* Four years after *Eisenstadt*, the Court in *Carey v. Population Services International*, 431 U.S. 678 (1977), reaffirmed and significantly expanded the constitutional right of individuals to use and obtain contraceptives, holding unconstitutional a law that made it a crime for any person "other than a licensed pharmacist to distribute contraceptives," for any person, including a licensed pharmacist, "to sell or distribute any contraceptive . . . to a minor under the age of 16 years," and for any person, including a licensed pharmacist, "to advertise or display contraceptives."

religious beliefs can enlist the authority of the state to prevent those who do not share their beliefs from deciding for themselves whether to use contraceptives, but whether the government can constitutionally compel religious organizations and employers whose religious beliefs condemn the use of contraceptives to provide contraceptive coverage to their employees.[43] We have, indeed, come a long way. Margaret Sanger would be pleased.

16

THE ROAD TO *ROE*

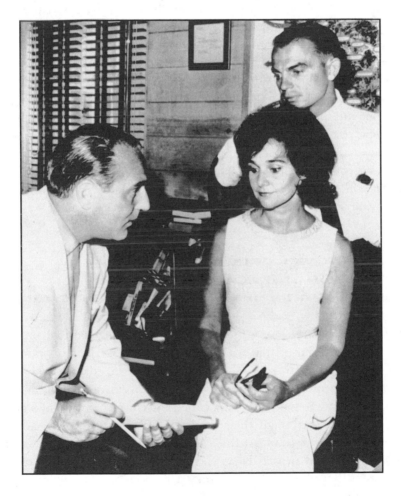

Sherri Finkbine, August 4, 1962

B Y THE EARLY 1960s, abortion had been illegal in the United
States for almost a century. Although a few states allowed abortion when necessary to prevent serious harm to a woman's
health, the vast majority permitted abortion only when necessary to save the woman's life. At this time, approximately eight thousand
women each year were able to obtain legal abortions, whereas approximately one million women resorted each year to illegal abortions.

In short, more than 99 percent of the women who terminated unwanted
pregnancies in the early 1960s were compelled to resort either to potentially dangerous self-abortions or to equally dangerous "back-alley" abortions. Opponents of abortion insisted that the issue was simple: If a woman
doesn't want a baby, she shouldn't "do anything to get pregnant."[1]

THE AMERICAN LAW INSTITUTE,
THE THALIDOMIDE SCARE, AND
THE DARK WORLD OF "BACK-ALLEY" ABORTIONS

BEGINNING IN THE 1950s, some members of the medical profession
began to express frustration with the nation's restrictive abortions laws,
which prevented them from serving the medical needs of their patients
and effectively compelled women to seek illegal, unregulated, and often
unsafe abortions. Some physicians called for change in the laws governing abortion, even though their advocacy of this position risked their
standing in the profession. At this time, those concerned about the issue
of abortion focused primarily on the rights of doctors to have the freedom to treat their patients in what they deemed a professionally responsi-

ble manner, rather than on the rights of women, which were not yet seen as "rights" at all.[2]

Driven in part by the concerns raised by members of the medical community, the American Law Institute (ALI), an independent organization of the nation's most distinguished lawyers, judges, and law professors, endorsed a reform proposal in 1962 as part of its Model Penal Code. The proposal called on states to legalize therapeutic* abortions whenever two or more doctors agreed that there was a "substantial risk that continuance of the pregnancy would gravely impair the physical or mental health of the mother," that "the child would be born with a grave physical or mental defect," or that "the pregnancy resulted from rape, incest, or other felonious intercourse."[3] The ALI's proposal carried considerable weight. Within a few years, twelve states amended their laws to adopt some or all of the ALI's recommendations.[4]

These reforms were driven in part by new medical concerns that first came to light as a result of the 1962 pregnancy of television star Sherri Finkbine, who played "Miss Sherri" on the popular children's show *Romper Room*. To alleviate her morning sickness, Finkbine took medicine containing the drug thalidomide, which her husband had brought back from England. Thereafter, Finkbine read an article that reported that thalidomide caused severe birth defects, including babies born without arms or legs, deafness, defects of the muscles of the eyes and face, severe deformities of the femur and tibia, and malformations of the heart, the bowel, the uterus, and the gallbladder.

Finkbine's doctor in Arizona recommended a therapeutic abortion and the hospital committee approved it. But before the abortion could be performed, Finkbine encouraged a reporter to write an article that would pass on the warning about thalidomide. After the reporter published the story, which mentioned Finkbine by name, the hospital refused to perform the abortion because Arizona law allowed therapeutic abortions only when necessary to save the life of the woman.†

When the public learned about Finkbine's effort to obtain an abortion, she was dismissed from her job and her husband was fired from his position as a high school teacher. Their children were hounded, anonymous death threats poured in by mail and by telephone, and the press swarmed

---

* The term "therapeutic" abortion refers to abortions that are deemed medically justified in order to protect the life or health of the woman.

† I am grateful to Justice Ruth Bader Ginsburg, who, after reading a draft of this chapter, correctly pointed out that I should change the last word of this sentence from "mother" to "woman."

around their home. After several weeks of very public controversy, Fink-bine finally secured a legal abortion in Sweden. The doctor who performed the abortion informed Finkbine and her husband that because of the thalidomide, the fetus had become nothing more than an "abnormal growth."[5]

The incident ignited broad public discussion about the nation's abortion laws. A Gallup poll found that 52 percent of Americans thought Finkbine, who was seen as a role model to children, had done the right thing, 32 percent thought she had done the wrong thing, and 16 percent had no opinion. Some of Finkbine's supporters called for outright repeal of laws prohibiting abortion, while others called for more modest reforms along the lines of the ALI recommendation.[6]

In addition to the thalidomide scare, an epidemic of German measles, known as rubella, spread throughout the United States from 1962 to 1965. Any pregnant woman who caught rubella ran a substantial risk of giving birth to a deformed fetus. The deformities included severe cardiac defects, blindness, deafness, hypospadias, microcephaly, and mental retardation. More than 80,000 pregnant women contracted rubella in these years, the vast majority of whom were denied abortions because of the restrictive laws in their states. In the end, some 15,000 severely deformed babies were born because their mothers were unable to obtain legal abortions.*[7]

SOME OF the approximately one million women who resorted each year to unlawful abortions were fortunate enough—and wealthy enough—to find doctors willing to perform such abortions. The going rate for an illegal abortion performed by a qualified physician was typically in the range of $1,000 to $1,500 (approximately $8,000 to $12,000 in today's dollars).† Most women who could afford to pay a doctor to perform an illegal abortion were married, wealthy, and well connected. Even for them, though, it was frequently difficult to find such physicians. Often, they would have to ask friends whether they "knew anyone who knew anyone," an inquiry that could be quite mortifying. To avoid that humiliation, some women who

---

* In 1969, a vaccine was discovered to prevent the spread of rubella.

† Some physicians, who believed women had a right to control their own bodies and destinies, performed illegal abortions for only a nominal fee. "Dr. S," in New York, for example, performed more than 30,000 illegal abortions during his career for an average fee of only $50 to $100.

could afford to do so, like Sherri Finkbine, left the country to get a legal abortion elsewhere.

The vast majority of women who found themselves facing the dilemma of an unwanted pregnancy could not afford either to leave the country or to pay a physician to perform an illegal abortion in the United States. Instead, they turned either to dangerous self-induced abortions or to the dark and often forbidding underworld of untrained and unreliable "back-alley" abortionists. Women who resorted to self-induced abortion typically relied on such methods as throwing themselves down a flight of stairs or ingesting, douching with, or inserting into themselves a chilling variety of chemicals and toxins ranging from bleach to potassium permanganate to turpentine to gunpowder to whiskey. Knitting needles, crochet hooks, scissors, and coat hangers were among the tools commonly used by women who attempted to self-abort. Approximately 30 percent of all illegal abortions were self-induced.

Women who sought abortions from "back-alley" abortionists encountered similar horrors. To find someone to perform an illegal abortion, women often had to rely on the advice of friends or acquaintances or on tips from elevator operators, taxicab drivers, salesmen, and the like. Because of the clandestine nature of illegal abortions, the very process of finding an abortionist was often dangerous and terrifying. Women who sought "back-alley" abortions were sometimes blindfolded, driven to remote areas, and passed off to people they did not know and could not even see during the entire process. Such abortions were performed not only in secret offices and hotel rooms, but also in bathrooms, in the backseats of cars, and literally in back alleys. The vast majority of these abortions were performed either by persons with only limited medical training, such as physiotherapists, midwives, and chiropractors, or by rank amateurs, including elevator operators, prostitutes, barbers, and unskilled laborers.

In the 1960s, an average of more than two hundred women died each year as a result of botched illegal abortions. The mortality rate for black and Hispanic women was twelve times higher than the mortality rate for white women. In addition to those who died in the course of illegal abortions, many thousands more suffered serious illness or permanent injury. Because of the humiliation associated with having an illegal abortion, many women who suffered complications were reluctant to visit a doctor for treatment. The stories of women who suffered through this nightmare are legion.

One woman recalled how a fellow college student who had had an illegal abortion was too frightened to tell anyone what she had done. She locked herself in the bathroom in her dorm and quietly bled to death. In another incident, 28-year-old Geraldine Santoro bled to death on the floor of a Connecticut hotel room after she and her former lover attempted an abortion on their own. The former lover, who had no medical experience, used a textbook and some borrowed tools. When things went terribly wrong, he fled the scene, and Santoro died alone.*[8]

RELIGION AND POLITICS

MANY RELIGIOUS ORGANIZATIONS that had previously been silent on abortion increasingly felt compelled to address the issue. Protestant churches varied in their opinions. Many supported some variation of the ALI's position, but some went even further. The United Methodist Church, for example, acknowledged "the sanctity of unborn human life," but nonetheless proclaimed that because "we are equally bound to respect the sacredness of the life and well-being of the mother, for whom devastating damage may result from an unacceptable pregnancy," we "support the removal of abortion from the criminal code, placing it instead under laws relating to other procedures of standard medical practice."[9]

Similarly, the American Baptist Convention came to the conclusion in 1968 that abortion should be a matter of "responsible personal decision" and should be available as an "elective medical procedure" at the "request of the individual" at any time before the end of the first trimester of pregnancy.[10]

Three years later, the more conservative evangelical Southern Baptist Convention endorsed the ALI's approach and called on Southern Baptists to support laws that would permit abortion "under such conditions as rape, incest, clear evidence of fetal deformity, and carefully ascertained evidence of the likelihood of damage to the emotional, mental, and physical health of the mother."[11] Although some evangelicals maintained that abortion was condemned in the Bible, most took a more moderate approach. The National Association of Evangelicals, for example, expressly endorsed "the necessity for therapeutic abortion to safeguard the health or the life of the mother."[12]

---

* The former lover pled no contest to manslaughter and served a year in prison.

The Catholic Church, on the other hand, continued to insist that abortion was always and unequivocally forbidden, even when necessary to save the life of the woman. As Pope Paul VI made clear in 1968, "abortion, even for therapeutic reasons," is "absolutely excluded."[13]

T HE POLITICS of abortion began to play out in surprising ways. Because Catholics had traditionally identified with the Democratic Party, and because Catholics were more likely than others to oppose abortion, Republicans in the 1960s were more "pro-abortion" than Democrats. As late as 1972, 68 percent of Republicans and only 59 percent of Democrats thought that "the decision to have an abortion should be made solely by a woman and her physician."

The Democratic Party, however, was officially more pro-abortion than the Republican Party. Republican leaders, seeing an opportunity to draw disaffected Catholics away from the Democrats, began to move toward a more anti-abortion stance. They knew that if they could succeed in this effort, they might bring about a profound shift in the future of American politics.

This strategy was clearly evident in President Richard Nixon's policies. In 1970, Nixon authorized all military hospitals to perform therapeutic abortions. A year later, however, with a clearer sense of the potential political ramifications of the abortion issue, Nixon revoked that policy. Influenced by Republican Party strategist Kevin Phillips's popular 1969 book *The Emerging Republican Majority*, Nixon now sharply attacked the Democrats for their support of abortion and embraced an increasingly strident anti-abortion stance in a determined effort to draw Catholic voters into the Republican camp.

Osn May 5, 1972, for example, Nixon publicly repudiated the pro-abortion recommendations of the Rockefeller Commission's *Report of the Commission on Population Growth and the American Future*. In light of the growing concern about overpopulation, Nixon had appointed the Commission, which was chaired by John D. Rockefeller III, to address the "serious challenges to human destiny" posed by the growth in world population. Noting the large number of deaths due to illegal abortions and the importance of a woman's freedom to control her own fertility and destiny, the Commission supported measures to bring abortion from "the backrooms to the hospitals and clinics of this country." The Commission concluded that "the matter of abortion should be left to the conscience of the individual concerned, in consultation with her physician."[14]

Nixon emphatically rejected the Commission's recommendations, declaring that more flexible "abortion policies would demean human life."[15] A few days later, Nixon underscored the point when he made public a letter to Terence Cardinal Cooke expressing his ardent support for the Cardinal's anti-abortion advocacy. Nixon proclaimed that more permissible abortion policies would be "impossible to reconcile with either our religious traditions or our Western heritage," and he applauded those who defended "the right to life of the unborn."[16]

Nixon knew what he was doing. Millions of Catholics who were prepared to cast single-issue votes on the abortion issue voted Republican for the first time in 1972, helping Nixon win a landslide victory over the Democrats' pro-choice candidate, George McGovern, in that year's presidential election.*[17]

THE RISING VOICE OF THE WOMEN'S MOVEMENT

THE PUSH TO REFORM abortion laws in the early-to-mid-1960s focused almost exclusively on the authority of doctors to make medical decisions in the best interests of their patients. The notion that women might themselves have an independent and legally protected right to control their own bodies and destinies had not yet surfaced. Women's rights groups still did not place abortion high on their agendas, focusing instead on promoting equal access to education, equal opportunities in the workplace, and other policies that would enhance the standing of women in society. Near the end of the decade, however, the rising voice of the women's movement began for the first time to shape the public discourse on abortion.[18]

This shift was energized by the often aggressive activism of student groups on college campuses in the late '60s. In 1969, for example, Heather

---

* Nixon's strategy proved quite successful. In the five presidential elections between 1952 and 1968, the Democratic nominee received an average of 65 percent of the Catholic vote. In the five presidential elections between 1972 and 1988, the Democratic nominee received an average of only 48 percent of the Catholic vote. By contrast, the percentage of Protestants voting Democratic in those elections dropped only slightly, from 42 percent to 39 percent. This dramatic change in Catholic voting patterns produced a shift of an average of more than three million Catholic votes from the Democratic to the Republican column in each presidential election between 1972 and 1988. This shift in Catholic voting patterns has remained more or less in place ever since. Indeed, no Democratic presidential candidate has received a majority of the votes of white Catholics since 1972.

Heather Booth and JANE

Booth, a student at the University of Chicago, created a women's organization using the code name JANE, an underground abortion-referral service that helped make illegal abortions available to women in need. Women would call a secret phone number and ask for JANE. A counselor would then instruct the woman to go to a designated apartment, where a physician or a trained member of JANE, often a student at the university, would discreetly perform the abortion. Between 1969 and 1973, JANE provided safe and inexpensive illegal abortions to more than 11,000 women in Chicago, most of them with no connection to the university.

Similarly, in California, Patricia Maginnis founded the Society for Humane Abortion (SHA) both to advocate for the legalization of abortion and to help women find a safe way to end unwanted pregnancies. The SHA offered secret classes on self-abortion and created an "underground railroad" network with several Mexican abortion clinics that helped more than 12,000 women obtain safe abortions across the border.[19]

In February 1969, Betty Friedan—who had risen to fame in 1963 as author of the best-selling book *The Feminine Mystique* and who in 1966 had served as the founding president of the National Organization for Women (NOW)—delivered a rousing address in Chicago at what was billed as the First National Conference on Abortion Laws. Friedan declared: "[T]here is no freedom, no equality . . . possible for women until we assert and demand the control over our own bodies, over our own reproductive process." She proclaimed that "the right of woman to control her reproductive process must be established as a basic and valuable human civil right not to be denied or abridged by the state." This right was essential, she maintained, to the full human "dignity of women."[20]

At the end of the conference the participants founded the National Association for Repeal of Abortion Laws (NARAL) on the premise that what was needed was not ALI-type reforms, but a complete overhaul of America's abortion laws. NARAL declared itself "dedicated to the elimination of all laws and practices that would compel any woman to bear a child against her will."[21] In November 1969, the American Public Health Association and Planned Parenthood, which had been founded in 1922 by Margaret Sanger, who had died three years earlier in 1966 at the age of eighty-two, called for repeal rather than reform of America's abortion laws and declared abortion to be a personal right of the woman.

The next year, NOW called for a "Women's Strike for Equality" on August 26, 1970, the fiftieth anniversary of the adoption of the Nineteenth Amendment, which had gained women the right to vote. Women across America marched, protested, and demonstrated in support of ratification of the Equal Rights Amendment,* gender equality in education and the workplace, government-financed health care, and recognition of a woman's right to control her own body's reproductive process as an inalienable human right. During the Women's Strike for Equality, the phrase "abortion on demand" appeared for the first time on a leaflet announcing the march in New York City.[22]

The campaign for abortion reform was now, for the first time, about the rights of women rather than the rights of doctors. These groups maintained that denial of a woman's right to control her own reproductive destiny violated her fundamental right to decide for herself whether—or not—"to bear or beget a child."[23]

THE BATTLE FOR LEGISLATIVE LEGALIZATION

THESE EARLY CALLS for reform generated a new momentum for change. By October 1971, 50 percent of Americans believed that, at least in the first trimester of pregnancy, abortion should be a decision for a woman and her doctor. Less than a year later, that figure had climbed to 64 percent.[24] In

---

* "Equality of rights under the law shall not be denied or abridged by the United States or by any state on account of sex."

1970, four states—Hawaii, Alaska, Washington, and New York—legalized abortion either in the first trimester or previability, thus moving the law back toward what it had been a century earlier.

On March 11, 1970, Hawaii became the first state to take this step, authorizing abortion by a doctor of a "nonviable fetus."[25] The struggle to enact this law took almost two years. Opposition to the proposed law came primarily from the Catholic Church and its affiliated organizations.[26] With polls showing citizens of Hawaii supporting legalization by a margin to 55 percent to 33 percent, the bill was ultimately approved by substantial margins in both houses of the state legislature. Governor John A. Burns, a Catholic, refused to sign the bill, however, explaining that after "sincere prayer to the Creator," he could not bring himself to do so. At the same time, though, he declined to veto the legislation, and under Hawaii law the bill went into effect without the governor's signature.[27]

Shortly thereafter, the Washington state legislature placed on the ballot a referendum proposal to legalize abortion in the first sixteen weeks of pregnancy. Seattle Archbishop Thomas A. Connolly immediately launched an aggressive campaign to defeat the proposal. Opponents of the proposal erected billboards depicting a four-month-old fetus with such captions as "Kill Referendum 20, Not Me." On November 3, 1970, with more than a million people voting, Washington enacted the proposal with more than 56 percent voting in favor of the reform.

Later that same year, after a fierce legislative battle, Alaska enacted legislation legalizing all abortions performed by a doctor during the first twenty weeks of pregnancy. The *New York Times* declared that "a dramatic liberalization of public attitudes and practices regarding abortions appears to be sweeping the country."[28]

THE BATTLE over legalization in New York was particularly tense. For almost a century, New York had prohibited abortion unless the procedure was necessary to save the life of the woman. Beginning in 1965, bills designed to move New York law toward the ALI position were introduced repeatedly in the state legislature, but despite broad public support the bills never made it out of committee because the New York State Catholic Conference succeeded each time in blocking them.[29]

In February 1969, a women's rights group known as the Redstockings demanded that the New York legislators "hear from some real experts . . . women."[30] After being shut out of the legislative hearing, the Redstockings took their protest to the streets, with the first-ever abortion "speak-out" in a

Washington Square church. The women spoke openly about their personal experiences and challenged the prevailing norms that "consigned abortion to silence and shame."[31]

Later that year, New York Assemblywoman Constance Cook, a Republican, introduced a bill to legalize abortion up to the twenty-fourth week of pregnancy. In introducing the legislation, Cook observed that illegal abortions were the leading cause of maternal death, that one-fifth of all women would have at least one abortion during their lives, and that most of the women who died in New York City from illegal abortions left children behind.[32]

The vote on Cook's bill was dramatic. Just as it appeared that the proposal would go down to defeat by a single vote, it was saved by Assemblyman George M. Michaels's last-minute change of heart. Michaels, who had served heroically in the Marine Corps during World War II, rose, called out to get the Speaker's attention, and then courageously reversed his initial vote against the bill, tearfully explaining: "I realize, Mr. Speaker, that I am terminating my political career, but I cannot in good conscience sit here and allow my vote to be the one that defeats this bill." And so, with Republican Governor Nelson Rockefeller's signature, the bill became law.[*33]

THE ANTI-ABORTION forces in New York quickly regrouped under the leadership of the Roman Catholic National Right to Life Committee (NRLC). Its goal, quite simply, was to overturn the new law and to reinstate the old one. Its approach had two distinct prongs—one legal, the other political.[34]

On the legal front, Robert Byrn, a law professor at Fordham University and a leader of New York's Catholic anti-abortion movement, immediately filed a lawsuit challenging the constitutionality of the new law. Byrn argued that from the moment of conception, the "unborn child" is a "person" within the meaning of the Constitution, and that the New York law unconstitutionally deprived "unborn children" of "life . . . without due process of law." The New York Court of Appeals, the state's highest court, rejected Byrn's argument, holding that a fetus is not a "person" within the meaning of the Constitution.[35]

On the political front, opponents of the new law mobilized their forces.

---

* Michaels was right in his prediction. He ran for a sixth term in the next election in 1970 but did not get the Democratic nomination because of his vote on this bill. He never again won an election.

Adding fuel to the fire, in early 1972 Congress approved the Equal Rights Amendment and submitted it to the states for ratification. This immediately tied the question of abortion to even larger issues about the "permissive" society, the meaning of sex roles in American culture, and the future of the traditional family. Phyllis Schlafly, a longtime conservative activist and an outspoken Catholic, immediately tied abortion to the ERA and reframed a woman's asserted right to abortion as women's abdication of motherhood. As opponents of the ERA and abortion linked arms in a "pro-family" union, Schlafly charged that the "women's libbers" were promoting "free sex" at the expense of motherhood and that they were encouraging "abortions instead of families."[36]

On April 16, 1972, designated by Terence Cardinal Cooke, the Archbishop of New York, as "Right to Life Sunday," thousands of people partici-

Terence Cardinal Cooke

pated in an anti-abortion rally in New York City. Meanwhile, the New York Right to Life Committee aggressively distributed anti-abortion mailings, and more than fifty anti-abortion organizations made phone calls, wrote letters, and threatened to defeat legislators who did not vote to repeal the new legislation. By rallying around a single issue in this manner and threatening to vote exclusively on this issue, the anti-abortion forces put extraordinary pressure on public officials to acquiesce, or risk losing their seats.

The debate in the New York legislature was highly emotional. At one point, a member of the Assembly leaped to his feet crying, "We forgot the voiceless victim," while waving aloft a jar containing what purported to be a dead fetus. Such antics, which drew enormous press attention, combined with incessant and determined lobbying, got the job done. The repeal bill passed the New York Assembly by a margin of two votes.[37]

New York's Republican governor, Nelson Rockefeller, who had promised to veto any law that reinstated the ban on abortion, courageously kept his promise. Noting "the extremes of personal vilification and political coercion" that had been brought to bear on members of the legislature, Rockefeller suggested that there were "serious doubts that the vote to repeal the reform represented the will of a majority of the people of New York State." He concluded: "I do not believe it right for one group to impose its vision of morality on an entire society. . . . The bill is disapproved."[38]

TURNING TO THE COURTS

AFTER A SERIES of legislative victories between 1967 and 1970, when thirteen states liberalized their abortion laws by enacting a version of the ALI proposal and four others legalized abortion in at least the first trimester, legislative progress suddenly ground to a halt. Despite increasing—and clear majority—public support for leaving the abortion decision to the woman and her doctor, no state legislature enacted reform legislation between 1970 and 1973.

Several factors contributed to this sudden legislative paralysis. The initial round of legislative victories both surprised and energized abortion opponents, especially the Catholic leadership, and after getting their act together they organized with extraordinary effectiveness. Moreover, those opposed to abortion threatened quite credibly to act as single-issue voters, and they communicated that intention to elected officials with perfect clarity. As a result, many legislators came to understand that although a majority of citizens supported legalizing abortion, when election day rolled around committed single-issue voters could nonetheless vote them out of office.[39]

Faced with paralysis in the legislative arena, pro-choice advocates began to think seriously about challenging the constitutionality of anti-abortion statutes in the courts. Initially, this seemed a long shot because, in the words of the *New York Times* Supreme Court columnist Linda Greenhouse, the idea of a constitutional right of abortion seemed "illusory." But with legislative change effectively blocked, the courts increasingly seemed the best alternative.[40]

THE SUPREME COURT's 1965 decision in *Griswold v. Connecticut* was a useful starting point.* Only two years after *Griswold* was decided, Roy Lucas, a student in his last year at NYU Law School, wrote a research paper for a class in which he argued that a woman's right to decide for herself whether or not to have a child should be understood as a fundamental constitutional right protected by the right of privacy recognized in *Griswold*. Although Lucas's professors thought the argument implausible, others did not.[41]

Harriet Pilpel, who had served as general counsel for both Planned Parenthood and the ACLU and had been involved in twenty-seven cases before the Supreme Court, was so intrigued by the idea of a direct constitutional challenge to anti-abortion laws that she and Lucas began to craft a test case to pose the question.[42] In early 1970, before the New York legislature amended its abortion law, a group of lawyers, relying in part on Lucas's theory, filed four separate cases in federal court challenging the constitutionality of the New York law.

The state's lawyers argued that *Griswold* was irrelevant because, when dealing with abortion, the state is protecting the interests of "a potential human being's life." Before the federal court could address the question, the New York legislature amended the state's abortion statute, thus rendering the cases moot.[43]

AT THE same time in Connecticut, after the legislature repeatedly refused even to consider reforming its nineteenth-century abortion statute, a group of women's liberation activists formed a new organization,

---

* See chapter 15.

"Women versus Connecticut," to challenge the constitutionality of the law. Their goal was to empower women by putting together a group of women plaintiffs, experts, and lawyers to mount their case. "We want control over our own bodies," they declared. "We are tired of being pressured to have children or not to have children. *It's our decision.*" Because getting a new law through Connecticut's heavily Catholic legislature was clearly implausible, they turned to the courts.[44]

On March 2, 1971, in *Abele v. Markle,* "Women versus Connecticut" filed its complaint in federal district court on behalf of 858 women plaintiffs. Six weeks later, a three-judge federal court, in a two-to-one decision, held the Connecticut statute unconstitutional. Judge Edward Lumbard, an Eisenhower appointee, held that in this law, "Connecticut trespasses unjustifiably on the personal privacy and liberty of its female citizens in violation of the Ninth Amendment and the Due Process Clause." Judge Lumbard was especially concerned with the dignitary, psychological, social, medical, and economic consequences of forcing pregnancy and motherhood on unwilling women. These consequences, he explained, could fundamentally alter a woman's life to such an extent that the woman's interest in making this decision for herself outweighed the state's interest in protecting potential life.[45]

Cases challenging state anti-abortion laws now started popping up everywhere. In Texas, Linda Coffee and Sarah Weddington, recent graduates of the University of Texas Law School, teamed up to bring a test case to challenge the constitutionality of the Texas anti-abortion statute. The Texas law, which had been enacted in 1854, outlawed abortion except when necessary to save the life of the woman. They chose as their plaintiff a woman named Norma McCorvey, an unmarried, pregnant, twenty-one-year-old. On March 3, 1970, Coffee and Weddington filed a complaint on behalf of McCorvey, now identified as "Jane Roe" in order to protect her anonymity, alleging that the Texas law unconstitutionally infringed the fundamental right of women to decide for themselves whether or not to bear children.[46]

On June 17, 1970, a three-judge federal district court ruled unanimously that the "fundamental right" of a woman to decide for herself "whether to have children is protected by the Ninth Amendment" and that the Texas anti-abortion statute therefore violated the United States Constitution.[47]

On May 3, 1971, the Supreme Court announced that it would take up *Roe v. Wade.*

ROE

WHEN *ROE V. WADE* REACHED the Supreme Court, the Court itself was in a state of flux. President Richard Nixon was in the process of remaking the Court. Two years earlier, Nixon had replaced Chief Justice Earl Warren and Justice Abe Fortas, two liberal stalwarts, with two conservative nominees—Chief Justice Warren Burger and Justice Harry Blackmun. Then, in September of 1971, just as the Court was about to take up the issue of abortion, Justices Hugo Black and John Marshall Harlan announced that for reasons of health, they too would step down.

Nixon appointed two more conservative justices, Lewis F. Powell and William Rehnquist, to succeed them. Because the confirmation process took several months and because neither Powell nor Rehnquist had been sworn in by the time the Court heard oral arguments in *Roe*, neither was eligible to participate in the consideration of the case.[48]

Roe was argued on December 13, 1971. In his opening argument in defense of the Texas law, Jay Floyd, representing the state, made one of the most inappropriate comments in the history of Supreme Court oral arguments. Appearing against two women lawyers, Floyd infamously began, "Mr. Chief Justice and may it please the Court. It's an old joke, but when a man argues against two beautiful ladies like this, they are going to have the last word." The justices were not amused.

Three days later, the seven participating justices met in conference to discuss the case and to cast their preliminary votes. After some deliberation, there seemed to be at least five votes to hold the Texas statute unconstitutional. There was uncertainty, however, about the precise rationales for the individual justices' positions. Justices Blackmun and Stewart indicated that they were inclined to join Justices Douglas, Brennan, and Marshall in striking down the statute, but they had reservations.

As the father of three daughters, Blackmun was attuned to the significance of the abortion issue. Moreover, in light of his experience for almost a decade as general counsel to the Mayo Clinic, he was sympathetic to the interests of doctors who wanted the freedom to act in what they believed to be the best interests of their patients. On the other hand, Blackmun had been nominated by Richard Nixon in no small part because of his long-standing record of judicial restraint. He was acutely aware that a decision striking down the Texas statute would be seen in many quarters as a classic example of judicial activism. This was not why he had been appointed. He was unsure how to proceed.

Justice Potter Stewart believed strongly that the Court should avoid issues with significant political implications. He had dissented in *Griswold* and he remained skeptical of the notion that there exists a wide-ranging constitutional right of privacy. Nonetheless, Stewart found the prohibition of abortion deeply troubling.

Justice White, who also had dissented in *Griswold*, voted in conference to uphold the Texas statute. Chief Justice Burger's position at the conference was unclear. To the dismay of some of his brethren, he assigned the task of writing the Court's opinion to Justice Blackmun,* in part because he was confident that he could count on his longtime friend and colleague to write a "narrowly focused" opinion that "would discharge the Court's duty without doing or saying anything more than necessary."[49]

Blackmun was both pleased and daunted by the assignment. He knew that whatever he did in *Roe*, he would make enemies. This early in his tenure on the Court, this prospect made him uneasy. At the same time, though, Blackmun was convinced that he was the only justice with the medical background necessary to deal with the scientific issues at stake.

Blackmun's initial draft sought to dispose of the case on vagueness grounds. What, he asked in his draft opinion, did it mean to say that a doctor can legally perform an abortion only to save the life of the woman? Did this mean that the doctor could perform an abortion "only when, without it, the patient will surely die? Or only when the odds are greater than even that she will die? Or when there is a mere possibility that she will not survive? . . . Must death be imminent?"

In effect, Blackmun argued that the statute was "insufficiently informative" to meet the demands of due process for the physician who would have to cope with these uncertainties at the risk of his medical career and his personal freedom. If the physician guessed wrong about the meaning of the law, he could land in jail. Although acknowledging that the case raised deeper issues, Blackmun's draft reasoned that the Court did not need to reach those larger issues because the particular law at issue in the case was unconstitutionally vague.

Blackmun's draft fell well short of what the Court's more liberal justices—

---

* Burger's decision to assign the task of writing the majority opinion rankled some of the other justices because, according to Supreme Court tradition, the chief justice has that authority only if he has voted with the majority. Because Burger had not clearly voted one way or the other at conference, Justice Douglas, as the senior justice in the majority, ordinarily would have had the prerogative of assigning the majority opinion. Douglas was furious with Burger for, in his view, usurping his authority.

Douglas, Brennan, and Marshall—had expected. There had been considerable discussion at conference and in exchanges among the justices about a broader approach, one that invoked the principles of *Griswold* and *Eisenstadt* and that recognized what they saw as a woman's constitutionally protected interest in making for herself the fundamental decision whether or not to bear an unwanted child. Blackmun's draft contained none of that. Although Blackmun was sympathetic to this approach, he was not yet ready to embrace such a right.[50]

As the Court's term drew to a close, and just after President Nixon started making his series of sharply anti-abortion speeches in the spring of 1972, Blackmun suggested that he needed more time to craft his opinion. The other justices acquiesced in this request and agreed to set the case for re-argument the following fall. Not only would that give Blackmun more time, but it would also enable Justices Powell and Rehnquist to participate.

D URING THE summer of 1972, Harry Blackmun spent much of his time at the Mayo Clinic library reviewing books and articles on the history and practice of abortion. Blackmun's handwritten notes suggest that he was struck particularly by an observation in the *American Journal of Public Health* that the "risk of legal abortion in the first trimester is less" than the risk of "carrying pregnancy to term"; by a June 1972 Gallup poll that showed that 64 percent of Americans thought that "abortion should be a matter for decision solely between a woman and her physician"; and by his realization that the criminalization of abortion was a "relatively recent phenomenon, without roots in the English common-law tradition."[51]

After *Roe* was reargued on October 11, 1972, the justices met again in conference, this time with Justices Powell and Rehnquist in attendance. To the surprise of the other justices, Lewis Powell, a courtly, soft-spoken, cautious conservative from Virginia, announced that he supported recognizing a constitutional right to abortion and he encouraged Blackmun to move beyond the vagueness rationale. Powell apparently first became sympathetic to the right of legal abortion after the girlfriend of one of the employees of his Richmond law firm bled to death while the couple attempted to perform an illegal hanger abortion. Powell was instrumental in persuading prosecutors not to file criminal charges against the boyfriend.

Although Justices White and Rehnquist made clear that they could not support a decision invalidating the Texas law, by the end of the conference it was clear that there were at least six, and probably seven (Burger was still not ready to commit) votes to invalidate the Texas statute and, more broadly, the anti-abortion statutes currently on the books in forty-five other states, on the ground that they failed to respect the fundamental constitutional right of a woman and her physician to decide for themselves whether to terminate an unwanted pregnancy.[52]

T HE SUPREME COURT announced its decision in *Roe v. Wade* on January 22, 1973.* The Court held the Texas abortion statute unconstitutional by a vote of seven-to-two. In his opinion for the Court, Justice Blackmun began by acknowledging "the sensitive and emotional nature of the abortion controversy" and the "deep and seemingly absolute convictions that the subject inspires." The Court's task, he explained, "is to resolve the issue by constitutional measurement, free of emotion." Blackmun added that to put the issue in its proper context, it was necessary to understand the historical evolution of attitudes toward abortion over the centuries.[53]

Turning to that history, Blackmun observed that the criminalization of abortion was a relatively recent phenomenon. Laws prohibiting the procedure, he explained, were not of ancient origin, but derived from legislation in the late nineteenth century. In the ancient world, he observed, particularly in Greece and Rome, neither law nor religion forbade abortion. Moreover, under the Anglo-American common law, abortion before quickening was not a crime. Indeed, a review of the common law precedents led him to conclude that even post-quickening abortion was rarely enforced as a common law crime.[54]

Blackmun noted further that it was only in the latter part of the nineteenth century that most states banned abortion unless necessary to preserve the life of the woman. It was thus apparent, he concluded, that "at the time of the adoption of our Constitution, and throughout the major portion of the 19th century, . . . a woman enjoyed a substantially broader right to terminate a pregnancy than she does in most States today."[55]

After reviewing the history of medical views on abortion,[56] Blackmun identified the three arguments that had most often been advanced in the late nineteenth century to justify strict criminal laws against abortion. First,

---

* Although the opinions were ready to be announced by mid-January, Chief Justice Burger dawdled while he drafted a brief concurring opinion. Justice Blackmun suspected, with good reason, that Burger was intentionally delaying the announcement of the decision until after President Nixon's second inauguration on January 20, because he wanted to save Nixon the embarrassment of seeing three of his appointees to the Court recognizing a constitutional right to abortion.

some anti-abortion advocates had insisted that such laws could be justified in terms "of a Victorian social concern to discourage illicit sexual conduct." Blackmun dismissed this justification as plainly inadequate, noting that no legal authority today takes this argument "seriously" as a legitimate justification for banning abortion.[57]

Second, some defenders of restrictive abortion laws had argued that such laws were necessary to protect pregnant women against the temptation to submit to dangerous procedures that might place their lives "in serious jeopardy." Although noting that abortion had indeed been risky prior to the "development of antisepsis," Blackmun emphasized that modern medical techniques had clearly altered this situation and that by 1973 it was well established that abortion prior to the end of the first trimester was generally a very safe procedure. At the same time, though, Blackmun noted that states have a legitimate interest in ensuring that abortion, like any other medical procedure, is performed under appropriate circumstances. He therefore concluded that states retain an interest in protecting the woman's own health and safety when an abortion is proposed "at a late stage of pregnancy," when the medical risks to the woman are potentially greater.[58]

Third, Blackmun noted that some defenders of anti-abortion laws had argued that such laws were necessary to protect the lives of unborn children. Without attempting to resolve the question of when human life begins, Blackmun acknowledged that the government has a legitimate interest at stake when "at least *potential* life is involved."[59]

HAVING THUS laid out the state interests in regulating abortion, Blackmun turned next to identifying the constitutional interests on the other side. Although noting that the Constitution does not explicitly enumerate a right to privacy, Blackmun pointed out that in a line of decisions going back to the 1890s, the Court had repeatedly recognized that "a right of personal privacy" exists under the Constitution.[60] As examples, Blackmun cited a long list of decisions, including *Skinner v. Oklahoma*,[61] in which the Court had recognized a fundamental right not to be sterilized; *Stanley v. Georgia*,[62] in which the Court had recognized a fundamental right to possess obscenity in the privacy of the home; *Griswold v. Connecticut*,[63] in which the Court had recognized a fundamental right of married couples to use contraceptives; *Loving v. Virginia*,[64] in which the Court had recognized a fundamental right to marry; and *Eisenstadt v. Baird*,[65] in which the Court had recognized a fundamental right of individuals to decide for themselves "whether to bear or beget a child."[66]

"This right of privacy," Blackmun maintained, whether grounded in the Ninth Amendment or in the Due Process Clause, "is broad enough to encompass a woman's decision whether or not to terminate her pregnancy." Blackmun explained that the harm that a state inflicts upon a woman when it denies her this choice is obvious:

> Specific and direct harm medically diagnosable even in early pregnancy may be involved. Maternity, or additional offspring, may force upon the woman a distressful life and future. Psychological harm may be imminent. Mental and physical health may be taxed by child care. There is also the distress, for all concerned, associated with the unwanted child, and there is the problem of bringing a child into a family already unable, psychologically and otherwise, to care for it. In other cases, as in this one, the additional difficulties and continuing stigma of unwed motherhood may be involved.[67]

On the other hand, Blackmun made clear that recognizing the existence of a right does not mean that the right is "absolute." Rather, as with other constitutional rights, there are circumstances when the right of privacy might be regulated, consistent with the Constitution, in the face of compelling government interests. Turning specifically to the regulation of abortion, Blackmun declared that, in at least some circumstances, the government's interests "in safeguarding health, in maintaining medical standards, and in protecting potential life" might be "sufficiently compelling" to justify restrictions on a woman's right to terminate an unwanted pregnancy. The next question, of course, was which, if any, of the state's asserted interests in regulating abortion met that standard.[68]

IN DEFENSE of its absolute prohibition on abortion except when necessary to save the life of the woman, Texas maintained that human life begins at conception and that its interest in preserving the life of unborn children was sufficiently compelling to override any constitutional right of the woman. Blackmun rejected this argument. Noting that even "those trained in the respective disciplines of medicine, philosophy, and theology are unable to arrive at any consensus" on the profound religious, moral, and scientific question of when human life begins, Blackmun reasoned that neither the state of Texas nor the Supreme Court is "in a position to speculate as to the answer." In such circumstances, he concluded, the state, by

Justice Harry A. Blackmun

merely asserting "one theory of life," cannot declare a purported interest to be "compelling" in order to set aside "the rights of the pregnant woman."[69]

Blackmun turned next to the government's interest in regulating abortion to protect the health of the woman. Although recognizing that this interest is clearly legitimate, Blackmun held that it becomes "compelling" only at the end of the first trimester. This was so, he explained, because until that point abortion was now a relatively safe and simple medical procedure—safer even than childbirth. Thus, during the first trimester the woman and her attending physician must be free to decide, without government interference, whether the pregnancy should be terminated.

Blackmun also held, however, that after the first trimester, as the possible health risks to the woman increase, the government can *reasonably* regulate the abortion procedure in order to protect the woman's health. He noted, for example, that after this point in a pregnancy the state can reasonably regulate such matters as the qualifications of those who are authorized to perform an abortion and the types of facilities in which an abortion may be performed.

Blackmun finally turned to the government's interest in protecting "potential life." This interest, he concluded, becomes compelling at the point of fetal viability. Blackmun explained that this made sense because, at this stage in a pregnancy, the fetus has the ability to live "outside the mother's womb," and the government can therefore protect fetal life at that point without intruding on the right of the woman not to be pregnant. Blackmun emphasized, however, that even after this point in pregnancy the government cannot constitutionally forbid a woman to have an abortion if the procedure "is necessary to preserve the life or health" of the woman.*[70]

J USTICE BYRON WHITE, joined by Justice William Rehnquist, dissented. White, a Kennedy appointee, was generally quite conservative on such issues as obscenity, contraception, and abortion. In a brief opinion, he declared that he found "nothing in the language or history of the

---

* In the initial draft of his opinion in *Roe*, Blackmun had limited the right to terminate a pregnancy, except when necessary to preserve the health or life of the woman, to the first trimester. Justices Powell and Marshall persuaded him to focus on the viability issue and to extend the right through the end of the second trimester. See Michael J. Graetz & Linda Greenhouse, *The Burger Court and The Rise of the Judicial Right* 144–45 (Simon & Schuster 2016).

Constitution to support the Court's judgment." In his view, the Court in *Roe* "simply fashions and announces a new constitutional right for pregnant mothers." White insisted that in an area as "sensitive" as abortion, the matter "should be left with the people and to the political processes the people have devised to govern their affairs."[71]

In a separate dissenting opinion, Rehnquist conceded that if "the Texas statute were to prohibit an abortion even where the mother's life is in jeopardy," it would be unconstitutional because it "would lack a rational relation to a valid state objective." But the very fact that a majority of the states "have had restrictions on abortions for at least a century," he reasoned, is a "strong indication" that the right to abortion "is not 'so rooted in the traditions and conscience of our people as to be ranked as fundamental.'" That being so, he concluded, there was no legitimate basis for the Court to find such a right in the Constitution.[72]

REACTION

MANY AMERICANS TODAY think of *Roe v. Wade* as a radical, left-wing decision. That was not the view at the time. By 1973, a substantial majority of Americans supported the right of a woman to terminate an unwanted pregnancy. Gallup polls showed that "two out of three Americans think abortion should be a matter for decision solely between a woman and her physician." Thus, at the time of the decision, the justices "had every reason to suppose that they were embracing a broad national consensus."[73] Moreover, as we have seen, lower courts were already moving in a direction that clearly anticipated *Roe*. Strikingly, three of the four justices appointed to the Supreme Court by President Richard Nixon joined the decision. In light of Nixon's determination to appoint "conservative" justices who, unlike their Warren Court predecessors, would be committed to a position of judicial restraint, it is telling that Blackmun, Powell, and Burger all voted as they did. Indeed, without the support of these three Nixon appointees, *Roe* would have come out the other way. That Burger, Blackmun, and Powell joined Douglas, Brennan, Stewart, and Marshall in *Roe* speaks volumes about the mainstream nature of the decision at the time.

Indeed, it is worth noting for the sake of comparison that at the very moment that the justices were contemplating *Roe*, they were also in the process of deciding the 1973 obscenity cases—*Miller* and *Paris Adult Theatre*—in which Burger, Blackmun, and Powell parted company with Douglas, Brennan, Stewart, and Marshall, and joined instead with Justices White and Rehnquist to embrace a sharply conservative view of the First Amendment right of sexual expression.*

The plain and simple fact is that at the time *Roe* was decided, Blackmun, Burger, and Powell did not view the abortion issue as posing a particularly *ideological* question. Although all of the justices understood that *Roe* addressed a highly emotional and important issue, none of them imagined that it would become a flash point of American politics or that it would continue to shape those politics for decades to come.

This understanding of *Roe* is consistent with both the news coverage and the public reaction at the time. Because Lyndon Johnson died on the same day that the Court announced its decision in *Roe*, newspapers, magazines, and news shows treated the Court's decision as only a secondary headline. The primary story was the death of the former president. *U.S. News & World Report,* for example, described *Roe* as "a historic resolution of a fiercely controversial issue," but did not even mention it on the front page of that week's issue. Forty years later, the editors observed correctly that "the far-reaching effects of the decision weren't evident at the time."[74]

The editorials and commentary about *Roe* in the days after the decision were generally approving. Even newspapers in Georgia and Texas, whose laws had been held unconstitutional, were supportive. The *Atlanta Constitution* characterized the decision as "realistic and appropriate," the *Houston Chronicle* called it "sound," the *San Angelo Standard-Times* applauded it as "wise and humane," and the *San Antonio Light* gushed that although the ruling was "not perfect, . . . it was as close to it as humanly possible."[75] These responses were not surprising in light of the fact that the American people clearly endorsed the decision. In polls taken at the time, Americans approved of *Roe* by a margin of 52 to 41 percent.[76]

To put that in perspective, it is instructive to compare the public's reaction to *Roe* with its reaction to other—more controversial—decisions. In 1962, for example, after the Supreme Court held prayer in public schools unconstitutional,[77] 79 percent of the American people disapproved of the decision. In 1967, after the Court held laws prohibiting interracial marriage unconstitutional,[78] 72 percent of Americans disapproved. In 2010, after the Court held laws limiting corporate campaign expenditures unconstitutional,[79] 80 percent of Americans disapproved.[80] But only 41 percent of Americans disapproved of *Roe*. Indeed, one measure of how uncontroversial

---

* See chapter 12.

Roe was at the time is that when President Gerald Ford nominated John Paul Stevens to succeed Justice William Douglas in 1975, not a single senator asked Stevens a question about *Roe* or about his views on abortion.[81]

Even evangelicals did not condemn the decision. In 1973, most evangelicals "regarded abortion as a Catholic issue." Moreover, even evangelicals who did not share that view did not make a fuss over the decision. Indeed, it was not until the end of the decade that the evangelical community finally changed its tune and began to focus negatively on *Roe* as an important religious, moral, and political issue as part of the emerging Culture Wars.[82]

T HE ONE group that did strongly condemn *Roe* from the very moment of the decision was Catholics, who disapproved of the decision by a margin of 56 to 40 percent.[83] This was hardly surprising, in light of the fierce legislative battles that had preceded *Roe* and that had often been driven by Catholic opposition to abortion. Within days of the decision, thousands of telegrams and letters of protest from Catholics inundated the Supreme Court. Whole classes of Catholic school students, directed by their teachers, wrote in an organized campaign to denounce the justices as "murderers" and "butchers." For several weeks, the letters arrived at the rate of 2,000 to 3,000 per day.

The vast majority were addressed either to Justice Blackmun, the author of the opinion, or to Justice Brennan, the Court's only Catholic justice. In Brennan's words, "The rhetoric and tone of the majority of the letters was extremely vitriolic."*[84] Some went so far as to call for Brennan's excommunication from the Church. Many of the letters to Justice Blackmun invoked God's wrath and attacked him as "a baby killer." Blackmun noted that he had "never before been so personally abused and castigated." For the next several years, anti-abortion picketers, often carrying ugly placards, picketed Blackmun and Brennan at all of their public appearances.[85]

---

* Justice Brennan had to reconcile his own personal religious views with his responsibilities as a justice of the Supreme Court. In 1987, he confided privately that "I wouldn't under any circumstances condone an abortion in my private life," but, he added, "that has nothing to do with whether or not those who have different views are entitled to have them and are entitled to be protected in their exercise of them. That's my job in applying and interpreting the Constitution." Brennan was quite sensitive to his fundamental responsibility to separate his religious views from his obligations as a justice of the Supreme Court. He later observed that "it never crossed my mind—never, not the slightest—that my faith had a damn thing to do with how I decided the abortion case."

New York's Terence Cardinal Cooke condemned the Court, asking, "How many millions of children . . . will never live to see the light of day because of the shocking action of the majority of the United States Supreme Court today?" John Joseph Cardinal Krol of Philadelphia, the president of the National Conference of Catholic Bishops, called *Roe* "an unspeakable tragedy" and declared that "it is hard to think of any decision in the two hundred years of our history which has had more disastrous implications for our stability as a civilized society." And the National Conference of Catholic Bishops declared that the decision in *Roe* corrupted "the moral order."[86]

In the years after *Roe*, the involvement of the Catholic hierarchy in American politics increased to an unprecedented level, with bishops devoting more time, energy, and money to abortion than to any other issue. Shortly after *Roe*, Catholic leaders created the National Right to Life Committee (NRLC), which recruited non-Catholics as well as Catholics and which eventually became the largest anti-abortion organization in the nation.

The first formal challenge to *Roe* came in the form of Catholic-sponsored proposed amendments to the Constitution to override the decision. On January 30, 1973, only eight days after *Roe* was announced, Republican Congressman Lawrence Hogan of Maryland introduced the first of many versions of a proposed "human life" amendment. Hogan's proposed amendment would have prohibited the United States or any state to "deprive any human being, from the moment of conception, of life without due process of law."[87] Over the course of the next several decades, many more such proposals were presented to Congress. The campaign to overturn *Roe v. Wade* was officially underway.

I N ADDITION to those who objected to *Roe* on religious grounds, there were other critics as well. Some shared the view of Justices White and Rehnquist that the Constitution simply does not protect either a general right of privacy or a more specific right of a woman to decide for herself whether "to bear or beget a child." Put simply, these critics disagreed with the Court's judgment that a constitutional right was at stake in *Roe*.[88]

Other critics argued that even if the Constitution protects a right of privacy, and even if that right is broad enough to encompass a woman's right to decide for herself whether to bear or beget a child, the state's interest in protecting human life or potential human life is sufficiently compelling to override that constitutional right.

Even among those who agreed with *Roe*'s conclusion that the Texas law was unconstitutional, there were critics of Justice Blackmun's *opinion*. One such criticism turned on Blackmun's emphasis on the role of the doctor and on the right to privacy, rather than on the way in which anti-abortion laws discriminate against women. On this view, the problem with laws prohibiting abortion was not so much that they impaired a woman's right to privacy, but that they reinforced traditional sex-role stereotypes and turned women's capacity to bear children into a serious personal, social, and economic disadvantage.*[89]

Another criticism lodged by some who agreed that the Texas law was unconstitutional was that the Court had gone too far, too fast. These critics maintained that the Court should have invalidated the Texas law because it allowed abortion only to save the life of the woman, but that it should have left the constitutionality of all other possible restrictions on abortion to the future. These critics argued that by overreaching, *Roe* unnecessarily ignited a destructive backlash. Justice Ruth Bader Ginsburg, for example, has consistently argued that by venturing "too far in the change it ordered" *Roe* "stimulated the mobilization of a right-to-life movement" and put an end to the legislative progress that was already underway.[90]

TO BOLDLY GO . . . OR NOT?

WHY DID THE COURT eschew this more modest approach? Why did it reach out beyond what was absolutely necessary to decide the case before it and address such issues as trimesters, viability, and medical regulations? Given that public opinion clearly supported the right of a woman to terminate an unwanted pregnancy, why did the justices feel the need to move so far, so fast? If the state legislatures would eventually have reached the same outcome themselves, shouldn't the justices have let the issue percolate through the political process and addressed the constitutional question in a more incremental manner, one issue and one case at a time, as they arose over the years?

Several considerations explain why the Court moved as boldly as it

---

* One reason why the justices did not take this approach in *Roe* is that at the very same time that the justices were putting the finishing touches on the opinion in *Roe*, they were wrestling— *inconclusively*—with the question of how to deal with constitutional challenges to laws that expressly discriminated against women. See *Frontiero v. Richardson*, 411 U.S. 677 (1973).

did. First, and perhaps most obviously, it was clear by 1973 that despite the state of public opinion most legislatures were unlikely to act on the majority view anytime soon. Only four states had enacted an approach similar to the one embraced in *Roe*, none had done so since 1970, the New York law had come within a hair's breadth of being repealed, and by 1973 no new laws like those enacted in Hawaii, Alaska, Washington, and New York were even remotely on the horizon. The plain and simple fact is that by 1973 the power of determined, passionate, single-issue voting had effectively frozen the legislative process. As scholars of the era have observed, even in states where the opponents of liberalizing abortion laws were substantially outnumbered, they were "single-issue focused and passionate in moral conviction." It was thus clear by 1973 that any further progress in the state legislatures was likely to be slow, painful, and halting, at best.[91]

Second, although patience may be a virtue in most circumstances, it is not necessarily a virtue when legislative paralysis denies millions of Americans a fundamental constitutional right and causes as many as a million women each year to resort to dangerous, degrading, and illegal back-alley abortions. It must have seemed clear to the justices that the option of sitting back and patiently letting the state legislatures dither over these issues for five, ten, or twenty years was not a *responsible* option.

Third, the justices may have felt impelled to act decisively in *Roe* because they recognized that many state legislatures were inhibited from carrying out the will of the majority in this context because of pressure from religious organizations. In its 1961 decision in *McGowan v. Maryland*,[92] the Court had made clear that the First Amendment prohibits legislation that has a predominantly religious purpose. Although the First Amendment vigorously protects the right of religious groups to try to persuade others to accept their beliefs and to act upon those beliefs in their personal capacities, it precludes them from enlisting the power of the state to *compel* others to act in accord with those beliefs. The justices clearly understood the central role that religion played in the opposition to abortion, and this concern may well have made them more reluctant than usual to defer to the "ordinary" workings of the legislative process.

In any event, and whatever the reason or combination of reasons for the Court's decision to act as decisively as it did in *Roe*, it is clear that the justices intended in *Roe* to settle the abortion issue then and there, once and for all.

It turned out not to be that simple.

17

ROE AND BEYOND

ALTHOUGH THE CRITICISMS of *Roe* were relatively muted at the time of the decision, this began to change over the course of the next decade. Indeed, over time *Roe* would come to be seen as perhaps the most polarizing issue in American politics. For those Americans who believe that abortion is immoral—or, worse, murder—the idea that *Roe* "ended" the debate was simply unacceptable. They would not sit quietly and allow the nation to slaughter millions of innocent children. Resistance was necessary. With this understanding, some commentators have assumed that the fierce political polarization we have seen over the abortion issue was an inevitable consequence of *Roe*.[1]

Other commentators maintain, though, that it was not *Roe* itself that triggered this backlash, but a calculated campaign by Republican Party operatives to exploit *Roe* for partisan political gain. These commentators point out that political strategists in the late 1970s leveraged *Roe* as part of a carefully crafted campaign to energize evangelicals and to bring them into the Republican Party. In their view, the centrality of *Roe* in American politics was not an inevitable consequence of the decision, but the result of a strategic campaign to turn *Roe* into a divisive and a highly emotional political symbol, along with the issues of pornography, homosexuality, and women's rights, in what would come to be known as the "Culture Wars."[2]

Whatever the cause or combination of causes, there is no doubt that in the decades since *Roe* was decided controversy over the decision has played a critical role in American politics, in the nomination and confirmation of Supreme Court justices, and in the continued evolution of American constitutional law.

RISE OF THE CHRISTIAN RIGHT

FOLLOWING THE LEAD of their forebears during the Second Great Awakening, Protestant fundamentalists remained active in American politics throughout the twentieth century. Alarmed by the widespread teaching of evolution (exemplified by the Scopes "monkey trial" in 1925), the rise of Catholics as a national political force (exemplified by the Democratic Party's nomination of a Catholic, Al Smith, for the presidency in 1928), and rapidly changing sexual mores and gender roles in the 1920s, evangelical Christians sought to reclaim the nation's institutions and to "make them a force for Protestantism and public morality." Despite their fervor, though, they had little impact on national politics because neither of the two major political parties was all that interested in their demands.

By mid-century, however, Protestant fundamentalists began increasingly to identify with the Republican Party as the party most likely to embrace a "Protestant-based moral order." In 1960, Southern Baptists, northern evangelicals, and independent fundamentalists came together in a rare moment of unity to try to prevent a Catholic—John F. Kennedy—from being elected president. It was only in the late 1960s, however, that Protestant fundamentalists began to influence the Republican agenda. By focusing on the emerging struggle over evolving gender roles and sexual and reproductive morals, and by presenting a united front in their campaign to attain meaningful political influence, what came to be known as the "Christian Right" aligned itself with the Republican Party in a concerted effort to resist what they perceived as the growing threat to American culture posed by "feminism, abortion, pornography, and gay rights."[3]

Opposition to the Equal Rights Amendment was a crystallizing force. In the 1960s, evangelicals worried about what they perceived as the disintegration of the American family. The divorce rate had doubled, out-of-wedlock births had increased, young people were now living openly together in sin, and the media increasingly suggested in movies, magazines, and television that single career women like Mary Richards of the Mary Tyler Moore Show could have satisfying sex lives. As the Rev. Billy Graham warned, the nation was facing "an assault on marriage such as man has never known." If that assault was not halted, he railed, America would be "finished."[4]

Evangelicals blamed the feminist movement, in particular, for what they saw as the demise of the American family. Feminists had already made important strides in the 1960s with the publication of Betty Friedan's *The Feminine Mystique* in 1963; the passage of Title VII of the Civil Rights Act of 1964, which for the first time prohibited employment discrimination against women; and the founding of the National Organization for Women in 1966. Six years later, the Equal Rights Amendment, which provided that "equality of rights under the law shall not be denied or abridged by the United States or any state on account of sex," passed both Houses of Congress by overwhelming majorities. At that time, the ERA was enthusiastically endorsed by Republicans and Democrats alike. Supporters anticipated quick ratification by the thirty-eight states necessary to approve the amendment.[5]

It was not to be. The ERA ignited an unexpected and furious response from social conservatives—including many socially conservative women—who saw the ERA as an assault on their "notions of femininity" and on what they regarded as the necessity of "separate spheres" for women and men. Socially conservative women did not want to be "equal" to men. They wanted to preserve what they firmly believed to be "God-given gender differences." Almost immediately after the ERA was approved by Congress, evangelicals denounced the proposed amendment as "an affront to God."

The individual who most effectively led the charge against the ERA was Phyllis Schlafly, a fiercely conservative lawyer, activist, author, and speaker who founded STOP ERA. By characterizing the ERA as a symbol of rampant feminism, Schlafly "transformed the debate over the amendment into a national referendum on 'women's lib.'" Her opposition to the ERA was more than political—it was holy. When Schlafly, who fervently believed that she had God at her back, declared that her campaign against the ERA was a "heavenly cause," she was in earnest.

Meanwhile, Beverly LaHaye, a leading evangelical voice in the anti-ERA movement, proclaimed that the "woman who is truly Spirit-filled will want to be totally submissive to her husband." She founded Concerned Women for America to "promote Biblical values for women and families—first through prayer, then education, and finally by influencing our elected leaders and society." She challenged her followers—those "truly committed to Jesus Christ"—to "wage warfare against those who would destroy our children, our families, our religious liberties."

The anti-ERA campaign brought together a broad array of previously divided Catholics, Mormons, Baptists, and Protestant evangelicals. In a few short years, the anti-ERA campaign swept into its fold millions of citizens who fervently opposed homosexuality, abortion, obscenity, and sexual license in a nationwide movement committed to restoring "family values." The abortion issue particularly inflamed these groups, not only because they thought abortion a moral wrong, but also because they saw abortion as a direct threat to traditional social and family relationships. Claiming to represent true American values and invoking the mantle of the United States as a "Christian nation," these advocates took a vehement stance on social issues and insisted more vigorously than any prior social or political movement in American history that life begins at conception.

As Republican Party strategist Richard Viguerie observed after the successful campaign in 1977 to repeal the Dade County, Florida, ordinance forbidding discrimination against gays and lesbians,* family issues were the engine propelling the rise of the Christian Right. "Conservatives can win," he declared, when they fight for "traditional family values." This movement brought Protestant fundamentalism back into American politics in a way that had not been seen since the Second Great Awakening.[6]

BEFORE THE 1970s, no one would have associated the Republican Party with opposition to abortion. Republican politicians had spearheaded some of the earliest efforts to liberalize abortion laws in California, Colorado, and New York; Barry Goldwater, one of the party's conservative icons and its 1964 presidential candidate, had supported abortion rights; and in 1967, California Governor Ronald Reagan signed a bill liberalizing that state's abortion laws. But as the anti-ERA movement energized the Christian Right, and as the focus expanded from the ERA to issues of sexuality, reproduction, obscenity, homosexuality, and abortion, Republican Party strategists saw a unique opportunity to bring a critical voting bloc into the fold.

The potential political gain was enormous. By the mid-1970s, polls showed that more than a third of all Americans self-identified as "born again." Evangelicals had become the nation's largest religious demographic. Christian bookstores sold millions of copies of books by James Dobson, Tim and Beverly LaHaye, and Billy Graham, and more than sixty nationally syndicated religious broadcasters, along with many more local TV preachers, filled the airwaves with evangelical messages. Influenced by its growing connection to the Christian Right, the Republican Party increasingly embraced the "right to life" as a central tenet of its program.[7]

When the Rev. Jerry Falwell, an evangelical Southern Baptist pastor, televangelist, and conservative political commentator, founded the Moral

---

* See chapter 11.

Majority in 1979, he brought together, through the engine of the Culture Wars, the many disparate elements of Christian fundamentalism into a single, unified political movement. In the tradition of Billy Sunday and Aimee Semple McPherson, Falwell established the Moral Majority to counteract what he deemed the "liberalizing" tendencies in American society. Falwell explained that, as in a Puritan chiliastic vision, *Roe* had awakened him from his slumber and showed him that preachers must not only speak out against sin to their flock, but must also strive to bring about political change. Falwell derided the Framers' commitment to the separation of church and state and insisted that if evangelicals worked together they had the power "to take control of the national government."[8]

The Moral Majority raised huge amounts of money to support political candidates, and in state after state its members wrested control of the state Republican apparatus from party regulars. As one observer noted,

Rev. Jerry Falwell

Falwell's "masterful use of publicity gained him access to corridors of power that other Christian Right activists had never dreamed of entering." By the summer of 1980, Republican Party leaders were treating Falwell, more than any other religious figure in American history, like the leader of a powerful political constituency.[9]

Evangelicals now realized that for the first time in more than a century they had "the voting power and the financial resources to change national politics." Christian broadcaster Pat Robertson, who railed that "the feminist agenda" was "a socialist, anti-family, political movement that encourages women to leave their husbands, kill their children, practice witchcraft, destroy capitalism, and become lesbians," boasted that the evangelical community now had "enough votes to run the country." Evangelical leaders were increasingly confident that conservative Christians were now in a position to compel the Republican Party to embrace their positions on obscenity, abortion, gay rights, and the ERA. They were now, in their view, the true "moral majority."[10]

In 1980, in his pursuit of the presidency, Ronald Reagan condemned abortion as immoral and advocated a constitutional amendment to overturn *Roe*. For the first time, the issue of abortion sharply divided the Republican and Democratic parties, and Reagan, despite his Hollywood roots, officially allied himself with the Christian Right. In August of 1980, he journeyed to Dallas to address fifteen thousand evangelical leaders who had gathered at the Religious Roundtable's National Affairs Briefing. The Christian Right viewed this event "as the beginning of a long-term alliance." The leaders of the Christian Right determined then and there that electing Ronald Reagan president was the key to getting the federal government to curb abortion rights, put women back in their place, roll back the gay rights movement, and "lead the nation back to morality."[11]

As part of this bargain, the Republican Party platform of 1980 promised the appointment of pro-life, socially conservative judges at all levels of the judiciary, thus ushering in a historic era of judicial nominations shaped in no small part by religious conceptions of constitutional law. Jerry Falwell called the 1980 Republican Party platform a "dream platform" that "could easily be the constitutional of a fundamentalist Baptist Church."

Abandoning any pretense of nonpartisanship, evangelical leaders for the first time in American history began to coordinate their activities in a concerted effort to elect a designated candidate for president. In the 1980 election, priests and pastors expressly endorsed "pro-life" candidates across the nation and the evangelical *Christian Voice* magazine issued a "moral report card" rating congressional candidates on abortion and other moral issues. Politicians across the nation suddenly realized that their position on *Roe* could well determine their political futures.

Jerry Falwell declared Ronald Reagan's election in November 1980 the greatest event for the cause of "morality in my adult life," and James Dobson, the founder of Focus on the Family, proclaimed that evangelicals had finally "come home" and that "home was the White House."[12]

RESISTING *ROE*

AS THE OPPOSITION to *Roe* crystalized and became more focused and energized, several responses to *Roe* emerged. The first, and most obvious, was to enact a constitutional amendment to overturn the decision. Only eight days after the Court announced its decision in *Roe*, Catholic members of Congress began introducing what came to be known as "human life" amendments.* These proposed constitutional amendments provided, in one form or another, that nothing in the Constitution should be understood to limit the authority of the state and federal governments to regulate or prohibit abortion.

These proposals attempted to recast abortion, not as a fundamental right of the woman, but as the murder of unborn children. The Catholic Church established the National Right to Life Committee, which enlisted priests to recruit supporters, raise money, and promote a popular movement to amend the Constitution.[13] In the mid-1970s, fifty different right to life amendments were put before Congress, but to no avail. None garnered the votes necessary to move the process forward. Frustrated, but undaunted, the pro-life forces next turned to the political process in an effort to elect more members of Congress who would support a human life amendment.[14]

At the end of the decade, with the founding of the Moral Majority, Protestant evangelicals, who in the past had divided on the issue of abortion, now joined forces with Catholics in their demand for a human life amendment. In an effort to court the Catholic and evangelical vote in the 1982 midterm election, President Reagan promised that he would "not rest . . . until a human life amendment becomes part of our Constitution."

In the 1984 election, Christian Right leaders dropped all pretense of nonpartisanship and, in an unprecedented effort to achieve the necessary majority in Congress, went all out for the Republican Party. Eighty per-

---

* See chapter 16.

cent of evangelicals voted for Republican candidates up and down the line. This represented a profound and historic shift in the American political landscape. Only a decade earlier, a majority of evangelicals had supported the Democratic Party. But despite their passion, their commitment, their resources, and the certainty of their convictions, even the Catholic Church and the Moral Majority *combined* could not muster enough votes to achieve the two-thirds majority that was necessary to get a human life amendment through Congress.[15]

A SECOND response to *Roe*, born out of outrage and frustration, was resort to obstruction and violence. Some anti-abortion activists directly interfered with the operation of abortion clinics by blocking entrances, harassing women who sought to enter, and publishing the names of women who obtained abortions. Others went further.[16]

In 1980, Joseph Scheidler founded the Pro-Life Action League, a national organization dedicated to confronting "abortionists" and their supporters. The Action League picketed abortion clinics, pro-choice organizations, and the homes of both those who performed legal abortions and those who had them. Scheidler's supporters jammed clinic telephone lines so patients could not make appointments and scheduled fraudulent appointments to overwhelm the schedules of abortion providers.[17]

Another tactic used by abortion opponents was to establish fraudulent abortion clinics, which advertised aggressively in an effort to lure in women seeking to exercise their right to terminate an unwanted pregnancy. The unsuspecting women were then greeted with harsh anti-abortion messages, shown gruesome slides of aborted fetuses, and given dire warnings about the supposed medical consequences of abortion. By 1988, there were between 800 and 2,000 fraudulent abortion clinics in the United States, and they managed to draw in—and to intimidate—almost half-a-million women annually.[18]

The anger generated by legal abortions triggered even more extreme responses. In 1978, a Cleveland clinic was firebombed, an act that elicited cheers from several anti-abortions organizations on the ground that violence was a necessary and morally appropriate response to the slaughter of unborn children. Anti-abortion violence soared in the mid-1980s, in part as a result of increasing frustration over the lack of progress on the political front. In 1984 alone there were 161 acts of violence against abortion clinics and twenty-one reported death threats against medical and other personnel.[19]

In 1986, the anti-abortion activist Randall Terry founded Operation Rescue, an organization dedicated to the proposition that "if you believe abortion is murder, act like it's murder." Doctors and other employees of abortion clinics were increasingly subjected to threats, harassment, and violence. In 1993, for example, Michael Griffin, a right-to-life activist, shot and killed a forty-seven-year-old physician, Dr. David Gunn, because he had performed legal abortions in Florida. Pro-life extremists applauded Griffin's act, proclaiming that by murdering Dr. Gunn, Griffin had saved the lives of many as-yet-unborn babies.

In part as a consequence of this violence, fewer and fewer doctors and hospitals were willing to perform abortions, making it ever more difficult for women to exercise their right to terminate unwanted pregnancies. By the mid-1990s, the number of doctors receiving abortion training in medical schools and residency programs had decreased dramatically; 84 percent of all counties in the United States, and 95 percent of all rural counties, had no abortion providers; and there were six hundred fewer hospitals offering abortion services than twenty years earlier.[20]

But despite these efforts, the core right recognized by the Court in *Roe* remained intact, and almost a million women each year still managed to have safe and *legal* abortions. Violence was not enough to stem the tide.

THE THIRD response to *Roe* was legal regulation. *Roe* did not prohibit all regulation of abortion. Although the Court held in *Roe* that the state cannot constitutionally interfere with a woman's decision to terminate a pregnancy during the first trimester, it also held that in the second trimester, as the possible health risks to the woman increase, the state can reasonably regulate the abortion procedure in order to protect the woman's health. Moreover, at the beginning of the third trimester, after the fetus is viable, the Court held that the state could constitutionally prohibit abortion, unless the procedure was necessary to preserve the life or health of the woman.

Although this structure seems reasonably clear, much was left unresolved. In the years since *Roe*, the federal and state governments have enacted hundreds, if not thousands, of laws testing the limits of this structure. Some of these laws reflect good faith efforts to exercise the authority left open by the Court to regulate abortion for appropriate reasons in the second and third trimesters. Others, however, were clearly designed to push the envelope and to see just how far the Court would push back.

Not surprisingly, the aggressiveness of these regulations has varied from state to state, depending largely on the political and religious makeup of the community. In states that are predominantly Republican or have large Catholic or evangelical populations, the efforts to restrict abortion have often been quite aggressive. Indeed, in many instances the legislative attitude was, in effect, "We *dare* you to hold this unconstitutional!"[21]

Thus, in the years since *Roe*, the state and federal governments have enacted a broad range of restrictions on the circumstances in which a woman can terminate an unwanted pregnancy. Illustrative restrictions include laws requiring first trimester abortions to be performed by a licensed physician, prohibiting any advertisement for abortion services, requiring a woman to wait several days before having an abortion, prohibiting a woman to have an abortion without first obtaining the father's consent, prohibiting a minor to have an abortion without first obtaining parental consent, requiring facilities that perform abortions to have all the features of ambulatory surgical centers, and prohibiting "partial-birth" abortions even when necessary to protect the life or health of the woman.[22]

These and similar laws have kept the Supreme Court very busy, indeed.

T HE FOURTH response to *Roe* focused on the makeup of the Supreme Court itself. Who, in short, would get the last word on the constitutionality of such laws? *Roe* raised the stakes dramatically in the Supreme Court nomination and confirmation process. Indeed, ever since the 1980 Republican Party platform promised the appointment of judges who respect "the sanctity of innocent human life," the question "What is your view of *Roe?*" has played a central role in both the president's choice of Supreme Court nominees and the often bitter struggles in the Senate over confirmation. If the anti-abortion movement could not muster the votes needed to overturn *Roe* by constitutional amendment, then perhaps it could achieve the same result by transforming the Court and thus getting the decision narrowed or even overruled.

REFINING ROE

IN THE YEARS after *Roe*, the Supreme Court took a generally firm stance in defense of the right of a woman to terminate an unwanted pregnancy. Thus, in a series of decisions between 1973 and 1990, the Court, often over sharply-worded dissents, invalidated laws requiring a woman's husband to give prior written consent before she could obtain an abortion; requiring second trimester abortions to be performed in a hospital; requiring a woman's physician to inform her of the availability of adoption services before allowing her to consent to an abortion; requiring a woman to wait twenty-four hours after signing a consent form before she could obtain an abortion; requiring parental consent before an unmarried woman under the age of eighteen could obtain an abortion; and prohibiting advertisements for abortions.[23]

At the same time, though, the Court in this era did uphold some regulations of abortion. For example, the Court sustained the constitutionality of requirements that records be kept about the performance of abortions, that tissue samples of aborted fetuses be submitted to certified pathologists, and that a minor who sought to have an abortion must first obtain either parental consent or judicial approval. In the Court's view, these were reasonable regulations that did not significantly interfere with the fundamental right recognized in *Roe*.[24]

More controversially, the Court in these years also upheld the constitutionality of laws prohibiting the use of public Medicaid funds to enable indigent women to pay for legal abortions. In 1977, for example, in a six-to-three decision in *Maher v. Roe*,[25] the Court rejected a constitutional challenge to a Connecticut statute which, like the laws in thirty-three other states, prohibited the use of state Medicaid funds to pay for indigent women's abortions unless the abortion was necessary to protect the life or health of the woman.

In an opinion by Justice Lewis Powell, who had joined the decision in *Roe*, the Court explained that although the government cannot constitutionally prohibit abortion, nothing in the Constitution requires the government to pay for the medical expenses of indigents, whether for abortion, foot surgery, prescription drugs, or any other medical matter. To the contrary, Powell reasoned, just as the government has no constitutional obligation to buy poor people megaphones so they can exercise the freedom of speech, and just as it has no constitutional obligation to buy poor people guns so they can exercise their rights under the Second Amendment, so too is it under no constitutional obligation to pay for poor women's abortions.

The dissenting justices—Brennan, Marshall, and Blackmun—objected that the issue in *Maher* was not that simple. They argued that because the state allowed Medicaid funds to be used to pay for the cost of childbirth but not for the cost of abortion, the Medicaid program unconstitutionally pressured indigent women to choose childbirth over abortion.[26] The Court rejected this argument, declaring that nothing in *Roe* prohibited the government from making "a value judgment favoring childbirth over abortion."[27]

Two years later, in *Harris v. McRae*,[28] the Court went even further and upheld the constitutionality of the so-called Hyde Amendment. Enacted in 1976, the Hyde Amendment was named after its chief sponsor, Republican Congressman Henry Hyde of Illinois. A vehement critic of *Roe*, Hyde proclaimed that "when a pregnant woman, who should be the natural protector of her unborn child, becomes its deadly adversary, then it is the duty of this legislature to intervene on behalf of defenseless human life." Unlike the Connecticut statute at issue in *Maher*, the Hyde Amendment expressly prohibited the use of federal Medicaid funds to pay for an indigent woman's abortion even if the abortion was medically necessary to protect the health of the woman.*[29]

In a sharply-divided five-to-four decision, the Court held that even when a woman's health is at risk, her "freedom of choice" does not carry with it a "constitutional entitlement" to government funds to enable her to exercise her right to abortion. The Court explained that the Hyde Amendment was constitutional because it furthered "the legitimate governmental objective of protecting potential life."[30]

In a furious dissenting opinion, Justice Thurgood Marshall, a liberal lion and the greatest civil rights advocate of the twentieth century, offered an impassioned critique of the Court's reasoning. The majority, Marshall argued, coldly ignored the fact that women too poor to pay for *medically necessary* abortions would now be left with no choice but to "resort to back-alley butchers, attempt to induce an abortion themselves by crude and dangerous methods, or suffer the serious medical consequences of attempting to carry the fetus to term." The Court's decision, Marshall fumed, "represents a cruel blow to the most powerless members of our society."†[31]

Despite these decisions on funding, which dealt with the admittedly complex issue of government subsidies for the exercise of constitutional rights, the core protections guaranteed by *Roe* remained largely intact. The makeup of the Court, however, was about to change.

---

* The Hyde Amendment permitted Medicaid funds to be used only if the woman's life was at stake or if she had been the victim of rape or incest.

† In subsequent decisions, the Court extended the principle of *Maher* and *Harris*, holding that government can constitutionally prohibit public hospitals from performing abortions and can even constitutionally prohibit doctors who receive public funds to support family planning programs to inform their patients about the availability of abortion. See *Webster v. Reproductive Health Services*, 492 U.S. 490 (1989); *Rust v. Sullivan*, 500 U.S. 173 (1991).

"OUR WORST FEARS HAVE JUST BEEN REALIZED"

A HISTORIC SHIFT significantly changed the direction of the Supreme Court in the years after *Roe*. In 1975, President Gerald Ford appointed John Paul Stevens to replace Justice William O. Douglas. In 1981, President Ronald Reagan appointed Sandra Day O'Connor to replace Justice Potter Stewart. In 1986, President Reagan promoted William Rehnquist to replace Chief Justice Warren Burger and then appointed Antonin Scalia to fill Justice Rehnquist's seat on the Court. In 1988, President Reagan appointed Anthony Kennedy to replace Justice Lewis Powell. In 1990, President George H. W. Bush appointed David Souter to replace Justice William Brennan. And in 1991, President George H. W. Bush appointed Clarence Thomas to replace Justice Thurgood Marshall. Thus, between 1975 and 1991 a succession of Republican presidents had made six consecutive appointments to the Supreme Court, transforming the institution and replacing six of the seven justices who had voted with the majority in *Roe*. Of those seven justices, only the author of *Roe*, Justice Harry Blackmun, remained on the Court.

Moreover, as *Roe* increasingly became a cultural and political lightning rod, a central theme in all five of the post-1980 nominations was the future of *Roe* itself. As the journalist Jan Crawford has observed, "For religious conservatives, the Supreme Court had become a battleground, and abortion was its defining war." From the moment Ronald Reagan assumed the presidency, the die was cast. In his 1980 campaign, he had pledged to appoint judges who would respect "the sanctity of innocent human life." The time soon came for him to honor that pledge.

In 1981, as the Reagan White House contemplated the nomination of Sandra Day O'Connor to replace Justice Powell, White House adviser Mike Uhlmann cautioned Ed Meese, then the counselor to the president, that "it is important to bear in mind the special significance that right-to-lifers attach to Supreme Court nominations." Although members of the Christian Right urged Reagan to nominate Phyllis Schlafly, he instead chose O'Connor, a little-known justice on the Arizona Supreme Court.

O'Connor grew up on a cattle ranch in Arizona. She went on to graduate near the top of her class from Stanford Law School in 1952, but found it almost impossible to secure a job with a law firm because she was a woman. She finally found employment as a deputy county attorney in San Mateo, California, but only after she agreed to work for no salary and without an office. Over the next quarter-century she served as assistant attorney general of Arizona, as the first woman majority leader of the Arizona Senate, and as a judge on the Arizona Court of Appeals.

Because O'Connor's views on abortion were unclear, and because she declined to state publicly that she would vote to overrule *Roe*, right-to-life groups vehemently opposed her nomination. Moral Majority leader Jerry Falwell called her nomination a "disaster," and the head of the National Right to Life Committee denounced it as a "betrayal." But those groups had not yet attained the influence they would later have, and Reagan satisfied himself with O'Connor's assurance to him that she was "personally opposed" to abortion. O'Connor was confirmed by a vote of 99–0.[32]

Each year, the Christian Right continued to gain political power and influence. In an inflammatory address in 1984, President Reagan declared that because of "our nation-wide policy of abortion on demand . . . more than 15 million unborn children have had their lives snuffed out by legalized abortion. That is over ten times the number of Americans lost in our nation's wars."[33] The following year, the Reagan Justice Department launched a full-scale attack on *Roe*, urging the Court to overrule the decision because it lacked any "textual, doctrinal or historical basis."[34] Although the Court was not yet ready to embrace that position, the argument was very much in the air.

The next year, Reagan nominated Antonin Scalia to the Supreme Court. A former law professor at the University of Chicago and judge on the United States Court of Appeals, Scalia was a leading proponent of "originalism" as a method of constitutional interpretation. Proponents of that approach argued that the right of a woman to terminate an unwanted pregnancy could not plausibly be found in the "original meaning" of the Constitution. The Reagan administration agreed. O'Connor's appointment had fulfilled a campaign promise to appoint a woman justice; Scalia's appointment was designed to further "Reagan's quest for a remade judiciary." In short, this was Reagan's "opportunity to shift the Court's direction."

In a memo on Scalia's nomination, White House staffer Patrick Buchanan referred to "the cruciality of the Supreme Court to the Right-to-Life Movement," a group that could help "provide the Republicans with the decisive Presidential Margins" in future elections. Scalia was perfect, because he was a "fervent antiabortion Catholic with street-fighter intensity."[35] Not surprisingly, *Roe* was a central focus of Scalia's confirmation hearings. Senator Edward Kennedy, a committed civil libertarian and a staunch advocate for a woman's right to choose, asked Scalia point-blank: "If you were confirmed, do you expect to overrule *Roe v. Wade*?" Exercising discretion, Scalia replied: "Senator, I do not think it would be proper for me to answer that question," but he assured Kennedy that "I am not going onto the Court with a list of things I want to do." The Senate confirmed Scalia by a vote of 98–0. In the first abortion case Justice Scalia heard as a member of the Supreme Court, he called for *Roe* to be overruled.[36]

T HEN, IN 1987, after Justice Lewis Powell announced his intention to retire, President Reagan nominated Robert Bork to replace him. Bork had been a distinguished law professor at Yale, solicitor general of the United States, and a judge on the United States Court of Appeals. Robert Bork first became a household name in the United States in 1973 when, as part of the "Saturday Night Massacre," he complied with Richard Nixon's directive to fire Watergate Special Prosecutor Archibald Cox after his two superiors in the Justice Department, Attorney General Elliot Richardson and Deputy Attorney General William Ruckelshaus, both resigned rather than do so.

Like Scalia, Bork was an originalist. He was strident in his criticism of the Warren Court, and across a range of issues he had staked out what many of his critics saw as extreme conservative positions. Perhaps most provocatively, Bork proclaimed in no uncertain terms that the Constitution had nothing at all to say about a right to privacy, a right to use contraceptives, or a right to abortion. Indeed, in testimony before a Senate Judiciary Committee subcommittee several years earlier, Bork had denounced *Roe* as "an unconstitutional decision."[37]

Among the pro-choice groups in Washington, Justice Powell's resignation set off alarm bells. They feared that with another conservative justice on the Court, *Roe* could be in serious jeopardy. When Kate Michelman, the executive director of the National Abortion Rights Action League (NARAL), learned of Powell's resignation, she exclaimed, "Our worst fears have just been realized."[38]

Shortly after Reagan named Bork as his nominee, Senator Edward Kennedy warned that "Robert Bork's America is a land in which women would be forced into back-alley abortions."[39] Unlike Antonin Scalia and most other nominees, Bork did not exercise restraint in his confirmation hearings. Instead, he attempted to conduct a seminar in constitutional theory, an admirable but ultimately disastrous course. At the center of the debate was the concern that, if confirmed, Bork would provide the critical fifth vote to overrule *Roe*. In the course of his hearings, Bork gave proponents of *Roe* plenty to worry about, insisting in his testimony that "*Roe v.*

Wade contains almost no legal reasoning." In the end, Bork's nomination went down to defeat by a vote of fifty-eight nays to forty-two ayes. Adding insult to injury, six Republican senators voted against confirmation. Many factors contributed to Robert Bork's defeat, but central among them was the sense that he was a sure bet to vote to overrule *Roe*.

O VER THE next three years, Presidents Reagan and George H. W. Bush appointed three more justices to the Court. By 1991, with the additions of Anthony Kennedy, David Souter, and Clarence Thomas, it seemed inevitable that *Roe* would be overruled. When Anthony Kennedy was vetted by lawyers in the Department of Justice, he implied that "he was solidly opposed to *Roe*"; when George H. W. Bush nominated David Souter, Eleanor Smeal, president of the Fund for the Feminist Majority, pronounced him "a devastating threat" on the issue of abortion; and no one believed Clarence Thomas's claim during his confirmation hearings that he "had never had time to discuss or debate *Roe v. Wade* with anyone in the eighteen years since the decision."[40]

The Court now included eight justices who had been appointed by Republican presidents. Moreover, Justice Byron White, the only justice appointed by a Democratic president, had dissented in *Roe*. Only Harry Blackmun, now a member of the Court for more than two decades, remained from the seven justices in the majority in *Roe*. Would *Roe* now be overruled? Justice Blackmun feared the worst, noting in his private papers that for the Court "to overthrow" *Roe* would turn millions "of American women into criminals" and would "return us to the back alley, and a number of these women, an unconscionable number, will die."

The question finally came to a head in 1992.[41]

PLANNED PARENTHOOD V. CASEY: "I FEAR FOR THE DARKNESS"

THE DRAMA LEADING UP to the Court's decision in *Planned Parenthood of Southeastern Pennsylvania v. Casey*[42] cannot be overstated. By 1992, several states, including Utah and Louisiana, had defiantly enacted laws that outlawed almost all abortions that were not necessary to save the life of the woman. Shortly before the argument in *Casey*, which involved the constitutionality of a series of Pennsylvania restrictions on abortion, more than half-a-million people marched on the nation's capital to demand that *Roe* be overturned. Once again, a Republican administration—this one led by President George H. W. Bush—urged the Court to overrule *Roe*.

In his brief for the United States in *Casey*, Solicitor General Kenneth Starr, who would later spearhead the impeachment of President Bill Clinton, left no doubt of the Bush administration's position: "*Roe v. Wade* was wrongly decided and should be overruled. . . . The protection of innocent human life—in and out of the womb—is certainly the most compelling interest that a State can advance. In our view, a State's interest in protecting fetal life throughout pregnancy . . . outweighs a woman's liberty interest in an abortion."[43]

With David Souter and Clarence Thomas now on the Court, the conventional wisdom assumed that the newly-constituted Court was finally poised to overrule *Roe*. Indeed, as the *New York Times* journalist Linda Greenhouse observed, "With the new makeup of the Court, *Roe* had never looked so imperiled."

At the Court's conference after the oral argument in *Casey*, Justices O'Connor and Souter seemed hesitant, but five justices seemed ready to change the course of history. With the support of Justices White, Scalia, Kennedy, and Thomas, Chief Justice Rehnquist assigned the opinion to himself. In the words of the legal journalist Jan Crawford, it was the opinion "he had waited eighteen years to write."

But two days after Rehnquist circulated his draft majority opinion to the other justices, Justice Anthony Kennedy sent Justice Blackmun a rather cryptic note. Kennedy, who was raised in an Irish Catholic family in Sacramento, California, earned his law degree from Harvard, and then practiced and taught law in California, had been nominated to the United States Court of Appeals by President Gerald Ford in 1975 on the recommendation of then-California Governor Ronald Reagan. Thirteen years later, Reagan, confident of Kennedy's conservative credentials and outlook, appointed him to the Supreme Court.

Kennedy's note to Blackmun read: "I need to see you as soon as you have a few free moments. I want to tell you about some developments in *Planned Parenthood v. Casey*, and at least part of what I say should come as welcome news." It was, for Blackmun, "welcome news" indeed. When the two justices met the following day, Kennedy informed Blackmun that he, O'Connor, and Souter "had been meeting privately and were jointly drafting an opinion that, far from overruling *Roe*, would save it." Ever after, pro-life conservatives would cast Kennedy in the "role of traitor."

This was a role Kennedy would come to play often in the Court's later decisions dealing with issues of sexual expression, sexual orientation, and same-sex marriage. Kennedy, a justice who cannot easily be pigeonholed ideologically, once boasted to his law clerks that rather than let a rigid ideology dictate his positions, he tries in each case "to get it right." Whether he succeeds is, of course, a matter of some dispute.[44]

IN A five-to-four decision, with Justices Blackmun, Stevens, O'Connor, Kennedy, and Souter in the majority—all five appointed by Republican presidents—the Court concluded, in a stunning turn of events, that "the essential holding of *Roe v. Wade* should be retained and once again reaffirmed."[45] After ratifying the underlying constitutional rationale of *Roe*, the Court explained that even if some members of the majority had reservations about *Roe*, there was no sufficient justification for overruling it. In short, none of the traditional reasons for overruling a precedent—that it had

Justice Sandra Day O'Connor

proved unworkable over time, that it could be jettisoned without upsetting settled expectations, or that subsequent decisions had eroded its rationale—was present in the case of *Roe*. Moreover, even if a justice were inclined to overrule *Roe*, there were important institutional reasons not to do so. This was so, the Court observed, because when viewed against the continuing political controversy over abortion, such a decision would inevitably be seen as "a surrender to political pressure" that "would subvert the Court's legitimacy."[46]

Although reaffirming "the essential holding" of *Roe*, Justices O'Connor, Kennedy, and Souter then parted company with Blackmun and Stevens and jettisoned the trimester framework of *Roe*. In an unusual opinion authored by the three of them jointly, O'Connor, Kennedy, and Souter maintained that the trimester framework was unduly "rigid" and was "unnecessary" to protect the core of the right guaranteed in *Roe*.

In their view, the critical "line should be drawn at viability," because viability marks "the time at which there is a realistic possibility of maintaining and nourishing a life outside the womb." At that point, which shifts over time with medical advances, the state's interest in protecting human life "overrides" the woman's interests in privacy and personal liberty. This is only fair, they reasoned, because "it might be said that a woman who fails to act before viability has consented to the State's intervention on behalf of the developing child."[47]

O'Connor, Kennedy, and Souter concluded further that although a woman has a right to decide for herself whether to terminate a pregnancy before viability, the government can constitutionally impose regulations "to ensure that this choice is thoughtful and informed." Even in the earliest stages of pregnancy, for example, the government may enact regulations designed to inform the woman that there are "arguments of great weight that can be brought to bear in favor of continuing the pregnancy" and that there are alternatives available to abortion, including adoption and, in some cases, financial assistance if the woman chooses to raise the child.

Thus, "only where state regulation imposes an *undue burden* on a woman's ability" to decide to terminate a pregnancy previability does it violate the Constitution. Government measures "designed to persuade" a pregnant woman "to choose childbirth over abortion" are therefore constitutional, unless they "constitute an undue burden" on her "freedom of choice."[48]

Applying this newly fashioned standard, O'Connor, Kennedy, and Souter, joined by the four dissenting justices—who called for *Roe* to be overruled—upheld the constitutionality of several statutory restrictions on the right of women to obtain previability abortions, including requirements that, except in a medical emergency, a person performing an abortion must inform the woman at least 24 hours before the abortion of "the health risks of the abortion" and of "the availability of printed materials published by the State describing the fetus and providing information about . . . agencies which provide adoption and other services as alternatives to abortion." In upholding these regulations, the Court in *Casey* overruled several earlier decisions that had held such restrictions unconstitutional.*[49]

Although dissenting from the Court's decision to uphold these restrictions, Justice Blackmun nonetheless commended O'Connor, Kennedy, and Souter for "an act of personal courage and constitutional principle" and for reaffirming that "the Constitution protects a woman's right to terminate her pregnancy in its early stages."[50]

CHIEF JUSTICE REHNQUIST, joined by Justices White, Scalia, and Thomas, declared that "*Roe* was wrongly decided" and "should be overruled." Reiterating his dissent in *Roe*, Rehnquist, who had been robbed of his opportunity to write the opinion finally overturning *Roe*, argued that unlike marriage, procreation, and contraception, which might plausibly be recognized as "fundamental" constitutional rights, abortion should never have been brought within the right of privacy because it "involves the purposeful termination of a potential life" and because there was no "deeply rooted tradition of relatively unrestricted abortion in our history."[51]

In a separate opinion, a furious Justice Scalia proclaimed in no uncertain terms that "the power of a woman to abort her unborn child" is not "a liberty protected by the Constitution." This was so, he explained, "because of two simple facts: (1) the Constitution says absolutely nothing about it, and (2) longstanding traditions of American society have permitted it to be legally proscribed." Scalia therefore concluded that the Court "should get out of this area, where we have no right to be."[52]

Although relieved, Justice Blackmun, looking to the future, saw much "to fear." "I fear for the darkness," he wrote, "as four Justices anxiously await the single vote necessary to extinguish the light. . . . I am 83 years old. I cannot remain on this Court forever, and when I do step down, the confirmation process for my successor well may focus on the issue before us today.

---

* The Court in *Casey* overruled parts of the decisions in *City of Akron v. Akron Center for Reproductive Health, Inc.*, 462 U.S. 416 (1983) and *Thornburgh v. American College of Obstetricians & Gynecologists*, 476 U.S. 747 (1986).

That, I regret, may be exactly where the choice between the two worlds will be made."[53]

"PARTIAL-BIRTH" ABORTION

ALTHOUGH THE CORE of *Roe* had been saved, the 1992 presidential election once again put the decision at risk. As Harry Blackmun had noted in *Casey*, his days on the Court were numbered. If George H. W. Bush was reelected, he might replace Blackmun with another conservative like Clarence Thomas or Antonin Scalia, and who knew where that might lead? When Bill Clinton defeated Bush, those in the pro-*Roe* camp were greatly relieved.

Shortly thereafter, Justice Byron White, who had opposed *Roe* for two decades, announced his retirement. Clinton's appointment of Ruth Bader Ginsburg, a staunch defender of the rights of women—even though a critic of Blackmun's opinion in *Roe*—meant that there would now be six likely supporters of *Roe* on the Court. In such circumstances, Justice Blackmun felt secure in announcing his own retirement the following year. When President Clinton appointed Stephen Breyer, a former Harvard law professor who had worked closely with Senator Edward Kennedy on the Senate Judiciary Committee, as Blackmun's successor, the six-justice majority to preserve *Roe* settled into place.

For the most part, the Supreme Court got out of the business of making headlines over abortion for the next decade. The most significant case the Court decided on the meaning of *Roe* and *Casey* in this era dealt with the question of so-called partial-birth abortion. In 2000, the Court, in *Stenberg v. Carhart*,[54] considered the constitutionality of a Nebraska statute banning partial-birth abortion, both pre- and post-viability, except when "necessary to save the life of the mother." The statute defined partial-birth abortion as "an abortion procedure in which the person performing the abortion partially delivers vaginally a living unborn child before killing the unborn child" in order to complete the delivery. Thirty-one states had similar laws at the time.

To understand the issue, some background is necessary. As the Court explained the situation in *Stenberg*, approximately 90 percent of all abortions performed in the United States take place in the first trimester of pregnancy, before twelve weeks of gestational age. During this period, the most common method of abortion is vacuum aspiration, which involves the insertion of a vacuum tube into the uterus to evacuate the contents. Such abortions, which are much safer than childbirth, are typically performed on an outpatient basis under local anesthesia.

Later in the gestation process, after about fifteen weeks, when vacuum aspiration is no longer effective, doctors most often use a procedure known as standard dilation and evacuation (standard D&E), in which the doctor dismembers the fetus in utero in order to remove it from the woman. In a small number of late-term abortions, however, estimated as less than 0.5 percent of all abortions annually, the doctor may use a procedure called intact dilation and extraction (intact D&E), which involves partially extracting a fetus from the uterus and then collapsing its skull in order to extract it from the woman in as intact a manner as possible. This is what is meant by "partial-birth abortion."

Doctors who use intact D&E typically do so because, in at least some cases, the standard D&E method can cause substantial blood loss in the woman, increase the risk of puncturing the cervix, and impair the woman's ability to have children in the future. There is substantial disagreement within the medical profession about the relative advantages and disadvantages of the two procedures, although the standard D&E is generally accepted as the preferred method of performing late-term abortions.

The Court, in a bitterly divided five-to-four decision, held the Nebraska law, which banned the use of intact D&E in all cases except when necessary to save the life of the woman, unconstitutional. Justice Breyer, joined by Justices Stevens, O'Connor, Souter, and Ginsburg, wrote the majority opinion. Breyer observed that although the medical profession was divided on the necessity for using partial-birth abortion, many medical authorities were of the view that for at least some mid- and late-term abortions the procedure was safer than other abortion procedures.

This being so, Breyer reasoned that the state had failed to demonstrate that partial-birth abortion was *never* necessary to preserve the health of the woman. Thus, under *Casey*, the Nebraska statute imposed an "undue burden" on the right of a woman to terminate an unwanted pregnancy previability, and violated the right of a woman to terminate a pregnancy post-viability in circumstances in which use of the procedure was, in appropriate medical judgment, necessary to preserve the woman's health. The law was therefore unconstitutional.

Chief Justice Rehnquist and Justices Kennedy, Scalia, and Thomas dissented. In a scathing opinion, Justice Scalia predicted that "one day" this decision "will be assigned its rightful place in the history of this Court's jurisprudence" beside what he described as two of the Court's most shameful decisions—*Korematsu v. United States*[55] (in which the Court had upheld the constitutionality of the Japanese internment during World War II) and *Dred Scott v. Sandford*[56] (in which the Court had held that African Americans could not be citizens of the United States). "The notion that the Constitution of the United States . . . prohibits the States from simply banning this visibly brutal means of eliminating our half-born posterity is," he declared, "quite simply absurd."[57]

Justice Kennedy, who had been the critical fifth vote in *Casey*, was livid. As one observer put the point, Kennedy now felt that in joining *Casey*, he had been "had."[58] In his view, in light of the medical disagreement over the necessity for what he regarded as a gruesome procedure, the government was entitled to find that the ban on partial-birth abortion advanced important state interests in safeguarding the sanctity of human life, without substantially interfering with "the rights of any woman." In such circumstances, he concluded, *Casey* required the Court to defer to what he deemed the reasonable judgment of the state, even if some medical authorities disagreed with that judgment. The Court's decision in *Stenberg* was clearly not what Justice Kennedy had had in mind when he cast his decisive vote in *Casey*.*[59]

"IN THE MOLD OF SCALIA AND THOMAS"

SIX MONTHS AFTER *Stenberg*, President George W. Bush took the oath of office after a bitterly contested election that was ultimately decided by the Supreme Court. During the 2000 campaign, Bush promised to appoint judges "in the mold of Scalia and Thomas," a vow that excited and energized his anti-abortion supporters. In his first term, however, Bush had no opportunities to appoint a justice to the Supreme Court. In his 2004 reelection campaign, Bush needed to stoke his conservative base, particularly evangelical Christians. He therefore went out of his way in his debates with Democratic nominee John Kerry to declare that in his view *Roe* was a "monstrous" decision that needed to be overturned.[60]

In 2005, Bush had his first opportunity to shape the direction of the Court when Justice O'Connor, a Reagan nominee who had deeply disap-

---

* In another dissenting opinion, Justice Thomas, joined by Chief Justice Rehnquist and Justice Scalia, reiterated their view that *Roe* "was grievously wrong" and should be overruled.

pointed the anti-*Roe* forces by playing a pivotal role in preserving the right to abortion in *Casey* and by joining the majority in *Stenberg*, announced her intention to retire. The first name floated by the White House was that of Attorney General Alberto Gonzales, a longtime ally of George W. Bush and a former justice on the Texas Supreme Court.

Although Gonzales was by every measure a committed conservative, the anti-abortion lobby was concerned that, in the words of Phyllis Schlafly, his "paper trail" did not establish that he would be a reliable vote on *Roe*. That "paper trail" consisted of a decision Gonzales had joined as a justice on the Texas Supreme Court in which he had dutifully applied the Supreme Court's precedents on abortion.[61] Although this revealed nothing about Gonzales's own views on abortion, the vehemence and influence of the anti-*Roe* forces were so powerful that Bush quickly dropped Gonzales from consideration.[62]

After reviewing several other possibilities, Bush and his advisers settled on John Roberts to replace O'Connor. Roberts, who had served as a law clerk to Justice William Rehnquist in 1980 and had then worked for several years in the Reagan White House, had been appointed to the United States Court of Appeals by Bush in 2003. Roberts had a long track record as a solid conservative, and he was able to garner the support of the pro-life lobby that had derailed Gonzales.

Before Roberts could be confirmed to replace O'Connor, however, Chief Justice Rehnquist suddenly died. Bush promptly nominated Roberts to succeed Rehnquist as chief justice. In his confirmation hearings, Roberts successfully ducked the issue of abortion. Although conceding that *Roe* was "settled as a precedent of the court," he also noted that the Court sometimes overruled its own decisions. Careful not to make the same mistake as Robert Bork, he declined to say how he himself might vote on that question. Because Roberts was now replacing Rehnquist rather than O'Connor, his confirmation would not affect the balance on the Court on the issue of abortion—even if it turned out that he was willing to overrule *Roe*. He was therefore easily confirmed by a vote of seventy-eight to twenty-two.[63]

B UT THAT left Bush with the task of finding a replacement for O'Connor. Bush wanted to appoint a woman and he quickly settled on Harriet Miers, his White House counsel. Miers's nomination turned out to be a "political black comedy." Although she almost surely would have been confirmed, her nomination was "vetoed by the most conservative elements of the Republican Party" in a move that shocked the White House. Miers was an evangelical Christian who had publicly supported a constitutional amendment to overrule *Roe*, but the anti-abortion faction was still skeptical. To address this concern, Karl Rove, Bush's closest adviser and deputy chief of staff, arranged a conference call with an alliance of sixty pro-life organizations. The central question was: "Do you believe she would vote to overturn *Roe v. Wade?*" The answer offered by Rove was: "Absolutely." But the pro-lifers remained unconvinced. They feared that Miers, who had no judicial track record, might turn out to be another "turncoat" like O'Connor, Kennedy, and Souter. In the end, Miers was forced to withdraw from consideration.[64]

It then fell to President Bush and his advisers to nominate "the most conservative possible Supreme Court justice, one who would be welcomed by the Republican Party's anti-abortion base." Within days, they had their man in Samuel Alito. Like Roberts, Scalia, and Thomas, Alito was a practicing Catholic. Moreover, like Roberts, Alito had been a star among the cadre of conservative young lawyers who had staffed the Reagan Justice Department. After spending six years in the Office of the Solicitor General and the Office of Legal Counsel, President Reagan appointed Alito to serve as United States attorney in his home state of New Jersey. Then, in 1990, President George H. W. Bush appointed him to the United States Court of Appeals.

In his first year as a judge, Alito voted to uphold the very same Pennsylvania anti-abortion statute that the Supreme Court later held unconstitutional in *Casey*. In his opinion, Alito went so far as to uphold a requirement that a wife must prove that she had notified her husband of her intention to have an abortion before she could exercise her constitutional right to do so. In their opinion in *Casey*, which overturned Alito's position, Justices O'Connor, Kennedy, and Souter famously called Alito's view "repugnant to our present understanding of marriage and of the nature of the rights secured by the Constitution. Women do not lose their constitutionally protected liberty when they marry."[65]

Now, thirteen years later, Samuel Alito "was getting a promotion to O'Connor's own seat—and largely because Alito had proved his conservative bona fides in that very case." Unlike Gonzales and Miers, there was no doubt about Alito's position on *Roe*. Indeed, referring to the briefs he had written for the Solicitor General's Office in the 1980s urging the Court to overrule *Roe*, Alito later stated that he was "particularly proud" to have been able to advance that position because he "personally believed" that "the Constitution does not protect a right of abortion."

Pro-choice forces, such as the Alliance for Justice, warned that if confirmed, Alito could tip the balance on the Court in a way that could "jeopardize our most cherished rights and freedoms," and women's rights groups marched in protest against his nomination. In the end, though, Alito was confirmed by a vote of fifty-eight to forty-two. Most Democrats—including then-Senator Barack Obama—voted against confirmation. Although the opponents of confirmation had enough votes successfully to block the nomination by a filibuster, they decided not to do so. After all, even with Roberts and Alito on the Court, there were still five Justices—Stevens, Kennedy, Souter, Ginsburg, and Breyer—who were committed to *Roe* and *Casey*.[66]

"PARTIAL-BIRTH" ABORTION REVISITED

TWO YEARS LATER, in *Gonzales v. Carhart*,[67] the newly-constituted Roberts Court revisited the issue of partial-birth abortion. Several years after the Court's decision in *Stenberg*, President George W. Bush signed into law the federal Partial-Birth Abortion Ban Act of 2003.* Like the Nebraska law invalidated in *Stenberg*, the federal law did not contain an exception that permitted the procedure when necessary to protect the health of the woman. Every federal court that considered the constitutionality of this statute held it unconstitutional. The Roberts Court, however, in a five-to-four decision, upheld the law. In effect, Justice Alito's replacement of Justice O'Connor flipped the outcome in the case.

In his opinion for the majority, Justice Anthony Kennedy effectively turned his *Stenberg* dissent into the majority opinion. In a now infamous passage in his opinion in *Gonzales*, Kennedy began by observing that although "we find no reliable data to measure the phenomenon, it seems unexceptional to conclude that some women come to regret their choice to abort the infant life they once created and sustained. Severe depression and loss of esteem can follow."† This grief, he declared, must surely be even more "pro-

---

* In 1997, Congress enacted a law banning partial-birth abortion, but it was vetoed by President Bill Clinton.

† It was noteworthy that Kennedy cited no authority for this assumption.

found" when the woman allows "a doctor to pierce the skull and vacuum the fast-developing brain of her unborn child."[68]

Nonetheless, Kennedy conceded that the government's paternalistic interest in protecting women from making such supposedly grievous errors of judgment would not in itself be sufficient justification to ban the use of partial-birth abortion, if use of the procedure was medically necessary to preserve the life or health of the woman. But, he concluded, this was not the case. Although acknowledging that medical opinion was divided on whether intact D&E abortions might be safer for some women in some circumstances, Kennedy noted that Congress had made a finding in enacting the challenged legislation that partial-birth abortion "is never medically necessary." Concluding that the Court should defer to that legislative finding, Kennedy held that the law did not impose an "undue burden" on the right of a woman to terminate an unwanted pregnancy.[*69]

JUSTICE RUTH BADER GINSBURG, who authored a dissenting opinion for herself and Justices Stevens, Souter, and Breyer, was as angry in *Gonzales* as Justice Kennedy had been in *Stenberg*. Ginsburg castigated the majority for upholding Congress's categorical ban on the use of a medical procedure deemed "necessary and proper" in many cases by the American College of Obstetricians and Gynecologists. This was, she observed, the first time since *Roe* that the Court had upheld "a prohibition with no exception safeguarding a woman's health."[70]

Moreover, Ginsburg insisted that the congressional finding relied upon by the majority could not "withstand inspection." To the contrary, she maintained, and as every other court that had considered the question had concluded, Congress's bare assertion that "there was a medical consensus that the banned procedure is never necessary" was completely inconsistent with the medical and scientific facts.[71]

Ginsburg was particularly irked by the majority's patronizing approach toward women. She noted that Justice Kennedy's assertions about the

---

* Kennedy left open the question whether the Partial-Birth Abortion Ban Act might be unconstitutional as applied to a particular woman who could demonstrate on the specific facts of her situation that the nature of the medical risk to her could be managed only with an intact D&E abortion.

decreased self-esteem of women who have had abortions lacked any empirical support and that this anachronistic and insulting perception of "women's fragile emotional state" could not possibly justify depriving "women of the right to make an autonomous choice," especially when the restriction comes at the expense of their own health and safety.[72]

A S JUSTICE GINSBURG pointedly observed in her dissenting opinion, the critical difference between *Stenberg* and *Gonzales* was that the Court in *Gonzales* was "differently composed" than it had been just a few years earlier. Indeed, it was clearly the substitution of Justice Alito for Justice O'Connor that was responsible for the Court's dramatic change of course. In *Casey* and *Stenberg*, the Court had made clear that if there was uncertainty about the medical necessity of an abortion procedure, "the tie would go to women's health." In *Gonzales*, the new majority declared instead that in such circumstances the tie must go "to those wishing to ban the procedure."[73]

The decision in *Gonzales* raised awkward questions about the possible influence of religious belief in judicial decisions. With the appointments of Roberts and Alito, the Court for the first time in its history had five Catholic justices—all of whom voted to uphold the federal ban on partial-birth abortion. In some sense, this could easily be explained by the fact that those five justices generally shared a "conservative" judicial philosophy that would naturally have made them skeptical of *Roe*. But what was jarring about *Gonzales* was that these five justices felt compelled even to hear the case, in light of the recent decision in *Stenberg* and the unanimous judgments of the lower courts, all of which had invalidated the challenged federal law. Ordinarily in such circumstances, even with a change in the makeup of the Court, one would expect the Court simply to follow its own recent precedent. That the five justices in the majority in *Gonzales* could not bring themselves to do so naturally gave rise to speculation that the religious beliefs of the justices might have influenced their judicial behavior.

The *Philadelphia Inquirer* published a cartoon that showed the justices in the majority wearing bishops' miters; the *Washington Post* ran a story that began with the question: "Is it significant that the five Supreme Court justices who voted to uphold the federal ban on a controversial abortion procedure also happen to be the Court's Roman Catholics?"; and the *New York Times* published an article observing that debate over

CHURCH & STATE

the influence of religion on the justices has now "moved from the theo-retical to the concrete."*[74]

ABORTION TODAY

EACH YEAR IN the United States, there are approximately 6.7 million pregnancies. Of these, roughly 50 percent, or 3.4 million, are unintended. More than half of all women experience an unintended pregnancy at least once during their lives. Forty percent of all unintended pregnancies end in abortion. Thirty percent of all women have at least one abortion.[†] One mil-lion abortions are performed in the United States each year.

Married women have 55 percent of all abortions. They end 7 percent of

---

* Shortly after the decision in *Gonzales*, I published an op-ed in the *Chicago Tribune* to similar effect. See Geoffrey R. Stone, *Our Faith-Based Justices*, Chicago Tribune (Apr. 30, 2007). This led to a bit of a flap between Justice Scalia, my former colleague at the University of Chicago Law School, and me. See Joan Biskupic, *American Original: The Life and Constitution of Supreme Court Justice Antonin Scalia* 204 (Farrar, Straus and Giroux 2009). Happily, Justice Scalia and I later resolved our differences.

† Fifty percent of women who have an abortion have two or more abortions during their lives.

their pregnancies with an abortion.* Unmarried women end 35 percent of their pregnancies with an abortion. They are therefore five times as likely as married women to terminate a pregnancy with an abortion. Teenage girls have almost one-fifth of all abortions in America today.

Not surprisingly, income inequality plays a large role in these data. Women living below the poverty line (defined as roughly $24,000 for a family of four) are five times more likely to have an unintended pregnancy than higher-income women (women with incomes of $48,000 or more for a family of four). Faced with an unintended pregnancy, higher-income women are three times more likely to have an abortion than women living below the poverty line, whereas women living below the poverty line are six times more likely to give birth to an unintended child.

Put differently, if we compare 1,000 women living under the poverty line with 1,000 higher-income women, in an average year 122 poor women will have an unintended pregnancy, compared to only 29 higher-income women; 52 poor women will have an abortion, compared to 17 higher-income women; and 70 poor women will have an unintended child compared to 12 higher-income women. Fifteen percent of women live at or below the poverty line, but they have 40 percent of all abortions and 50 percent of all unintended children.[75]

T HE ANNUAL abortion rate has declined significantly over the past thirty-five years, from 29 per 1,000 women of childbearing age in 1981 to 17 per 1,000 women of childbearing age in 2016. Similarly, the number of abortions performed annually has declined from a high of 1.6 million in 1990 to approximately 1 million in 2016. This decline is due primarily to two factors. First, women—both married and unmarried—are less likely to get pregnant. There was an 11 percent decline in the pregnancy rate from 1990 to 2016. Second, women who get pregnant are less likely to have an abortion. In 1990, married women had abortions in 8 percent of their pregnancies; in 2016 they had abortions in 5 percent of their pregnancies. In 1990, unmarried women had abortions in 47 percent of their pregnancies; in 2016 they had abortions in 31 percent of their pregnancies.

The shift is especially dramatic among teenagers. The rate of pregnancy among teenage girls declined 44 percent from 1990 to 2016, from

---

* All of the data concerning the percentage of pregnancies that end in abortion refer to pregnancies that do not end in miscarriage.

117 pregnancies per 1,000 girls in 1990 to 65 pregnancies per 1,000 girls in 2016. The annual abortion rate among teenage girls declined 60 percent in this era, from 40 abortions per 1,000 in 1990 to 16 abortions per 1,000 in 2016. This was due both to a reduction in the pregnancy rate among teenage girls and a reduction in the abortion rate among teenage girls who got pregnant. Among teenage girls who got pregnant, 35 percent had abortions in 1990, compared to 25 percent in 2016. As a result, teenage girls who got pregnant (almost all unmarried) were 29 percent more likely to give birth to an unintended child in 2016 than in 1990.[76]

THESE DATA suggest that at least three important factors are at work. First, because the pregnancy rate has declined, it is reasonable to infer that the combination of better sex education, easier access to contraception, and the availability of more effective contraception has reduced both the number of unintended pregnancies and, as a result, the number and rate of abortions. This is hardly surprising, because there is a strong correlation between the failure to use contraception and the likelihood of an unintended pregnancy.

The 65 percent of women who use contraception consistently and correctly account for only 5 percent of all unintended pregnancies. The 35 percent of women who use contraception inconsistently or not at all account for 95 percent of all unintended pregnancies. Those who correctly use the contraceptive implant, IUD, oral contraceptive pills, the hormonal patch, or the vaginal ring have less than a 1 percent chance of experiencing an unintended pregnancy over the course of a year. Those who use the male condom correctly have a 2 percent chance of experiencing an unintended pregnancy over the course of a year. Those who do not use any method of contraception have an 85 percent chance of experiencing an unintended pregnancy over the course of a year.

For those who want to reduce the number of abortions, easy access to effective contraception and guidance in the use of contraception is critical. Indeed, if all people used contraception consistently and correctly, the number of abortions per year in the United States would drop from one million to approximately 75,000.*

---

* If all people used contraception consistently and correctly, the total number of unintended pregnancies annually would be reduced from 3.4 million to approximately 250,000. Because 30 percent of unintended pregnancies result in abortion, this would reduce the number of abortions annually from one million to approximately 75,000.

· · ·

Second, between 1992 and 2016, it became increasingly difficult for many women who experienced an unintended pregnancy to obtain a legal abortion. This was so in part because the Supreme Court in *Casey* and subsequent decisions opened the door to greater regulation of abortion, and this resulted in a broad range of new restrictions that significantly constricted the ability of women to exercise their constitutional right to terminate an unwanted pregnancy. The nature and extent of these regulations varies considerably from state to state. The states that have been the most aggressive in restricting abortion since *Casey* are Alabama, Arizona, Arkansas, Idaho, Indiana, Kansas, Kentucky, Missouri, Nebraska, North Carolina, North Dakota, Oklahoma, Texas, and Utah. Not surprisingly, these are all among the most religious states in the nation.

Here are some examples of these restrictions as of 2016:

Eleven states prohibit coverage of medically necessary abortions even in *private* medical insurance plans, unless the woman's life is in danger or the pregnancy was the result of rape or incest;

Thirty-five states require a woman to submit to "counseling" before she may elect to have an abortion;

Twenty-eight states require a woman to wait a period of time, usually twenty-four hours, between her "counseling" and when the procedure may be performed;

Thirteen states effectively require a woman to make two separate trips to the clinic or hospital before she may have an abortion;

Twenty-two states require facilities that perform early-term abortions to meet the requirements for ambulatory surgical centers;

Eleven states require abortion facilities that perform early-term abortions to be located within a short distance of a hospital;

Sixteen states have burdensome regulations governing the size of procedure rooms and the width of corridors in facilities that perform abortions;

Thirteen states require abortion providers to have an affiliation with a local hospital (many of which are unwilling to have an affiliation with any doctor or clinic that performs abortions).

According to the Guttmacher Institute, between the years 2000 and 2016 the number of states with substantial and "unnecessary" abortion restrictions (that is, restrictions that are intended to make abortion more difficult, rather than genuinely to protect either the health of the woman or fetal life post-viability) nearly doubled, from thirteen to twenty-four. Largely as a result of these restrictions, by 2016, 89 percent of all counties in the United States did not have a clinic or hospital that could perform a legal abortion. As a consequence, women who reside in these counties often have to travel substantial distances in order to exercise their constitutional right to terminate an unwanted pregnancy, often at considerable cost. Not surprisingly, these restrictions have a particularly severe impact on poor women.[77]

A THIRD explanation for the decline in abortion rates might be that people have become less accepting of abortion. In light of the Christian Right's campaign to characterize abortion as murder and to condemn and shame those who "kill" their "unborn children," it would be surprising if public attitudes about abortion had not grown more negative over the years. As Carole Joffe, a historian of abortion, has observed, although the effects of these efforts are difficult to measure, the anti-abortion movement has been "successful at stigmatizing abortion," and this would seem logically to have influenced the downward trend in the rate of abortions.[78]

In fact, however, the evidence is ambiguous. On some measures, the public's attitude toward abortion has remained strikingly constant. In 1975, 22 percent of Americans thought abortion should be illegal in all circumstances; 19 percent think that today. In 1989, 31 percent of Americans wanted the Supreme Court to overturn *Roe*; 29 percent of Americans want that today. On the question of whether the Court's decision in *Roe* has been good for the nation, 53 percent of Americans say "yes," and only 30 percent say "no." And on the question whether abortion should be legal in "most or all cases," 58 percent of Americans say "yes" and only a third believe that abortion laws should be stricter than they are now.

On balance, then, it does not appear that there has been a significant shift in Americans' acceptance of abortion in the years since *Roe*. The decline in the rate of abortion therefore seems due more to other changes in society, such as greater access to better methods of contraception and the sharp restrictions some states have enacted in an effort to make abortion less available, than to any dramatic change in public opinion about abortion itself.*[79]

P OVERTY IS a central factor in the incidence of abortion in America. Although seventeen states cover medically necessary abortions for poor women, the remaining thirty-three states, the District of Columbia, and the federal government make such funds available only if the abortion is necessary to save the woman's life or the pregnancy was caused by rape or incest.† In all other circumstances, indigent women are left to their own devices in dealing with the consequences of unwanted pregnancies.

For many poor women, the challenge of raising the funds necessary to pay for an abortion is simply insurmountable. Although women living at or below the poverty line have 42 percent of all abortions (even though they represent only 15 percent of the population), a quarter of poor women who *want* to terminate unintended pregnancies are unable to raise the funds necessary to do so and therefore give birth to unplanned—and often unwanted children. The consequences for such women, and for their families, are often severe.

As demonstrated by the significant decline in the abortion rate among higher-income women in recent decades, a critically important response to the dilemma of poor women would be greater access to effective methods of contraception. Indeed, if poor women used contraception in the same manner and to the same degree as other women in society, they would have approximately 600,000 fewer unintended pregnancies and 300,000 fewer abortions each year. But many religious and other morality-based groups oppose programs designed to promote sex education and contraceptive use among the poor, either because they deem contraception immoral or because they fear that greater access to contraception will lead to greater promiscuity. The cost of those beliefs is literally *hundreds of thousands* of otherwise avoidable abortions each year.[80]

---

* As noted, though, the evidence is ambiguous. One poll, for example, suggests that the percentage of Americans who view themselves as pro-life has increased from 37 percent in 1996 to 46 percent today.

† The seventeen states that cover medically necessary abortions for indigent women are Alaska, Arizona, California, Connecticut, Hawaii, Illinois, Maryland, Massachusetts, Minnesota, Montana, New Jersey, New Mexico, New York, Oregon, Vermont, Washington, and West Virginia.

"UNDUE BURDEN" AND THE FUTURE OF ABORTION

THE 2010 ELECTIONS, in which Republicans swept into office in many state legislatures, led to a dramatic surge in anti-abortion legislation. Between 2010 and 2016, more than half the states enacted laws that pushed and sometimes clearly exceeded the limits of constitutionally permissible restrictions on access to abortion. In 2013 alone, twenty-two states adopted seventy different restrictions, including bans on abortion after twenty weeks of pregnancy, stringent restrictions on the physical structure of clinics, new requirements that doctors who perform abortions must be admitted to practice in nearby hospitals, prohibitions on clinics if they are not located in close proximity to a hospital, requirements that clinics have all the attributes of ambulatory surgical centers, requirements that women considering an abortion view an ultrasound of the fetus, strict limitations on medication-induced abortions, and additional bans on private insurance coverage for abortion.

Defenders of these restrictions insisted that they were designed to ensure that women considering an abortion make "informed" decisions, that they restricted abortions that might cause unnecessary pain to the fetus, and that they protected women against unsafe facilities and procedures. Opponents of these restrictions maintained that they were unconstitutionally paternalistic, that they were based on medical assertions without scientific foundation, and that their real purpose was not to protect women's health, but to make abortion more expensive, more difficult, and less accessible.

A key question raised by these regulations was whether, in light of *Casey* and *Gonzales,* these sorts of restrictions were constitutional. There are two central questions: First, do these laws impose an "undue burden" on a woman's constitutional right to terminate an unwanted pregnancy? And second, how much deference must a court give to the legislature in assessing the reasonableness and credibility of the asserted justifications for these restrictions?

After *Casey,* the Court's doctrine made clear that such laws could pass constitutional muster only if they reasonably served a legitimate state interest and did not pose an "undue burden" on the right to abortion. Applying the *Casey* standard, most of these laws could not withstand constitutional scrutiny. After *Gonzales,* however, the governing doctrine became less clear. In light of the Court's suggestion in *Gonzales* that courts should give some measure of deference to the judgments of the legislature, it became less certain that such restrictions were unconstitutional.

Not surprisingly, lower courts divided on these issues.[81] In *Planned Parenthood v. Abbott*,[82] for example, the United States Court of Appeals for the Fifth Circuit upheld the constitutionality of a Texas law that prohibited any doctor to perform an abortion unless she had admitting privileges at a hospital no more than 30 miles from the clinic in which she performed the abortion. The court held that even though this requirement would put many abortion providers out of business and would therefore cause some women to have to travel as far as 150 miles in order to reach a facility that could perform an abortion, it did not impose an "undue burden" on a woman's right to an abortion because the legislature could reasonably believe that the regulation promoted better medical care for women and because "an increase of travel" in order to obtain an abortion "is not an undue burden."[83]

On the other hand, in *Planned Parenthood v. Schimel*,[84] the United States Court of Appeals for the Seventh Circuit invalidated a Wisconsin law quite similar to the Texas law upheld in *Abbott*. In an opinion by Judge Richard Posner, one of the most influential legal scholars of the past half-century, the court concluded that the state's purported justifications for the law were "spurious." This was so, the court reasoned, because "complications from an abortion are both rare and rarely dangerous," and because Wisconsin had not imposed similar restrictions on other—often more dangerous—medical procedures that are also "performed outside a hospital." The court concluded that the challenged statute violated the Constitution because it substantially curtailed the availability of abortion in Wisconsin "without conferring an offsetting benefit (or indeed any benefit) on women's health."[85]

Although most lower court judges agreed with Judge Posner's analysis, there was a clear difference of opinion. At some point, the Supreme Court would have to step in to resolve the uncertainty.

O N JUNE 27, 2016, in *Whole Woman's Health v. Hellerstedt*,[86] the Supreme Court, in a landmark decision, embraced Judge Posner's approach and clarified the meaning of the undue burden standard. At issue were two highly controversial Texas restrictions on abortion. The "admitting privileges requirement" provided that any physician who performs an abortion must have admitting privileges at a hospital located within thirty miles of the facility where the abortion is performed. The "surgical center requirement" provided that any facility performing an abortion must meet the standards required by the state for ambulatory surgical centers.

When the bill incorporating these provisions was first considered by the Texas legislature in June 2013, Texas state senator Wendy Davis from

Fort Worth donned a pair of pink running shoes and boldly launched a dramatic eleven-hour filibuster against the legislation, which she deemed unconstitutional. During her filibuster, Davis was forbidden to eat, drink, use the restroom, sit, or even lean against her desk. Her protest galvanized supporters across the nation and had millions of Americans biting their collective nails as the drama streamed online and the clock ticked down to midnight, which marked the end of the legislative session. When all the dust settled, Davis had successfully blocked enactment of the legislation, to the fury of Texas Republicans. During the next legislative session, however, the legislature succeeded in enacting the restrictions, and Republican Governor Rick Perry triumphantly signed the bill into law, prompting one commentator to observe that "Wendy Davis won the battle, but Rick Perry won the war."[87]

After the Supreme Court agreed to hear the case, Justice Antonin Scalia suddenly died of natural causes on February 13, 2016. One of the Court's harshest critics of *Roe v. Wade* was now gone. With only eight justices participating in the case, most observers reasoned that there were now two more or less equally probable outcomes. Given their past positions on the abortion issue, it seemed clear that Chief Justice Roberts and Justices Thomas and Alito would vote to uphold the challenged provisions, whereas Justices Ginsburg, Breyer, Sotomayor, and Kagan would vote to strike them down.

The unknown was Anthony Kennedy. Would he apply the "undue burden" standard as a test with real bite, as he and Justices O'Connor and Souter had first articulated it in *Casey*, or would he apply it in a more deferential manner, giving the benefit of the doubt to the state, as he had reinterpreted the standard fifteen years later in his opinion for the Court in *Gonzales*?

In a five-to-three decision, with Justices Kennedy, Ginsburg, Sotomayor, and Kagan joining Justice Stephen Breyer's majority opinion, the Court invalidated both of the Texas provisions and cast doubt upon the constitutionality of many of the similar restrictions that had been enacted by states across the nation. Chief Justice Roberts and Justices Thomas and Alito dissented.

J USTICE BREYER concluded that both of the challenged restrictions placed "a substantial obstacle" in the path of women seeking to exercise their constitutional right to abortion, that neither restriction provided any "medical benefits" sufficient to justify the burdens they imposed, and that both restrictions therefore imposed "an undue burden" on the right of women to terminate unwanted pregnancies.

In reaching this result, Breyer cited the following findings of the federal district court judge in the case: (1) the implementation of these two requirements would cause most abortion facilities in the state to go out of business, reducing the number from forty to only seven; (2) with such a dramatic reduction of the number of abortion providers, approximately 1.3 million women of reproductive age would live more than 100 miles from the nearest abortion provider, and more than 750,000 would live more than 200 miles from the nearest abortion provider; (3) the claim that the seven surviving facilities could meet the needs of the 60,000 to 72,000 women who sought abortions each year in Texas "stretches credulity"; (4) the impact of these restrictions would be particularly severe on poor, rural, and disadvantaged women; (5) abortion even without these restrictions is "extremely safe" and has very low rates of medical complication; and (6) abortion is a much safer medical procedure than many other common medical procedures, including childbirth, colonoscopy, vasectomy, and liposuction, for which Texas did not impose these requirements.[88]

After reviewing the record, Breyer concluded that Texas had failed to present any credible evidence that the admitting privileges requirement advanced in any meaningful way "Texas' legitimate interest in protecting women's health." Moreover, he found that by causing the closure of so many abortion facilities, the challenged law placed a "substantial obstacle in the path of a woman's choice." In such circumstances, he held that the admitting privileges requirement imposed an "undue burden" on the ability of women to exercise their constitutional right to obtain safe and legal abortions.

Applying a similar analysis, Breyer also held that the surgical center provision, which required abortion service providers to have very costly physical facilities and elaborate nursing staffs, violated the undue burden standard, particularly in light of the fact that Texas did not impose a similar requirement on the performance of many riskier medical procedures.

The plain and simple fact, he concluded, was that the evidence clearly established that "the surgical center requirement is not necessary" to protect the health of the woman, despite the state's claims to the contrary. Indeed, "in the face of no threat to women's health," Texas seeks "to force women to travel long distances to get abortions in crammed-to-capacity" facilities where they are less likely to "get the kind of individualized attention" they might need. In short, the effect of the ambulatory surgical center requirement would, if anything, "be harmful to, not supportive of, women's health."*[89]

U PON LEARNING of the Court's decision in *Hellerstedt*, Wendy Davis burst into tears of "relief, happiness, and gratitude." "There was so much at stake," she proclaimed, as she lauded "the wisdom of the five justices who came together and understood the sham nature of this law and the disingenuous arguments" of its proponents who claimed falsely that its purpose was to "protect women's health."[90]

Chief Justice Roberts and Justices Thomas and Alito did not join in the celebration. In a separate dissenting opinion, Clarence Thomas declared once again that "I remain fundamentally opposed to the Court's abortion jurisprudence." Beyond that, though, and even taking *Casey* as stating the proper standard, Thomas charged that in this decision "the majority radically rewrites the undue-burden test." Most fundamentally, Thomas insisted that *Casey* did not invite courts to "balance the benefits and burdens" of laws restricting abortion, but required them to give legislatures "wide discretion to pass legislation in areas where there is medical and scientific uncertainty." In Thomas's view, both the Court's precedents and common sense require courts "to leave disputed medical science to the legislature." Invoking Justice Scalia, Thomas concluded by asserting that, with this decision, "the entire Nation has lost something essential," for we have now "passed the point where 'law,' properly speaking, has any further application."[91]

Justice Alito, joined by Roberts and Thomas, also filed a dissenting opinion. Alito focused primarily on several procedural issues in the case. He insisted that, in light of those issues, the Court should not have reached the merits of the case at all. Alito fumed that the majority's refusal to dispose of the case on procedural grounds was yet another example of its willingness to bend the rules in order to protect the purported right of abortion, and that its behavior in this regard was so "indefensible" that

---

* In her separate concurring opinion, Justice Ruth Bader Ginsburg added that "when a State severely limits access to safe and legal procedures, women in desperate circumstances may resort to unlicensed rogue practitioners, *faute de mieux*, at great risk to their health and safety." 136 S. Ct. at 2321 (Ginsburg, J., concurring).

it "will undermine public confidence in the Court as a fair and neutral arbiter."*92

Turning to the merits, Alito challenged both the federal district court's and the majority's analyses of the facts. He maintained, for example, that it was not clear that the surgical center and admitting privileges requirements were responsible for the closing of particular clinics; that the closing of particular clinics would inconvenience women seeking abortions and in what numbers; and that the decrease in the number of clinics performing abortions would make it impossible for the remaining clinics to meet the demand for abortion, either statewide or in particular areas of the state.

In response, Justice Breyer emphatically rejected this argument, holding that nothing requires the Court to proceed in so "piecemeal" a fashion "when we have found the statutory provisions at issue facially unconstitutional."93

*H*ELLERSTEDT WAS the most significant victory for abortion rights in almost a quarter-of-a-century. Moreover, the decision was clearly correct. As the Court had held in *Casey*, "Unnecessary health regulations that have the purpose or effect of presenting a substantial obstacle to a woman seeking an abortion" impose an "undue" and therefore unconstitutional burden on the exercise of the right. The Texas laws invalidated in *Hellerstedt*, as recognized not only by the majority of the Supreme Court but also by the vast majority of lower court judges who had addressed the question, were perfect examples of such constitutionally impermissible regulations.

Indeed, the standard applied by the majority in *Hellerstedt* was very much in line with its approach to laws that substantially interfere with the exercise of other constitutional rights, whether the freedom of speech, the freedom of the press, the freedom of religion, the right to bear arms, the right to due process, or the right to equal protection of the laws. As long as *Roe* remains the law of the land, the Court in *Hellerstedt* clearly reached the constitutionally correct outcome. If anyone was guilty of manipulating the ordinary rules of constitutional jurisprudence because of their views of abortion, it was not the justices in the majority, but the three dissenters.†

---

* Justice Alito's primary procedural objection was his claim that the case was barred by the doctrine of *res judicata*, which provides that once a case has been litigated it cannot thereafter be re-litigated. In his opinion for the Court, Justice Breyer reasoned that the doctrine was inapplicable to the situation in *Hellerstedt*.

† An interesting question is why Justice Kennedy voted as he did in *Hellerstedt*. My own guess, for what it's worth, is that *Casey* in fact best reflects Kennedy's own view of the right, and that he

Hellerstedt was a truly pivotal decision. Opponents of abortion quickly condemned the Court's action. The Texas attorney general, Ken Paxton, raged that the Court had eviscerated what he described as a perfectly sensible set of regulations that had been designed "to improve minimum safety standards and ensure capable care for Texas women." Clarke Forsythe, acting president of Americans United for Life, castigated the Court for accepting "the abortion industry's argument that it should be allowed to keep its profits high and patient care standards low," thus endangering "women nationwide." And Robin Vos, the Speaker of the Wisconsin assembly, declared that "today the Court has put women's health and safety on the back burner for the profits of Planned Parenthood."[94]

Needless to say, the concerted efforts to restrict the right of abortion will not end with *Hellerstedt*. Although the decision reinvigorated *Roe* and made clear that extreme and disingenuous efforts to restrict the right, exemplified by the admitting privileges and surgical center provisions, will not pass constitutional muster, *Hellerstedt* left many other restrictions in constitutional limbo. For example, can a state constitutionally prohibit private medical insurers to cover medically necessary abortions? Can it require a woman to submit to counseling before electing to have an abortion? Can it require a woman to wait twenty-four hours between her counseling and the procedure, even if she has to travel long distances to get to the abortion provider? Can it restrict abortions with medication? Can it ban specific surgical procedures to perform abortions? What, in other words, will the "undue burden" standard mean in practice as courts attempt to assess the constitutionality of these and other restrictions on abortion that states will inevitably continue to impose in the future?

As Suzanne Goldberg, the director of the Center for Gender and Sexuality Law at Columbia Law School, observed immediately after the Court handed down its decision in *Hellerstadt*, "The ruling deals a crushing blow to this most recent wave of state efforts to shut off access to abortion through hyper-regulation," but it still leaves unresolved many difficult questions for the future. The struggle will no doubt continue, and much will depend on the future makeup of the Court.[95]

---

shifted from that view in *Gonzales* largely because he was so personally revolted by what he saw as the particular brutality of partial-birth abortion. On the general issue of regulating abortion, however, Kennedy made clear in *Hellerstedt*, by joining Justice Breyer's opinion, that it was *Casey* that best captured his overall understanding of the right.

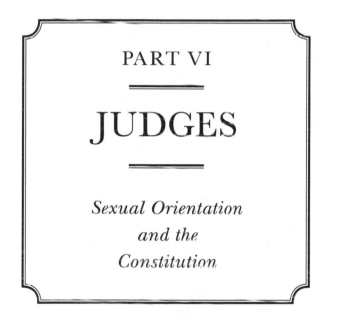

PART VI

JUDGES

*Sexual Orientation
and the
Constitution*

18

"THE GAY MOMENT"

AIDS Memorial Quilt

T HE YEARS AFTER 1980 saw a profound transformation in the standing of gays and lesbians in American society. The AIDS epidemic wreaked horror and havoc on the gay community, but it also brought homosexuality into the light. As tens of thousands of gay men died horrible deaths, people had to take notice—often, though not always, with sympathy and concern. Gradually, one person at a time, in often awkward and sometimes excruciatingly painful conversations with family, friends, and acquaintances, the previously secret lives of homosexuals became visible, first out of necessity and desperation, then out of candor and pride. Slowly, the world changed.

As the journalist Andrew Kopkind wrote in *The Nation*, by 1993 the "Gay Moment" had arrived. "The gay moment," he explained, "fills the media, charges politics, saturates popular and elite culture. It is the stuff of everyday conversation and public discourse." As if in a dream, gays and lesbians woke up "to headlines alternately disputing their claim to equality" and "affirming their social identity." "Gay invisibility" was suddenly melting away.[1]

By 1993, national newspapers were regularly publishing articles on gay and lesbian life, and books, plays, and movies by openly gay authors about openly gay subjects were earning public acclaim. Tony Kushner's play *Angels in America* won the Tony Award in 1993, and the following year Jonathan Demme's movie *Philadelphia*, which addressed the AIDS epidemic, became the top-grossing film in the nation. Martina Navratilova, who had won four U.S. Open tennis championships, came out as a lesbian, and at the Gay and Lesbian March on Washington in 1993, hundreds of thousands of people marched from the Ellipse past the White House in support of equality. Four years later, Ellen DeGeneres, star of the popular ABC television show *Ellen*, came out as a lesbian. Shortly thereafter, some forty-two million viewers tuned in to watch DeGeneres's character, Ellen Morgan, reveal that she, too, was a lesbian.[2]

The response of the Christian Right was fierce. Religious conservatives fumed that perversion, immorality, and degeneracy were now being spewed across the land. The Reverend Jerry Falwell called Ellen DeGeneres "Ellen DeGenerate," and Donald Wildmon, the founder and president of the American Family Association, railed that homosexuality was "a sin grievous to God and repulsive to Christians." This struggle, he declared, was a matter life and death, because if we fail, "we fear the judgment of God on our nation."[3]

"THE PLAGUE OF THE CENTURY"

IN JANUARY 1981, a thirty-one-year-old gay man rushed to the emergency room at the UCLA Medical Center because he had a fungal infection that nearly blocked his esophagus. Two weeks later, the patient developed *Pneumocystis carinii* pneumonia, or PCP, a form of lung infection that had previously been found almost exclusively in cancer and transplant patients. The patient had had neither cancer nor a transplant. It was a mystery.

Around the same time, Dr. Alvin Friedman-Kien, a dermatologist at New York University, treated a patient with equally mystifying symptoms. He was examining a gay man for Hodgkin's disease when he noticed a number of purplish-red spots on the man's legs. Friedman-Kien thought they looked like Kaposi's sarcoma, a rare type of skin cancer usually found in older men. Two weeks later, he examined another man with similar symptoms. This man was also gay. Friedman-Kien called a colleague in San Francisco who reported two similar cases there. Soon, more than forty homosexual men had been diagnosed with Kaposi's sarcoma.[4]

When news of the mysterious illness reached the national Centers for Disease Control and Prevention (CDC), its highly-regarded virologist, Don Francis, recognized that what was being reported was a possible crisis in the making. He was then working on sexually-transmitted hepatitis in gay men, and he suspected that the outbreak might be due to another sexually-transmitted virus. According to Francis, in such circumstances the CDC usually took immediate steps to address the spread of a new disease. In this instance, though, the "White House told us to 'look pretty and do as little as we can.'"

It soon became clear that the Reagan administration was "not interested in a disease that affects gay men." By the end of the year, 121 people had died from the mysterious disease, which gradually took on the name "acquired immune deficiency syndrome," or AIDS. It was not until 1983 that scientists determined that a virus called HIV, or human immunodeficiency virus, caused the disease.*[5]

Although we now know that HIV/AIDS is not directly connected either to homosexuality or to same-sex sexual behavior, it quickly came to be known as the "gay plague." That association had grave consequences. It made gay sex, which was already stigmatized, synonymous with a fatal illness. Fearful of infection, cities and towns across the nation feverishly enacted a wave of new laws discriminating against homosexuals in employment, housing, insurance, and education in order to keep them away from "normal" people. To make matters worse, because homosexuals were already perceived as freaks, perverts, and outsiders, neither the government nor the media made an effort to educate either gays or the public about the disease.[6]

Religious conservatives aggressively exploited the HIV/AIDS epidemic in their ongoing campaign to crush the burgeoning call for "gay rights." On July 4, 1983, the Moral Majority held a rally in Cincinnati to address what the main speaker, Jerry Falwell, described as the "plague of the century." AIDS, Falwell proclaimed, was "the judgment of God." The Moral Majority insisted that the government should not spend any public funds on AIDS research, because a cure would "allow these diseased homosexuals to go back to their perverted practices without any standards of accountability."

For the Christian Right, AIDS proved to be a godsend. The conservative organizations that had railed earlier against the evils of obscenity, abortion, and the Equal Rights Amendment now exploited the AIDS crisis to demonize homosexuals. As Falwell put the point, "AIDS is not just God's punishment for homosexuals. It is God's punishment for the society that tolerates homosexuals."[7]

Ronald Reagan's reelection in 1984 did not bode well for the gay community. Reagan did not even acknowledge the AIDS epidemic publicly until 1985, after his friend and fellow actor Rock Hudson died from the disease. But even then, the Reagan administration, fearful of upsetting the Christian Right, refused to commit any meaningful resources to AIDS research.[8]

---

* The Reagan administration's position on AIDS was hardly a surprise. Upon assuming office, and at the behest of the Moral Majority, Reagan nominated to the nation's Office of Personnel Management a Philadelphia minister who had declared that "the majority of Americans, particularly the godly among us, see homosexuality as sinful," and Reagan's surgeon general, C. Everett Koop, was an evangelical Christian who had denounced homosexuality as a sin.

"WE DIE/THEY DO NOTHING"

MEANWHILE, THE LIST of those dying of AIDS grew ever longer. In 1987, gay rights activist Cleve Jones created the NAMES Project AIDS Memorial Quilt. Each patch in the quilt represented a person who had died of AIDS. When the NAMES Project first took the quilt to Washington, D.C., and spread it on the National Mall for the nation's lawmakers to see, it contained two thousand squares. It would soon get *much* larger.[9]

At another event that year, the playwright Larry Kramer, speaking at the Gay and Lesbian Community Center in New York City, informed his audience that doctors had several drugs ready to be tested, but that the Federal Drug Administration (FDA) refused to approve the tests. Shortly thereafter, members of the Community Center established the AIDS Coalition to Unleash Power (ACT UP). ACT UP chapters soon sprang up in cities across the nation. ACT UP members were tired of being ignored. As one member observed, "We [need] to draw attention to ourselves and to our problem." ACT UP soon got the opportunity to do just that.

Burroughs Wellcome, the manufacturer of the only drug approved to treat AIDS, announced that a one-year supply of AZT would cost the patient $10,000. Outraged, ACT UP members wearing T-shirts emblazoned with the message "Silence=Death," and carrying signs saying "One AIDS Death Every 8 Minutes," flooded Wall Street to protest the corporation's indifference to human suffering. They hung an effigy of the FDA commissioner, distributed leaflets condemning Burroughs Wellcome for its exploitative pricing of the drug, and demanded that the FDA immediately release several other drugs that had been identified as having the potential to treat AIDS. The ACT UP members and their supporters then sat down in the middle of Wall Street, completely stopping traffic. The next day, every major newspaper in the nation published photographs of the protestors being carried away by the police.

Fueled by the Reagan administration's indifference to the plight of homosexuals and by the media's reluctance even to address the issue, ACT UP represented the dawn of a new, more aggressive era in the gay rights movement. The organization's dramatic and often confrontational demonstrations across the country attracted widespread public attention. If the media were too shy to tell the truth about AIDS and about the intransigence of the Reagan administration, then ACT UP would make them do so.[10]

448 · SEX AND THE CONSTITUTION

· · ·

BY THE end of 1987, more than twenty thousand people had died of AIDS. Faced with an ever-growing and ever more visible crisis, government spending on AIDS finally began to increase. Progress was slow, though, and the death toll continued to mount. One of ACT UP's most effective demonstrations was its "Seize Control of the FDA" initiative on October 11, 1988. More than a thousand ACT UP demonstrators protested outside the Rockville, Maryland, headquarters of the FDA, chanting, "Where is the FDA? . . . Release the drugs now. . . . We die/they do nothing. We die/they do nothing." Some two hundred demonstrators were arrested, and the protest again gained national attention. Embarrassed, the FDA reluctantly agreed to speed up the process for developing and approving AIDS drugs.[11]

After Ronald Reagan left the White House, things began to improve. In 1990, Dr. Anthony Fauci, head of the National Institute of Allergy and Infectious Diseases under President George H. W. Bush, authorized the use of several new medications for the treatment of AIDS. Thereafter, medical researchers gradually made progress. Finally, in 1996, a new and much more effective type of AIDS medication, the protease inhibitor, was introduced. As the *New York Times*, which finally dared use the word "gay" in print, explained in an article titled "When Plagues End," with the development of these new medications "a diagnosis of H.I.V. infection . . . no longer signifies death. It merely signifies illness."[12]

"WE ARE LESS THAN WE OUGHT TO BE"

SINCE 1981, MORE THAN a quarter-of-a-million gay men have died from AIDS. Despite—or perhaps because of—this horrific statistic, the AIDS crisis strengthened the gay rights movement. As one commentator observed, a diagnosis of AIDS could be the ultimate "outing."[13] Suddenly, it became impossible for hundreds of thousands of gay men to lead their lives in the closet. People learned for the first time that their sons, their brothers, their friends, their neighbors, their co-workers, their fellow churchgoers, their doctors, their teachers, and their plumbers were . . . gay.

With these revelations, it became increasingly apparent to millions of Americans that gays were not "strange freaks of nature," but people pretty much just like them. The more that gay men and lesbians learned that they could come out safely, the more they did. The notion of "gay rights" was no longer a claim to equal treatment for creepy perverts, but a claim to equal treatment for the people we knew, cared about, and even loved. It was, truly, a "great awakening."*

The question, though, was whether their fellow citizens were willing to grant gays and lesbians rights equal to those enjoyed by other citizens—most obviously, the right not to be discriminated against in employment, housing, public accommodations, education, military service, child custody, adoption, and marriage.

By 1992, there was cause for optimism. During that year's presidential campaign, candidate Bill Clinton proclaimed that "we can't afford to waste the hearts, abilities and minds of the gay and lesbian people, for every day that we refuse to avail ourselves of the potential of any group of Americans, we are less than we ought to be." Moreover, at that year's Democratic National Convention, more than a hundred openly gay and lesbian delegates, alternates, and party officials participated, and the Democratic Party platform called for the first time for the enactment of legislation guaranteeing the equal rights of gays and lesbians.[14]

The Republican National Convention took a rather different stance. Patrick Buchanan, the arch-conservative political commentator and politician who had served as a senior adviser to Presidents Nixon, Ford, and Reagan, and who had then unsuccessfully sought the Republican presidential nomination in 1992, set the tone in his opening address. He ridiculed the leaders of the gay rights movement and declared that "there is a religious war going on in this country for the soul of America." As conceived by Buchanan, this "war" pitted Christian moralists on one side, and radical feminists, abortionists, libertines, and homosexuals on the other.

Echoing Buchanan's vision, the theme of the Republican Convention was the need to protect "family values," a term that clearly excluded homosexuals. Forty percent of the delegates were evangelical Christians. Delegates enthusiastically waved signs declaring, "FAMILY RIGHTS FOREVER, GAY RIGHTS NEVER," and the party platform expressly opposed equal rights for homosexuals. Phyllis Schlafly and Jerry Falwell exulted that this was "the best Republican convention ever."[15]

After the votes were counted in November and Bill Clinton had defeated George H. W. Bush, the *New York Times* proclaimed that gays were "jubilant." Gay rights activists put together a transition team to send

---

* By 2013, 75 percent of Americans had been told personally by friends, relatives, neighbors, or co-workers that they were gay or lesbian.

résumés of gays and lesbians to the White House for government positions. Their hopes, at least at first, were met. Bill Clinton was the first president to appoint openly gay officials to his administration. Long excluded from American politics, gays and lesbians rejoiced that they had finally found an advocate in the White House. They were hopeful that after twelve consecutive years of openly hostile Republican administrations, they, like other loyal Americans, would finally be granted the right, the privilege, and the dignity of being accorded equal treatment under the core precepts of American law.[16]

"QUIT DISCRIMINATING AGAINST PEOPLE JUST BECAUSE THEY'RE GAY"

THE FOURTEENTH AMENDMENT provides that "no *state* shall . . . deny to any person . . . the equal protection of the laws," but it does not prohibit *private* individuals or businesses from discriminating.* Historically, the law permitted private individuals and businesses to discriminate without legal restraint. If they did not want to hire African Americans, or Jews, or Catholics, or women, or persons of Irish descent, or short persons, they were free not to do so. Such private discrimination was traditionally thought not to be any of the government's business.

In 1945, New York became the first state to pass a law prohibiting private discrimination in employment on the basis of race, creed, color, or national origin. Over the next two decades, many cities and states enacted similar legislation, sometimes extending the prohibition to cover discrimination in housing as well as employment. In 1964, Congress enacted the landmark Civil Rights Act, which prohibited discrimination on the basis of race, color, religion, national origin, or sex in employment, education, and public accommodations, such as restaurants and hotels. Four years later, in the Fair Housing Act, Congress prohibited discrimination in the sale, rental, or financing of housing on the basis of race, religion, or national origin.†[17]

A major goal of the gay rights movement has been to extend the protections of these laws to discrimination on the basis of sexual orientation and

---

* Whether and to what extent the Constitution prohibits government to discriminate on the basis of sexual orientation is addressed in chapters 19 and 20.

† In 1974, Congress extended this prohibition to cover discrimination in housing on the basis of sex.

gender identity. Today, twenty-two states and many cities have laws prohibiting private employment discrimination on the basis of sexual orientation.*[18]

The battles over the adoption of these laws have often been fierce. When the Houston city council considered a gay rights ordinance in 1984, the city's religious leaders poured into the city council chamber in protest and sang "Onward Christian Soldiers." After the council nonetheless voted in favor of the ordinance, the city's religious leaders demanded that voters be given an opportunity to decide the issue. When the question was put to a popular vote, the citizens of Houston, fired up by the objections of the Christian Right, rejected the gay rights ordinance by a margin of almost four-to-one.

The following summer, the city council of Providence, Rhode Island, reluctantly removed a reference to sexual orientation from its civil rights ordinance after Bishop Louis E. Gelineau aggressively campaigned against it, charging that "homosexual acts are contrary to God's command." In Chicago, Joseph Cardinal Bernardin successfully demanded that the city council reject a proposed gay rights ordinance by insisting that lawmakers had a solemn obligation to "protect the rights . . . of those who are offended by gay lifestyles." Similar efforts to defeat or repeal laws forbidding discrimination on the basis of sexual orientation have been waged, often successfully, in cities and states across the nation.[19]

Despite this opposition, twenty-two states now have laws prohibiting employment discrimination on the basis of sexual orientation, a fact that would have been unimaginable half a century earlier. But it remains the case that twenty-eight states still do not have such laws. Thus, in a majority of the states, private employers can still legally fire or refuse to hire individuals because of their sexual orientation.

There is a direct correlation between religious belief and a state's policies on discrimination against gays and lesbians. Only one of the nation's eighteen most religious states (Utah) has enacted a law forbidding such discrimination, whereas all of the nation's eleven most secular states have done so.†

---

* The twenty-two states are: Wisconsin (1982), Massachusetts (1989), Connecticut (1991), Hawaii (1991), California (1992), New Jersey (1992), Vermont (1992), Minnesota (1993), Rhode Island (1995), New Hampshire (1997), Nevada (1999), Maryland (2001), New York (2002), New Mexico (2003), Maine (2005), Illinois (2006), Washington (2006), Colorado (2007), Iowa (2007), Oregon (2007), Delaware (2009), and Utah (2015).

† According to the Gallup organization the eighteen most religious states are Mississippi, Utah, Alabama, Louisiana, South Carolina, Tennessee, Georgia, Arkansas, North Carolina, Oklahoma, Kentucky, Texas, Idaho, Nebraska, Kansas, South Dakota, North Dakota, and Indi-

It is striking that only one state has enacted legislation prohibiting employment discrimination on the basis of sexual orientation since 2009. In effect, we have reached a point, similar to the point we had reached with respect to private racial discrimination in 1964, where the states have more or less sorted themselves out in a manner that does not promise much change at the state level in the foreseeable future.

In such circumstances, as was the case in 1964 when Congress enacted the federal Civil Rights Act, the focus naturally turns to the possibility of federal legislation, especially if a substantial majority of all Americans have concluded that employment discrimination on the basis of sexual orientation should no longer be legal. That is, in fact, the case today.

According to recent polls, 89 percent of Americans now believe that gays and lesbians should have equal rights in employment, and 63 percent now support federal legislation prohibiting employment discrimination on the basis of sexual orientation.[20] Thus, just as the Civil Rights Act of 1964 adopted a *national* ban on private employment discrimination on the basis of race, religion, sex, and national origin, it would seem that similar national legislation should now be enacted to prohibit employment discrimination on the basis of sexual orientation.

That battle has been going on now for more than two decades.

THE EMPLOYMENT NON-DISCRIMINATION ACT (ENDA) was first introduced in Congress on June 23, 1994. Its central purpose was to prohibit private employment discrimination on the basis of sexual orientation. Senator Edward M. Kennedy (D-Massachusetts), a passionate champion of equal rights and civil liberties, first introduced the bill in the Senate. He explained at the time that the proposed legislation paralleled protections against job discrimination that were already provided to other groups under the Civil Rights Act of 1964.

Because the Christian Right had vehemently objected to proposed state and local laws prohibiting employment discrimination against gays and lesbians on the ground that such laws would unfairly grant "special rights for homosexuals," Kennedy insisted from the outset that "this bill is not

---

ana, and the twelve most secular states are Vermont, New Hampshire, Maine, Massachusetts, Oregon, Nevada, Washington, Connecticut, Hawaii, New York, California, and Rhode Island. Roughly half of the moderately religious states have enacted laws prohibiting employment discrimination on the basis of sexual orientation.

about granting special rights—it is about righting senseless wrongs." "What it requires," he declared, "is simple justice for gay men and lesbians who deserve to be judged in their job settings—like all other Americans—by their ability to do the work."[21]

The conservative icon Barry Goldwater, the 1964 Republican nominee for president who went so far right in that campaign that he embraced the John Birch Society, shocked Republicans by endorsing Kennedy's bill. In a *Washington Post* editorial, Goldwater declared: "It's time America realized that there was no gay exemption in the right to 'life, liberty and the pursuit of happiness.'" Goldwater insisted that people should "quit discriminating against people just because they're gay."*[22]

Opponents of the bill objected that ENDA would violate the First Amendment's guarantee of "free exercise of religion" because it would require employers whose religion teaches that homosexuality is a sin to hire homosexuals.[23] They objected further that unlike race, sex, and national origin, which were appropriately protected against discrimination by the Civil Rights Act, homosexuality is a choice, rather than an inherent personal characteristic, and it is therefore not deserving of civil rights protection. The most frequently and fervently voiced objection to the proposed legislation, though, was that for Congress to extend the protections of the Civil Rights Act to homosexuals would wrongly imply that homosexuality is normal and acceptable behavior and would therefore encourage further depravity and immorality.

After the proposed bill was sent to committees in the Senate and House, no further action was taken.[24]

TWO YEARS later, Senator Kennedy struck a deal with Senate Republicans to allow ENDA to come to a vote. The bill's supporters insisted that there was no evidence that sexual orientation relates in any way to job performance, and they invoked a government study that showed that employment discrimination against gays and lesbians cost the nation's economy $1.4 billion per year.[25] Opposition to the bill was once again fierce, echoing the objections that had been voiced two years earlier.[26]

On September 10, 1996, a bitterly divided Senate rejected ENDA by a

---

* Goldwater had a gay grandson, Ty Ross. According to Ross, he never talked to Goldwater about his sexual orientation, but his homosexuality was never a secret. When he visited Goldwater with his partner, Goldwater would say, "It's good that you're standing up for what you believe in. I'm proud of you, Goddammit." Frank Rich, *The Right Stuff*, New York Times (June 3, 1998).

single vote—50 to 49. Once again, religion played a central role. Only 17 percent of the senators from the twenty most religious states voted in favor of ENDA, whereas 70 percent of all other members of the Senate supported the legislation.[27]

Nine months later, Senator James Jeffords (R-Vermont) introduced a revised version of ENDA. Specifically, the new version of ENDA exempted religious organizations from its coverage. Under this exemption, a Catholic hospital, for example, could refuse to hire a nurse who is gay or lesbian, and a Mormon child-care agency could refuse to hire a gay or lesbian social worker.[28] With this exemption in place, supporters hoped that the legislation finally would pass, but to no avail. The bill was referred to committee, where it languished once again.[29] And so it went, year after year after year.

A DECADE later, in 2007, members of Congress introduced the first version of ENDA that prohibited discrimination on the basis of gender identity as well as sexual orientation. Once again, the bill died in committee. Representative Barney Frank (D-Massachusetts), the nation's first openly gay member of Congress, then made a second attempt at moving the bill, this time without the provision protecting transgender persons. Once again, religious conservatives blocked the bill. Ed Vitagliano, the spokesman for the American Family Association, declared that there was "no real problem of discrimination against homosexuals" and that what homosexuals were really after was "the ideological surrender of . . . Christians." Other voices of the Christian Right warned that if ENDA was enacted, it would mark the end of religious freedom in America.[30]

Despite these and similar objections, the Democratic-controlled House of Representatives voted in favor of ENDA by a margin of 235 to 184. But, after President George W. Bush threatened to veto the bill, it never made it to the floor of the Senate.[31]

B Y 2013, almost 80 percent of Americans, including a substantial majority of Republicans and a majority of citizens in every state in the nation, had come to the view that Congress should finally enact ENDA. This was based on two widely shared beliefs: that discrimination against gays and lesbians was unfair, and that individuals should be judged in the employment context on the basis of their ability to perform.[32]

Against this background, a Senate committee approved ENDA by an overwhelming vote in 2013. Faced with a threatened filibuster by Senate

Republicans, a cloture vote was held and sixty-one senators, including seven Republicans, voted to override the filibuster. Several days later, the Senate voted sixty-four to thirty-two to enact ENDA. Ten Republicans broke ranks with their party's line and supported the legislation.

President Barack Obama promised to sign the bill into law as soon as it passed the House, but that was not to be. Just minutes after the Senate approved the measure, Speaker of the House John Boehner (R-Ohio) and House Majority Leader Eric Cantor (R-Virginia) made clear that the bill would be dead-on-arrival in the Republican-controlled House of Representatives. And so it was.[33]

Thus, despite overwhelming public support for ENDA, the bill still languishes in the Republican-controlled Congress. The fierce objections of the Christian Right, a powerful political force, continue to paralyze the leaders of the Republican Party, even over the wishes of a majority of their own supporters. And so it remains to this day.[*]

"THE RIGHT TO SERVE THE COUNTRY THEY LOVE"

DURING AND AFTER World War II, the United States adopted a firm policy prohibiting homosexuals to serve in the military.[†] According to a 1982 Department of Defense statement, the presence of homosexuals in the armed forces "adversely affects" military discipline, good order, and morale and therefore "seriously impairs the accomplishment of the military mission." Although the statement cited no evidence in support of its assertion, its accuracy was assumed to be obvious by military leaders and politicians alike.[34]

A decade later, during the 1992 presidential campaign, the issue of "gays in the military" moved to center stage. By this time, Americans were evenly divided on the question. In a speech at Harvard University in 1991, candidate Bill Clinton announced that if elected, he would lift the ban against homosexuals in the military. At the 1992 Democratic National Conven-

---

[*] Through the use of executive orders, Presidents Bill Clinton and Barack Obama have prohibited discrimination on the basis of sexual orientation and gender identity in the federal civilian workforce and by federal contractors. Although the Christian Right has vehemently disparaged and challenged these executive orders, it has not managed to muster sufficient support in Congress to override them.

[†] See chapter 11.

tion, the party platform expressly embraced that policy.* The Republican National Convention took precisely the opposite position. Nonetheless, after Clinton was elected, gays and lesbians rejoiced in the hope that they, like other patriotic Americans, would finally be granted the right to serve their nation in the armed forces.[35]

S HORTLY AFTER the 1992 election, though, and before Clinton could sign a planned executive order ending the ban on homosexuals in the military, the opposition mobilized with a vengeance. The Christian Right organized passionate phone calls and letters to members of Congress condemning the proposed change. Pat Robertson charged that allowing gays in the military would give "preferred status to evil," Jerry Falwell rallied support on the *Old Time Gospel Hour*, and Beverly LaHaye, president of Concerned Women for America, castigated homosexuals on her radio broadcasts, which were played on more than a thousand stations nationwide. Faced with such a bitterly divisive issue, and seeking to avoid conflict in the early weeks of his presidency, Clinton looked for a compromise.[36]

After reflection, he announced that the ban would remain in place for six months, during which time the Pentagon would study the question.[37] Among the most influential opponents of ending the ban were General Colin Powell, the first African American chairman of the Joint Chiefs of Staff, and Senator Sam Nunn (D-Georgia), the chairman of the powerful Senate Armed Services Committee. They argued against changing the policy because, in their view, the presence of gays and lesbians would undermine order in the military and impair the troops' sense of privacy.[38]

On July 19, 1993, after a heated and sometimes bitter public debate, Clinton announced that the policy governing gays in the military would change—but only sort of. His proposal was that the military would no longer inquire into the sexual orientation of members of the armed forces, but it could still discharge service members who either engaged in homosexual conduct or revealed their sexual orientation to others. This policy became known as "Don't Ask, Don't Tell," or "DADT."

Almost no one was happy with the compromise. Supporters of gay rights were appalled that gay and lesbian service members would have to hide

---

* Between 1980 and 1990, approximately 17,000 servicemen and women were separated from the military for reasons of "homosexuality."

their sexual orientation in order to serve their country, and the Christian Right was appalled that gays and lesbians could now legally serve in the armed forces as long as they masked their "propensity to engage in homosexual acts."[39]

W HEN GEORGE W. BUSH entered the White House in 2001, gay rights supporters were uneasy. Although Bush had campaigned as a "compassionate conservative," as governor of Texas he had both defended the state's anti-sodomy law and supported a measure that banned gay couples from becoming foster parents. Moreover, several of Bush's early cabinet appointments, such as Senator John Ashcroft (R-Missouri) as attorney general, had vehemently opposed the recognition of gay rights.

Most observers therefore expected Bush to revoke Don't Ask, Don't Tell and to reinstate the earlier policy. Indeed, this seemed inevitable, because it had been the demand of the 2000 Republican Party platform and because Bush's new secretary of state, Colin Powell, had strongly supported the prior policy in 1993. But Bush, who had other priorities, left the matter alone.

Four years later, the American Psychological Association, which a quarter-century earlier had determined that homosexuality is not a mental illness, issued a report concluding that "empirical evidence fails to show that sexual orientation is germane to any aspect of military effectiveness."[40] Moreover, it had become increasingly clear to military leaders during the Iraq War that the cost to the nation of discharging gay and lesbian service members—both financially and in the loss of expertise (most dramatically in the discharge of more than sixty Arabic- and Persian-speaking translators)—had significantly damaged the nation's effectiveness in the war.[41]

Against this background, in 2007 former Chairman of the Joint Chiefs of Staff John Shalikashvili and former Secretary of Defense William Cohen called for the repeal of Don't Ask, Don't Tell. Later that year, more than one hundred retired generals and admirals issued a statement urging the government to repeal the policy. Bush, however, nearing the end of his presidency, did nothing.[42]

D URING THE 2008 presidential campaign, candidate Barack Obama called for the repeal of all laws barring gays and lesbians from serving openly in the military. Nineteen days after his election, though, Obama's advisers announced that plans to repeal the policy would be put on hold while the new president conferred with military leaders before presenting any legislation on this issue to Congress.[43]

By this time, even Colin Powell conceded that "a lot has changed with respect to attitudes within our country," and that it was time for the policy to be "reviewed." Attitudes had, indeed, changed. Although there were still those who defended Don't Ask, Don't Tell, and even those who insisted that the nation should return to its pre-1993 policy, the American people had clearly moved on. Seventy-seven percent of Americans now thought that gays and lesbians should be permitted to serve openly in the military, and even most Republicans (74 percent) and conservatives (67 percent) agreed.[44]

In his 2010 State of the Union address, President Obama promised that "this year, I will work with Congress and our military to finally repeal the law that denies gay Americans the right to serve the country they love."[45] Shortly thereafter, the Joint Chiefs of Staff released a report concluding that there was a low risk of disruption if gays, lesbians, and bisexuals were permitted to serve openly in the armed forces. On December 15, 2010, a bill to repeal Don't Ask, Don't Tell passed the House by a vote of 250 to 175, and the Senate by a vote of 65 to 31. On September 20, 2011, the policy of Don't Ask, Don't Tell was officially terminated.*

During the seventeen years that DADT remained in effect, the military discharged approximately 13,000 gay and lesbian service members. The effect on many of these individuals was devastating. Their only "offense" had been their desire to serve their nation.

In the days and weeks after DADT was repealed, a series of memorable and often moving events took place across the nation. Reservist Jeremy Johnson became the first person discharged under DADT to openly reenlist. Air Force intelligence officer Ginger Wallace became the first openly LGBT service member to have a same-sex partner participate in the "pinning-on" ceremony that marked her promotion to colonel. After 80 days at sea, Navy Petty Officer Marissa Gaeta won the right to the traditional "first kiss" when her ship returned to port. She shared it with her previously secret same-sex partner. And at the very moment that the repeal of DADT took effect, Navy Lieutenant Gary C. Ross married his previ-

---

* The repeal of DADT did not lift the ban on transgender persons in the military, because they are considered medically unfit for service. In 2015, Secretary of Defense Ashton Carter announced that the continuation of that policy would be placed under review. It is estimated that, as of 2016, approximately 15,000 transgender persons serve in the U.S. military.

"First Kiss," Petty Officers Marissa Gaeta and Citlalic Snell, December 21, 2011

ously secret same-sex partner of eleven-and-a-half years, making them the first same-sex military couple to openly marry in the history of the United States.[46]

"GOING TO THE CHAPEL"?

FOR MOST OF American history, the notion that a man could marry a man or a woman could marry a woman would have seemed utterly absurd, if anyone even thought to consider the question. Indeed, before the 1980s no one bothered to poll on the question of same-sex marriage. Marriage was a union between a man and a woman, period. Moreover, even after the issue of same-sex marriage finally came to the fore, the gay community was divided on the question. Many members of the gay community saw the institution of marriage as an unjust and "patriarchal system" that was grounded in the "dominance of men over women." Why, they asked, should they want to enter into such a morally corrupt institution?[47]

Despite the strong traditional assumptions about the meaning of marriage as involving a man and a woman, and despite the gay community's own ambivalence about the issue, by 2015, 60 percent of Americans had come to the view that "marriages between same-sex couples should be recognized by the law as valid"—a stunning shift from twenty years earlier, when only a tiny fraction of Americans held that view. Several factors contributed to this revolution in public attitudes.

Perhaps most important was the impact of AIDS. Not only did the AIDS crisis help draw millions of gay men out of the closet, but it also changed the nature of gay sexual relations. The realization that HIV was spread by sex was destabilizing. To avoid the transmission of HIV, it became necessary for gay men to alter their prior sexual practices. The concept of "safe sex" soon emerged. Gay men increasingly recognized that by avoiding high-risk behavior, they could still have a satisfying, but much safer sex life. The need for self-protection, combined with the increased ability to step out of the closet, encouraged the creation of more stable and more committed relationships.[48]

But as the AIDS epidemic made dramatically clear, those relationships, no matter how committed they might be, had no *legal* standing. Committed same-sex partners were considered by the state and by the medical profession as legal strangers to one another. Hospitals denied them the right to play a role in the treatment and care of their ill and often dying partners, and the law denied them a vast array of benefits, routinely available to married couples, dealing with such matters as health insurance, income taxes, health care deductions, property rights, inheritance rights, and estate tax exemptions. It became increasingly clear that committed gay couples needed to secure some legal recognition of their relationships.[49]

Another factor that spurred the movement for legal recognition of same-sex relationships came from within the lesbian community. By the 1980s, many lesbians had come to resent the idea that in order to have children they had to marry a man. In 1982, a group of lesbians who were considering motherhood founded the organization "Baby Maybe" in Washington, D.C., to explore the ways in which lesbian couples could have children. The primary options included adoption, artificial insemination, and having sex with a male friend. As the issue gradually came into the open, conferences for lesbian couples considering motherhood were held in cities across the nation.

Lesbian couples who had children in this era faced serious legal challenges. If the biological mother died and her relatives contested the right of the surviving partner to have custody over the child, courts saw the non-biological mother as a legal stranger to the child and therefore granted custody to the biological mother's relatives. Similarly, if the women in a lesbian relationship separated after one of them gave birth to a child who was raised by both of them, the ordinary rules governing custody disputes in a divorce did not apply. Because the non-biological mother had no legally recognized connection to the child, she had little, if any, recourse if her ex-partner chose to deny her access to their child. And, of course, like gay male couples, lesbian couples faced severe challenges when it came to such issues as taxes, inheritance, property rights, and health care.

For all of these reasons, as well as for reasons of simple dignity and equality, it became increasingly clear that committed same-sex couples, like committed opposite-sex couples, should have access to the rights and protections of marriage. At the 1987 March on Washington for Lesbian and Gay Rights, two thousand same-sex couples demonstrated their support for same-sex marriage by participating in a mass "wedding." Aleta Fence-roy, who "married" her partner Jean Mayberry at the ceremony, recalled that "the whole subway tunnel burst out with people singing 'Going to the Chapel.' It was one of those moments that still gives me goose bumps when I think of it."

But no one at the time thought that the legalization of same-sex marriage was a realistic goal in the foreseeable future.[50]

I N THE meantime, San Francisco gay rights attorney Matt Coles, who would later go on to serve as deputy national legal director of the ACLU, and several colleagues in the local gay community came up with a somewhat less ambitious idea: the "domestic partnership." Their hope was that the domestic partnership would serve as an alternative means of achieving at least some degree of protection for committed same-sex couples.* In 1982, the San Francisco Board of Supervisors passed an ordinance recognizing domestic partnerships for municipal employees, but in the face of intense opposition from the Catholic Church, which called the measure "severely inimical to marriage and the family," Liberal mayor Dianne Feinstein vetoed the measure.[51]

Two years later, Berkeley, California, became the first city in the nation

---

* The difference between civil unions, which did not yet exist, and domestic partnerships is that civil unions usually grant couples all of the rights associated with marriage, whereas domestic partnerships are more selective in the specific rights they grant.

to establish a registry where both same-sex and opposite-sex couples could record their domestic partnerships. A registered couple was entitled to modest benefits from the local government. A decade later, approximately twenty-five cities and counties across the nation offered domestic partnership benefits to municipal employees. In the private sector, a few companies, led by the software company Lotus, and a few universities, led by the University of Chicago and Stanford, also provided the committed same-sex partners of their employees and students some or all of the benefits they provided to married couples. But such examples were still few and far between.[52]

In many cities across the nation, efforts to enact domestic partnership programs for same-sex couples were fiercely resisted. In the relatively progressive community of Austin, Texas, for example, voters in a 1993 referendum overturned the city council's decision to offer domestic partnership benefits to city employees by a two-to-one margin. In 1996, after Philadelphia mayor Ed Rendell issued an executive order extending health care benefits to the domestic partners of city employees, the Catholic Church proclaimed that Rendell's action would lead "to the deterioration of our own civilization," and the president of the Black Clergy of Philadelphia charged that Rendell had put the city at risk of becoming "a modern day Sodom and Gomorrah."[53]

It was not until 1999 that a state—California—finally enacted domestic partnership benefits for same-sex couples. The California law granted a limited set of rights, such as hospital visitation, to domestic partners. But this was still a far cry from marriage equality.*[54]

BOMBSHELLS ACROSS AMERICA

IN 1990, THREE GAY COUPLES in Hawaii applied for marriage licenses, which were, of course, denied. They then filed suit in state court claiming that the state's refusal to allow same-sex couples to marry violated the Hawaii constitution. None of the major national gay rights organizations supported the litigation. They were certain that the plaintiffs would lose and that both the lawsuit and the loss would damage the cause of gay rights

---

* Later that year, the Vermont Supreme Court ruled that under the state constitution, same-sex couples were entitled to the same legal rights as married couples. But rather than extend marriage to same-sex couples, the state legislature authorized them to enter into "civil unions," which carried the same legal rights as marriage, but not the name.

nationally. As predicted, both the state trial court and the state court of appeals rejected the plaintiffs' claim.

But then, to almost everyone's surprise, the Hawaii Supreme Court ruled in 1993 in *Baehr v. Lewin* that the law restricting marriage to a man and a woman implicated Hawaii's constitutional guarantee forbidding discrimination on the basis of sex.*[55] The court therefore held that the restriction was unconstitutional unless it was "necessary to serve a compelling government interest." It sent the case back to the trial court to explore that issue.[56]

The Hawaii Supreme Court's decision in *Baehr* provoked a furious response. Although Hawaii was one of the most liberal states in the nation, and was one of the first states to enact a law forbidding employment discrimination on the basis of sexual orientation, same-sex marriage was something else entirely. At the time of the decision, 70 percent of Hawaiians opposed same-sex marriage, the state's usually "gay-friendly" governor condemned the decision, the hierarchy of the Catholic Church expressed outrage, the Mormon Church poured more than $600,000 into a campaign to overturn the decision, and an organization called Stop Promoting Homosexuality Hawaii castigated the court for "shoving gay marriage down the throats of Hawaiians." In 1998, before anyone could actually be married under the Hawaii Supreme Court's decision, Hawaii amended its state constitution to define marriage as only between a man and a woman, thus overriding the decision in *Baehr*.[57]

B Y OPENING the door to even the possibility of same-sex marriage, the Hawaii Supreme Court's decision became not only a local, but a national, sensation. After the court announced its decision, an Associated Press article warned that it could "throw bombshells across America." Lambda Legal, the nation's oldest LGBT civil rights organization, inflamed moral conservatives with a widely publicized suggestion that same-sex couples should immediately travel to Hawaii in the hope of getting married, because if they could do so their home states would then be legally obligated to recognize their marriages. The very suggestion of such a strategy triggered a ferocious national response.

The *Los Angeles Times* warned that "homosexual marriage had

---

* The theory was that because a man could legally marry a woman but not a man, and because a woman could marry a man but not a woman, the law discriminated on the basis of sex.

abruptly emerged as an emotional flashpoint" in the nation's Culture Wars, and a Gallup poll revealed that Americans opposed same-sex marriage by an overwhelming margin of 68 to 27 percent. Utah promptly enacted a statute expressly providing that same-sex marriages performed in other states would *not* be recognized in Utah.[58]

For Republicans, the Hawaii decision was a political gift, because it both mobilized their base of religious conservatives and aligned them on this issue with most swing voters. In the spring of 1996, Republican legislators in thirty-four state legislatures introduced "defense of marriage" bills similar to the one enacted in Utah. Within a year, twenty-two states had enacted such laws.*

Moreover, and importantly, most of these laws were adopted not by legislation, but by amending the state constitution. This served two critical purposes. First, it made it impossible for the state's supreme court ever to hold that the state's limitation of marriage to opposite-sex couples violated the state's constitution. Second, it tied the hands of future generations, for in the unlikely event that at some point in the future a majority of the state's citizens should come to favor same-sex marriage, they still would not be able to enact that policy into law without first undertaking the much more onerous task of re-amending the state constitution.†[59]

T HE CENTRAL role that religion played in the enactment of these laws is well illustrated by the events in California. After the decision of the Hawaii Supreme Court in *Baehr*, the California legislature enacted the California Defense of Marriage Act, which declared that "only marriage between a man and a woman" could be valid in California.[60] In 2008, however, the California Supreme Court held that the California Defense of Marriage Act violated the state constitution and that same-sex couples in California had a state constitutional right to marry.[61]

Six months later, after the most expensive referendum campaign in American history, California voters adopted Proposition 8, which amended

---

* By 2009, eleven more states had enacted such laws.

† The states that adopted state constitutional amendments banning same-sex marriage are Alabama, Alaska, Arizona, Arkansas, California, Colorado, Florida, Georgia, Idaho, Kansas, Kentucky, Louisiana, Michigan, Mississippi, Missouri, Montana, Nebraska, Nevada, North Carolina, North Dakota, Ohio, Oklahoma, Oregon, South Carolina, South Dakota, Tennessee, Texas, Utah, Virginia, and Wisconsin. In addition, Indiana, West Virginia, and Wyoming have enacted statutes banning same-sex marriage.

the California constitution to overrule the decision of the California Supreme Court. Those supporting Proposition 8 were energetically supported and lavishly funded by religious organizations. The bishops of the California Catholic Conference aggressively supported Proposition 8; the Knights of Columbus, a Roman Catholic fraternal organization, donated more than $1.2 million in support of the measure; the archbishop of San Francisco campaigned vigorously in favor of Proposition 8; and the Mormon Church contributed more than $20 million to get Proposition 8 enacted. Other religious leaders and conservative organizations also campaigned energetically to persuade California voters to enact Proposition 8, including the American Family Association, Focus on the Family, and Rick Warren, the pastor of Saddleback Church, one of the nation's largest megachurches.[62]

Proposition 8 was approved in the referendum by a slim margin of 52 to 48 percent. The breakdown in the vote was revealing. Those who identified themselves as evangelicals supported Proposition 8 by a margin of 81 to 19 percent, and those who attended church weekly supported Proposition 8 by a margin of 84 to 16 percent. Non-Christians, on the other hand, opposed Proposition 8 by a margin of 85 to 15 percent, and voters who did not attend church regularly opposed Proposition 8 by a vote of 83 to 17 percent.

Thus, although the proponents of Proposition 8, like the proponents of Sunday-closing laws and blasphemy laws during the Second Great Awakening, invoked a variety of nonreligious "justifications" for the prohibition of same-sex marriage, including arguments about tradition, morality, the interests of children, and family values, the voting patterns made crystal clear that Proposition 8 was, "in practical effect, a successful effort by persons holding a specific religious belief to use the authority of the law to impose their belief on their fellow citizens."[63]

DEFENSE OF MARRIAGE

THE CAMPAIGN OF religious conservatives against marriage equality for gays and lesbians played out in the national government, as well as in the states. In 1994, the Republican Party gained control of the House of Representatives for the first time in forty years. Central to this achievement was the effort of Pat Robertson's Christian Coalition to turn out the evangelical vote. The Christian Coalition, which distributed more than thirty million voter guides in churches across the nation, was now one of the nation's most powerful lobbying groups. As the 1996 presidential election approached,

Christian Right leaders like Gary Bauer of the Family Research Council and James Dobson of Focus on the Family made clear to Republican candidates that to gain their support they would have to toe the line on issues like abortion and homosexuality.

The anti-gay rhetoric was ugly. Dick Armey (R-Texas), the Republican whip in the House, publicly referred to openly gay Democratic Congressman Barney Frank as "Barney Fag." Senator Bob Dole (R-Kansas), the front-runner for the party's nomination for president, actively courted the Christian Right, and six of the seven Republican presidential candidates, including Dole, signed a "marriage protection resolution" that harshly condemned the morality of same-sex marriage. One candidate, Patrick Buchanan, derided "the false god of gay rights," and another, Alan Keyes, who would later disown his own daughter after she came out as a lesbian, charged that the homosexual agenda was "destroying the integrity" of the United States.[64]

In the spring of 1996, Republican Speaker of the House Newt Gingrich (R-Georgia) instructed Congressman Bob Barr (R-Georgia) to draft a law that would forbid the federal government from recognizing the legality of same-sex marriages, even if they were recognized as legal by a state. Titled the "Defense of Marriage Act," or DOMA, Barr's bill not only empowered states to deny the legality of same-sex marriages recognized as legal by other states, but also denied individuals who had entered into valid same-sex marriages under state law the multitude of federal benefits that were otherwise available to married couples, including the right to file joint tax returns, social security survivorship benefits, immigration rights, and the like.[65]

In May, Barr's bill was sent to the House Judiciary Committee, which was chaired by Congressman Henry Hyde (R-Illinois), who twenty years earlier had sponsored the Hyde Amendment that denied impoverished women Medicaid funding that would have enabled them to pay for legal abortions.* The hearings quickly turned "openly homophobic."[66] As the legal scholar Dale Carpenter has observed, members of Congress "evidenced deep hostility" to gays and lesbians, "described the effects of same-sex marriage in apocalyptic and paranoid terms," and repeatedly described gays and lesbians "as sick, perverted, and dangerous."[67]

Congressman Charles Canady (R-Florida) declared that only opposite-sex marriage "comports with . . . our Judeo-Christian moral heritage"; Congressman David Funderburk (R-North Carolina) derided homosexual-

---

* See chapter 17.

ity as "inherently wrong and harmful"; Senator Jesse Helms (R-North Carolina) insisted that DOMA was essential to protect the nation from those who were attempting "to tear apart America's moral fabric"; and Congressman Bob Barr (R-Georgia) warned that "the flames of hedonism . . . are licking at the very foundations of our society."[68]

The House passed the bill by an overwhelming majority of 342 to 67, and the Senate approved it by a veto-proof margin of 85 to 14, with all but one Republican, and even a majority of Democrats, supporting the measure.[69]

With a presidential election just around the corner, and with the American people opposed to same-sex marriage by a margin of 68 to 27 percent, President Bill Clinton reluctantly signed DOMA into law on September 21, 1996. He released an awkward and somewhat ironic statement warning that the new law "should not, despite the fierce and at times divisive rhetoric surrounding it, be understood to provide an excuse for discrimination . . . against any person on the basis of sexual orientation."[70] And thus did the president who had promised to be an advocate for the gay community sign into law one of the most insultingly homophobic federal laws in American history.

THUS, DESPITE the occasional successes of the ongoing effort to win equal rights for gays and lesbians through the political process, the repeated defeats and frustrations at both the state and federal levels made it increasingly clear that at some point, as with the abortion issue, a turn to the courts—and to the United States Constitution—might be necessary. As the Hawaii Supreme Court had demonstrated, it was not impossible to imagine that constitutional law might offer protection even to homosexuals. This might not have been what the Framers had envisioned when they drafted the Constitution, but that was not necessarily the end of the inquiry.

19

A RIGHT TO
"RETAIN THEIR DIGNITY"

S UPPOSE SEVERAL POLICE officers lawfully search a married couple's home for illegal drugs. Upon entering the home they find no drugs, but they see the couple engaging in oral sex in their bedroom. The couple are prosecuted and convicted for violating the state's anti-sodomy law, which prohibits any person to engage in oral or anal sex. The couple maintains that this law, and especially in its application to them, violates the Constitution.

The first thing to notice is that the Constitution nowhere expressly guarantees a right to engage in sodomy. So why might this law be unconstitutional? One possible argument might be that the anti-sodomy law does not rationally further a legitimate government interest. As a general rule, a law that does not rationally further a legitimate government interest will be held to violate the Constitution.[1] But anti-sodomy laws have been a part of Anglo-American law for hundreds of years. They have traditionally been thought to reflect moral standards of behavior. Does a law that enforces long-standing moral precepts rationally serve a legitimate government interest?

Another possible argument might be that the Constitution implicitly protects the privacy of the marriage relation and that for the government to prohibit a married couple to engage in intimate sexual conduct even of this nature implicates the unenumerated but fundamental right of marital privacy. A strong precedent for this argument might be *Griswold*, in which the Court held unconstitutional a law making it a crime for married couples to use contraceptives. Whether or not that law was rational, the Court invalidated it because, by invading the most private intimacies of the marriage relation, it infringed "a right of privacy older than the Bill of Rights."[2] Perhaps application of the anti-sodomy statute to our married couple is similarly unconstitutional, on the theory that it too invades the intimacies of the marriage relation.

Suppose now, however, that the couple in the home is not married. Even if the sodomy statute could not constitutionally be applied to a married couple, is the same true for unmarried persons? In *Eisenstadt,* the Court extended the principle of *Griswold* from married to unmarried persons. The Court explained that "if the right of privacy means anything, it is the right of the individual, married or single, to be free from unwarranted governmental intrusion into matters so fundamentally affecting a person as the decision whether to bear or beget a child."*[3]

But that does not necessarily help our unmarried couple, because oral sex is not about bearing or begetting a child. Of course, one might argue that oral sex is in fact related to that fundamental decision, because oral sex is a way of having sex while avoiding the risk of pregnancy. But that seems a bit strained. Is there, then, a right of individuals to shape their own sexual intimacies wholly apart from the issue of reproduction? But even if there is such a right, does it extend to *homosexual* sodomy? In light of our long history of condemning such behavior, can homosexual sodomy now, suddenly, be deemed a constitutional right?

And there is one final twist. Suppose the state prohibits *only* homosexual sodomy? Even if there is no constitutional right to engage in sodomy generally, does such a law violate the Equal Protection Clause because it discriminates against gays and lesbians?

BOWERS: "HOMOSEXUAL SODOMY IS IMMORAL"

IN AUGUST 1982, an Atlanta police officer went to the home of Michael Hardwick to serve an arrest warrant for public drinking. Upon entering the home, the officer observed Hardwick and another man engaged in consensual oral sex. The officer placed both men under arrest for the crime of sodomy, which was defined by Georgia law as oral or anal sex between two individuals, whether of the same or opposite sex. Although the local district attorney decided not to pursue the charges, Hardwick filed suit against Michael Bowers, the attorney general of Georgia, seeking

---

* *Griswold* and *Eisenstadt* are discussed in chapter 15.

a judicial declaration that the state's sodomy law violated the United States Constitution.*

At the time the Constitution was adopted, every state made sodomy a crime, although these laws were rarely enforced. In 1961, the American Law Institute recommended the decriminalization of sodomy, and by the mid-1980s a majority of states had adopted this recommendation. But twenty-three states, including Georgia, still made sodomy a crime. It remained the case, though, that these laws were rarely enforced. Indeed, the state of Georgia had not invoked its sodomy statute for several decades before the arrest of Michael Hardwick.[4]

In *Bowers v. Hardwick*,[5] decided in 1986, the Supreme Court, in a sharply-divided five-to-four decision, held that the Georgia statute, as applied to homosexual sodomy, was not unconstitutional. Justice Byron White, joined by Chief Justice Burger and Justices Powell, Rehnquist, and O'Connor, wrote the opinion of the Court.

At the outset, Justice White rejected the contention that the Court's prior decisions in such cases as *Skinner, Griswold, Eisenstadt*, and *Roe*[†6] recognized a constitutional right of privacy broad enough to encompass a right to engage in homosexual sodomy. Rather, he reasoned, those cases dealt with fundamental issues of "family, marriage, or procreation," issues that have "no connection" to homosexual activity.[7]

White turned next to the question whether, independent of those precedents, the Constitution *should* be understood to protect such a right. He answered that question in the negative. Proscriptions against homosexuality, he noted, "have ancient roots" and have existed in the United States from the very founding of the nation. Against that background, he reasoned, "to claim that a right to engage in such conduct is 'deeply rooted in this Nation's history and tradition' . . . is, at best, facetious." White therefore concluded that unlike the implied fundamental rights recognized in the earlier decisions, there was no basis for granting constitutional status to the asserted right to engage in homosexual sodomy.[8]

Finally, White turned to the question whether, even if no fundamental right was at issue, the statute should nonetheless be deemed unconstitu-

---

* The Georgia sodomy statute provided that a "person commits the offense of sodomy when he performs or submits to any sexual act involving the sex organs of one person and the mouth or anus of another." The act provided further that a "person convicted of the offense of sodomy shall be punished by imprisonment for not less than one nor more than 20 years." Ga. Code Ann. 16-6-2 (1984).

† *Skinner, Griswold*, and *Eisenstadt* are discussed in chapter 15; *Roe* is discussed in chapter 16.

Justice Byron R. White

tional because it served no legitimate state interest. Hardwick maintained that the state's prohibition of homosexual sodomy was based on nothing more than the belief "of a majority of the electorate in Georgia that homosexual sodomy is immoral." White rejected the contention that this was an insufficient justification for the law. "Law," he observed, "is constantly based on notions of morality, and if all laws representing essentially moral choices are to be invalidated . . . the courts will be very busy indeed."[9]

In a separate concurring opinion, Chief Justice Burger, in the final days of his tenure on the Court, went out of his way to insist that under the United States Constitution, there is "no such thing as a fundamental right to commit homosexual sodomy." A lifelong Presbyterian who was clearly disturbed by the very existence of Hardwick's claim, Burger declared that condemnation of homosexual conduct "is firmly rooted in

Judeo-Christian moral and ethical standards." To underscore his point, he invoked Sir William Blackstone, the eighteenth-century English jurist and scholar, who had described "the infamous crime against nature" as "a crime not fit to be named" among Christians. In light of that history, Burger concluded that "to hold that the act of homosexual sodomy is somehow protected as a fundamental right would be to cast aside millennia of moral teaching."[10]

"JUDEO-CHRISTIAN VALUES . . . CANNOT PROVIDE AN ADEQUATE JUSTIFICATION"

IN A BITING dissenting opinion, Justice Harry Blackmun, joined by Justices Brennan, Marshall, and Stevens, began by chastising the majority for framing the issue as if the case was about nothing more than whether there is "a fundamental right to engage in homosexual sodomy." To the contrary, he argued, "this case is about 'the most comprehensive of rights and the right most valued by civilized men,' namely, 'the right to be let alone.'"[11]

The Georgia statute, Blackmun insisted, denies individuals the fundamental "right to decide for themselves whether to engage in particular forms of private, consensual sexual activity." Blackmun added that, as the Court had observed in *Paris Adult Theatre*, the conservative 1973 decision that redefined the law of obscenity, sexual intimacy is a vital part of "human existence" and is central to "the development of human personality."*[12]

Moreover, Blackmun reasoned, in a nation "as diverse as ours, . . . there may be many 'right' ways" of having intimate relationships, and much of the richness and meaning of those relationships comes "from the freedom an individual has to choose the form and nature of these intensely personal bonds." Thus, Blackmun reasoned, the interest all individuals have in controlling the "nature of their intimate associations" is every bit as fundamental as the individual's interest in making decisions about such matters as marriage, contraception, sterilization, and abortion.[13]

Blackmun then turned to the majority's argument that the Georgia law was constitutional because sodomy had long been deemed immoral. Invoking his opinion for the Court thirteen years earlier in *Roe*, Black-

---

* *Paris Adult Theatre* is discussed in chapter 12.

mun responded that the mere fact that certain moral judgments may be long-standing does not dictate the meaning of the Constitution.[14] Quoting Justice Oliver Wendell Holmes, Blackmun declared that it "'is revolting to have no better reason for a rule of law than that so it was laid down in the time of Henry IV.'"[15]

Turning to the issue of religion, Blackmun conceded that "traditional Judeo-Christian values" had, indeed, historically proscribed homosexual intimacy. But, Blackmun insisted, that fact could not justify the Georgia law. That certain "religious groups condemn" certain behavior, he reasoned, "gives the State no license to impose their judgments on the entire citizenry." To the contrary, the legitimacy of legislation depends on "whether the State can advance some justification for its law beyond its conformity to religious doctrine." Blackmun therefore concluded that if the right to privacy means anything, "it means that, before Georgia can prosecute its citizens for making choices about the most intimate aspects of their lives, it must do more than assert that the choice they have made is an 'abominable crime not fit to be named among Christians.'"[16]

In closing, Blackmun expressed his hope that, before the passage of too many years, the Court would reconsider its analysis and "conclude that depriving individuals of the right to choose for themselves how to conduct their intimate relationships poses a far greater threat to the values most deeply rooted in our Nation's history than tolerance of nonconformity could ever do."[17]

*B*OWERS WAS a bitter disappointment to the gay community. Thousands of gays and lesbians protested in front of the Supreme Court building after the decision was announced. Reflecting the prejudices and fears of the moment, the protestors were met by several hundred police officers wearing black visors and latex gloves to keep themselves "safe" from AIDS. For six hours, the demonstrators chanted "Equal Justice Under Law," pointing to the words emblazoned on the Supreme Court building; scattered thousands of pink paper triangles; and shouted "Shame! Shame! Shame!" at the justices who were inside the marble edifice. By the end of the day, six hundred protestors had been arrested, more than at any other protest in the history of the Supreme Court.

While Christian conservatives regarded the decision in *Bowers* as "a great reaffirmation of moral values in American life," leaders of the gay community compared it to two of the most despised and discredited decisions in the history of the Supreme Court—*Dred Scott v. Sanford* and *Plessy v. Ferguson*, which had held, respectively, that African Americans could not be citizens of the United States and that state-sponsored racial segregation was constitutional.

The issue for the gay community was not so much the fear of prosecution, which was rare, but the dignitary, liberty, and equality implications of a legal regime that demeaned same-sex sexual intimacy as sinful, abhorrent, and even criminal. And, indeed, in the years after *Bowers*, state and federal courts regularly invoked the decision to uphold all manner of laws discriminating against gays and lesbians. After all, if homosexuals were criminals, then they, like other criminals, could lawfully be denied all sorts of rights and privileges to which other citizens were routinely entitled.[18]

A LTHOUGH *BOWERS* dealt a serious blow to the gay community, it is noteworthy that as early as 1986 the Supreme Court came within a single vote of holding that gays and lesbians have a constitutional right to engage in homosexual sodomy. Twenty years earlier, that would have been unimaginable. Indeed, at the time Justices Blackmun, Brennan, Marshall, and Stevens took the position they did in *Bowers*, the Reagan administration still refused to devote any resources to combat the "gay plague"; there were few laws anywhere in the United States protecting gays and lesbians against discrimination in housing, employment, education, or adoption; gays and lesbians were still absolutely excluded from serving in the military; the idea that gays and lesbians might someday be permitted to marry was no more than a glimmer in anyone's mind; and less than a third of all Americans thought that homosexual sodomy should be legal. That four justices of the Supreme Court were prepared at that moment to hold laws forbidding homosexual sodomy unconstitutional was truly remarkable.

In fact, though, the vote was even closer than that. The critical "swing" justice in *Bowers*—that is, the justice who expressed the greatest uncertainty about which way to vote in the case—was Lewis Powell. A conservative Southern gentleman from Virginia who had been appointed by President Richard Nixon in 1972, Powell had joined both the liberal majority in *Roe* and the conservative majority in the Court's 1973 obscenity decisions. Although personally uncomfortable dealing with issues about sex, Powell struggled to put aside his own discomfort and to apply the law in a fair and evenhanded manner.

Before *Bowers* was argued to the Court, Justice Powell struck up a conversation about the case with one of his law clerks, Carter Chinnis. After discussing the constitutional question, Powell remarked that, as far as he knew, he had never met a homosexual. Unbeknownst to Powell, he was speaking to one. Powell, who was quite naïve about homosexuality, expressed puzzlement about why homosexuals did not date and marry women. Chinnis, who did not reveal that he was gay, answered, "Justice Powell, a gay man cannot have an erection to perform intercourse with a woman." "But doesn't sodomy require an erection?" Powell asked, confused. "Yes," Chinnis explained, but "gay men have erections with men rather than with women."[19]

Shortly thereafter, at the Court's conference after oral argument in *Bowers*, Justice Powell voted with Brennan, Marshall, Blackmun, and Stevens to hold the Georgia statute unconstitutional. Powell explained that Hardwick should not be punished "for private conduct based on a natural sexual urge and with a consenting partner." In the weeks that followed, however, Powell continued to dither. Ultimately, and after considerable badgering by his more conservative colleagues, he was persuaded to switch sides, thus determining the outcome of the case. In later years, Powell would publicly express regret that he had voted the way he had in *Bowers*.[20]

ROMER: "A BARE DESIRE TO HARM"

BEGINNING IN THE MID-1980S, several cities enacted ordinances prohibiting discrimination on the basis of sexual orientation. This generated a sharp backlash from the Christian Right, which often succeeded in getting these laws repealed.* In Colorado, the cities of Denver, Boulder, and Aspen all enacted such ordinances. The Denver ordinance, for example, which was enacted in 1990, prohibited discrimination on the basis of sexual orientation in employment, education, housing, and public accommodations.[21]

Soon thereafter, conservative Christians in Colorado established Colorado for Family Values (CFV) with the goal of amending the Colorado constitution to override the Denver ordinance. The group soon gained national support from such figures as Pat Robertson, Jerry Falwell, James Dobson, and Phyllis Schlafly and from a broad range of Christian Right organizations. After CFV gathered the necessary signatures, what became known as Amendment 2 was placed on the ballot for a statewide referendum.[22]

Amendment 2 forbade the state of Colorado and all of its agencies, political subdivisions, municipalities, universities, and school districts to enact or

---

* See chapter 14.

enforce any law, regulation, or policy that prohibited discrimination against gays, lesbians, or bisexuals.[23] In an aggressive campaign, the proponents of Amendment 2 insisted that the amendment was necessary because homosexuals were impious, immoral, and destructive to society, and that it would therefore be improper and immoral for the state or any of its subdivisions to shield them from discrimination. When the votes were counted on November 3, 1992, Amendment 2 received 53 percent of the vote and therefore became part of the Colorado constitution.[24]

Nine days later, lawyers from Lambda Legal and the American Civil Liberties Union filed suit claiming that Amendment 2 violated the United States Constitution. The case eventually worked its way up to the Supreme Court, which handed down its decision in *Romer v. Evans*[25] on May 20, 1996.

I N LIGHT of the Court's decision ten years earlier in *Bowers, Romer* seemed an easy case. After all, if a state can constitutionally declare certain conduct a crime, then it seems only logical that it can also constitutionally refuse to prohibit discrimination against persons who engage in that conduct. A state, for example, has no constitutional obligation to forbid individuals from discriminating against robbers, rapists, and burglars.

By the time the Court addressed *Romer*, however, its makeup had changed substantially. Six of the nine justices who had participated in *Bowers* were now gone (Burger, Brennan, White, Marshall, Blackmun, and Powell). The six new justices had been appointed by Ronald Reagan (Scalia and Kennedy), George H. W. Bush (Thomas and Souter), and Bill Clinton (Ginsburg and Breyer). Ten years after *Bowers*, in a society whose views of homosexuality were clearly evolving, it was unclear how this newly-constituted Court would approach the question.

Most commentators thought it likely that Rehnquist, Scalia, and Thomas would vote to uphold Amendment 2, and that Stevens (who had dissented in *Bowers*), Ginsburg, and Breyer would vote to strike it down. The most uncertain votes were O'Connor, Kennedy, and Souter. Four years earlier, those same three justices, all appointed by Republican presidents, had authored the critical opinion in *Planned Parenthood v. Casey*[26] that had saved the essence of *Roe v. Wade* and infuriated the Christian Right.*

The central question now was: How would these three moderate conservative justices approach the issue of gay rights? Gay rights advocates were

---

* See chapter 17 .

wary of them all. O'Connor had voted with the majority in *Bowers*; Kennedy had upheld the constitutionality of several laws that discriminated against gays and lesbians when he was a judge on the federal Court of Appeals; and Souter had upheld a state law that prohibited gays and lesbians from adopting when he was a justice on the New Hampshire Supreme Court.[27]

Y ET IN a stunning six-to-three decision the Supreme Court held Amendment 2 unconstitutional. Justice Anthony Kennedy delivered the opinion of the Court, which was joined by Justices Stevens, O'Connor, Souter, Ginsburg, and Breyer. In Kennedy's view, the problem with Amendment 2 was that it imposed "a special disability" *only* upon homosexuals. This was so because under Amendment 2 every group in Colorado, including African Americans, Catholics, the elderly, Hispanics, persons of Irish descent, women, veterans, disabled persons, Republicans, unmarried persons, and persons convicted of crime was free to try to persuade a city council, a state university, a state agency, or the state legislature to enact laws or regulations that would protect them against discrimination—*except* homosexuals. Because of Amendment 2, *only* homosexuals had to amend the State Constitution in order to obtain legal protection against discrimination.[28]

With that fact firmly in mind, Kennedy turned to the Equal Protection Clause of the Fourteenth Amendment, which provides that "no state shall . . . deny to any person . . . the equal protection of the laws." Kennedy explained that under that guarantee, if a law treats some people differently than others, it ordinarily will satisfy the demands of equal protection if it bears a rational relation to some legitimate state interest. Although almost every law passes that highly deferential standard, Kennedy concluded that Amendment 2 did not.

In reaching that result, Kennedy observed that a law making it "more difficult for one group of citizens than for all others to seek aid from the government" was virtually "unprecedented" in American history, and that it was therefore impossible to escape the inference that the special disadvantage imposed on homosexuals by Amendment 2 was born, not out of any rational effort to further a legitimate state interest, but out of "animosity" toward gays and lesbians. Indeed, Kennedy reasoned, Amendment 2 seemed "inexplicable by anything but animus toward the class it affects," and as the Court had previously established, "'a bare . . . desire to harm a politically unpopular group cannot constitute a *legitimate* governmental interest.'"[29] In such circumstances, Kennedy concluded that Amendment 2 violated the United States Constitution.

. . .

JUSTICE ANTONIN SCALIA, joined by Chief Justice Rehnquist and Justice Thomas, was of a rather different view. Amendment 2, he maintained, did not manifest a "'bare . . . desire to harm' homosexuals," but was rather a modest attempt by "Coloradans to preserve traditional sexual mores." In Scalia's view, that objective was perfectly permissible under any sensible constitutional doctrine. Moreover, he observed, the Court's claim that homosexuality could not be "singled out for disfavorable treatment" directly contradicted *Bowers*. This was so, he reasoned, because if a state could constitutionally criminalize homosexual conduct, then it necessary followed that it could "enact other laws merely *disfavoring* homosexual conduct."[30]

Scalia vigorously rejected Justice Kennedy's assertion that the enactment of Amendment 2 was premised on an impermissible "animus" toward homosexuals. To the contrary, he argued, it was entirely appropriate for the citizens of a state to "consider certain conduct reprehensible—murder, for example, or polygamy, or cruelty to animals," and it was therefore entirely appropriate for the state to exhibit animus toward such conduct. Coloradans, he insisted, were "*entitled* to be hostile toward homosexual conduct," and that, in itself, was sufficient to justify Amendment 2.

The Court's decision, Scalia fumed, was "an act, not of judicial judgment, but of political will." In a speech a year later, Justice Scalia openly mocked the Court's opinion in *Romer*, sarcastically declaring that his brethren had struck down Amendment 2 "under, I don't know, the Homosexuality Clause of the Bill of Rights."[31]

WHAT WAS going on in *Romer*? The central disagreement between Justices Kennedy and Scalia was on the issue of animus. Although all the justices agreed in principle that mere animus toward a group is not in itself a constitutionally legitimate basis for government action, what *Romer* demonstrated was that it is not always easy to spot animus, or even to know what the term means. In some sense, the core question is whether disadvantaging individuals because citizens morally disapprove of their conduct is different constitutionally from disadvantaging those individuals because citizens despise them. Like Justice Potter Stewart in the obscenity context, Justice Kennedy seemed to be suggesting in *Romer*, with respect to animus, "I know it when I see it." This would become an increasingly pivotal issue in later decisions.

Romer was an important victory for the gay rights movement. Matt Coles of the ACLU's Lesbian and Gay Rights Project declared that it marked "a sea change in the struggle" for gay and lesbian equality, and Suzanne Goldberg of Lambda Legal celebrated the decision as "the most important victory ever for lesbian and gay rights."

At the same time, though, *Romer* was a very narrow decision. Although it seemed to reject moral disapproval of homosexuality as a sufficient justification for discrimination against gays, the specific issue presented in the case was, as Justice Kennedy emphasized throughout his opinion, "unprecedented." Colorado was the only state in the nation with a law like Amendment 2, and it therefore wasn't clear just how far *Romer* would extend.[32]

LAWRENCE: "AN EMERGING AWARENESS"

ON SEPTEMBER 17, 1998, officers of the Harris County Police Department in Houston, Texas, were dispatched to a private residence in response to a reported disturbance. After they entered the residence, they allegedly saw John Geddes Lawrence and Tyron Garner, a white man and a black man, engaging in anal sex. Lawrence and Garner were arrested, charged, and convicted of violating a rarely enforced Texas law making it a crime for any person to engage "in deviate sexual intercourse with another individual of the same sex."[33] Lawrence and Garner maintained that the statute was unconstitutional. The Texas Court of Appeals rejected the constitutional challenge, citing *Bowers v. Hardwick*.

Lawrence v. Texas reached the Supreme Court in 2003. As the Harvard constitutional law scholar Laurence Tribe, who authored the ACLU's brief in *Lawrence*, later observed, for seventeen years *Bowers* "had loomed like a thundercloud over claims to gay and lesbian equality." *Bowers* had been invoked by politicians, legislators, and judges to justify discrimination against gays and lesbians in deportation hearings, adoption proceedings, dishonorable military discharges, and a host of other contexts.[34]

Much had changed, though, in the years between *Bowers* and *Lawrence*. Several state courts had held that their state sodomy laws violated state constitutional provisions, and a number of state legislatures had repealed their sodomy statutes, so that by 2003 only thirteen states still had laws criminalizing sodomy between consenting adults.

Moreover, as gays and lesbians increasingly came out to their friends, families, acquaintances, and colleagues, public opinion changed as well. When *Bowers* was decided, only 32 percent of Americans thought same-sex sex should be legal. Seventeen years later, 60 percent of Americans held that view. In addition, there had been a substantial change in the makeup of the Court, as reflected in *Romer*. Indeed, by the time *Lawrence* reached the Court, only three of the justices who had participated in *Bowers*—Rehnquist, Stevens, and O'Connor—were still there.

Of course, none of that meant that the outcome in *Lawrence* would be any different than the outcome in *Bowers*, but possibility was in the air.[35]

I N A dramatic and in some quarters quite horrifying six-to-three decision, the Supreme Court in *Lawrence* overruled *Bowers v. Hardwick* and held that the Texas anti-sodomy statute violated the United States Constitution.[36] Justice Anthony Kennedy, the key player in both *Casey* and *Romer*, again wrote the opinion of the Court.* Invoking the Court's earlier decisions in *Griswold, Eisenstadt,* and *Roe*, Kennedy concluded that Lawrence and Garner had a constitutional right to engage in the private sexual conduct involved in this case.[37]

Kennedy dismissed out of hand the Court's reasoning in *Bowers*, charging that it had been distorted by its "failure to appreciate the extent of the liberty at stake" in same-sex relationships. Kennedy explained that laws prohibiting homosexual sex touch "upon the most private human conduct" and intrude upon the freedom of individuals to enter into intimate sexual and personal relationships without surrendering "their dignity as free persons." Thus, he declared, the "liberty protected by the Constitution allows homosexual persons the right to make this choice."[38]

Kennedy then embarked upon a biting critique of the Court's assertions in *Bowers* about the history of laws prohibiting same-sex sex. He traced that history in great detail, arguing that the Court's claim in *Bowers* that proscriptions against homosexual conduct have "ancient roots" was both simplistic and erroneous. Moreover, Kennedy noted that as a matter of actual practice, laws against sodomy were rarely, if ever, enforced against consenting adults acting in private. Thus, he concluded, the historical claims relied upon in *Bowers* to support the Court's assumptions about the legal system's long-standing condemnation of homosexual sex were in fact much more doubtful than the Court's opinion, and Chief Justice Burger's concurring opinion, had suggested.[39]

At the same time, though, Kennedy acknowledged that, as the Court had observed in *Bowers*, "for centuries there have been powerful voices to condemn homosexual conduct as immoral." That condemnation, he noted,

---

* Kennedy's opinion was joined by Justices Stevens, Souter, Ginsburg, and Breyer.

had been shaped in large part by sincerely held "religious beliefs" that for many persons reflected "profound and deep" convictions about morality and personal relations. As Chief Justice Burger had argued in his concurring opinion in *Bowers*, condemnation of homosexuality was "firmly rooted in Judeo-Christian moral and ethical standards." But Kennedy declared that whatever the sincerity and depth of those beliefs, the Constitution forbids the majority to use the power of the state to enforce the majority's religious views on the whole of society.[40]

Moreover, Kennedy explained that even if it were true that there had been a long-standing condemnation of homosexual sex, that history would not necessarily control the constitutional inquiry, because history and tradition are only the starting point of that analysis. In the context of same-sex sex, he maintained, more recent understandings are "of most relevance," because there has been "an emerging awareness that liberty gives substantial protection to adult persons in deciding how to conduct their private lives in matters pertaining to sex." To support this view, Kennedy pointed, for example, to the fact that many states had repealed their laws against consensual sodomy, to the fact that even those states that retained such prohibitions did not enforce them, and to the fact that many nations had eliminated their laws against consensual sodomy.[41]

In holding the Texas law unconstitutional, Kennedy conceded that the Framers of the Constitution had not expressly guaranteed the right of adults to engage in homosexual sodomy. Thus, under a strictly originalist approach to the Constitution, the Texas law might have to be upheld. But, Kennedy explained, the Framers intentionally left some constitutional guarantees open-ended precisely because they understood that later generations might sometimes come to understand that laws once thought "necessary and proper" in fact served only to oppress individuals and to deny them their most basic freedoms. That, Kennedy concluded, was the situation in *Lawrence*.[42]

I T IS noteworthy that the Court in *Lawrence* invalidated the Texas law on substantive due process rather than equal protection grounds. That is, the Court held that the state could not constitutionally prohibit adults from engaging in private consensual sex because it did not have a legitimate interest in doing so. But because the Texas statute prohibited *only* homosexual sodomy, the Court might instead have invalidated the law on the ground that even if the state could constitutionally ban *all* adult consensual sodomy, it could not constitutionally discriminate in this manner against homosexuals.

In her concurring opinion in *Lawrence*, Justice Sandra Day O'Connor embraced this approach. Having joined the Court's opinion in *Bowers*, O'Connor thought it unnecessary to reconsider that decision. Rather, in her view, the Texas sodomy statute at issue in *Lawrence*, which prohibited deviate sexual intercourse *only* by homosexuals, violated the Equal Protection Clause because it made "homosexuals unequal in the eyes of the law." [43] This interplay between substantive due process and equal protection would continue to engage the justices in the years, and cases, to come.

THE COURT AND THE "HOMOSEXUAL AGENDA"

IN AN EVEN more angry opinion than the one he had written in *Romer*, Justice Antonin Scalia, joined once again by Chief Justice Rehnquist and Justice Thomas, dissented. Scalia focused on two questions: Did the state's prohibition of homosexual sodomy rationally further a legitimate state interest? Did the state's prohibition of homosexual sodomy implicate a constitutional right to engage in such conduct?

On the first of these questions, Scalia emphatically rejected the Court's conclusion that the Texas statute did not rationally further a legitimate state interest. Scalia insisted that the Texas law was clearly designed to further what he deemed to be the perfectly rational and legitimate judgment that certain forms of sexual behavior are immoral. Scalia noted scornfully that although the Court in *Bowers* had held this to be a legitimate state interest, it "today reaches the opposite conclusion." By so doing, Scalia warned, the Court "effectively decrees the end of all morals legislation."[44]

On the second question, Scalia vigorously contested the notion that individuals have a constitutional right to engage in homosexual sodomy. An unenumerated right merits constitutional protection, he maintained, only if it is "'deeply rooted in this Nation's history and tradition.'" He insisted that, as the Court had held in *Bowers*, the purported right to engage in homosexual sodomy clearly fails this test. Indeed, *Bowers'* conclusion on this point, he declared, "is utterly unassailable."[*45]

---

* Applying the "deeply rooted" principle, Justice Scalia might hold, for example, that laws forbidding people who are convicted of a crime to marry, or forbidding married couples to have sex except for purposes of procreation, or forbidding married couples to have more than two children violate the unenumerated rights to marry, to marital privacy, and to have children, because such rights are both fundamental to our values and are "deeply rooted" in our nation's history, in the sense that the government has never before placed such restrictions on these rights. On this view, only departures from long-established traditions can be held to violate unenumerated rights.

Justice Antonin Scalia

Scalia scoffed at Justice Kennedy's argument that even if the asserted right to engage in homosexual sodomy was not "deeply rooted" in our nation's history, it was nonetheless worthy of protection because of an "emerging awareness" that the Constitution should be understood to guarantee individuals the right to decide for themselves how to "conduct their private lives in matters pertaining to sex." Scalia insisted both that there was no such emerging awareness and that even if there was, it could not in itself establish a right as fundamental.

On this question, both sides could find support in the precedents. There are certainly Supreme Court opinions that suggest that the concept of fundamental rights applies only to those unenumerated rights that are "deeply rooted" in our nation's traditions,[46] but there are other opinions, such as *Griswold*, *Eisenstadt*, and *Roe*, that clearly embrace a much broader conception of fundamental rights than the one articulated by Justice Scalia.[47]

In closing, Scalia accused the Court of signing on to what he derisively called the "homosexual agenda," by which he meant a left-wing campaign to eliminate "the moral opprobrium that has traditionally attached to homosexual conduct." Scalia charged that the Court had once again "taken sides in the culture war." Because, in his view, the Texas statute was "well within the range of traditional democratic action," that action should not be thwarted by "the invention of a brand-new 'constitutional right.' "[48]

Justice Scalia's annoyance with the Court's decision in *Lawrence* was evident when he warned in dire tones in his dissenting opinion that the majority's reasoning would inevitably open the door to a constitutional right to same-sex marriage. Indeed, he snarled, "if, as the Court coos (casting aside all pretense of neutrality)," moral disapproval of homosexual sodomy is not a "legitimate state interest" that justifies proscribing such conduct, then "what justification could there possibly be for denying the benefits of marriage to homosexual couples?"[49]

Over the next several months, Justice Scalia gave a series of public speeches that caustically mocked Justice Kennedy's opinion in *Lawrence*. Commenting on these orations, the legal commentator Dahlia Lithwick observed that Scalia at this point must have been "feeling besieged and marginalized by the constitutional wall that's been erected between church and state," a wall, she added, that "keeps the devout" from dictating the rules of behavior to all other citizens.[50]

· · ·

D ESPITE JUSTICE SCALIA'S objections, Justice Kennedy's concerns about unconstitutional animus in *Lawrence,* as in *Romer,* were well founded. Only a decade before the arrests of Lawrence and Garner in Houston, for example, outraged Christian conservatives launched an all-out campaign to repeal a recently enacted Houston ordinance that prohibited discrimination on the basis of sexual orientation. One advocate for repeal charged that homosexuality was "a disease that destroys the individual and society," while another declared that because "homosexuals don't reproduce," they must recruit young people into their "cult" of "sexual perversion." The Reverend C. Anderson Davis compared homosexuals to "drug addicts," and a widely circulated brochure falsely charged that "you are 15 times more apt to be killed by a gay than a heterosexual" and that "half of all sex murderers are homosexuals."*[51]

Similarly, in the briefs filed in the Supreme Court in *Lawrence,* defenders of the Texas anti-sodomy statute repeatedly expressed "revulsion against homosexuality." Steeped in "religious devotion," many of these briefs described homosexuality as a "dangerous and unnatural maladjustment" and as "a contagious and filthy thing" that must be stamped out of existence. Several briefs went so far as to claim that gay men with HIV "were deliberately infecting the heterosexual population."[52]

In short, there was plenty of reason to see raw, unadulterated animus in the positions of those who defended the Texas anti-sodomy statute. Justice Kennedy was not making it up.

AN OCCASION FOR DANCING IN THE STREETS

WHEN IT CAME TIME for Justice Kennedy to announce the Court's decision in *Lawrence,* he read a brief statement explaining the outcome from the bench. At the end he declared: "*Bowers* was not correct when it was decided, and it is not correct today. It ought not to remain binding precedent. *Bowers v. Hardwick* should be, and now is, overruled." It was a remarkable moment. Overwhelmed by emotion, many of the gay and lesbian lawyers sitting in the courtroom openly sobbed.[53]

Christian conservatives throughout the nation were furious. This was an insult to the very morality of their nation. Visions of Sodom and Gomorrah were invoked in churches across the land. The United States Conference

---

* The referendum to repeal the ordinance passed.

of Catholic Bishops condemned the decision as "deplorable." Lou Sheldon of the Traditional Values Coalition compared *Lawrence* to the September 11 terrorist attack on the United States and warned that "the enemy is at our doorsteps." Pat Robertson denounced the Court for rending the "moral fabric of the nation," Jerry Falwell predicted that *Lawrence* would lead to bestiality, and a pastor in Kansas fumed that it was "the death knell of American civilization." Taking Justice Scalia's warning seriously, the Family Research Council, Jerry Falwell, the Conference of Catholic Bishops, and President George W. Bush all called for a constitutional amendment to define marriage as exclusively the union of a man and a woman.[54]

For the gay and lesbian community, though, it was an occasion for dancing in the streets. Joyous demonstrations erupted in cities across the nation. In San Francisco, a group of veterans who had been expelled from military service because of their sexual orientation proudly saluted as a huge Rainbow Flag, which had flown atop an eighty-foot pole for more than five years, was lowered and an American flag was raised in its place.

For the gay community, *Lawrence* meant much more than that rarely enforced anti-sodomy laws could no longer be legally enforced. Rather, as the legal scholar Dale Carpenter eloquently observed, *Lawrence* meant that "never again would their rights be dismissed by the highest tribunal in the land as, 'at best, facetious,'" and "never again would they wonder whether the words engraved on the pediment of the Supreme Court building, 'Equal Justice Under Law,' included them. The Constitution was now their constitution, too."[55]

B UT WHAT, really, did *Lawrence* mean? Did it, as Justice Scalia charged, embrace the so-called "homosexual agenda"? After *Lawrence*, were state laws precluding gays and lesbians from working as teachers or adopting children now unconstitutional? Was Don't Ask, Don't Tell unconstitutional? How about DOMA? And what about state laws limiting marriage to one man and one woman? Did *Lawrence*, as Justice Scalia asserted, threaten to render all morals legislation unconstitutional, including laws against polygamy, bestiality, necrophilia, cannibalism, and incest?

Some commentators read *Lawrence* broadly as endorsing an aggressively civil libertarian approach to the Constitution, whereas others read it in a more minimalist manner, as narrowly invalidating laws against homosexual sodomy, but leaving everything else up for future consideration.[56] Although Justice Kennedy's opinion was vague on its precise rationale and scope, the

EQUAL·JUSTICE·UNDER·LAW·

best understanding of *Lawrence* was that it opened the door to the possibility of expansion in the future, but did not commit the Court to walk through the door.

In the years immediately after *Lawrence*, courts tended to take a narrow view of the decision and continued to uphold laws denying gay couples the right to adopt, discriminating against gay and lesbian parents in custody disputes, and denying gay couples the right to marry.[57]

But the door was still open.

20

SAME-SEX MARRIAGE AND THE CONSTITUTION

Edie Windsor and Thea Spyer at Their Wedding

AMONG THE MANY THINGS that infuriated Justice Antonin Scalia about *Lawrence v. Texas,* perhaps the most galling was what he saw as the implication that the Court would next hold that same-sex couples have a constitutional right to marry. Indeed, Scalia blasted Justice Kennedy's opinion for even implicitly calling into question the traditional view that marriage was only between a man and a woman.[1]

Scalia was certainly right that *Lawrence* carried the seed of an argument that could be extended to laws against same-sex marriage. As several commentators observed at the time, "The merged threads of liberty, equality, and dignity that constituted the core of Kennedy's reasoning could easily be read as gesturing toward marriage equality."[2] Scalia insisted that this seed should be crushed out of existence. In his view, if states choose to permit homosexuals to marry, that is none of the Court's business. But, conversely, if they choose *not* to allow homosexuals to marry, that, too, is none of the Court's business. The Constitution, he maintained, does not speak to the issue one way or the other.

Even some commentators who were sympathetic to the idea that same-sex couples should have a constitutional right to marry argued after *Lawrence* that the Court should take its time before addressing the question. As the Yale legal scholar William Eskridge, a strong proponent of same-sex marriage, opined in 2008, the Court should go slow because in the vast majority of states a Supreme Court decision mandating the recognition of same-sex marriage would almost certainly create a backlash that would be "catastrophic . . . for gay people."*

---

* This argument was most often made by those who held to the view that had the Court gone more slowly on the abortion issue, much of the backlash to *Roe* might have been avoided.

It was Eskridge's hope that, with time, people would gradually come to have a more accepting attitude toward same-sex marriage, therefore making the long-term transition easier for society, less risky for gays and lesbians, and less precarious for the Court as an institution. Indeed, this was precisely the course the Supreme Court had followed on the issue of interracial marriage, where it hedged for thirteen years after *Brown v. Board of Education*[3] before finally holding laws against miscegenation unconstitutional in 1967 in *Loving v. Virginia*.[4]

BUT MANY gay rights advocates objected to this strategy on at least two grounds. First, by 2008 a majority of states had enacted state constitutional amendments that defined marriage as only between a man and a woman. The purpose of those amendments was both to prevent the state's own supreme court from recognizing a state constitutional right to same-sex marriage and to make it impossible for citizens of the state to legalize same-sex marriage through the ordinary legislative process. In effect, these amendments meant that if future majorities wanted to legalize marriage between two persons of the same sex, they could do so only by undertaking the much more onerous process of re-amending their state's constitution, a process that often requires the support of a supermajority of the state's voters.[5]

Second, the democratic process does not trump the Constitution. If a proper interpretation of the Constitution guarantees same-sex couples the right to marry, then a strategy of intentionally hesitating arguably amounts to a form of constitutional abdication. Advocates for a more aggressive judicial approach maintained that gays and lesbians should not be expected to wait patiently in the face of oppressive and unconstitutional laws while the justices dithered.

Rather, just as the Court had recognized in *Roe v. Wade* that a woman has a constitutional right to abortion even though many citizens vehemently opposed such a right, and just as the Court had held in *Loving v. Virginia* that interracial couples have a constitutional right to marry even though three-quarters of Americans then opposed such a right,[6] so too should the Court protect the constitutional right of same-sex couples to marry without regard to the popularity or unpopularity of the right with segments of the American people.

Of course, that still left the question whether the Constitution *should* be construed to guarantee a right of same-sex couples to marry. *Lawrence* may have raised the question but, despite Justice Scalia's alarm, it did not resolve it.

THE TERMS OF THE DEBATE

IN 1983, EVAN WOLFSON, a student at the Harvard Law School who would eventually go on to found the organization Freedom to Marry, proposed writing an independent research paper exploring the question whether the Constitution guarantees same-sex couples the right to marry. The constitutional law professors at Harvard dismissed Wolfson's proposed inquiry as so outlandish that none would supervise the project. Wolfson finally persuaded a trusts and estates professor to take on the task. In the end, Wolfson produced a lengthy analysis arguing that the refusal to permit same-sex couples the freedom to marry violated the Constitution. At the time, it was an interesting, though largely pointless, thought experiment.[7]

Decades later, in what was no longer a mere thought experiment, those who argued that same-sex couples had a constitutional right to marry advanced three primary arguments to support their position. First, building on *Romer* and *Lawrence*, they maintained that laws forbidding same-sex couples to marry are unconstitutional because they do not rationally further a legitimate state interest. They contended that such laws serve no purpose other than to denigrate a despised class of citizens and that, like the laws invalidated in *Romer* and *Lawrence*, they therefore violate both the Due Process and Equal Protection Clauses of the Constitution.

Those on the other side responded that there are clearly legitimate justifications for laws limiting marriage to one man and one women, including morality, tradition, and the state's interests in encouraging procreation, promoting family stability, and preserving respect for the institution of marriage. They rejected as absurd the suggestion that laws limiting marriage to a man and a woman are in any way irrational or grounded in animus toward gays and lesbians. To the contrary, they insisted that such laws reflect a long-standing conception of the proper definition of marriage that was grounded in concerns about procreation and that has nothing whatever to do with any animus toward homosexuals.[8]

SECOND, BUILDING upon cases like *Skinner, Griswold, Eisenstadt, Loving,* and *Roe,** those who questioned the constitutionality of laws limiting marriage to opposite-sex couples maintained that because the Court

---

* These cases are discussed in chapters 15 and 16.

has long recognized that marriage is an unenumerated fundamental right,[9] laws denying individuals the freedom to marry must be tested not by rational basis review, but by a much more demanding standard. They reasoned that even if such laws are rational, they cannot possibly satisfy the much more rigorous standard of justification that applies to laws that deny individuals the fundamental freedom to marry.

Those on the other side responded that even if the right to marry is a fundamental right, that right applies *only* to opposite-sex couples. This is so, they argued, because for an unenumerated right to be recognized as fundamental it must be deeply rooted in "our Nation's history, legal traditions, and practices."[10] Although agreeing that the right of opposite-sex couples to marry is fundamental under that standard,* they insisted that there is no analogous fundamental right of same-sex couples to marry, because that practice could hardly be said to be deeply rooted in "our Nation's history."

In response, those who contended that same-sex couples have a fundamental right to marry maintained that just as the meaning of express constitutional rights—like freedom of speech, equal protection of the laws, and freedom from unreasonable searches and seizures—necessarily evolves over time as circumstances and society change, so too must the meaning of unenumerated fundamental rights evolve over time. Indeed, they pointed out that this was precisely what explained the Court's decisions in cases like *Skinner, Griswold, Eisenstadt, Loving, Roe,* and *Lawrence,* all of which involved contemporary, rather than narrowly traditional, understandings of deeply rooted fundamental rights.[11]

THIRD, THOSE challenging the constitutionality of laws limiting marriage to one man and one woman argued that because such laws discriminate on the basis of sexual orientation they are analogous to laws that discriminate against individuals on the basis of race, national origin, and sex and therefore call forth heightened scrutiny under the Equal Protection Clause. Although most laws that treat people differently from one another are constitutional under the Equal Protection Clause as long as the

---

* Even Justice Scalia, for example, would presumably invalidate a law that limited marriage only to persons who are capable of reproducing, because such a law would be a radical departure from "our Nation's history, legal traditions, and practices" with respect to an interest that is fundamental.

differential treatment is rationally related to a legitimate state interest,* the Supreme Court has long held that laws discriminating against individuals on the basis of certain "suspect" criteria are especially problematic and therefore violate the Equal Protection Clause unless they satisfy a much more demanding standard of justification.[12]

Because laws discriminating against African Americans are the paradigm of a violation of the Equal Protection Clause, the Court generally considers four factors in determining whether discrimination against any particular group should be deemed "suspect": whether the group has experienced a history of invidious discrimination; whether the defining characteristic of the group is essentially immutable; whether the group can effectively protect itself against discrimination in the majoritarian political process; and whether the discrimination is based on a stereotyped characteristic that is not truly indicative of the group's abilities.[13] Those who contested the constitutionality of laws limiting marriage to a man and a woman maintained that discrimination against gays and lesbians meets these criteria and that such laws therefore must be tested by heightened scrutiny.

In response, those who defended the constitutionality of laws discriminating against gays and lesbians asserted that homosexuality is a choice, that what homosexuals call a history of discrimination is no different than a history of "discrimination" against any other group of individuals who choose to violate society's moral norms and legal strictures, that gays and lesbians have ample political power, and that homosexuality is relevant to a host of legal considerations, most obviously to marriage. Thus, in their view, laws that discriminate against homosexuals are no different than laws that discriminate against people who commit incest, or bestiality, or polygamy. Such laws, they insisted, are completely different constitutionally from laws that discriminate against African Americans, women, or Japanese Americans.[14]

With the arguments so aligned, what would the courts do?

---

* For example, a law limiting drivers' licenses to people over the age of sixteen, limiting the practice of medicine to those with a medical degree, and imposing higher income tax rates on wealthier individuals are all consistent with the Equal Protection Clause because the distinctions rationally serve legitimate state interests.

"THE RIGHT TO MARRY THE PERSON OF ONE'S CHOICE"

IN 2001, MARY BONAUTO, who had been working on behalf of marriage equality with Gay and Lesbian Advocates and Defenders (GLAD) since 1990, filed an action in Massachusetts on behalf of seven same-sex couples challenging the constitutionality of the state's law limiting marriage only to opposite-sex couples. Years later, Barney Frank, the nation's first openly gay member of Congress, aptly described Bonauto as the "Thurgood Marshall of our movement." Although many gay rights activists were uneasy about the litigation, fearing that it came too soon, Bonauto decided that Massachusetts posed a good test case because the state had already taken a series of legislative steps to recognize the equal status of gays and lesbians.[15]

In 2003, only five months after the Supreme Court handed down its decision in *Lawrence*, the Supreme Judicial Court of Massachusetts held in *Goodridge v. Department of Public Health*[16] that the Massachusetts constitution guarantees the right of same-sex couples to marry. In her landmark opinion in *Goodridge*, Chief Justice Margaret Marshall, drawing an analogy to laws

Mary Bonauto

prohibiting interracial marriage, reasoned that "the right to marry means little if it does not include the right to marry the person of one's choice," and that at least in this context tradition must yield to a contemporary understanding of the "invidious quality of the discrimination" here at issue. [17]

Justice Marshall was herself an interesting figure. She was born in South Africa where, as a young woman, she courageously led an organization dedicated to ending apartheid and achieving equal justice for all South Africans. She eventually emigrated to the United States in order to escape political persecution by the South African government, earned a law degree from Yale, and in 1999 was appointed the first woman Chief Justice of Massachusetts by Republican Governor Paul Cellucci. Marshall's experience in South Africa instilled in her a deep skepticism of government efforts to classify people on the basis of immutable characteristics, such as race, sex, national origin, and sexual orientation.

Marshall found it unnecessary to decide in *Goodridge* whether same-sex marriage was a fundamental right or whether homosexuals were a suspect class, concluding instead that the ban on same-sex marriage could not survive even rational basis review. She dismissed as implausible the state's arguments that limiting marriage to opposite-sex couples ensured that children would be raised in "optimal" families and that making marriage available to same-sex couples would "trivialize or destroy the institution of marriage."[18] With the decision in *Goodridge*, Massachusetts became the first state in the nation to allow same-sex marriage.*

That night, supporters of gay marriage held a huge rally at Boston's Old South Meeting House, the historic Quaker house of worship where the Boston Tea Party had been planned in 1773. As one celebrant who shared in the festivities that evening later recalled, the "building was electric, the joy palpable, and the cheers raucous; a new freedom movement was gaining strength."[19]

The backlash to *Goodridge* in Massachusetts, a heavily Catholic state, was fierce. Archbishop Sean Patrick O'Malley denounced the decision, the Catholic Action League of Massachusetts called for Chief Justice Marshall to be impeached, Focus on the Family rounded up more than four thousand members of the clergy to protest the court's action, Governor Mitt Romney compared the decision to the United States Supreme Court's discredited 1857 decision in *Dred Scott v. Sandford*, and the Catholic Bishops of Massa-

---

* Massachusetts was the fifth jurisdiction in the world (after Ontario, British Columbia, Belgium, and the Netherlands) to permit same-sex marriage.

chusetts declared *Goodridge* a "national tragedy" and called for a state constitutional amendment to overturn the decision. Over the next five years,
a furious battle over the proposed state constitutional amendment raged
across Massachusetts.

Meanwhile, at the national level, the Christian Right made *Goodridge* a
pivotal issue in the 2004 elections. James Dobson, the evangelical Christian founder of Focus on the Family, roared that the fight against gay marriage would be "our D-Day," the 2004 Republican Party platform called
for adoption of a proposed federal marriage amendment limiting marriage
nationwide to one man and one woman, and President George W. Bush
repeatedly endorsed that amendment during his reelection campaign,
declaring that the amendment was necessary to "defend the sanctity of
marriage."

An official of the Southern Baptist Convention observed that nothing
had ever "energized and provoked our grass roots" like this issue, including even *Roe v. Wade.* Indeed, before *Goodridge,* only three states—Alaska,
Nebraska, and Nevada—had amended their state constitutions to forbid
same-sex marriage. In the five years after *Goodridge,* twenty-five additional
states did so.[20] Moreover, in the five years after *Goodridge* not a single state
supreme court followed *Goodridge*'s lead, but the state supreme courts in
Georgia, Maryland, New Jersey, New York, and Washington all rejected
claims that laws prohibiting same-sex marriage violated either the state or
federal constitution.[21]

In light of these fierce reactions to *Goodridge,* many observers concluded
that the decision did the gay rights movement "more harm than good."
Indeed, the University of Chicago political scientist Gerald Rosenberg
concluded that the nationwide backlash sparked by *Goodridge* was "nothing
short of disastrous for the right to same-sex marriage."[22]

"WE'RE GOING TO TAKE YOU OUT"

ON THE OTHER HAND, there is a difference between the short and the
long run. Although *Goodridge* triggered a powerful negative response both
in Massachusetts and across the nation, it also focused attention on the
issue and generated much needed debate and discussion. When Chief
Justice Margaret Marshall handed down her controversial decision in
Goodridge in 2003, Massachusetts voters opposed same-sex marriage by
a margin of 53 to 35 percent. But after five years of bitter and often divisive debate, public opinion shifted markedly. By the time the campaign

to amend the state constitution ended in defeat in 2008, 60 percent of Massachusetts voters supported same-sex marriage and only 30 percent were opposed.

During those five years, more than twelve thousand same-sex couples were married in Massachusetts, and neighbors, friends, relatives, and co-workers began to get used to the idea that same-sex couples actually *can* marry. By 2010, Massachusetts Republican Senator Scott Brown, who had run for office in 2004 on an aggressive anti-gay platform, calmly observed that gay marriage is now "settled law" and that "the people have moved on." As the experience in Massachusetts proved, sometimes familiarity breeds, not contempt, but acceptance.[23]

Moreover, in 2008 and 2009, the state supreme courts of Connecticut, California, and Iowa, following Chief Justice Marshall's lead, held that their state constitutions also guaranteed same-sex couples the right to marry.[24] And then in 2009, Vermont became the first state in the nation to enact same-sex marriage by legislation. Shortly thereafter, New Hampshire, Maine, and New York followed suit.

Thus, despite fierce religious opposition, public opinion nationally was now moving in support of same-sex marriage. A series of polls in 2009 found that as many as 49 percent of Americans supported same-sex marriage, a sharp increase from only a few years earlier. Even some conservatives were beginning to hedge on whether Republicans should continue to oppose same-sex marriage. The conservative political commentator Glenn Beck, for example, declared that "same-sex marriage isn't hurting anybody," and former Vice President Dick Cheney, whose daughter is a lesbian, came out publicly in favor of gay marriage.[25]

T HE PUSHBACK against same-sex marriage continued to be furious, however. In California, for example, the state supreme court's decision holding that the state constitution guaranteed same-sex couples the freedom to marry led to an epic battle over a proposed amendment to the state's constitution.* A coalition of religious organizations succeeded in an aggressive campaign to enact Proposition 8, which amended the state constitution to provide that "only marriage between a man and a woman is valid or recognized in California." The vote broke down almost entirely along religious lines, and Proposition 8 could fairly be characterized as a

---

* See chapter 18.

"successful effort by persons holding a specific religious belief to use the authority of the law to impose their belief on their fellow citizens."[26]

In Maine, the day after the governor signed the bill granting same-sex couples the freedom to marry, a coalition including the Catholic archdiocese of Portland and evangelicals from the Maine Family Policy Council launched a vigorous drive to amend the state constitution to override the new law. Heavily funded by the Catholic and Mormon churches, the campaign was successful, and in late 2009 Maine voters approved the constitutional amendment by a vote of 53 to 47 percent.

The following year, voters in Iowa voted out of office three of the state supreme court justices who had voted to recognize a state constitutional right to same-sex marriage. The failure of sitting justices to win retention in Iowa was almost unprecedented, but in a campaign backed by the National Organization for Marriage, the American Family Association, and a coalition of pastors from conservative churches throughout the state, all three of the justices were ousted. This sent a powerful message to elected state court judges throughout the nation. As the executive director of the American Family Association warned, "Those who impose what we perceive as an amoral agenda, we're going to take [you] out."[27]

THE LONG AND WINDING ROAD TO . . .
THE SUPREME COURT

THUS, DESPITE SEVERAL landmark victories, by 2010 the movement for same-sex marriage was struggling. DOMA remained the law nationally and more than thirty states had enacted constitutional amendments outlawing same sex marriage. One way for advocates of same sex marriage to get past the political obstacles in the states was to head to the Supreme Court. Supporters of same-sex marriage were uneasy, however, about pursuing that route.

Since the Court's 2003 decision in *Lawrence*, President George W. Bush had replaced William Rehnquist and Sandra Day O'Connor with John Roberts and Samuel Alito. Because O'Connor had voted with the majority in both *Romer* and *Lawrence*, and because it was generally assumed that Roberts and Alito would side with Scalia and Thomas on these issues, the outcome in a case challenging the constitutionality of laws banning same-sex marriage was uncertain. Although Justice Kennedy, who was seen as the critical "swing" vote on these issues, had authored both *Romer* and *Lawrence*, he had written those opinions quite narrowly, and it was unclear whether he would be willing to go any further. It was possible that in a case directly posing the issue of same-sex marriage, Justice Kennedy would back off and join Roberts, Scalia, Thomas, and Alito.

A loss in such a case, creating a clear precedent that same-sex couples have no federal constitutional right to marry, would be devastating. Most members of the gay rights community therefore favored a cautious approach, challenging state laws prohibiting same-sex marriage only in those states where the state supreme court seemed likely to be sympathetic, seeking legislative action on a state-by-state basis where that seemed possible, and leaving the federal constitutional challenge to another day. That clearly seemed the safest—and wisest—course of action.

T HAT STRATEGY was upended, however, when two of the most prominent American lawyers at the turn of the twentieth-first century— David Boies and Ted Olson—decided to team up in 2009 to challenge the constitutionality of California's Proposition 8. Boies and Olson had faced off against each other in the Supreme Court in 2000 in *Bush v. Gore*,[28] with Boies representing Al Gore and Olson representing George W. Bush. Although they came from opposite ends of the political divide, they decided that, together, they could bring home a victory.

It was surprising that Olson had signed on to this challenge. A renowned conservative, Olson had served as a high-ranking official of Ronald Reagan's Justice Department and as George W. Bush's solicitor general. Nonetheless, his personal and professional relationships with gays and lesbians had given him a sense of the pain that they experienced in the face of such discrimination. This, he concluded, was a cause worth fighting for.

Most national gay rights organizations opposed the filing of the Boies-Olson lawsuit, *Perry v. Schwarzenegger*. They saw it as reckless, arrogant, self-centered, and premature. A loss in the Supreme Court could set back the equality movement for decades. A group of gay rights organizations, including Lambda Legal, the ACLU, and the Human Rights Campaign, issued a press release criticizing the lawsuit. Olson confidently responded, "We know what we're doing."[29]

After the *Perry* case was filed, California's Democratic Attorney General Jerry Brown and Republican Governor Arnold Schwarzenegger jointly announced that the state would not defend the constitutionality of Proposition 8, declaring that, in their view, it violated the United States Constitution. This created a procedural dilemma, because no party to the litigation was now in a position to defend the constitutionality of Proposition 8. Judge

Vaughn Walker, the federal district court judge assigned to the case, solved the problem by ruling that the proponents of Proposition 8 could intervene in the litigation to defend its constitutionality.[30]

Having resolved that issue, Judge Walker then went on to declare Proposition 8 unconstitutional because it denied individuals the fundamental right to marry "without a legitimate (much less compelling) reason."[*31] The defenders of Proposition 8 promptly appealed to the United State Court of Appeals, which held Proposition 8 unconstitutional because it failed to satisfy even rational basis review.[32]

The Supreme Court then agreed to hear the case. The stakes were huge. But then, after all the excitement and angst surrounding the initiation of the litigation by Olson and Boies, the Court concluded that the issue was not properly before it because the proponents of Proposition 8 should not have been permitted to defend its constitutionality. The Court therefore held that the matter should be dismissed.[33]

The net effect of the Court's resolution in *Perry* was to leave Judge Walker's decision invalidating Proposition 8 in place. The result was to reinstate the pre-Proposition 8 law in California, which permitted same-sex couples to marry. Olson and Boies had therefore won an important victory for gays and lesbians in California, but they had not succeeded in transforming the law nationally. Unsure what the justices would have done had they reached the merits of the case, most gay rights advocates breathed a deep sigh of relief.

A T THE same time that all this was going on, lawsuits were being filed across the country challenging the constitutionality of the federal Defense of Marriage Act. The central claim in these actions was that the federal government could not constitutionally withhold social security, health care, veterans, tax, and other federal marriage benefits from same-sex couples who were legally married under state law. This was a significantly narrower claim than the one in *Perry*, because the argument in these cases was not that states were constitutionally obligated to permit same-sex

---

* Judge Walker was a long-closeted homosexual. Ironically, when President George H. W. Bush first nominated him to the federal bench, gay groups opposed his appointment because he had represented interests that were hostile to the interests of gays. After Walker's ruling in *Perry*, conservatives, including the National Organization for Marriage, the American Family Association, and Patrick Buchanan, denounced him for failing to disqualify himself from the case because he was a homosexual.

marriage, but only that if they chose to do so, the federal government could not then constitutionally discriminate against same-sex marriages that had been lawfully recognized by a state.[34]

In 2009, Mary Bonauto, who had litigated *Goodridge*, filed an action in Massachusetts challenging the constitutionality of DOMA. Bonauto argued that any law that discriminated against gays and lesbians should be deemed "suspect" under the Equal Protection Clause, and must therefore be tested by heightened scrutiny rather than rational basis review. Most gay rights advocates were uneasy, fearing that Bonauto was moving too quickly.

On July 8, 2010, however, in *Gill v. Office of Personnel Management*, federal judge Joseph Tauro, an eighty-year-old Nixon appointee, declared DOMA unconstitutional. Without addressing the heightened scrutiny issue, Judge Tauro, invoking *Romer* and *Lawrence*, explained that he could "conceive of no way" in which the difference between legally married same-sex couples and legally married opposite-sex couples could rationally be thought relevant to their eligibility for federal marriage benefits. He therefore concluded that only "irrational prejudice" could have motivated Congress to enact DOMA.[35]

Meanwhile, public opinion continued to evolve. By the spring of 2011, for the first time in American history, a majority of Americans, by a margin of 53 to 45 percent, approved of same-sex marriage.* The Obama administration now decided that enough was enough and, after much internal wrangling, Attorney General Eric Holder informed Congress in early 2011 that the Department of Justice could no longer in good conscience defend the constitutionality of DOMA.[36]

House Republicans, livid that the Obama administration would not argue that DOMA was constitutional, promptly volunteered to take on the task. Speaker of the House John Boehner (R-Ohio) announced that Paul Clement, a former solicitor general in the George W. Bush administration, would represent the House of Representatives in defending the constitutionality of DOMA.[37]

Soon thereafter, the United States Court of Appeals affirmed Judge Tauro's ruling that DOMA was unconstitutional.[38] Clement promptly sought review in the Supreme Court, but the Court decided not to hear the case, most likely because Justice Elena Kagan, who had served as solicitor

---

* Moreover, in 2011 and 2012, four more state legislatures—in New York, Washington, New Jersey, and Maryland—enacted legislation legalizing same-sex marriage.

general while the case was being litigated, would not be able to participate. Once again, the gay rights community breathed a sigh of relief.

But there were other cases in the wings.

WINDSOR: DOMA'S DEMISE

EDITH WINDSOR AND Thea Spyer met in New York City in 1963 and began a long-term relationship. Windsor was a math whiz who had worked as a senior systems programmer at IBM and Spyer was a clinical psychologist. They registered as domestic partners in 1993 when New York City first gave that option to same-sex couples. Then in 2007, more than forty years after they first became a couple, they married in Ontario, Canada. Thereafter, their marriage was recognized as legal by the state of New York.[39]

After Spyer passed away in 2009 at the age of seventy-seven, Windsor sought to claim the standard federal estate tax exemption for surviving spouses. She was barred from doing so, though, by section 3 of DOMA, which denied federal marriage benefits to any married couple other than a man and a woman. Windsor took her case to court, arguing that section 3 was unconstitutional.

Three years later, in *Windsor v. United States*, federal district court Judge Barbara Jones, following the precedent set by Judge Tauro in *Gill*, held DOMA unconstitutional, concluding that there was no rational justification for the federal government's discrimination against legally recognized same-sex marriages.[40]

Soon thereafter, the United States Court of Appeals affirmed Judge Jones's decision. Chief Judge Dennis Jacobs, who had been appointed to the court by President George H. W. Bush, held that laws that discriminate against gays and lesbians are constitutionally "suspect" and that DOMA therefore denied legally married same-sex couples the equal protection of the law because its discrimination against them did not substantially further an important government interest.[41]

On December 7, 2012, the Supreme Court announced that it would decide *Windsor*. As Roberta Kaplan, the lawyer for Edie Windsor, later recalled, "jubilation broke out" and we cracked open the champagne because "we were heading to the Supreme Court." For years, Kaplan observed, Edie Windsor had suffered "the crushing indignity of having her marital relationship denied," but now "her case would be heard by the highest court in the land."[42]

. . .

THE SUPREME COURT handed down its decision in *United States v. Windsor*[43] on June 26, 2013—ten years to the day after *Lawrence*. In a bitterly divided five-to-four decision, the Court invalidated section 3 of DOMA. As in *Romer* and *Lawrence,* Justice Kennedy authored the opinion of the Court. He was joined by Justices Ginsburg, Breyer, Sotomayor, and Kagan. Chief Justice Roberts and Justices Scalia, Thomas, and Alito dissented.

Justice Kennedy began by emphasizing that the question before the Court was not whether states were constitutionally obligated to recognize same-sex marriages, but whether the federal government could constitutionally discriminate against couples who were legally married in a state because those individuals happened to be of the same sex. In approaching that question, Kennedy observed that the definition of marriage had traditionally been treated as within the authority of the individual states. He therefore characterized DOMA as wholly "unprecedented" because of its radical departure from that tradition.[44]

Looking for an explanation for this departure, Kennedy turned to the legislative history of DOMA. What he found disturbed him. The House Report on DOMA, for example, made clear that the legislation was intended to express "both moral disapproval of homosexuality, and a moral conviction" that homosexuality is incompatible with "Judeo-Christian" morality. Kennedy concluded that a central purpose of DOMA was to undermine "the equal dignity of same-sex marriages" and to tell "same-sex couples, and all the world, that their otherwise valid marriages are unworthy" of respect. By so doing, he observed, DOMA "demeans the couple" and "humiliates tens of thousands of children now being raised by same-sex couples."[45]

As in *Romer* and *Lawrence*, Kennedy explained that " 'a bare . . . desire to harm a politically unpopular group cannot' " justify discriminatory treatment of that group. Because the principal purpose and inevitable effect of DOMA was to "disparage and to injure those whom the State, by its marriage laws, sought to protect in personhood and dignity," Kennedy concluded that DOMA violated the liberty and equality guaranteed to all Americans by the United States Constitution.[46]

AS IN *Lawrence*, the dissenting justices were furious. Justice Antonin Scalia, joined by Justice Clarence Thomas, characterized the majority opinion as nothing short of "remarkable." At various points, Scalia dismissed Justice Kennedy's analysis as "perplexing," "confusing," "absurd," "overcooked," and "legalistic argle-bargle." Scalia reiterated what he had proclaimed in *Lawrence*: "The Constitution does not forbid the government to enforce traditional moral and sexual norms." The Constitution, he insisted, no more requires society to approve of same-sex marriage than it requires it to approve of no-fault divorce or polygamy. That, in itself, he maintained, was sufficient justification for the federal government's decision not to recognize same-sex marriages.

But even setting aside the issue of "traditional moral disapproval," Scalia insisted that there were several "perfectly valid—indeed, downright boring" justifications for DOMA, including, for example, Congress's desire to avoid complicating the administration of the federal code by extending marital benefits to same-sex couples. Scalia charged that Kennedy had simply ignored such justifications in an effort to create the "illusion" that the members of Congress who passed this legislation were "unhinged members of a wild-eyed mob" who sought to "disparage and to injure same-sex couples," to "brand gay people as 'unworthy,'" and "to 'humiliat[e]' their children." Such "accusations," Scalia insisted, "are quite untrue."[47]

Finally, echoing his admonition in *Lawrence*, Scalia warned that *Windsor* would surely lead to recognition of a constitutional right to same-sex marriage. In short, he charged, if the Court believed that DOMA was the product of unconstitutional animus against homosexuals, then it would inevitably make the same assertion about state laws limiting marriage to a man and a woman. "As far as this Court is concerned," he seethed, "no one should be fooled; it is just a matter of . . . waiting for the other shoe."[*48]

A FTER LEARNING of the Court's decision, Edie Windsor, who had just marked her eighty-fourth birthday, exclaimed that she wanted to go to the Stonewall Inn with her lawyer, Roberta Kaplan, to celebrate. By the time Windsor and Kaplan arrived at the Stonewall, hundreds of people had already gathered there, at the place where the modern era of gay rights activism had begun almost half a century earlier. When Windsor stepped out of the car, the crowd went crazy. Kaplan, who is gay, then spoke from the heart. Today's decision, she said, reminds us why "we have

---

* Chief Justice Roberts and Justice Alito, who were joined by Justice Thomas, also filed dissenting opinions.

a Constitution—to bind us together as citizens of one nation each of whom is entitled to equal protection of the law."

That moment no doubt meant a lot to Kaplan, not only because she had won a momentous victory in the Supreme Court, but also because of her own life story. As she recalls it: "Ever since high school I had suspected that I might be gay, but I couldn't really confront the issue until 1991 when I was in my third year of law school, in part because I was terrified. . . . The consequences seemed clear: Being gay meant losing the support of your family. It meant never being able to get married or to start a family of your own. It meant living a covert life on the fringes of society, a life where none of the promises of a happy, secure adulthood applied."

When Kaplan finally decided to come out in 1991 she felt not relief, but despair. Her mother's sharply negative reaction to her announcement sent her into a deep depression. In a remarkable twist of fate, the therapist she saw for guidance, a quarter-century before the decision in *Windsor*, was Thea Spyer.[49]

IN THE WAKE OF *WINDSOR*

IT IS STRIKING how far the Court had moved in the twenty-seven years from *Bowers* to *Windsor*. This was due to several factors, one of which was *not* an overall move of the Court in a more "liberal" direction. To the contrary, on a broad range of issues, including affirmative action, campaign finance, gun regulation, and voting rights, the Court, with the additions of Justices Scalia, Kennedy, Thomas, Roberts, and Alito, had grown, if anything, notably more "conservative" than the Court that decided *Bowers*.

What had changed in those years was the new awareness of gays and lesbians in society and the new public and legal understanding of the morality and wisdom of laws discriminating against homosexuals. In 1986, no one even bothered to poll on the question of same-sex marriage. The inquiry would have seemed absurd. It wasn't until 1996 that Gallup finally thought to ask people about same-sex marriage. At that time, only 27 percent of Americans thought same-sex marriage should be legal. By 2013, when *Windsor* was decided, 54 percent of Americans held that view.[50]

This shift was due to many factors, but most important was the profound change in the visibility of gays and lesbians in American society. This transformation affected not only everyday citizens, but also legislators, mayors, governors, presidents, and judges. With these changes, the traditional understandings of such fundamental legal concepts as liberty, equality, and due process—as applied to gays and lesbians—were suddenly called into question, and rightly so.

It is important to note, though, that these changes in public attitudes and understandings did not in themselves *dictate* any particular change in constitutional doctrine. *Bowers* and *Windsor* were both five-to-four decisions. Only one vote had "changed" over the course of those twenty-seven years. Had Robert Bork been confirmed, and had Anthony Kennedy therefore never been appointed to the Court, the outcome in *Windsor* might well have been five-to-four the other way.

The divergent outcomes in these cases were thus shaped by at least two critical factors: the general social and public understanding of homosexuality at the time of the decision, and the particular interpretative approaches and values of the individual justices who just happened to be on the Court at the specific moment when the issues arose.

B UT WHAT did the Court actually *do* in *Windsor?* Both the precise rationale and the implications of the decision were unclear. In the immediate aftermath of *Windsor*, commentators were "deeply fractured" in their views of Kennedy's opinion and somewhat perplexed at its meaning. No doubt, this was intentional on the part of Justice Kennedy. Wary of a backlash if the Court went too far, too fast, Kennedy hedged his bets. Although his opinion arguably laid the groundwork for the Court to move toward recognition of a constitutional right to same-sex marriage, it also "left the door open just wide enough to retreat from the field."[51]

Despite this ambiguity, in the aftermath of *Windsor* there was a virtual avalanche of judicial decisions invalidating state laws and state constitutional provisions denying same-sex couples the freedom to marry. Within a year, more than twenty courts across the nation had reached that conclusion. Judges, apparently, caught the drift of Kennedy's meaning.

In *Bostic v. Schaefer*,[52] for example, the Court of Appeals for the Fourth Circuit invalidated Virginia's state constitutional provision limiting marriage to one man and one woman. In his opinion for the court, Judge Henry Floyd, who had been appointed to the federal bench by President George W. Bush, argued that because the Virginia law denied individuals the fundamental right to marry, it had to be tested by heightened scrutiny. Judge Floyd concluded that the state's asserted justifications of tradition, morality, responsible procreation, and optimal child-rearing were simply too attenuated to meet the demands of the Constitution.

In *Baskin v. Bogan*,[53] the Court of Appeals for the Seventh Circuit invalidated the Indiana and Wisconsin laws that denied same-sex couples the freedom to marry. In a scathing opinion by Judge Richard Posner, one of the nation's most distinguished and influential legal scholars, who had been appointed to the bench by President Reagan, the court noted that these laws discriminated "along suspect lines" because "homosexuals are among the most stigmatized, misunderstood, and discriminated-against minorities in the history of the world," and because there is no longer any doubt that "homosexuality is not a voluntary condition."

But beyond that, Judge Posner added that laws denying same-sex couples the freedom to marry failed even rational basis review, because the states' arguments in defense of these laws were "so full of holes" that they could not "be taken seriously." Indeed, Posner dismissed the only rationale that the states put forth with any conviction—that same-sex couples don't need marriage because they can't produce children—as "totally implausible."[54]

And so it went, in case after case, with judges of all stripes holding unconstitutional state laws denying same-sex couples the freedom to marry in Arkansas, Colorado, Florida, Idaho, Illinois, Indiana, Kentucky, Michigan, New Jersey, New Mexico, Ohio, Oklahoma, Oregon, Pennsylvania, Tennessee, Texas, Virginia, and Wisconsin.* In short, judges across the nation, at both the state and federal levels, agreed almost without exception with Justice Scalia's angry warning in *Windsor* that Justice Kennedy's opinion had profoundly changed the legal and constitutional landscape. Before *Windsor*, the vast majority of all judges who addressed this question held that laws limiting marriage to opposite-sex couples were constitutional. After *Windsor*, the overwhelming majority held such laws unconstitutional. The shift was sudden and it was seismic.[†55]

Not surprisingly, though, in light of the somewhat obscure nature of the

---

* Moreover, in several of these states, governors—including the Republican governors of New Jersey and Nevada—agreed that their state's laws were unconstitutional and declined to defend them in court.

† There were a few exceptions. In *DeBoer v. Snyder*, 772 F.3d 388 (6th Cir. 2014), for example, the Court of Appeals for the Sixth Circuit, in a sharply-divided decision, upheld the constitutionality of a law denying same-sex couples the freedom to marry.

Supreme Court's reasoning in *Romer*, *Lawrence*, and *Windsor*, the courts that invalidated these laws did so on a variety of grounds. Some argued that they violated the fundamental right to marry, some relied on the argument that discrimination on the basis of sexual orientation is constitutionally "suspect," and some concluded that these laws were either wholly irrational or tainted by a constitutionally impermissible animus toward gays and lesbians.

By the spring of 2015, 60 percent of all Americans approved of same-sex marriage and same-sex couples could legally marry in thirty-eight states and the District of Columbia. After some hesitation, the Supreme Court finally announced that it was ready to address the constitutional issue. Because the vast majority of the states that permitted same-sex marriage at this time did so because of judicial decisions holding that a state's refusal to allow same-sex couples to marry violated the United States Constitution, the stakes were high, indeed. A decision holding that such laws were *not* unconstitutional would turn pretty much everything upside down.

In Justice Scalia's words in *Windsor*, the "other shoe" was about to fall.

"THE OTHER SHOE"

JAMES OBERGEFELL AND John Arthur had lived together in a long-term committed relationship for more than twenty years in Cincinnati, Ohio. After John became terminally ill with amyotrophic lateral sclerosis, commonly known as ALS, a fatal disease that paralyzes the body, they decided they wanted the dignity of marrying before John died. Because Ohio law forbade same-sex couples to marry, on July 11, 2013, they chartered a medical plane to Maryland, where they could legally marry. Only a few minutes after the plane landed, Arthur's Aunt Paulette performed the ceremony on the tarmac of the Baltimore-Washington International Airport. Three months later, John died and Jim brought suit to compel the state of Ohio to recognize him as John's husband on the death certificate. The state, of course, refused.

When the Supreme Court heard argument in *Obergefell v. Hodges*[56] on April 28, 2015, the lawyer representing Jim Obergefell was, appropriately, Mary Bonauto, who had argued *Goodridge* to the Massachusetts Supreme Court twelve years earlier. Among those present in the courtroom were Robbie Kaplan, who had argued *Windsor*; Evan Wolfson, who thirty years earlier had first advanced the implausible idea that same-sex couples had a constitutional right to marry; Paul Smith, who had argued *Lawrence v. Texas*; now-retired Massachusetts Chief Justice Margaret Marshall; and many other lawyers, historians, and activists who had played key roles in helping to get the Supreme Court—and the nation—to this moment.

During oral argument, Justice Anthony Kennedy, whom everyone expected to be the critical swing vote in the case, raised some eyebrows— and stirred some angst—when he asked during oral argument whether it was appropriate for the Court to intervene this quickly in what he described as an ongoing social movement. The definition of marriage as involving a man and a woman, he observed, "has been with us for millennia." Was it really appropriate, he asked, "for the Court to say, oh, well, we know better?" Solicitor General Donald Verilli, representing the Obama administration and, more importantly, the United States, responded directly to Justice Kennedy's question. "Gay and lesbian people are equal," he declared. "They deserve equal protection of the laws, and they deserve it *now*."[57]

On June 26, 2015, the anniversary of the decisions in both *Lawrence* and *Windsor*, the Supreme Court announced its decision in *Obergefell* to an anxiously awaiting nation.

A S IN *Romer*, *Lawrence*, and *Windsor*, Justice Anthony Kennedy delivered the opinion of the Court. Once again, the Court was sharply divided. As in *Windsor*, Justices Ginsburg, Breyer, Sotomayor, and Kagan joined Justice Kennedy's opinion, and Chief Justice Roberts and Justices Scalia, Thomas, and Alito dissented.

At the outset, Justice Kennedy emphasized that the Court had long held that marriage, although not expressly enumerated in the Constitution, is a right of fundamental importance. Noting the "transcendent importance" of marriage throughout human history, Kennedy observed that marriage has always been understood to promise "dignity" to committed couples. For that reason, he observed, the Court had held over the course of many years that a state cannot constitutionally deny married couples the freedom to use contraception, prohibit interracial couples from marrying, forbid fathers who are late on their child support payments from marrying, or prohibit prisoners from marrying.[58]

Although conceding that the Court's prior decisions protecting marriage as a fundamental right had all dealt with relationships between opposite-sex partners, Kennedy explained that that did not in any way foreclose the

Justice Anthony Kennedy

Court's responsibility to determine whether same-sex couples should also benefit from the right. This was so, he explained, because although history and tradition guide constitutional interpretation, when "new insight" reveals an evolution in society's understanding of the fundamental guarantees of the Constitution, the meaning of those guarantees must evolve as well. Thus, he reasoned, although the limitation of marriage to opposite-sex couples "may long have seemed natural and just," its "inconsistency with the central meaning of the fundamental right to marry is now manifest."*[59]

Kennedy then addressed the issue he himself had raised during oral argument: In considering such a politically sensitive issue as same-sex marriage, should the Court "proceed with caution" and stay its hand while awaiting further public debate, litigation, and legislation? Although affirming that the Constitution contemplates that the democratic process is ordinarily the appropriate mechanism for political change, Kennedy declared that when fundamental rights are violated, "the Constitution requires redress by the courts." Echoing the Framers of our Constitution, Kennedy explained that the very idea of the Constitution "was to withdraw certain subjects from the vicissitudes of political controversy" and "to place them beyond the reach of majorities" and public officials.

Thus, echoing the Court's stance in *Roe v. Wade* forty years earlier, Kennedy declared that "were the Court to stay its hand to allow slower, case-by-case determination," it would effectively, and irresponsibly, empower states to deny to gays and lesbians a fundamental freedom that is guaranteed to them by the Constitution.[60]

In the final paragraphs of his opinion, Justice Kennedy turned to the lurking issue of religion. Kennedy recognized that the Constitution protects the freedom of those who adhere to certain religious doctrines to argue that same-sex marriage is sinful and that people should not enter into such relationships. But, he insisted, as he had in *Romer, Lawrence,* and *Windsor,* the Constitution does not permit the state to deny individuals the freedoms guaranteed them by the Constitution in order to accommodate the religious beliefs of others.[61]

---

* Invoking such decisions as *Skinner v. Oklahoma,* and *Eisenstadt v. Baird,* Kennedy explained further that a state's decision to deny same-sex couples the freedom to marry implicates not only the liberty guaranteed by the Due Process Clause, but also the equality guaranteed by the Equal Protection Clause. Indeed, he explained, the "interrelation" of these two principles is essential, because the "denial to same-sex couples of the right to marry works a grave and continuing harm" on those who are unfairly denied this right.

"THE CONSTITUTION . . . HAD NOTHING TO DO WITH IT"

THE DISSENTING JUSTICES were irate. Although acknowledging that many people "will rejoice" at the Court's decision, Chief Justice John Roberts, joined by Justices Scalia and Thomas, declared that "for those who believe in a government of laws, not of men," the Court's decision must be "disheartening." It was, he complained, "an act of will," rather than an act of "legal judgment," because the right it announced "has no basis in the Constitution."

Although Roberts agreed that the Constitution protects an implied right to marry, he insisted that that right extends only to unions of a man and a woman. This is so, he argued, because that definition of marriage "has existed for millennia and across civilizations." Characterizing the Court's approach as "unprincipled" and "indefensible," Roberts maintained that an unenumerated right can legitimately be deemed fundamental only if it is deeply "rooted in the traditions and conscience of our people," a test that does not in any way describe the asserted right to same-sex marriage. This limitation is essential, he opined, because it is necessary to cabin the discretion of judges. Indeed, he warned, the Court's unrestrained reasoning could apply with equal force to the claim that "plural marriage" is also a fundamental right.

Roberts concluded by acknowledging that those who favor the recognition of same-sex marriage would no doubt "celebrate today's decision." But, he cautioned, "do not celebrate the Constitution. It had nothing to do with it."[62]

JUSTICE SCALIA, joined by Justice Thomas, embraced Roberts's opinion in full but felt the need to write separately to underscore the magnitude of the Court's "threat to American democracy." Insisting that it was not a matter of much importance to him one way or the other whether same-sex couples can or cannot marry, Scalia maintained that what really galled him about the Court's decision was what he described as "the hubris reflected in today's judicial Putsch." Scalia was brutal in his attack on Kennedy's opinion, mocking it as "pretentious," "egotistic," "profoundly incoherent," and "lacking even a thin veneer of law."

Invoking his "originalist" approach to constitutional interpretation, Justice Scalia noted that when the Fourteenth Amendment was ratified after the Civil War, every state "limited marriage to one man and one woman, and no one doubted the constitutionality of doing so." That unimpeachable fact, he maintained, ought to resolve the issue once and for all. The Court, he declared, had no legitimate authority to invalidate these laws on constitutional grounds, and "the public debate over same-sex marriage must be allowed to continue."*[63]

Justice Thomas, joined by Justice Scalia, emphasized that the Court's decision "threatens the religious liberty our Nation has long sought to protect." Indeed, he warned, because marriage is a religious as well as a government institution, it "appears all but inevitable" that these two versions of marriage will now "come into conflict" as individuals and churches are confronted with demands that they participate in and endorse marriages between same-sex couples. Given that reality, Thomas charged that the Court's decision will have "potentially ruinous consequences for religious liberty."†[64]

SO, WHO IS RIGHT?

A PERSISTENT OBJECTION of the four dissenting justices in *Obergefell* was their emphatic assertion that the justices in the majority were unabashedly—and illegitimately—distorting the "true" meaning of the Constitution to suit their own personal values and beliefs. Perhaps making the point most emphatically, Justice Scalia sneered that "today's decree says that my Ruler, and the Ruler of 320 million Americans coast-to-coast, is a majority of the nine lawyers on the Supreme Court." Such a system, he fumed, "does not deserve to be called a democracy."[65] In their separate dissenting opinions, Chief Justice Roberts and Justices Thomas and Alito each chimed in with similar denunciations of the Court's usurpation of the "right of the people" to govern themselves.[66]

Charges of this sort might have been warranted if they had been made by justices who were themselves committed to the principle of judicial restraint. There have, in fact, been justices in our history—Felix Frankfurter and John Marshall Harlan are examples—who sincerely believed in

---

* Following this same line of reasoning, Justice Scalia once suggested that the Equal Protection Clause, properly understood, also had nothing to say about laws discriminating against women.

† Justice Alito, joined by Justices Scalia and Thomas, also filed a dissenting opinion.

judicial restraint. In their view, justices of the Supreme Court should be modest in their interpretation of the Constitution, always giving the benefit of the doubt to the elected branches of government, unless their actions clearly and unequivocally violated the Constitution.

If justices like Frankfurter and Harlan had condemned the majority opinion in *Obergefell* for violating the principle of judicial restraint, one would at least have had to respect the sincerity of their commitment to that principle. But Chief Justice Roberts and Justices Scalia, Thomas, and Alito are in no way adherents to this principle. To the contrary, in decision after decision they have exercised an often fierce form of judicial activism, a form of activism that is completely incompatible with their self-righteous paeans to judicial restraint in *Obergefell*.

These four justices, for example, have embraced aggressive interpretations of the Constitution in order to hold unconstitutional laws regulating campaign expenditures and contributions, authorizing affirmative action programs, regulating the availability of guns, protecting the voting rights of racial minorities, and promoting racial integration. Put simply, these four justices are not in any principled way committed to the doctrine of judicial restraint.[67]

Although there were certainly plausible arguments they could and did make in opposition to the Court's decision, their exaggerated accusations that *Obergefell* violated the legitimate constitutional role of the Court and intruded in some egregious manner on the norms of American democracy are, at best, facetious. It is one thing to disagree with the Court's reasoning. It is quite another to charge that, in this decision in particular, the justices in the majority betrayed the respect the Court owes to the democratic process. Quite simply, they did not.

What the vehemence of these attacks suggests is that, their protestations to the contrary notwithstanding, the four dissenting justices were deeply and morally offended by the very idea of same-sex marriage, and their fury got the better of them. In this sense, it would be fair to say that, more than the justices in the majority, the dissenters in *Obergefell* were responding to the case not in a calm, measured, dispassionate, professional manner, but in a fit of pique.

THIS IS not to say, however, that there were not reasonable grounds on which to disagree with the Court's analysis. In invalidating laws limiting marriage to a man and a woman, Justice Kennedy relied on the argument that marriage is a fundamental right and that government therefore cannot constitutionally deny the right of same-sex couples to marry without a compelling justification. The very notion that the Constitution protects unenumerated fundamental rights has always been somewhat vexing, although clearly anticipated by the Ninth Amendment.* As James Madison observed, the recognition in the Constitution "of particular rights, shall not be so construed as to diminish the just importance of other rights retained by the people."[68] Over the years, the Court has recognized that several such rights exist, including, for example, the right not to be sterilized, the right to use contraception, the right to privacy, the right to vote, the right to travel, the right to terminate an unwanted pregnancy, the right to learn a foreign language, the right to educate one's own children, and the right to marry.[69]

But the recognition of unenumerated rights is always a tricky business, because it gives the justices potentially broad authority to override the democratic process by imposing on the people their own judgments about what rights are fundamental. Thus, as the dissenters in *Obergefell* argued, one constraint the Court has sometimes imposed on this inquiry is that an unenumerated right should be recognized as fundamental only if it is one that is "deeply rooted in the Nation's history and tradition." On this view, the Court should hold a law unconstitutional because it restricts an unenumerated right only when the law departs sharply from long-settled tradition. This might be the case, for example, if a state enacted a law forbidding unemployed people from marrying.

As the dissenters argued, this standard, so understood, was not met in *Obergefell*. Although the Court has long recognized marriage as a fundamental right, what is "deeply rooted in the Nation's history and tradition" is marriage between two people of the opposite sex, not marriage between two people of the same sex. Thus, the decision of states not to permit same-sex couples to marry was not a departure from the established, well-settled understanding of the historic contours of the right. Hence, in the view of the dissenters, the Court in *Obergefell* was not protecting a right that is "deeply rooted in the Nation's history and tradition," but was instead creating an entirely new right out of whole cloth, an act that was beyond the legitimate authority of the Court.

Although this is a plausible argument as a matter of first principles, it is not in fact consistent with the actual practice of the Court over time.

---

* The adoption of the Ninth Amendment is discussed in chapter 6.

Indeed, many of the unenumerated fundamental rights that the Court has recognized clearly involved new applications of traditionally-recognized rights in light of evolving social understandings and values.

This was so, for example, when the Court held in *Skinner v. Oklahoma* that the right to procreate includes the fundamental right not to be sterilized, when it held in *Griswold v. Connecticut* that the right of "marital privacy" includes the fundamental right of married couples to use contraceptives, when it held in *Eisenstadt v. Baird* that the right of individuals to decide for themselves whether "to bear or beget a child" includes the fundamental right of unmarried individuals to use contraceptives, when it held in *Loving v. Virginia* that the right to marry includes the fundamental right of interracial couples to marry, and when it held in *Roe v. Wade* that the right of privacy includes the fundamental right of a woman to decide for herself whether to terminate a pregnancy.

In all of these instances, and in many others besides, the Court did *not* limit itself to protecting fundamental rights only when the challenged law represented a departure from narrowly-defined conceptions of traditionally-recognized rights. Rather, it asked whether the general understanding of the right was "deeply rooted in the Nation's history and tradition," and then determined whether a particular restriction violated evolving and contemporary understandings of that more general fundamental right.*

This mode of analysis invites greater judicial discretion than the more constrained approach, but the Court has sensibly decided over time that just as expressly guaranteed constitutional rights must evolve over time in order to preserve their vitality, the same must be true of unenumerated rights. Indeed, given the Court's traditional approach to this question, which does not comport with the claims of the dissenters, it is not surprising that the vast majority of the lower court judges who considered this question in the years between *Windsor* and *Obergefell* fully anticipated the Court's approach.

As the legal scholar David Cole has astutely observed, the Court in

---

* Perhaps the strongest precedent for the dissenters' position on this question was *Washington v. Glucksberg*, 521 U.S. 702 (1997), in which the Court, in an opinion by Chief Justice Rehnquist, rejected the argument that a law prohibiting physician-assisted suicide violated an individual's asserted fundamental right to decide for himself whether to continue his life. On the other hand, in earlier decisions, such as *Cruzan v. Director, Missouri Department of Health*, 497 U.S. 261 (1990), the Court affirmed that individuals do have a fundamental right under the Constitution to control their own bodily integrity and thus to refuse the administration of even lifesaving medications.

Obergefell "did not so much rewrite constitutional law as recognize that it had been rewritten."[70] The profound shift in public opinion, legal understanding, and constitutional analysis on this issue was the result of decades of determined advocacy by dedicated individuals and organizations including, among many others, Frank Kameny, Mary Bonauto, Evan Wolfson, Roberta Kaplan, the Mattachine Society, GLAD, Lambda Legal, Freedom to Marry, the Human Rights Campaign, and the ACLU.

It was their often courageous efforts, combined with the willingness of innumerable legislators, governors, mayors, scholars, and private citizens to question the accepted wisdom, to reconceptualize the core American principles of equality and individual dignity, and to then work tirelessly to open the minds and hearts of their fellow citizens that brought about the profound evolution of constitutional doctrine that was recognized by the Supreme Court in *Obergefell.*

IT IS important to note that, as in *Lawrence* and *Windsor,* Justice Kennedy again premised his decision on relatively narrow grounds in *Obergefell.* A broader, and even more compelling rationale for the Court's decision would have been the argument, adopted by several lower courts post-*Windsor,* that discrimination against gays and lesbians demands heightened scrutiny under the Equal Protection Clause. The argument is straightforward: Gays and lesbians have been subjected to a long history of invidious discrimination, sexual orientation is not a matter of choice, gays and lesbians have consistently had their interests dismissed and overridden in the majoritarian political process, and sexual orientation has nothing to do with an individual's ability to perform in society.

This being so, laws that discriminate against gays and lesbians, like laws that discriminate on the basis of race, gender, and national origin, whether in marriage, child custody proceedings, adoption proceedings, government employment, or any other context, should properly be understood as constitutionally "suspect," in the sense that such discrimination is likely to be tainted by considerations of animus, hostility, ignorance, and prejudice. This is the most compelling reason for invalidating laws that discriminate against gays and lesbians. Moreover, unlike the "marriage is a fundamental interest" argument, the suspect classification argument would render *all* government discrimination against gays and lesbians presumptively unconstitutional—as it should be. Why the Court, and more precisely Justice Kennedy, chose to emphasize that marriage is a fundamental right rather than the "suspect" classification rationale for the decision in *Obergefell* is not clear, but presumably it was because Justice Kennedy, and perhaps others in the majority, wanted to leave those other issues for another day.

LOOKING TO THE FUTURE

UPON EXITING THE Supreme Court building on June 26, 2015, Jim Obergefell, in tears, observed that "today's ruling . . . affirms that our love is equal" and that "all Americans deserve equal dignity, respect and treatment." He was surrounded by hundreds of supporters beaming with joy and pride, waving rainbow flags, and chanting "Love Conquers." On the second floor of a six-story walk-up in New York City, in the offices of the organization Freedom to Marry, the group's founder, Evan Wolfson, wept as he read Justice Kennedy's opinion.

At the same time, several blocks away, Sarah Kate Ellis, the president

James Obergefell

of GLAAD (Gay and Lesbian Alliance Against Defamation), declared that "today our nation became a more perfect union," while throngs of couples and families—gay and straight—flocked to the Stonewall Inn to rejoice and to pay tribute to the determined gay rights activists whose efforts over the years had opened the door to the Court's decision. For most of those who gathered at the Stonewall, this was a moment they had never thought possible in their lifetime.[71]

This enthusiasm reflected the views of a clear majority of the American people. Indeed, despite the complaints of the dissenting justices that the Court's decision in *Obergefell* had been foisted upon the American people, 58 percent of Americans supported the decision.

In a statement issued only moments after the Court announced its judgment, President Barack Obama hailed *Obergefell* as "a victory for America," declaring that it "affirms what millions of Americans already know in their hearts." "When all Americans are treated as equal," he said, choking with emotion, "we are all more free." The President exulted that "America should be very proud."

In the four months after the Court's decision, some 200,000 gays and lesbians entered into same-sex marriages in states across the nation, bringing to one million the number of gays and lesbians in same-sex marriages. More than a quarter of these families were already raising their own children.[72]

N OT EVERYONE was celebrating. To a person, the Republican presidential candidates in the summer of 2015, already in the throes of a heated campaign for the nomination, condemned the decision. Texas Senator Ted Cruz, for example, described *Obergefell* as among "the darkest hours in our nation's history." He railed that impeachment was a fitting response and called for a constitutional amendment to overturn the Court's ruling. Former Arkansas Governor Mike Huckabee declared that "the Supreme Court can no more repeal the laws of nature or of nature's God on marriage than it can the laws of gravity," and Florida Senator Marco Rubio promised that if elected president, he would nominate justices who would overturn the decision.[73]

The Christian Right was livid. Tony Perkins, the President of the Family Research Council, declared that "no court can overturn nature's law." Truth, he proclaimed, is decided not by five justices of the Supreme Court, "but by the One who created time and everything that exists therein."

Brian S. Brown, the President of the National Organization for Marriage, compared the Court's decision in *Obergefell* with its decision in *Dred Scott v. Sandford*, and warned that "today's decision" is "only the beginning of the next phase of the struggle."[74]

Across the nation, bishops of the Catholic Church deplored the Court's action. Archbishop Joseph Kurtz of Louisville, Kentucky, decried *Obergefell* as a "tragic error." Boston's Cardinal Sean O'Malley warned that the decision posed grave dangers to our nation's future. Bishop Richard Malone of Buffalo, New York, declared that the traditional understanding of marriage as involving one man and one woman "is rooted in creation: God created marriage in the very same breath as He created the human person." Bishop Thomas Tobin of Providence, Rhode Island, proclaimed that Justice Kennedy's opinion was nothing less than "an attempt to destroy God's plan."[75]

Despite all the fuss, though, public officials in almost every state in the nation quickly acknowledged that it was their duty to obey the Constitution, whether or not they agreed with the Court, and they set out to do so. In Mississippi, Attorney General Jim Hood authorized county clerks to issue marriage licenses to same-sex couples, noting that this is now "the law of the land." In Louisiana, Governor Bobby Jindal, although condemning the Court's decision, announced that the state would comply with the ruling. Shortly thereafter, in a suburb of New Orleans, Alesia LeBoeuf and Celeste Autin became the first same-sex couple ever to marry in Louisiana. As LeBoeuf observed, her hands still shaking with excitement, "I'm just speechless. I never thought I'd see the day."[76]

And so, with but a few exceptions,* the transition to this brave new world went astonishingly smoothly. Unlike the furious resistance in the South to *Brown v. Board of Education*,[77] which raged for more than a decade, within a few days of the Court's decision in *Obergefell* same-sex couples were joyously marrying even in states that had bitterly opposed same-sex marriage. To echo the words of President Obama, it was a remarkable moment in our history, and a moment of which "America should be very proud."

---

* The incident that garnered the most publicity was triggered by Kim Davis, a county clerk in Kentucky who refused to issue marriage licenses either to same-sex or opposite-sex couples, claiming that for her to issue marriage licenses to same-sex couples would violate her religious beliefs. After defying a federal court order she was jailed for five days for contempt of court. In the end, the matter was resolved when she authorized her assistants to issue the licenses in her stead.

• • •

WHAT, THOUGH, of the future? Despite the extraordinary achievements reflected in *Romer, Lawrence, Windsor,* and *Obergefell,* many questions remain. Perhaps the most obvious question is whether, with a change in the makeup of the Court, a new majority might overrule *Obergefell.* In light of the vehemence of the dissenting justices and their harsh condemnation of the legitimacy of the decision, it is certainly possible that at some point down the road a majority of justices holding similar views might jettison the precedent and cast the states back into the chaotic pre-*Windsor* state of affairs. But given the settled expectations of more than a million married gays and lesbians and their children, even justices holding that view would likely be reluctant to call the legitimacy of all those families into question.

But even if *Obergefell* remains in place, it is important to recognize that it does not address the broader question of government discrimination on the basis of sexual orientation. Suppose, for example, that a public school district refuses to hire gay, lesbian, or transgender teachers, arguing that such individuals are distracting and upsetting to children in the district, whose residents do not approve of such behavior. Because of its emphasis on the fundamental right to marry, *Obergefell* does not address this issue. The question would be whether such discrimination violates the Equal Protection Clause.

In all likelihood, the five justices in the majority in *Obergefell* would invalidate such a policy, either on the ground that such discrimination does not rationally further a legitimate state interest and is motivated by constitutionally impermissible animus, or on the ground that discrimination on the basis of sexual orientation is constitutionally suspect and must therefore be tested by a heightened level of scrutiny.

Once again, though, given the intensity of the dissenters in *Obergefell,* and given the fact that neither *Obergefell* nor any of the Court's prior decisions necessarily controls this situation, a change in the makeup of the Court could easily result in a decision that limits *Obergefell* to the right to marry and upholds the discriminatory policy—and, indeed, all other forms of non-marital governmental discrimination against gays and lesbians. This remains a question for the future.

ANOTHER UNRESOLVED question, not at the constitutional level, concerns private discrimination on the basis of sexual orientation and gender identity. In light of current and evolving attitudes on this issue, will the federal government at some point enact the Employment Non-Discrimination Act (ENDA)? Such legislation would prohibit *private* discrimination on the basis of sexual orientation, in much the same way that the federal Civil Rights Act now prohibits such private discrimination on the basis of race, sex, national origin, religion, veterans' status, and so on. Despite the overall state of public opinion on this issue, which strongly favors the enactment of ENDA, the realities of national politics and the blocking power of the filibuster suggest that it is unlikely, though not impossible, that Congress will enact ENDA anytime soon.*

Then there is the question of state law. As of 2016, twenty-two states had laws prohibiting private discrimination on the basis of sexual orientation in employment, housing, and public accommodations.† Twenty-eight states, though, had no such laws.‡ In those twenty-eight states, except insofar as individual municipalities might have anti-discrimination ordinances of their own, private discrimination against gays and lesbians remains perfectly legal. Thus, in those states, a barber who does not want gay men in his shop is free to exclude them; a hotel that does not want married same-sex couples staying as guests is free to exclude them; and a manufacturer who does not want to employ homosexuals is free not to hire them. In these states, the individual who discriminates on the basis of sexual orientation or gender identity is free to do so for any reason at all, including just plain hatred of homosexuals.

But what about the twenty-two states with laws prohibiting private discrimination on the basis of sexual orientation? In such states the question inevitably arises whether individuals who discriminate against gays and lesbians *because of their religious beliefs* have either a constitutional or statutory right to do.

• • •

---

* See chapter 18 for a discussion of ENDA.

† California, Colorado, Connecticut, Delaware, Hawaii, Illinois, Iowa, Maine, Maryland, Massachusetts, Minnesota, Nevada, New Jersey, New Mexico, Oregon, Rhode Island, Utah, Vermont, and Washington have laws prohibiting discrimination on the basis of either sexual orientation or gender identity, and New Hampshire, New York, and Wisconsin have laws prohibiting discrimination only on the basis of sexual orientation. Several states, including Kansas, Kentucky, Louisiana, and Virginia, at one time had such laws, but then later repealed them.

‡ Alabama, Alaska, Arizona, Arkansas, Florida, Georgia, Idaho, Indiana, Kansas, Kentucky, Louisiana, Michigan, Mississippi, Missouri, Montana, Nebraska, North Carolina, North Dakota, Ohio, Oklahoma, Pennsylvania, South Carolina, South Dakota, Tennessee, Texas, Virginia, West Virginia, Wyoming.

NOT SURPRISINGLY, in the days and weeks after the Supreme Court announced its judgment in *Obergefell*, this was a central theme of those who denounced the decision. The concern, foreshadowed in Justice Clarence Thomas's dissenting opinion, was that the decision would have "potentially ruinous consequences for religious liberty." Russell Moore of the Southern Baptist Convention warned, for example, that religious freedom would be "the next front" in the war that homosexuals were waging on the liberty of American citizens; and Jim Daly, the president of Focus on the Family, charged that *Obergefell* would subject God-fearing Christians to "prejudice and persecution" if they had the courage to take a stand against same-sex marriage.[78]

Critics of *Obergefell* identified a broad range of situations in which they feared that such conflicts would arise. Would religiously-affiliated hospitals, universities, schools, charities, adoption agencies, and shelters now be compelled to recognize same-sex marriages in ways that violated their religious beliefs? Would religiously-affiliated businesses, such as hotels, restaurants, florists, bakers, musicians, and photographers now be compelled to participate in same-sex weddings that they deemed sinful? Would public officials who hold religious beliefs incompatible with the Court's ruling, such as clerks who issue marriage licenses, now be compelled to act in ways that betray their faith?

How are we to reconcile these competing claims to individual dignity and equality, on the one hand, and religious liberty, on the other?

Put simply, do people of faith have a right to discriminate against gays and lesbians? There are at least two possible sources for such a right. First, the individual might insist that for the state to compel her to act in a way that she deems incompatible with her religious beliefs violates her rights under the First Amendment, which prohibits government to make any law "prohibiting the free exercise of religion." This guarantee clearly forbids the government from making a law that *expressly* disadvantages the members of a particular religion. This would be the case, for example, if a law expressly prohibited Muslims to be school teachers or expressly prohibited Jews to wear yarmulkes.

The more difficult question, and the one raised here, is whether a law that is not *directed* at religion, but has an *incidental* effect on the ability of an individual to act in accord with her religious beliefs, is for that reason unconstitutional as applied to her. This is the issue raised, for example, by the application of a law prohibiting discrimination on the basis of sexual orientation to a florist who claims that her religion forbids her to provide flowers for a same-sex wedding. This is the type of situation the critics of *Obergefell* were worried about.

For a time, the Supreme Court, during the liberal heyday of the Warren Court, held that such laws, even though not intended to interfere with anyone's religious liberty, were nonetheless unconstitutional if they substantially burdened an individual's free exercise of religion, unless the application of the law to that person served a compelling government interest. If the law did not satisfy that standard, the individual was entitled to a constitutional exemption from the law.

In the pivotal decision, *Sherbert v. Verner*,[79] Adeil Sherbert, a member of the Seventh-Day Adventist Church, was fired from her job after she refused to work on Saturday, the Sabbath Day of her faith. The South Carolina Employment Security Commission denied her unemployment benefits, finding unacceptable her religious justification for refusing to work on Saturdays. The Supreme Court, in a landmark 1963 opinion by Justice William Brennan, held that in these circumstances, the state could not constitutionally deny Sherbert the unemployment benefits.

Under this doctrine, in the florist example the question today would be whether the non-discrimination requirement that the florist must provide flowers for the same-sex wedding substantially burdens her religious liberty and, if so, whether the government has a compelling interest in requiring the florist not to discriminate against persons planning same-sex weddings.

B UT THAT is no longer the law. In 1990, after the Supreme Court had moved in a sharply more conservative direction with the appointments of eight consecutive justices by Presidents Nixon, Ford, and Reagan, the Court overturned the *Sherbert* doctrine in *Employment Division v. Smith*.[80] The issue in *Smith* was whether a state could constitutionally deny unemployment benefits to individuals who had been dismissed from their jobs because of their unlawful use of peyote, a naturally occurring psychoactive drug. For these individuals, the use of peyote was an essential element of the religious rituals of their Native American Church. The members of the church maintained that just as Prohibition had exempted the use of wine by Catholics for sacramental purposes, the anti-peyote law should have exempted the use of peyote by members of the Native American Church for similar religious purposes. Because it didn't, they argued that under settled law, the First Amendment required such an exemption.

In an opinion by Justice Antonin Scalia, the Court flat-out rejected the proposition that the Free Exercise Clause gives individuals a constitutional right to violate "a generally applicable law that requires (or forbids) the performance of an act that his religious belief forbids (or requires)." Scalia explained that "the government's ability to enforce generally applicable prohibitions of socially harmful conduct . . . cannot depend on measuring the effects of a governmental action on a religious objector's spiritual development." Indeed, he declared, "to make an individual's obligation to obey such a law contingent upon the law's coincidence with his religious beliefs" contradicts "common sense."[81]

The more liberal justices who had fashioned the prior doctrine several decades earlier had been concerned that unlike mainstream religions, which can protect themselves in the political process and would not need a constitutionally-based exemption to safeguard their religious freedom, minority religions needed this principle to protect their religious freedom against the indifference—or hostility—of the majority. The more conservative justices who joined Justice Scalia's analysis in *Smith* rejected this justification for the earlier doctrine.

Under the current state of the law established by Justice Scalia in *Smith*, then, it would seem that individuals who have a religious objection to providing flowers, cakes, or marriage licenses for same-sex weddings in states or cities that forbid discrimination on the basis of sexual orientation have no constitutional leg to stand on—unless, of course, the Court, seeing whose ox is now being gored, once again reconsiders its interpretation of the First Amendment.*

BUT *SMITH* was not the end of the story. Three years later, Congress, annoyed by Justice Scalia's opinion in *Smith*, enacted the Religious Freedom Restoration Act of 1993 (RFRA), which as a *statutory* matter now prohibits the federal government from "substantially burdening" a person's exercise of religion, even if the burden results from a mere incidental effect, unless the government can demonstrate that the law is narrowly drawn to

---

* It is noteworthy that ten years after *Smith*, the Supreme Court, again in an opinion by Justice Scalia, held that a state law prohibiting discrimination against gays and lesbians could not constitutionally be applied to the Boy Scouts because the requirement that the Boy Scouts have gay scoutmasters had an incidental effect on the Boy Scouts' *free speech* right to teach that homosexuality is immoral. See *Boy Scouts of America v. Dale*, 530 U.S. 640 (2000).

further a compelling governmental interest. Moreover, as of 2016, following Congress's lead, twenty-one states had enacted similar legislation.*

Perhaps not surprisingly given the religious differences among the states, there is very little overlap between the twenty-two states that have laws prohibiting private discrimination on the basis of sexual orientation and the twenty-one states that have enacted state RFRAs. Indeed, only four states both prohibit such discrimination *and* exempt religious objectors from laws prohibiting such discrimination. In the remaining forty-six states, either discrimination against gays and lesbians is legal, and therefore no religious exemptions are necessary, or such discrimination is illegal and no religious exemptions exist.

More precisely, as of 2016, thirty-two states permit discrimination against gays and lesbians for religious reasons either because they do not forbid such discrimination at all (twenty-eight states) or because they forbid such discrimination but then exempt those who discriminate for religious reasons (four states). And as of 2016, eighteen states prohibit discrimination against gays and lesbians without exempting individuals who do so for religious reasons. In those eighteen states, the constitutional question, currently settled by *Smith*, leaves religious objectors without an exemption.

A central question for the future, at both the legislative and constitutional level, is which of the three following scenarios is the "right" one: (1) Private individuals and institutions can legally discriminate against people based on their sexual orientation or gender identity. (2) Private individuals and institutions cannot legally discriminate against people based on their sexual orientation or gender identity. (3) Private individuals and institutions can legally discriminate against people based on their sexual orientation or gender identity if such discrimination is "justified" by their religious beliefs.

This is the issue for the future.

---

* Alabama, Arizona, Arkansas, Connecticut, Florida, Idaho, Illinois, Indiana, Kansas, Kentucky, Louisiana, Mississippi, Missouri, New Mexico, Oklahoma, Pennsylvania, Rhode Island, South Carolina, Tennessee, Texas, and Virginia had enacted state Religious Freedom Restoration Acts.

EPILOGUE

*Sex, a great and mysterious motive force in human life,
has indisputably been a subject of absorbing interest to
mankind through the ages.*

—ROTH V. UNITED STATES, 354 U.S. 476, 487 (1957)

W E ARE IN the midst of a constitutional revolution. It is a revolution that has tested the most fundamental values of the American people and shaken constitutional law to its very roots. It has divided citizens, politicians, and judges. It has dominated politics, inflamed religious passions, and challenged Americans to rethink and reexamine their positions on issues once thought settled.

Over the grand sweep of history, social, religious, and legal attitudes toward sex have shifted dramatically over time. These shifts have not been in any one direction. Rather, they have swung back and forth, depending on a range of influences and circumstances. Whereas the Greeks and Romans did not attach any religious significance to sex, the early Christians came to view sex as inherently sinful. For more than a millennium, the Church imposed its beliefs about sex on the faithful, but left those who did not share the faith to their own destinies.

This began to change in the late Middle Ages, as first the Church and then Protestant Reformers turned increasingly to the secular law to require *all* people to conform their behavior to the dictates of the dominant religion. As time passed, though, Enlightenment thinkers, such as Locke, Voltaire, and Rousseau, came to reject many of the dogmas of traditional Christianity and, more broadly, the assumption that the dominant religion can legitimately conscript the power of the state to impose its own notions of sin on others.

This view shaped the understandings of the Framers of our Constitution and led ultimately to the principle of separation of church and state, which the Framers embodied in the First Amendment. This guarantee made clear that although religions have a right to set their own rules of behavior for those who share the faith, they cannot constitutionally enlist the authority of the state to compel others to conform their behavior to the commands of a religion that they do not accept as their own.

At the time the Constitution was adopted, there were no laws in the United States forbidding sexual expression, contraception, or pre-quickening abortion, and the long-standing laws against consensual sodomy were rarely, if ever, enforced. This was a reflection of the core values of the Enlightenment that both inspired and informed the founding of the American republic.

But then, with the Second Great Awakening, the religious moralism of the Victorian era, the impact of the social purity movement, and the reign of Anthony Comstock, religious forces throughout the nineteenth century imposed harsh new restraints on sexual expression, contraception, abortion, and homosexuality. Religious leaders unabashedly invoked the Bible as justification for secular laws that sharply restricted the freedom of individuals.

Although there was always opposition to this radical transformation of American law, it was not until the twentieth century that bold leaders like Margaret Sanger, Horace Liveright, and Frank Kameny began successfully to challenge this campaign to engraft religious dogma into our nation's laws. As the decades passed, social movements demanding a more robust freedom of expression, the right of women to control their own reproductive destinies, and the dignity and equality of gays and lesbians gradually gained steam. These social movements insisted that the laws they now challenged were incompatible with the most fundamental guarantees of the American Constitution.

THROUGHOUT THIS history, political, legal, and constitutional battles over obscenity, contraception, abortion, sodomy, and same-sex marriage sharply divided Americans along religious lines. Those holding certain religious beliefs about the sinfulness of such behavior, ranging from Lyman Beecher to Anthony Comstock to Jerry Falwell, vigorously insisted that such conduct must be forbidden as "immoral," whereas those holding a different set of beliefs, ranging from Samuel Roth to Estelle Griswold to Mary Bonauto, insisted with equal vigor that government cannot constitutionally restrict the freedom of American citizens merely because some—or even most—people believe their conduct to be "sinful."

Although the dominant influence of religion in these controversies has been pervasive, the justices of the Supreme Court have been reluctant to invoke the Establishment Clause to invalidate such laws. This is so because those who defend these laws invariably advance nonreligious justifications in their defense. For example, laws forbidding the sale of contraceptives were defended, not on the ground that contraception is inconsistent with certain religious beliefs, but on the ground that the availability of contraceptives would encourage promiscuity among women and thus undermine family stability. In such circumstances, the justices of the Supreme Court have understandably been hesitant to accuse the other branches of government of behaving in a disingenuous manner in order to get away with violating the Constitution. But in evaluating the constitutionality of laws restricting contraception, sexual expression, abortion, sodomy, and same-sex marriage under *other* provisions of the Constitution, whether the Equal Protection Clause, the Free Speech Clause, the Due Process Clause, or the Ninth Amendment, the justices—or at least some of them—have no doubt been aware, as they should be, of the underlying realities.

U NTIL 1957, the Supreme Court avoided any direct engagement with the constitutionality of laws regulating sexual expression, contraception, abortion, or homosexuality. This was not because the opportunities for such engagement did not exist. To the contrary, from the late nineteenth century forward, for example, the federal Comstock Act clearly raised potential constitutional questions about both obscenity and contraception. But the justices sidestepped these questions, in part because they did not yet take these issues seriously and in part because they were no doubt uneasy about the prospect of addressing such unseemly matters in the somber confines of the Supreme Court.

Beginning with the issue of obscenity in the *Roth* case in 1957, however, the Court found itself immersed in a stream of challenging and controversial cases posing complex issues about the regulation of sexually-related behavior. Eight years after *Roth*, the Court in *Griswold* held that married couples could not constitutionally be denied access to contraceptives. A few years later, in *Eisenstadt*, the Court extended this principle to unmarried persons and expressly recognized the unenumerated but fundamental right of individuals to decide for themselves whether "to bear or beget a child." Then, in 1973, the Court went even further and held in *Roe v. Wade* that the Constitution guarantees the fundamental right of a woman to decide for herself whether to carry an unwanted pregnancy to term.

In these decisions, a diverse set of justices, appointed by presidents from both political parties, recognized that some choices in life are so central to individual dignity and so deeply personal that the government cannot constitutionally interfere with them without an overriding justification. At the very heart of these decisions was the Court's consistent rejection of the argument that mere invocations of "morality" can constitutionally justify such intrusive restrictions of individual liberty.

Over the next four decades, the Court continued to wrestle with these issues, eventually turning its attention to the rights of gays and lesbians. In a series of dramatic decisions in *Romer, Lawrence, Windsor,* and *Obergefell,* the Court invoked the same basic principles it had embraced in the earlier cases to hold that sodomy cannot constitutionally be made a crime and that same-sex couples have a constitutional right to marry.

Thus, from 1957 to the present we have seen a profound transformation in American constitutional law. Sexually-explicit material is now readily available to consenting adults, contraceptives can now openly be purchased at drugstores across the land, women can now legally obtain an abortion, and gay and lesbian couples can now rejoice openly in their freedom to marry.

This revolution, though, is in no sense complete. Many states still impose serious and highly invasive restrictions on abortion, and most states and the federal government still permit discrimination on the basis of sexual orientation and gender identity. Indeed, we now face new questions about the constitutionality of laws discriminating against transgender individuals in such contexts as access to public bathrooms. But although these issues still remain to be resolved, the revolution in constitutional law is real, and it has had a dramatic impact on American society.

Is this revolution here to stay? It would be easy to say "of course," but we know that attitudes and laws governing sex often shift over time, and those who celebrate this revolution today should not for a moment take it for granted. Indeed, a change in the makeup of the Supreme Court could cause a dramatic shift in the extent to which the Constitution is understood in the future to guarantee the freedoms that have thus far been recognized.

Of course, these changes in American law and culture were not brought about by the Supreme Court alone. They resulted from the actions of individuals and organizations with the courage and determination to challenge the conventional wisdom. They raised questions that, at first, were dismissed out of hand. But because of their persistence, their insight, and their conviction, they changed minds and mores in a way that made constitutional change possible. The justices of the Supreme Court do not operate in a vacuum. As intended by the Framers of our Constitution, they operate in a world of evolving social, political, legal, and constitutional values and understandings.

The meaning of such vague phrases as "the freedom of speech," "equal protection of the laws," "due process of law," and "the rights retained by the people" inevitably change over time. It is the responsibility of the justices of the Supreme Court to give content to these phrases, not by imposing their own personal values on the nation, but by understanding how the American people themselves have come to understand their most fundamental freedoms. In this respect, the Supreme Court in these decisions, despite the vehement dissents of some justices, has truly fulfilled its core mission. By protecting the rights of individuals in the face of fierce religious opposition, the Court has done its job well, and for this we should all be grateful.

B UT WE now find ourselves in a puzzling and unprecedented situation. For much of American history, those who espoused traditional Christian values have had their way. Whether in the realm of sexual expression, contraception, abortion, or homosexuality, government has imposed religious beliefs and values on individuals who did not share them. Although we are not a "Christian Nation," for more than a century our laws in the realm of sex embodied a set of religious tenets and insisted that all citizens must live their lives in accord with those beliefs.

But now, for the first time in our history, it is the *religious* groups and individuals who are on the defensive. Religious employers now seek the freedom not to be compelled to provide contraceptive coverage to women employees as part of their health insurance. Religious florists, bakers, hotel owners, and restaurant owners now seek the freedom not to be compelled to participate in same-sex weddings. Religious landlords now seek the freedom not to be compelled to rent to same-sex couples. Religious public officials now seek the freedom not to be compelled to sanction same-sex marriages. These demands present complex policy, legislative, and constitutional issues. They raise serious—and difficult—questions about the meaning of religious freedom, the meaning of discrimination, and the meaning of equality.

The remarkable thing is that these are the issues that are *now* before us. Individuals with strong religious beliefs about these matters are no longer in a position to impose their beliefs on others, but they now seek the freedom to act in accord with their own religious beliefs. This is a stunning and, indeed, historic, shift in our culture and in our law.

. . .

A S WE HAVE seen throughout this history, the makeup of the Supreme Court matters. In this respect, the 2016 presidential election was pivotal. After the death of Antonin Scalia in February of 2016, President Barack Obama nominated Chief Judge Merrick Garland to succeed him. In choosing Garland, President Obama clearly offered a compromise to the Republicans, who controlled the Senate. Rather than putting forth a much younger nominee who was known to be a committed liberal—like his two earlier nominations of Sonia Sotomayor and Elena Kagan—Obama nominated a sixty-four-year-old judge who was well known for being only moderately liberal. Indeed, it is noteworthy that Garland was thirteen years older than the average of the four most recent nominees (Roberts, Alito, Sotomayor, and Kagan) and that his track record was clearly more moderate than any of them. He was, in short, a highly qualified, clearly ethical, and reasonably moderate nominee.

But knowing that a Court with Justice Garland rather than Justice Scalia on it would clearly tilt in a more liberal direction, Senate Republicans refused even to give Garland a hearing. Although they purported to justify this action on the ground that the Senate should not confirm a Supreme Court nominee in the last year of a president's term, this position was clearly disingenuous. Indeed, a long list of presidents, including George Washington, Thomas Jefferson, Andrew Jackson, Abraham Lincoln, William Howard Taft, Woodrow Wilson, Herbert Hoover, Franklin Roosevelt, and Ronald Reagan, have had Supreme Court nominees confirmed in the last year of their presidencies. Nonetheless, with issues like abortion and gay rights firmly in mind, the Senate Republicans chose power over principle. This was unconscionable—but it worked.

With the election of Donald J. Trump, it was he, rather than Barack Obama or Hillary Clinton, who would get to nominate Antonin Scalia's successor. And beyond that, with the three oldest sitting justices—Ruth Bader Ginsburg, Stephen Breyer, and Anthony Kennedy—all supportive of both abortion and gay rights, if and when President Trump gets to replace any one or more of them, we will likely have a more conservative Supreme Court than at any time in almost a century. What will then happen to decisions like *Hellerstedt*, *Lawrence*, *Obergefell*, and *Roe* remains to be seen.

. . .

PERHAPS THE central lesson of *Sex and the Constitution* is this: We can and should rejoice that our nation has taken an important step in our protection of human dignity and equality. We have many steps left to take, but this is one we should celebrate—however much some justices and some individuals might think we are on the road to perdition.

As we strive to fulfill the obligations of citizenship in the society our Framers envisioned, we must have the courage and the integrity to challenge the accepted wisdom, and we must fully embrace our moral, legal, and constitutional responsibility to respect the rights of others. This was, after all, what the founders of our nation counted on us to do.

NOTES

CHAPTER 1

1   David Cohen, *Law, Sexuality and Society* 123 (Cambridge 1991); Marguerite Johnson & Terry Ryan, *Sexuality in Greek and Roman Society and Literature* 1 (Routledge 2005).

2   See Robert Flacelière, *Love in Ancient Greece* 134 (Crown Publishers 1962); Reay Tannahill, *Sex in History* 84–85 (Scarborough House 1992); Johnson & Ryan, *Sexuality in Greek and Roman Society* at 1 (cited in note 1); K. J. Dover, *Greek Popular Morality in the Time of Plato and Aristotle* 205–6 (Blackwell 1974); Strabo, *Geography* 8.6. 20–21 (Harvard 1932); Scott, *"Into Whose Hands"* 17 18 (Gerald G. Swan 1945).

3   See Vern L. Bullough, *Sexual Variance in Society and History* 99–100 (Chicago 1976); Scott, *"Into Whose Hands"* at 17–18 (cited in note 2); Hans Licht, *Sexual Life in Ancient Greece* 87–89, 139–50, 314 (J. H. Freese trans.; Lawrence H. Dawson ed., Dorset 1993); Norman St. John-Stevas, *Obscenity and the Law* 2–3 (Secker & Warburg 1956); H. A. Shapiro, *Leagros and Euphronios: Painting Pederasty in Athens*, in *Greek Love Reconsidered* 12 (Thomas K. Hubbard ed., Wallace Hamilton 2000); Robert F. Sutton Jr., *Pornography and Persuasion on Attic Pottery*, in *Pornography and Representation in Greece and Rome* 3–35 (Amy Richlin ed., Oxford 1992).

4   Aristophanes, *The Knights* lines 24–29, 164–67, 1241–42 (Henderson trans., Loeb 2000).

5   See Licht, *Sexual Life in Ancient Greece* at 314–15 (cited in note 3); K. J. Dover, *Greek Homosexuality* 102 (Harvard 1978); St. John-Stevas, *Obscenity and the Law* at 2–3 (cited in note 3); Holt N. Parker, *Love's Body Anatomized*, in Richlin, *Pornography and Representation* at 90–111 (cited in note 3).

6   See Johnson & Ryan, *Sexuality in Greek and Roman Society* at 1–3 (cited in note 1); Tannahill, *Sex in History* at 100–105 (cited in note 2).

7   See Bullough, *Sexual Variance* at 98 (cited in note 3), quoting Xenophon, *Memorabilia*, II, 2, 4.

8   See Licht, *Sexual Life in Ancient Greece* at 329–42 (cited in note 3); Ira L. Reiss, *Premarital Sexual Standards in America* 45–46 (Free Press 1960); Flacelière, *Love in Ancient Greece* at 133–61 (cited in note 2); Dover, *Greek Homosexuality* at 132 (cited in note 5); Tannahill, *Sex in History* at 100–105 (cited in note 2); Johnson & Ryan, *Sexuality in Greek and Roman Society* at 1–2 (cited in note 1).

9   Xenarchus, *The Pentathlete* (fr. 4), quoted in David M. Halperin, *One Hundred Years of Homosexuality* 92–93 (Routledge 1990).

10   See John M. Riddle, *Contraception and Abortion from the Ancient World to the Renaissance* 18 (Harvard 1992); Norman E. Himes, *Medical History of Contraception* 79–82 (Gamut

1963); Bullough, *Sexual Variance* at 99 (cited in note 3); Jerome E. Bates & Edward S. Zawadzki, *Criminal Abortion* 16–17 (Thomas 1964).

11 Plutarch, *The Dialogue on Love*, in Vol. IX of the *Moralia*, 751C, quoted in Bullough. *Sexual Variance* at 102 (cited in note 3).

12 See Halperin, *One Hundred Years of Homosexuality* at 33 (cited in note 9); John Boswell, *Christianity, Social Tolerance, and Homosexuality* 58–59 (Chicago 1980); Craig A. Williams, *Roman Homosexuality* 6–7 (Oxford 1992); David F. Greenberg, *The Construction of Homosexuality* 14 (Chicago 1988); Michel Foucault, *The History of Sexuality* (R. Hurley trans., Random House 1978); Dover, *Greek Homosexuality* at 60–68, 81–109 (cited in note 5); Kyle Harper, *From Shame to Sin: The Christian Transformation of Sexual Morality in Late Antiquity* 22–24 (Harvard 2013).

13 Plato, *Symposium* 183a, quoted in Flacelière, *Love in Ancient Greece* at 71 (cited in note 2); Licht, *Sexual Life in Ancient Greece* at 416–18 (cited in note 3). See Dover, *Greek Homosexuality* at 91–92 (cited in note 5); Reiss, *Premarital Sexual Standards* at 46 (cited in note 8); Arno Karlen, *Sexuality and Homosexuality: A New View* 21–27 (Norton 1971); Halperin, *One Hundred Years of Homosexuality* at 5, 47 (cited in note 9); Bullough, *Sexual Variance* at 100–103 (cited in note 3); Dover, *Greek Popular Morality* at 213–15 (cited in note 2); Tannahill, *Sex in History* at 85–89 (cited in note 2); Flacelière, *Love in Ancient Greece* at 72 (cited in note 2); Williams, *Roman Homosexuality* at 63–64 (cited in note 12).

14 Flacelière, *Love in Ancient Greece* at 88 (cited in note 2); Bullough, *Sexual Variance* at 108–9 (cited in note 3); Tannahill, *Sex in History* at 86–88 (cited in note 2); Johnson & Ryan, *Sexuality in Greek and Roman Society* at 4 (cited in note 1).

15 See Plato, *Symposium* 182b–d, 178c; Bullough, *Sexual Variance* at 102–3 (cited in note 3); Boswell, *Christianity, Social Tolerance* at 27, 49–51 (cited in note 12); Dover, *Greek Homosexuality* at 39–49 (cited in note 5); Halperin, *One Hundred Years of Homosexuality* at 56–59 (cited in note 9); Harper, *From Shame to Sin* at 30 (cited in note 12).

16 Aristophanes, *Knights* at lines 991, 1045 (cited in note 4); Plato, *Laws* 836e, 841d; Aristotle, *Rhetoric* 1384a. See Thomas K. Hubbard, *Pederasty and Democracy* in Hubbard, *Greek Love Reconsidered* at 7–11 (cited in note 3); Cohen, *Law, Sexuality and Society* at 187–88 (cited in note 1); Harper, *From Shame to Sin* at 33 (cited in note 12).

17 Jérôme Carcopino, *De Pythagore aux Apôtres* 27 (Flammarion 1956), quoted in Flacelière, *Love in Ancient Greece* at 98 (cited in note 2). See Hubbard, *Greek Love Reconsidered* at 29–35 (cited in note 3).

18 See Dover, *Greek Popular Morality* at 205–16 (cited in note 2); Licht, *Sexual Life in Ancient Greece* at 523–25 (cited in note 3); Johnson & Ryan, *Sexuality in Greek and Roman Society* at 5 (cited in note 1); Flacelière, *Love in Ancient Greece* at 219 (cited in note 2); Dover, *Greek Homosexuality* at 170 (cited in note 5); Himes, *Medical History of Contraception* at 79–82 (cited in note 10); Bullough, *Sexual Variance* at 99 (cited in note 3); Bates & Zawadzki, *Criminal Abortion* at 16–17 (cited in note 10); Michel Foucault, *The Use of Pleasure* 143–65 (Pantheon 1985).

19 Karlen, *Sexuality and Homosexuality* at 45 (cited in note 13).

20 See Boswell, *Christianity, Social Tolerance* at 63–71 (cited in note 12); Otto Kiefer, *Sexual Life in Ancient Rome* 4–6, 148–49 (Routledge 2012); Bullough, *Sexual Variance* at

130, 137 (cited in note 3); Licht, *Sexual Life in Ancient Greece* at 90 (cited in note 3); Holt
N. Parker, *The Teratogenic Grid*, in *Roman Sexualities* 47–65 (Judith P. Hallett & Marilyn
B. Skinner eds., Princeton 1997); Williams, *Roman Homosexuality* at 4–5, 69–70 (cited in
note 12).

21   See Pliny, *Naturalis Historiæ* xxviii, 4 [7], quoted in Kiefer, *Sexual Life in Ancient Rome*
at 115 (cited in note 20). See Bullough, *Sexual Variance* at 130 (cited in note 3); Williams,
Roman Homosexuality at 86–92 (cited in note 12).

22   See Richard A. Posner, *Sex and Reason* 45 (Harvard 1992); Kiefer, *Sexual Life in
Ancient Rome* at 56–63 (cited in note 20); Boswell, *Christianity, Social Tolerance* at 77 (cited in
note 12); Williams, *Roman Homosexuality* at 38–47 (cited in note 12); Reiss, *Premarital Sexual Standards* at 47 (cited in note 8); Harper, *From Shame to Sin* at 46–47 (cited in note 12).

23   See Boswell, *Christianity, Social Tolerance* at 73–83 (cited in note 12); Parker, *Teratogenic
Grid* at 47–65 (cited in note 20); Williams, *Roman Homosexuality* at 4–8, 18–31, 60–61,
77–78, 96–128, 172–81 (cited in note 12); David M. Friedman, *A Mind of Its Own* 25 (Free
Press 2001); Johnson & Ryan, *Sexuality in Greek and Roman Society* at 8–9 (cited in note 1);
Harper, *From Shame to Sin* at 25, 150–51 (cited in note 12).

24   Paterculus (ii, 1), quoted in Kiefer, *Sexual Life in Ancient Rome* at 42 (cited in note 20).
See Reiss, *Premarital Sexual Standards* at 48–49 (cited in note 8).

25   Quoted in Amy Richlin, *Pliny's Brasserie*, in Hallett & Skinner, *Roman Sexualities* at
210 (cited in note 20); Livy, *Introduction*, quoted in Kiefer, *Sexual Life in Ancient Rome* at 4
(cited in note 20); Sallust, *Cat.* 13, quoted in Kiefer, *Sexual Life in Ancient Rome* at 45 (cited
in note 20); Propertius (ii, 32, 41m ff.), quoted in Kiefer, *Sexual Life in Ancient Rome* at
45 (cited in note 20). See Amy Richlin, *Garden of Priapus* 1–2 (Yale 1984); Harper, *From
Shame to Sin* at 163 (cited in note 12); Bates & Zawadzki, *Criminal Abortion* at 17–18 (cited
in note 10); John T. Noonan Jr., *Contraception: A History of Its Treatment by the Catholic Theologians and Canonists* 13–20, 28–29, 85–86 (Harvard 1965); Tannahill, *Sex in History* at 121,
127–30 (cited in note 2); Himes, *Medical History of Contraception* at 79–96 (cited in note 10);
Williams, *Roman Homosexuality* at 245–52 (cited in note 12); Friedman, *Mind of Its Own* at
31 (cited in note 23).

26   Ovid, *The Art of Love*, part II, elegy 19, quoted in Kiefer, *Sexual Life in Ancient Rome* at
221 (cited in note 20). See Ovid, *Amores* (book III, elegy ii); Ovid, *Amores* (book II, elegy
x); Ovid, *Amores* (book III, elegy vii); Ovid, *Amores* (book II, 683 et seq.).

27   See Boswell, *Christianity, Social Tolerance* at 84–85 (cited in note 12); Williams, *Roman
Homosexuality* at 60–61, 194 (cited in note 12).

28   See Augustine, *De civitate Dei* (vi, 9). See Harper, *From Shame to Sin* at 173 (cited in
note 12).

29   See Karlen, *Sexuality and Homosexuality* at 66 (cited in note 13); Noonan, *Contraception*
at 32, 86 (cited in note 25). Tikva Frymer-Kensky, *Virginity in the Bible*, in *Gender and Law
in the Hebrew Bible and the Ancient Near East* 80 (Victor H. Matthews, Bernard M. Levinson,
& Tikva Frymer-Kensky eds., Sheffield 1998); Bullough, *Sexual Variance* at 78 (cited in
note 3); Jonathan Klawans, *Impurity and Sin in Ancient Judaism* 26–27 (Oxford 2000); Tannahill, *Sex in History* at 74–75 (cited in note 2); Noonan, *Contraception* at 11, 50–52 (cited in
note 25); Roland de Vaux, *Ancient Israel: Its Life and Institutions* 36–37 (Eerdmans 1997).

30 *Proverbs* 5:19 (Hebrew Bible). See Calum M. Carmichael, *The Laws of Deuteronomy* 167 (Cornell 1974); Klawans, *Impurity and Sin* at 26–27 (cited in note 29); de Vaux, *Ancient Israel* at 36–37 (cited in note 29); Bullough, *Sexual Variance* at 76–81 (cited in note 3); Phillip J. King & Lawrence E. Stager, *Life in Biblical Israel* 60 (Westminster 2002); Max Weber, *Ancient Judaism* 191 (Free Press 1952); William E. Phipps, *Was Jesus Married?* 23 (Harper & Row 1970); Noonan, *Contraception* at 32, 86 (cited in note 25); *Leviticus* 20:10; *Exodus* 21:22–23 (both in Hebrew Bible).

31 See Klawans, *Impurity and Sin* (cited in note 29); Tikva Frymer-Kensky, *Pollution, Purification, and Purgation in Biblical Israel*, in *The Word of the Lord Shall Go Forth* 399–410 (Carol L. Meyers & M. O'Connor eds., Eisenbrauns 1983).

32 *Leviticus* 20:13 (King James Version). See also *Leviticus* 18:22, "Thou shalt not lie with mankind, as with womankind: it is abomination" (King James Version).

33 See Daniel A. Helminiak, *What the Bible Really Says about Homosexuality* ch. 4 (Alamo Square 2000); Steven Greenberg, *Wrestling with God and Men: Homosexuality in the Jewish Tradition* 82 (Wisconsin 2004); Bullough, *Sexual Variance* at 75, 85, 181 (cited in note 3); Derrick Sherwin Bailey, *Homosexuality and the Western Christian Tradition* 43–45 (Longmans Green 1955); Boswell, *Christianity, Social Tolerance* at 97–101 (cited in note 12); King & Stager, *Life in Biblical Israel* at 59 (cited in note 30). For an analysis of the differences among the many Old Testament rules dealing with diet, rituals, sexuality, and so on, see generally Klawans, *Impurity and Sin* (cited in note 29); Mary Douglas, *Leviticus as Literature* 238–39 (Oxford 2001).

34 *Genesis* 38:8–10 (Hebrew Bible).

35 Although Talmudic scholars occasionally interpreted the story of Onan in terms of coitus interruptus, this was not the prevailing view, and the practice was commonly used as a means of contraception in biblical times, along with vaginal cups, occlusive pessaries, postcoital ejection, and a wide variety of potions. See King & Stager, *Life in Biblical Israel* at 56–57 (cited in note 30); Noonan, *Contraception* at 10–12, 34–36 (cited in note 25); Tannahill, *Sex in History* at 74–75 (cited in note 2); de Vaux, *Ancient Israel* at 37–38 (cited in note 29); Bullough, *Sexual Variance* at 78 (cited in note 3); David M. Feldman, *Birth Control in Jewish Law* ch. 8 (NYU 1968); Linda Gordon, *Woman's Body, Woman's Right* 5 (Grossman 1976); Phipps, *Was Jesus Married?* at 25 (cited in note 30).

36 *Genesis* 13:13; 18–19 (King James Version).

37 See Helminiak, *What the Bible Really Says* at 45 (cited in note 33); Greenberg, *Wrestling with God and Men* at 64–69 (cited in note 33).

38 *Judges* ch. 19–20 (King James Version).

39 de Vaux, *Ancient Israel* at 10 (cited in note 29).

40 See *Ezekiel* 16: 49–50 (King James Version).

41 *Matthew* 10:14–15 (King James Version). See *Deuteronomy* 29:23, 32:32; *Ezekiel* 16:46–48, 51–56; *Isaiah* 3:8–9, 13, 19; *Jeremiah* 23:14, 49; *Luke* 17:26–29; 2 *Peter* 2:6–8; *Jude* 1:4, 7, 8. *Lamentations* 4:6; *Amos* 4:11; *Romans* 9:29; 2 *Peter* 2:6; *Jude* 7. See Mark D. Jordan, *The Invention of Sodomy in Christian Theology* 32 (Chicago 1997); Boswell, *Christianity, Social Tolerance* at 93 (cited in note 12); Bullough, *Sexual Variance* at 83 (cited in note 3). Two passages in the New Testament associated Sodom with sexual sins, but neither mentions homosexuality. See 2 *Peter* 2:10; *Jude* 7–8.

42   *Homilia V in Genesim* (PG 12:188–89), quoted in Greenberg, *Wrestling with God and Men* at 67 (cited in note 33).

43   *Judges* 19:22 ff. (King James Version). See Boswell, *Christianity, Social Tolerance* at 92–98, 113–14 (cited in note 12); Bailey, *Homosexuality and the Western Christian Tradition* at 2–6 (cited in note 33); Greenberg, *Wrestling with God and Men* at 64–73 (cited in note 33); de Vaux, *Ancient Israel* at 10 (cited in note 29).

44   See Bullough, *Sexual Variance* at 159–60 (cited in note 3); J. N. D. Kelly, *Early Christian Doctrines* 11–13 (Harper Collins 1978); Kiefer, *Sexual Life in Ancient Rome* at 108 (cited in note 20).

45   *Matthew* 5:28 (King James Version). See also *Matthew* 19:9; *Matthew* 5:32; *Mark* 10:11–12. See Bullough, *Sexual Variance* at 175–76 (cited in note 3).

46   *Matthew* 19:10–12 (King James Version).

47   See Bullough, *Sexual Variance* at 179 (cited in note 3); Derrick Sherwin Bailey, *Sexual Relation in Christian Thought* 72 n.11 (Harper 1959); Karlen, *Sexuality and Homosexuality* at 70 (cited in note 13); Boswell, *Christianity, Social Tolerance* at 114–15 (cited in note 12); Phipps, *Was Jesus Married?* at 72–73 (cited in note 30).

48   *Romans* 1:26 (King James Version).

49   *Romans* 1:26–28 (King James Version).

50   1 *Corinthians* 6:9–10 (King James Version). See 1 *Corinthians* 7:1–9.

51   1 *Corinthians* 7:6; 1 *Corinthians* 7:29–30 (both King James Version). See Bailey, *Sexual Relation in Christian Thought* at 13 (cited in note 47); Bullough, *Sexual Variance* at 178–81 (cited in note 3); Henry Chadwick, *The Early Church* 19–20 (Penguin 1993); Boswell, *Christianity, Social Tolerance* at 115 (cited in note 12); Phipps, *Was Jesus Married?* at 114–17 (cited in note 30).

52   See Kelly, *Early Christian Doctrines* at 5–6 (cited in note 44); Chadwick, *Early Church* at 19–20 (cited in note 51).

53   See Elaine Pagels, *The Gnostic Gospels* (Vintage Books ed. 1989).

54   Bullough, *Sexual Variance* at 166–67 (cited in note 3). See Martha C. Nussbaum, *The Incomplete Feminism of Musonius Rufus: Platonist, Stoic, and Roman*, in *Sleep of Reason: Erotic Experience and Sexual Ethics in Ancient Greece and Rome* 283–326 (Martha C. Nussbaum & Juha Sihvola eds., Chicago 2002); Lucretius, *De Rerum natura*, IV, 1052–1120, quoted in Bullough, *Sexual Variance* at 166 (cited in note 3).

55   See Kelly *Early Christian Doctrines* at 15–27 (cited in note 44); Chadwick, *Early Church* at 34–37, 70–78, 97–101, 285–86 (cited in note 51); Bullough, *Sexual Variance* at 150–51, 182–92 (cited in note 3); Noonan, *Contraception* at 46 (cited in note 25); Phipps, *Was Jesus Married?* at 128–33 (cited in note 30); Bailey, *Sexual Relation in Christian Thought* at 36–37 (cited in note 47); Harper, *From Shame to Sin* at 103, 109–12 (cited in note 12).

56   Augustine, *Confessions* 2.1–2, quoted in Karlen, *Sexuality and Homosexuality* at 73 (cited in note 13).

57   See Noonan, *Contraception* at 107–12 (cited in note 25); Bullough, *Sexual Variance* at 190–92 (cited in note 3); Kelly, *Early Christian Doctrines* at 13–14 (cited in note 44); Boswell, *Christianity, Social Tolerance* at 128–29 (cited in note 12).

58   Augustine, *Confessions* VIII, vii. See Bullough, *Sexual Variance* at 193 (cited in note 3);

Phipps, *Was Jesus Married?* at 167–69 (cited in note 30); Bailey, *Sexual Relation in Christian Thought* at 49–53 (cited in note 47); James J. O'Donnell, *Augustine: A New Biography* 44–45, 49, 69–74 (Harper Perennial 2005); Robin Lane Fox, *Augustine: Conversions to Confessions* 62–64 (Basic Books 2015).

59   See Kelly, *Early Christian Doctrines* at 15–22 (cited in note 44); Bullough, *Sexual Variance* at 150–51 (cited in note 3); Fox, *Augustine* at 225–40 (cited in note 58).

60   Augustine, *Confessions* VIII, vii. See Augustine, *Soliloquies* 1.10; Noonan, *Contraception* at 122 (cited in note 25).

61   Augustine was not the first to make this leap. Philo, a Jew born in Alexandria near the end of the first century B.C., linked Stoicism with Judaism. He argued that the fall of Adam and Eve had been the result of sexual desire, and that this was the Stoics' Original Sin. See Bullough, *Sexual Variance* at 160–70 (cited in note 3); Kelly, *Early Christian Doctrines* at 15–19 (cited in note 44); Chadwick, *Early Church* at 56 (cited in note 51).

62   See Augustine, *City of God* XIV, 17, 19; Bailey, *Sexual Relation in Christian Thought* at 54 (cited in note 47); Augustine, *c. duas epist. Pelag* I 34 17; Augustine, *De nupt. Et concup.* II 8, 12–13, 22; Augustine, *de civ. Dei* XIII 13, XIV 17; Augustine, *de pecc. Merit. Et remiss.* II 36 22; Augustine, *c. duas epist. Pelag.* I 31; Tannahill, *Sex in History* at 141–42 (cited in note 2); Bullough, *Sexual Variance* at 193–94 (cited in note 3); Noonan, *Contraception* at 131–39 (cited in note 25); Glanville Williams, *The Sanctity of Life and the Criminal Law* 51–57 (Knopf 1957); Fox, *Augustine* at 401–5 (cited in note 58); Kelly, *Early Christian Doctrines* at 354–55, 364 (cited in note 44); Phipps, *Was Jesus Married?* at 171–72 (cited in note 30); Harper, *From Shame to Sin* at 99 (cited in note 12).

63   See Merry E. Wiesner-Hanks, *Christianity and Sexuality in the Early Modern World* 31–32 (Routledge 2010); Doron S. Ben-Atar & Richard D. Brown, *Taming Lust: Crimes Against Nature in the Early Republic* 14 (Pennsylvania 2014).

64   Augustine, *Against Faustus* 22.30, quoted in Noonan, *Contraception* at 121 (cited in note 25). See Augustine, *De nuptiis et concupiscentia* I, 17 (xv); Bullough, *Sexual Variance* at 193–94 (cited in note 3); Tannahill, *Sex in History* at 142–43 (cited in note 2); Noonan, *Contraception* at 119–39 (cited in note 25); Gordon, *Woman's Body* at 6–7 (cited in note 35); Kelly, *Early Christian Doctrines* at 363–69 (cited in note 44); Boswell, *Christianity, Social Tolerance* at 165 (cited in note 12); Reiss, *Premarital Sexual Standards* at 50 (cited in note 8); Karlen, *Sexuality and Homosexuality* at 75–76 (cited in note 13); Phipps, *Was Jesus Married?* at 172–73 (cited in note 30); Bailey, *Sexual Relation in Christian Thought* at 49–59 (cited in note 47).

65   Augustine, *De perfect. iustit. hom.* 9; Augustine, *Enarr. in ps.* 89, 4.

66   Pelagius, *De vita christ.* 6 (PL 40, 1037). See Chadwick, *Early Church* at 227–28 (cited in note 51); Kelly, *Early Christian Doctrines* at 361 (cited in note 44).

67   Chadwick, *Early Church* at 232–33 (cited in note 51). See Kelly, *Early Christian Doctrines* at 361 (cited in note 44).

68   See Augustine, *De peccatorum meritis et remissione libri*; Augustine, *De spiritu et litera*; Augustine, *De perfectione justitiae hominis*; Augustine, *De natura et gratia*; Augustine, *De gestis Pelagii*.

69   See Kelly, *Early Christian Doctrines* at 361–70 (cited in note 44); Chadwick, *Early*

Church at 227–32 (cited in note 51); O'Donnell, *Augustine: A New Biography* at 253, 264 (cited in note 58).

70 Tannahill, *Sex in History* at 136 (cited in note 2). See Chadwick, *Early Church* at 120–28, 152–53, 166, 287–88 (cited in note 51); Kelly, *Early Christian Doctrines* at 5 (cited in note 44); Karlen, *Sexuality and Homosexuality* at 67 (cited in note 13); Boswell, *Christianity, Social Tolerance* at 119–21 (cited in note 12).

71 See Chadwick, *Early Church* at 120–28, 152–53, 166, 287–88 (cited in note 51); Kelly, *Early Christian Doctrines* at 5 (cited in note 44); Karlen, *Sexuality and Homosexuality* at 67–68 (cited in note 13); Tannahill, *Sex in History* at 136 (cited in note 2).

72 Kiefer, *Sexual Life in Ancient Rome* at 349–55 (cited in note 20); Karlen, *Sexuality and Homosexuality* at 68 (cited in note 13); Boswell, *Christianity, Social Tolerance* at 119–20 (cited in note 12).

73 See Kelly, *Early Christian Doctrines* at 371–74 (cited in note 44); Tannahill, *Sex in History* at 160–61 (cited in note 2).

CHAPTER 2

1 See Henry Chadwick, *The Early Church* 288 (Penguin 1993); Reay Tannahill, *Sex in History* 137–38 (Scarborough House 1992); Ruth Mazo Karras, *Sexuality in Medieval Europe: Doing Unto Others* 20 (Routledge 2005); John Boswell, *Christianity, Social Tolerance, and Homosexuality* 169–70 (Chicago 1980); Arno Karlen, *Sexuality and Homosexuality: A New View* 85–90 (Norton 1971).

2 Chadwick, *Early Church* at 177 (cited in note 1); Merry E. Wiesner-Hanks, *Christianity and Sexuality in the Early Modern World* 35 (Routledge 2000).

3 See Dyan Elliott, *Fallen Bodies: Pollution, Sexuality, & Demonology in the Middle Ages* 14–16, 30–31 (Pennsylvania 1999); Michael Goodich, *The Unmentionable Vice: Homosexuality in the Later Medieval Period* 64–66 (ABC-Clio 1979).

4 St Basil, *De renuntiatione saeculi*, quoted in Vern L. Bullough, *Sexual Variance in Society and History* 195 (Chicago 1976).

5 See Chadwick, *Early Church* at 175–80 (cited in note 1); Boswell, *Christianity, Social Tolerance* at 156–60, 172–77, 187–91 (cited in note 1); Bullough, *Sexual Variance* at 195 (cited in note 4); Ira L. Reiss, *Premarital Sexual Standards in America* 50–51 (Free Press 1960); Tannahill, *Sex in History* at 156–57 (cited in note 1); Goodich, *Unmentionable Vice* at 46 (cited in note 3); Judith C. Brown, *Immodest Acts: The Life of a Lesbian Nun in Renaissance Italy* 8 (Oxford 1986).

6 Tannahill, *Sex in History* at 143 (cited in note 1).

7 See Goodich, *Unmentionable Vice* at 23–25 (cited in note 3); Reiss, *Premarital Sexual Standards* at 50–51 (cited in note 5); Bullough, *Sexual Variance* at 189–92 (cited in note 4); Tannahill, *Sex in History* at 143–47 (cited in note 1); James A. Brundage, *Sin, Crime, and the Pleasures of the Flesh: The Medieval Church Judges Sexual Offences*, in *The Medieval World* 294–300 (Peter Linehan & Janet L. Nelson eds., Routledge 2001); Elliott, *Fallen Bodies* at 82–106 (cited in note 3); Derrick Sherwin Bailey, *Sexual Relation in Christian Thought* 30–33, 148–51 (Literary 2011); Karras, *Sexuality in Medieval Europe* at 42–45 (cited in note

1); Margaret McGlynn & Richard J. Moll, *Chaste Marriage in the Middle Ages*, in *Handbook of Medieval Sexuality* 105–7 (Vern L. Bullough & James A. Brundage eds., Garland 1996).

8   Barbara W. Tuchman, *A Distant Mirror: The Calamitous Fourteenth Century* 30–31 (Ballantine Books 1978). See Tannahill, *Sex in History* at 145 (cited in note 1); Karras, *Sexuality in Medieval Europe* at 44, 100–101 (cited in note 1); Goodich, *Unmentionable Vice* at 43 (cited in note 3); Brundage, *Sin, Crime* at 299–300 (cited in note 7).

9   Jeffrey Richards, *Sex, Dissidence and Damnation* 140–41 (Routledge 1994). See Boswell, *Christianity, Social Tolerance* at 187–91 (cited in note 1); Mary McLaughlin, *Survivors and Surrogates: Children and Parents from the Ninth to the Tenth Centuries*, in *The History of Childhood* 130–31 (Lloyd deMause ed., New York 1974); Karlen, *Sexuality and Homosexuality* at 86 (cited in note 1); Karras, *Sexuality in Medieval Europe* at 135–36 (cited in note 1); Mark D. Jordan, *The Invention of Sodomy in Christian Theology* 45–47, 50 (Chicago 1997).

10   See Boswell, *Christianity, Social Tolerance* at 182, 210–11 (cited in note 1); Tannahill, *Sex in History* at 156–60 (cited in note 1); Goodich, *Unmentionable Vice* at 18–19, 28–31, 44–46 (cited in note 3); Bailey, *Sexual Relation in Christian Thought* at 152–53 (cited in note 7); Warren Johansson & William A. Percy, *Homosexuality*, in Bullough & Brundage, *Handbook of Medieval Sexuality* at 168–69 (cited in note 7); Brundage, *Sin, Crime* at 299–300 (cited in note 7); Christopher Kleinhenz, *Texts, Naked and Thinly Veiled: Erotic Elements in Medieval Italian Literature*, in *Sex in the Middle Ages: A Book of Essays* 102 (Joyce E. Salisbury ed., Garland 1991); Richards, *Sex, Dissidence* at 138–43 (cited in note 9).

11   See Bullough & Brundage, *Handbook of Medieval Sexuality* at ix–xv (cited in note 7); Karras, *Sexuality in Medieval Europe* at 5–9, 17–22 (cited in note 1).

12   Karras, *Sexuality in Medieval Europe* at 22 (cited in note 1). See James A. Brundage, *Sex and the Canon Law* in Bullough & Brundage, *Handbook of Medieval Sexuality* at 42 (cited in note 7).

13   Synod of Angers (c. 1217), quoted in Pierre J. Payer, *Sex and Confession in the Thirteenth Century*, in Salisbury, *Sex in the Middle Ages* at 130 (cited in note 10).

14   Paul of Hungary, *De Confessione* 210b, quoted in Payer, *Sex and Confession*, in Salisbury, *Sex in the Middle Ages* at 135 (cited in note 13).

15   Tuchman, *Distant Mirror* at 34 (cited in note 8).

16   See Jordan, *Invention of Sodomy in Christian Theology* at 104 (cited in note 9); John J. Noonan Jr., *Contraception: A History of Its Treatment by the Catholic Theologians and Canonists* 154–55 (Harvard 1965); Pierre J. Payer, *Confession and the Study of Sex in the Middle Ages*, in Bullough & Brundage, *Handbook of Medieval Sexuality* at 4 (cited in note 7); Boswell, *Christianity, Social Tolerance* at 182 (cited in note 1); Karlen, *Sexuality and Homosexuality* at 80–81 (cited in note 1); *Penitential of Cummean*; Payer, *Sex and Confession* at 128–29 (cited in note 13); Vern L. Bullough, *The Sin Against Nature and Homosexuality*, in *Sexual Practices and the Medieval Church* 60–61 (Vern L. Bullough & James A Brundage eds., Prometheus 1982); Jordan, *Invention of Sodomy in Christian Theology* at 45–51 (cited in note 9); Brundage, *Sin, Crime* at 305 (cited in note 7); Goodich, *Unmentionable Vice* at 25–31, 51–52 (cited in note 3).

17   Elliott, *Fallen Bodies* at 22 (cited in note 3). See Payer, *Sex and Confession* at 127 (cited in note 13); Elliott, *Fallen Bodies* at 22–23 (cited in note 3); Jordan, *Invention of Sodomy in*

Christian Theology at 92–93, 106–7, 109, 111 (cited in note 9); Noonan, *Contraception* at 258–60, 268–74 (cited in note 16).

18 Quoted in Jordan, *Invention of Sodomy in Christian Theology* at 111 (cited in note 9).

19 See Tannahill, *Sex in History* at 152 (cited in note 1); Karras, *Sexuality in Medieval Europe* at 123 (cited in note 1); Brundage, *Sin, Crime* at 294 (cited in note 7); Joyce E. Salisbury, *Bestiality in the Middle Ages*, in Salisbury, *Sex in the Middle Ages* at 182 (cited in note 10); Brundage, *Sex and the Canon Law* at 41 (cited in note 12); Doron S. Ben-Atar & Richard D. Brown, *Taming Lust: Crimes Against Nature in the Early Republic* 16–17 (Pennsylvania 2014).

20 Quoted in Karlen, *Sexuality and Homosexuality* at 80 (cited in note 1).

21 Jerome, *Against Jovinianus* 367, quoted in Joyce E. Salisbury, *Church Fathers, Independent Virgins* 23 (Verso 1991).

22 Elliott, *Fallen Bodies* at 36–37 (cited in note 3).

23 See Elliot, *Fallen Bodies* at 45–47 (cited in note 3). See Joyce E. Salisbury, *Gendered Sexuality*, in Bullough & Brundage, *Handbook of Medieval Sexuality* at 85–87 (cited in note 7); Geoffrey May, *Social Control of Sex Expression* 53–54 (New York 1931); Salisbury, *Church Fathers* at 21, 26 (cited in note 21).

24 See Karras, *Sexuality in Medieval Europe* at 120 (cited in note 1).

25 See James A. Brundage, *Adultery and Fornication*, in Bullough & Brundage, *Sexual Practices* at 130–31 (cited in note 16); Payer, *Confession and the Study of Sex* at 13 (cited in note 16); Brundage, *Sin, Crime* at 298 (cited in note 7).

26 Quoted in Payer, *Sex and Confession* at 130 (cited in note 13).

27 Saint Gregory the Great, *Pastoral Rule* 3.27, PL, 77:102, quoted in Noonan, *Contraception* at 150 (cited in note 16).

28 Huguccio, *Summa* 2.32.2.1, quoted in Noonan, *Contraception* at 197 (cited in note 16). See Wiesner-Hanks, *Christianity and Sexuality* at 37 (cited in note 2).

29 Saint Thomas Aquinas, *On the Sentences* 4.31.2.1, 4.31.1.1, quoted in Noonan, *Contraception* at 293–94 (cited in note 16).

30 Quoted in Jane Tibbetts Schulenburg, *Saints and Sex*, in Salisbury, *Sex in the Middle Ages* at 225 (cited in note 10). See Brundage, *Sex and the Canon Law* at 35–40 (cited in note 12); Karras, *Sexuality in Medieval Europe* at 59, 73 (cited in note 1); Brundage, *Sin, Crime* 294 (cited in note 7); Albert the Great, *Animals* 10.2; Albert the Great, *On the Sentences* 4.31.24; Noonan, *Contraception* at 238–39 (cited in note 16); James A. Brundage, *Law, Sex, and Christian Society in Medieval Europe* 452 (Chicago 1987); Tannahill, *Sex in History* at 152, 158–59 (cited in note 1); Noonan, *Contraception* at 163, 193–99, 238–39, 292–95 (cited in note 16); Payer, *Sex and Confession* at 130–31 (cited in note 13).

31 Bernardine, *The Eternal Gospel* 15.2.1, quoted in Noonan, *Contraception* at 237 (cited in note 16). See Helen Rodnite Lemay, *Human Sexuality in Twelfth through Fifteenth-Century Scientific Writings*, in Bullough & Brundage, *Sexual Practices* at 200 (cited in note 16); Tannahill, *Sex in History* at 152 (cited in note 1); Noonan, *Contraception* at 100–101, 143–44, 162–68, 178, 200–236, 258 (cited in note 16); Karras, *Sexuality in Medieval Europe* at 72–74 (cited in note 1); Linda Gordon, *Woman's Body, Woman's Right* 6–7 (Grossman 1976); John

M. Riddle, *Contraception and Early Abortion in the Middle Ages*, in Bullough & Brundage, *Handbook of Medieval Sexuality* at 261–68 (cited in note 7).

32 See Lemay, *Human Sexuality* at 200 (cited in note 31). A late medieval law in England made it unlawful for any person to assist a woman in committing a late-term abortion, but abortion itself was not unlawful. See Tannahill, *Sex in History* at 152 (cited in note 1); Riddle, *Contraception and Early Abortion* at 264–73 (cited in note 31); Noonan, *Contraception* at 162–67 (cited in note 16).

33 *Romans* 1:24–27 (King James Version).

34 Justinian, *Novella* 77 1–2, quoted in Tannahill, *Sex in History* at 156 (cited in note 1). See Tannahill, *Sex in History* at 155–56 (cited in note 1); Boswell, *Christianity, Social Tolerance* at 171 (cited in note 1); Derrick Sherwin Bailey, *Homosexuality and the Western Christian Tradition* 73–79 (London 1955); Bullough, *Sin Against Nature* at 58 (cited in note 16); Karlen, *Sexuality and Homosexuality* at 77–78 (cited in note 1); Goodich, *Unmentionable Vice* at 75–76 (cited in note 3).

35 See Boswell, *Christianity, Social Tolerance* at 183–84, 194–97, 202–4 (cited in note 1); Goodich, *Unmentionable Vice* at 3–4 (cited in note 3).

36 Similarly, the seventh-century Cummean penitential set forth its penances without regard to whether the acts were committed heterosexually or homosexually. See Boswell, *Christianity, Social Tolerance* at 179–80, 198–205 (cited in note 1); Tannahill, *Sex in History* at 158–59 (cited in note 1); Bailey, *Homosexuality and the Western Christian Tradition* at 100–110 (cited in note 34).

37 Quoted in Jordan, *Invention of Sodomy in Christian Theology* at 49 (cited in note 9). See Goodich, *Unmentionable Vice* at 29–31, 51–52 (cited in note 3); Jordan, *Invention of Sodomy in Christian Theology* at 29, 43–48, 55, 57 (cited in note 9); Bullough, *Sin Against Nature* at 62 (cited in note 16).

38 Bullough, *Sin Against Nature* at 62 (cited in note 16). See Brundage, *Sex and the Canon Law* at 40–41 (cited in note 12); Goodich, *Unmentionable Vice* at 32–33, 43 (cited in note 3).

39 Paul of Hungary, *Summa* 207b, 208b–209a, quoted in Jordan, *Invention of Sodomy in Christian Theology* at 97, 100–101 (cited in note 9). See Jordan, *Invention of Sodomy in Christian Theology* at 93–101 (cited in note 9); Goodich, *Unmentionable Vice* at 60–61 (cited in note 3).

40 Karlen, *Sexuality and Homosexuality* at 76–77 (cited in note 1); Tannahill, *Sex in History* at 159–60 (cited in note 1); Jordan, *Invention of Sodomy in Christian Theology* at 138–40 (cited in note 9); Goodich, *Unmentionable Vice* at 35–36, 59–61 (cited in note 3).

41 See Thomas Aquinas, *Summa Theologica* 154.12; Jordan, *Invention of Sodomy in Christian Theology* at 143–45 (cited in note 9); Bailey, *Sexual Relation in Christian Thought* at 159–61 (cited in note 7); Karlen, *Sexuality and Homosexuality* at 76–77 (cited in note 1); Bullough, *Sin Against Nature* at 65 (cited in note 16); Goodich, *Unmentionable Vice* at 62–63 (cited in note 3); Noonan, *Contraception* at 226–27 (cited in note 16). Bestiality was sometimes treated quite leniently, but in some times and places it was dealt with harshly. In England, men were burned at the stake "with such paramours as dogs, goats, cows, pigs, and geese." Karlen, *Sexuality and Homosexuality* at 88 (cited in note 1). See Salisbury, *Besti-*

ality in the Middle Ages 181–82 (cited in note 19); Noonan, *Contraception* at 239–46 (cited in note 16).

42 Karlen, *Sexuality and Homosexuality* at 77 (cited in note 1). See Jordan, *Invention of Sodomy in Christian Theology* at 136–37 (cited in note 9); Boswell, *Christianity, Social Tolerance* at 303–34 (cited in note 1).

43 Goodich, *Unmentionable Vice* at 21 (cited in note 3). See Vern L. Bullough, *Heresy, Witchcraft, and Sexuality*, 1 J. of Homosexuality 94 (1976).

44 See Johansson & Percy, *Homosexuality* at 175 (cited in note 10); Karras, *Sexuality in Medieval Europe* at 136–42 (cited in note 1); Bullough, *Sin Against Nature* at 70 (cited in note 16); Karlen, *Sexuality and Homosexuality* at 85–89, 93–96 (cited in note 1); Goodich, *Unmentionable Vice* at 7–15, 77–88, 123 (cited in note 3).

45 Quoted in Boswell, *Christianity, Social Tolerance* at 288 (cited in note 1) (quoting *Fuero Real* [promulgated by Alfonso X] 4.9.2, in *Los codigos espanoles* [Madrid, 1847], 1:409).

46 Goodich, *Unmentionable Vice* at 7 (cited in note 3).

47 See Bullough, *Heresy, Witchcraft, and Sexuality* at 76–77 (cited in note 43); Karlen, *Sexuality and Homosexuality* at 93–94 (cited in note 1); Goodich, *Unmentionable Vice* at 9–12, 75–79 (cited in note 3); Boswell, *Christianity, Social Tolerance* at 269–302 (cited in note 1).

48 See Brown, *Immodest Acts* at 6, 9, 19 (cited in note 5).

49 Quoted in Brown, *Immodest Acts* at 11 (cited in note 5). See Karras, *Sexuality in Medieval Europe* at 110–11 (cited in note 1); Brown, *Immodest Acts* at 9–17 (cited in note 5).

50 Quoted in Brown, *Immodest Acts* at 7 (cited in note 5). See Karras, *Sexuality in Medieval Europe* at 53–54, 109–11 (cited in note 1).

51 See Helmut Puff, *Female Sodomy: The Trial of Katherina Hetzeldorfer (1477)*, 30 J. Medieval and Early Modern Studies 30, 57–61 (2000); Karras, *Sexuality in Medieval Europe* at 110–11 (cited in note 1); Brown, *Immodest Acts* at 9 (cited in note 5).

52 *Exodus* 22:18 (King James Version); Karlen, *Sexuality and Homosexuality* at 96–98 (cited in note 1). See Bullough, *Heresy, Witchcraft, and Sexuality* at 87–90 (cited in note 43).

53 Brundage, *Sex and the Canon Law* at 42 (cited in note 12).

54 See Karras, *Sexuality in Medieval Europe* at 20 (cited in note 1); Goodich, *Unmentionable Vice* at xiii–xiv, 67–68 (cited in note 3); Richards, *Sex, Dissidence* at 36–40 (cited in note 9); Brundage, *Sex and the Canon Law* at 42 (cited in note 12); Brundage, *Law, Sex, and Christian Society* at 436–37 (cited in note 30).

55 Quoted in Bailey, *Sexual Relation in Christian Thought* at 166 (cited in note 7).

56 Quoted in 15 *Encyclopædia Britannica* 661 (15th ed. 1978).

57 Patrick Collinson, *The Reformation* 17 (Modern Library 2006).

58 Martin Luther, *Lectures on Titus*, in Martin Luther, 29 *Luther's Works* 18 (Jaroslav Pelikan & Helmut Lehmann eds., Muhlenberg and Concordia 1955–1967).

59 Martin Luther, *Lectures on Romans*, in 15 *Library of Christian Classics* 32 (William Pauck ed., Westminster 1961); Martin Luther, *Letters of Spiritual Counsel*, in 18 *Library of Christian Classics* 273–74 (Theodore G. Tappert ed., Westminster 1955); Tannahill, *Sex in History* at 327 (cited in note 1). See Martin Luther, *Letter to Wolfgang Reissenbusch*, in Martin Luther, *Letters of Spiritual Counsel* 274 (T. G. Tappert ed. and trans., London 1955);

Wiesner-Hanks, *Christianity and Sexuality* at 60–63 (cited in note 2); Bailey, *Sexual Relation in Christian Thought* at 169 (cited in note 7).

60 Jeremy Taylor, *Holy Living* ii 3, in III *Works of Jeremy Taylor* 62–64 (London 1847–1856), quoted in Tannahill, *Sex in History* at 328 (cited in note 1).

61 Jeremy Taylor, *Ductor Dubitantium* I v 8 par 17, in IX *Works* 246–47 (London 1847–1856), quoted in Tannahill, *Sex in History* at 328 (cited in note 1); Martin Luther, *Letter to Nicholas Gerbel*, in 48 *Luther's Works* 321–22 (cited in note 58).

62 Noonan, *Contraception* at 383 (cited in note 16). See Gordon, *Woman's Body* at 15–16 (cited in note 31).

63 Quoted in Guido Ruggiero, *The Boundaries of Eros* 109, 117–19 (Oxford 1989). See William Naphy, *Sex Crimes: From Renaissance to Enlightenment* 141 (Tempus 2004); Karlen, *Sexuality and Homosexuality* at 120–21 (cited in note 1).

64 Kenneth Borris, *Same-Sex Desire in the English Renaissance* 20, 23, 58–59 (Routledge 2015). See Karlen, *Sexuality and Homosexuality* at 120–21 (cited in note 1).

65 Quoted in Collinson, *Reformation* at 61 (cited in note 57); John Bale, *The Acts of English Votaries* (London 1560), quoted in Borris, *Same-Sex Desire* at 25 (cited in note 64). See David F. Greenberg, *The Construction of Homosexuality* 283–92 (Chicago 1988); Brown, *Immodest Acts* at 19–20 (cited in note 5); Goodich, *Unmentionable Vice* at 87 (cited in note 3); Vern L. Bullough, *Sex, Society, and History* 74 (Watson 1976); Boswell, *Christianity, Social Tolerance* at 283–86 (cited in note 1); Borris, *Same-Sex Desire* at 72 (cited in note 64).

66 Luther, *Letters of Spiritual Counsel* at 293 (cited in note 59). See W. D. J. Cargill Thompson, *The Political Thought of Martin Luther* 120, 131–35 (Barnes & Noble 1984); Bernhard Lohse, *Martin Luther: An Introduction to His Life and Work* 186–93 (Fortress 1986); Gerhard Ebeling, *Luther: An Introduction to His Thought* 177–91 (Collins 1970); Harold J. Berman, *Law and Revolution II* 40–45 (Harvard 2003); Thomas Wilson, *A Commentary upon the Most Divine Epistle of St. Paul to the Romans* 93 (London 1614), quoted in Borris, *Same-Sex Desire* at 28 (cited in note 64).

CHAPTER 3

1 See Patrick Collinson, *The Reformation* (Modern Library 2006); Norman Hampson, *The Enlightenment* (Penguin 1991); Peter Gay, *The Enlightenment* 265 (Norton 1966); Ernst Cassirer, *The Philosophy of the Enlightenment* (Princeton University 1968); Doron S. Ben-Atar & Richard D. Brown, *Taming Lust: Crimes Against Nature in the Early Republic* 76 (Pennsylvania 2014).

2 Lawrence Stone, *The Family, Sex and Marriage in England, 1500–1800* 139 (Harper & Row 1977).

3 Stone, *Family, Sex and Marriage* at 135 (cited in note 2); Diarmaid MacCulloch, *Thomas Cranmer* 421 (Yale 1996). See John Milton, *The Doctrine and Discipline of Divorce*, in John Milton, III *The Complete Prose Works of John Milton* 394, 510 (New York 1931); Thomas Wilson, *A Commentary upon the Most Divine Epistle of St. Paul to the Romans* 93 (London 1614), quoted in *Same-Sex Desire in the English Renaissance* 28 (Kenneth Borris, *Same Sex Desire* at ed., Routledge 2004); *A Homily Against Disobedience and Wilful Rebellion* (1570), quoted in Borris, *Same-Sex Desire* at 31 (cited in this note); *A Sermon Against Whoredom and Uncleanness* (1623), quoted in *Sexuality and Gender in the English Renaissance* 5–12 (Lloyd Davis ed., Garland 1998); Collinson, *Reformation* at 130 (cited in note 1).

4 Quoted in Stuart Banner, *When Christianity Was Part of the Common Law*, 16 Law and History Review 27, 30 (1998); quoted in G. R. Quaife, *Wanton Wenches and Wayward Wives* 61 (Rutgers 1979). See A. D. Harvey, *Sex in Georgian England* 84–85 (St. Martins 1994); Stone, *Family, Sex and Marriage* at 519 (cited in note 2); Merry E. Wiesner-Hanks, *Christianity and Sexuality in the Early Modern World* 81–82 (Routledge 2010); William Naphy, *Sex Crimes: From Renaissance to Enlightenment* 22 (Tempus 2004); Quaife, *Wanton Wenches and Wayward Wives* at 225 (cited in this note); Richard Adair, *Courtship, Illegitimacy, and Marriage in Early Modern England* 13–38, 89, 131 (Manchester 1996); Randolph Trumbach, *Sex and the Gender Revolution* 231 (Chicago 1998).

5 William Lambarde, *The Duties of Constables, Borsholders, Tithing Men, and Such Other Low Ministers of the Peace* 18 (London 1583), quoted in Gregory Durston, *Crime and Justice in Early Modern England: 1500–1750* 175 (Barry Rose 2004). See Durston, *Crime and Justice* at 174–76 (cited in this note); Morris Ploscowe, *Sex and the Law* 140–43 (New York Prentice-Hall 1951); Quaife, *Wanton Wenches and Wayward Wives* at 192, 197–98 (cited in note 4).

6 See 25 Henry VIII, ch. 6 (1533). See Isabel Drummond, *The Sex Paradox* 19 (G. P. Putnam's Sons 1953); Durston, *Crime and Justice* at 176 77 (cited in note 5); Ploscowe, *Sex and the Law* at 140–43, 198 (cited in note 5); Quaife, *Wanton Wenches and Wayward Wives* at 197–98 (cited in note 4); Vern L. Bullough, *Sexual Variance in Society and History* 461–66 (Chicago 1976); Stone, *Family, Sex and Marriage* at 627 (cited in note 2); 25 Henry VIII, ch. 6 (1533).

7 Stone, *Family, Sex and Marriage* at 530–33 (cited in note 2). See Roger Thompson, *Unfit for Modest Ears* 210 (Rowman & Littlefield 1979); Caroline Bingham, *Seventeenth-Century Attitudes towards Deviant Sex*, 1 J. Interdisciplinary Hist. 447, 466–69 (1971); Terry Castle, *The Culture of Travesty: Sexuality and Masquerade in Eighteenth-Century England*, in *Sexual Underworlds of the Enlightenment* 158–71 (G. S. Rousseau & Roy Porter eds., UNC Press 1988); Norman St. John-Stevas, *Obscenity and the Law* 15 (Secker & Warburg 1956).

8 David M. Vieth ed., *The Complete Poems of John Wilmot Earl of Rochester* xvii, 54–59 (Yale 1962); Trumbach, *Sex and the Gender Revolution* at 73–74 (cited in note 4).

9 Trumbach, *Sex and the Gender Revolution* at 72 (cited in note 4). See Naphy, *Sex Crimes* at 62–63, 79–80 (cited in note 4); Harvey, *Sex in Georgian England* at 90, 98–101 (cited in note 4); Julie Peakman, *Lascivious Bodies: A Sexual History of the Eighteenth Century* 17–19 (Atlantic Books 2004); Frank McLynn, *Crime and Punishment in Eighteenth-Century England* 97–101 (Routledge 1989); Stone, *Family, Sex and Marriage* at 615–19 (cited in note 2); Trumbach, *Sex and the Gender Revolution* at 69–72 (cited in note 4).

10 McLynn, *Crime and Punishment* at 99 (cited in note 9). See Durston, *Crime and Justice* at 349–53 (cited in note 5).

11 Trumbach, *Sex and the Gender Revolution* at 183, 157 (cited in note 4); Stone, *Family, Sex and Marriage* at 539 (cited in note 2). See Vern L. Bullough, *Prostitution and Reform in Eighteenth-Century England*, in *'Tis Nature's Fault* 62–63 (Robert Purks Maccubbin ed., Cambridge 1987).

12   Quoted in Reay Tannahill, *Sex in History* 336 (Stein and Day 1980). See Trumbach, *Sex and the Gender Revolution* at 203 (cited in note 4); Adair, *Courtship, Illegitimacy, and Marriage* at 42 (cited in note 4); Quaife, *Wanton Wenches and Wayward Wives* at 171 (cited in note 4); Angus McLaren, *Reproductive Rituals* 66–85 (Methuen 1984); Stone, *Family, Sex and Marriage* at 536–37 (cited in note 2); Bullough, *Sexual Variance* at 443–44 (cited in note 6); Linda Gordon, *Woman's Body, Woman's Right* 15–16 (Grossman 1976); John T. Noonan Jr., *Contraception: A History of Its Treatment by the Catholic Theologians and Canonists* 303–40 (Harvard University Press 1965).

13   Quoted in McLaren, *Reproductive Rituals* at 95 (cited in note 12). Abortifacients were well known in early modern England. See Julie Peakman, *Mighty Lewd Books* 84 (Palgrave 2003).

14   Abortion prior to quickening was not made a statutory offense in England until the nineteenth century. See McLaren, *Reproductive Rituals* at 90–111 (cited in note 12); Quaife, *Wanton Wenches and Wayward Wives* at 118–20 (cited in note 4); Drummond, *The Sex Paradox* at 24–25 (cited in note 6); Wiesner-Hanks, *Christianity and Sexuality* at 83 (cited in note 4).

15   Quoted in Borris, *Same-Sex Desire* at 104 (cited in note 3). See Ben-Atar & Brown, *Taming Lust* at 17 (cited in note 1).

16   Edward Coke, *The Third Part of the Institutes of the Laws on England* ch. 10 (London 1644), quoted in Borris, *Same-Sex Desire* at 96–97 (cited in note 3). See An Act for the Punishment of the Vice of Buggery, 25 Henry VIII, ch. 6 (1533–1534); An Act for the Punishment of the Vice of Buggery, 5 Elizabeth, ch. 17 (1563). See also Drummond, *Sex Paradox* at 120 (cited in note 6); Borris, *Same-Sex Desire* at 86–90 (cited in note 3); Bullough, *Sexual Variance* at 437 (cited in note 6); Harvey, *Sex in Georgian England* at 122–23 (cited in note 4); Wiesner-Hanks, *Christianity and Sexuality* at 87–89 (cited in note 4); Arno Karlen, *Sexuality and Homosexuality* 121 (Norton 1971); Donald N. Mager, *John Bale and Early Tudor Sodomy Discourse*, in *Queering the Renaissance* 141–43 (Jonathan Goldberg ed., Duke University 1994); Bruce R. Smith, *Homosexual Desire in Shakespeare's England* 43–45 (Chicago 1991); Alan Bray, *Homosexuality and the Signs of Male Friendship in Elizabethan England*, in Goldberg, *Queering the Renaissance* at 40–42 (cited in this note); Ben-Atar & Brown, *Taming Lust* at 18 (cited in note 1).

17   For an example of such a prosecution, see Borris, *Same-Sex Desire* at 99–101 (cited in note 3); Edward Coke, *A Book of Entries: Containing Perfect and Approved Presidents of Counts, Declarations, Informations, Pleints* (London 1614), quoted in Borris, *Same-Sex Desire* at 95–96 (cited in note 3).

18   Alan Bray, *Homosexuality in Renaissance England* 34 (Columbia 1996); Trumbach, *Sex and the Gender Revolution* at 5 (cited in note 4); Naphy, *Sex Crimes* at 104–5 (cited in note 4).

19   Randolph Trumbach, *Sodomitical Assaults, Gender Role, and Sexual Development in Eighteenth-Century London*, in *The Pursuit of Sodomy* 407, 408 (Kent Gerard & Gert Hekma eds., Routledge 1989); Simonds D'Ewes, *Diary* 92–93 (Elisabeth Bourcier ed., Didier 1974), quoted in Borris, *Same-Sex Desire* at 12 (cited in note 3).

20   See Bray, *Homosexuality in Renaissance England* at 82–86 (cited in note 18); Dennis Rubini, *Sexuality and Augustan England: Sodomy, Politics, Elite Circles and Society*, in Gerard & Hekma, *Pursuit of Sodomy* at 349–50 (cited in note 19); Trumbach, *Sodomitical Assaults* at 408 (cited in note 19); Trumbach, *Sex and the Gender Revolution* at 3–8 (cited in note 4); Bullough, *Sexual Variance* at 480–81 (cited in note 6); Durston, *Crime and Justice* at 180–81 (cited in note 5); Michel Delon, *The Priest, the Philosopher, and Homosexuality in Enlightenment France* in Maccubbin, *'Tis Nature's Fault* at 122–23 (cited in note 11).

21   Quoted in Harvey, *Sex in Georgian England* at 133 (cited in note 4); Borris, *Same-Sex Desire* at 85 (cited in note 3); Rubini, *Sexuality and Augustan England* at 352 (cited in note 20); Thomas Bray, *For God, or for Satan: Being a Sermon Preached at St. Mary Le Bow, Before the Society for Reformation of Manners, 27 December 1708* 30 (1709), quoted in Rubini, *Sexuality and Augustan England* at 352 (cited in note 20).

22   Borris, *Same-Sex Desire* at 86 (cited in note 3). See Naphy, *Sex Crimes* at 125 (cited in note 4). David F. Greenberg, *The Construction of Homosexuality* 337–41 (Chicago 1988); Bray, *Homosexuality in Renaissance England* at 82–91 (cited in note 18); Peakman, *Lascivious Bodies* at 166 (cited in note 9); Rubini, *Sexuality and Augustan England* at 350–58 (cited in note 20); Trumbach, *Sodomitical Assaults* at 408–9 (cited in note 19); Trumbach, *Sex and the Gender Revolution* at 6–8, 91–92 (cited in note 4); Wiesner-Hanks, *Christianity and Sexuality* at 87–89 (cited in note 4).

23   Naphy, *Sex Crimes* at 167 (cited in note 4). See Lillian Faderman, *Surpassing the Love of Men* 52–53 (Morrow 1981); Emma Donoghue, *Passions Between Women* 18 (Harper Collins 1993); Trumbach, *Sex and the Gender Revolution* at 8 (cited in note 4); Borris, *Same-Sex Desire* at 12, 19, 78 (cited in note 3); Judith C. Brown, *Immodest Acts: The Life of a Lesbian Nun in Renaissance Italy* 6 (Oxford 1986); Harvey, *Sex in Georgian England* at 113 (cited in note 4).

24   See Donoghue, *Passions Between Women* at 25–27, 59–69 (cited in note 23); Faderman, *Surpassing the Love of Men* at 27, 33 34 (cited in note 23); Valerie Traub, *The Renaissance of Lesbianism in Early Modern England* 194 (Cambridge 2002); Naphy, *Sex Crimes* at 163 (cited in note 4); Brown, *Immodest Acts* at 19 (cited in note 23); Peakman, *Lascivious Bodies* at ch. 8 (cited in note 9); Bullough, *Sexual Variance* at 485–87 (cited in note 6).

25   See Joan DeJean, *The Reinvention of Obscenity: Sex, Lies, and Tabloids in Early Modern France* 8 (Chicago 2002); Frederick F. Schauer, *The Law of Obscenity* 1–2 (Bureau of National Affairs 1976); George Ryley Scott, *"Into Whose Hands"* 17–18 (Gerald G. Swan 1945); St. John-Stevas, *Obscenity and the Law* at 2–5 (cited in note 7).

26   See Jürgen Beyer, *The Morality of the Amoral*, in *The Humor of the Fabliaux* 32–33 (Thomas D. Cooke & Benjamin L. Honeycutt eds., Missouri 1974); Barbara W. Tuchman, *A Distant Mirror: The Calamitous Fourteenth Century* 62, 162–63, 210–11 (Random House 1987); Michael Goodich, *The Unmentionable Vice: Homosexuality in the Later Medieval Period* 10 (ABC-Clio 1979).

27   See Tuchman, *Distant Mirror* at 103–4 (cited in note 26).

28   Giovanni Boccaccio, *The Decameron* (Mark Musa & Peter Bondanella, trans.) 660–62 (Signet 1982).

29   Geoffrey Chaucer, *The Miller's Tale*, in *The Canterbury Tales* 93–110 (Franklin Library 1974).

30   See James Cleugh, *The Divine Aretino* (Stein and Day 1966); Ian Frederick Moulton, *Before Pornography: Erotic Writing in Early Modern England* 120–35 (Oxford 2000); Karlen,

Sexuality and Homosexuality at 106–8 (cited in note 16); Borris, *Same-Sex Desire* at 355–64 (cited in note 3).

31 Pietro Aretino, *The School of Whoredom* 10–12 (Hesperus 2003).

32 See C. H. Rolph, *Books in the Dock* 29–31 (Andre Deutsch 1969); Schauer, *Law of Obscenity* at 2–3 (cited in note 25); Richard Findlater, *Banned! A Review of Theatrical Censorship in Britain* 10–35 (MacGibbon & Kee 1967); St. John-Stevas, *Obscenity and the Law* at 9 (cited in note 7); Peakman, *Mighty Lewd Books* at 39 (cited in note 13).

33 St. John-Stevas, *Obscenity and the Law* at 10–11 (cited in note 7). See Rolph, *Books in the Dock* at 29–30 (cited in note 32).

34 See Rolph, *Books in the Dock* at 31–32 (cited in note 32); St. John-Stevas, *Obscenity and the Law* at 11–12 (cited in note 7).

35 Quoted in Albert B. Gerber, *Sex, Pornography, and Justice* 57–63 (Lyle Stuart 1965).

36 *Queen v. Read*, Fortesque's Reports 98, 92 Eng. Rep. 777, 11 Mod. Rep. 142, 88 Eng. Rep. 953 (K.B. 1708). See Edward De Grazia, *Censorship Landmarks* 3 (R. R. Bowker 1969); Schauer, *Law of Obscenity* at 5 (cited in note 25); Alec Craig, *Suppressed Books* 25 (World Publishing Co. 1963); Peakman, *Mighty Lewd Books* at 39–40 (cited in note 13); Peter Wagner, *Eros Revived: Erotica of the Enlightenment in England and America* 152–55 (Secker & Warburg 1988).

37 2 Stra. 788 (1727).

38 Craig, *Suppressed Books* at 26–29 (cited in note 36). See Gerber, *Sex, Pornography, and Justice* at 64–65 (cited in note 35); Ralph Straus, *The Unspeakable Curll* (Robert M. McBride 1928); Pat Rogers & Paul Baines, *The Prosecutions of Edmund Curll*, 5 Library: The Transactions of the Bibliographical Society 176 (2004); Leo M. Alpert, *Judicial Censorship of Obscene Literature*, 52 Harv. L. Rev. 40, 43–44 (1938).

39 Quoted in Gerber, *Sex, Pornography, and Justice* at 64–66 (cited in note 35). See Wagner, *Eros Revived* at 72–73, 229–31 (cited in note 36); Peter Naumann, *Keyhole und Candle* 43–50 (Heidelburg 1976); Peakman, *Mighty Lewd Books* at 148–49 (cited in note 13).

40 De Grazia, *Censorship Landmarks* at 4 (cited in note 36). See Rogers & Baines, *Prosecutions of Edmund Curll* at 189 (cited in note 38); Peakman, *Mighty Lewd Books* at 39–40 (cited in note 13); Craig, *Suppressed Books* at 29–32 (cited in note 36); Scott, *"Into Whose Hands"* at 21–22, 83–84 (cited in note 25); Schauer, *Law of Obscenity* at 5–6 (cited in note 25); Gerber, *Sex, Pornography, and Justice* at 66–67 (cited in note 35).

41 Scott, *"Into Whose Hands"* at 142 (cited in note 25).

42 Wagner, *Eros Revived* at 6 (cited in note 36). See Stone, *Family, Sex and Marriage* at 539–40 (cited in note 2).

43 See McLaren, *Reproductive Rituals* at 19–21 (cited in note 12); Roy Porter, *"The Secrets of Generation Display'd,"* in Maccubbin, *'Tis Nature's Fault* at 1–15 (cited in note 11); Wagner, *Eros Revived* at 8–29, 167–70 (cited in note 36); Stone, *Family, Sex and Marriage* at 493–94 (cited in note 2); Bullough, *Sexual Variance* at 472 (cited in note 6); Thompson, *Unfit for Modest Ears* 164–66 (cited in note 7); Ben-Atar & Brown, *Taming Lust* at 76 (cited in note 1); Roy Porter, *Mixed Feelings*, in *Sexuality in Eighteenth-Century Britain* 8 (Paul-Gabriel Boucé ed., Manchester 1982); Mary Pardo, *Artifice as Seduction in Titian*, in *Sexuality and Gender in Early Modern Europe* 69 (James Grantham Turner ed., Cambridge 1993);

Randolph Trumbach, *Erotic Fantasy and Male Libertinism in Enlightenment England*, in *Invention of Pornography, 1500–1800: Obscenity and the Origins of Modernity* 262–63 (Lynn Hunt ed., Zone 1996); Wagner, *Eros Revived* at 117–18 (cited in note 36).

44   See Wagner, *Eros Revived* at 73 (cited in note 36); Peakman, *Mighty Lewd Books* at 126 (cited in note 13).

45   Quoted in Wagner, *Eros Revived* at 234, 236 (cited in note 36).

46   See Porter, *Mixed Feelings*, in *Sexuality in Eighteenth-Century Britain* at 8 (cited in note 43); Wagner, *Eros Revived* at 87–109, 248–55 (cited in note 36); Stone, *Family, Sex and Marriage* at 537–40 (cited in note 2).

47   Quoted in Wagner, *Eros Revived* at 209 (cited in note 36). See St. John-Stevas, *Obscenity and the Law* at 19–20 (cited in note 7); Wagner, *Eros Revived* at 209–16 (cited in note 36).

48   Gerber, *Sex, Pornography, and Justice* at 89 (cited in note 35). See Scott, *"Into Whose Hands"* at 145 (cited in note 25); Gerald W. Johnson, *Hod-Carrier* 67 (Morrow 1964); Craig, *Suppressed Books* at 33–34 (cited in note 36); Schauer, *Law of Obscenity* at 6 (cited in note 25).

49   See Craig, *Suppressed Books* at 33–34 (cited in note 36); Schauer, *Law of Obscenity* at 6 (cited in note 25); Scott, *"Into Whose Hands"* at 143 (cited in note 25); Johnson, *Hod-Carrier* at 67 (cited in note 48); Gerber, *Sex, Pornography, and Justice* at 89 (cited in note 35); Faderman, *Surpassing the Love of Men* at 28 (cited in note 23); Wagner, *Eros Revived* at 240–44 (cited in note 36).

50   See Peakman, *Mighty Lewd Books* at 12, 24 (cited in note 13).

51   See Trumbach, *Sex and the Gender Revolution* at 83–86 (cited in note 4); Bullough, *Sexual Variance* at 480–81 (cited in note 6). See Wagner, *Eros Revived* at 48–49, 54 (cited in note 36); Donald McCormick, *The Hell-Fire Club* (Jarrolds 1958); Daniel P. Mannix, *The Hell-Fire Club* (Ballantine 1961).

52   Quoted in Peakman, *Mighty Lewd Books* at 171–72 (cited in note 13). See Bullough, *Sexual Variance* at 480–81 (cited in note 6); Harvey, *Sex in Georgian England* at 36–37 (cited in note 4); Karlen, *Sexuality and Homosexuality* at 141–43 (cited in note 16); Naphy, *Sex Crimes* at 200–201 (cited in note 4); Trumbach, *Sex and the Gender Revolution* at 158–60 (cited in note 4); Peakman, *Mighty Lewd Books* at 161–72 (cited in note 13).

53   Wagner, *Eros Revived* at 214–16 (cited in note 36); Alan Corkhill, *Kant, Sade and the Libertine Enlightenment*, in *Libertine Enlightenment* 61, 66 (Peter Cryle & Lisa O'Connell eds., Palgrave 2003). See Karlen, *Sexuality and Homosexuality* at 155–57 (cited in note 16); Ben-Atar & Brown, *Taming Lust* at 13 (cited in note 1).

54   Trumbach, *Sex and the Gender Revolution* at 88 (cited in note 4). See Richard Payne Knight, *Discourse on the Worship of Priapus* (London 1786); Giancarlo Carabelli, *In the Image of Priapus* (Duckworth 1996); Peter Gay, *The Enlightenment: The Rise of Modern Paganism* 84 (Norton 1995).

55   See Kathleen Wilson, *The Female Rake*, in Cryle & O'Connell, *Libertine Enlightenment* at 105–9 (cited in note 54); Jonathan Lamb, *Preserving the Self in the South Seas, 1680–1840* (Chicago 2001); Smith, *Homosexual Desire in Shakespeare's England* at 3 (cited in note 16).

56   Rousseau & Porter, *Sexual Underworlds* at 1–2 (cited in note 7).

57   Gay, *Enlightenment: Rise of Modern Paganism* at 3 (cited in note 54), quoting Immanuel Kant, *Beantwortung der Frage: Was Ist Aufklärung?* in IV *Werke* 169.

58   Peter Cryle & Lisa O'Connell, *Sex, Liberty and Licence in the Eighteenth Century*, in Cryle & O'Connell, *Libertine Enlightenment* at 1 (cited in note 53); Porter, *Mixed Feelings* at 2 (cited in note 43); Gay, *Enlightenment: Rise of Modern Paganism* at 35 (cited in note 54); Edward Gibbon, I *The Decline and Fall of the Roman Empire* 30, quoted in Gay, *Enlightenment: Rise of Modern Paganism* at 73 (cited in note 54); Condorcet, *Esquisse*, in VI *Œuvres* 103, quoted in Gay, *Enlightenment: Rise of Modern Paganism* at 212 (cited in note 54); Rousseau, *Discours sur les sciences et les arts*, in III *Œuvres* 6, quoted in Gay, *Enlightenment: Rise of Modern Paganism* at 208 (cited in note 54).

59   Porter, *Mixed Feelings* 4 (cited in note 43); Rousseau & Porter, *Sexual Underworlds* at 1–2 (cited in note 7); Holbach, I *Système de la nature* 357, quoted in Peter Gay, *The Enlightenment: The Science of Freedom* 194 (Norton 1996). See Wagner, *Eros Revived* at 54 (cited in note 36); Norman L. Torrey, *The Spirit of Voltaire* 22 (Marston 1968).

60   Quoted in G. Rattray Taylor, *The Angel Makers* 7 (Dutton 1974); Cryle & O'Connell, *Sex, Liberty and Licence* at 4, 13 (cited in note 58). See Porter, *Mixed Feelings* at 7 (cited in note 43).

61   Denis Diderot, *Supplément au voyage de Bougainville* 26–29 (1772); Gay, *Enlightenment: Science of Freedom* at 199 (cited in note 59). See Gay, *Enlightenment: Science of Freedom* at 201–7 (cited in note 59).

62   Wagner, *Eros Revived* at 303 (cited in note 36). See Porter, *Mixed Feelings* at 8, 13–14 (cited in note 43); Alpert, *Judicial Censorship* at 47 (cited in note 38).

63   Wagner, *Eros Revived* at 303 (cited in note 36); Aphra Behn, *The Disappointment*, in *Selected Writings of the Ingenious Mrs. Aphra Behn* 235–40 (Robert Phelps ed., Grove Press 1950); Stone, *Family, Sex and Marriage* at 529 (cited in note 2). See Roy Porter & Lesley Hall, *The Facts of Life: The Creation of Sexual Knowledge in Britain, 1650–1950* 21–28 (Yale 1995).

64   See Porter, *Mixed Feelings* at 6–10 (cited in note 43); Trumbach, *Sex and the Gender Revolution* at 108–9, 158 (cited in note 4); Peakman, *Mighty Lewd Books* at 12–24 (cited in note 13); Stone, *Family, Sex and Marriage* at 494, 535–36, 537 (cited in note 2); Bullough, *Sexual Variance* at 472 (cited in note 6); Wagner, *Eros Revived* at 120–28 (cited in note 36); Porter & Hall, *Facts of Life* at 21–22, 36–97 (cited in note 63); Porter, *Secrets of Generation Display'd* at 1–2 (cited in note 43).

65   See Porter, *Mixed Feelings* at 9–13 (cited in note 43); Bullough, *Prostitution and Reform* at 61 (cited in note 11).

66   Stone, *Family, Sex and Marriage* at 501 (cited in note 2); Cryle & O'Connell, *Sex, Liberty and Licence* at 11 (cited in note 58); Porter, *Mixed Feelings* at 15 (cited in note 43). See Ben-Atar & Brown, *Taming Lust* at 78 (cited in note 1); Wilson, *Female Rake* at 95–105 (cited in note 55); McLaren, *Reproductive Rituals* at 29 (cited in note 12); Porter, *Mixed Feelings* at 18–19 (cited in note 43); Porter & Hall, *Facts of Life* at 28 (cited in note 63).

67   See Harvey, *Sex in Georgian England* at 124, 136, 144 (cited in note 4); Porter, *Mixed Feelings* at 13, 17–18 (cited in note 43); Rousseau & Porter, *Sexual Underworlds* at 3 (cited in note 7); Porter & Hall, *Facts of Life* at 32 (cited in note 63); Wagner, *Eros Revived* at 37 (cited in note 36); Randolph Trumbach, *Sodomitical Subcultures, Sodomitical Roles, and the Gender Revolution of the Eighteenth Century: The Recent Historiography*, in Maccubbin, *'Tis Nature's Fault* 111 (cited in note 11).

68 Quoted in Michel Rey, *Police and Sodomy in Eighteenth-Century Paris: From Sin to Disorder*, 16 J. Homosexuality 129, 145 (1989). See Gay, *Enlightenment: Science of Freedom* at 431 (cited in note 59); Wagner, *Eros Revived* at 34–35 (cited in note 36); Harvey, *Sex in Georgian England* at 125 (cited in note 4); Ben-Atar & Brown, *Taming Lust* at 24 (cited in note 1).

69 See Naphy, *Sex Crimes* at 166 (cited in note 4); Trumbach, *Sex and the Gender Revolution* at 8 (cited in note 4); Wagner, *Eros Revived* at 39, 41, 240–42 (cited in note 36).

70 Quoted in Harvey, *Sex in Georgian England* at 119 (cited in note 4). See Rousseau & Porter, *Sexual Underworlds* at 2–3 (cited in note 7); Peakman, *Mighty Lewd Books* at 45 (cited in note 13); Harvey, *Sex in Georgian England* at 118 (cited in note 4); Porter & Hall, *Facts of Life* at 96–105 (cited in note 63); Naphy, *Sex Crimes* at 180–85 (cited in note 4); Ben-Atar & Brown, *Taming Lust* at 76 (cited in note 1).

71 See S. A. D. Tissot, *Onanism; or, A Treatise Upon the Disorders Produced by Masturbation* (A. Hume trans., J. Pridden 1766); Bullough, *Sexual Variance* at 498–99 (cited in note 6); Peakman, *Mighty Lewd Books* at 45, 56 (cited in note 13); Stone, *Family, Sex and Marriage* at 495 (cited in note 2); Peakman, *Lascivious Bodies* at 276 (cited in note 9); Harvey, *Sex in Georgian England* at 121 (cited in note 4). Rousseau & Porter, *Sexual Underworlds* at 3 (cited in note 7); Harvey, *Sex in Georgian England* at 44, 119 (cited in note 4); Ben-Atar & Brown, *Taming Lust* at 76 (cited in note 1).

CHAPTER 4

1 See Richard Godbeer, *Sexual Revolution in Early America* 10–11 (John Hopkins 2002); Kermit L. Hall & Peter Karsten, *The Magic Mirror: Law in American History* 12–15, 32–33 (Oxford 1989); John D'Emilio & Estelle B. Freedman, *Intimate Matters: A History of Sexuality in America* 4–14 (Harper & Row 1988); Lawrence Stone, *The Family, Sex and Marriage in England, 1500–1800* 630–32 (Harper & Row 1977).

2 Hall & Karsten, *Magic Mirror* at 30–31, 34 (cited in note 1).

3 John Davenport, *A Sermon Preach'd at the Election of the Governour of Boston in New-England* 4 (1669), quoted in Hall & Karsten, *Magic Mirror* at 15 (cited in note 1); Jonathan Mayhew, *Sermons: Of the Nature and Principle of Evangelical Obedience* 258 (Richard Draper 1755); John D. Cushing ed., *The Laws and Liberties of Massachusetts, 1641–1691* xvi (1976). See Mark A. Noll, *The Bible in Revolutionary America*, in *The Bible in American Law, Politics, and Political Rhetoric* 39–40 (James Turner Johnson ed., Fortress 1985); John W. Welch, *Biblical Law in America*, 2002 BYU L. Rev. 611, 619–35; David H. Flaherty, *Law and the Enforcement of Morals in Early America*, in V *Perspectives in American History* 201, 206–9 (Donald Fleming & Bernard Bailyn eds., Harvard 1971); Max Farrand ed., *The Law and Liberties of Massachusetts* preamble (Cambridge 1929); Hall & Karsten, *Magic Mirror* at 16, 31 (cited in note 1).

4 Quoted in Welch, *Biblical Law in America* at 620–21 (cited in note 3).

5 *New Haven's Settling in New-England and Some Lawes for Government* (1656), in *The Earliest Laws of the New Haven and Connecticut Colonies 1639–1673* 11 (John D. Cushing ed., Glazier 1977). See Welch, *Biblical Law in America* at 626 (cited in note 3); Flaherty, *Law and the Enforcement of Morals* at 206–9, 221–22 (cited in note 3); Hall & Karsten, *Magic Mirror* at 26–27 (cited in note 1); Lawrence M. Friedman, *A History of American Law* 33 (3d ed., Simon & Schuster 2005); Jonathan Ned Katz ed., *Gay/Lesbian Almanac* 66–133 (Harper & Row 1983).

6 Hall & Karsten, *Magic Mirror* at 15 (cited in note 1).

7 Nathaniel Philbrick, *Mayflower: A Story of Courage, Community, and War* 3 (Viking 2006).

8 Philbrick, *Mayflower* at 3–6 (cited in note 7).

9 John Winthrop, *A Model of Christian Charity*, in Winthrop Papers 293–95 (Massachusetts Historical Society 1931), quoted in Perry Miller, *Errand into the Wilderness* 5 (Belknap 1964); Miller, *Errand into the Wilderness* at 5, 144 (cited in this note). On the Puritan covenant, see Miller, *Errand into the Wilderness* at 60–63, 71–74 (cited in this note).

10 Winthrop, *Model of Christian Charity* at 293–95 (cited in note 9), quoted in Miller, *Errand into the Wilderness* at 11–12 (cited in note 9).

11 Kai Erikson, *Wayward Puritans* 52, 57 (Prentice Hall 2004); Thomas Hooker, *The Application of Redemption* 684 (London 1659), quoted in Edmund S. Morgan, *Puritan Family* 6 (Harper & Row 1966); Morgan, *Puritan Family* at 6–7 (cited in note 11). See Sydney E. Ahlstrom, *A Religious History of the American People* 129 (Yale 2004).

12 Perry Miller, *The New England Mind* 35 (Belknap 1983). See Doron S. Ben-Atar & Richard D. Brown, *Taming Lust: Crimes Against Nature in the Early Republic* 21 (Pennsylvania 2014).

13 Samuel Willard, *A Compleat Body of Divinity* 609 (Boston 1726), quoted in Richard Godbeer, "*The Cry of Sodom*," 52 Wm. & M. Q. 259, 263 (1995). See Morgan, *Puritan Family* at 33–64, 166 (cited in note 11); Godbeer, *Sexual Revolution* at 56–62 (cited in note 1); Peter Wagner, *Eros Revived* 293 (Secker & Warburg 1988); Lyle Koehler, *A Search for Power: The "Weaker Sex" in Seventeenth-Century New England* 73–76 (Illinois 1980); Kathleen Verduin, "*Our Cursed Natures*": *Sexuality and the Puritan Conscience* 56 New Eng. Q. 220, 223–26 (1983).

14 Milton Rugoff, *Prudery and Passion* 15–16 (Putnam 1971); D'Emilio & Friedman, *Intimate Matters* at 15–16, xvii (cited in note 1); William E. Nelson, *Emerging Notions of Modern Criminal Law in the Revolutionary Era*, 42 N.Y.U. L. Rev. 450, 451 (1967). See Godbeer, *Cry of Sodom* at 262–63 (cited in note 13); Edmund S. Morgan, *The Puritans and Sex*, 15 New Eng. Q. 593–94 (1942); Douglas Greenberg, *Crime, Law Enforcement, and Social Control in Colonial America*, 28 Am. J. Leg. Hist. 293, 297 (1982).

15 Farrand, *Law and Liberties of Massachusetts* at 23 (cited in note 3). See Godbeer, *Sexual Revolution* at 33–38 (cited in note 1); Laurel Thatcher Ulrich, *Good Wives* 6, 31, 94–98 (Knopf 1982); Flaherty, *Law and the Enforcement of Morals* at 213–14 (cited in note 3); Koehler, *Search for Power* at 146–52 (cited in note 13); Rugoff, *Prudery and Passion* at 17–18, 22–23 (cited in note 14).

16 Godbeer, *Cry of Sodom* at 263–64 (cited in note 13); Cotton Mather, *An Holy Rebuke to the Unclean Spirit* 44 (Boston 1693), quoted in Godbeer, *Cry of Sodom* at 264 (cited in note 13); John Cotton, *An Abstract of the Laws of New England as They Are Now Established* (1641), quoted in Godbeer, *Cry of Sodom* at 264 (cited in note 13); Samuel Whiting, *Abraham's Humble Intercession for Sodom* 46 (1666), quoted in Godbeer, *Cry of Sodom* at 264 (cited in note 13).

17 Samuel Danforth, *The Cry of Sodom Enquired Into* 9 (1674), reprinted in Katz, *Gay/*

Lesbian Almanac at 108–9 (cited in note 5). See Godbeer, *Cry of Sodom* at 262–67 (cited in note 13); Louis Crompton, *Homosexuals and the Death Penalty in Colonial America*, 1 J. of Homosexuality 277, 279 (1976); Kenneth Borris, *Same-Sex Desire in the English Renaissance* 81 (Routledge 2004).

18   See Katz, *Gay/Lesbian Almanac* at 69–70, 90 (cited in note 5); Godbeer, *Sexual Revolution* at 104–11 (cited in note 1); Welch, *Biblical Law in America* at 620–22 (cited in note 3); Cushing, *Earliest Laws of New Haven* at 19 (cited in note 5); Vern L. Bullough, *Sexual Variance in Society and History* 519–22 (John Wiley & Sons 1976); Martin Baum Duberman, *Reclaiming the Gay Past*, 16 Rev. in Am. Hist. 515, 516–17 (1988); Crompton, *Homosexuals and the Death Penalty* at 277–81 (cited in note 17); Ben-Atar & Brown, *Taming Lust* at 83 (cited in note 12).

19   Samuel Danforth, *Cry of Sodom Enquired Into* 5 (cited in note 17). See Godbeer, *Sexual Revolution* at 67 (cited in note 1); D'Emilio & Freedman, *Intimate Matters* at 17 (cited in note 1); Stephen Botein, *Early American Law and Society* 26 (Borzoi 1983); Hall & Karsten, *Magic Mirror* at 32–33 (cited in note 1); Katz, *Gay/Lesbian Almanac* at 87, 111 (cited in note 5); Ulrich, *Good Wives* at 95 (cited in note 15); Emil Oberholzer Jr., *Delinquent Saints* 142–50 (Columbia 1956).

20   Bradley Chapin, *Criminal Justice in Colonial America, 1606–1660* 128–29 (Georgia 1983); Hall & Karsten, *Magic Mirror* at 33 (cited in note 1); John M. Murrin, *"Things Fearful to Name,"* 65 J. Penn. Hist. 8, 30–31 (1998); Ben-Atar & Brown, *Taming Lust* at 22–23 (cited in note 12). In 1673, Benjamin Goad was sentenced to death in Massachusetts for committing the "unnatural and horrid act of Bestialitie on a mare in the highway or field." Friedman, *History of American Law* at 72 (cited in note 5).

21   William Bradford, *History of Plymouth Plantation* 363–67 (William T. Davis ed., 1908); Michael Wigglesworth, *God's Controversy with New England* (1662), quoted in Rugoff, *Prudery and Passion* at 18 (cited in note 14). See Rugoff, *Prudery and Passion* at 17–18 (cited in note 14); Flaherty, *Law and the Enforcement of Morals* at 217 (cited in note 3); Oberholzer, *Delinquent Saints* at 150 (cited in note 19); Erikson, *Wayward Puritans* at 169–70 (cited in note 11); Perry Miller ed., *The American Puritans* 294–300 (Columbia 1956).

22   William Bradford, *Of Plymouth Plantation* 367 (McGraw-Hill 1981); Morgan, *Puritan Family* at 170–71, 173 (cited in note 11). See Samuel E. Morison, *Builders of the Bay Colony* 339–46 (Boston 1930); *The Puritans* 191 (Perry Miller & Thomas H. Johnson eds., New York 1938).

23   Miller, *Errand into the Wilderness* at 6 (cited in note 9).

24   Godbeer, *Sexual Revolution* at 23 (cited in note 1); quoted in Edwin Powers, *Crime and Punishment in Early Massachusetts* 179–80 (Beacon 1966); Bullough, *Sexual Variance* at 515 (cited in note 18).

25   Morgan, *Puritan Family* at 173, 185 (cited in note 11); quoted in Sanford Fleming, *Children and Puritanism* 11 (Yale 1933); Oberholzer, *Delinquent Saints* at 235 (cited in note 19). See Godbeer, *Sexual Revolution* at 29 (cited in note 1); Morgan, *Puritans and Sex* at 602–3 (cited in note 14); Hall & Karsten, *Magic Mirror* at 33 (cited in note 1); Ahlstrom, *Religious History* 158–65 (cited in note 11); Frank Lambert, *The Founding Fathers and the Place of Religion in America* 81 (Princeton 2006).

26   See Jules Paul Seigel, *Puritan Light Reading*, 37 New Eng. Q. 185, 188–94 (1964); W. C. Ford, *The Boston Book Market* 89, 106, 116, 128 (Boston 1917); George Emery Littlefield, *Early Boston Booksellers* (Boston 1900); James D. Hart, *The Popular Book: A History of America's Literary Taste* 16–17 (Oxford 1950); Thomas A. Foster, *Sex and the Eighteenth-Century Man* 179 (Beacon Press 2006).

27   Erikson, *Wayward Puritans* at 155–56 (cited in note 11).

28   Crane Brinton, *A History of Western Morals* 384–85 (Harcourt Brace 1959); Flaherty, *Law and the Enforcement of Morals* at 236–37 (cited in note 3).

29   See Godbeer, *Sexual Revolution* at 227–29 (cited in note 1); Greenberg, *Crime, Law Enforcement, and Social Control* at 315 (cited in note 14); Nelson, *Emerging Notions* at 455–59 (cited in note 14); D'Emilio & Freedman, *Intimate Matters* at 42 (cited in note 1); Flaherty, *Law and the Enforcement of Morals* at 232–33 (cited in note 3).

30   See Godbeer, *Sexual Revolution* at 230–34 (cited in note 1); Foster, *Sex and the Eighteenth-Century Man* at xvii (cited in note 26); Charles Francis Adams, *Some Phases of Sexual Morality and Church Discipline in Colonial New England*, 6 Proc. of Mass. Hist. Soc., 2d Ser., 486–90 (1891); Christopher Jedrey, *The World of John Cleaveland* 152 (Norton 1979).

31   Jonathan Edwards, *Joseph's Great Temptation and Gracious Deliverance*, in *The Works of Jonathan Edwards* 231–32 (Edward Hickman ed., London 1835); Jonathan Edwards, *A Faithful Narrative*, in *The Works of Jonathan Edwards: The Great Awakening* 144, 146 (C. C. Goen ed., Yale 1972); *The Testimony and Advice of an Assembly of Pastors of Churches in New England*, July 7, 1743, in *The Great Awakening* 129–30 (Richard L. Bushman ed., North Carolina 1989); *The Testimony of the Pastors of the Churches in the Province of the Massachusetts Bay*, May 25, 1743, in Bushman, *Great Awakening* at 127–28 (cited in this note).

32   David L. Holmes, *The Faiths of the Founding Fathers* 28 (Oxford 2006). See Henry F. May, *The Enlightenment in America* 42–51 (Oxford 1976); Lambert, *Founding Fathers* at 8, 124–29, 157–58 (cited in note 25); Oberholzer, *Delinquent Saints* at 136 (cited in note 19); Godbeer, *Sexual Revolution* at 234–36 (cited in note 1).

33   See Foster, *Sex and the Eighteenth-Century Man* at 96, 155–74 (cited in note 26).

34   Tobias Smollett, *The Adventures of Roderick Random* 312 (Oxford 1979).

35   John Urmston to Secretary, July 7, 1711, and July 21, 1721, in *The Colonial Records of North Carolina*, 1st Ser., 10 vols. (William F. Saunders ed., Raleigh 1886–90) 1:767; 2: 371–72, 431–32. See Godbeer, *Sexual Revolution* at 119–20 (cited in note 1); Richard J. Hooker ed., *The Carolina Backcountry on the Eve of Revolution* 15, 52, 56, 61 (North Carolina 1953); Gordon S. Wood, *The Radicalism of the American Revolution* 132–33 (Vintage 1991); Holmes, *Faiths of Founding Fathers* at 23 (cited in note 32).

36   Ahlstrom, *Religious History* at 196–97 (cited in note 11); Godbeer, *Sexual Revolution* at 121, 129 (cited in note 1).

37   See Frank J. Klingberg ed., *The Carolina Chronicle of Dr. Francis Le Jau, 1706–1717* 94 (Berkeley 1956); Godbeer, *Sexual Revolution* at 132–38, 147–50 (cited in note 1); Franklin Steiner, *The Religious Beliefs of Our Presidents* 86 (Haldeman-Julius 1936); May, *Enlightenment in America* at 69 (cited in note 32); Hooker, *Carolina Backcountry* at 6–64 (cited in note 35); Wood, *Radicalism* at 132–33 (cited in note 35).

38   See Katz, *Gay/Lesbian Almanac* at 119–20 (cited in note 5); Rugoff, *Prudery and Passion*

at 25–26 (cited in note 14); Flaherty, *Law and the Enforcement of Morals* at 214–15, 226–27 (cited in note 3); Greenberg, *Crime, Law Enforcement, and Social Control* at 301, 303, 310 (cited in note 14); Kathleen M. Brown, *Good Wives, Nasty Wenches, and Anxious Patriarchs* 189 (North Carolina 1996); Ahlstrom, *Religious History* at 184–99 (cited in note 11); D'Emilio & Freedman, *Intimate Matters* at 11–12, 22–23, 28, 38 (cited in note 1); Peter C. Hoffer & William B. Scott eds., *Criminal Proceedings in Colonial Virginia* 19–20, 71, 77 (Georgia 1984).

39   See Wagner, *Eros Revived* at 292–96 (cited in note 13); Richard Beale Davis, *A Colonial Southern Bookshelf* 11, 114–26 (Georgia 1979); Richard Beale Davis, *Literature and Society in Early Virginia, 1608–1840* 89–93 (Louisiana State 1973); E. M. Sowerby, 4 *Catalogue of the Library of Thomas Jefferson* 433–66 (Washington, DC 1952–1959); Hart, *Popular Book* at 16, 56–58 (cited in note 26); Howard Mumford Jones, *The Importation of French Books in Philadelphia*, 32 Mod. Phil. 157 (1934 35).

40   Wagner, *Eros Revived* at 301–2 (cited in note 13). See Hart, *Popular Book* at 16 (cited in note 26); Wagner, *Eros Revived* at 295–96 (cited in note 13); D'Emilio & Freedman, *Intimate Matters* at 19 (cited in note 1); Vern L. Bullough, *An Early American Sex Manual, Or, Aristotle Who?* in Vern L. Bullough, *Sex, Society, and History* 93 (Science History 1976); *The Catalogue of All the Books Printed in the United States* (Boston 1804); Wagner, *Eros Revived* at 296 (cited in note 13); Otho T. Beall Jr., *Aristotle's Master-Piece in America*, 20 Wm. & M. Q. 207, 208 (1963).

41   See Frederick F. Schauer, *The Law of Obscenity* 5–6, 8–9 (Bureau of National Affairs 1976); *Report of the Commission on Obscenity and Pornography* 352 (New York Times ed. 1970); Albert B. Gerber, *Sex, Pornography, and Justice* 88 (Lyle Stuart 1965); Wagner, *Eros Revived* at 297 (cited in note 13); Alec Craig, *Suppressed Books* 127 (World Publishing 1963); Leon M. Alpert, *Judicial Censorship of Obscene Literature*, 52 Harv. L. Rev. 40, 53 (1938); *Commonwealth v. Sharpless*, 2 Serg. & Rawle 91 (1815).

42   Ahlstrom, *Religious History* at 208 (cited in note 11); William Penn, *Frame of Government* (1682), in *Church and State in the Modern Age* 52 (J. F. Maclear ed., Oxford 1995). See Ahlstrom, *Religious History* at 208–13 (cited in note 11); Lambert, *Founding Fathers* at 100–122 (cited in note 25); May, *Enlightenment in America* at 80, 197–98, 202 (cited in note 32); William Frost, *A Perfect Freedom: Religious Liberty in Pennsylvania* (Pennsylvania State 1993); Edwin B. Bronner, *William Penn's "Holy Experiment"* (Temple 1962).

43   Godbeer, *Sexual Revolution* at 300 (cited in note 1). See Clare A. Lyons, *Sex Among the Rabble* 6–7, 61–62, 72–77, 83 (North Carolina 2006); Billy G. Smith, *The "Lower Sort": Philadelphia's Laboring People, 1750–1800* 178–80, 191–92 (Cornell 1990).

44   Godbeer, *Sexual Revolution* at 301 (cited in note 1). See Lyons, *Sex Among the Rabble* at 15–67 (cited in note 43); Kenneth Roberts & Anna M. Roberts eds. and trans., *Moreau de St. Méry's American Journey* 311–15 (Country Life 1947); Godbeer, *Sexual Revolution* at 302–7, 311–18 (cited in note 1); Lyons, *Sex Among the Rabble* at 72–83, 188–98 (cited in note 43); Susan Klepp, *Philadelphia in Transition* 87–88 (Garland 1989); D'Emilio & Freedman, *Intimate Matters* at 21–23 (cited in note 1).

45   Lyons, *Sex Among the Rabble* at 192 (cited in note 43). See Godbeer, *Sexual Revolution* at 302–8 (cited in note 1); Roberts & Roberts, *Moreau de St. Méry's American Journey* at 311–15 (cited in note 44); Lyons, *Sex Among the Rabble* at 188–95 (cited in note 43).

46 See Godbeer, *Sexual Revolution* at 301, 321–33 (cited in note 1); Lyons, *Sex Among the Rabble* at 101–12, 193–95, 321–33 (cited in note 43).

47 Lyons, *Sex Among the Rabble* at 218, 72–73 (cited in note 43). See Godbeer, *Sexual Revolution* at 301–8 (cited in note 1); Lyons, *Sex Among the Rabble* at 196–223 (cited in note 43).

48 See Clare A. Lyons, *Mapping an Atlantic Sexual Culture*, 60 Wm. & M. Q. 119, 121, 127–50 (2003).

49 Lyons, *Sex Among the Rabble* at 118–51 (cited in note 43).

50 Godbeer, *Sexual Revolution* at 263 (cited in note 1). See Godbeer, *Sexual Revolution* at 229–30, 264–98 (cited in note 1).

51 See Godbeer, *Sexual Revolution* at 245–47 (cited in note 1); D'Emilio & Freedman, *Intimate Matters* at 22, 46–47 (cited in note 1); Rugoff, *Prudery and Passion* at 19–20 (cited in note 14); Oberholzer, *Delinquent Saints* at 141 (cited in note 19); Samuel Peters, *General History of Connecticut* 327–30 (London 1781); Godbeer, *Sexual Revolution* at 247–55 (cited in note 1); Henry Reed Stiles, *Bundling: Its Origins, Progress, and Decline in America* 84, 108 (Knickerbocker 1871); Dana Doten, *The Art of Bundling* (Countryman Press 1938); Bullough, *Sexual Variance* at 512–13 (cited in note 18).

52 See Joseph J. Kelly Jr., *Life and Times in Colonial Philadelphia* 177–83 (Penn State 1973); Lyons, *Sex Among the Rabble* at 183–88 (cited in note 43).

53 Lyons, *Sex Among the Rabble* at 225–26 (cited in note 43). See Godbeer, *Sexual Revolution* at 295 (cited in note 1); Gordon S. Wood, *The Creation of the American Republic* 114–18, 508, 517–18 (North Carolina 1969).

54 Benjamin Rush, *An Address to the People of the United States on the Defects of the Confederation*, quoted in Ronald Takaki, *Iron Cages: Race and Culture in 19th-Century America* 19 (Alfred A. 1979); Benjamin Rush, *An Address to the Ministers*, quoted in Lyons, *Sex Among the Rabble* at 227–28 (cited in note 43). See D'Emilio & Freedman, *Intimate Matters* at 45 (cited in note 1).

CHAPTER 5

1 See Jerry Falwell, *Listen, America!* 25 (Doubleday 1980); Isaac Kramnick & R. Laurence Moore, *The Godless Constitution* 22–23 (Norton 1996); Tim LaHaye, *Faith of Our Founding Fathers* 29 (Master Books 1996).

2 Sydney E. Ahlstrom, *A Religious History of the American People* 264, 362 (Yale 2004). See Henry F. May, *The Enlightenment in America* 88 (Oxford 1976); Gordon S. Wood, *The Radicalism of the American Revolution* 96 (Vintage 1993); Bernard Bailyn, *The Ideological Origins of the American Revolution* 26–30 (Belknap 1992).

3 Thomas Paine, Letter to the Abbe Raynal (1782), in II *The Complete Writings of Thomas Paine* 243, 244 (Philip S. Foner ed., Citadel Press 1945). See Frank Lambert, *The Founding Fathers and the Place of Religion in America* 171 (Princeton 2003); Bernard Bailyn, *To Begin the World Anew* 5 (Vintage 2004).

4 The Fundamental Orders of Connecticut, January 14, 1639, in *Documents of American History* 23 (Henry S. Commager ed., 7th ed., Prentice-Hall 1963); Mark A. Noll, *Evangelicals in the American Founding and Evangelical Political Mobilization Today*, in *Religion* *and the New Republic* 137, 146 (James H. Hutson ed., Rowman & Littlefield 2000); Hutson, *Religion and New Republic* at 137, 146 (cited in this note). See Ahlstrom, *Religious History* at 365 (cited in note 2); Kramnick & Moore, *Godless Constitution* at 17 (cited in note 1); Lambert, *Founding Fathers* at 282 (cited in note 3); Jon Butler, *Why Revolutionary America Wasn't a "Christian Nation,"* in Hutson, *Religion and New Republic* at 187, 191 (cited in this note); Rodney Stark & Roger Finke, *American Religion in 1776* 49 Sociological Analysis 39 (1988).

5   Wood, *Radicalism* at 158 (cited in note 2).

6   Lambert, *Founding Fathers* at 161–62 (cited in note 3).

7   Lambert, *Founding Fathers* at 1–2 (cited in note 3); Butler, *Revolutionary America* at 196 (cited in note 4).

8   Voltaire, 26 *Oeuvres Completes* 298 (Louis Moland ed., Paris 1877–1885). See Michael Novak, *The Influence of Judaism and Christianity on the American Founding*, in Hutson, *Religion and New Republic* at 162 (cited in note 4); Brooke Allen, *Moral Minority: Our Skeptical Founding Fathers* 174 (Ivan R. Dee 2006).

9   See Wood, *Radicalism* at 330 (cited in note 2); David L. Holmes, *The Faiths of the Founding Fathers* 134 (Oxford 2006).

10   Thomas Woolston, *A Second Discourse on the Miracles of Our Saviour*, in Woolston, *Six Discourses on the Miracles of Our Saviour and Defences of His Discourses* 18 (Rene Wellek ed., Garland 1979). See Allen, *Moral Minority* at xii–xiii, 172–73 (cited in note 8); Holmes, *Faiths of Founding Fathers* at 40 (cited in note 9); Kerry Walters, *Revolutionary Deists* 23 (Prometheus 2010).

11   See Holmes *Faiths of Founding Fathers* at 47 (cited in note 9); Matthew Stewart, *Nature's God: The Heretical Origins of the American Republic* 88 (Norton 2014).

12   Walters, *Revolutionary Deists* at ix–xi (cited in note 10). See Stewart, *Nature's God* at 91–92 (cited in note 11); Holmes, *Faiths of Founding Fathers* at 47 (cited in note 9).

13   See Ahlstrom, *Religious History* at 356 58 (cited in note 2); Holmes, *Faiths of Founding Fathers* at 41, 46–48 (cited in note 9); Allen, *Moral Minority* at 172–73 (cited in note 8); May, *Enlightenment* at 21–22 (cited in note 2); Lambert, *Founding Fathers* at 168–75 (cited in note 3); Walters, *Revolutionary Deists* at ix–xii, 5, 102 (cited in note 10).

14   See Allen, *Moral Minority* at 172–73 (cited in note 8); Ahlstrom, *Religious History* at 358–59 (cited in note 2); Lambert, *Founding Fathers* at 161–62 (cited in note 3); Walters, *Revolutionary Deists* at xii (cited in note 10); Holmes, *Faiths of Founding Fathers* at 133–41 (cited in note 9).

15   Lambert, *Founding Fathers* at 161 (cited in note 3). See Walters, *Revolutionary Deists* at ix (cited in note 10); Holmes, *Faiths of Founding Fathers* at 49 (cited in note 9).

16   See Holmes, *Faiths of Founding Fathers* at 143–60 (cited in note 9); Allen, *Moral Minority* at 102 (cited in note 8).

17   Gordon S. Wood, *Revolutionary Characters* 69 (Penguin 2006); Benjamin Franklin, *Autobiography* 59, 97, 96, 117, in *A Benjamin Franklin Reader* (Nathan G. Goodman ed., Thomas Y. Crowell 1945); Benjamin Franklin, Letter to the Printer of the London Packet, June 3, 1772, in William B. Wilcox ed., XIX *Papers of Benjamin Franklin* 164 (Yale 1975). See Wood, *Revolutionary Characters* at 68–69 (cited in this note); John G. West Jr.,

The Politics of Revelation and Reason 21 (Kansas 1996); Stewart, *Nature's God* at 27–28 (cited in note 11).

18 Benjamin Franklin to Ezra Stiles, March 9, 1790, in 3 *The Literary Diary of Ezra Stiles* 387 (Franklin Bowditch-Dexter ed., Charles Scribner's Sons 1901).

19 Benjamin Franklin to Ezra Stiles, March 9, 1790, in Bowditch-Dexter, *Literary Diary of Ezra Stiles* at 387 (cited in note 18).

20 Benjamin Franklin, *A Man of Sense*, in Labaree, 2 *The Papers of Benjamin Franklin* 16 (Yale 1961); Benjamin Franklin, *Articles of Belief and Acts of Religion*, in Labaree, 1 *Papers of Franklin* at 103 (cited in this note). See Stewart, *Nature's God* at 300 (cited in note 11); Benjamin Franklin, to Rev. George Whitfield, June 6, 1753, in *The Life of Benjamin Franklin* 76–77 (Leonard Woods ed., London 1826).

21 Joseph Priestley, *Autobiography* 117 (Fairleigh Dickinson 1970). On Franklin's religious beliefs, see Walters, *Revolutionary Deists* at 44–81 (cited in note 10); Allen, *Moral Minority* at 9–11 (cited in note 8); Wood, *Revolutionary Characters* at 69 (cited in note 17); Lambert, *Founding Fathers* at 159–60 (cited in note 3); Holmes, *Faiths of Founding Fathers* at 53–56 (cited in note 9); Walter Isaacson ed., *A Benjamin Franklin Reader* 376–78 (Simon & Schuster 2003); Jon Meacham, *American Gospel: God, the Founding Fathers, and the Making of a Nation* 20–22 (Random House 2006); May, *Enlightenment* at 126–29 (cited in note 2); Steven Waldman, *Founding Faith* 18–26 (Random House 2008).

22 Wood, *Revolutionary Characters* at 93 (cited in note 17); Abraham Lincoln to H. L. Pierce and others, April 6, 1859, in *Abraham Lincoln: His Speeches and Writings* 489 (Roy P. Basler ed., World Publishing 1946); Allen, *Moral Minority* at 70 (cited in note 8).

23 Thomas Jefferson to Peter Carr, August 10, 1787, in *Thomas Jefferson: Writings* 902 (Merrill D. Peterson ed., Library of America 1984). See Stewart, *Nature's God* at 198 (cited in note 11).

24 Thomas Jefferson to John Adams, October 12, 1813, in 2 *The Adams-Jefferson Letters* 384 (Lester J. Cappon ed., North Carolina 1959); Thomas Jefferson to Joseph Priestley, April 9, 1803, in Peterson, *Jefferson: Writings* at 1120 (cited in note 23). See Thomas Jefferson to William Short, April 13, 1820, and Thomas Jefferson to Benjamin Waterhouse, June 26, 1822, in Albert Ellery Bergh, 15 *The Writings of Thomas Jefferson* 244, 383–85 (Thomas Jefferson Memorial Association 1907); Holmes, *Faiths of Founding Fathers* at 82–84 (cited in note 9).

25 Thomas Jefferson to Benjamin Rush (1803), in 9 *The Works of Thomas Jefferson* 457 (Paul Ford ed., G. P. Putnam's Sons 1904). See Thomas Jefferson to William Short, August 4, 1820, in Peterson, *Jefferson: Writings* at 1437–38 (cited in note 23). 26 Thomas Jefferson to Benjamin Rush, April 21, 1803, in Bergh, 10 *Writings of Jefferson* at 379–80 (cited in note 24); Holmes, *Faiths of Founding Fathers* at 82–87 (cited in note 9); Thomas Jefferson to Benjamin Waterhouse, June 26, 1822, in Dickinson W. Adams, *Jefferson's Extracts from the Gospels* 405 (Princeton 1983). Thomas Jefferson to William Short, April 13, 1820; Thomas Jefferson to Jared Sparks, November 4, 1820; Thomas Jefferson to James Smith, December 8, 1822; Thomas Jefferson to Benjamin Waterhouse, June 26, 1822; Thomas Jefferson to Benjamin Waterhouse, July 19, 1822; all in Bergh, 15 *Writings of Jefferson* at 243–45, 287–88, 408–10, 383–85, 390–92 (cited in note 24).

27   Thomas Jefferson to John Davis, January 18, 1824, in *Jefferson and Madison on the Separation of Church and State* 373 (Lenni Brenner ed., Barricade Books 2004); Thomas Jefferson to William Short, April 13, 1820, in Brenner, *Jefferson and Madison* at 336 (cited in this note); Thomas Jefferson to Benjamin Waterhouse, June 26, 1822, in Adams, *Jefferson's Extracts* at 405 (cited in note 26); Thomas Jefferson to Francis Adrian Van der Kemp, July 30, 1816, in Adams, *Jefferson's Extracts* at 375 (cited in note 26). See West, *Politics of Revelation* at 60 (cited in note 17).

28   Allen, *Moral Minority* at 78 (cited in note 8). See Kramnick & Moore, *Godless Constitution* at 95–96 (cited in note 1).

29   Thomas Jefferson to Benjamin Rush, April 21, 1803, in Bergh, 10 *Writings of Jefferson* at 379–80 (cited in note 24).

30   Thomas Jefferson to James Fishback, September 27, 1809, in Brenner, *Jefferson and Madison* at 195 (cited in note 27); Thomas Jefferson to John Adams, January 22, 1821, in Cappon, *Adams-Jefferson Letters* at 569 (cited in note 24). See Thomas Jefferson to Matthew Carey, November 11, 1816, in Gabriel Richard Mason, *Great American Liberals* 21 (Starr King 1956).

31   Thomas Jefferson to John Adams, October 14, 1816, in Cappon, *Adams-Jefferson Letters* at 492 (cited in note 24); Thomas Jefferson to Peter Carr, August 10, 1787, in 12 *The Papers of Thomas Jefferson* 15 (Julian P. Boyd et al. eds., Princeton 1955); Thomas Jefferson to Thomas Law, June 13, 1814, in Peterson, *Jefferson: Writings* at 1337 (cited in note 23); Thomas Jefferson, *Opinion on the French Treaties*, April 28, 1793, in 6 *The Writings of Thomas Jefferson* 220–21 (Paul Leicester Ford ed., G. P. Putnam's Sons 1895); Thomas Jefferson to Thomas Law, June 13, 1814, in Adams, *Jefferson's Extracts* at 357 (cited in note 26).

32   Allen, *Moral Minority* at 180 (cited in note 8). See Stewart, *Nature's God* at 300 (cited in note 11). See Thomas Jefferson to Thomas Law, June 13, 1814, in Peterson, *Jefferson: Writings* at 1336 (cited in note 23).

33   Thomas Jefferson to John Adams, October 14, 1816, in Cappon, *Adams-Jefferson Letters* at 490, 492 (cited in note 24). See Stewart, *Nature's God* at 308 (cited in note 11).

34   On Jefferson's religious beliefs, see Meacham, *American Gospel* at 3–4 (cited in note 21); Allen, *Moral Minority* at 70–87 (cited in note 8); Kramnick & Moore, *Godless Constitution* at 95–96 (cited in note 1); Wood, *Revolutionary Characters* at 107 (cited in note 17); Holmes, *Faiths of Founding Fathers* at 80 (cited in note 9); Lambert, *Founding Fathers* at 174–77, 279 (cited in note 3); John M. Murrin, *Religion and Politics in America from the First Settlements to the Civil War*, in *Religion and American Politics* 19, 32–33 (Mark A. Noll ed., Oxford 1990); Ahlstrom, *Religious History* at 367–68 (cited in note 2); Stewart, *Nature's God* at 328–29 (cited in note 11).

35   Bailyn, *To Begin the World Anew* at 64 (cited in note 3). See Wood, *Revolutionary Characters* at 178–79 (cited in note 17).

36   Allen, *Moral Minority* at 59 (cited in note 8); John Adams to Benjamin Rush, June 12, 1812, in *The Spur of Fame* 244 (John A. Schutz & Douglass Adair eds., Indiana 2001). See Ahlstrom, *Religious History* at 367–68 (cited in note 2).

37   1 *Diary and Autobiography of John Adams*, ser. 1, in *The Adams Papers* at 42–44 (Lyman H. Butterfield ed., Belknap 1961); John Adams to F. A. Van der Kamp, December 27,

1816, in 10 *The Works of John Adams* 234 (Charles Francis Adams ed., Little, Brown 1856); West, *Politics of Revelation* at 50, 49 (cited in note 17). See Wood, *Radicalism* at 330 (cited in note 2); Stewart, *Nature's God* at 62 (cited in note 11); Holmes, *Faiths of Founding Fathers* at 73–74, 78 (cited in note 9).

38 John Adams to Thomas Jefferson, December 12, 1816, in Cappon, *Adams-Jefferson Letters* at 499 (cited in note 24); Sunday, August 14, 1796, 3 *Diary and Autobiography of John Adams* in Butterfield, *Adams Papers* at 240–41 (cited in note 37). See Anne Holt, *A Life of Joseph Priestley* 140 (Oxford 1931); Ahlstrom, *Religious History* at 358–59, 391–92 (cited in note 2).

39 John Adams to Benjamin Rush, June 12, 1812, in Schutz & Adair, *Spur of Fame* at 244 (cited in note 36); John Adams to Benjamin Rush, April 12, 1809, in Schutz & Adair, *Spur of Fame* at 155 (cited in note 36); John Witte Jr., *"A Most Mild and Equitable Establishment of Religion"* in Hutson, *Religion and New Republic* at 1, 18–19 (cited in note 4); Joseph J. Ellis, *Passionate Sage: The Character and Legacy of John Adams* 123 (Norton 1993).

40 John Adams to Abigail Adams, September 17, 1775, in *The Letters of John and Abigail Adams* 97 (Frank Shuffelton ed., Penguin 2004); *The Boston Price-Current and Marine Intelligencer*, June 26, 1797, quoted in Allen, *Moral Minority* at 142 (cited in note 8).

41 John Adams to Thomas Jefferson, April 19, 1817, quoted in Holmes, *Faiths of Founding Fathers* at 78 (cited in note 9).

42 Quoted in Adams, 5 *Works of John Adams* at 488 (cited in note 37); *id.* at 4: 406; *id.* at 6: 10. See Wood, *Revolutionary Characters* at 182, 188 (cited in note 17); John Adams to Mercy Warren, April 16, 1776, in 1 *The Founders' Constitution* 670 (Philip B. Kurland & Ralph Lerner eds., Chicago 1987). See Wood, *Revolutionary Characters* at 180 (cited in note 17); James H. Hutson ed., *The Founders on Religion* 146–47 (Princeton 2007).

43 John Adams, *Dissertation on the Canon and Feudal Law* (1765), in Adams, 3 *Works of John Adams* at 455–57 (cited in note 37); John Adams to Mercy Warren, January 8, April 16, 1776, in 1 *Correspondence Between John Adams and Mercy Warren* 201–2, 223 (Arno 1972); John Adams to Zabdiel Adams, June 21, 1776, 2 *Adams Family Correspondence*, ser. 2, in *The Adams Papers* at 21 (Lyman H. Butterfield ed., Belknap 1963). See Wood, *Revolutionary Characters* at 181 (cited in note 17); Adams, *A Defence of the Constitution of the United States of America (1787–1788)*, in *The Portable John Adams* xxv–xxvi (John Patrick Diggins ed., Penguin 2004); Meacham, *American Gospel* at 27–28 (cited in note 21).

44 John Adams to Thomas Jefferson, December 12, 1816, in Cappon, 2 *Adams-Jefferson Letters* at 499 (cited in note 24); Thomas Jefferson to John Adams, January 11, 1817, in Cappon, 2 *Adams-Jefferson Letters* at 506 (cited in note 24).

45 Jean-Jacques Rousseau, *On the Social Contract* 131 (Roger D. Masters ed., Judith R. Masters trans., St. Martin's 1978). See West, *Politics of Revelation* at 76–77 (cited in note 17); Lambert, *Founding Fathers* at 282 (cited in note 3); Ahlstrom, *Religious History* at 363 (cited in note 2).

46 George Washington to Marquis de Lafayette, August 15, 1787, in 29 *The Writings of George Washington* 259 (John C. Fitzpatrick ed., U.S. Government Printing Office 1939); William J. Johnson, *George Washington the Christian* 288–91 (Abington Press 1919). See

Wood, *Revolutionary Characters* at 34–35 (cited in note 17); Peter R. Henriques, *Realistic Visionary: A Portrait of George Washington* 170 (Virginia 2006).

47 Paul K. Longmore, *The Invention of George Washington* 169, 288–90 (Virginia 1999); Edwin S. Gaustad, *Disciples of Reason*, Christian History (Spring 1996), quoted in Allen, *Moral Minority* at 40 (cited in note 8); Joseph J. Ellis, *His Excellency: George Washington* 269 (Vintage 2004). See Henriques, *Realistic Visionary* at 168–69, 175 (cited in note 46); May, *Enlightenment* at 72 (cited in note 2); Paul F. Boller Jr., *George Washington and Religion* 31, 67 (Southern Methodist 1963).

48 See A. W. Greely, *Washington's Domestic and Religious Life*, Ladies Home Journal, April 1896, quoted in Allen, *Moral Minority* at 35 (cited in note 8); Barry Schwartz, *George Washington: The Making of an American Symbol* 175 (Free Press 1987); West, *Politics of Revelation* at 39 (cited in note 17).

49 Quoted in Rupert Hughes, *George Washington: The Savior of the States, 1777–1781* 286, 287 (William Morrow 1930); Henriques, *Realistic Visionary* at 177 (cited in note 46). See Meacham, *American Gospel* at 78 (cited in note 21); Boller, *George Washington and Religion* at 89 (cited in note 47); Kramnick & Moore, *Godless Constitution* at 101 (cited in note 1); Henriques, *Realistic Visionary* at 170–75, 182–83 (cited in note 46); Allen, *Moral Minority* at 36 (cited in note 8); Holmes, *Faiths of Founding Fathers* at 140–41 (cited in note 9).

50 Douglas Southall Freeman, *Washington* 500 (Charles Scribner's Sons 1952); Henriques, *Realistic Visionary* at 182 (cited in note 46).

51 See Meacham, *American Gospel* at 77–78 (cited in note 21); Don Higginbotham, *George Washington: Uniting a Nation* 53–60 (Rowman & Littlefield 2002); *George Washington: Writings* 767 (John Rhodehamel ed., Library of America 1997); Allen, *Moral Minority* at 40 (cited in note 8); Wood, *Revolutionary Characters* at 59 (cited in note 17); Holmes, *Faiths of Founding Fathers* at 65 (cited in note 9); May, *Enlightenment* at 72 (cited in note 2); Lambert, *Founding Fathers* at 282 (cited in note 3); Henriques, *Realistic Visionary* at 174 (cited in note 46); Allen, *Moral Minority* at xiii (cited in note 8). There were only two public occasions on which Washington referred to Christianity—a 1779 statement in which he urged the Delaware Chiefs "to learn. . . the religion of Jesus Christ" and a 1783 statement about the disbanding of the army in which he referred to "our blessed religion." George Washington, Speech to the Delaware Chiefs, May 12, 1779, in Fitzpatrick, *Writings of George Washington* at 53–55 (cited in note 46); George Washington, *Circular Letter to the Governors of All the States on Disbanding the Army*, in *The Washington Papers* 213–14 (Saul K. Padover ed., 1955). See Samuel W. Calhoun, *Getting the Framers Wrong: A Response to Professor Geoffrey Stone*, 57 UCLA L. Rev. Disc. 1 (2009).

52 See Boller, *George Washington and Religion* at 64 (cited in note 47); Wood, *Revolutionary Characters* at 34–35 (cited in note 17); Holmes, *Faiths of Founding Fathers* at 66–68 (cited in note 9); Henriques, *Realistic Visionary* at 182–83 (cited in note 46); West, *Politics of Revelation* at 37 (cited in note 17).

53 Walters, *Revolutionary Deists* at 122–23, 125 (cited in note 10). See Stewart, *Nature's God* at 334–35 (cited in note 11).

54 Thomas Paine, *The Age of Reason* pt. 1, in 8 *The Life and Works of Thomas Paine* 4–5

(William M. Van der Weyde ed., 1925); Thomas Paine, *The Age of Reason* pt. 1, in *Common Sense and Other Writings* 245 (Gordon S. Wood ed., Modern Library 2003).

55 Thomas Paine, *Of the Religion of Deism Compared with the Christian Religion, and the Superiority of the Former Over the Latter*, in 4 *The Writings of Thomas Paine* 322 (Moncure Conway ed., G. P. Putnam's Sons 1896). See Holmes, *Faiths of Founding Fathers* at 39 (cited in note 9).

56 Thomas Paine, *The Age of Reason* 55, 182 (Philip S. Foner ed., Citadel Press 1974); Thomas Paine, 1 *The Age of Reason* 132 (Centennial ed., Boston 1908). See May, *Enlightenment* at 174 (cited in note 2).

57 Thomas Paine, *The Age of Reason* pt. 2, in Van der Weyde, 8 *Life and Works* at 269 (cited in note 54). See Stewart, *Nature's God* at 225 (cited in note 11).

58 Thomas Paine, *The Age of Reason* pt. 2, in Van der Weyde, *Life and Works* at 278 (cited in note 54).

59 Thomas Paine, *The Age of Reason* pt.1, in Van der Weyde, *Life and Works* at 50 (cited in note 54); Holmes, *Faiths of Founding Fathers* at 42 (cited in note 9). See John Keane, *Tom Paine: A Political Life* xiv–xiii (Little, Brown 1995); Wood, *Revolutionary Characters* at 207 (cited in note 17); May, *Enlightenment* at 124 (cited in note 2); Lambert, *Founding Fathers* at 175 (cited in note 3).

60 See Holmes, *Faiths of Founding Fathers* at 49 (cited in note 9); Walters, *Revolutionary Deists* at 8–9, 11 (cited in note 10); Ahlstrom, *Religious History* at 365–67 (cited in note 2); May, *Enlightenment* at 121–23, 136–37 (cited in note 2).

61 Timothy Dwight, *Triumph of Infidelity* 23–24 (New York 1788), quoted in Walters, *Revolutionary Deists* at 92 (cited in note 10); Jonathan Edwards, *A History of the Work of Redemption* 347 (American Tract Society 1816); Charles A. Jellison, *Ethan Allen: Frontier Rebel* 311, 331 (Syracuse 1969); Ezra Stiles to Thomas Clap, August 6, 1759, quoted in I. Woodbridge Riley, *American Philosophy: The Early Schools* 217 (Dodd, Mead 1907); Walters, *Revolutionary Deists* at 8–9, 11 (cited in note 10). See Walters *Revolutionary Deists* at 24–25, 84–114 (cited in note 10); Ahlstrom, *Religious History* at 364, 367 (cited in note 2); Allen, *Moral Minority* at 159 (cited in note 8); Holmes, *Faiths of Founding Fathers* at 44–49 (cited in note 9); May, *Enlightenment* at 123, 184–90 (cited in note 2); Lambert, *Founding Fathers* at 160 (cited in note 3); Stewart, *Nature's God* at 11–12, 22 (cited in note 11).

62 Among the members of the Revolutionary generation who did not entertain deist beliefs and might properly be described as "traditional Christians" were Patrick Henry, Samuel Adams, and John Jay. See Holmes, *Faiths of Founding Fathers* at 143–60 (cited in note 9); Allen, *Moral Minority* at 102 (cited in note 8).

63 James Madison, *Federalist* No. 55, February 13, 1788, in *Federalists and Antifederalists* 58, 62 (John P. Kaminski & Richard Leffler eds., Rowman & Littlefield 1998); James Madison, *Federalist* No. 55, February 13, 1788, in Kaminski & Leffler, *Federalists and Antifederalists* at 58, 62 (cited in this note); Allen, *Moral Minority* at 179 (cited in note 8). See Noll, *Evangelicals in American Founding* at 146–47 (cited in note 4); Murrin, *Religion and Politics* at 31 (cited in note 34); Patricia U. Bonomi, *Under the Cope of Heaven: Religion, Society, and Politics in Colonial America* 102–4 (Oxford 1986); Meacham, *American Gospel* at 22–23, 75–78 (cited in note 21); Lambert, *Founding Fathers* at 161, 178 (cited in note 3); Holmes,

Faiths of Founding Fathers at 143–60 (cited in note 9); Allen, *Moral Minority* at xv (cited in note 8); Stewart, *Nature's God* at 72–73 (cited in note 11).

64 Phillips Payson, *Election Sermon of 1778*, in 1 *American Political Writing During the Founding Era* 529–30 (Charles S. Hyneman & Donald S. Lutz eds., Liberty Press 1983); John Witherspoon, *The Dominion of Providence over the Passions of Man* (May 17, 1776), in 3 *The Works of the Reverend John Witherspoon* 41 (Massachusetts Historical Society 1917–1925), quoted in Hutson, *Founders on Religion* at 148 (cited in note 42); Benjamin Rush to Noah Webster, July 20, 1798, in 2 *Letters of Benjamin Rush* 799 (Lyman H. Butterfield ed., Princeton 1951).

65 John Adams to Zabdiel Adams, June 21, 1776, in Adams, 9 *Works of John Adams* at 401 (cited in note 37). John Adams to Benjamin Rush, August 28, 1811, in *Old Family Letters* 354 (Alexander Biddle ed., Lippincott 1892); Alexander Hamilton, *The Stand No. III* (Apr. 7, 1798), in 21 *The Papers of Alexander Hamilton* 405 (Harold C. Syrett ed., Columbia 1974). See West, *Politics of Revelation* at 45–51 (cited in note 17); John Adams, *To the Officers of the First Brigade of the Third Division of the Militia of Massachusetts*, October 11, 1798, in Adams, 9 *Works of John Adams* at 229 (cited in note 37).

66 Benjamin Franklin to Unknown Recipient, December 13, 1757, in 7 *The Papers of Benjamin Franklin* 294–95 (Leonard W. Labaree ed., Yale 1963). See West, *Politics of Revelation* at 24–25 (cited in note 17).

67 Kramnick & Moore, *Godless Constitution* at 24 (cited in note 1).

68 Meacham, *American Gospel* at 22–23 (cited in note 21).

CHAPTER 6

1 John Locke, *A Letter Concerning Toleration*, in 6 John Locke, *Works* 40 (1823).

2 See Frank Lambert, *The Founding Fathers and the Place of Religion in America* 219–20 (Princeton 2003).

3 *Virginia Statute for Religion Freedom*, in Jack N. Rakove, *Declaring Rights: A Brief History with Documents* 95–96 (Bedford 1998); Thomas Jefferson, *Notes on Locke and Shaftesbury*, October 11–November 19, 1776, in *Jefferson and Madison on Separation of Church and State* 28 (Lenni Brenner ed., Barricade Books 2004); Jefferson, *Notes on the State of Virginia*, in *The Life and Selected Writings of Thomas Jefferson* 275 (Adrienne Koch & William Peden eds., Modern Library 1944); Thomas Jefferson, *Autobiography* (1821) in *The Complete Jefferson* 1147 (Saul K. Padover ed., Duell, Sloan & Pearce 1943).

4 James Madison, *Memorial and Remonstrance Against Religious Assessments* (June 20, 1785), in *James Madison: Writings* 32 (Jack N. Rakove ed., Library of America 1999).

5 See Merrill D. Peterson & Robert C. Vaughan eds., *The Virginia Statute for Religious Freedom* (Cambridge 1988); Lambert, *Founding Fathers* at 209 (cited in note 2); Brooke Allen, *Moral Minority: Our Skeptical Founding Fathers* 70–71 (Ivan R. Dee 2006); Jon Meacham, *American Gospel: God, The Founding Fathers, and the Making of a Nation* 85–86 (Random House 2006).

6 Lambert, *Founding Fathers* at 238 (cited in note 2). See Lambert, *Founding Fathers* at 235 (cited in note 2); Mark A. Noll, *Evangelicals in the American Founding and Evangelical*

Political Mobilization Today, in *Religion and the New Republic* 137, 146–47 (James H. Hutson ed., Rowman & Littlefield 2000); Patricia U. Bonomi, *Under the Cope of Heaven: Religion, Society, and Politics in Colonial America* 102–4 (Oxford 1986); John M. Murrin, *Religion and Politics in America from the First Settlements to the Civil War,* in *Religion and American Politics: From the Colonial Period to the 1980s* 19, 31 (Mark A. Noll ed., Oxford 1990).

7   James Madison, *Federalist* No. 10, in Rakove, *Madison: Writings* at 162 (cited in note 4). See Gordon S. Wood, *Revolutionary Characters* 143 (Penguin 2006).

8   U.S. Const., art. VI, § 3.

9   Philip B. Kurland & Ralph Lerner eds., 4 *The Founders' Constitution* 643 (Chicago 1987); Jonathan Elliot, ed., 4 *The Debates in the Several State Conventions on the Adoption of the Federal Constitution* 199, 215 (Philadelphia 1888); Isaac Kramnick & R. Laurence Moore, *The Godless Constitution* 32–36 (Norton 1996). See Henry F. May, *The Enlightenment in America* 97, 371 n.20 (Oxford 1976); Harry S. Stout, *Rhetoric and Reality in the Early Republic,* in Noll, *Religion and American Politics* at 62, 74 n.1 (cited in note 6); Isaac Kramnick, *The "Great National Discussion,"* in Edward Countryman, *What Did the Constitution Mean to Early Americans?* 31, 42–43 (Bedford/St. Martin's 1999).

10   Kramnick & Moore, *Godless Constitution* at 38–39, 27–28 (cited in note 9).

11   See Gordon S. Wood, *The Radicalism of the American Revolution* 229 (Vintage 1991); Bernard Bailyn, *The Ideological Origins of the American Revolution* 142 (Belknap 1992).

12   John Adams to Mercy Warren, January 8, April 16, 1776, in 1 *Warren-Adams Letters* 201–2, 222 (Worthington C. Ford ed., Massachusetts Historical Society 1917, 1925).

13   Wood, *Radicalism* at 104, 195–96 (cited in note 11). See William Livingston, *The Independent Reflector* 220 (Milton M. Klein ed., Belknap 1963). See Bailyn, *Ideological Origins* at 302–3 (cited in note 11); Wood, *Revolutionary Characters* at 107 (cited in note 7).

14   *Madison's Observations on Jefferson's Draft of a Constitution for Virginia* (1788), in Julian P. Boyd, 6 *The Papers of Thomas Jefferson* 308–9 (Princeton 1965); James Madison, *Federalist* No. 10, November 22, 1787, in *Federalists and Antifederalists* 26, 27 (John P. Kaminski & Richard Leffler eds., Rowman & Littlefield 1998); James Madison, *Vices of the Political System of the United States* (Apr. 1787), in Rakove, *Madison: Writings* at 69–75 (cited in note 4). See Wood, *Radicalism* at 250–51, 229–30 (cited in note 11); Rakove, *Declaring Rights* at 103–4 (cited in note 3); Countryman, *What Did the Constitution Mean* at 18–19 (cited in note 9).

15   See May, *Enlightenment* at 98 (cited in note 9); Wood, *Radicalism* at 252–53, 48–50 (cited in note 11).

16   Wood, *Revolutionary Characters* at 145 (cited in note 7). See Drew R. McCoy, *The Last of the Fathers: James Madison and the Republican Legacy* 45–64 (Cambridge 1989); Bernard Bailyn, *To Begin the World Anew* at 97, 108–9 (Vintage 2004).

17   Providence Gazette, January 5, 1788, quoted in Wood, *Radicalism* at 255 (cited in note 11); Elliot, 2 *Debates in the State Conventions* at 260, 13 (cited in note 9). See Wood, *Radicalism* at 255 (cited in note 11).

18   Bernard Bailyn, *Faces of Revolution: Personalities and Themes in the Struggle for American Independence* 245 (Vintage 1992); Richard Henry Lee to Governor Edmund Randolph, October 16, 1787, in Kaminski & Leffler, *Federalists and Antifederalists* at 156 (cited in note

14). See *Federal Farmer*, in 14 *The Documentary History of the Ratification of the Constitution* 242 (John P. Kaminski & Gaspare J. Saladino eds., State Historical Society of Wisconsin 1981); *An Old Whig*, in Kaminski & Saladino, 13 *Documentary History* at 541 (cited in this note); *An Old Whig IV*, Philadelphia Independent Gazetteer (Oct. 27, 1787), in Kaminski & Leffler, *Federalists and Antifederalists* at 19 (cited in note 14).

19 See A Countryman (Roger Sherman), New Haven Gazette, November 22, 1787, in Kaminski & Leffler, *Federalists and Antifederalists* 170 (cited in note 14); James Wilson, Speech in Pennsylvania Ratifying Convention, November 24, 1787, in Kaminski & Leffler, *Federalists and Antifederalists* 170–71 (cited in note 14); Leonard W. Levy, *Origins of the Bill of Rights* 1–43 (Yale 1999); Jack N. Rakove, *Original Meanings: Politics and Ideas in the Making of the Constitution* 327 (Knopf 1996).

20 Rakove, *Declaring Rights* at 2–3 (cited in note 3); Bailyn, *Ideological Origins* at 184–85 (cited in note 11).

21 John Dickinson, *An Address to the Committee of Correspondence in Barbados* (Philadelphia 1766), in *Writings of John Dickinson* 262 (Paul Leicester Ford ed., Philadelphia 1895) (XIV, Memoirs of the Historical Society of Pennsylvania); Alexander Hamilton, *The Farmer Refuted, &c.* (New York 1775), in 1 *The Papers of Alexander Hamilton* 122 (Harold C. Syrett & Jacob E. Cooke eds., Columbia 1961); Philip Livingston, *The Other Side of the Question . . .* (New York 1774), quoted in Bailyn, *Ideological Origins* at 188 (cited in note 11).

22 Rakove, *Declaring Rights* at 3 (cited in note 3).

23 See Gordon S. Wood, *The Creation of the American Republic, 1776–1787* 271 (North Carolina 1986); Rakove, *Declaring Rights* at 36–38, 75–78 (cited in note 3); John Phillip Reid, *Constitutional History of the American Revolution: The Authority of Rights* 65–66 (Wisconsin 1986); Rakove, *Original Meanings* at 306–10 (cited in note 19); Larry D. Kramer, *The People Themselves: Popular Constitutionalism and Judicial Review* 39–40 (Oxford 2004). For more on the state bills of rights, see Bernard Schwartz, *The Great Rights of Mankind: A History of the American Bill of Rights* 53–91 (Madison House 1992).

24 James Madison, *Memorandum on the Vices of the Political System of the United States*, April 1787, in 9 *The Papers of James Madison* 355 (Robert A. Rutland & William M. E. Rachal eds., Chicago 1975); James Madison to Thomas Jefferson, October 24, 1787, in Rakove, *Declaring Rights* at 150, 152 (cited in note 3). See Rakove, *Declaring Rights* at 103–5 (cited in note 3).

25 See Rakove, *Declaring Rights* at 106–7 (cited in note 3).

26 Thomas Jefferson to James Madison, December 20, 1787, in Rakove, *Declaring Rights* at 154, 156 (cited in note 3).

27 James Madison to Thomas Jefferson, October 17, 1788, in Rakove, *Declaring Rights* at 160–62 (cited in note 3). See Rakove, *Original Meanings* at 330–36 (cited in note 19).

28 Thomas Jefferson to James Madison, March 15, 1789, in Rakove, *Declaring Rights* at 165 (cited in note 3).

29 James Madison, Speech to the House of Representatives, June 8, 1789, in 12 *The Papers of James Madison* 204 (Charles F. Hobson, Robert A. Rutland, & William M. E. Rachal eds., Virginia 1979).

30 James Madison, Speech to the House of Representatives, June 8, 1789, in Rakove, *Declaring Rights* at 170, 179 (cited in note 3).

31 James Madison, Speech to the House of Representatives, June 8, 1789, in Rakove, *Declaring Rights* at 170, 179 (cited in note 3).

32 James Madison, Speech to the House of Representatives, June 8, 1789, in Rakove, *Declaring Rights* at 170, 179 (cited in note 3). See Bailyn, *To Begin the World Anew* at 47–48 (cited in note 16); Levy, *Origins of Bill of Rights* at 25–43 (cited in note 19); Dumas Malone, 3 *Jefferson and His Time: Jefferson and the Ordeal of Liberty* 401–5 (Little, Brown 1962); Boyd, 12 *Papers of Jefferson* at 449 (cited in note 14); Boyd, 14 *Papers of Jefferson* at 18–19 (cited in note 14).

33 John Adams, Letter to the People of Pennsylvania 7 (Philadelphia 1760), quoted in Bailyn, *Ideological Origins* at 74–75 (cited in note 11). See Rakove, *Declaring Rights* at 164 (cited in note 3); Bailyn, *Ideological Origins* at 74–75, 105–7 (cited in note 11).

34 *To the Public*, in 2 Griffith J. McRee, *Life and Correspondence of James Iredell* 148 (Appelton 1858).

35 Kramer, *The People Themselves* at 79 (cited in note 23).

36 *Federalist* No. 78. See Rakove, *Original Meanings* at 328–29 (cited in note 19).

37 Jack Rakove, *The Origins of Judicial Review* 49 Stan. L. Rev. 1031, 1047 (1997). See Kramer, *The People Themselves* at 35–92 (cited in note 23); Kermit L. Hall & Peter Karsten, *The Magic Mirror: Law in American History* 64 (Oxford 2009).

38 See Bailyn, *Ideological Origins* at 78, 85 (cited in note 11); Daniel A. Farber, *Retained by the People* 21–44 (Basic Books 2007).

39 James Iredell, Speech in the North Carolina Ratification Convention, July 28, 1788, in Rakove, *Declaring Rights* at 145, 146 (cited in note 3).

40 Thomas Jefferson to James Madison, March 15, 1789, in Rakove, *Declaring Rights* at 165, 166 (cited in note 3); James Madison, Speech to the House of Representatives, June 8, 1789, in Rakove, *Declaring Rights* at 170, 174 (cited in note 3); United States House of Representatives, Constitutional Amendments Proposed to the Senate, August 24, 1789, in Rakove, *Declaring Rights* at 183, 185 (cited in note 3).

41 For commentary on the meaning of the Ninth Amendment, see the essays collected in Randy E. Barnett ed., *The Rights Retained by the People: The History and Meaning of the Ninth Amendment* (George Mason University 1989); Thomas C. Grey, *Do We Have an Unwritten Constitution?* 27 Stan. L. Rev. 703, 709, 716 (1975); Thomas C. Grey, *The Origins of the Unwritten Constitution: Fundamental Law in American Revolutionary Thought*, 30 Stan. L. Rev. 843 (1978); Suzanna Sherry, *The Founders' Unwritten Constitution*, 54 U. Chi. L. Rev. 1127, 1163–67 (1987).

42 William E. Nelson, *Emerging Notions of Modern Criminal Law in the Revolutionary Era: An Historical Perspective*, 42 N.Y.U. L. Rev. 450, 451 (1967); William E. Nelson, *Americanization of the Common Law: The Impact of Legal Change on Massachusetts Society, 1760–1830* 5, 39, 68 (Georgia 1994). See John E. O'Connor, *Legal Reform in the Early Republic: The New Jersey Experience*, 22 Am. J. Leg. Hist. 95, 100 (1978); David J. Rothman, *The Discovery of the Asylum: Social Order and Disorder in the New Republic* 59–62 (Little, Brown 1971); Lawrence M. Friedman, *A History of American Law* 207–12 (3d ed., Simon & Schuster 2005); Wood, *Radicalism* at 193, 300–301 (cited in note 11); David H. Flaherty, *Law and the Enforcement* *of Morals in Early America*, 5 Perspectives in Am. Hist. 203, 245–53 (1971); Kramnick & Moore, *Godless Constitution* at 77–78 (cited in note 9).

43   Nelson, *Americanization of the Common Law* at 36–37 (cited in note 42); William Blackstone, 4 *Commentaries on the Laws of England* 41 (Oxford 1769). See Nelson, *Americanization of the Common Law* at 37–38 (cited in note 42); Friedman, *History of American Law* at 36 (cited in note 42).

44   Nelson, *Americanization of the Common Law* at 6, 111, 118 (cited in note 42). See Nelson, *Americanization of the Common Law* at 89, 110 (cited in note 42); Nelson, *Emerging Notions* at 455–66 (cited in note 42); Cecelia M. Kenyon ed., *The Antifederalists* 122 (Bobbs-Merrill 1966); O'Connor, *Legal Reform* at 108 (cited in note 42); Flaherty, *Law and Enforcement of Morals* at 246–49 (cited in note 42); John D'Emilio & Estelle B. Freedman, *Intimate Matters: A History of Sexuality in America* 49 (Chicago 1997).

45   Leonard W. Levy, *The Establishment Clause: Religion and the First Amendment* 84, 92 (Macmillan 1986). See Rakove, *Original Meanings* at 290 (cited in note 19); Thomas J. Curry, *The First Freedoms* 202 (Oxford 1986); Levy, *Origins of Bill of Rights* at 81–82 (cited in note 19).

46   Curry, *First Freedoms* at 194, 199, 205, 216 (cited in note 45).

47   James Madison to Edward Livingston, July 10, 1822, in Rakove, *Madison: Writings* at 788–89 (cited in note 4); James Madison to Jasper Adams, September 1833, in Daniel L. Dreisbach, *Religion and Politics in the Early Republic* 120 (Kentucky 1996). See George Washington to the Hebrew Congregation in Newport, Rhode Island (Aug. 17, 1790), in Paul F. Boller Jr., *George Washington and Religion* 170 (Southern Methodist 1963).

48   Thomas Jefferson, Letter to a Committee of the Danbury Baptist Association, January 1, 1802, in *Thomas Jefferson: Writings* 510 (Merrill D. Peterson ed., Library of America 1984).

49   Allen, *Moral Minority* at 181 (cited in note 5). See Wood, *Radicalism* at 231 (cited in note 11); Allen, *Moral Minority* at 143 (cited in note 5).

50   Wood, *Revolutionary Characters* at 116–17 (cited in note 7).

CHAPTER 7

1   John G. West Jr., *The Politics of Revelation and Reason* 119–21 (Kansas 1996).

2   Benjamin Rush, Letter from Benjamin Rush to Noah Webster, July 20, 1798, in 2 *Letters of Benjamin Rush* 799 (L. H. Butterfield ed., Princeton 1951); Perry Miller, *The Life of the Mind in America: From the Revolution to the Civil War* 3–4 (Harcourt, Brace & World 1965). See Robert H. Abzug, *Cosmos Crumbling: American Reform and the Religious Imagination* 27 (Oxford 1994); West, *Politics of Revelation* at 9 (cited in note 1). On the causes of the Second Great Awakening, see Paul E. Johnson, *A Shopkeeper's Millennium: Society and Revivals in Rochester, New York, 1815–1837* 9, 53–57 (Hill and Wang 1978); Abzug, *Cosmos Crumbling* at 5–6 (cited in this note); Sydney E. Ahlstrom, *A Religious History of the American People* 474–75 (Yale 1972); Nancy F. Cott, *Young Women in the Second Great Awakening in New England*, 3 Feminist Stud. 15 (1975).

3 See Ahlstrom, *Religious History* at 387, 416, 433 (cited in note 2); Perry Miller, *Life of the Mind* at 6 (cited in note 2).

4 Barton Warren Stone, *A Short History of the Life of Barton W. Stone Written by Himself*, in *Voices from Cane Ridge* 68, 69–72 (Rhodes Thompson ed., Bethany Press 1954), quoted in Ahlstrom, *Religious History* at 434–35 (cited in note 2).

5 See Daniel Walker Howe, *What Hath God Wrought: The Transformation of America, 1815–1848* 286 (Oxford 2007); Francis Wayland, *The Duties of an American Citizen: Two Discourses* 19, 34, 44 (James Loring 1825), quoted in Howe, *What Hath God Wrought* at 288 (cited in this note); Ahlstrom, *Religious History* at 387 (cited in note 2); Howe, *What Hath God Wrought* at 156–59, 286, 292 (cited in this note); Abzug, *Cosmos Crumbling* at 40 (cited in note 2); Miller, *Life of the Mind* at 3–95 (cited in note 2); Richard J. Carwardine, *Evangelicals and Politics in Antebellum America*, 52–53 (Yale 1993).

6 Ahlstrom, *Religious History* at 416 (cited in note 2); Abzug, *Cosmos Crumbling* at 36 (cited in note 2). See Abzug, *Cosmos Crumbling* at 35 (cited in note 2); Doron S. Ben-Atar & Richard D. Brown, *Taming Lust: Crimes Against Nature in the Early Republic* 68 (Pennsylvania 2014).

7 West, *Politics of Revelation* at 86 (cited in note 1); Lyman Beecher, *The Practicality of Suppressing Vice by Means of Societies Instituted for That Purpose* 27 (Samuel Green 1804), quoted in West, *Politics of Revelation* at 86 (cited in note 1); Howe, *What Hath God Wrought* at 166 (cited in note 5).

8 Abzug, *Cosmos Crumbling* at 40–41 (cited in note 2); Beecher, *Practicality of Suppressing Vice* at 12 (cited in note 7), quoted in West, *Politics of Revelation* at 87 (cited in note 1); Beecher, *Practicality of Suppressing Vice* at 17–20 (cited in note 7), quoted in Abzug, *Cosmos Crumbling* at 40–41 (cited in note 2). See West, *Politics of Revelation* at 87, 97–99 (cited in note 1).

9 Abzug, *Cosmos Crumbling* at 44 (cited in note 2); Lyman Beecher, *A Reformation of Morals Practicable and Indispensable*, in 2 *The Works of Lyman Beecher* 17–19, 77–80, 93–95 (Jewett 1852) (1812), quoted in Abzug, *Cosmos Crumbling* at 45 (cited in note 2); Lyman Beecher, *Resources of the Adversary and Means of their Destruction: A Sermon Preached October 12, 1827, Before the American Board of Missions at New York* (Boston 1827), quoted in Abzug, *Cosmos Crumbling* at 53 (cited in note 2). See Abzug, *Cosmos Crumbling* at 45–46 (cited in note 2).

10 Miller, *Life of the Mind* at 32 (cited in note 2). Howe, *What Hath God Wrought* at 172 (cited in note 5). See Bruce J. Kuklick, *Churchmen and Philosophers: From Jonathan Edwards to John Dewey* 94–111 (Yale 1985).

11 Johnson, *Shopkeeper's Millennium* at 3–8 (cited in note 2). See James D. Bratt ed., *Antirevivalism in Antebellum America* xvi, 61 (Rutgers 2006).

12 Johnson, *Shopkeeper's Millennium* at 95, 98, 100–102 109–11 (cited in note 2); Howe, *What Hath God Wrought* at 172 (cited in note 5); Miller, *Life of the Mind* at 28 (cited in note 2).

13 Howe, *What Hath God Wrought* at 192 (cited in note 5). See Anson Phelps Stokes & Leo Pfeffer, *Church and State in the United States* 3–84 (Greenwood 1975); Miller, *Life of the Mind* at 47 (cited in note 2); Ahlstrom, *Religious History* at 422–25 (cited in note 2); West, *Politics of Revelation* at 100–101 (cited in note 1); Johnson, *Shopkeeper's Millennium* at 6 (cited in note 2).

14   West, *Politics of Revelation* at 117, 121, 126 (cited in note 1); Lyman Beecher, *The Memory of Our Fathers: A Sermon Delivered*, in 1 *The Works of Lyman Beecher* at 341 (cited in note 9). See Howe, *What Hath God Wrought* at 447 (cited in note 5); James Turner Johnson ed., *The Bible in American Law, Politics, and Political Rhetoric* (Fortress 1985); West, *Politics of Revelation* at 128–29 (cited in note 1).

15   West, *Politics of Revelation* at 133–34 (cited in note 1).

16   Frances Wright D'Arusmont, *Life, Letters, and Lectures, 1834–1844* vii–viii (Arno 1972).

17   Catharine Esther Beecher, *Letters on the Difficulties of Religion* (1836), quoted in Lori D. Ginzberg, *"The Hearts of Your Readers Will Shudder,"* 46 Am. Q. 195, 215, 216 (1994); Francis Wright D'Arusmont, Lecture, in D'Arusmont, *Life, Letters, and Lectures* 65–66 (cited in note 16). See Celia Morris Eckhardt, *Fanny Wright: Rebel in America* 249–50 (Harvard 1984); West, *Politics of Revelation* at 134 (cited in note 1).

18   Abzug, *Cosmos Crumbling* at 41 (cited in note 2).

19   An Act Regulating the Post-Office Establishment, § 9, 11th Cong., 2d Sess. (1810).

20   Lyman Beecher, *The Memory of Our Fathers: A Sermon Delivered* (1828), quoted in Abzug, *Cosmos Crumbling* at 111 (cited in note 2); Abzug, *Cosmos Crumbling* at 114 (cited in note 2); West, *Politics of Revelation* at 141–45 (cited in note 1).

21   West, *Politics of Revelation* at 148, 150 (cited in note 1); Petition of Inhabitants of Hanover, Pennsylvania (Mar. 1, 1830), quoted in West, *Politics of Revelation* at 150 (cited in note 1).

22   Senate Comm., 20th Cong., Senate Report on Sunday Mails, Communicated to the Senate, January 19, 1829, quoted in West, *Politics of Revelation* at 154–55 (cited in note 1).

23   21st Cong., No. 87, Sunday Mails, Communicated to the House of Representatives, March 4–5, 1830, in *American State Papers: Documents, Legislative and Executive, of the Congress of the United States* 230–31 (1834), quoted in West, *Politics of Revelation* at 159 (cited in note 1); Report of Mr. Johnson (Mar. 4–5, 1830), in 1 *American State Papers, Class 7: Post Office* 230–31, quoted in West, *Politics of Revelation* at 159 (cited in note 1).

24   West, *Politics of Revelation* at 159, 140, 157 (cited in note 1).

25   Carwardine, *Evangelicals and Politics* at 100 (cited in note 5). See Arthur M. Schlesinger Jr., *The Age of Jackson* 143 (J.J. Little & Ives 1945); Charles Miles Snow, *Religious Liberty in America* 239–54 (Review and Herald 1914); Stokes & Pfeffer, *Church and State* at 254–55 (cited in note 13); West, *Politics of Revelation* at 137–61 (cited in note 1).

26   West, *Politics of Revelation* at 161, 123 (cited in note 1); Leonard W. Levy, *Blasphemy: Verbal Offense Against the Sacred* 3 (Knopf 1993).

27   See Levy, *Blasphemy* at 44, 49 (cited in note 26). See Saint Augustine, 87. Augustine to His Cherished and Beloved Brother Emeritus (c. 405; before 411), in Saint Augustine, 2 *Letters* at 12 (Wilfred Parsons, trans., Fathers of the Church 1955); Saint Augustine, 93. Augustine to His Beloved Brother, Vincent (408), in 2 *Letters* at 56 (cited in this note); Saint Augustine, 173. Augustine, Bishop of the Catholic Church, to Donatus, Priest of the Donatist Sect (c. 416), in Saint Augustine 4 *Letters* at 73 (cited in this note); Saint Augustine, 185. Augustine to Boniface, Tribune and Count in Africa (417), in 4 *Letters* at 141 (cited in this note).

28   St. Thomas Aquinas, *Summa Theologica* (Fathers of the English Dominican Province

trans., London 1912–1929, 22 volumes), vol. 9, 168–69, quoted in Levy, *Blasphemy* at 52 (cited in note 26). See Levy, *Blasphemy* at 46–237 (cited in note 26).

29 Levy, *Blasphemy* at 400 (cited in note 26); see *id.* at 238–271.

30 *People v. Ruggles*, 8 Johns. (N.Y.) 290 (1811); Miller, *Life of the Mind* at 66 (cited in note 2). See Levy, *Blasphemy* at 400–406 (cited in note 26).

31 *Updegraph v. The Commonwealth*, 11 Serg. & R. (Pa.) 394 (1824). See Sarah Barringer Gordon, *Blasphemy and the Law of Religious Liberty in Nineteenth-Century America*, 52 Am. Q. 682, 693 (2000).

32 Miller, *Life of the Mind* at 206 (cited in note 2); John Adams to Thomas Jefferson, January 23, 1825, in *The Adams-Jefferson Letters* 607–9 (Lester J. Cappon ed., North Carolina 1971); Thomas Jefferson to John Cartwright, June 5, 1824, in 15 *The Writings of Thomas Jefferson* 48–51 (Albert Ellery Bergh ed., Arkose 1907). See Miller, *Life of the Mind* at 192–93 (cited in note 2).

33 John Davison Lawson ed., 13 *American State Trials* 536–37 (1921); *Commonwealth v. Kneeland*, 37 Mass. 206, 220 (1838). See Miller, *Life of the Mind* at 195 (cited in note 2).

34 See Ahlstrom, *Religious History* at 425–26 (cited in note 2); Abzug, *Cosmos Crumbling* at 82 (cited in note 2); Howe, *What Hath God Wrought* at 166–68 (cited in note 5); W. J. Rorabaugh, *The Alcoholic Republic* 1–146 (Oxford 1979); Joyce Appleby, *Inheriting the Revolution* 204–15 (Belknap 2000); Mark Edward Lender & James Kirby Martin, *Drinking in America: A History* 16–21, 41–46 (Free Press 1987).

35 Lyman Beecher, *Six Sermons on the Nature, Occasions, Signs, Evils, and Remedy of Intemperance* 10, 53, 49, 64 (6th ed., Boston, Marvin 1828), quoted in Abzug, *Cosmos Crumbling* at 86–88 (cited in note 2).

36 See Ahlstrom, *Religious History* at 425–26 (cited in note 2); West, *Politics of Revelation* at 107 (cited in note 1); Abzug, *Cosmos Crumbling* at 82–93 (cited in note 2).

37 Abzug, *Cosmos Crumbling* at 83, 84–85 (cited in note 2). See Ahlstrom, *Religious History* at 425–27 (cited in note 2); Johnson, *Shopkeeper's Millennium* at 55–61, 79–85 (cited in note 2); Abzug, *Cosmos Crumbling* at 82–102 (cited in note 2); Timothy L. Smith, *Revivalism and Social Reform in Mid-Nineteenth-Century America* 167–68 (Abingdon Press 1957).

38 Abzug, *Cosmos Crumbling* at 131–32, 135 (cited in note 2). See Howe, *What Hath God Wrought* at 478–80 (cited in note 5); Carwardine, *Evangelicals and Politics* at 56–58 (cited in note 5).

39 See West, *Politics of Revelation* at 110 (cited in note 1); Abzug, *Cosmos Crumbling* at 133 (cited in note 2).

40 George Fredrickson ed., *William Lloyd Garrison* 14–15 (Prentice-Hall 1968); Abzug, *Cosmos Crumbling* at 129, 135–36, 143 (cited in note 2). See Fredrickson, *William Lloyd Garrison* at 14–15 (cited in this note); Smith, *Revivalism and Social Reform* at 183 (cited in note 37).

41 Abzug, *Cosmos Crumbling* at 151–52 (cited in note 2); Samuel J. May, *Some Recollections of Our Antislavery Conflict* 19 (Fields, Osgood 1869), quoted in Abzug, *Cosmos Crumbling* at 153 (cited in note 2). See Abzug, *Cosmos Crumbling* at 151–52 (cited in note 2).

42 *Acts* 17:26 (King James Version); *Genesis* 9:25 (King James Version); Howe, *What Hath God Wrought* at 475–80 (cited in note 5). See Mason I. Lowance Jr. ed., *A House*

Divided: The Antebellum Slavery Debates in America, 1776–1865 63–67, 92–96 (Princeton 2003); Drew Gilpin Faust, *Southern Stories: Slaveholders in Peace and War* 72–87 (Missouri 1992); Richard Hofstadter, *The American Political Tradition* 68 (Knopf 1989).

43　Patricia Cline Cohen, Timothy J. Gilfoyle, & Helen Lefkowitz Horowitz, *The Flash Press: Sporting Male Weeklies in 1840s New York* 9 (Chicago 2008); Helen Lefkowitz Horowitz, *Rereading Sex: Battles Over Sexual Knowledge and Suppression in Nineteenth-Century America* 5–6 (Knopf 2002). See Cohen, Gilfoyle, & Horowitz, *Flash Press* at 109 (cited in this note).

44　2 Str. 788 (1727).

45　*Commonwealth of Pennsylvania v. Sharpless*, 2 Serg. & R. 91, 92, 94 (Pa. 1815).

46　*Commonwealth v. Holmes*, 17 Mass. 336 (1821).

47　Horowitz, *Rereading Sex* at 48–49, 67–68 (cited in note 43).

48　Horowitz, *Rereading Sex* at 75 (cited in note 43); Charles Knowlton, *Fruits of Philosophy* (F. P. Rogers 1839), quoted in Horowitz, *Rereading Sex* at 75, 76 (cited in note 43). See Janet Farrell Brodie, *Contraception and Abortion in 19th-Century America* 97–104 (Cornell 1994); Norman E. Himes, *Medical History of Contraception* 226–30 (Gamut 1963).

49　See Horowitz, *Rereading Sex* at 73–77 (cited in note 43).

50　Horowitz, *Rereading Sex* at 102–3 (cited in note 43); Luther V. Bell, *An Hour's Conference with Fathers and Sons, in Relation to a Common and Fatal Indulgence of Youth* 26–27 (Whipple and Damrell 1840), quoted in Horowitz, *Rereading Sex* at 102 (cited in note 43); Michael S. Patton, *Masturbation from Judaism to Victorianism*, 24 J. Relig. & Health, 133–46, 142 (1985).

51　See Cohen, Gilfoyle, & Horowitz, *Flash Press* at 90–91 (cited in note 43).

52　See Hal D. Sears, *The Sex Radicals: Free Love in High Victorian America* 34 (Kansas 1977); Albert Post, *Popular Freethought in America, 1825–1850* 53–61, 122–26 (Octagon 1974); Eckhardt, *Fanny Wright* at 180 (cited in note 17).

53　Frances Wright, *Views of Society and Manners in America* 219 (1821), quoted in Eckhardt, *Fanny Wright* at 83 (cited in note 17); Frances Wright, *Free Enquirer*, April 29, 1829; quoted in Eckhardt, *Fanny Wright* at 194 (cited in note 17). See Ginzberg, *Hearts of Your Readers* at 212 (cited in note 17).

54　Quoted in Roderick S. French, *Liberation from Man and God in Boston*, 32 Amer. Q. 202, 206 (1980); John Spurlock, *The Free Love Network in America, 1850 to 1860*, 21 J. Soc. Hist. 765 (1988). See Howe, *What Hath God Wrought?* at 293–95 (cited in note 5).

55　Frances Wright, *Nashoba, Explanatory Notes and Continued*, New-Harmony Gazette (Feb. 6, 1828) 132, quoted in Horowitz, *Rereading Sex* at 54–55 (cited in note 43); Robert Dale Owen, *Moral Physiology* 13, 55 (1830), quoted in Horowitz, *Rereading Sex* at 58–60 (cited in note 43). See Eckhardt, *Fanny Wright* at 156–58 (cited in note 17); Horowitz, *Rereading Sex* at 61–67 (cited in note 43).

56　Horowitz, *Rereading Sex* at 61 (cited in note 43); Lyman Beecher, *Lectures on Political Atheism and Kindred Subjects* at 91, 97–99 (1852), quoted in Horowitz, *Rereading Sex* at 62–63 (cited in note 43); John Spurlock, *Free Love Network* at 765, 768 (cited in note 54).

57　See Spurlock, *Free Love Network* at 771, 774–75 (cited in note 54); Martin Blatt, *Free Love and Anarchism: The Biography of Ezra Heywood* 174 (Illinois 1990); Sears, *Sex Radicals* at 22 (cited in note 52); Brodie, *Contraception and Abortion* at 61 (cited in note 48).

58   See Johnson, *Shopkeeper's Millennium* at 4–5 (cited in note 2); Miller, *Life of the Mind* at 38 (cited in note 2); Howe, *What Hath God Wrought?* at 172–73, 186, 190–91 (cited in note 5); Miller, *Life of the Mind* at 3–95 (cited in note 2); Nancy F. Cott, *The Bonds of Womanhood* 141 (Yale 1997); Johnson, *Shopkeeper's Millennium* at 5 (cited in note 2); West, *Politics of Revelation* at 207–8 (cited in note 1).

59   West, *Politics of Revelation* at 207–8, 210 (cited in note 1); Johnson, *Shopkeeper's Millennium* at 7 (cited in note 2).

60   Calvin Colton, *Thoughts on the Religious State of the Country* (1836) in Bratt, *Antirevivalism in Antebellum America* at 108 (cited in note 11); West, *Politics of Revelation* at 207–8, 210 (cited in note 1). See Howe, *What Hath God Wrought* at 448–49 (cited in note 5); Stokes & Pfeffer, *Church and State* at 47–72 (cited in note 13).

CHAPTER 8

1   See Frederick F. Schauer, *The Law of Obscenity* 3 (Bureau of National Affairs 1976); Timothy J. Gilfoyle, *City of Eros* 29–31, 59–60, 70, 164 (Norton 1992); Kat Long, *The Forbidden Apple: A Century of Sex and Sin in New York City* 22 (Ig 2009); Patricia Cline Cohen, Timothy J. Gilfoyle, & Helen Lefkowitz Horowitz, *The Flash Press: Sporting Male Weeklies in 1840s New York* 7 (Chicago 2008); Helen Lefkowitz Horowitz, *Rereading Sex: Battles Over Sexual Knowledge and Suppression in Nineteenth-Century America* 146–47 (Knopf 2002); Milton Rugoff, *Prudery and Passion* ch. 11 (Hart-Davis 1971).

2   Gilfoyle, *City of Eros* at 99 (cited in note 1); Cohen, Gilfoyle, & Horowitz, *Flash Press* at 62–63 (cited in note 1). See Donna Dennis, *Licentious Gotham: Erotic Publishing and Its Prosecution in Nineteenth-Century New York* 45–50 (Harvard 2009); Frederick S. Lane III, *Obscene Profits: The Entrepreneurs of Pornography in the Cyber Age* 43 (Routledge 2000).

3   Horowitz, *Rereading Sex* at 171–72 (cited in note 1).

4   Francis Ludlow Holt, *The Law of Libel* (1816), quoted in Cohen, Gilfoyle, & Horowitz, *The Flash Press* at 84 (cited in note 1).

5   William Snelling, *Our Indictments*, in Flash (Dec. 11, 1841) (vol. 1, no. 16), quoted in Cohen, Gilfoyle, & Horowitz, *The Flash Press* at 106 (cited in note 1).

6   Horowitz, *Rereading Sex* at 213, 218–23 (cited in note 1). See Dennis, *Licentious Gotham* at 108 (cited in note 2).

7   See Horowitz, *Rereading Sex* at 319–22 (cited in note 1); Gilfoyle, *City of Eros* at 225 (cited in note 1).

8   Horowitz, *Rereading Sex* at 301 (cited in note 1). See Jocelyn Elise Crowley & Theda Skocpol, *The Rush to Organize*, 45 Am. J. Pol. Sci. 813, 815 (2001); Horowitz, *Rereading Sex* at 310–12 (cited in note 1).

9   See Horowitz, *Rereading Sex* at 361 (cited in note 1); Dennis, *Licentious Gotham* at 255–57 (cited in note 2).

10   See Schauer, *Law of Obscenity* at 10 (cited in note 1); Horowitz, *Rereading Sex* at 361–62 (cited in note 1).

11   Gilfoyle, *City of Eros* at 187 (cited in note 1).

12 Dennis, *Licentious Gotham* at 233 (cited in note 2); Heywood Broun & Margaret Leech, *Anthony Comstock: Roundsman of the Lord* 45–49 (New York 1927).

13 Horowitz, *Rereading Sex* at 369 (cited in note 1). See Dennis, *Licentious Gotham* at 234 (cited in note 2); Broun & Leech, *Anthony Comstock* at 81 (cited in note 12); Long, *Forbidden Apple* at 15 (cited in note 1).

14 See Broun & Leech, *Anthony Comstock* at 84–85 (cited in note 12); Dennis, *Licentious Gotham* at 242 (cited in note 2).

15 Comstock, *Frauds Exposed* 8 (J. H. Brown 1880), quoted in Broun & Leech, *Anthony Comstock* at 86 (cited in note 12). See Horowitz, *Rereading Sex* at 374–75, 381 (cited in note 1); Broun & Leech, *Anthony Comstock* at 81 (cited in note 12); Dennis, *Licentious Gotham* at 252 (cited in note 2); James C. N. Paul & Murray L. Schwartz, *Federal Censorship: Obscenity in the Mail* 21 (Free Press 1961); Dorothy Ganfield Fowler, *Unmailable: Congress and the Post Office* 60–61 (Georgia 1977).

16 Comstock Act, 42 Cong. ch. 258, 17 Stat. 598 (1873). See Horowitz, *Rereading Sex* at 382 (cited in note 1); Hal D. Sears, *The Sex Radicals: Free Love in High Victorian America* 71 (Kansas 1977); Fowler, *Unmailable* at 62 (cited in note 15).

17 See Schauer, *Law of Obscenity* at 21 (cited in note 1); Dennis, *Licentious Gotham* at 276, 280, 294–95 (cited in note 2); Paul & Schwartz, *Federal Censorship* at 19 (cited in note 15); Lane, *Obscene Profits* at 15 (cited in note 2); Broun & Leech, *Anthony Comstock* at 153 (cited in note 12); Walter Kendrick, *The Secret Museum: Pornography in Modern Culture* 130 (Viking 1987).

18 Charles Rembar, *The End of Obscenity* 21 (Random House 1968); Long, *Forbidden Apple* at 25 (cited in note 1); Comstock, *Frauds Exposed* at 416 (cited in note 15).

19 Anthony Comstock, *Traps for the Young* 8, 10, 6, 240, 14 (Harvard 1967). See Martin Blatt, *Free Love and Anarchism: The Biography of Ezra Heywood* 78 (Illinois 1989); Robert H. Bremmer, *Editor's Introduction*, in Comstock, *Traps for the Young* at xvi (cited in this note).

20 Comstock, *Frauds Exposed* at 390 (cited in note 15); Broun & Leech, *Anthony Comstock* at 259 (cited in note 12).

21 Morris L. Ernst, *Reflections on the* Ulysses *Trial and Censorship*, 3 James Joyce Q. 3 (1965); Arthur Garfield Hays, *Let Freedom Ring* 170 (Liveright 1928); Dennis, *Licentious Gotham* at 292–93 (cited in note 2). See Sears, *Sex Radicals* at 73 (cited in note 16).

22 See Sears, *Sex Radicals* at 79 (cited in note 16); Leigh Ann Wheeler, *Against Obscenity: Reform and the Politics of Womanhood in America, 1873–1935* 11 (John Hopkins 2004).

23 Horowitz, *Rereading Sex* at 337 (cited in note 1).

24 Ezra H. Heywood, *Cupid's Yokes: or, The Binding Forces of Conjugal Life* 21 (Co-operative Pub. 1876). See David M. Rabban, *Free Speech in Its Forgotten Years: 1870–1920* 35 (Cambridge 1997); Blatt, *Free Love and Anarchism* at 105 (cited in note 19).

25 Sears, *Sex Radicals* at 167 (cited in note 16); Comstock, *Traps for the Young* at 163–64 (cited in note 19).

26 L.R. 3 Q. B. 360, 371 (1868). See Stephen Gillers, *A Tendency to Deprave and Corrupt*, 85 Wash. U. L. Rev. 215, 228 (2007); Schauer, *The Law of Obscenity* at 7 (cited in note 1). See Albert B. Gerber, *Sex, Pornography, and Justice* 82 (Lyle Stuart 1965).

27 *United States v. Bennett*, 24 F. Cas. 1093, 1104 (C.C.S.D. N.Y. 1879).

28 *United States v. Harmon*, 45 F. 414, 417 (D. Kan. 1891). See *Bennett*, 24 F. Cas. at 1093 (cited in note 27).

29 See Blatt, *Free Love and Anarchism* at 114–19 (cited in note 19); *Bennett*, 24 F. Cas. at 1101 (cited in note 27).

30 Sears, *Sex Radicals* at 169 (cited in note 16).

31 See *Bennett*, 24 F. Cas. at 1101 (cited in note 27).

32 Bremmer, *Editor's Introduction*, in Comstock, *Traps for the Young* at xviii (cited in note 19); National Defense Association, *Words of Warning to Those Who Aid and Abet in the Suppression of Free Speech and Free Press* (New York 1879), quoted in Paul S. Boyer, *Purity in Print* 9 (Wisconsin 2002).

33 Quoted in Comstock, *Traps for the Young* at 189–90 (cited in note 19), quoted in Boyer, *Purity in Print* at 9 (cited in note 32); Paul & Schwartz, *Federal Censorship* at 29 (cited in note 15). See Comstock, *Traps for the Young* at 192–96 (cited in note 19).

34 Sears, *Sex Radicals* at 75 (cited in note 16).

35 *United States v. Harmon*, 45 F. 414 (D. Kan. 1891). See Sears, *Sex Radicals* at 74 (cited in note 16); Jesse F. Battan, *"The Word Made Flesh": Language, Authority, and Sexual Desire in Late Nineteenth-Century America* 3 J. Hist. Sexuality 223, 225 (1992).

36 See Rabban, *Free Speech* at 41 (cited in note 24); Sears, *Sex Radicals* at 110–11, 172 (cited in note 16); David M. Rabban, *The Free Speech League, the ACLU, and Changing Conceptions of Free Speech in American History*, 45 Stan. L. Rev. 47, 89 (1992); Horowitz, *Rereading Sex* at 409 (cited in note 1).

37 George Bernard Shaw, Letter to Robert W. Welch (ca. September 22–23, 1905), in *Bernard Shaw: Collected Letters 1898–1910* 559–61 (Dan H. Laurence ed., Reinhardt 1972); Lane, *Obscene Profits* at 16 (cited in note 2); Kendrick, *Secret Museum* at 147–48 (cited in note 17).

38 Lincoln Steffens, *An Answer and an Answer*, 25 Everybody's Mag 717, 718 (1911); Rabban, *The Free Speech League* at 80 (cited in note 36). See Rabban, *The Free Speech League* at 71, 53, 83, 88–90 (cited in note 36).

39 *Theodore Schroeder: A Very Wise Man*, in *Theodore Schroeder's Last Will* (Leslie Kuhn ed., 1958) (quoting H. L. Mencken), quoted in Rabban, *The Free Speech League* at 77 (cited in note 36). See Rabban, *The Free Speech League* at 88, 91–96 (cited in note 36); Theodore Schroeder, *"Obscene" Literature and Constitutional Law* 12–14 (New York 1911).

40 Malcolm Cowley, *After the Genteel Tradition: American Writers, 1910–1930* 10–11 (Southern Illinois 1964), quoted in Felice Flanery Lewis, *Literature, Obscenity, and Law* 19–20 (Southern Illinois 1976); Arthur E. Bostwick, *The Librarian as Censor*, 33 Library J. 257, 264 (1908), quoted in Boyer, *Purity in Print* at 31 (cited in note 32). See Tom Dardis, *Firebrand at Work*, 53 Antioch Rev. 338, 342 (1995); Boyer, *Purity in Print* at 16 (cited in note 32); Rugoff, *Prudery and Passion* at 76 (cited in note 1).

41 Anthony Comstock, *Vampire Literature*, CLIII N. Amer. Rev. 165 (1891), quoted in Boyer, *Purity in Print* at 21 (cited in note 32).

42 See Boyer, *Purity in Print* at 19, 45, 66–67 (cited in note 32); Lewis, *Literature, Obscenity, and Law* at 1, 54–56 (cited in note 40); Rugoff, *Prudery and Passion* at 314 (cited in note 1); Broun & Leech, *Anthony Comstock* at 232 (cited in note 12).

43 *United States v. Kennerley*, 209 F. 119 (S.D.N.Y. 1913).

44 *Id.* at 121.

45 See Paul S. Boyer, *Boston Book Censorship in the Twenties*, 15 Amer. Quart. 3, 11 (1963); Thomas F. O'Connor, *The National Organization for Decent Literature*, 65 Lib. Q. 390 (1995); William B. Lockhart & Robert C. McClure, *Literature, the Law of Obscenity, and the Constitution*, 38 Minn. L. Rev. 295, 304 and n.64 (1954); Lane, *Obscene Profits* at 98–99 (cited in note 2).

46 See Boyer, *Boston Book Censorship* at 5–6, 13 (cited in note 45); Robert T. Bushnell, *Banned in Boston*, 229 N. Amer. Rev. 518, 521 (1930).

47 See H. L. Mencken, *Puritanism as a Literary Force*, in H. L. Mencken, *A Book of Prefaces* 277 (Knopf 1917); Boyer, *Purity in Print* at 9 (cited in note 32).

48 *Halsey v. New York Society for Suppression of Vice*, 234 N.Y. 1, 4, 136 N.E. 219 (1922). See Gillers, *A Tendency to Deprave* at 266–67 (cited in note 26).

49 Lewis, *Literature, Obscenity, and Law* at 84 (cited in note 40). See Boyer, *Purity in Print* at 80–81 (cited in note 32).

50 Dardis, *Firebrand at Work* at 345–46 (cited in note 40). See Boyer, *Purity in Print* at 82–83 (cited in note 32); Gillers, *A Tendency to Deprave* at 267–68 (cited in note 26).

51 See Boyer, *Purity in Print* at 100–105 (cited in note 32); Dardis, *Firebrand at Work* at 348 (cited in note 40).

52 See Dardis, *Firebrand at Work* at 350 (cited in note 40); Boyer, *Purity in Print* at 108–9 (cited in note 32).

53 Quoted in Dardis, *Firebrand at Work* at 351, 353 (cited in note 40).

54 George Jean Nathan, *The Theatre*, American Mercury 373 (Mar. 1927), quoted in Kaier Curtin, *"We Can Always Call Them Bulgarians"* 62 (Alyson 1987); quoted in Hays, *Let Freedom Ring* at 244 (cited in note 21). See Jonathan Ned Katz, *Gay American History* 82–91 (rev. ed. Meridian 1992); Thomas B. Leary & J. Roger Noall, *Entertainment: Public Pressures and the Law: Official and Unofficial Control of the Content and Distribution of Motion Pictures and Magazines*, 71 Harv. L. Rev. 326 (1957); Barry B. Witham, *The Play Jury*, 24 Educ. Theatre J. 430, 431–32 (1972); Marybeth Hamilton, *Mae West Live: SEX, The Drag, and 1920s Broadway*, 36 The Drama Rev. 82 (1988); Sherrie A. Inness, *Who's Afraid of Stephen Gordon?* 4 Natl. Women's Stud. Assn. J. 305 (1992); Hays, *Let Freedom Ring* at 239–48 (cited in note 21).

55 See Hamilton, *Mae West Live* at 90–94 (cited in note 54); Gail Finney, *Queering the Stage*, 40 Comp. Lit. Stud. 54, 64–65 (2003); Section 1140-a New York Penal Code (Apr. 5, 1927), quoted in Hays, *Let Freedom Ring* at 264 (cited in note 21).

56 Quoted in Hamilton, *Mae West Live* at 85–87 (cited in note 54); New York World (Mar. 31, 1927), quoted in Hamilton, *Mae West Live* at 98 (cited in note 54). See Finney, *Queering the Stage* at 63 (cited in note 55); Witham, *The Play Jury* at 430 (cited in note 54).

57 Hays, *Let Freedom Ring* at 268 (cited in note 21). See Note, *Motion Pictures and the First Amendment*, 60 Yale L.J. 696 (1951); Leary & Noall, *Entertainment: Public Pressures and the Law* at 328 (cited in note 54); *Block v. City of Chicago*, 87 N.E. 1011, 1013 (Ill. 1909).

58 Gregory D. Black, *Hollywood Censored*, 3 Film Hist. 167, 171 (1989). See Leary & Noall, *Entertainment: Public Pressures and the Law* at 354 (cited in note 54); Marjorie Heins, *Sex, Sin, and Blasphemy* 39–48 (New Press 1993).

59   Black, *Hollywood Censored* at 172 (cited in note 58).

60   *How to Judge a Motion Picture*, 65 The Irish Monthly 359, 360 (1937). See William E. Berchtold, *The Hollywood Purge*, 238 N. Amer. Rev. 503, 506–7 (1934); Wheeler, *Against Obscenity* at 163–71 (cited in note 22).

61   Black, *Hollywood Censored* at 167 (cited in note 58). See Ruth A. Inglis, *Need for Voluntary Self-Regulation*, 254 Annals of the Am. Acad. of Polit. and Soc. Sci. 153 (1947); Gregory D. Black, *The Catholic Crusade Against the Movies: 1940–1975* 1–2 (Cambridge 1997).

62   *People v. Vanguard Press, Inc.*, 192 Misc. 127, 129–30 (N.Y. Magis. Ct. 1947) citing *People v. Eastman*, 188 N.Y. 478, 480, 81 N.E. 459 (1907) (Cullen, J., concurring); *People v. Wendling*, 258 N.Y. 451, 453 (Ct. App. 1932); *People v. Muller*, 96 N.Y. 408 (N.Y. 1884); *People ex rel. Sumner v. Miller*, 155 Misc. 446, 447–48 (N.Y. Magis. Ct. 1935); *People ex rel. Savery v. Gotham Book Mart, Inc.*, 158 Misc. 240 (N.Y. Magis. Ct. 1936); *People v. Berg*, 241 A.D. 543, 544–45 (N.Y. App. Div. 1934); *United States v. One Book Called "Ulysses,"* 5 F. Supp. 182, 184 (D.N.Y. 1933).

63   *Commonwealth v. Friede*, 271 Mass. 318, 171 N.E. 472, 473–474 (Sup. Jud. Ct. Mass. 1930).

64   *United States v. Dennett*, 39 F. 2d 564, 565–66 (2d Cir. 1930).

65   See Leigh Ann Wheeler, *How Sex Became a Civil Liberty* 40–43 (Oxford 2013); Gerber, *Sex, Pornography, and Justice* at 95 (cited in note 26); Hays, *Let Freedom Ring* at 464 (cited in note 21).

66   Hays, *Let Freedom Ring* at 465 (cited in note 21). See Laura M. Weinrib, *The Sex Side of Civil Liberties*, 30 Law & Hist. Rev. 325, 351–56 (2012).

67   *United States v. Dennett*, 39 F. 2d 564 (1930); Lewis Gannett, *Books and Things*, New York Herald Tribune (Mar. 20, 1930). See Weinrib, *Sex Side of Civil Liberties* at 356–63 (cited in note 66).

68   See Terrence J. Murphy, *Censorship: Government and Obscenity* 4 (Helicon 1963).

69   *United States v. One Book Called "Ulysses,"* 5 F. Supp. 182, 184 (D.N.Y. 1933).

70   *United States v. One Book Entitled Ulysses by James Joyce*, 72 F.2d 705, 706–7 (2d Cir. 1934). See Weinrib, *Sex Side of Civil Liberties* at 375–77 (cited in note 66).

71   *Parmelee v. United States*, 113 F.2d 729, 731 (D.C. Cir. 1940).

72   Henry Miller, *Tropic of Cancer* 4 (Grove 2004). See Jay Martin, *"The King of Smut":*
Henry Miller's Tragical History, 35 Antioch Rev. 342, 346–47 (1977).

73   George Orwell, *Inside the Whale* 187 (Victor Gollancz Ltd. 1940). See Martin, *"The King of Smut"* at 348 (cited in note 72).

74   *United States v. Two Obscene Books*, 99 F. Supp. 760, 762 (N.D. Cal. 1951), aff'd *Besig v. United States*, 208 F.2d 142 (9th Cir. 1953).

75   *Near v. Minnesota*, 283 U.S. 697, 716 (1931).

76   *Chaplinsky v. New Hampshire*, 315 U.S. 568, 571–72 (1942). See also *Winters v. New York*, 333 U.S. 507, 515 (1948); *Beauharnais v. Illinois*, 343 U.S. 250, 266 (1952). See Lockhart and McClure, *Literature, Law of Obscenity, and the Constitution* at 352–58 (cited in note 45).

77   See *Roth v. United States*, 354 U.S. 476 (1957), and chapter 12.

CHAPTER 9

1 *"The Other Side of the Question,"* The Nation 317 (Oct. 17, 1867); Peter Fryer, *The Birth Controllers* 113 (Secker & Warburg 1965). See R. Sauer, *Attitudes to Abortion in America 1800–1973*, 28 Popul. Stud. 53 (1974); Janet Farrell Brodie, *Contraception and Abortion in 19th-Century America* 39, 41, 42–43, 112 (Cornell 1994); Linda Gordon, *Woman's Body, Woman's Right* 54 (2d ed., Penguin 1990); David M. Kennedy, *Birth Control in America: The Career of Margaret Sanger* 42 (Yale 1971); Rosalind Pollack Petchesky, *Abortion and Woman's Choice* 68 (Longman 1984); Nanette J. Davis, *From Crime to Choice: The Transformation of Abortion in America* 26 (Contributions in Women's Studies ser., no. 60, Greenwood 1985); Linda Gordon, *The Moral Property of Women* 4 (3d ed., Illinois 2002); Paul S. Boyer, Clifford E. Clark Jr., Joseph F. Kett, Neal Salisbury, Harvard Sitkoff, & Nancy Woloch, *The Enduring Vision* 274 (6th ed., Houghton Mifflin 2008); Dallas A. Blanchard, *The Anti-Abortion Movement and the Rise of the Religious Right* 13 (Twayne 1994); Faye D. Ginsburg, *Contested Lives: The Abortion Debate in an American Community* 28, 230 (2d ed., California 1998).

2 See Fryer, *Birth Controllers* at 74 (cited in note 1); Brodie, *Contraception and Abortion* at 91 (cited in note 1).

3 James C. Mohr, *Abortion in America* 86 (Oxford 1978).

4 See Sauer, *Attitudes to Abortion* at 54 (cited in note 1); Ginsburg, *Contested Lives* at 24 (cited in note 1); Petchesky, *Abortion and Woman's Choice* at 76 (cited in note 1); Ginsburg, *Contested Lives* at 26 (cited in note 1); Marvin Olasky, *Abortion Rites: A Social History of Abortion in America* 48–49 (Crossway 1992).

5 Ginsburg, *Contested Lives* at 228 (cited in note 1). See Barbara Leslie Epstein, *The Politics of Domesticity* 24–47 (Wesleyan 1981).

6 Gordon, *Moral Property of Women* at 58 (cited in note 1).

7 Brodie, *Contraception and Abortion* at 88 (cited in note 1). See Gordon, *Moral Property of Women* at 10–12, 58 (cited in note 1); Ginsburg, *Contested Lives* at 26 (cited in note 1); Brodie, *Contraception and Abortion* at 88 (cited in note 1).

8 James Reed, *The Birth Control Movement and American Society: From Private Vice to Public Virtue* 7 (Princeton 1978); Brodie, *Contraception and Abortion* at 98, 91 (cited in note 1). See Norman E. Himes, *Medical History of Contraception* 227 (Gamut 1963); Peter C. Engelman, *A History of the Birth Control Movement in America* 6 (Praeger 2011); Fryer, *Birth Controllers* at 94 (cited in note 1); Brodie, *Contraception and Abortion* at 88, 91, 107 (cited in note 1); Reed, *Birth Control Movement* at 7, 11 (cited in this note).

9 Reed, *Birth Control Movement* at 8 (cited in note 8); Brodie, *Contraception and Abortion* at 99 (cited in note 1). See Brodie, *Contraception and Abortion* at 90, 99, 109, 278 (cited in note 1); Fryer, *Birth Controllers* at 103 (cited in note 1); Himes, *Medical History of Contraception* at 227–29, 264–79 (cited in note 8); Engelman, *History of the Birth Control Movement* at 6–8 (cited in note 8).

10 See Helen Lefkowitz Horowitz, *Rereading Sex: Battles Over Sexual Knowledge and Suppression in Nineteenth-Century America* 73–77 (Knopf 2002). Reed, *Birth Control Movement* at 9 (cited in note 8); Fryer, *Birth Controllers* at 103–5 (cited in note 1); Brodie, *Contraception and*

Abortion at 95–96 (cited in note 1); C. Thomas Dienes, *Law, Politics, and Birth Control* 25 (Illinois 1972).

11   See Donna I. Dennis, *Obscenity Law and Its Consequences in Mid-Nineteenth-Century America*, 16 Colum. J. Gender & L. 43 (2007); Dienes, *Law, Politics, and Birth Control* at 25–31 (cited in note 10).

12   Engelman, *History of the Birth Control Movement* at 10–11 (cited in note 8). See Mohr, *Abortion in America* at 46–60, 239 (cited in note 3); Gordon, *Moral Property of Women* at 31 (cited in note 1); Gordon, *Woman's Body* at 61 (cited in note 1).

13   Clifford Browder, *The Wickedest Woman in New York: Madame Restell, the Abortionist* 9 (Archon Books 1988). See Lawrence Lader, *Abortion* 85 (Bobbs-Merrill 1966).

14   Quoted in Browder, *Madame Restell* at 17–18, 74 (cited in note 13). See Carroll Smith-Rosenberg, *Disorderly Conduct: Visions of Gender in Victorian America* 226 (Knopf 1985).

15   Blackstone, 1 *Commentaries* 129 (1765); James Wilson, *Of the Natural Rights of Individuals* (1790–1791). See Mohr, *Abortion in America* at 3–4 (cited in note 3). See Gordon, *Woman's Body* at 52 (cited in note 1); Leslie J. Reagan, *When Abortion Was a Crime* 8 (California 1997); Gordon, *Moral Property of Women* at 26 (cited in note 1); Lader, *Abortion* at 86 (cited in note 13); Mohr, *Abortion in America* at 45 (cited in note 3); Olasky, *Abortion Rites* at 83 (cited in note 4).

16   See Mohr, *Abortion in America* at 6–16 (cited in note 3).

17   *The Public Statute Laws of the State of Connecticut* 152–53 (1821), quoted in Mohr, *Abortion in America* at 21 (cited in note 3).

18   Suzanne M. Alford, *Is Self-Abortion a Fundamental Right?* 52 Duke L.J. 1011, 1022 (2003); Mohr, *Abortion in America* at 43 (cited in note 3). See Ginsburg, *Contested Lives* at 24 (cited in note 1); Reagan, *When Abortion Was a Crime* at 10 (cited in note 15); Sauer, *Attitudes to Abortion* at 57 (cited in note 1); Mohr, *Abortion in America* at 20–45, 120–28 (cited in note 3); Blanchard, *Anti-Abortion Movement* at 12 (cited in note 1); Lader, *Abortion* at 86 (cited in note 13).

19   Act of May 13, 1845, ch. 260, § 3, 1845 N.Y. Laws 285–86, quoted in Cyril C. Means Jr., *The Law of New York Concerning Abortion and the Status of the Foetus*, 14 N.Y.L.F. 411, 454 n.101 (1968). See Mohr, *Abortion in America* at 24, 119–46 (cited in note 3).

20   See Engelman, *History of the Birth Control Movement* at 17 (cited in note 8); Fryer, *Birth Controllers* at 117–18 (cited in note 1); Dienes, *Law, Politics, and Birth Control* at 58–59 (cited in note 10); Brodie, *Contraception and Abortion* at 281 (cited in note 1).

21   Gordon, *Woman's Body* at 52 (cited in note 1); Mohr, *Abortion in America* at 47 (cited in note 3). See Mohr, *Abortion in America* at 46–85 (cited in note 3).

22   Joseph F. Kett, *Growing Up in Rural New England, 1800–1840*, in *Anonymous Americans* 10–11 (Tamara K. Hareven ed., Prentice-Hall 1971); Sauer, *Attitudes to Abortion* at 58 (cited in note 1).

23   Brodie, *Contraception and Abortion* at 266 (cited in note 1); Hugh Lenox Hodge, *An Introductory Lecture to the Course on Obstetrics and Diseases of Women and Children* (1839), quoted in Eva R. Rubin, *Abortion, Politics, and the Courts* 12 (Greenwood 1982). See Kristin Luker, *Abortion and the Politics of Motherhood* 15–16 (California 1984).

24   See Petchesky, *Abortion and Woman's Choice* at 81 (cited in note 1); Luker, *Abortion and the Politics of Motherhood* at 32–33 (cited in note 23); Petchesky, *Abortion and Woman's Choice* at 81 (cited in note 1); Ginsburg, *Contested Lives* at 26–32 (cited in note 1); Reagan, *When Abortion Was a Crime* at 10, 42–43 (cited in note 15); Mohr, *Abortion in America* at 160–61 (cited in note 3); Luker, *Abortion and the Politics of Motherhood* at 15–16 (cited in note 23).

25   *Report of the Committee on Criminal Abortion*, American Medical Association (1859). See Ginsburg, *Contested Lives* at 32 (cited in note 1); Luker, *Abortion and the Politics of Motherhood* at 32–33 (cited in note 23); Mohr, *Abortion in America* at 148–57 (cited in note 3).

26   See Luker, *Abortion and the Politics of Motherhood* at 21–26 (cited in note 23); Ginsburg, *Contested Lives* at 26–31 (cited in note 1); Petchesky, *Abortion and Woman's Choice* at 28 (cited in note 1); Brodie, *Contraception and Abortion* at 266–67 (cited in note 1); Engelman, *History of the Birth Control Movement* at 12–13 (cited in note 8); Mohr, *Abortion in America* at 158–59 (cited in note 3).

27   Horatio Robinson Storer, *Why Not? A Book for Every Woman* (1866).

28   See Ginsburg, *Contested Lives* at 33 (cited in note 1); Petchesky, *Abortion and Woman's Choice* at 80–82 (cited in note 1).

29   Horatio Robinson Storer, *Is It I?: A Book for Every Man* 67 (Lee and Shepard 1867), quoted in Mohr, *Abortion in America* at 168 (cited in note 3); J. C. Stone, *Report on the Subject of Criminal Abortion*, 1 Transactions of the Iowa State Medical Society 34 (1871), quoted in Mohr, *Abortion in America* at 169 (cited in note 3). See Gordon, *Moral Property of Women* at 73–75 (cited in note 1); Christine Rosen, *Preaching Eugenics* 17, 26 (Oxford 2004); Brodie, *Contraception and Abortion* at 262, 270 (cited in note 1); Ginsburg, *Contested Lives* at 23–28, 232 (cited in note 1); Martin E. Marty, 1 *Modern American Religion* 210 (Chicago 1986); Sauer, *Attitudes to Abortion* at 53–55 (cited in note 1); John Todd, *Serpents in the Doves' Nest* 4 (Lee and Shepard 1867); Carl N. Degler, *At Odds: Women and the Family in America from the Revolution to the Present* 280–85 (Oxford 1981); Mohr, *Abortion in America* at 128 (cited in note 3); Luker, *Abortion and the Politics of Motherhood* at 22 (cited in note 23).

30   See Mohr, *Abortion in America* at 145–46, 200–225 (cited in note 3); Ginsburg, *Contested Lives* at 24–25 (cited in note 1); Sauer, *Attitudes to Abortion* at 57 (cited in note 1); Brodie, *Contraception and Abortion* at 254 (cited in note 1); Blanchard, *Anti-Abortion Movement* at 15 (cited in note 1); Gordon, *Woman's Body* at 57 (cited in note 1).

31   See Gordon, *Woman's Body* at 53 (cited in note 1); Blanchard, *Anti-Abortion Movement* at 17 (cited in note 1); Sauer, *Attitudes to Abortion* at 55 (cited in note 1).

32   F. Barham Zincke, *Last Winter in the United States* 293–94 (John Murray 1868), quoted in Engelman, *History of the Birth Control Movement* at 11 (cited in note 8). See Andrea Tone, *Devices and Desires: A History of Contraceptives in America* 14–20, 53–54 (Hill and Wang 2001); Reed, *Birth Control Movement* at 13–16 (cited in note 8); Fryer, *Birth Controllers* at 113–16 (cited in note 1); Brodie, *Contraception and Abortion* at 180–81, 201 (cited in note 1); Engelman, *History of the Birth Control Movement* at 10–11 (cited in note 8).

33   An Act for the Suppression of Trade in, and Circulation of, Obscene Literature and Articles of Immoral Use, 17 Stat. 598 (1873).

34   Anthony Comstock, *Vampire Literature*, 153 N. Amer. Rev. 162, 171 (Aug. 1891); Anthony Comstock, *Lotteries and Gambling*, 154 N. Amer. Rev. 217 (Feb. 1892). See Brodie, *Contraception and Abortion* at 255–66 (cited in note 1); Gordon, *Woman's Body* at 57

(cited in note 1); Ginsburg, *Contested Lives* at 29 (cited in note 1); Fryer, *Birth Controllers* at 117 (cited in note 1); Dienes, *Law, Politics, and Birth Control* at 32 (cited in note 10); Engelman, *History of the Birth Control Movement* at 14–16 (cited in note 8).

35   Brodie, *Contraception and Abortion* at 256–57 (cited in note 1). See Dienes, *Law, Politics, and Birth Control* at 42–47 (cited in note 10); Tone, *Devices and Desires* at 23–24 (cited in note 32).

36   See Ginsburg, *Contested Lives* at 29 (cited in note 1); Olasky, *Abortion Rites* at 161 (cited in note 4); Engelman, *History of the Birth Control Movement* at 17, 24 (cited in note 8); Tone, *Devices and Desires* at 33–34 (cited in note 32).

37   Brodie, *Contraception and Abortion* at 261, 281 (cited in note 1); Engelman, *History of the Birth Control Movement* at 17 (cited in note 8). See Fryer, *Birth Controllers* at 117 (cited in note 1).

38   See Gordon, *Woman's Body* at 53, 61–62, 150 (cited in note 1); Tone, *Devices and Desires* at 31–32, 48 (cited in note 32); Himes, *Medical History of Contraception* at 286–89 (cited in note 8).

39   Elizabeth Cady Stanton, Revolution (1868), quoted in Ginsburg, *Contested Lives* at 29 (cited in note 1). See Sauer, *Attitudes to Abortion* at 56 (cited in note 1); Ginsburg, *Contested Lives* at 29 (cited in note 1).

40   See Linda Gordon, *Voluntary Motherhood: The Beginnings of Feminist Birth Control Ideas in the United States*, in *Women and Health in America* 104 (Judith Walzer Leavitt ed., 2d ed., Wisconsin 1999); Gordon, *Moral Property of Women* at 75–83 (cited in note 1); Mohr, *Abortion in America* at 107–13 (cited in note 3).

41   Margaret Sanger, *The Aim*, The Woman Rebel, vol. 1, no. 1 (Mar. 1914), quoted in Engelman, *History of the Birth Control Movement* at xvi (cited in note 8); Engelman, *History of the Birth Control Movement* at xvi–xvii (cited in note 8). See Margaret Sanger, *My Fight for Birth Control* 83 (Farrar & Rinehart 1931); Margaret Sanger, *Woman and the New Race* 1 (Brentano's 1920); Gordon, *Moral Property of Women* at 139, 149 (cited in note 1); Tone, *Devices and Desires* at 25–32, 38 (cited in note 32); Brodie, *Contraception and Abortion* at 281–86 (cited in note 1); Engelman, *History of the Birth Control Movement* at 18–19 (cited in note 8).

42   Margaret Sanger, *An Autobiography* 21, 69, 88 (Norton 1938); Sanger, *My Fight for Birth Control* at 47, 49, 56 (cited in note 41). See Engelman, *History of the Birth Control Movement* at 27–29 (cited in note 8); John W. Johnson, *Griswold v. Connecticut: Birth Control and the Constitutional Right of Privacy* 8–10 (Kansas 2005); Gordon, *Moral Property of Women* at 143 (cited in note 1).

43   Margaret Sanger, *The Pivot of Civilization* 209–10 (Kessinger 2004); and Sanger, *Woman and the New Race* at 6–8 (cited in note 41). See Carole R. McCann, *Birth Control Politics in the United States, 1916–1945* 10 (Cornell 1999).

44   Emma Goldman, 1 *Living My Life* 137, 170–74, 185–86, 187, 272–73, 274–78 (Knopf 1931); Emma Goldman, 2 *Living My Life* 552–53 (Knopf 1931). See Reed, *Birth Control Movement* at 47–48 (cited in note 8); Engelman, *History of the Birth Control Movement* at 24–27 (cited in note 8).

45   Havelock Ellis, *Studies in the Psychology of Sex* (vol. 1): *The Evolution of Modesty* vi (F.A. Davis 1910); Havelock Ellis, *Studies in the Psychology of Sex* (vol. 6): *Sex in Relation to Society* 601 (F.A. Davis 1913). See John D'Emilio & Estelle B. Freedman, *Intimate Matters: A*

History of Sexuality in America 223–26 (Harper & Row 1988); *Gordon, Moral Property of Women* at 126 (cited in note 1); Engelman, *History of the Birth Control Movement* at 30–31 (cited in note 8).

46 See Engelman, *History of the Birth Control Movement* at 31–32 (cited in note 8); Ellen Chesler, *Woman of Valor* 66 (Simon & Schuster 1992); The Call (Mar. 2, 1913); Gordon, *Moral Property of Women* at 143 (cited in note 1).

47 Engelman, *History of the Birth Control Movement* at 38 (cited in note 8). See Tone, *Devices and Desires* at 81–82 (cited in note 32); Sanger, *My Fight for Birth Control* at 65–78 (cited in note 41); Robert Jütte, *Contraception: A History* 166–67 (Polity Press 2008); Gordon, *Moral Property of Women* at 144–45 (cited in note 1).

48 Margaret Sanger, The Woman Rebel (Mar. 1914), quoted in Engelman, *History of the Birth Control Movement* at 39–41 (cited in note 8); and Dienes, *Law, Politics, and Birth Control* at 80 (cited in note 10).

49 Margaret Sanger, The Woman Rebel (Mar. 1914), quoted in Dienes, *Law, Politics, and Birth Control* at 80 (cited in note 10). See Sanger, *An Autobiography* at 110 (cited in note 42).

50 Gordon, *Moral Property of Women* at 150 (cited in note 1); Engelman, *History of the Birth Control Movement* at 45 (cited in note 8). See David M. Rabban, *Free Speech in Its Forgotten Years, 1870–1920* 50 (Cambridge 1997); Engelman, *History of the Birth Control Movement* at 41–46 (cited in note 8); Gordon, *Moral Property of Women* at 150–51 (cited in note 1).

51 *The Control of Births*, The New Republic 2 (Mar. 6, 1915); New York Tribune (May 21, 1915); Daily Herald (Apr. 15, 1915) (Biloxi, Mississippi). See Engelman, *History of the Birth Control Movement* at 49–51 (cited in note 8).

52 New York Times (May 27, 1915); New York Tribune (May 27, 1915). See Engelman, *History of the Birth Control Movement* at 51–52 (cited in note 8).

53 New York Tribune (May 22, 1915); Mary Alden Hopkins, *The Catholic Church and Birth Control*, 60 Harper's Weekly 609–10 (June 26, 1915); Engelman, *History of the Birth Control Movement* at 52–54 (cited in note 8).

54 Ben Reitman, *The Tour*, 10 Mother Earth 269–70 (Sept. 1915); New York Times (Aug. 8, 1915); Engelman, *History of the Birth Control Movement* at 54–55 (cited in note 8). See Roger A. Bruns, *The Damndest Radical: The Life and World of Ben Reitman* 168 71 (Illinois 1987); Gordon, *Moral Property of Women* at 148 (cited in note 1); D'Emilio & Freedman, *Intimate Matters* at 230–31 (cited in note 45).

55 New York Times (Sept. 11, 1915); New York Tribune (Sept. 11, 1915); Engelman, *History of the Birth Control Movement* at 56 (cited in note 8).

56 The Masses 6 (Sept. 1915); Engelman, *History of the Birth Control Movement* at 56–57, 62 (cited in note 8).

57 See Engelman, *History of the Birth Control Movement* at 56–57, 62 (cited in note 8); Dienes, *Law, Politics, and Birth Control* at 80–84 (cited in note 10).

58 Alexander Berkman, *The Birth Control Fight*, The Blast 1 (July 1, 1916), quoted in Engelman, *History of the Birth Control Movement* at 75 (cited in note 8).

59 See Sanger, *An Autobiography* at 178–80, 210–18 (cited in note 42); Sanger, *My Fight for Birth Control* at 153–56 (cited in note 41); Tone, *Devices and Desire* at 55–77 (cited in note 32); Abraham Stone & Norman E. Himes, *Planned Parenthood* 123–40 (Macmillan 1951);

Gordon, *Moral Property of Women* at 150–57, 167–68 (cited in note 1); Dienes, *Law, Politics, and Birth Control* at 84–88 (cited in note 10); Chesler, *Woman of Valor* at 151 (cited in note 46); Engelman, *History of the Birth Control Movement* at 75–83 (cited in note 8).

60   See Sanger, *An Autobiography* at 212, 225–29 (cited in note 42); Gordon, *Moral Property of Women* at 156 (cited in note 1); Engelman, *History of the Birth Control Movement* at 83–87, 90–91 (cited in note 8); Cathy Moran Hajo, *Birth Control on Main Street: Organizing Clinics in the United States, 1916–1939* 24–25 (Illinois 2010); David J. Garrow, *Liberty and Sexuality* 12–13 (California 1994); Dienes, *Law, Politics, and Birth Control* at 84–88 (cited in note 10); Chesler, *Woman of Valor* at 152–53 (cited in note 46); Johnson, *Griswold v. Connecticut* at 10 (cited in note 42).

61   Quoted in Engelman, *History of the Birth Control Movement* at 92 (cited in note 8).

62   John T. Noonan Jr., *Contraception: A History of Its Treatment by the Catholic Theologians and Canonists* 406 (2d ed., Belknap 1986) citing Gury, *Compendium of Moral Theology* 2.703. See Noonan, *Contraception* at 387–437 (cited in this note); Leslie Woodcock Tentler, *Catholics and Contraception* 16–17 (Cornell 2004).

63   John A. Ryan, *Family Limitation*, 54 Ecclesiastical Rev. 684 (1916), quoted in Noonan, *Contraception* at 423 (cited in note 62); *Pastoral Letter of the Archbishops and Bishops of the United States* (Sept. 26, 1919), quoted in Noonan, *Contraception* at 423–24 (cited in note 62).

64   See Tentler, *Catholics and Contraception* at 16–40 (cited in note 62); Engelman, *History of the Birth Control Movement* at 96–97 (cited in note 8).

65   Sanger, *Woman and the New Race* (cited in note 41), quoted in Petchesky, *Abortion and Woman's Choice* at 89 (cited in note 1), and Lader, *Abortion* at 167 (cited in note 13). See Nancy F. Cott, *The Grounding of Modern Feminism* 68–69 (Yale 1987); Engelman, *History of the Birth Control Movement* at 120–21 (cited in note 8); McCann, *Birth Control Politics* at 40–49 (cited in note 43).

66   See Sanger, *An Autobiography* at 290–305 (cited in note 42); Cott, *Grounding of Modern Feminism* at 68–69 (cited in note 65); Engelman, *History of the Birth Control Movement* at 121–27 (cited in note 8); Kennedy, *Birth Control in America* at 181–82 (cited in note 1).

67   See Sanger, *An Autobiography* at 297–315 (cited in note 42); New York Times (Nov. 12–25 1921); New York Times (Dec. 3, 4, 8. 18, 1921); New York Tribune (Nov. 14–22, 1921); New York Tribune (Dec. 18, 20, 1921); Engelman, *History of the Birth Control Movement* at 124–29 (cited in note 8); Kennedy, *Birth Control in America* at 181–82 (cited in note 1).

68   Sanger, *An Autobiography* at 315 (cited in note 42); Sanger, *My Fight for Birth Control* at 237 (cited in note 41); Engelman, *History of the Birth Control Movement* at 129 (cited in note 8). See Tentler, *Catholics and Contraception* at 53 (cited in note 62).

69   Annie G. Porritt, *Publicity in the Birth Control Movement*, 7 Birth Control Rev. 88–89 (Apr. 1923), quoted in Engelman, *History of the Birth Control Movement* at 141 (cited in note 8).

70   Edwina Davis, *Birth Control of the Seas*, Life Magazine 5 (Aug. 2, 1923), quoted in Engelman, *History of the Birth Control Movement* at 141 (cited in note 8).

71   Engelman, *History of the Birth Control Movement* at 141–42 (cited in note 8). See D'Emilio & Freedman, *Intimate Matters* at 239–41 (cited in note 45); Reed, *Birth Control Movement* at 60 (cited in note 8); Tone, *Devices and Desires* at 136–37 (cited in note 32);

Engelman, *History of the Birth Control Movement* at 141–43 (cited in note 8); Luker, *Abortion and the Politics of Motherhood* at 48–54 (cited in note 23).

72   *Romans* 3:8, quoted in *Encyclical on Marriage*, authorized English text of the Encyclical Letter of His Holiness Pope Pius XI 26–27, 22 (Washington, DC: National Catholic Welfare Conference, 1931); Engelman, *History of the Birth Control Movement* at 146–49 (cited in note 8). See Tentler, *Catholics and Contraception* at 86 (cited in note 62); Rosen, *Preaching Eugenics* at 157–60 (cited in note 29); Sanger, *My Fight for Birth Control* at 200–202 (cited in note 41); Sanger, *An Autobiography* at 411 (cited in note 42); Constance M. Chen, *"The Sex Side of Life": Mary Ware Dennett's Pioneering Battle* 230–38 (New Press 1996).

73   Walter Lippmann, *A Preface to Morals* 89 (6th ed., Rutgers 2009); 7 Birth Control Rev. 179.

74   Harry Emerson Fosdick to John Elwood, 8 January 1930 (Harry Emerson Fosdick Papers, Union Theological Seminary Library). See Rosen, *Preaching Eugenics* at 122, 156–57 (cited in note 29); *Bishop Stearly Defends Birth Control Clinics*, Chicago Daily Tribune 10 (May 13, 1931).

75   Engelman, *History of the Birth Control Movement* at 162–63 (cited in note 8); Sanger, *An Autobiography* at 417–27 (cited in note 42). See Dienes, *Law, Politics, and Birth Control* at 103–8 (cited in note 10).

76   Chicago Daily Tribune (Jan. 19, 1934); Sanger, *An Autobiography* at 424–26 (cited in note 42); Engelman, *History of the Birth Control Movement* at 162–64 (cited in note 8). See Noonan, *Contraception* at 442–47 (cited in note 62).

77   See Petchesky, *Abortion and Woman's Choice* at 112 (cited in note 1); McCann, *Birth Control Politics* at 178–79 (cited in note 43); Garrow, *Liberty and Sexuality* at 26 (cited in note 60).

78   See *Youngs Rubber Corporation v. C. I. Lee and Co., Inc.*, 45 F.2d 103 (2d Cir. 1930); Dienes, *Law, Politics, and Birth Control* at 110–11 (cited in note 10); Laura M. Weinrib, *The Sex Side of Civil Liberties*, 30 Law & Hist. Rev. 325, 379 (2012); *Davis v. United States*, 62 F.2d 473 (6th Cir. 1933).

79   19 U.S.C.A. § 1305(a).

80   86 F.2d 737 (2d Cir. 1936).

81   86 F.2d 740 (Hand, J., concurring).

82   See Garrow, *Liberty and Sexuality* at 91, 42–43 (cited in note 60); Engelman, *History of the Birth Control Movement* at 169–72 (cited in note 8).

83   See Luker, *Abortion and the Politics of Motherhood* at 49 (cited in note 23); Jerome E. Bates & Edward S. Zawadzki, *Criminal Abortion* 3, 44–45 (Thomas 1964); Davis, *From Crime to Choice* at 4 (cited in note 1); Susan Cotts Watkins & Angela D. Danzi, *Women's Gossip and Social Change: Childbirth and Fertility Control Among Italian and Jewish Women in the United States, 1920–1940*, 9 Gender & Society 469, 477–79, 482–485 (1995); Endre Kopperl Brunner & Louis Newton, *Abortions in Relation to Viable Births in 10,609 Pregnancies*, 38 Am. J. of Obstetrics and Gynecology 82–90 (1939).

84   See Leslie J. Reagan, *"About to Meet Her Maker,"* 77 J. of Amer. Hist. 1240, 1242, 1244–48, 1261 (1991); Luker, *Abortion and the Politics of Motherhood* at 53–54 (cited in note 23); Bates & Zawadzki, *Criminal Abortion* at 4–5 (cited in note 83).

85   See Bates & Zawadzki, *Criminal Abortion* at 3–11, 36–60 (cited in note 83).

CHAPTER **10**

1   See William N. Eskridge Jr., *Dishonorable Passions: Sodomy Laws in America, 1861–2003* 19–20 (Viking 2008); Clare A. Lyons, *Mapping an Atlantic Sexual Culture*, 60 Wm. & Mary Q. 119, 138 (2003); *Bowers v. Hardwick*, 478 U.S. 186, 192 n.5 (1986).

2   See Jonathan Ned Katz, *Gay American History* at 26–33, 40–42 (rev. ed. Meridian 1992); Eskridge, *Dishonorable Passions* at 19–22 (cited in note 1); Jonathan Ned Katz, *Love Stories: Sex Between Men Before Homosexuality* 45–55, 402–6 (Chicago 2001); *Davis v. State*, 3 H.&J. 154 (MD Ct. of App 1810); Timothy J. Gilfoyle, *City of Eros* 135–38 (Norton 1992); John D'Emilio & Estelle B. Freedman, *Intimate Matters: A History of Sexuality in America* 123 (Harper & Row 1988).

3   Robert K. Martin, *Knights-Errant and Gothic Seducers*, in *Hidden from History: Reclaiming the Gay and Lesbian Past* 169–82, 170, 173, 181 (Martin Duberman, Martha Vicinus, & George Chauncey Jr. eds., New American Library 1989); Walt Whitman, *The Complete Poetry and Prose of Walt Whitman* 129 (Pellegrini & Cudahy 1948); Nicholas C. Edsall, *Toward Stonewall: Homosexuality and Society in the Modern Western World* 70, 75 (Virginia 2003).

4   Colin Scott, *Sex and Art*, 7 Am. J. of Psychology 216 (Jan. 1896), quoted in Katz, *Gay American History* at 44 (cited in note 2). See Katz, *Gay American History* at 47 (cited in note 2).

5   See Lillian Faderman, *Surpassing the Love of Men* 152–73, 220–25 (Morrow 1981); Katz, *Gay American History* at 450 (cited in note 2); Carroll Smith-Rosenberg, *Discourses of Sexuality and Subjectivity*, in Duberman et al., *Hidden from History* at 264–80 (cited in note 3).

6   See Neil Miller, *Out of the Past: Gay and Lesbian History from 1869 to the Present* xvii–xviii (Alyson Books 2006); Michael Bronski, *A Queer History of the United States* 106–7 (Beacon 2011); George Chauncey, *Gay New York* 118 (Basic Books 1994); Faderman, *Surpassing the Love of Men* at 184–206, 237–38 (cited in note 5); Barry D. Adam, *The Rise of a Gay and Lesbian Movement* 45 (Twayne 1995); Eskridge, *Dishonorable Passions* at 41–43 (cited in note 1); Lillian Faderman, *Odd Girls and Twilight Lovers: A History of Lesbian Life in Twentieth-Century America* 13–28 (Columbia 1991).

7   Richard von Krafft-Ebing, *Perversion of the Sexual Instinct—Report of Cases*, 9 Alienist and Neurologist 564, 565 (1888), quoted in Jonathan Ned Katz, *Gay/Lesbian Almanac* 205 (Carroll & Graf 1994); Eskridge, *Dishonorable Passions* at 47 (cited in note 1). See John Lauritsen & David Thorstad, *The Early Homosexual Rights Movement (1864–1935)* 7 (Times Change Press 1995); Duberman et al., *Hidden from History* at 1–13 (cited in note 3); Jonathan Ned Katz, *The Invention of Heterosexuality* 19–21, 207–8 (Dutton 1995); Eskridge, *Dishonorable Passions* at 15–16 (cited in note 1); Jeffrey Weeks, *Discourse, Desire and Sexual Deviance*, in *The Making of the Modern Homosexual* 83, 181 (Kenneth Plummer ed., Hutchinson 1981); Bronski, *Queer History* at 95–96 (cited in note 6).

8   E. C. Spitzka, *A Historical Case of Sexual Perversion*, 4 Chicago Med. Rev. 378–79 (1881), quoted in Katz, *Gay/Lesbian Almanac* at 179 (cited in note 7).

9   Katz, *Gay/Lesbian Almanac* at 139–42 (cited in note 7). See Faderman, *Odd Girls* at 40 (cited in note 6). Jeffrey Weeks, *Inverts, Perverts, and Mary-Annes*, in Duberman et al., *Hidden from History* at 195–211, 205 (cited in note 3); David M. Halperin, *One Hundred Years of Homosexuality* 15 (Routledge 1990).

10 William Lee Howard, *Sexual Perversion in America*, 8 Am. J. of Dermatology and Genito-Urinary Diseases 10 (1904), quoted in Chauncey, *Gay New York* at 48–49 (cited in note 6); Katz, *Gay/Lesbian Almanac* at 145 (cited in note 7); Miller, *Out of the Past* at 15 (cited in note 6).

11 George F. Shrady, *Perverted Sexual Instinct*, 26 Med. Rec. 70 (1884), quoted in Katz, *Gay/Lesbian Almanac* at 197 (cited in note 7). See Faderman, *Surpassing the Love of Men* at 243 (cited in note 5); Miller, *Out of the Past* at 14–15 (cited in note 6); Weeks, *Discourse, Desire and Sexual Deviance* at 86 (cited in note 7); Katz, *Gay/Lesbian Almanac* at 179–99 (cited in note 7); Katz, *Gay American History* at 148 (cited in note 2); Eskridge, *Dishonorable Passions* at 47–49 (cited in note 1).

12 See Katz, *Gay/Lesbian Almanac* at 144–50 (cited in note 7); Adam, *Rise of a Gay and Lesbian Movement* at 42 (cited in note 6); Chauncey, *Gay New York* at 100, 121 (cited in note 6); John Marshall, *Pansies, Perverts and Macho Men*, in Plummer, *Making of the Modern Homosexual* at 136 (cited in note 7); Weeks, *Inverts, Perverts, and Mary-Annes* at 204 (cited in note 9); Halperin, *One Hundred Years of Homosexuality* at 16 (cited in note 9).

13 James Weir Jr., *The Effects of Female Suffrage on Posterity*, 29 Am. Naturalist 819 (1895), quoted in Eskridge, *Dishonorable Passions* at 47–48 (cited in note 1). See Katz, *Gay/Lesbian Almanac* at 151, 379 (cited in note 7); Miller, *Out of the Past* at 19–20 (cited in note 6); Eskridge, *Dishonorable Passions* at 43 (cited in note 1); Faderman, *Odd Girls* at 45–46 (cited in note 6).

14 Smith-Rosenberg, *Discourses of Sexuality* at 270–71 (cited in note 5). On the evolution of the medical understanding of homosexuality, see Vern L. Bullough, *Homosexuality and the Medical Model*, 1 J. of Homosexuality 99 (1974); Paul A. Robinson, *The Modernization of Sex* 1–41 (Cornell 1989); Jeffrey Weeks, *Coming Out* 23–32 (Quartet 1977); Katz, *Gay American History* at 129–207 (cited in note 2).

15 Katz, *Gay/Lesbian Almanac* at 196 (cited in note 7); Xavier Mayne, pseud., *The Intersexes: A History of Similisexualism as a Problem in Social Life* 119–22 (Arno 1975), quoted in Katz, *Gay American History* at 146–47 (cited in note 2).

16 See Katz, *Gay/Lesbian Almanac* at 186–87, 201, 228 (cited in note 7); Katz, *Gay American History* at 134–55, 167–70, 590 n.5 (cited in note 2).

17 Katz, *Gay/Lesbian Almanac* at 242 (cited in note 7). See Miller, *Out of the Past* at 23 (cited in note 6); Katz, *Gay American History* at 137, 143 (cited in note 2); Adam, *Rise of a Gay and Lesbian Movement* at 241–43 (cited in note 6); Katz, *Gay/Lesbian Almanac* at 536 (cited in note 7); Dave King, *Gender Confusions*, in Plummer, *Making of the Modern Homosexual* at 161 (cited in note 7).

18 Miller, *Out of the Past* at 20 (cited in note 6); Katz, *Gay/Lesbian Almanac* at 154, 231, 247 (cited in note 7).

19 Miller, *Out of the Past* at 24 (cited in note 6).

20 Ronald Bayer, *Homosexuality and American Psychiatry: The Politics of Diagnosis* 22 (Basic Books 1981); Sigmund Freud, *Letters of Sigmund Freud* 423–24 (Basic Books 1960). See Katz, *Gay American History* at 155–58 (cited in note 2).

21 Wilhelm Stekel, *Is Homosexuality Curable?* 17 Psychoanalytic Rev. 443, 447–48 (1930), quoted in Katz, *Gay American History* at 159 (cited in note 2). See Miller, *Out of the Past* at 23–25 (cited in note 6); Eskridge, *Dishonorable Passions* at 61–65 (cited in note 1); Edsall,

Toward Stonewall at 241–48 (cited in note 3); John D'Emilio, *Sexual Politics, Sexual Communities* 16 (Chicago 1983).

22 D'Emilio, *Sexual Politics* at 13 (cited in note 21); quoted in Bronski, *Queer History* at 97 (cited in note 6). See Chauncey, *Gay New York* at 6–8, 60–61, 101–6, 187–88 (cited in note 6); Katz, *Gay/Lesbian Almanac* at 257 (cited in note 7).

23 Chauncey, *Gay New York* at 1 (cited in note 6). See Katz, *Gay/Lesbian Almanac* at 335 (cited in note 7); Lauritsen & Thorstad, *Early Homosexual Rights Movement* at 40 (cited in note 7); Adam, *Rise of a Gay and Lesbian Movement* at 43 (cited in note 6); Chauncey, *Gay New York* at 132–36 (cited in note 6); Katz, *Gay/Lesbian Almanac* at 258, 367 (cited in note 7); Mayne, *The Intersexes* at 638–40 (cited in note 15); Eskridge, *Dishonorable Passions* at 45–46 (cited in note 1).

24 See Chauncey, *Gay New York* at 16, 20, 47–56 (cited in note 6); Eskridge, *Dishonorable Passions* at 45, 64–65 (cited in note 1).

25 Quoted in Eskridge, *Dishonorable Passions* at 46 (cited in note 1).

26 Chauncey, *Gay New York* at 100 (cited in note 6). See Chauncey, *Gay New York* at 66–67, 99–111 (cited in note 6).

27 Gene S., quoted in George W. Henry, *Sex Variants: A Study of Homosexual Patterns* 254–55 (Paul B. Hoeber 1941).

28 Chauncey, *Gay New York* at 2 (cited in note 6). See Chauncey, *Gay New York* at 100–106 (cited in note 6).

29 See Chauncey, *Gay New York* at 65–97 (cited in note 6); Eskridge, *Dishonorable Passions* at 63–64 (cited in note 1).

30 See Nan Alamilla Boyd, *Wide Open Town: A History of Queer San Francisco to 1965* at 25–29 (California 2003); Chauncey, *Gay New York* at 34–45 (cited in note 6); Eskridge, *Dishonorable Passions* at 63–65, 70–72 (cited in note 1); Bronski, *Queer History* at 121–23 (cited in note 6); Miller, *Out of the Past* at 135–44 (cited in note 6); Eric Garber, *A Spectacle in Color*, in Duberman et al., *Hidden from History* at 318–31 (cited in note 3); Faderman, *Odd Girls* at 59 (cited in note 6).

31 E. S. Shepherd, *Contribution to the Study of Intermediacy*, 14 Am. J. of Urology and Sexology 242, 245 (1918), quoted in Chauncey, *Gay New York* at 4 (cited in note 6); Chauncey, *Gay New York* at 37 (cited in note 6). See Katz, *Gay/Lesbian Almanac* at 218–19 (cited in note 7); Chauncey, *Gay New York* at 38–39 (cited in note 6).

32 See Kat Long, *The Forbidden Apple: A Century of Sex and Sin in New York City* 23 (Ig 2009); Katz, *Gay/Lesbian Almanac* at 298 (cited in note 7); Eskridge, *Dishonorable Passions* at 45, 55–59 (cited in note 1); Chauncey, *Gay New York* at 146, 215 (cited in note 6).

33 Chauncey, *Gay New York* at 142 (cited in note 6).

34 See Chauncey, *Gay New York* at 45, 141–47, 168–76, 172–73, 183–86, 196–98, 200, 214–16 (cited in note 6); Katz, *Gay/Lesbian Almanac* at 452 (cited in note 7).

35 Chauncey, *Gay New York* at 156 (cited in note 6). See Edsall, *Toward Stonewall* at 254–55 (cited in note 3); Miller, *Out of the Past* at 130 (cited in note 6); Chauncey, *Gay New York* at 154–56 (cited in note 6); David K. Johnson, *The Lavender Scare* 49 (Chicago 2004); Bronski, *Queer History* at 111 (cited in note 6).

36 Langston Hughes, *The Big Sea: An Autobiography* 273 (Knopf 1940). See Chauncey,

Gay New York at 7, 301 (cited in note 6); Faderman, *Odd Girls* at 67–79 (cited in note 6); Edsall, *Toward Stonewall* at 253–55 (cited in note 3); Miller, *Out of the Past* at 130–31 (cited in note 6).

37 Faderman, *Odd Girls* at 65 (cited in note 6); Harvey Warren Zorbaugh, *The Gold Coast and the Slum* 100 (Chicago 1929). See Chauncey, *Gay New York* at 318–25 (cited in note 6); Eskridge, *Dishonorable Passions* at 67–69 (cited in note 1).

38 Faderman, *Odd Girls* at 82 (cited in note 6); Max Eastman, *Great Companions* 91 (Farrar, Straus, Cudahy 1959). See Faderman, *Odd Girls* at 62–92 (cited in note 6); Bronski, *Queer History* at 125–26 (cited in note 6).

39 Joseph Collins, *The Doctor Looks at Love and Life* 64–68 (Doran 1926). See San Francisco Lesbian and Gay History Project, *"She Even Chewed Tobacco,"* in Duberman et al., *Hidden from History* at 183–94, 185 (cited in note 3); Katz, *Gay/Lesbian Almanac* at 452 (cited in note 7); Eskridge, *Dishonorable Passions* at 41–43, 45 (cited in note 1); Katz, *Gay American History* at 209–79 (cited in note 2); D'Emilio, *Sexual Politics* at 97 (cited in note 21).

40 Miller, *Out of the Past* at 166–67 (cited in note 6); Weeks, *Coming Out* at 107 (cited in note 14).

41 Radclyffe Hall, *The Well of Loneliness* 447 (Sun Dial Press 1928).

42 Hall, *The Well of Loneliness* at 506 (cited in note 41). See Miller, *Out of the Past* at 166–75 (cited in note 6); Katz, *Gay/Lesbian Almanac* at 448–52 (cited in note 7); Katz, *Gay American History* at 397–405 (cited in note 2); Adam, *Rise of a Gay and Lesbian Movement* at 42, 47 (cited in note 6); Eskridge, *Dishonorable Passions* at 69 (cited in note 1).

43 Edsall, *Toward Stonewall* at 260 (cited in note 3).

44 See Chauncey, *Gay New York* at 331–39, 348 (cited in note 6); Long, *Forbidden Apple* at 84–86 (cited in note 32); Lewis A. Erenberg, *From New York to Middletown*, 38 Am. Q. 761 (1986); Mark H. Moore & Dean R. Gerstein eds., *Alcohol and Public Policy* 61–75 (National Academy Press 1981).

45 See Boyd, *Wide Open Town* at 35–38 (cited in note 30); D'Emilio, *Sexual Politics* at 19 (cited in note 21).

46 D'Emilio, *Sexual Politics* at 19 (cited in note 21). See Adam, *Rise of a Gay and Lesbian Movement* at 47 (cited in note 6); Faderman, *Odd Girls* at 103 (cited in note 6); Edsall, *Toward Stonewall* at 257 (cited in note 3).

47 Quoted in Faderman, *Odd Girls* at 101 (cited in note 6).

48 Faderman, *Odd Girls* at 93, 97–98 (cited in note 6).

49 Ralph H. Major Jr., *New Moral Menace to Our Youth*, 28 Coronet 104 (Sept. 1950), quoted in Chauncey, *Gay New York* at 359 (cited in note 6); Allan Bérubé, *Coming Out Under Fire: The History of Gay Men and Women in World War Two* 258 (Free Press 1990); Eskridge, *Dishonorable Passions* at 77 (cited in note 1). Adam, *Rise of a Gay and Lesbian Movement* at 47–48 (cited in note 6).

50 Chauncey, *Gay New York* at 9 (cited in note 6). See Vito Russo, *The Celluloid Closet* 31 (Harper & Row 1981); Robert Sklar, *Movie-Made America* 173–74 (Random House 1975); Chauncey, *Gay New York* at 352–53, 359–60 (cited in note 6); Eskridge, *Dishonorable Passions* at 55–59, 63, 66–67 (cited in note 1); Bronski, *Queer History* at 119, 125 (cited in note 6); Faderman, *Odd Girls* at 101–10 (cited in note 6).

CHAPTER **11**

1   Emma Goldman, 2 *Living My Life* 555–56 (Dover 1970); quoted in John Lauritsen & David Thorstad, *The Early Homosexual Rights Movement (1864–1935)* 40 (Times Change Press 1995). See Michael Bronski, *A Queer History of the United States* 93–94 (Beacon 2011); Jonathan Ned Katz, *Gay/Lesbian Almanac* 160 (Carroll & Graf 1994).

2   Henry Gerber, *The Society for Human Rights—1925*, 10 ONE Magazine 5–10 (Sept. 1962), quoted in Jonathan Ned Katz, *Gay American History* 388–93 (rev. ed. Meridian 1992). See Katz, *Gay/Lesbian Almanac* at 418–21 (cited in note 1); Barry D. Adam, *The Rise of a Gay and Lesbian Movement* 46–47 (Twayne 1995); Nicholas C. Edsall, *Toward Stonewall: Homosexuality and Society in the Modern Western World* 252–53 (Virginia 2003); Jim Kepner & Stephen O. Murray, *Henry Gerber (1895–1972)* in *Before Stonewall: Activists for Gay and Lesbian Rights in Historical Context* 24 (Vern L. Bullough ed., Harrington Park 2002).

3   John D'Emilio, *Sexual Politics, Sexual Communities* 20–22 (Chicago 1983).

4   10 U.S.C. § 925(a) (1950).

5   See Margot Canaday, *The Straight State: Sexuality and Citizenship in Twentieth-Century America* 57–59, 77–85 (Princeton 2011).

6   Allan Bérubé, *Marching to a Different Drummer*, in *Hidden from History: Reclaiming the Gay and Lesbian Past* 383, 387 and n.11 (Martin Duberman, Martha Vicinus, & George Chauncey Jr. eds., New American Library 1989). See Allan Bérubé, *Coming Out Under Fire: The History of Gay Men and Women in World War Two* 12, 19 (Free Press 1990); Bronski, *Queer History* at 158–59 (cited in note 1); Neil Miller, *Out of the Past: Gay and Lesbian History from 1869 to the Present* 210–11 (Alyson 2006); D'Emilio, *Sexual Politics* at 24–25 (cited in note 3); Canaday, *Straight State* at 87–89 (cited in note 5).

7   Quoted in Bérubé, *Coming Out* at 8 (cited in note 6). See Bronski, *Queer History* at 159 (cited in note 1); Miller, *Out of the Past* at 211 (cited in note 6); Edsall, *Toward Stonewall* at 262–63 (cited in note 2); Merle Miller, *On Being Different* 19–20 (Random House 1971); Katz, *Gay/Lesbian Almanac* at 616–18 (cited in note 1).

8   Miller, *Out of the Past* at 212 (cited in note 6); Lillian Faderman, *Odd Girls and Twilight Lovers: A History of Lesbian Life in Twentieth-Century America* 120 (Columbia 1991). See Miller, *Out of the Past* at 214 (cited in note 6); D'Emilio, *Sexual Politics* at 27–30 (cited in note 3); Randy Shilts, *Conduct Unbecoming: Gays and Lesbians in the U.S. Military* 140 (St. Martin's 1993).

9   See Bronski, *Queer History* at 161, 164 (cited in note 1); National Research Council, *Psychology for the Fighting Man* 34 (Infantry Journal 1943), quoted in Bronski, *Queer History* at 165–66 (cited in note 1); Bérubé, *Marching to a Different Drummer* at 384–86 (cited in note 6); Faderman, *Odd Girls* at 123 (cited in note 8).

10   See Bérubé, *Marching to a Different Drummer* at 388 (cited in note 6); Katz, *Gay/Lesbian Almanac* at 616–18 (cited in note 1).

11   *Cong. Rec.*, 78th Cong., 2d Sess. 4454 (May 12, 1944). See Bronski, *Queer History* at 165 (cited in note 1); Bérubé, *Marching to a Different Drummer* at 388 (cited in note 6); Katz, *Gay/Lesbian Almanac* at 616–18, 634–39 (cited in note 1). For an excellent account of the

use of blue discharges and its consequences for returning veterans, see Canaday, *Straight State* at 142–73 (cited in note 5).

12   See Bérubé, *Marching to a Different Drummer* at 391–92 (cited in note 6).

13   Marvin Liebman, *Coming Out Conservative* 45 (Chronicle 1992). See Bérubé, *Marching to a Different Drummer* at 392 (cited in note 6).

14   Canaday, *Straight State* at 191–98 (cited in note 5).

15   Nancy Adair & Casey Adair, *Word Is Out* 61 (Delacorte 1978).

16   See Miller, *Out of the Past* at 215–17 (cited in note 6); Bronski, *Queer History* at 166 (cited in note 1); Canaday, *Straight State* at 174–213 (cited in note 5); Bérubé, *Marching to a Different Drummer* at 392 (cited in note 6); Katz, *Gay/Lesbian Almanac* at 616–18, 634–39 (cited in note 1); Faderman, *Odd Girls* at 154–55 (cited in note 8).

17   Quoted in Geoffrey R. Stone, *Perilous Times* 331 (Norton 2004).

18   *Never Condoned Disloyalty, Says Acheson of His Stand*, New York Times (Mar. 1, 1950). See David K. Johnson, *The Lavender Scare* 1, 15–39 (Chicago 2004).

19   New York Times (Mar. 9, 1950). See Miller, *Out of the Past* at 234 (cited in note 6); Katz, *Gay American History* at 91 (cited in note 2); Adam, *Rise of a Gay and Lesbian Movement* at 62 (cited in note 2); D'Emilio, *Sexual Politics* at 41 (cited in note 3).

20   New York Times (Mar. 20, 1950). See *Cong. Rec.*, 81st Cong., 2d Sess. 5699 (Apr. 25, 1950), New York Times (May 5, 1950); *Perverts Called Government Peril*, New York Times (Apr. 19, 1950); Katz, *Gay American History* at 91–92 (cited in note 2); Miller, *Out of the Past* at 235 (cited in note 6); Katz, *Gay American History* at 92–93 (cited in note 2); Adam, *Rise of a Gay and Lesbian Movement* at 62 (cited in note 2); Johnson, *Lavender Scare* at 18–20, 28–30 (cited in note 18); D'Emilio, *Sexual Politics* at 41–42 (cited in note 3); Kat Long, *The Forbidden Apple: A Century of Sex and Sin in New York City* 106 (Ig 2009); William N. Eskridge Jr., *Dishonorable Passions: Sodomy Laws in America, 1861–2003* 100 (Viking 2008).

21   *Inquiry by Senate on Perverts Asked*, New York Times (May 20, 1950); *The Senator and the Purge*, New York Post (July 17, 1950). See Katz, *Gay American History* at 95–96 (cited in note 2); D'Emilio, *Sexual Politics* at 41–43 (cited in note 3); Long, *Forbidden Apple* at 107 (cited in note 20); Faderman, *Odd Girls* at 143 (cited in note 8); Edsall, *Toward Stonewall* at 278 (cited in note 2).

22   Quoted in Johnson, *Lavender Scare* at 31, 36, 37, 28 (cited in note 18).

23   Quoted in Nicholas Von Hoffman, *Citizen Cohn* 127 (Doubleday 1988). See Miller, *Out of the Past* at 235 (cited in note 6); Bronski, *Queer History* at 180 (cited in note 1).

24   New York Times (July 13, 1950). See Katz, *Gay American History* at 95 (cited in note 2); *Federal Vigilance on Perverts Asked*, New York Times (Dec. 16, 1950). See U.S. Congress, Senate Committee on Expenditures in the Executive Departments, *Employment of Homosexuals and Other Sex Perverts in Government; Interim Report Submitted to the Committee on Expenditures in the Executive Departments by Its Subcommittee on Investigations Pursuant to S. Res 280*, 81st Cong., 2d Sess., Sen. doc. 241 (Dec. 15, 1950); Katz, *Gay American History* at 99 (cited in note 2); D'Emilio, *Sexual Politics* at 42–43 (cited in note 3); Edsall, *Toward Stonewall* at 277 (cited in note 2).

25   New York Times (Apr. 28, 1951). See Katz, *Gay American History* at 100 (cited in note

2); D'Emilio, *Sexual Politics* at 46–47 (cited in note 3); Miller, *Out of the Past* at 239 (cited in note 6); New York Times (Dec. 20, 1951); Johnson, *Lavender Scare* at 128 (cited in note 18); Faderman, *Odd Girls* at 142–43 (cited in note 8); Edsall, *Toward Stonewall* at 278 (cited in note 2).

26 Quoted in Bronski, *Queer History* at 124 (cited in note 1).

27 Jack Lait & Lee Mortimer, *Washington Confidential* 90–91, 98 (Crown 1951). See Miller, *Out of the Past* at 236 (cited in note 6); Katz, *Gay American History* at 100–101 (cited in note 2); Johnson, *Lavender Scare* at 89–92 (cited in note 18).

28 Eskridge, *Dishonorable Passions* at 75, 102 (cited in note 20); Miller, *Out of the Past* at 237 (cited in note 6); Gregory B. Lewis & Marc A. Rogers, *Does the Public Support Equal Employment Rights for Gays and Lesbians?* in *Gays and Lesbians in the Democratic Process* 118, 119 (Ellen D. B. Riggle & Barry L. Tadlock eds., Columbia 1999).

29 Johnson, *Lavender Scare* at 149, 151 (cited in note 18). See Miller, *Out of the Past* at 238 (cited in note 6); Johnson, *Lavender Scare* at 157, 166 (cited in note 18); D'Emilio, *Sexual Politics* at 43–45 (cited in note 3).

30 Quoted in Faderman, *Odd Girls* at 151 (cited in note 8). See Pub. L. 82–414, 66 Stat. 163, 183 (June 27, 1952); Canaday, *Straight State* at 214–54 (cited in note 5).

31 *Raids Continue on S.F. Sex Deviates*, San Francisco Examiner 1 (June 28, 1954); *Needed: A Cleanup*, San Francisco Examiner 12 (June 28, 1954); *Police Jail, Warn Sex Deviates in Full Scale Drive*, San Francisco Examiner 1 (June 27, 1954); *Raids here Lauded*, San Francisco Examiner 1 (June 29, 1954); Nan Alamilla Boyd, *Wide-Open Town: A History of Queer San Francisco to 1965* 93 (California 2003).

32 Clark Taylor, *Folk Taxonomy and Justice in Dade County, Florida, 1954*, 4 *Anthropological Research Group on Homosexuality Newsletter* 9 (1983), quoted in Adam, *Rise of a Gay and Lesbian Movement* at 63 (cited in note 2); *Florida Reviews an Era of Fear*, New York Times (July 4, 1993); Adam, *Rise of a Gay and Lesbian Movement* at 63 (cited in note 2). See Miller, *Out of the Past* at 247–48 (cited in note 6); D'Emilio, *Sexual Politics* at 48 (cited in note 3); Eskridge, *Dishonorable Passions* at 103–4 (cited in note 20).

33 Adam, *Rise of a Gay and Lesbian Movement* at 64 (cited in note 2); quoted in Faderman, *Odd Girls* at 139 (cited in note 8).

34 Quoted in Faderman, *Odd Girls* at 146 (cited in note 8).

35 See Miller, *Out of the Past* at 250 (cited in note 6); John D'Emilio, *Making Trouble: Essays on Gay History, Politics, and the University* 159 (Routledge 1992); D'Emilio, *Sexual Politics* at 112 (cited in note 3); Adam, *Rise of a Gay and Lesbian Movement* at 64 (cited in note 2); Allan Bérubé & John D'Emilio, *The Military and Lesbians During the McCarthy Years*, 9 Signs: J. Women in Cult. and Soc. 759, 764, 770–75 (1984); Faderman, *Odd Girls* at 134–37, 144–45 (cited in note 8).

36 Donald Webster Cory (pseud.), *The Homosexual in America* 14 (Greenberg 1951).

37 Mattachine Society, *Missions and Purposes* (July 20, 1951), quoted in Katz, *Gay American History* at 412 (cited in note 2). See Adam, *Rise of a Gay and Lesbian Movement* at 67–68 (cited in note 2); Miller, *Out of the Past* at 302–3 (cited in note 6).

38 John D'Emilio, *Sexual Politics* at 58, 66 (cited in note 3). See Katz, *Gay American History* at 406–14 (cited in note 2); Johnson, *Lavender Scare* at 169–71 (cited in note 18); Boyd, *Wide-Open Town* at 165–68 (cited in note 31); Edsall, *Toward Stonewall* at 269–75 (cited in note 2).

39   Quoted in D'Emilio, *Sexual Politics* at 67 (cited in note 3).

40   See Miller, *Out of the Past* at 303–5 (cited in note 6); D'Emilio, *Sexual Politics* at 68, 71–73 (cited in note 3); Lillian Faderman, *The Gay Revolution* at 53–73 (Simon & Schuster 2015).

41   See D'Emilio, *Sexual Politics* at 103, 104, 110–11, 119 (cited in note 3); Adam, *Rise of a Gay and Lesbian Movement* at 69–70 (cited in note 2); Lillian Faderman, *Surpassing the Love of Men* 378–82 (Morrow 1981); Boyd, *Wide-Open Town* at 168–79 (cited in note 31); Miller, *Out of the Past* at 307–11 (cited in note 6); Katz, *Gay American History* at 420–33 (cited in note 2); Faderman, *Odd Girls* at 148–50 (cited in note 8); Faderman, *Gay Revolution* at 74–90 (cited in note 40); Edsall, *Toward Stonewall* at 282–84 (cited in note 2).

42   See Adam, *Rise of a Gay and Lesbian Movement* at 74–75 (cited in note 2); D'Emilio, *Sexual Politics* at 115, 122–25 (cited in note 3).

43   Alfred C. Kinsey, Wardell B. Pomeroy, & Clyde E. Martin, *Sexual Behavior in the Human Male* (W.B. Saunders 1948).

44   Kinsey et al., *Sexual Behavior in the Human Male* at 623, 639, 650–51, 656, 659 (cited in note 43); Eskridge, *Dishonorable Passions* at 110 (cited in note 20). See Bronski, *Queer History* at 177–78 (cited in note 1); Boyd, *Wide-Open Town* at 187 (cited in note 31); D'Emilio, *Sexual Politics* at 33–36 (cited in note 3); Edsall, *Toward Stonewall* at 265–67 (cited in note 2); Eskridge, *Dishonorable Passions* at 116 (cited in note 20).

45   Johnson, *Lavender Scare* at 54 (cited in note 18). See Katz, *Gay/Lesbian Almanac* at 630–33 (cited in note 1).

46   Edmund Bergler, *The Myth of a New National Disease: Homosexuality and the Kinsey Report*, 22 Psychiatric Q. 66, 86 (1948); Henry Van Dusen, *The Moratorium on Moral Revulsion*, 8 Christianity and Crisis 81 (June 21, 1948). See *About the Kinsey Report* 109–10 (Donald Porter Geddes & Enid Curie eds., New American Library 1948); Johnson, *Lavender Scare* at 54 (cited in note 18); Bronski, *Queer History* at 179 (cited in note 1); D'Emilio, *Sexual Politics* at 36 (cited in note 3).

47   Alfred C. Kinsey, Wardell B. Pomeroy, Clyde E. Martin, & Paul Gebhard, *Sexual Behavior in the Human Female* (Indiana 1998) (1953).

48   Kinsey et al, *Sexual Behavior in the Human Female* at 474–75 (cited in note 47). See Eskridge, *Dishonorable Passions* at 116–17 (cited in note 20).

49   Reinhold Niebuhr, *Sex and Religion in the Kinsey Report*, 8 Christianity and Crisis 140 (Nov. 2, 1953); Billy Graham, *The Bible and Dr. Kinsey*, Moody Monthly 13 (Nov. 1953). See James H. Jones, *Alfred C. Kinsey* 727–37 (Norton 1997); Eskridge, *Dishonorable Passions* at 115 (cited in note 20); D'Emilio, *Sexual Politics* at 36 (cited in note 3).

50   See Eric Marcus, *Making Gay History: The Half-Century Fight for Lesbian and Gay Equal Rights* 35–37 (Harper 2002); Faderman, *Gay Revolution* at 98–102 (cited in note 40); Boyd, *Wide-Open Town* at 187–89 (cited in note 31); D'Emilio, *Sexual Politics* at 37 (cited in note 3); Edsall, *Toward Stonewall* at 310 (cited in note 2); Evelyn Hooker, *The Adjustment of the Male Overt Homosexual*, 21 J. of Projective Techniques 18 (1957).

51   See Model Penal Code (American Law Institute 1962); Eskridge, *Dishonorable Passions* at 122 (cited in note 20); D'Emilio, *Sexual Politics* at 144–45 (cited in note 3).

52   Model Penal Code § 207.1, comment at 207 (Tent. Draft No. 4, 1955).

53   Model Penal Code § 207.5, comment at 277–78 (Tent. Draft No. 4, 1955); Louis B. Schwartz, *Morals Offenses and the Model Penal Code*, 63 Colum. L. Rev. 669, 669–70, 676 (1963). See Eskridge, *Dishonorable Passions* at 121–24 (cited in note 20).

54   Eskridge, *Dishonorable Passions* at 125, 127 (cited in note 20).

55   Cory, *Homosexual in America* at 54 (cited in note 36). See Eskridge, *Dishonorable Passions* at 127–29 (cited in note 20).

56   See D'Emilio, *Sexual Politics* at 145–47 (cited in note 3); Adam, *Rise of a Gay and Lesbian Movement* at 72–73 (cited in note 2); Edsall, *Toward Stonewall* at 314–16 (cited in note 2); Eskridge, *Dishonorable Passions* at 145–47, 161–63 (cited in note 20).

57   Quoted in D'Emilio, *Sexual Politics* at 153 (cited in note 3).

58   Douglass Shand-Tucci, *The Crimson Letter: Harvard, Homosexuality, and the Shaping of American Culture* 268 (St. Martin's 2003); D'Emilio, *Sexual Politics* at 198 (cited in note 3). See Marcus, *Making Gay History* at 80–84 (cited in note 50); Linda Hirshman, *Victory: The Triumphant Gay Revolution* 68 (Harper 2012); Faderman, *Gay Revolution* at 128–68 (cited in note 40); Edsall, *Toward Stonewall* at 325–26 (cited in note 2); D'Emilio, *Sexual Politics* at 150–55, 164 (cited in note 3); Eskridge, *Dishonorable Passions* at 136–38, 140, 171, 213–14 (cited in note 20); Johnson, *Lavender Scare* at 199 (cited in note 18).

59   Quoted in Marcus, *Making Gay History* at 75–76 (cited in note 50). See Marcus, *Making Gay History* at 79–87 (cited in note 50); Hirshman, *Victory* at xvi (cited in note 58); D'Emilio, *Sexual Politics* at 198–99 (cited in note 3).

60   Carl Wittman, *A Gay Manifesto*, http://library.gayhomeland.org/0006/EN/A_Gay_Manifesto.htm.

61   Bronski, *Queer History* at 209 (cited in note 1). See Hirshman, *Victory* at 68, 90–92 (cited in note 58); Edsall, *Toward Stonewall* at 329–30 (cited in note 2); D'Emilio, *Sexual Politics* at 150 (cited in note 3); Eskridge, *Dishonorable Passions* at 139 (cited in note 20); Bronski, *Queer History* at 208–9 (cited in note 1); Miller, *Out of the Past* at 339–41, 355–58 (cited in note 6).

62   D'Emilio, *Sexual Politics* at 219, 146 (cited in note 3). See Eskridge, *Dishonorable Passions* at 139 (cited in note 20); D'Emilio, *Sexual Politics* at 201–5 (cited in note 3).

63   Hirshman, *Victory* at 96 (cited in note 58). See David Carter, *Stonewall: The Riots That Sparked the Gay Revolution* 67–88 (Griffin ed., St. Martin's 2005); Adam, *Rise of a Gay and Lesbian Movement* at 81 (cited in note 2); Edsall, *Toward Stonewall* at 333 (cited in note 2); Miller, *Out of the Past* at 335–36 (cited in note 6).

64   Miller, *Out of the Past* at 336 (cited in note 6); Eskridge, *Dishonorable Passions* at 167 (cited in note 20); Kenneth Sherrill, *The Youth of the Movement*, in Riggle & Tadlock, *Gays and Lesbians* at 269, 272 (cited in note 28). See Hirshman, *Victory* at 93–95, 103–4 (cited in note 58); Carter, *Stonewall* at 129–205 (cited in note 63); Marcus, *Making Gay History* at 126–30 (cited in note 50); Faderman, *Gay Revolution* at 171–87 (cited in note 40); Bronski, *Queer History* at 209–10 (cited in note 1); Martin Duberman, *Stonewall* at 201 (Plume 1993).

65   Quoted in Carter, *Stonewall* at 199 (cited in note 63); Eskridge, *Dishonorable Passions* at 167 (cited in note 20).

66   Eskridge, *Dishonorable Passions* at 167–68 (cited in note 20); Martha Shelley, *Gay Is Good*, in *Out of the Closets: Voices of Gay Liberation* 32, 34 (Karla Jay & Allen Young eds., NYU 1992). See Marcus, *Making Gay History* at 131–35 (cited in note 50); Miller, *Out of the Past* at 336–39 (cited in note 6); Faderman, *Gay Revolution* at 188–209 (cited in note 40).

67   Quoted in Hirshman, *Victory* at 127 (cited in note 58). See Duberman, *Stonewall* at 276–80 (cited in note 64); Carter, *Stonewall* at 253–55 (cited in note 63); Adam, *Rise of a Gay and Lesbian Movement* at 81, 85–88 (cited in note 2); Hirshman, *Victory* at 123–27 (cited in note 58); Marcus, *Making Gay History* at 143 (cited in note 50); Faderman, *Gay Revolution* at 210–26 (cited in note 40); Miller, *Out of the Past* at 353–54 (cited in note 6).

68   Bronski, *Queer History* at 216 (cited in note 1). See Adam, *Rise of a Gay and Lesbian Movement* at 86 (cited in note 2).

69   Adam, *Rise of a Gay and Lesbian Movement* at 97–98 (cited in note 2). See Miller, *Out of the Past* at 344–48 (cited in note 6); Faderman, *Gay Revolution* at 227–46 (cited in note 40); Sidney Abbott & Barbara Love, *Sappho Was a Right-On Woman* 119–23, 134 (Stein and Day 1972).

70   See Adam, *Rise of a Gay and Lesbian Movement* at 87–88 (cited in note 2); Bronski, *Queer History* at 218–19 (cited in note 1); D'Emilio, *Sexual Politics* at 163, 217 (cited in note 3); Hirshman, *Victory* at 131–40 (cited in note 58); Eskridge, *Dishonorable Passions* at 170–84, 197–203 (cited in note 20); Johnson, *Lavender Scare* at 207–10 (cited in note 18); Adam, *Rise of a Gay and Lesbian Movement* at 88 (cited in note 2); Donald P. Haider-Markel, *Creating Change*, in Riggle & Tadlock, *Gays and Lesbians* at 248–49 (cited in note 28); Miller, *Out of the Past* at 366, 385–86 (cited in note 6); Faderman, *Odd Girls* at 202 (cited in note 8); Nan D. Hunter & Nancy D. Polikoff, *Custody Rights of Lesbian Mothers: Legal Theory and Litigation Strategy*, 25 Buffalo L. Rev. 691 (1976).

71   See Haider-Markel, *Creating Change* at 248 (cited in note 70).

72   Eskridge, *Dishonorable Passions* at 210 (cited in note 20); Fred Fejes, *Gay Rights and Moral Panic* 96 (Palgrave Macmillan 2008); Bronski, *Queer History* at 220 (cited in note 1).

73   See Adam, *Rise of a Gay and Lesbian Movement* at 110 (cited in note 2); Bronski, *Queer History* at 220 (cited in note 1); Miller, *Out of the Past* at 372–73 (cited in note 6); Faderman, *Gay Revolution* at 321–54 (cited in note 40).

74   See Adam, *Rise of a Gay and Lesbian Movement* at 109–11, 133 (cited in note 2); Bronski, *Queer History* at 220 (cited in note 1).

75   Adam, *Rise of a Gay and Lesbian Movement* at 111, 121 (cited in note 2); Bronski, *Queer History* at 223 (cited in note 1). See Eskridge, *Dishonorable Passions* at 209–12 (cited in note 20).

76   Eskridge, *Dishonorable Passions* at 197 (cited in note 20). See Faderman, *Odd Girls* at 271–72 (cited in note 8).

77   See Didi Herman, *The Antigay Agenda: Orthodox Vision and the Christian Right* 44–54 (Chicago 1997); Oran P. Smith, *The Rise of Baptist Republicanism* 171, 218–31 (NYU 1997); Adam, *Rise of a Gay and Lesbian Movement* at 115 (cited in note 2); Eskridge, *Dishonorable Passions* at 203–9 (cited in note 20); Tim F. LaHaye, *The Unhappy Gays: What Everyone*

Should Know about Homosexuality (Tyndale House 1978); Donald T. Critchlow, *Phyllis Schlafly and Grassroots Conservatism* 225, 229 (Princeton 2005).

78 Hirshman, *Victory* at 174 (cited in note 58); Charles Perrow & Mauro F. Guillén, *The AIDS Disaster* 50–54 (Yale 1990); Bronski, *Queer History* at 225 (cited in note 1). See Hirshman, *Victory* at 170–81 (cited in note 58); Marcus, *Making Gay History* at 255–56, 268–70 (cited in note 50); Adam, *Rise of a Gay and Lesbian Movement* at 155–57 (cited in note 2); Miller, *Out of the Past* at 409–10, 421–22 (cited in note 6); Bronski, *Queer History* at 224–35 (cited in note 1).

CHAPTER 12

1 William B. Lockhart & Robert C. McClure, *Literature, the Law of Obscenity, and the Constitution*, 38 Minn. L. Rev. 295, 304 and n.64 (1954).

2 See Seth Stern & Stephen Wermiel, *Justice Brennan: Liberal Champion* 122 (Houghton Mifflin Harcourt 2010); John D'Emilio & Estelle B. Freedman, *Intimate Matters: A History of Sexuality in America* 282–88 (Chicago 1988); Whitney Strub, *Perversion for Profit* 23–24 (Columbia 2010); Frederick S. Lane III, *Obscene Profits* xvi, 22–24, 81–82 (Routledge 2000); Edward de Grazia & Roger K. Newman, *Banned Films: Movies, Censors and the First Amendment* 68 (Bowker 1982); Kenneth C. Davis, *Two-Bit Culture* 135–41, 219–39 (Mariner 1984); Marjorie Heins, *Not in Front of the Children* 50–52 (Rutgers 2001); Terrence J. Murphy, *Censorship: Government and Obscenity* 66, 84–88 (Helicon 1963); *New American Library of World Literature v. Allen*, 114 F. Supp. 823, 826 (1953).

3 See D'Emilio & Freedman, *Intimate Matters* at 284 (cited in note 2). *The Spread of Smut*, Newsweek 41–42 (Apr. 27, 1957); Howard Whitman, *Smut: The Poison that Preys on Our Children*, Good Housekeeping 64–65, 101–4, 173–75 (Nov. 1961), quoted in Strub, *Perversion for Profit* at 25 (cited in note 2).

4 H.R. Rep. No. 2510, 82nd Cong., 2d Sess. 1 (1952) quoted in Lockhart & McClure, *Literature, the Law of Obscenity, and the Constitution* at 306–7 (cited in note 1); See de Grazia & Newman, *Banned Films* at 75 (cited in note 2); Murphy, *Censorship* at 98–100 (cited in note 2); Neil Miller, *Banned in Boston* 176 (Beacon 2010).

5 See D'Emilio & Freedman, *Intimate Matters* at 281–82 (cited in note 2); Lockhart & McClure, *Literature, The Law of Obscenity, and the Constitution* at 295–320 (cited in note 1).

6 See de Grazia & Newman, *Banned Films* at 86, 78 (cited in note 2); Heins, *Not in Front of the Children* at 92–93 (cited in note 2); Lili Levi, *The FCC's Regulation of Indecency* 4 (The First Amendment Center, April 2008); Jennifer Poole Hayward, *Consuming Pleasures* 131–33 (Kentucky 1997).

7 See Lockhart & McClure, *Literature, The Law of Obscenity, and the Constitution* at 320, 323 (cited in note 1); D'Emilio & Freedman, *Intimate Matters* at 285 (cited in note 2); Davis, *Two-Bit Culture* at 135–41, 219–39 (cited in note 2).

8 Anthony Lewis, *Sex and the Supreme Court*, Esquire 82 (June 1963), quoted in Stern & Wermiel, *Justice Brennan* at 121 (cited in note 2).

9 See *Schenck v. United States*, 249 U.S. 47, 52 (1919).

10 See *Shaffer v. United States*, 255 F. 886 (9th Cir. 1919); Geoffrey R. Stone, *The Origins* *of the Bad Tendency Test*, 2002 Sup. Ct. Rev. 411; David Rabban, *The Emergence of Modern First Amendment Doctrine*, 50 U. Chi. L. Rev. 1205 (1983).

11 *Abrams v. United States*, 250 U.S. 616, 630 (1919) (Holmes, J., dissenting).

12 *Whitney v. California*, 274 U.S. 357, 377 (1927) (Brandeis, J., concurring).

13 See, e.g., *Thornhill v. Alabama*, 310 U.S. 88 (1940); *Cantwell v. Connecticut*, 310 U.S. 296 (1940); *Bridges v. California*, 314 U.S. 252 (1941); *Chaplinsky v. New Hampshire* 315 U.S. 568 (1942); *Kovacs v. Cooper*, 335 U.S. 77 (1949); *Feiner v. New York*, 340 U.S. 315 (1951); *Dennis v. United States*, 341 U.S. 494 (1951).

14 360 U.S. 684 (1959).

15 *Id.* at 685, 688–89.

16 See *Near v. Minnesota*, 283 U.S. 697, 716 (1931); *Chaplinsky v. New Hampshire*, 315 U.S. 568, 571–72 (1942); *Winters v. New York*, 333 U.S. 507, 510 (1948); *Beauharnais v. Illinois*, 343 U.S. 250, 266 (1952).

17 See Leo Hamalian, *Nobody Knows My Names: Samuel Roth and the Underside of Modern Letters*, 3 J. of Mod. Lit., 889–918 (Apr. 1974); Frederick F. Schauer, *The Law of Obscenity* 33 (Bureau of National Affairs 1976).

18 *United States v. Roth* 237 F.2d 796, 798–99 (2d Cir. 1956).

19 *Id.* at 802, 804–5, 808–9 (Frank, J., concurring).

20 354 U.S. 476 (1957).

21 See Stern & Wermiel, *Justice Brennan* at 130 (cited in note 2).

22 354 U.S. at 481 (cited in note 20).

23 *Id.* at 482–83.

24 *Id.* at 484, 497, 485, quoting *Chaplinsky v. New Hampshire*, 315 U.S. 568, 571–72 (1942).

25 *Id.* at 486–87.

26 *Id.* at 488–89.

27 *Id.* at 490.

28 *Id.* at 491, quoting *United States v. Petrillo*, 332 U.S. 1, 7–8 (1947).

29 Hugo Black, *The Bill of Rights*, 35 N.Y.U. L. Rev. 865, 874, 879 (1960).

30 354 U.S. at 509, 512–14 (cited in note 20) (Douglas, J. dissenting).

31 See *High Court Rule Bars Obscenity*, Washington Post (June 25, 1957); Stern & Wermiel, *Justice Brennan* at 125, 252 (cited in note 2).

32 Louis Henkin, *Morals and the Constitution: The Sin of Obscenity*, 63 Colum. L. Rev. 393–95, 402 (1963).

33 William J. Brennan to John Marshall Harlan (June 9, 1962), quoted in Stern & Wermiel, *Justice Brennan* at 252 (cited in note 2).

34 378 U.S. 184 (1964).

35 *Id.* at 197 (Stewart, J., concurring).

36 See Strub, *Perversion for Profit* at 146–48 (cited in note 2); Leonard J. Leff & Jerold L. Simmons, *The Dame in the Kimono: Hollywood, Censorship, and the Production Code* 250–66 (Grove Weidenfeld 1990).

37 *A Book Named "John Cleland's Memoirs of a Woman of Pleasure" v. Attorney General of Massachusetts*, 383 U.S. 413 (1966).

38 *Id.* at 502.

39 *Id.* at 463.

40 *Id.* at 418.

41 *Attorney General v. Memoirs,* 206 N.E. 2d 403, 406 (1965), quoted in *Memoirs,* 383 U.S. at 419.

42 383 U.S. at 419–20 (cited in note 37) (Black, J., dissenting).

43 Harry M. Clor, *Obscenity and Public Morality* 78 (Chicago 1975).

44 383 U.S. at 456, 458, 460 (cited in note 37) (Harlan, J., dissenting).

45 *Id.* at 505.

46 *Id.* at 508.

47 *Id.* at 467–70.

48 Andrew Kopkind, *May It Please the Court,* New Republic 9 (Dec. 9, 1965), quoted in Stern & Wermiel, *Justice Brennan* at 256 (cited in note 2).

49 New York Penal Law § 484-h as enacted by L. 1965, c. 327.

50 390 U.S. 629 (1968).

51 *Id.* at 635, 638–41.

52 394 U.S. 557 (1969).

53 *Id.* at 559, 564, quoting *Olmstead v. United States,* 277 U. S. 438, 478 (1928) (Brandeis, J., dissenting).

54 394 U.S. at 565–68 (cited in note 52).

55 Bob Woodward & Scott Armstrong, *The Brethren: Inside the Supreme Court* 235 (Simon and Schuster 1979). See Harry Kalven Jr., *A Worthy Tradition: Freedom of Speech in America* 47 (Harper & Row 1988); Al Katz, *Privacy and Pornography: Stanley v. Georgia,* 1969 Sup. Ct. Rev. 203; Bryan K. McCarthy, *Obscenity from Stanley to Karalexis,* 23 Vand. L. Rev. 369 (1970); *Karalexis v. Byrne,* 306 F. Supp. 1363 (D. Mass. 1969).

56 386 U.S. 767 (1967).

57 398 U.S. 434 (1970).

58 Richard F. Hixson, *Pornography and the Justices: The Supreme Court and the Intractable Obscenity Problem* ix (Southern Illinois 1996); *Paris Adult Theatre I v. Slaton,* 413 U.S. 49, 83 (1973) (Brennan, J., dissenting).

59 Lewis, *Sex and the Supreme Court* at 82 (cited in note 8), quoted in Stern & Wermiel, *Justice Brennan* at 121 (cited in note 2).

60 Woodward & Armstrong, *The Brethren* at 239 (cited in note 55).

61 *The Report of the Commission on Obscenity and Pornography* 1, 10, 11, 18 (1970).

62 *Id.* at 23–32.

63 *Id.* at 59, 47–49.

64 *Id.* at 63, 67. See Ian Hunter, David Saunders, & Dugald Williamson, *On Pornography: Literature, Sexuality and Obscenity Law* 203 (Macmillan 1993); Heins, *Not in Front of the Children* at 10 (cited in note 2).

65 Statement of Commissioner Charles H. Keating Jr., in *Report of Commission on Obscenity* at 578, 580–82 (cited in note 61). See *Court Enjoins Publication of Obscenity Report,* Publishers Weekly 37 (Sept. 21, 1970).

66   Statement of Commissioners Morton A. Hill & Winfrey C. Link, in *Report of Commission on Obscenity* at 456–58 (cited in note 61).

67   *Porno Report Becomes Political Football*, Publishers Weekly 34–35 (Oct. 12, 1970).

68   Richard M. Nixon, *Statement About the Report of the Commission on Obscenity and Pornography* (Oct. 24, 1970); Michael J. Graetz & Linda Greenhouse, *The Burger Court and the Rise of the Judicial Right* 195 (Simon & Schuster 2016).

69   See Kalven, *Worthy Tradition* at 48 (cited in note 55).

70   Graetz & Greenhouse, *The Burger Court* at 4 (cited in note 68).

71   Woodward & Armstrong, *The Brethren* at 233, 236, 295 (cited in note 55); William J. Brennan Jr., *Notes* xvi–xvii (October Term 1972) (unpublished document).

72   413 U.S. 15 (1973).

73   *Id.* at 73.

74   *Id.* at 52–53.

75   Woodward & Armstrong, *The Brethren* at 236, 239–40 (cited in note 55); Stern & Wermiel, *Justice Brennan* at 367 (cited in note 2).

76   413 U.S. 22, 16, 24 (1973).

77   *Id.* at 41, 44–45 (Douglas, J., dissenting).

78   *Paris Adult Theatre*, 413 U.S. at 97 (Brennan, J., dissenting).

79   413 U.S. at 58–61, 63, 66–69.

80   *Id.* at 107–8, quoting *Whitney v. California*, 274 U.S. 357, 378 (1927) (Brandeis, J., concurring).

81   410 U.S. 113 (1973).

82   413 U.S. 108–10 (1973) (Brennan, J., dissenting).

83   Kalven, *Worthy Tradition* at 48, 50, 53 (cited in note 55).

CHAPTER 13

1   See Stephen Gillers, *A Tendency to Deprave and Corrupt*, 85 Wash. U. L. Rev. 215, 295–96 (2007).

2   See David Domke & Kevin Coe, *The God Strategy: How Religion Became a Political Weapon in America* (Oxford 2008).

3   Attorney General's Commission on Pornography, *Final Report* 215 (1986) (hereinafter cited as *Meese Commission Report*).

4   *Meese Commission Report* at 247–48, 366–67, 229 (cited in note 3); Frederick S. Lane III, *Obscene Profits* 52 (Routledge 2000); Whitney Strub, *Perversion for Profit* 166–68, 173 (Columbia 2011).

5   *Meese Commission Report* at 323–27 (cited in note 3).

6   *Id.* at 376–77.

7   Patrick A. Trueman, *Hearing on Obscenity Prosecution and the Constitution, Subcommittee on the Constitution, Civil Rights and Property Rights, United States Senate Committee on the Judiciary* 3 (Mar. 16, 2005); Jason Krause, *The End of the Net Porn Wars*, A.B.A. J. (Feb. 2008). See Trueman, *Hearing on Obscenity Prosecution* at 3 (cited in this note).

8 See Lane, *Obscene Profits* at 48–49 (cited in note 4); Eric Schlosser, *The Bill Gates of Porn*, U.S. News & World Report (Feb. 10, 1997).

9 Trueman, *Hearing on Obscenity Prosecution* at 4 (cited in note 7).

10 Mike Mosedale, *The Porn Warrior at Rest: Ferris Alexander's Legacy*, City Pages News (Mar. 12, 2003).

11 See *Alexander v. United States*, 509 U.S. 544 (1993).

12 Mosedale, *Porn Warrior* (cited in note 10), quoting John Weston.

13 See Krause, *End of the Net Porn Wars* (cited in note 7).

14 See James M Fottrell, Steve DeBrota, & Francey Hakes, *Statement for the Record before the United States Sentencing Commission Hearing on the Child Pornography Guidelines* 1–2 (Feb. 15, 2012).

15 See *New York v. Ferber*, 458 U.S. 747, 749 n.1 (1982); Strub, *Perversion for Profit* at 194–97 (cited in note 4).

16 Protection of Children Against Sexual Exploitation Act, Pub. L. 95–225, 92 Stat. 7 § 2 (1978) (codified at 18 U.S.C. §§ 2251–53).

17 See *Meese Commission Report* at 413 (cited in note 3); Child Sexual Abuse and Pornography Act of 1986, Pub. L. 99–628, 100 Stat. 3510 (1986); Child Abuse Victims' Rights Act, Pub. L. 99–500, 100 Stat. 1783, Title I, § 101(b) [Title VII, §§ 701–05 (1986)] and amended by Pub. L. 99–591, 100 Stat. 3341–75, Title I, §101(b) [Title VII, §§ 701–05] (1986).

18 See http://www.cwfa.org/familyvoice/2000–11/20–25.asp; http://www.bpnews.net/BPnews.asp?ID=5935.

19 *Review of Child Pornography and Obscenity Crimes*, Rept. No. I-2001-07, tables 1, 3, 6 and 8 (July 19, 2001). See Tim Wu, *American Lawbreaking*, Slate (Oct. 14, 2007).

20 Quoted in Wu, *American Lawbreaking* (cited in note 19). See Krause, *End of the Net Porn Wars* (cited in note 7).

21 Christian Bourge, *Ashcroft's Obscenity Crusade* (Dec. 4, 2003).

22 Quoted in Robert D. Richards & Clay Calvert, *Obscenity Prosecutions and the Bush Administration*, 14 Vill. Sports & Ent. L.J. 233, 237–38 (2007); Eric Lichtblau, *Justice Dept. Fights Ruling on Obscenity*, New York Times A25 (Feb. 17, 2005).

23 Trueman, *Hearing on Obscenity Prosecution* at 1, 2, 5 (cited in note 7); See *ACLU v. Gonzales*, 478 F. Supp. 2d 775 ¶ 132 (E.D. Pa. 2007).

24 *Prepared Remarks of Attorney General Alberto R. Gonzales, Hoover Institution Board of Overseers Conference* (Feb. 28, 2005); Scott Glover, *Trial to Gauge What L.A. Sees as Obscene*, Los Angeles Times (June 9, 2008) quoted in Clay Calvert, Wendy Brunner, Karla Kennedy, & Kara Murrhee, *Judicial Erosion of Protection for Defendants in Obscenity Prosecutions?* Harv. J. Sports & Enter. L. 7, 9 (2010); Wu, *American Lawbreaking* (cited in note 19). See Krause, *End of the Net Porn Wars* (cited in note 7).

25 Quoted in Krause, *End of the Net Porn Wars* (cited in note 7).

26 Krause, *End of the Net Porn Wars* (cited in note 7) (quoting Trueman). See *ACLU v. Gonzales* at 133 (cited in note 23).

27 Jan LaRue, *Budgeting Wars Part II: Feds Fail Obscenity Enforcement*, Concerned Women for America (Feb. 26, 2007); http://www.ccv.org/; Dustin McNab, *Government Failing in*

Obscenity Fight, Baptist Press (Mar. 16, 2007); *U.S. Justice Department's Record of Enforcing Obscenity Laws May Be Disappointing, but Latest Obscenity Prosecution Success Proves Again That Most Adults Do Not Accept the Proliferation of Obscenity*, Christian News Wire (June 6, 2008).

28   *United States v. Ragsdale*, 426 F.3d 765, 769 (5th Cir. 2005).

29   See *United States v. Little A/K/A "Max Hardcore,"* CCH-GDCL P 49494 (C.C.H.) (M.D. Fla. 2009), aff'd *United States v. Little, a.k.a. Max Hardcore*, 365 Fed. Appx. 159 (11th Cir. 2010). Richards & Calvert, *Obscenity Prosecutions* at 546 (cited in note 22).

30   *Oversight of the U.S. Department of Justice: Hearing Before the Committee on the Judiciary, United States Senate*, 110th Cong., 2d Sess., 15–16 (July 9, 2008).

31   See Calvert, Brunner, Kennedy, & Murrhee, *Judicial Erosion* at 8 n.2 (cited in note 24).

32   Wu, *American Lawbreaking* (cited in note 19).

33   Quoted in Richards & Calvert, *Obscenity Prosecutions* at 580 (cited in note 22).

34   House Committee on Appropriations, H. Rept. 112–69, *Commerce, Justice, Science, and Related Agencies Appropriations Bill, 2012*, 112th Cong., 1st Sess. 46 (2012).

35   Letter from Forty-Two Senators to Attorney General Eric Holder Calling for Enforcement of Federal Obscenity Laws (Apr. 4, 2011).

36   George Weaver, *Obama Administration Fails Obscenity Test*, World (Apr. 24, 2013); Nicola Menzie, *Attorney General Eric Holder No. 1 on Morality in Media's List of "Sex Exploiters,"* The Christian Post (Apr. 3, 2013), David Baumann, *Folding of Anti Smut Unit Revives Debate on How to Fight Porn*, Main Justice (May 4, 2011).

37   Quoted in Baumann, *Folding of Anti-Smut Unit* (cited in note 36).

38   Quoted in *Holder Accused of Neglecting Porn Fight*, Politico (May 2, 2011).

39   See, e.g., Nathan Stubbs, *Out of Sight*, The Independent (Jan. 12, 2005); Jill Barton, *Runaway Grand Jury*, 77 UMKC L. Rev. 249 (2008); Jennifer M. Kinsley, *The Myth of Obsolete Obscenity*, Cardozo Arts & Ent. L.J. (2015); *Varkonyi v. State*, 276 S.W. 3d 27 (Tex. 2008); *Melton v. State*, 69 So. 3d 916 (Ala. 2010); *Ex parte Dave*, 220 S.W. 3d 154 (Tex. 2007).

40   Baylor University Counseling Center, *Exposing Pornography*, http://www. promisekeepers.org/about/core-values. See Benjamin Edelman, *Red Light States: Who Buys Online Adult Entertainment?* 23 J. of Econ. Perspect. at 212, 217–19 (2009); Lane, *Obscene Profits* at 105 (cited in note 4); Andrew Ross, *No Respect: Intellectuals and Popular Culture* (Routledge 1989); Gilbert Wondracek, Thorsten Holz, Christian Platzer, Engin Kirda, & Christopher Kruegel, *Is the Internet for Porn? An Insight Into the Online Adult Industry*, Ninth Workshop on the Economics of Information Security (WEIS 2010).

41   Robert Lopez & Jeff Marx, *The Internet Is for Porn*, Avenue Q (2003).

42   Testimony of Charles H. Keating, *Mailing of Obscene Matter: Hearings Before Subcommittee No. 1*, House Committee on the Judiciary 72 (Government Printing Office 1958), quoted in Strub, *Perversion for Profit* at 83–90 (cited in note 4); See Lane, *Obscene Profits* at 106 (cited in note 4); Kenneth T. Jackson, *Crabgrass Frontier: The Suburbanization of the United States* 231–82 (Oxford 1987); Thomas J. Sugrue, *The Origins of the Urban Crisis* 209–29 (Princeton 1996).

43   New York Times (Sept. 13, 1970); 116 *Cong. Rec.* 33829–30 (Sept. 25, 1970); 116 *Cong. Rec.* 34012 (Sept. 28, 1970); 116 *Cong. Rec.* 34016 (Sept. 28, 1970); 116 *Cong. Rec.* 37081 (Oct. 14, 1970); Richard M. Nixon, *Statement About the Report of the Commission on*

Obscenity and Pornography, October 24, 1970, American Presidency Project; Strub, *Perversion for Profit* at 134 (cited in note 4).

44 Strub, *Perversion for Profit* at 143–44 (cited in note 4). See Richard M. Nixon, *Remarks to Newsmen in Denver, Colorado*, August 3, 1970, American Presidency Project; Richard M. Nixon, *Special Message to the Congress Resubmitting Legislative Proposals*, January 26, 1971, American Presidency Project.

45 Jerry Falwell, *Listen, America!* 200–201 (Doubleday 2000). See Tim LaHaye, *The Battle for the Family* 18, 73 (Revell 1982); Tim LaHaye, *The Battle for the Mind* 20–21 (Revell 1980); Robert C. Liebman, *Mobilizing the Moral Majority*, in *The New Christian Right* 50–73 (Robert C. Liebman & Robert Wuthnow eds., Aldine 1983); Strub, *Perversion for Profit* at 179, 187–88 (cited in note 4); Lane, *Obscene Profits* at 99 (cited in note 4).

46 Ronald Reagan, *Remarks at the Annual Convention of the National Association of Evangelicals in Orlando, Florida*, March 8, 1983, American Presidency Project. See William Martin, *With God on Our Side: The Rise of the Religious Right in America* 208 (Broadway 1996); Strub, *Perversion for Profit* at 180, 191, 194, 198–99, 206–8 (cited in note 4); Philip Nobile & Eric Nadler, *United States of America v. Sex: How the Meese Commission Lied About Pornography* 16–22 (Minotaur 1986); Carole S. Vance, *Negotiating Sex and Gender in the Attorney General's Commission on Pornography*, in *Sex Exposed: Sexuality and the Pornography Debate* 29–49 (Lynne Segal & Mary McIntosh eds., Rutgers 1993); Beth Spring, *How Harmful Is Pornography?* Christianity Today 26–27 (July 11, 1986); Phyllis Schlafly, *The New Pornography Commission Report*, Phyllis Schlafly Report (July 1986); Edward Donnerstein, Daniel Linz, & Steven Penrod, *The Question of Pornography: Research Findings and Policy Implications* 172, 179 (Free Press 1987).

CHAPTER 14

1 390 U.S. 629 (1968).

2 352 U.S. 380 (1957).

3 *Id.* at 383.

4 403 U.S. 15 (1971).

5 Bob Woodward & Scott Armstrong, *The Brethren: Inside the Supreme Court* 153–54 (Simon & Schuster 1979).

6 422 U.S. 205 (1975).

7 *Id.* at 212–14.

8 438 U.S. 726 (1978).

9 See Pub. L. 632, Act of February 23, 1927, 69th Congress, codified as 18 U.S.C. §1464 (Radio Act of 1927); Pub. L. 416, Act of June 19, 1934, ch. 652, 48 Stat. 1064, 73rd Congress, codified as ch. 5 of Title 47 of the United States Code, 47 U.S.C. § 151 et seq. (Communications Act of 1934); Robert L. Hilliard & Michael C. Keith, *Dirty Discourse: Sex and Indecency in Broadcasting* 3, 12–13 (Iowa State 2003).

10 438 U.S. at 729–30, 747–51 (cited in note 8), quoting *Village of Euclid v. Ambler Realty Co.*, 272 U. S. 365, 388 (1926).

11 *Id.* at 764–66 (Brennan, J., dissenting), quoting *Cohen v. California*, 403 U.S. 21 (1971).

12 Federal Communications Commission Fact Sheet, *FCC Takes Strong Stand on Enforcement of Prohibition Against Obscene and Indecent Broadcasts* (Nov. 1987), quoted in Hilliard & Keith, *Dirty Discourse* at 4 (cited in note 9). See Hilliard & Keith, *Dirty Discourse* at 4, 33–42 (cited in note 9); Lili Levi, *The Hard Case of Broadcast Indecency*, 20 N.Y.U. Rev. L & Soc. Change 49, 90–91 (1992–1993); *Action for Children Television v. FCC* (ACT III), 58 F.3d 654 (D.C. Cir. 1995); Lili Levi, *The FCC's Regulation of Indecency*, 7 First Reports 1, 12–13 (First Amendment Center 2008); *In re Infinity Broadcasting Corp.*, 3 F.C.C. Rcd. 930 (1987); *In re Application of WGBH Educ. Foundation*, 69 F.C.C. 2d 1250, 1254 (1978) (FCC declares it "intend[s] strictly to observe the narrowness of the Pacifica holding"); *FCC v. Fox Television Stations*, 132 S. Ct. 2307 (2012).

13 Levi, *FCC's Regulation of Indecency* at 13 (cited in note 12). See Kevin J. Martin, *Family-Friendly Programming*, 55 Fed. Comm. L.J. 553, 557 n.18 (2003); Broadcast Decency Enforcement Act, 47 U.S.C. 503 (2005); Levi, *FCC's Regulation of Indecency* at 13–14 (cited in note 12).

14 See *In re Complaints Against Various Broadcast Licensees Regarding Their Airing of the "Golden Globe Awards" Program*, 19 F.C.C. Rcd. 4976, 4980 and n.32 (2004); *Omnibus Remand Order*, 21 F.C.C. Rcd. 13300 ¶ 3, 13, et seq. (2006); *Complaints Against Various Television Licensees Concerning Their February 1, 2004, Broadcast of the Super Bowl XXXVIII Halftime Show*, 21 F.C.C. Rcd. 6653, 6654, 6656 ¶ 5, ¶ 9 (2006); Levi, *FCC's Regulation of Indecency* at 14–16, 24–25 (cited in note 12).

15 *In re Industry Guidance On the Commission's Case Law Interpreting 18 U.S.C. § 1464 and Enforcement Policies Regarding Broadcast Indecency*, 16 F.C.C. Rcd. 8003 ¶ 10, 8008 ¶ 17 (2001); *In re Complaints Against Various Broadcast Licensees*, 19 F.C.C. Rcd. 4976, 4979 ¶ 9, 4980 ¶ 11 (cited in note 14); *In re Complaints Regarding Various Television Broadcasts Between February 2, 2002, and March 8, 2005*, 21 F.C.C. Rcd. 13299 (2006) (Remand Order); *FCC v. Fox Television Stations*, 132 S. Ct. 2307 (2012).

16 556 U.S. 502 (2009).

17 *FCC v. Fox Television Stations*, 132 S. Ct. 2307, 2317–18, 2320 (2012).

18 § 505 of the Telecommunications Act of 1996, Pub. L. 104–104, 110 Stat. 136, 47 U. S. C. § 561 (1994 ed., Supp. III).

19 529 U.S. 803 (2000).

20 *Id.* at 813, 826–27.

21 Communications Decency Act of 1996, Title 47 U.S.C.A. § 223(a)(1)(B)(ii) (Supp. 1997).

22 521 U.S. 844 (1997).

23 *Id.* at 867, 874.

24 47 U.S.C. § 231(c)(1).

25 542 U.S. 656 (2004).

26 *Id.* at 657, 668.

27 *Butler v. Michigan*, 352 U.S. 380, 383 (1957).

28 See *United States v. O'Brien*, 391 U.S. 367 (1968); *Branzburg v. Hayes*, 408 U.S. 665 (1972). Geoffrey R. Stone, *Free Speech in the Twenty-First Century: Ten Lessons from the Twentieth Century*, 36 Pepperdine L. Rev. 273, 297–98 (2009); Michael C. Dorf, *Incidental Burdens on Fundamental Rights*, 109 Harv. L. Rev. 1175 (1996); Jed Rubenfeld, *The First Amendment's Purpose*, 53 Stan. L. Rev. 767, 769 (2001); Elena Kagan, *Private Speech, Public Purpose: The Role of Government Motive in First Amendment Doctrine*, 63 U. Chi. L. Rev. 415, 494–508 (1996); Geoffrey R. Stone, *Content-Neutral Restrictions*, 54 U. Chi. L. Rev. 46, 114 (1987). In a few instances, the Court has held incidental effects on speech unconstitutional when the incidental effect on speech is especially severe. See, e.g., *NAACP v. Alabama*, 357 U.S. 449 (1958).

29 501 U.S. 560 (1991).

30 See Lucinda Jarrett, *Stripping in Time: A History of Erotic Dancing* (HarperCollins 1997); Rachel Shteir, *Striptease: The Untold History of the Girlie Show* (Oxford 2004); Dita Von Teese, *Burlesque and the Art of the Teese* (Regan Books 2006); Curt Sachs, *World History of the Dance* (Norton 1937); Peter Webb, *The Erotic Arts* 297–306 (Martin Secker & Warburg 1983); Walter Sorell, *Dance in Its Time* (Anchor 1981). Annotation, *Topless or Bottomless Dancing or Similar Conduct as Offense*, 49 A.L.R. 3d 1084 (1973), 49 A.L.R. 3d Supp. 59 (1989); *Miller v. Civil City of South Bend*, 904 F.2d 1081, 1089 (7th Cir. 1990) (Posner, J., concurring); *Schad v. Borough of Mt. Ephraim*, 452 U.S. 61 (1981).

31 501 U.S. at 566, 568–69, 571 (cited in note 29).

32 *Id.* at 591–92 (White, J., dissenting).

33 Irvin Molotsky, *The Supreme Court: Man in the News; Judge with Tenacity and Charm: Antonin Scalia*, New York Times (June 18, 1986). See Joan Biskupic, *American Original: The Life and Constitution of Supreme Court Justice Antonin Scalia* 121 (Sarah Crichton Books 2009); Bruce Allen Murphy, *Scalia: A Court of One* 1–20 (Simon & Schuster 2014).

34 501 U.S. at 575 (cited in note 29) (Scalia, J., dissenting).

35 *McGowan v. Maryland*, 366 U.S. 420, 453 (1961).

36 458 U.S. 747 (1982).

37 N.Y. Penal Law § 263 (1977).

38 422 N.E.2d 523 (1981).

39 458 U.S. at 753.

40 *Id.* at 756–57, quoting *Globe Newspaper Co. v. Superior Court*, 457 U.S. 596, 607 (1982).

41 *Id.* at 759–63.

42 *Statement for the Record of James M. Fottrell, Steve DeBrota, and Francey Hakes, Department of Justice*, before the United States Sentencing Commission Hearing on the Child Pornography Guidelines 1, 3, 5 (Feb. 15, 2012). See Marty Klein, *America's War on Sex* 138 (Praeger 2006); Chauntelle Anne Tibbals, *When Law Moves Quicker than Culture* 15 Scholar 213, 231–33 (2013); Mary Graw Leary, *Self-Produced Child Pornography*, 15 Va. J. Soc. Pol'y. & L. 1, 4–5 (2007).

43 See, e.g., *Board of Education, Island Trees Union Free School District No. 26 v. Pico*, 457 U.S. 853 (1982); *Rosenberger v. Rector and Visitors of the University of Virginia*, 515 U.S. 819 (1995); *Perry Education Association v. Perry Local Educators' Association*, 460 U.S. 37 (1983); *National Endowment for the Arts v. Finley*, 524 U.S. 569 (1998); *FCC v. Pacifica Foundation*, 438

U.S. 726 (1978); *Bethel School District No. 403 v. Fraser*, 478 U.S. 675 (1986); *Morse v. Frederick*, 551 U.S. 393 (2007).

44   See, e.g., *Board of Education, Island Trees Union Free School District v. Pico*, 457 U.S. 853 (1982) (school library); *Perry Education Association v. Perry Local Educators' Association*, 460 U.S. 37 (1983) (access to public school interschool mail system); *National Endowment for the Arts v. Finley*, 524 U.S. 569 (1998) (program to fund the arts).

45   457 U.S. at 853.

46   *Id.* at 870–71, 890.

47   20 U.S.C. §§ 953(b), 951(7) (1965); Marjorie Heins, *Sin, Sex, and Blasphemy: A Guide to America's Censorship Wars* 117–18 (New Press 1993).

48   Peggy Phelan, *Serrano, Mapplethorpe, the NEA, and You*, 34 Drama Review 6–7 (1990). See 135 *Cong. Rec.* S5594 (May 18, 1989) (Sen. D'Amato); 135 *Cong. Rec.* S5805 (May 31, 1989) (Sen. Gorton); Frederick S. Lane III, *Obscene Profits* 108–9 (Routledge 2000); Heins, *Sin, Sex, and Blasphemy* at 124–25 (cited in note 47).

49   Heins, *Sin, Sex, and Blasphemy* at 125 (cited in note 47).

50   135 *Cong. Rec.* S5594 (May 18, 1989), in *Culture Wars* 28 (Richard Bolton ed., New Press 1992); Hilton Kramer, *Is Art Above the Laws of Decency?* New York Times (July 2, 1989), in Bolton, *Culture Wars* at 51 (cited in this note); American Family Association, Press Release on the NEA (July 25, 1989), in Bolton, *Culture Wars* at 71–72 (cited in this note).

51   135 *Cong. Rec.* S16278 (July 26, 1989), in Bolton, *Culture Wars* at 77 (cited in note 50); Department of the Interior and Related Agencies Appropriations Act, 1990, Pub. L. 101–121, 103 Stat. 738, 738–42; Jesse Helms, *It's the Job of Congress to Define What's Art*, USA Today (Sept. 8, 1989), in Bolton, *Culture Wars* at 101 (cited in note 50); See 135 *Cong. Rec.* 22372 (1989), in Bolton, *Culture Wars* at 121 (cited in note 50).

52   The Independent Commission, Recommendations on the Issue of Obscenity and Other Content Restrictions, from *A Report to Congress on the National Endowment for the Arts* (Sept. 11, 1990), quoted in Bolton, *Culture Wars* at 261, 262–64 (cited in note 50).

53   20 U. S. C. § 954(d)(1) (1990).

54   Larissa Holmes, *Progress Through Provocations: Analyzing the Work of Karen Finley*, 3 CUJAH (2006–2007). See Heins, *Sex, Sin, and Blasphemy* at 132–33 (cited in note 47).

55   See Holly Hughes & Richard Elovich, *Homophobia at the N.E.A.*, New York Times (July 28, 1990), in Bolton, *Culture Wars* at 254–55 (cited in note 50).

56   524 U.S. 569 (1998).

57   *Id.* at 580, 582; *id.* at 587, quoting *Regan v. Taxation with Representation of Washington*, 461 U.S. 540, 550 (1983).

58   Mary Eberstadt & Mary Anne Layden, *The Social Costs of Pornography* 17–18 (Witherspoon Institute 2010). See Alvin Cooper, Coralie R. Scherer, Sylvain C. Boies, & Barry L Gordon, *Sexuality on the Internet*, 30 Prof. Psychol.: Res. & Pract. 154 (1999).

59   Eberstadt & Layden, *Social Costs of Pornography* at 23 (cited in note 58).

60   See Jill C. Manning, *The Impact of Internet Pornography on Marriage and the Family*, 13 Sexual Addiction & Compulsivity 131 (2006); Steven Stack, Ira Wasserman, & Roger Kern, *Adult Social Bonds and Use of Internet Pornography*, 85 Soc. Sci. Q. 75 (Mar. 2004); Eberstadt & Layden, *Social Costs of Pornography* at 23–25 (cited in note 58).

61   Quoted in Eberstadt & Layden, *Social Costs of Pornography* at 31 (cited in note 58). See Michele L. Ybarra & Kimberly J. Mitchell, *Exposure to Internet Pornography among Children and Adolescents* 8 CyberPsychology & Behavior 473 (2005); National Center on Addiction and Substance Abuse, *National Survey of American Attitudes on Substance Abuse IX: Teen Dating Practices and Sexual Activity* 6 (Columbia 2004); Christina Rogala & Tanya Tydén, *Does Pornography Influence Young Women's Sexual Behavior?* 13 Women's Health Issues 39 (Jan./ Feb. 2003); Manning, *Impact of Internet Pornography* at 106–7 (cited in note 60); Kimberly J. Mitchell, David Finkelhor, & Janice Wolak, *The Exposure of Youth to Unwanted Sexual Material on the Internet*, 34 Youth & Society 330 (2003); Eberstadt & Layden, *Social Costs of Pornography* at 27–28, 33–36 (cited in note 58).

62   See Stone, *Free Speech in the Twenty-First Century* at 280–82 (cited in note 28); *Brandenburg v. Ohio*, 395 U.S. 444 (1969); *New York Times Co. v. United States*, 403 U.S. 713 (1971).

63   274 U.S. 357, 375–77 (1927) (Brandeis, J., concurring).

CHAPTER 15

1   See C. Thomas Dienes, *Law, Politics, and Birth Control* 148 (Illinois 1972); Linda Gordon, *The Moral Property of Women* 247, 255–57, 298 (3d. ed., Illinois 2002); Linda Gordon, *Woman's Body, Woman's Right* 401 (2d ed., Penguin 1990); Leslie J. Reagan, *When Abortion Was a Crime* 194, 196 (California 1997); James Reed, *The Birth Control Movement and American Society: From Private Vice to Public Virtue* 294 (Princeton 1978); John W. Johnson, *Griswold v. Connecticut: Birth Control and the Constitutional Right of Privacy* 5–6 (Kansas 2005); Rosalind Pollack Petchesky, *Abortion and Woman's Choice* 103–12 (Northeastern 1984).

2   Paul R. Ehrlich, *The Population Bomb* (Ballantine 1968).

3   Nanette J. Davis, *From Crime to Choice: The Transformation of Abortion in America* 24 (Greenwood 1985).

4   See Gordon, *Moral Property of Women* at 247–55, 279–86 (cited in note 1); Reed, *Birth Control Movement* at 281–88, 303 (cited in note 1); Zad Leavy & Jerome M. Kummer, *Abortion and the Population Crisis: Therapeutic Abortion and the Law*, 27 Ohio St. L.J. 647 (1966); Davis, *From Crime to Choice* at 22–24 (cited in note 3); Linda Greenhouse and Reva B. Siegel, *Before Roe v. Wade* 3 (Kaplan 2010).

5   See Greenhouse & Siegel, *Before Roe* at 73–74 (cited in note 4).

6   *Casti Connubii*, Encyclical Letter of the Supreme Pontiff Pius XI (Dec. 31, 1930).

7   *Humanae Vitae*, Encyclical Letter of the Supreme Pontiff Paul VI (July 25, 1968).

8   See Dienes, *Law, Politics, and Birth Control* at 146–48 (cited in note 1); Christopher Z. Mooney & Mei-Hsien Lee, *Legislative Morality in the American States*, 39 Am. J. Polit. Sci. 599, 603–4, 606 (1995); Petchesky, *Abortion and Woman's Choice* at 120 (cited in note 1); Reed, *Birth Control Movement* at 371 (cited in note 1).

9   262 U.S. 390, 399 (1923).

10   Stat. §§ 53–32 and 54–196 of the General Statutes of Connecticut (1958 rev.).

11   David E. Bernstein, *Lochner Era Revisionism, Revised*, 92 Geo. L.J. 1, 55 (2003).

12   See David J. Garrow, *Liberty and Sexuality* 120–42, 196–225 (California 1994); Dienes, *Law, Politics, and Birth Control* at 187–88 (cited in note 1); Johnson, *Griswold v.*

Connecticut at 36, 77–96 (cited in note 1); Seth Stern & Stephen Wermiel, *Justice Brennan: Liberal Champion* 279–80 (Houghton Mifflin Harcourt 2010).

13   381 U.S. 479 (1965).

14   274 U.S. 200 (1927).

15   197 U.S. 11 (1905).

16   274 U.S. at 207.

17   316 U.S. 535 (1942).

18   Okla. Stat. Ann. Tit. 57, §§ 171, et seq.; L. 1935, pp. 94 et seq. See Victoria F. Nourse, *In Reckless Hands* 147–51 (Norton 2008).

19   316 U.S. at 536, 538, 541.

20   *Id.* at 541, 542.

21   367 U.S. 497 (1961).

22   See Garrow, *Liberty and Sexuality* at 152–54 (cited in note 12); Dienes, *Law, Politics, and Birth Control* at 152–53 (cited in note 1); Johnson, *Griswold v. Connecticut* at 38–40 (cited in note 1).

23   367 U.S. at 539–42 (cited in note 21), quoting *Corfield v. Coryell*, 4 Wash. C. C. 371, 380 (C.C.E.D. Pa. 1823).

24   *Id.* at 545, quoting *Skinner v. Oklahoma*, 316 U.S. 535, 541 (1942).

25   See Garrow, *Liberty and Sexuality* at 188–99 (cited in note 12); Johnson, *Griswold v. Connecticut* at 77–81, 97–99 (cited in note 1).

26   381 U.S. at 482–83 (cited in note 13). To support this statement, Douglas cited the Court's decisions in *NAACP v. Alabama*, 357 U.S. 449 (1958) (right of association); *Pierce v. Society of Sisters*, 268 U.S. 510 (1925) (right to send one's child to a private school); *Meyer v. Nebraska*, 262 U.S. 390 (1923) (right to teach a child a foreign language); *Martin v. City of Struthers*, 319 U.S. 141 (1943) (right to read); *Sweezy v. New Hampshire*, 354 U.S. 234 (1957) (right to academic freedom).

27   *Id.* at 484–86, quoting *Boyd v. United States*, 116 U.S. 616, 630 (1886).

28   *Id.* at 489–90, 493–96 (Goldberg, J., concurring), quoting *Snyder v. Massachusetts*, 291 U.S. 97, 105 (1934), and *Powell v. Alabama*, 287 U.S. 45, 67 (1932).

29   *Id.* at 507–13, 518–20 (Black, J., dissenting).

30   Stern & Wermiel, *Justice Brennan* at 286 (cited in note 12); See Garrow, *Liberty and Sexuality* at 256–57 (cited in note 12); Leslie Woodcock Tentler, *Catholics and Contraception* 203 (Cornell 2004).

31   See Greenhouse & Siegel, *Before Roe* at 58–67 (cited in note 4); Gordon, *Woman's Body* at 396–400 (cited in note 1); Reagan, *When Abortion Was a Crime* at 228–29 (cited in note 1); Kristin Luker, *Abortion and the Politics of Motherhood* 92–93, 100–112 (California 1984); Petchesky, *Abortion and Woman's Choice* at 125–26 (cited in note 1); Irving J. Sloan, *The Law Governing Abortion, Contraception and Sterilization* 9 (Oceana Publications 1988); Gordon, *Moral Property of Women* at 295–99 (cited in note 1); Eva Rubin, *Abortion, Politics, and the Courts* 23–25 (Greenwood 1982); Marvin Olasky, *Abortion Rites: A Social History of Abortion in America* 295–96 (Crossway 1992); Dienes, *Law, Politics, and Birth Control* at 151 (cited in note 1); Garrow, *Liberty and Sexuality* at 229, 256 (cited in note 12).

32   See Dienes, *Law, Politics, and Birth Control* at 188–91 (cited in note 1); Garrow, *Liberty*

and Sexuality at 471 (cited in note 12); Johnson, *Griswold v. Connecticut* at 189–90 (cited in note 1).

33 See Reed, *Birth Control Movement* at 377 (cited in note 1); Dienes, *Law, Politics, and Birth Control* at 193–99 (cited in note 1); Gordon, *Moral Property of Women* at 289 (cited in note 1); Andrea Tone, *Devices and Desires: A History of Contraceptives in America* 262 (Hill and Wang 2001).

34 Mass. Gen. Laws ch. 272, § 21.

35 Massachusetts General Laws Ann., ch. 272, § 21.

36 See Dienes, *Law, Politics, and Birth Control* at 200–206, 210–12 (cited in note 1); Johnson, *Griswold v. Connecticut* at 190 (cited in note 1); Reed, *Birth Control Movement* at 377 (cited in note 1); Roy Lucas, *New Historical Insights on the Curious Case of Baird v. Eisenstadt*, 9 Roger Williams U. L. Rev. 9, 14–15 (2003).

37 See Barbara J. Love ed., *Feminists Who Changed America, 1963–1975* 25 (Illinois 2006); Bill Baird & Joni Scott, *In Memory of Spurgeon LeRoy "Roy" Lucas Jr.*, 9 Roger Williams U. Law Rev. 1, 1–3 (2003); Lucas, *New Historical Insights* at 28–30 (cited in note 36); Garrow, *Liberty and Sexuality* at 320–21, 372–73 (cited in note 12); Dienes, *Law, Politics, and Birth Control* at 211–13 (cited in note 1); Johnson, *Griswold v. Connecticut* at 198–99 (cited in note 1).

38 405 U.S. 438 (1972).

39 *Id.* at 442, 448.

40 *Id.* at 453–55.

41 410 U.S. 113 (1973).

42 See Lucas, *New Historical Insights* at 43–44 (cited in note 36); Stern & Wermiel, *Justice Brennan* at 370–71 (cited in note 12).

43 See, e.g., *Burwell v. Hobby Lobby Stores, Inc.*, 134 S. Ct. 2751 (2014).

CHAPTER 16

1 Testimony of Mrs. Richard Albright, Hearing on Abortion before the Joint Standing Committee on Public Health and Safety of the Connecticut Legislature (May 19, 1972), quoted in Linda Greenhouse & Reva B. Siegel, *Before Roe v. Wade* 188 (Kaplan 2010). See Leslie J. Reagan, *When Abortion Was a Crime* 173–81, 190–93, 205, 211–13 (California 1997); Linda Gordon, *The Moral Property of Women* 299–308 (3d ed., Illinois 2002); Lawrence Lader, *Abortion* 3, 28–29 (Bobbs-Merrill 1966). Kristin Luker, *Abortion and the Politics of Motherhood* 55–56, 66–67 (California 1984); Greenhouse & Siegel, *Before Roe* at 3 (cited in this note); Rachel Benson Gold, *Lessons from Before Roe* 6; *The Guttmacher Report on Public Policy* 8 (Mar. 2003); Herbert L. Packer & Ralph J. Gampell, *Therapeutic Abortion*, 11 Stan. L. Rev. 417, 418 (1959).

2 See Reagan, *When Abortion Was a Crime* at 216–22 (cited in note 1); Rosalind Pollack Petchesky, *Abortion and Woman's Choice* 124–25 (rev. ed., Northeastern 1990); Lader, *Abortion* at 4–7 (cited in note 1); Luker, *Abortion and the Politics of Motherhood* at 66–74 (cited in note 1); David J. Garrow, *Liberty and Sexuality* at 275–80 (California 1994); Jerome E. Bates & Edward S. Zawadzki, *Criminal Abortion* 117–18 (Thomas 1964); Eva R. Rubin, *Abortion, Politics, and the Courts: Roe v. Wade and Its Aftermath* 16 (Greenwood 1982).

3   American Law Institute, Model Penal Code (1962), quoted in Greenhouse & Siegel, *Before Roe* at 24–25 (cited in note 1).

4   The twelve states were Arkansas, California, Colorado, Delaware, Georgia, Kansas, Maryland, Mississippi, New Mexico, North Carolina, South Carolina, and Virginia. See Greenhouse & Siegel, *Before Roe* at 24 (cited in note 1); Garrow, *Liberty and Sexuality* at 277, 281–85 (cited in note 2); Reagan, *When Abortion Was a Crime* at 220–21 (cited in note 1); Irving J. Sloan, *The Law Governing Abortion, Contraception and Sterilization* 8 (Oceana 1988); Rubin, *Abortion, Politics, and the Courts* at 16 (cited in note 2); Luker, *Abortion and the Politics of Motherhood* at 69 (cited in note 1); Rubin, *Abortion, Politics, and the Courts* at 20–22 (cited in note 2); Bates & Zawadzki, *Criminal Abortion* at 137 (cited in note 2).

5   Lader, *Abortion* at 16 (cited in note 1). See Linda Gordon, *Woman's Body, Woman's Right* 403 (rev. ed., Penguin 1990); Marvin Olasky, *Abortion Rites: A Social History of Abortion in America* 278–80 (Crossway 1992); Luker, *Abortion and the Politics of Motherhood* at 78–80 (cited in note 1); Gordon, *Moral Property of Women* at 299 300 (cited in note 1); Garrow, *Liberty and Sexuality* at 285–89 (cited in note 2); Lader, *Abortion* at 10–15 (cited in note 1); Greenhouse & Siegel, *Before Roe* at 11–18 (cited in note 1).

6   See Rubin, *Abortion, Politics, and the Courts* at 20–21 (cited in note 2); Olasky, *Abortion Rites* at 281–82 (cited in note 5); Luker, *Abortion and the Politics of Motherhood* at 78–79, 95–96 (cited in note 1); Garrow, *Liberty and Sexuality* at 285–95 (cited in note 2); Gordon, *Moral Property of Women* at 299–300 (cited in note 1); Greenhouse & Siegel, *Before Roe* at 15 16 (cited in note 1).

7   See Garrow, *Liberty and Sexuality* at 300–301 (cited in note 2); Greenhouse & Siegel, *Before Roe* at 15–24 (cited in note 1); Sloan, *Law Governing Abortion, Contraception, and Sterilization* at 9 (cited in note 4); Lader, *Abortion* at 44 (cited in note 1); Luker, *Abortion and the Politics of Motherhood* at 81–82 (cited in note 1).

8   See Lader, *Abortion* at 2, 43–65 (cited in note 1); Bates & Zawadzki, *Criminal Abortion* at 3 6, 35, 42–43 (cited in note 2); Gordon, *Moral Property of Women* at 298–99 (cited in note 1); Olasky, *Abortion Rites* at 276–78 (cited in note 5); Luker, *Abortion and the Politics of Motherhood* at 74–75, 104–5 (cited in note 1); Petchesky, *Abortion and Woman's Choice* at 113, 126–27 (cited in note 2); Greenhouse & Siegel, *Before Roe* at 23 (cited in note 1); Gold, *Lessons from Before Roe* at 8, 10 (cited in note 1).

9   United Methodist Church, *Statement of Social Principles* (1972), quoted in Greenhouse & Siegel, *Before Roe* at 70–71 (cited in note 1).

10   Quoted in Greenhouse & Siegel, *Before Roe* at 71 (cited in note 1).

11   Southern Baptist Convention, *Resolution on Abortion* (June 1971), quoted in Greenhouse & Siegel, *Before Roe* at 71 (cited in note 1).

12   National Association of Evangelicals, *Statement on Abortion* (1971), quoted in Greenhouse & Siegel, *Before Roe* at 72 (cited in note 1). See Linda Greenhouse, *Public Opinion and the Supreme Court*, Dædalus 69, 77 (Fall 2012); Daniel K. Williams, *God's Own Party: The Making of the Christian Right* 113–16 (Oxford 2010).

13   *Humanae Vitae*, Encyclical Letter of the Supreme Pontiff Paul VI (July 29, 1968), quoted in Greenhouse & Siegel, *Before Roe* at 73, 76 (cited in note 1). See Sloan, *Law Governing Abortion, Contraception, and Sterilization* at 11 (cited in note 4); Bates & Zawadzki,

Criminal Abortion at 24 (cited in note 2); Lader, *Abortion* at 7, 94–95 (cited in note 1); Gordon, *Moral Property of Women* at 303 (cited in note 1); Luker, *Abortion and the Politics of Motherhood* at 130–32 (cited in note 1); Williams, *God's Own Party* at 113–14 (cited in note 12).

14   The Report of the Commission on Population Growth and the American Future, *Population and the American Future* (Mar. 27, 1972), quoted in Greenhouse & Siegel, *Before Roe* at 201–7 (cited in note 1). See Michael J. Graetz & Linda Greenhouse, *The Burger Court and the Rise of the Judicial Right* 147 (Simon & Schuster 2016).

15   Richard M. Nixon, *Statement about the Report of the Commission on Population Growth and the American Future* (May 5, 1972), quoted in Greenhouse & Siegel, *Before Roe* at 210–12 (cited in note 1).

16   *Letter from President Richard Nixon to Terence Cardinal Cooke* (May 16, 1972), quoted in Greenhouse & Siegel, *Before Roe* at 157–58 (cited in note 1).

17   See Petchesky, *Abortion and Woman's Choice* at 120–22 (cited in note 2); Greenhouse & Siegel, *Before Roe* at 113–15, 120–21, 157–58, 202, 207–10, 215–18 (cited in note 1).

18   See Greenhouse & Siegel, *Before Roe* at 35 (cited in note 1); Don Harper Mills, *A Medicolegal Analysis of Abortion Statutes,* 31 S. Cal. L. Rev. 181, 181–83 (1958); Luker, *Abortion and the Politics of Motherhood* at 71–74 (cited in note 1); Garrow, *Liberty and Sexuality* at 297–300 (cited in note 2); Graetz & Greenhouse, *The Burger Court* at 136 (cited in note 14).

19   See Reagan, *When Abortion Was a Crime* at 223–26 (cited in note 1); Garrow, *Liberty and Sexuality* at 486–87 (cited in note 2); Gordon, *Woman's Body* at 405 (cited in note 5); Petchesky, *Abortion and Woman's Choice* at 128–29 (cited in note 2); Gordon, *Moral Property of Women* at 301 (cited in note 1); Luker, *Abortion and the Politics of Motherhood* at 96–99 (cited in note 1).

20   Speech by Betty Friedan, *Abortion: A Woman's Civil Right* (Feb. 1969), quoted in Greenhouse & Siegel, *Before Roe* at 38–40 (cited in note 1).

21   National Association for Repeal of Abortion Laws, *NARAL Policy Statement* (1969), quoted in Greenhouse & Siegel, *Before Roe* at 40–41 (cited in note 1).

22   Betty Friedan, *Call to Women's Strike for Equality* (Aug. 26, 1970), quoted in Greenhouse & Siegel, *Before Roe* at 41–44 (cited in note 1).

23   See Petchesky, *Abortion and Woman's Choice* at 103–26 (cited in note 2); Luker, *Abortion and the Politics of Motherhood* at 92–121 (cited in note 1); Greenhouse & Siegel, *Before Roe* at 35–40 (cited in note 1); Reagan, *When Abortion Was a Crime* at 227–33 (cited in note 1); Gordon, *Woman's Body* at 399–404 (cited in note 5); Rubin, *Abortion, Politics, and the Courts* at 23–25 (cited in note 2); Olasky, *Abortion Rites* at 295 (cited in note 5); Gordon, *Moral Property of Women* at 295–300 (cited in note 1); William N. Eskridge Jr., *Some Effects of Identity-Based Social Movements on Constitutional Law in the Twentieth Century,* 100 Mich. L. Rev. 2062, 2128–33 (2002); Andrea Tone, *Devices and Desires: A History of Contraceptives in America* 247 (Hill and Wang 2001); Garrow, *Liberty and Sexuality* at 357 (cited in note 2).

24   See Garrow, *Liberty and Sexuality* at 513, 562 (cited in note 2); Petchesky, *Abortion and Woman's Choice* at 113 (cited in note 2).

25   Hawaii Rev. Stat. § 453–16.

26   Hawaii State Legislature, Fifth Legislature, Senate Committee on Public Health, Welfare and Housing, Public Hearing on H.B. 61 (Feb. 3 and 4, 1970), written testimony

of Gerri Madden 3, quoted in Patricia G. Steinhoff & Milton Diamond, *Abortion Politics: The Hawaii Experience* 110 (Hawaii 1977).

27   Quoted in A. A. Smyser, *Hawaii's World: Hawaii's Abortion Law 30 Years Old*, Honolulu Star-Bulletin (Mar. 21, 2000). See Haw. Rev. Stat. § 453–16, Revised Statutes of Hawaii; Garrow, *Liberty and Sexuality* at 414 (cited in note 2); Steinhoff & Diamond, *Abortion Politics* at 42–44, 48, 63, 73–87, 96–113, 167–73 (cited in note 26).

28   *Washington Early-term Abortion, Referendum 20 (1970)*, http://ballotpedia.org/Washington_Early-term_Abortion_Referendum_20_(1970); Garrow, *Liberty and Sexuality* at 431–32, 457 (cited in note 2). See Garrow, *Liberty and Sexuality* at 411, 466 (cited in note 2); Sloan, *Law Governing Abortion, Contraception, and Sterilization* at 12 (cited in note 4).

29   Linda Greenhouse, *Constitutional Question: Is There a Right to Abortion?* New York Times Magazine (Jan. 25, 1970), quoted in Greenhouse & Siegel, *Before Roe* at 130–31 (cited in note 1). See Garrow, *Liberty and Sexuality* at 310–15 (cited in note 2).

30   Susan Brownmiller, *Everywoman's Abortions*, Village Voice (Mar. 27, 1969), quoted in Greenhouse & Siegel, *Before Roe* at 128 (cited in note 1). See Garrow, *Liberty and Sexuality* at 367 (cited in note 2).

31   Brownmiller, *Everywoman's Abortions* (cited in note 30), quoted in Greenhouse & Siegel, *Before Roe* at 127–28 (cited in note 1); Petchesky, *Abortion and Woman's Choice* at 129 (cited in note 2).

32   Memorandum of Assemblywoman Constance E. Cook, *New York State Legislative Annual* (1970), quoted in Greenhouse & Siegel, *Before Roe* at 147–49 (cited in note 1).

33   Greenhouse & Siegel, *Before Roe* at 150 (cited in note 1). See Garrow, *Liberty and Sexuality* at 420–21 (cited in note 2); Rubin, *Abortion, Politics, and the Courts* at 51 (cited in note 2); Petchesky, *Abortion and Woman's Choice* at 127–28 (cited in note 2).

34   See Sloan, *Law Governing Abortion, Contraception, and Sterilization* at 12 (cited in note 4); Garrow, *Liberty and Sexuality* at 483–84, 495–96, 546–47 (cited in note 2); Gordon, *Woman's Body* at 407 (cited in note 5); Gordon, *Moral Property of Women* at 302–3 (cited in note 1).

35   *Byrn v. New York City Health and Hospitals Corporation*, 31 N.Y.2d 194, 203, 286 N.E.2d 887, 890 (N.Y. Ct. App. 1972). See Greenhouse & Siegel, *Before Roe* at 150–51 (cited in note 1).

36   Phyllis Schlafly, *Women's Libbers Do NOT Speak for Us*, 5 Phyllis Schlafly Report (Feb. 1972), quoted in Greenhouse & Siegel, *Before Roe* at 218–19 (cited in note 1); See Gordon, *Woman's Body* at 406–7 (cited in note 5); Luker, *Abortion and the Politics of Motherhood* at 133–37 (cited in note 1); Gordon, *Moral Property of Women* at 300–301, 302–3 (cited in note 1); Greenhouse & Siegel, *Before Roe* at 218–20 (cited in note 1).

37   Hope Spencer, *The City Politic: The Case of the Missing Abortion Lobbyists*, New York Magazine (May 29, 1972), quoted in Greenhouse & Siegel, *Before Roe* at 160–62 (cited in note 1). See Greenhouse & Siegel, *Before Roe* at 157, 160–62 (cited in note 1); Graetz & Greenhouse, *The Burger Court* at 139 (cited in note 14).

38   Nelson A. Rockefeller, *Veto Message* (May 13, 1972), quoted in Greenhouse & Siegel, *Before Roe* at 158–60 (cited in note 1).

39   See Louis Cassels, *Swing to Right Seen Among Catholics, Jews* (Aug. 5, 1972), quoted in Greenhouse & Siegel, *Before Roe* at 212–15 (cited in note 1).

40   Linda Greenhouse, *Constitutional Question: Is There a Right to Abortion?* New York Times Magazine (Jan. 25, 1970), quoted in Greenhouse & Siegel, *Before Roe* at 132 (cited in note 1). See Garrow, *Liberty and Sexuality* at 374–85 (cited in note 2); Reagan, *When Abortion Was a Crime* at 234–39 (cited in note 1).

41   See Roy Lucas, *Federal Constitutional Limitations on the Enforcement and Administration of State Abortion Statutes*, 46 N.C. L. Rev. 730 (1967–1968); Garrow, *Liberty and Sexuality* at 334–39 (cited in note 2); Rubin, *Abortion, Politics, and the Courts* at 41–42 (cited in note 2); Greenhouse, *Constitutional Question* at 132–36 (cited in note 40).

42   Garrow, *Liberty and Sexuality* at 334, 337–39 (cited in note 2); Rubin, *Abortion, Politics, and the Courts* at 41–42 (cited in note 2); Greenhouse, *Constitutional Question* at 132–36 (cited in note 40).

43   Greenhouse, *Constitutional Question* (cited in note 40), quoted in Greenhouse & Siegel, *Before Roe* at 133–34, 138 (cited in note 1). See Greenhouse & Siegel, *Before Roe* at 133–38, 150 (cited in note 1); Garrow, *Liberty and Sexuality* at 379–81, 421 (cited in note 2); Rubin, *Abortion, Politics, and the Courts* at 42 (cited in note 2); Greenhouse, *Constitutional Question* (cited in note 40), quoted in Greenhouse & Siegel, *Before Roe* at 132–36 (cited in note 1).

44   Women versus Connecticut, *Organizing Pamphlet* (circa Nov. 1970), quoted in Greenhouse & Siegel, *Before Roe* at 169, 171–72 (cited in note 1).

45   *Abele v. Markle*, 342 F. Supp. 800, 801–4 (D. Conn. 1972) (Lumbard, J.).

46   See Garrow, *Liberty and Sexuality* at 402–6 (cited in note 2); Greenhouse & Siegel, *Before Roe* at 224 (cited in note 1).

47   *Roe v. Wade*, 314 F. Supp. 1217, 1225 (N.D. Tex. 1970). See Garrow, *Liberty and Sexuality* at 451–55 (cited in note 2); Greenhouse & Siegel *Before Roe* at 224–25 (cited in note 1).

48   See Rubin, *Abortion, Politics, and the Courts* at 55 (cited in note 2); Garrow, *Liberty and Sexuality* at 507, 512, 522 (cited in note 2); Greenhouse & Siegel, *Before Roe* at 226 (cited in note 1).

49   Linda Greenhouse, *Becoming Justice Blackmun* 82 (Henry Holt 2005). See Bob Woodward & Scott Armstrong, *The Brethren: Inside the Supreme Court* 200–204 (Simon & Schuster 1979); Greenhouse, *Becoming Justice Blackmun* at 80–81 (cited in this note); Garrow, *Liberty and Sexuality* at 531–32 (cited in note 2).

50   Justice Harry Blackmun's Draft Opinion in *Roe v. Wade* (1972), quoted in Greenhouse, *Becoming Justice Blackmun* at 88 (cited in note 49). See Woodward & Armstrong, *The Brethren* at 206–7 (cited in note 49); Graetz & Greenhouse, *The Burger Court* at 141 (cited in note 14).

51   George Gallup, *Abortion Seen Up to Woman, Doctor*, Washington Post (Aug. 25, 1972), quoted in Greenhouse & Siegel, *Before Roe* at 207–10 (cited in note 1). See Greenhouse, *Becoming Justice Blackmun* at 90–92 (cited in note 49); Rubin, *Abortion, Politics, and the Courts* at 63 (cited in note 2); Garrow, *Liberty and Sexuality* at 554–58, 563 (cited in note 2); Woodward & Armstrong, *The Brethren* at 224, 225 (cited in note 49).

52   Garrow, *Liberty and Sexuality* at 573–76 (cited in note 2).

53   410 U.S. 116–17 (1973).

54   *Id.* at 129–36.

55   *Id.* at 136–41.

56   See *id.* at 141–47.

57   *Id.* at. 147–48.

58   *Id.* at 148–50.

59   *Id.* at 150–51 (emphasis added).

60   *Id.* at 152–53.

61   316 U.S. 535, 541–42 (1942).

62   394 U.S. 557, 564 (1969).

63   381 U.S. 479, 484–85 (1965).

64   388 U.S. 1, 12 (1967).

65   405 U.S. 438, 453–54 (1972).

66   *Id.* at 453. See 410 U.S. 152–53 (1973).

67   410 U.S. 153.

68   *Id.*at 153–54.

69   *Id.* at 159–60, 162.

70   *Id.* at 163–64.

71   *Doe v. Bolton,* 410 U.S. at 221–22 (White, J., dissenting).

72   *Roe v. Wade* 410 U.S. at 173–77 (Rehnquist, J., dissenting), quoting *Snyder v. Massachusetts,* 291 U.S. 97, 105 (1934).

73   George Gallup, *Abortion Seen Up to Woman, Doctor* (cited in note 51), quoted in Greenhouse & Siegel, *Before Roe* at 207–10 (cited in note 1); Gractz & Greenhouse, *The Burger Court* at 139 (cited in note 14). See Greenhouse & Siegel, *Before Roe* at 256, 266 (cited in note 1).

74   Debra Bell, *Four Decades Ago, U.S. News Barely Acknowledged Roe v. Wade,* U.S. News & World Report Press Past (Jan. 22, 2013).

75   Quoted in Garrow, *Liberty and Sexuality* at 606, 911 n.8 (cited in note 2).

76   See Louis Harris, *Majority Agree with Supreme Court Decision on Abortion,* Harris Survey (Apr. 19, 1973).

77   See *Engel v. Vitale,* 370 U.S. 421 (1962).

78   See *Loving v. Virginia,* 388 U.S. 1 (1967).

79   See *Citizens United v. Federal Election Commission,* 558 U.S. 310 (2010).

80   See Linda Lyons, *The Gallup Brain: Prayer in Public Schools,* Gallup (Dec. 10, 2002) (school prayer); Jeffrey M. Jones, *Record-High 86% Approve of Black-White Marriages,* Gallup (Sept. 12, 2011) (interracial marriage); Dan Eggen, *Poll: Large Majority Opposes Supreme Court Decision on Campaign Financing,* Washington Post (Feb. 17, 2010) (campaign finance).

81   See Linda Greenhouse, *Justice John Paul Stevens as Abortion-Rights Strategist,* 43 U.C. Davis L. Rev. 749, 751 (2010).

82   Linda Greenhouse, *Public Opinion and the Supreme Court* 77–78 (cited in note 12). See Greenhouse & Siegel, *Before Roe* at 258–59 (cited in note 1).

83   See Louis Harris, *Majority Agree with Supreme Court Decision on Abortion,* Harris Survey (Apr. 19, 1973).

84   William J. Brennan Jr., *Notes* lxix (October Term 1972) (unpublished document).

85   Quoted in Greenhouse, *Becoming Justice Blackmun* at 134–35 (cited in note 49). See Woodward & Armstrong, *The Brethren* at 287 (cited in note 49); Seth Stern & Stephen Wermiel, *Justice Brennan: Liberal Champion* 369, 375–76 (Houghton Mifflin Harcourt 2010).

86 Quoted in Greenhouse & Siegel, *Before Roe* at 258 (cited in note 1).

87 H.J.Res. 261, 93rd Cong., 1st Sess. (1973).

88 John Hart Ely, for example, a distinguished constitutional law scholar at Harvard, charged that Blackmun's opinion in *Roe* lacked "even colorable support in the constitutional text, history, or any other appropriate source of constitutional doctrine." John Hart Ely, *The Wages of Crying Wolf*, 82 Yale L.J. 920, 943 (1973). For a response to Ely, see Philip B. Heymann & Douglas E. Barzelay, *The Forest and the Trees*, 53 B.U. L. Rev. 765 (1973).

89 See Ruth Bader Ginsburg, *Some Thoughts on Autonomy and Equality in Relation to Roe v. Wade*, 63 N.C. L. Rev. 375, 382–83 (1985); Laurence H. Tribe, *Constitutional Choices* 243 (Harvard 1985); Greenhouse & Siegel, *Before Roe* at 254 (cited in note 1); Sylvia A. Law, *Rethinking Sex and the Constitution*, 132 U. Pa. L. Rev. 955 (1984); Catharine A. MacKinnon, *Reflections on Sex Equality under Law*, 100 Yale L.J. 1281, 1308–24 (1991); Reva Siegel, *Reasoning from the Body*, 44 Stan. L. Rev. 261 (1992).

90 Ginsburg, *Some Thoughts* at 381, 385 (cited in note 89). See Paul A. Freund, *Storms Over the Supreme Court*, 69 A.B.A. J. 1474, 1480 (1983); Robert A. Burt, *The Burger Court and the Family*, in *The Burger Court: The Counter-Revolution That Wasn't* 92 (Vincent Blasi ed., Yale 1983).

91 Greenhouse & Siegel, *Before Roe* at 256 (cited in note 1). See Gene Burns, *The Moral Veto: Framing Contraception, Abortion, and Cultural Pluralism in the United States* 227–28 (Cambridge 2005); Laurence H. Tribe, *Abortion: The Clash of Absolutes* 50–51 (Norton 1990); David J. Garrow, *Abortion Before and After Roe v. Wade*, 62 Albany L. Rev. 833, 840–41 (1999); Graetz & Greenhouse, *The Burger Court* at 146–47 (cited in note 14).

92 366 U.S. 420 (1961).

CHAPTER 17

1 See Gene Burns, *The Moral Veto* 225 (Cambridge 2005); N. E. H. Hull & Peter Charles Hoffer, *Roe v. Wade: The Abortion Rights Controversy in American History* 182–85 (Kansas 2010); Allen Pusey, *Ginsburg: Court Should have Avoided Broad-Based Decision in Roe v. Wade*, A.B.A. J. (May 13, 2013); Jason Keyser, *Liberal Supreme Court Justice Ruth Bader Ginsburg Criticizes Roe v. Wade*, Associated Press (May 13, 2013); Ruth Bader Ginsburg, *Some Thoughts on Autonomy and Equality in Relation to Roe v. Wade*, 63 N.C. L. Rev. 375 (1985).

2 Linda Greenhouse & Reva B. Siegel, *Before Roe v. Wade* 267–68, 294–95 (Kaplan 2010).

3 Daniel K. Williams, *God's Own Party: The Making of the Christian Right* 2–5 (Oxford 2010). See George M. Marsden, *Fundamentalism and American Culture* 242–47 (2d. ed., Oxford 2006); Kenneth K. Bailey, *Southern White Protestantism in the Twentieth Century* 45–106 (Harper & Row 1964); Mark A. Noll, *America's God* 170, 197 (Oxford 2002).

4 Williams, *God's Own Party* at 106–7 (cited in note 3). See Steven Mintz & Susan Kellogg, *Domestic Revolutions: A Social History of American Family Life* 203–10 (Free Press 1988); David Allyn, *Make Love, Not War* 274 (Routledge 2001); Natasha Zaretsky, *No Direction Home*, 231–39 (North Carolina 2007).

5   See Flora Davis, *Moving the Mountain: The Women's Movement in America Since 1960* 133–36 (2d ed., Illinois 1999); Jane J. Mansbridge, *Why We Lost the ERA* 1–15 (Chicago 1986); Williams, *God's Own Party* at 107 (cited in note 3).

6   Williams, *God's Own Party* at 108–11 (cited in note 3); Beverly LaHaye, *The New Spirit-Controlled Woman* 71 (Harvest House 2005). See Donald T. Critchlow, *Phyllis Schlafly and Grassroots Conservatism* 213–42 (Princeton 2005); Ruth Murray Brown, *For a "Christian America": A History of the Religious Right* 47–76 (Prometheus 2002); Carol Felsenthal, *The Sweetheart of the Silent Majority* 54–178, 240 (Doubleday 1981); Catherine E. Rymph, *Republican Women* 205 (North Carolina 2006); Linda Gordon, *The Moral Property of Women* 303–4 (Illinois 2007); Kristin Luker, *Abortion and the Politics of Motherhood* 141–47, 156–65, 172–79 (California 1984); Eva R. Rubin, *Abortion, Politics, and the Courts* 165–67 (rev. ed., Praeger 1987).

7   See Lee Edwards, *Goldwater: The Man Who Made a Revolution* 420–21 (Regnery 1995); *Reagan Reluctantly Signs Bill Easing Abortions*, New York Times (June 16, 1967); David Domke & Kevin Coe, *The God Strategy: How Religion Became a Political Weapon in America* 17 (Oxford 2010); Williams, *God's Own Party* at 111–19, 160–61 (cited in note 3); Gordon, *The Moral Property of Women* at 306 (cited in note 6); Linda Gordon, *Woman's Body, Woman's Right* 407–8 (Penguin 1990); Domke & Coe, *The God Strategy* at 17–18 (cited in this note); Rosalind Pollack Petchesky, *Abortion and Woman's Choice* 242–52 (rev. ed., Northeastern 1990); Hull & Hoffer, *Abortion Rights Controversy* at 187, 192–93 (cited in note 1); Leslie J. Reagan, *When Abortion Was a Crime* 248 (California 1997); Rubin, *Abortion, Politics, and the Courts* at 112–13, 165 (cited in note 6); Greenhouse & Siegel, *Before Roe* at 259 (cited in note 2).

8   Dallas A. Blanchard, *The Anti-Abortion Movement and the Rise of the Religious Right* 75 (Twayne 1994); Hull & Hoffer, *Abortion Rights Controversy* at 187 (cited in note 1).

9   Williams, *God's Own Party* at 171, 178–79 (cited in note 3). See Blanchard, *Anti-Abortion Movement* at 42, 75–77 (cited in note 8); Hull & Hoffer, *Abortion Rights Controversy* at 187 (cited in note 1); Malcolm L. Goggin, *Understanding the New Politics of Abortion* 154 (SAGE 1993).

10   Williams, *God's Own Party* at 159–60 (cited in note 3). See Allan J. Lichtman, *White Protestant Nation* 343–49 (Atlantic Monthly 2008); Critchlow, *Phyllis Schlafly and Grassroots Conservatism* at 263–64 (cited in note 6); Bruce J. Schulman, *The Seventies: The Great Shift in American Culture, Society, and Politics* 23–52 (Free Press 2001).

11   Williams, *God's Own Party* at 187 (cited in note 3); Howell Raines, *Reagan Backs Evangelicals in Their Political Activities*, New York Times (Aug. 23, 1980). See Blanchard, *Anti-Abortion Movement* at 73 (cited in note 8); Hull & Hoffer, *Abortion Rights Controversy* at 207 (cited in note 1); Rubin, *Abortion, Politics, and the Courts* at 112 (cited in note 6); Domke & Coe, *The God Strategy* at 3, 22 (cited in note 7); Gene Burns, *Moral Veto* at 229–31 (cited in note 1); David J. Garrow, *Liberty and Sexuality* 637 (California 1994).

12   Williams, *God's Own Party* at 188–91, 194 (cited in note 3); Kenneth A. Briggs, *Dispute on Religion Raised by Campaign*, New York Times (Nov. 9, 1980). See Hull & Hoffer, *Abortion Rights Controversy* at 187–89 (cited in note 1); Gordon, *Woman's Body* at 407–8 (cited in note 7); Petchesky, *Abortion and Woman's Choice* at 255–56 (cited in note 7); Reagan, *When Abortion Was a Crime* at 248 (cited in note 7); Greenhouse & Siegel, *Before Roe* at 259 (cited in note 2); Blanchard, *Anti-Abortion Movement* at 83 (cited in note 8).

13 Blanchard, *Anti-Abortion Movement* at 32 (cited in note 8). See Hull & Hoffer, *Abortion Rights Controversy* at 186 (cited in note 1); Garrow, *Liberty and Sexuality* at 609, 617 (cited in note 11); Gordon, *Moral Property of Women* at 302–3 (cited in note 6); Gordon, *Woman's Body* at 407–10 (cited in note 7); Blanchard, *Anti-Abortion Movement* at 32, 52, 82–84 (cited in note 8); Petchesky, *Abortion and Woman 's Choice* at 242, 252 (cited in note 7); Rubin, *Abortion, Politics, and the Courts* at 115, 168 (cited in note 6); Greenhouse & Siegel, *Before Roe* at 258 (cited in note 2); Reagan, *When Abortion Was a Crime* at 248 (cited in note 7); Reva Siegel, *Reasoning from the Body*, 44 Stan. L. Rev. 261, 325 (1992).

14 See Hull & Hoffer, *Abortion Rights Controversy* at 186 (cited in note 1); Garrow, *Liberty and Sexuality* at 617, 630–31 (cited in note 11); Luker, *Abortion and the Politics of Motherhood* at 216 (cited in note 6); Rubin, *Abortion, Politics, and the Courts* at 141–44 (cited in note 6); Blanchard, *Anti-Abortion Movement* at 85 (cited in note 8); Goggin, *Understanding the New Politics of Abortion* at 170 (cited in note 9).

15 Williams, *God's Own Party* at 200, 203, 206–7, 210 (cited in note 3). See Domke & Coe, *The God Strategy* at 22 (cited in note 7).

16 See Blanchard, *Anti-Abortion Movement* at 53 (cited in note 8); Gordon, *Moral Property of Women* at 308–9 (cited in note 6); Reagan, *When Abortion Was a Crime* at 248 (cited in note 7).

17 See Blanchard, *Anti-Abortion Movement* at 85–86 (cited in note 8); Hull & Hoffer, *Abortion Rights Controversy* at 211–12 (cited in note 1); Gordon, *Moral Property of Women* at 309 (cited in note 6); Gordon, *Woman's Body* at 412 (cited in note 7).

18 See Blanchard, *Anti-Abortion Movement* at 53 (cited in note 8); Gordon, *Woman's Body* at 412–13 (cited in note 7); Gordon, *Moral Property of Women* at 309 (cited in note 6).

19 See Garrow, *Liberty and Sexuality* at 630–31, 657 (cited in note 11); Blanchard, *Anti-Abortion Movement* at 42, 58, 78–79, 87–91 (cited in note 8); Hull & Hoffer, *Abortion Rights Controversy* at 210–11 (cited in note 1); Gordon, *Moral Property of Women* at 309 (cited in note 6); Gordon, *Woman's Body* at 412 (cited in note 7).

20 See Blanchard, *Anti-Abortion Movement* at 48, 54, 87, 90 (cited in note 8); Hull & Hoffer, *Abortion Rights Controversy* at 209–13 (cited in note 1); Garrow, *Liberty and Sexuality* at 688–89, 714–18 (cited in note 11); Gordon, *Moral Property of Women* at 309–10, 318–19 (cited in note 6); Reagan, *When Abortion Was a Crime* at 252 (cited in note 7); Gordon, *Woman's Body* at 411 (cited in note 7).

21 See Rubin, *Abortion, Politics, and the Courts* at 116–18, 125–26 (cited in note 6); Gordon, *Moral Property of Women* at 310–11 (cited in note 6); Irving J. Sloan, *The Law Governing Abortion, Contraception and Sterilization* 16–21 (Oceana 1988); Reagan, *When Abortion was a Crime* at 252 (cited in note 7).

22 See Rubin, *Abortion, Politics, and the Courts* at 116–17, 125–29 (cited in note 6); Gordon, *Moral Property of Women* at 310–11 (cited in note 6); Sloan, *Law Governing Abortion* at 16–25 (cited in note 21); Reagan, *When Abortion was a Crime* at 252 (cited in note 7).

23 See *Bigelow v. Virginia*, 421 U.S. 809 (1975); *Planned Parenthood of Central Missouri v. Danforth*, 428 U.S. 52 (1976); *Bellotti v. Baird*, 443 U.S. 622 (1979); *City of Akron v. Akron Cen-*

ter for Reproductive Health, Inc., 462 U.S. 416 (1983); *Thornburgh v. American College of Obstetricians & Gynecologists*, 476 U.S. 747 (1986).

24 See *Planned Parenthood of Central Missouri v. Danforth*, 428 U.S. 52 (1976) (record keeping); *Planned Parenthood Association of Kansas City, Missouri, Inc. v. Ashcroft*, 462 U.S. 476 (1983) (tissue sample); *Bellotti v. Baird*, 443 U.S. 622 (1979).

25 432 U.S. 464 (1977). See Rubin, *Abortion, Politics, and the Courts* at 148–49 (cited in note 6); Gordon, *Moral Property of Women* at 311–12 (cited in note 6); Gordon, *Woman's Body* at 410 (cited in note 7).

26 432 U.S. at 483, 485 (Brennan, J., dissenting).

27 *Id.* at. 469–70, 474, 480.

28 448 U.S. 297 (1980).

29 Quoted in Eric J. Segall, *Supreme Myths* 64 (Praeger 2012). See Garrow, *Liberty and Sexuality* at 626–27 (cited in note 11); Rubin, *Abortion, Politics, and the Courts* at 136, 155 (cited in note 6); Petchesky, *Abortion and Woman' Choice* at 160, 242 (cited in note 7); Reagan, *When Abortion Was a Crime* at 248 (cited in note 7); Gordon, *Moral Property of Women* at 311–12 (cited in note 6); Gordon, *Woman's Body* at 410 (cited in note 7).

30 448 U.S. at 316, 325 (cited in note 28).

31 432 U.S. at 336 (Marshall, J., dissenting). See Garrow, *Liberty and Sexuality* at 634–36 (cited in note 11); Petchesky, *Abortion and Woman's Choice* at 297–99 (cited in note 7); Rubin, *Abortion, Politics, and the Courts* at 157–61 (cited in note 6); Michael J. Graetz & Linda Greenhouse, *The Burger Court and the Rise of the Judicial Right* 158–61 (Simon & Schuster 2016).

32 Jan Crawford Greenburg, *Supreme Conflict: The Inside Story of the Struggle for Control of the United States Supreme Court* 222–23 (Penguin Press 2007); David G. Savage, *Turning Right: The Making of the Rehnquist Supreme Court* 114, 266 (John Wiley & Sons 1992); Williams, *God's Own Party* at 210 (cited in note 3); Garrow, *Liberty and Sexuality* at 640 (cited in note 11); Linda Hirshman, *Sisters in Law* 134 (HarperCollins 2015).

33 Quoted in Segall, *Supreme Myths* at 65 (cited in note 29).

34 Amicus Curiae Brief of the United States in *Thornburgh v. American College of Obstetricians and Gynecologists*, No. 84–495, quoted in Joan Biskupic, *American Original: The Life and Constitution of Supreme Court Justice Antonin Scalia* 103 (Farrar, Straus and Giroux 2009). See Garrow, *Liberty and Sexuality* at 652 (cited in note 11).

35 Biskupic, *American Original* at 105–7 (cited in note 34).

36 Biskupic, *American Original* at 112–15, 121 (cited in note 34); Bruce Allen Murphy, *Scalia: A Court of One* 129 (Simon & Schuster 2014). See *Webster v. Reproductive Health Services*, 492 U.S. 490, 532 (1989) (Scalia, J., concurring).

37 Robert H. Bork, *The Tempting of America: The Political Seduction of the Law* 130 (Free Press 1990); Linda Greenhouse, *Becoming Justice Blackmun* 188 (Henry Holt 2005).

38 Quoted in Savage, *Turning Right* at 134 (cited in note 32). See Garrow, *Liberty and Sexuality* at 668–72 (cited in note 11).

39 Quoted in James Reston, *Kennedy and Bork*, New York Times (July 5, 1987).

40 Greenburg, *Supreme Conflict* at 79, 103 (cited in note 32) (Kennedy and Souter); Sav-

age, *Turning Right* at 461 (cited in note 32) (Thomas). See Greenhouse, *Becoming Justice Blackmun* at 199 (cited in note 37).

41   Quoted in Greenhouse, *Becoming Justice Blackmun* at 190 (cited in note 37). See Garrow, *Liberty and Sexuality* at 684, 689 (cited in note 11).

42   *Planned Parenthood of Southeastern Pennsylvania v. Casey*, 505 U.S. 833 (1992).

43   Brief for the United States as Amicus Curiae in *Planned Parenthood of Southeastern Pennsylvania v. Casey*, quoted in Savage, *Turning Right* at 456 (cited in note 32). See Segall, *Supreme Myths* at 67 (cited in note 29); Garrow, *Liberty and Sexuality* at 689 (cited in note 11); William N. Eskridge Jr., *Some Effects of Identity-Based Social Movements on Constitutional Law in the Twentieth Century*, 100 Mich. L. Rev. 2062, 2150 (2002); Jon F. Merz, Catherine A. Jackson, & Jacob A. Klerman, *A Review of Abortion Policy*, 17 Women's Rts. L. Rep. 1, 3 (1995); Greenhouse & Siegel, *Before Roe* at 260 (cited in note 2).

44   Greenburg, *Supreme Conflict* at 137, 154–55, 162 (cited in note 32); Greenhouse, *Becoming Justice Blackmun* at 190 (cited in note 37); Biskupic, *American Original* at 197 (cited in note 34); Murphy, *Scalia: A Court of One* at 207–8 (cited in note 36).

45   505 U.S. at 845–46 (cited in note 42).

46   *Id.* at 836.

47   *Id.* at 872, 870 (opinion of O'Connor, Kennedy, and Souter, JJ).

48   *Id.* at 870–72, 874, 877–78 (opinion of O'Connor, Kennedy, and Souter, JJ).

49   *Id.* at 881.

50   *Id.* at 923 (opinion of Blackmun, J.).

51   *Id.* at 944, 952–55 (opinion of Rehnquist, C. J.).

52   *Id.* at 980, 1002 (opinion of Scalia, J.).

53   *Id.* at 923, 943 (opinion of Blackmun, J.). See Eskridge, *Some Effects* at 2151 (cited in note 43); Gordon, *Moral Property of Women* at 312 (cited in note 6); Reagan, *When Abortion Was a Crime* at 251 (cited in note 7): Greenhouse & Siegel, *Before Roe* at 260–61 (cited in note 2); John W. Johnson, *Griswold v. Connecticut: Birth Control and the Constitutional Right of Privacy* 205 (Kansas 2005).

54   530 U.S. 914 (2000).

55   *Korematsu v. United States*, 323 U.S. 214 (1944).

56   *Dred Scott v. Sandford*, 60 U.S. 393 (1857).

57   530 U.S. at 953 (cited in note 54) (Scalia, J., dissenting).

58   Greenburg, *Supreme Conflict* at 178 (cited in note 32). See Hirshman, *Sisters in Law* at 250–53 (cited in note 32).

59   530 U.S. at 965, 968 (cited in note 54) (Kennedy, J., dissenting).

60   Jeffrey Toobin, *The Nine: Inside the Secret World of the Supreme Court* 302–3, 308 (Anchor 2007).

61   *In re Doe*, 19 S.W.3d 346 (Tex. 2000).

62   See Greenburg, *Supreme Conflict* at 225–26 (cited in note 32); Toobin, *The Nine* at 311–14 (cited in note 60).

63   See Toobin, *The Nine* at 322–24 (cited in note 60).

64   Toobin, *The Nine* at 330, 338 (cited in note 60). See Toobin, *The Nine* at 332–45 (cited in note 60).

65 505 U.S. at 833, 898 (cited in note 42) (O'Connor, J., concurring).

66 Toobin, *The Nine* at 347–49, 362 (cited in note 60); Greenburg, *Supreme Conflict* at 301, 308 (cited in note 32). See Marcia Coyle, *The Roberts Court: The Struggle for the Constitution* 67–68 (Simon & Schuster 2013); Murphy, *Scalia: A Court of One* at 359 (cited in note 36).

67 550 U.S. 124 (2007).

68 *Id.* at 159.

69 *Id.* at 161, 164.

70 *Id.* at 170 (Ginsburg, J., dissenting).

71 *Id.* at 171–76 (Ginsburg, J., dissenting).

72 *Id.* at 181–85 (Ginsburg, J., dissenting). See Hirshman, *Sisters in Law* at 268–70 (cited in note 32).

73 Segall, *Supreme Myths* at 74, 76–77 (cited in note 29).

74 Robert Barnes, *Did Justices' Catholicism Play Part in Abortion Ruling?* Washington Post (Apr. 30, 2007); Robin Toner, *The Supreme Court's Catholic Majority*, New York Times (Apr. 25, 2007). See Biskupic, *American Original* at 203–6 (cited in note 34).

75 See Guttmacher Institute, *Induced Abortion in the United States* (July 2014); Lawrence B. Finer & Mia R. Zolna, *Shifts in Intended and Unintended Pregnancies in the United States, 2001–2008*, 104 Am. J. Pub. Health S43 (Feb. 2014); Rachel K. Jones & Jenna Jerman, *Abortion Incidence and Service Availability in the United States, 2011*, Persp. on Sexual & Reprod. Health (2014); Rachel K. Jones & Megan L. Kavanaugh, *Changes in Abortion Rates Between 2000 and 2008 and Lifetime Incidence of Abortion*, 117 Obstet. Gynecol. 1358 (2011); Lawrence B. Finer & Mia R. Zolna, *Unintended Pregnancy in the United States: Incidence and Disparities, 2006*, 84 Contraception 478 (2011); Rebecca Wind, *U.S. Abortion Rate Hits Lowest Level Since 1973*, Guttmacher Institute (Feb. 3, 2014); Guttmacher Institute, *Fact Sheet: Unintended Pregnancy in the United States* (Dec. 2013); Stephanie J. Ventura, Sally C. Curtin, Joyce C. Abma, & Stanley K. Henshaw, *Estimated Pregnancy Rates and Rates of Pregnancy Outcomes for the United States, 1990–2008*, 60 National Vital Statistics Reports No. 7 (June 20, 2012) (U.S. Dept. of Health and Human Services).

76 See Wind, *U.S. Abortion Rate* (cited in note 75); Guttmacher Institute, *Trends in Abortion in the United States 1973–2011* (Jan. 2014); Sally S. Curtin, Joyce C. Abma, Stephanie J. Ventura, & Stanley K. Henshaw, *Data Brief 136: Pregnancy Rates for U.S. Women Continue to Drop* (Dec. 2013) (U.S. Dept. of Health and Human Services).

77 See Guttmacher Institute, *State Policies in Brief: Targeted Regulation of Abortion Providers* (July 1, 2015); Guttmacher Institute, *Induced Abortion* (cited in note 75); Guttmacher Institute, *State Policies in Brief: An Overview of Abortion Laws* (Oct. 1, 2014); James Trussell, *Contraceptive Failure in the United States*, 83 Contraception 397 (2011); Wind, *U.S. Abortion Rate* (cited in note 75); Heather D. Boonstra & Elizabeth Nash, *A Surge of State Abortion Restrictions Puts Providers—And the Women they Serve—in the Crosshairs*, 17 Guttmacher Policy Rev. 10 (Winter 2014); Ventura, Curtin, Abma, & Henshaw, *Estimated Pregnancy Rates* (cited in note 75); Guttmacher Institute, *Contraceptive Use in the United States* (Aug. 2013); Guttmacher Institute, *Unintended Pregnancy in the United States* (cited in note 75).

78 Quoted in Erik Eckholm, *Abortions Declining in U.S., Study Finds*, New York Times (Feb. 2, 2014).

79   See Gallup, *Abortion* (2015), http://www.gallup.com/poll/1576/abortion.aspx#1.

80   See Jones & Kavanaugh, *Changes in Abortion Rates Between 2000 and 2008* at (cited in note 75); Boonstra, *Insurance Coverage* at (cited in note 77); Finer & Zolna, *Unintended Pregnancy* at 478 (cited in note 75); Stanley K. Henshaw, Theodore J. Joyce, Amanda Dennis, Lawrence B. Finer, & Kelly Blanchard, *Restrictions on Medicaid Funding for Abortions* (Guttmacher Institute 2009); Rachel K. Jones, Ushma D. Upadhyay, & Tracy A. Weitz, *At What Cost? Payment for Abortion Care by U.S. Women*, 23 Women's Health Issues 173 (May-June 2013); Rachel K. Jones & Kathryn Kooistra, *Abortion Incidence and Access to Services in the United States, 2008* 43 Persp. on Sexual & Reprod. Health 41 (2011); Lorraine E. Ferris, Margot McMain-Klein, Nikki Colodny, G. Fraser Fellows, & John Lamont, *Factors Associated with Immediate Abortion Complications*, 154 Canadian Medical Assn. J. 1677 (1996); Guttmacher Institute, *State Policies in Brief: State Funding of Abortion Under Medicaid* (Oct. 1, 2013); Guttmacher Institute, *Induced Abortion* (cited in note 75).

81   See, e.g., *Planned Parenthood of Wisconsin v. Van Hollen*, 738 F.3d 786 (7th Cir. 2013); *Planned Parenthood of Greater Texas Surgical Health Services v. Abbott*, 748 F.3d 583 (5th Cir. 2014); *Jackson Women's Health Organization v. Currier*, 760 F.3d 448 (5th Cir. 2014); *Whole Woman's Health v. Lakey*, 46 F. Supp. 3d 673 (W.D. Tex. 2014); *Planned Parenthood of Wisconsin v. Schimel*, 806 F.3d 908 (7th Cir. 2015); *Whole Woman's Health v. Cole*, 790 F.3d 563 (5th Cir. 2015).

82   748 F.3d 583 (5th Cir. 2014).

83   *Id.* at 598.

84   806 F.3d 908 (7th Cir. 2015).

85   *Id.* at 920, 912, 914, 916.

86   136 S. Ct., 2292 (2016).

87   Betsy Woodruff, *Texas: How Pro-Lifers Won*, National Review (July 15, 2013).

88   136 S. Ct., at 2301–3.

89   *Id.* at 2318.

90   Asher Price, *Wendy Davis Celebrates Supreme Court Abortion Ruling with Tears*, Austin American-Statesman (June 27, 2016).

91   136 S. Ct., at 2330 (Thomas, J., dissenting), quoting Antonin Scalia, *The Rule of Law as a Law of Rules*, 56 U. Chi. L. Rev. 1175, 1182 (1989).

92   *Id.* at 2331 (Alito, J., dissenting).

93   *Id.* at 2319 (majority opinion).

94   Manny Fernandez & Abby Goodnough, *Opinion Transforms Texas' Abortion Landscape*, New York Times (June 27, 2016); *Reactions to the Supreme Court Ruling on Texas' Abortion Law*, New York Times (June 27, 2016); Erik Eckholm, *Abortion Ruling Could Create Waves of Legal Challenges*, New York Times (June 27, 2016).

95   Eckholm, *Abortion Ruling* (cited in note 94).

CHAPTER 18

1   Andrew Kopkind, *The Gay Moment*, Nation (May 3, 1993), in Andrew Kopkind, *The Thirty Years' Wars* 501 (Verso 1996). See Neil Miller, *Out of the Past: Gay and Lesbian History from 1869 to the Present* 430–31, 503–4 (Alyson 2006).

2   See Miller, *Out of the Past* at 506 (cited in note 1); George Chauncey, *Why Marriage?: The History Shaping Today's Debate Over Gay Equality* 53, 57 (Basic Books 2004); Gerald N. Rosenberg, *The Hollow Hope: Can Courts Bring About Social Change?* 413–15 (Chicago 2008); Miller, *Out of the Past* at 504–5, 556–59 (cited in note 1).

3   Quoted in Miller, *Out of the Past* at 557 (cited in note 1); Donald E. Wildmon, *Principles Which Guide AFA's Opposition to the Homosexual Agenda*, Free Republic (Dec. 14, 2001). See Miller, *Out of the Past* at 557 (cited in note 1); John Gallagher & Chris Bull, *Perfect Enemies: The Battle between the Religious Right and the Gay Movement* 31–38 (Madison Books 2001); Tina Fetner, *How the Religious Right Shaped Lesbian and Gay Activism* 56–73 (University of Minnesota 2008).

4   See Dudley Clendinen & Adam Nagourney, *Out for Good* 451–52 (Simon & Schuster 1999); Linda Hirshman, *Victory: The Triumphant Gay Revolution*, 172–73 (HarperCollins 2012); Miller, *Out of the Past* at 409 (cited in note 1).

5   Quoted in Hirshman, *Victory* at 174, 175 (cited in note 4). See Michael Bronski, *A Queer History of the United States* 224–25 (Beacon 2011); Hirshman, *Victory* at 173–75 (cited in note 4); Kat Long, *The Forbidden Apple: A Century of Sex and Sin in New York City* 185 (Ig 2009); Miller, *Out of the Past* at 410 (cited in note 1); Michael J. Klarman, *From the Closet to the Altar* 35 (Oxford 2013).

6   See Bronski, *Queer History* at 225–26 (cited in note 5).

7   Quoted in Clendinen & Nagourney, *Out for Good* at 487–88 (cited in note 4); Klarman, *From the Closet to the Altar* at 34 (cited in note 5); Bronski, *Queer History* at 226 (cited in note 5). See Fetner, *How the Religious Right Shaped Lesbian and Gay Activism* at 60 (cited in note 3).

8   See Barry D. Adam, *The Rise of a Gay and Lesbian Movement* 162 (Twayne 1995); Clendinen & Nagourney, *Out for Good* at 506–8 (cited in note 4).

9   See Hirshman, *Victory* at 211–12 (cited in note 4).

10   Quoted in Hirshman, *Victory* at 196 (cited in note 4). See Miller, *Out of the Past* at 426–27 (cited in note 1); Hirshman, *Victory* at 197–201 (cited in note 4); Walter Frank, *Law and the Gay Rights Story* 69–74 (Rutgers 2014); Bronski, *Queer History* at 231–33 (cited in note 5); Adam, *Rise of a Gay and Lesbian Movement* at 163 (cited in note 8); Fetner, *How the Religious Right Shaped Lesbian and Gay Activism* at 86 (cited in note 3).

11   See Miller, *Out of the Past* at 427–28 (cited in note 1); Hirshman, *Victory* at 192, 202–5 (cited in note 4); Lillian Faderman, *The Gay Revolution* 428–41 (Simon & Schuster 2015).

12   See Hirshman, *Victory* at 207–9 (cited in note 4); Gallagher & Bull, *Perfect Enemies* at 269 (cited in note 3); Miller, *Out of the Past* at 428, 550–51 (cited in note 1); Centers for Disease Control and Prevention, *HIV in the United States: At a Glance* (June 2016), http://www.cdc.gov/hiv/statistics/basics/ataglance.html.

13   Miller, *Out of the Past* at 444 (cited in note 1). See Klarman, *From the Closet to the Altar* at 39 (cited in note 5).

14   Quoted in Hirshman, *Victory* at 223 (cited in note 4). See Chauncey, *Why Marriage* at 49 (cited in note 2); Hirshman, *Victory* at 222 (cited in note 4); Miller, *Out of the Past* at 497–501 (cited in note 1); Clendinen & Nagourney, *Out for Good* at 571–72 (cited in note 4); Klarman, *From the Closet to the Altar* at 43–44 (cited in note 5); Gallagher & Bull, *Perfect Enemies* at 85–86 (cited in note 3).

15   Quoted in Fetner, *How the Religious Right Shaped Lesbian and Gay Activism* at 79–80 (cited in note 3); Gallagher & Bull, *Perfect Enemies* at 79, 88 (cited in note 3); Miller, *Out of the Past* at 498 (cited in note 1). See Fetner, *How the Religious Right Shaped Lesbian and Gay Activism* at 79–80 (cited in note 3); Miller, *Out of the Past* at 498–99 (cited in note 1); Gallagher & Bull, *Perfect Enemies* at 79, 88, 91 (cited in note 3); Klarman, *From the Closet to the Altar* at 44 (cited in note 5).

16   See Miller, *Out of the Past* at 499 (cited in note 1); Gallagher & Bull, *Perfect Enemies* at 95–96 (cited in note 3); Chauncey, *Why Marriage* at 52 (cited in note 2).

17   Civil Rights Act of 1964, Pub. L. 88–352, 78 Stat. 241 (1964); Civil Rights Act of 1968, Pub. L. 90–284, 82 Stat. 73 (1968).

18   William B. Turner, *"The Gay Rights State": Wisconsin's Pioneering Legislation to Prohibit Discrimination Based on Sexual Orientation*, 22 Wisc. Women's L.J. 91, 116–17 (2007). See Clendinen & Nagourney, *Out for Good* at 526 (cited in note 4); Adam, *Rise of a Gay and Lesbian Movement* at 131 (cited in note 8); Klarman, *From the Closet to the Altar* at 35, 42 (cited in note 5). See also Act of Mar. 2, 1982, ch. 112, sec. 3, § 21.35, 1981 Wisc. Sess. Laws 901 (codified as amended Wisc. Stat. § 21.35).

19   See Clendinen & Nagourney, *Out for Good* at 526–29 (cited in note 4); Gallagher & Bull, *Perfect Enemies* at 40–43 (cited in note 3); Miller, *Out of the Past* at 424 (cited in note 1); Adam, *Rise of a Gay and Lesbian Movement* at 133 (cited in note 8).

20   See *Gay and Lesbian Rights*, Gallup, http://www.gallup.com/poll/1651/gay-lesbian-rights .aspx#1; Frank Newport, *Senate Vote on ENDA Remarkably Close to Public Sentiment*, Gallup, http://pollingmatters.gallup.com/2013/11/senate-vote-on-enda-remarkably-close-to.html.

21   *Statements on Introduced Bills and Joint Resolutions*, 140 Cong. Rec. S7561, 103rd Congress (June 23, 1994).

22   Bart Barnes, *Barry Goldwater, GOP Hero, Dies*, Washington Post (May 30, 1998); *HRC Mourns Death of Barry Goldwater*, Oasis Magazine (1998).

23   Mark Eddy, *Sexual Orientation Discrimination in Employment* 3 (Cong. Res. S., July 25, 1994).

24   See Eddy, *Sexual Orientation Discrimination* at 3–6 (cited in note 23); H.R. Rep. 110–406 pt. 1, 110th Congress (2007–2008).

25   See H.R. Rep. 110–406 pt. 1, 110th Congress (2007–2008); Jill D. Weinberg, *Gender Nonconformity*, 44 U. S.F. L. Rev. 1, 10 (2009); Pat P. Putignano, *Why Doma and Not Enda?* 15 Hofstra Labor & Employ. L.J. 177 197, 199 (1997).

26   Quoted in Chauncey, *Why Marriage* at 154 (cited in note 2) (Ashcroft); Employment Nondiscrimination Act of 1996, 142 Cong. Rec. S10129, 104th Congress (Sept. 10, 1996); *Statements on Introduced Bills and Joint Resolutions*, 141 Cong. Rec. S8493, 104th Congress (June 15, 1995); Putignano, *Why Doma and Not Enda?* at 194–95 (cited in note 25); Jeremy S. Barber, *Re-Orienting Sexual Harassment*, 52 Amer. U. L. Rev. 493, 527–28 (2002).

27   See Weinberg, *Gender Nonconformity* at 9 (cited in note 25); Gallagher & Bull, *Perfect Enemies* at 263–68 (cited in note 3); Chauncey, *Why Marriage* at 126, 154 (cited in note 2); H.R. Rep. 110–406 pt. 1, 110th Congress (2007–2008).

28   *Statements on Introduced Bills and Joint Resolutions*, 143 Cong. Rec. S5444, 105th Con-

gress (June 10, 1997). See H.R. Rep. 110–406 pt. 1, 110th Cong. (2007–2008); Shannon H. Tan, *When Steve Is Fired for Becoming Susan*, 37 Stetson L. Rev. 579, 605 (2008).

29 Employment Non-Discrimination Act, 143 *Cong. Rec.* S5630, 105th Congress (June 12, 1997) (Murray); *Statements on Introduced Bills and Joint Resolutions*, 143 *Cong. Rec.* S5444, 105th Congress (June 10, 1997) (Jeffords). See H.R. Rep. 110–406 pt. 1, 110th Congress (2007–2008).

30 Ed Vitagliano, *Will Congress Fall for Gay Histrionics?* Am. Fam. Assoc. J. (Aug. 2007); Ed Vitagliano, *How ENDA Could Begin an UNcivil War*, Am. Fam. Assoc. J. (Sept. 2007).

31 *Final Vote Results for Roll Call 1057*, http://clerk.house.gov/evs/2007/roll1057.xml; Executive Office of the President, Office of Management and Budget, *Statement of Administration Policy, H.R. 3685—The Employment Non-Discrimination Act* (Oct. 23, 2007).

32 See Jeff Lax & Justin Phillips, *Memo to Senate Republicans: Your Constituents Want You to Vote for ENDA*, Washington Post (Nov. 3, 2013).

33 Employment Non-Discrimination Act of 2013, S. Rep. 113–105 (Sept. 12, 2013); Jacqueline Klimas, *Senate Passes Gay-Rights Bill to Prevent Workplace Discrimination*, Washington Times (Nov. 7, 2013); *U. S. Senate Roll Call Votes*, 113th Cong., 1st Sess., Motion to Invoke Cloture (Nov. 4, 2013).

34 United States General Accounting Office, *Homosexuals in the Armed Forces* (June 12, 1992).

35 See Chauncey, *Why Marriage* at 49–52 (cited in note 2); Hirshman, *Victory* at 222–23 (cited in note 4); Miller, *Out of the Past* at 497–501 (cited in note 1); Clendinen & Nagourney, *Out for Good* at 571–72 (cited in note 4); Klarman, *From the Closet to the Altar* at 43–44 (cited in note 5); Gallagher & Bull, *Perfect Enemies* at 85–86, 95–96 (cited in note 3); Fetner, *How the Religious Right Shaped Lesbian and Gay Activism* at 79–80 (cited in note 3); Gallagher & Bull, *Perfect Enemies* at 79, 88 (cited in note 3).

36 Quoted in Gallagher & Bull, *Perfect Enemies* at 132 (cited in note 3). See Miller, *Out of the Past* at 501 (cited in note 1); Gallagher & Bull, *Perfect Enemies* at 132 (cited in note 3).

37 Quoted in Miller, *Out of the Past* at 502 (cited in note 1). See Miller, *Out of the Past* at 502–3 (cited in note 1).

38 See Hirshman, *Victory* at 227–28 (cited in note 4); Gallagher & Bull, *Perfect Enemies* at 149 (cited in note 3); Klarman, *From the Closet to the Altar* at 46 (cited in note 5); Faderman, *Gay Revolution* at 495–501 (cited in note 11).

39 Pub. L. 103–160, 10 U.S.C. § 654(b) (Nov. 30, 1993). See Hirshman, *Victory* at 224 (cited in note 4); Miller, *Out of the Past* at 510 (cited in note 1); Faderman, *Gay Revolution* at 501–4 (cited in note 11); Gallagher & Bull, *Perfect Enemies* at 157 (cited in note 3); Department of Defense Directive 1304.26 (Dec. 21, 1993).

40 American Psychological Association, *Sexual Orientation and Military Service* (July 28 and 30, 2004). See Miller, *Out of the Past* at 534 (cited in note 1).

41 See *Report: "Don't Ask, Don't Tell" Costs $363M*, USA Today (Feb. 14, 2006); Daniel Nasaw, *Don't Ask, Don't Tell: Gay Veteran of Iraq Takes on US Army*, Guardian (June 29, 2009); Stephen Benjamin, *Don't Ask, Don't Translate*, New York Times (June 8, 2007); Miller, *Out of the Past* at 534 (cited in note 1).

42 Associated Press, *Admirals, Generals: Let Gays Serve Openly*, MSNBC (Nov. 18,

2008). See John M. Shalikashvili, *Second Thoughts on Gays in the Military*, New York Times (Jan. 2, 2007); Thom Shanker & Patrick Healy, *A New Push to Roll Back "Don't Ask, Don't Tell,"* New York Times (Nov. 30, 2007); *Former Defense Secretary William Cohen Says Congress Should Re-Visit "Don't Ask, Don't Tell,"* Servicemembers Legal Defense Network (Jan. 3, 2007).

43 Rowan Scarborough, *Obama to Delay Repeal of "Don't Ask, Don't Tell": Advisers See Consensus Building Before Lifting Ban on Gays*, Washington Times (Nov. 21, 2008); See Associated Press, *Obama: Repeal of "Don't Ask, Don't Tell" Possible*, NBC News (Apr. 10, 2008).

44 *Time to Review Policy on Gays in U.S. Military: Powell*, Reuters (July 5, 2009). See Leo Shane III, *Obama Wants to End Don't Ask, Don't Tell Policy*, Stars and Stripes (Jan. 16, 2009); Bryan Bender, *Continued Discharges Anger "Don't Ask, Don't Tell" Critics*, Boston Globe (May 20, 2009); Ed O'Keefe & Jon Cohen, *Most Back Repealing "Don't Ask, Don't Tell," Poll Says*, Washington Post (Dec. 15, 2010).

45 Barack Obama, *Remarks by the President in State of the Union Address* (Jan. 27, 2010). See H.R. 5136, 111th Cong. (May 27, 2010); David M. Herszenhorn & Carl Hulse, *House Votes to Allow "Don't Ask, Don't Tell" Repeal*, New York Times (May 27, 2010); Ted Barrett & Dana Bash, *Senate Halts "Don't Ask, Don't Tell" Repeal*, CNN (Sept. 22, 2010).

46 See Department of Defense, *Report of the Comprehensive Review of the Issues Associated with a Repeal of "Don't Ask, Don't Tell"* (Nov. 30, 2010); Carl Hulse, *Senate Repeals Ban Against Openly Gay Military Personnel*, New York Times (Dec. 18, 2010); Don't Ask, Don't Tell Repeal Act of 2010, H.R. 2965, S. 4023, 10 U.S.C. § 654; *Obama Certifies End of Military's Gay Ban*, NBC News (July 22, 2011); Viola Gienger & Flavia Krause-Jackson, *Obama, Pentagon Certify End of Gay Ban Won't Harm Military*, Bloomberg News (July 22, 2011); Faderman, *Gay Revolution* at 533–34 (cited in note 11).

47 Quoted in Klarman, *From the Closet to the Altar* at 49 (cited in note 5). See Katherine Franke, *Wedlocked: The Perils of Marriage Equality* (NYU 2015); *Gay and Lesbian Rights*, Gallup, http://www.gallup.com/poll/1651/gay-lesbian-rights.aspx#1; Ellen Ann Andersen, *Out of the Closets and into the Courts* 177 (Michigan 2005); Daniel R. Pinello, *America's Struggle for Same-Sex Marriage* 24–25 (Cambridge 2006); Chauncey, *Why Marriage* at 120 (cited in note 2); Klarman, *From the Closet to the Altar* at 48–49 (cited in note 5); William N. Eskridge Jr. & Darren R. Spedale, *Gay Marriage: For Better or For Worse?* 18 (Oxford 2006); Hirshman, *Victory* at 231–33 (cited in note 4).

48 See *Marriage*, Gallup, http://www.gallup.com/poll/117328/marriage.aspx; Bronski, *Queer History* at 229 (cited in note 5); Miller, *Out of the Past* at 419 (cited in note 1); Richard Berkowitz & Michael Callen, *How to Have Sex in an Epidemic* (News From The Front Publications 1983).

49 See Chauncey, *Why Marriage* at 95–104 (cited in note 2); Rhonda R. Rivera, *Lawyers, Clients, and AIDS*, 49 Ohio St. L.J. 883 (1989); David L. Chambers, *Tales of Two Cities: AIDS and the Legal Recognition of Domestic Partnerships in San Francisco and New York*, 2 L. & Sexuality 181, 184–85 (1992); Klarman, *From the Closet to the Altar* at 49–50 (cited in note 5); William N. Eskridge Jr., *The Case for Same-Sex Marriage* 53–54 (Free Press 1996).

50 Quoted in Miller, *Out of the Past* at 529 (cited in note 1); See Chauncey, *Why Marriage* at 105–10 (cited in note 2); Klarman, *From the Closet to the Altar* at 51–52 (cited in note 5);

Gallagher & Bull, *Perfect Enemies* at 223–24 (cited in note 3); Eskridge & Spedale, *Gay Marriage* at 18 (cited in note 47); Hirshman, *Victory* at 231–33 (cited in note 4); Miller, *Out of the Past* at 529 (cited in note 1).

51 Klarman, *From the Closet to the Altar* at 45 (cited in note 5). See William N. Eskridge Jr., *Equality Practice* 13 (Routledge 2002); Chambers, *Tales of Two Cities* at 183 (cited in note 49); Katherine Bishop, *San Francisco Grants Recognition to Couples Who Aren't Married*, New York Times (May 31, 1989).

52 See Chauncey, *Why Marriage* at 116 (cited in note 2); Klarman, *From the Closet to the Altar* at 45–46 (cited in note 5).

53 Quoted in Klarman, *From the Closet to the Altar* at 45, 59–60 (cited in note 5). See Chambers, *Tales of Two Cities* at 183, 201 (cited in note 49); Chauncey, *Why Marriage* at 151 (cited in note 2); Eskridge, *Case for Same-Sex Marriage* at 59 (cited in note 49); Gallagher & Bull, *Perfect Enemies* at 194–95 (cited in note 3); Pinello, *America's Struggle for Same-Sex Marriage* at 34–35 (cited in note 47); Eskridge & Spedale, *Gay Marriage* at 18 (cited in note 47).

54 See National Conference of State Legislatures, *Civil Unions and Domestic Partnership Statutes* (Nov. 18, 2014).

55 74 Haw. 530 (1993).

56 See Gallagher & Bull, *Perfect Enemies* at 203–4 (cited in note 3); Chauncey, *Why Marriage* at 124–25 (cited in note 2); Miller, *Out of the Past* at 530 (cited in note 1); Klarman, *From the Closet to the Altar* at 55–56 (cited in note 5); Pinello, *America's Struggle for Same-Sex Marriage* at 26 (cited in note 47).

57 See Klarman, *From the Closet to the Altar* at 56–57 (cited in note 5); Miller, *Out of the Past* at 530 (cited in note 1); Gallagher & Bull, *Perfect Enemies* at 204–6 (cited in note 3); Eskridge, *Equality Practice* at 3, 26, 40 (cited in note 51); Andersen, *Out of the Closets* at 194 (cited in note 47); David Cole, *Engines of Liberty* 25–29 (Basic Books 2016).

58 Arlene Levinson, *States Face Legal Quandary if Hawaii Allows Homosexual Marriages*, Associated Press (May 17, 1993); Bob Sipchen, *Same-Sex Marriage Moves to Forefront of Cultural Debate*, Los Angeles Times (Apr. 10, 1996). See Klarman, *From the Closet to the Altar* at 57–60 (cited in note 5); *Gay and Lesbian Rights*, Gallup, http://www.gallup.com/poll/1651/gay-lesbian-rights.aspx.

59 Klarman, *From the Closet to the Altar* at 59 (cited in note 5). See Gallagher & Bull, *Perfect Enemies* at 199 (cited in note 3); Eskridge, *Equality Practice* at 27–28 (cited in note 51); Katie Lofton & Donald P. Haider-Markel, *The Politics of Same-Sex Marriage Versus the Politics of Gay Civil Rights*, in *The Politics of Same-Sex Marriage* 313, 320–23 (Craig A. Rimmerman & Clyde Wilcox eds., Chicago 2007); Kenneth D. Wald & Graham B. Glover, *Theological Perspectives on Gay Unions*, in Rimmerman & Wilcox, *The Politics of Same-Sex Marriage* at 105, 121 (cited in this note); Klarman, *From the Closet to the Altar* at 58–59 (cited in note 5).

60 Cal. Fam. Code § 308.5 (West 2004).

61 See *In re Marriage Cases*, 183 P.3d 384 (Cal. Sup. Ct. 2008).

62 See Joe Okonkwo, *Catholic Bishops Endorse Prop 8*, Advocate (Aug. 8, 2008); *Proposition 8 to Protect Marriage Receives $1 Million Donation from the Knights of Columbus Catholic Organization*, Christian News Wire (Aug. 19, 2008); California Catholic Conference, *A*

Statement of the Catholic Bishops of California in Support of Proposition 8 (Aug. 1, 2008); *Bishop of Fresno Removes Priest Who Opposes Prop. 8*, Catholic New Agency (Oct. 14, 2008); Matthai Kuruvila, *Catholics, Mormons Allied to Pass Prop. 8*, San Francisco Chronicle (Nov. 10, 2008); *California and Same-Sex Marriage*, Newsroom of the Church of Jesus Christ of Latter-Day Saints (June 30, 2008); *Church Readies Members on Proposition 8*, Newsroom of the Church of Jesus Christ of Latter-Day Saints (Oct. 8, 2008); Mike Swift, *Opponents of Gay Marriage Ban Ride Wave of Donations*, San Jose Mercury News (Oct. 24, 2008); Jesse McKinley & Kirk Johnson, *Mormons Tipped Scale in Ban on Gay Marriage*, New York Times (Nov. 14, 2008).

63   Geoffrey R. Stone, *Same-Sex Marriage and the Establishment Clause*, 54 Villanova L. Rev. 617, 620, 621 (2009). See Debra Bowen, *Statement of Vote, November 4, 2008, General Election* 7, 13 (2008), available at http://www.sos.ca.gov/elections/sov/2008_general/sov_complete.pdf; CNN, *California General Exit Poll* 6 (2008), available at http://media.sacbee.com/smedia/2008/11/05/18/prop8.source.prod_affiliate.4.pdf.

64   Jerry Gray, *No. 2 House Leader Refers to Colleague with Anti-Gay Slur*, New York Times (Jan. 28, 1995) ("Barney Fag"); Ann Hartman, *The Long Road to Equality: Lesbians and Social Policy*, in *Lesbians and Lesbian Families* 91 (Joan Laird ed., Columbia 1999) (Buchanan); Derrick Z. Jackson, *Antigay Bias Hits Home for Keyes Family*, Boston Globe (Feb. 19, 2005) (Keyes). See Klarman, *From the Closet to the Altar* at 60–61 (cited in note 5); Andersen, *Out of the Closets* at 180 (cited in note 47); Gallagher & Bull, *Perfect Enemies* at 229–30, 248–54 (cited in note 3).

65   See Fetner, *How the Religious Right Shaped Lesbian and Gay Activism* at 112 (cited in note 3); Hirshman, *Victory* at 234 (cited in note 4); Klarman, *From the Closet to the Altar* at 61 (cited in note 5); Chauncey, *Why Marriage* at 125 (cited in note 2).

66   Hirshman, *Victory* at 235 (cited in note 4). See Klarman, *From the Closet to the Altar* at 61 (cited in note 5).

67   Dale Carpenter, *Windsor Products: Equal Protection from Animus*, 2013 Sup. Ct. Rev. 183, 264, 266. See *Defense of Marriage Act, Hearing Before the Subcommittee on the Constitution of the House Judiciary Committee*, 104th Cong., 2d Sess. 37 (1996).

68   Quoted in Carpenter, *Windsor Products* at 265–66, 268, 271 (cited in note 67); Hirshman, *Victory* at 235 (cited in note 4); Klarman, *From the Closet to the Altar* at 61 (cited in note 5).

69   Quoted in Eskridge & Spedale, *Gay Marriage* at 26–29 (cited in note 47). See Chauncey, *Why Marriage* at 126 (cited in note 2); Miller, *Out of the Past* at 531 (cited in note 1); Carpenter, *Windsor Products* at 257–78 (cited in note 67).

70   Quoted in Carpenter, *Windsor Products* at 194 (cited in note 67); See Defense of Marriage Act, Pub. L. 104–199, 110 S. 2419 (1996), codified 28 U.S.C. § 1738C; Chauncey, *Why Marriage* at 126 (cited in note 2); Miller, *Out of the Past* at 531 (cited in note 1); Weinberg, *Gender Nonconformity* at 10 (cited in note 25); *Gay and Lesbian Rights*, Gallup, http://www.gallup.com/poll/1651/gay-lesbian-rights.aspx.

CHAPTER **19**

1 See, e.g., *Fitzgerald v. Racing Association of Central Iowa*, 539 U.S. 103 (2003); *New York City Transit Authority v. Beazer*, 440 U.S. 568 (1979); *Williamson v. Lee Optical Co.*, 348 U.S. 483 (1955); *Railway Express Agency v. New York*, 336 U.S. 106 (1949).

2 381 U.S. 479, 486 (1965).

3 405 U.S. 438, 454–55 (1972).

4 See *Bowers v. Hardwick*, 478 U.S. 186, 198 n.2 (1986) (Powell, J., concurring).

5 *Id.* at 186.

6 See *Skinner v. Oklahoma*, 316 U.S. 535 (1942) (sterilization); *Griswold v. Connecticut*, 381 U.S. 479 (1965) (contraception); *Eisenstadt v. Baird*, 405 U.S. 438 (1972) (contraception); *Roe v. Wade*, 410 U.S. 113 (1973) (abortion).

7 478 U.S. at 190–91.

8 *Id.* at 191–92, 194, quoting *Moore v. City of East Cleveland*, 431 U. S. 494, 503 (1977) and *Palko v. Connecticut*, 302 U. S. 319, 325–26 (1937).

9 *Id.* at 196.

10 *Id.* at 196–97 (Burger, C.J., concurring), quoting 4 William Blackstone, *Commentaries on the Laws of England* 215 (Oxford 1769).

11 *Id.* at 199 (Blackmun, J., dissenting,), quoting *Olmstead v. United States*, 277 U.S. 438, 478 (1928) (Brandeis, J., dissenting).

12 *Id.* at 205 (Blackmun, J., dissenting), quoting *Paris Adult Theatre I v. Slaton*, 413 U.S. 49, 63 (1973).

13 *Id.* at 205–6 (Blackmun, J., dissenting).

14 *Id.* at 199 (Blackmun, J., dissenting), quoting *Roe v. Wade*, 410 U.S. 113, 117 (1973), quoting *Lochner v. New York*, 198 U.S. 45, 76 (1905) (Holmes, J., dissenting).

15 *Id.* at 199 (Blackmun, J., dissenting), quoting Oliver Wendell Holmes Jr., *The Path of the Law*, 10 Harv. L. Rev. 457, 469 (1897).

16 *Id.* at 199–200 (Blackmun, J., dissenting), quoting *Herring v. State*, 119 Ga. 709, 721, 46 S. E. 876, 882 (1904).

17 *Id.* at 211–12, 214 (Blackmun, J., dissenting).

18 Lillian Faderman, *The Gay Revolution* 429 (Simon & Schuster 2015); William N. Eskridge Jr., *Dishonorable Passions: Sodomy Laws in America, 1861–2003* 252 (Viking 2008). See Joyce Murdoch & Deb Price, *Courting Justice: Gay Men and Lesbians v. the Supreme Court* 330–34 (Basic Books 2002); Dudley Clendinen & Adam Nagourney, *Out for Good* 536–38 (Simon & Schuster 1999); Michael J. Klarman, *From the Closet to the Altar* 37–38 (Oxford 2013); Linda Hirshman, *Victory: The Triumphant Gay Revolution* 194–95 (HarperCollins 2012); David A. J. Richards, *The Sodomy Cases* 108–9 (Kansas 2009); Eskridge, *Dishonorable Passions* at 249–52 (cited in this note). For examples of cases invoking *Bowers* to uphold laws discriminating against gays and lesbians, see *Ben-Shalom v. Marsh*, 881 F.2d 454 (7th Cir. 1989); *High Tech Gays v. Def. Indus. Sec. Clearance Office*, 895 F.2d 563 (9th Cir. 1990); *Equality Foundation of Greater Cincinnati v. City of Cincinnati*, 54 F.3d 261 (6th Cir. 1995); *In re Opinion of the Justices*, 530 A.2d 21 (N.H. 1987).

19 Quoted in Murdoch & Price, *Courting Justice* at 274 (cited in note 18). See Jeffrey Toobin, *The Nine: Inside the Secret World of the Supreme Court* 218–19 (Anchor 2008); Dale Carpenter, *Flagrant Conduct: The Story of Lawrence v. Texas* 212–13 (Norton 2012); Richards, *Sodomy Cases* at 85–92 (cited in note 18); Murdoch & Price, *Courting Justice* at 305–6 (cited in note 18); Eskridge, *Dishonorable Passions* at 243–47 (cited in note 18); *Gay and Lesbian Rights*, Gallup, available at http://www.gallup.com/poll/1651/gay-lesbian-rights.aspx.

20 Quoted in Murdoch & Price, *Courting Justice* at 307 (cited in note 18). See Carpenter, *Flagrant Conduct* at 213 (cited in note 19); Eskridge, *Dishonorable Passions* at 243–47 (cited in note 18); Linda Greenhouse, *Becoming Justice Blackmun* 150–51 (Henry Holt 2005); Richards, *Sodomy Cases* at 104–7 (cited in note 18); Toobin, *The Nine* at 28, 218–19 (cited in note 19); Clendinen & Nagourney, *Out for Good* at 539 (cited in note 18); Hirshman, *Victory* at 194 (cited in note 18); Klarman, *From the Closet to the Altar* at 36–37 (cited in note 18); Murdoch & Price, *Courting Justice* at 274–75, 307–14 (cited in note 18).

21 See Denver Rev. Municipal Code, Art. IV; §§ 28–91 to 28–116 (1991); Aspen Municipal Code § 13–98 (1977); Boulder Rev. Code §§ 12–1–1 to 12–1–11 (1987).

22 Quoted in Hirshman, *Victory* at 249 (cited in note 18). See John Gallagher & Chris Bull, *Perfect Enemies: The Battle between the Religious Right and the Gay Movement* 103–10 (Madison Books 2001); Hirshman, *Victory* at 248–49 (cited in note 18); Barry D. Adam, *The Rise of a Gay and Lesbian Movement* 133 (Twayne 1995); Faderman, *Gay Revolution* at 455–63 (cited in note 18).

23 See Colo. Const., Art. II, § 30b.

24 Quoted in Eskridge, *Dishonorable Passions* at 280 (cited in note 18). See Hirshman, *Victory* at 249–51 (cited in note 18); Gallagher & Bull, *Perfect Enemies* at 112–19 (cited in note 22); Faderman, *Gay Revolution* at 455–63 (cited in note 18); Murdoch & Price, *Courting Justice* at 454 (cited in note 18); Adam, *Rise of a Gay and Lesbian Movement* at 133 (cited in note 22).

25 517 U.S. 620 (1996).

26 505 U.S. 833 (1992).

27 See Faderman, *Gay Revolution* at 464 (cited in note 18).

28 517 U.S. at 631.

29 *Id.* at 631–35, quoting *Department of Agriculture v. Moreno*, 413 U. S. 528, 534 (1973).

30 *Id.* at 636, 639–42 (Scalia, J., dissenting).

31 *Id.* at 644, 652–53 (Scalia, J., dissenting); Joan Biskupic, *American Original: The Life and Constitution of Supreme Court Justice Antonin Scalia* 221 (Farrar, Straus & Giroux 2009).

32 Klarman, *From the Closet to the Altar* at 69–70 (cited in note 18).

33 Tex. Penal Code Ann. § 21.06(a) (2003).

34 Laurence Tribe & Joshua Matz, *Uncertain Justice: The Roberts Court and the Constitution* 42 (Henry Holt 2014).

35 *Commonwealth v. Wasson*, 842 S.W.2d 487, 501 (Ky. 1992). See Klarman, *From the Closet to the Altar* at 85 (cited in note 18); Tribe & Matz, *Uncertain Justice* at 42 (cited in note 34); Eskridge, *Dishonorable Passions* at 289–308 (cited in note 18); *Gay and Lesbian Rights*, Gallup, available at http://www.gallup.com/poll/1651/gay-lesbian-rights.aspx.

36 *Lawrence v. Texas*, 539 U.S. 558 (2003).

37 *Id.* at 564–65.

38 *Id.* at 567.

39 *Id.* at 567–71, quoting *Bowers v. Hardwick*, 478 U.S. at 192 (1986).

40 *Id.* at 571, quoting *Bowers v. Hardwick*, 478 U.S. at 196 (1986) (Burger, C.J., concurring).

41 *Id.* at 571–72, 574, quoting *County of Sacramento v. Lewis*, 523 U.S. 833, 857 (1998). See American Law Institute, Model Penal Code § 213.2 (1980).

42 *Id.* at 578–79.

43 *Id.* at 581–82 (O'Connor, J., concurring).

44 *Id.* at 599 (Scalia, J., dissenting), quoting *Bowers v. Hardwick*, 478 U.S. at 196 (1986).

45 *Id.* at 592, 593, 596–98 (Scalia, J., dissenting), quoting *Washington v. Glucksberg*, 521 U. S. 702, 721 (1997).

46 See, e.g., *Washington v. Glucksberg*, 521 U.S. 707, 720–28 (1997).

47 539 U.S. at 593, 596–98 (Scalia, J., dissenting). See Eskridge, *Dishonorable Passions* at 328 (cited in note 18).

48 *Id.* at 602–3 (Scalia, J., dissenting).

49 *Id.* at 604–5 (Scalia, J., dissenting).

50 Dalia Lithwick, *Scaliapalooza*, Slate (Oct. 30, 2003). See Bruce Allen Murphy, *Scalia: A Court of One* 294–97 (Simon & Schuster 2014).

51 Quoted in Carpenter, *Flagrant Conduct* at 29–34 (cited in note 19).

52 Quoted in Carpenter, *Flagrant Conduct* at 204–6 (cited in note 19).

53 See Carpenter, *Flagrant Conduct* at 259 (cited in note 19); Eskridge, *Dishonorable Passions* at 325–26 (cited in note 18).

54 Quoted in Klarman, *From the Closet to the Altar* at 87–88 (cited in note 18); Carpenter, *Flagrant Conduct* at 268–69 (cited in note 19). See Craig A. Rimmerman, *The Presidency, Congress, and Same-Sex Marriage*, in *The Politics of Same-Sex Marriage* 273, 280, 282–84 (Craig A. Rimmerman & Clyde Wilcox eds., Chicago 2007); Hirshman, *Victory* at 295 (cited in note 18).

55 Quoted in Carpenter, *Flagrant Conduct* at 282 (cited in note 19). See Carpenter, *Flagrant Conduct* at 271–72 (cited in note 19); Hirshman, *Victory* at 269 (cited in note 18); Toobin, *The Nine* at 222 (cited in note 19).

56 See Randy E. Barnett, *Justice Kennedy's Libertarian Revolution*, 2002–2003 Cato Sup. Ct. Rev. 21 (broad reading); Laurence H. Tribe, *Lawrence v. Texas: The "Fundamental Right" That Dare Not Speak Its Name*, 117 Harv. L. Rev. 1898 (2004) (broad reading); Dale Carpenter, *Is Lawrence Libertarian?* 88 Minn. L. Rev. 1140 (2004) (narrow reading); Cass R. Sunstein, *What Did Lawrence Hold?* 2003 Sup. Ct. Rev. 27 (narrow reading); Eskridge, *Dishonorable Passions* at 331–34 (cited in note 18) (narrow reading).

57 See *Li v. State*, 110 P.3d 91 (Ore. Sup. Ct. 2005) (upholding law denying same-sex couples the right to marry); *Alaska Civil Liberties Union v. State*, 122 P.3d 781 (Alaska Sup. Ct. 2005) (upholding law prohibiting incest); *Lofton v. Secretary of Department of Children and Family Services*, 358 F.3d 804 (11th Cir. 2004) (upholding law denying gays and lesbians the right to adopt); *United States v. Orellana*, 62 M.J. 595 (N.M. Ct. Crim. App. 2005) (upholding law prohibiting adultery).

CHAPTER **20**

1   See *Lawrence v. Texas*, 539 U.S. 558, 604 (2003) (Scalia, J., dissenting).

2   Laurence Tribe & Joshua Matz, *Uncertain Justice: The Roberts Court and the Constitution* 44 (Henry Holt 2014).

3   347 U.S. 483 (1954).

4   *Loving v. Virginia*, 388 U.S. 1 (1967); William N. Eskridge Jr., *Dishonorable Passions: Sodomy Laws in America, 1861–2003* 355–58 (Viking 2008). For a range of views on this issue, see Michael J. Klarman, *From the Closet to the Altar* (Oxford 2013); Gerald N. Rosenberg, *The Hollow Hope* (Chicago 2008); Laurence H. Tribe & Joshua Matz, *The Constitutional Inevitability of Same-Sex Marriage*, 71 Md. L. Rev. 471 (2012); Martha C. Nussbaum, *A Right to Marry?* Dissent 43 (Summer 2009); Richard A. Posner, *Should There Be Homosexual Marriage?* 95 Mich. L. Rev. 1578 (1997).

5   See Steve Sanders, *Mini-DOMAs as Political Process Failures*, 109 Nw. U. L. Rev. 12, 14 (2014).

6   See Eric M. Uslaner & Ronald E. Weber, *Public Support for Pro-Choice Abortion Policies in the Nation and States*, 77 Mich. L. Rev. 1772, 1783–84 (1979); Jon Ponder, *Gay Marriage Has Twice the Support Today That Interracial Marriage Had When It Was Legalized in the 1960s*, Pensito Review (2010).

7   See David Cole, *Engines of Liberty* 1, 22–23 (Basic Books 2016); Marc Solomon, *Winning Marriage* 91–92 (ForeEdge 2014).

8   On the animus issue, see *Romer v. Evans*, 517 U.S. 620 (1996); *City of Cleburne v. Cleburne Living Center*, 473 U.S. 432 (1985); *Department of Agriculture v. Moreno*, 413 U.S. 528 (1973); Dale Carpenter, *Windsor Products: Equal Protection from Animus*, 2013 Sup. Ct. Rev. 183.

9   See, e.g., *Maynard v. Hill*, 125 U.S. 190, 205, 211 (1888); *Meyer v. Nebraska*, 262 U.S. 390, 399 (1923); *Griswold v. Connecticut*, 381 U.S. 479, 486 (1965); *Loving v. Virginia*, 388 U.S. 1, 12 (1967); *Boddie v. Connecticut*, 401 U.S. 371, 376, 383 (1971); *Cleveland Board of Education v. LaFleur*, 414 U.S. 632, 639–40 (1974); *Zablocki v. Redhail*, 434 U.S. 374, 384 (1978); *Turner v. Safley*, 482 U.S. 78, 95 (1987).

10   *Washington v. Glucksberg*, 521 U.S. 702, 710 (1997).

11   See Daniel O. Conkle, *Evolving Values, Animus, and Same-Sex Marriage*, 89 Ind. L.J. 27, 30–33 (2014).

12   See, e.g., *Strauder v. West Virginia*, 100 U.S. 303 (1880) (race); *United States v. Virginia*, 518 U.S. 515 (1996) (sex); *Sugarman v. Dougall*, 413 U.S. 634 (1973) (alienage); *Korematsu v. United States*, 323 U.S. 214 (1944) (national origin); *Levy v. Louisiana*, 391 U.S. 68 (1968) (non-marital children).

13   See, e.g., *Massachusetts Board of Retirement v. Murgia*, 427 U.S. 307, 313 (1976); *Bowen v. Gilliard*, 483 U.S. 587, 602 (1987); *Lyng v. Castillo*, 477 U.S. 635, 638 (1986).

14   See Cary Franklin, *Marrying Liberty and Equality: The New Jurisprudence of Gay Rights*, 100 Va. L. Rev. 817 (2014).

15   Roberta Kaplan, *Then Comes Marriage: United States v. Windsor and the Defeat of DOMA* 48 (Norton 2015). See Cole, *Engines of Liberty* at 45 (cited in note 7).

16   440 Mass. 309 (Sup. Jud. Ct. Mass. 2003).

17   *Id.* at 326–28, quoting *Baker v. State*, 170 Vt. 194, 229 (Vt. Sup. Ct. 1999).

18   *Id.* at 333, 336–37. See Klarman, *From the Closet to the Altar* at 90–91 (cited in note 4); George Chauncey, *Why Marriage* 129–35 (Basic Books 2004); Cole, *Engines of Liberty* at 47–48 (cited in note 7).

19   Solomon, *Winning Marriage* at 8 (cited in note 7).

20   See Klarman, *From the Closet to the Altar* at 105–6, (cited in note 4); Linda Hirshman, *Victory: The Triumphant Gay Revolution* 295 (HarperCollins 2012); Rosenberg, *Hollow Hope* at 369–70 (cited in note 4); Daniello R. Pinello, *America's Struggle for Same-Sex Marriage* 44, 175 (Cambridge 2006); Solomon, *Winning Marriage* at 7, 13–21 (cited in note 7).

21   See *Hernandez v. Robles*, 855 N.E.2d 1 (N.Y. 2006); *Andersen v. King County*, 138 P.3d 963 (Wash. 2006); *Lewis v. Harris*, 908 A.2d 196 (N.J. 2006); *Conaway v. Deane*, 932 A.2d 571 (Md. 2007); *Perdue v. O'Kelley*, 632 S.E.2d 110 (Ga. 2006); *Citizens for Equal Protection v. Bruning*, 455 F.3d 859 (8th Cir. 2006); Klarman, *From the Closet to the Altar* at 116 (cited in note 4).

22   Klarman, *From the Closet to the Altar* at 104–6, 111 (cited in note 4); Kaplan, *Then Comes Marriage* at 55 (cited in note 15); Cole, *Engines of Liberty* at 49 (cited in note 7); Gerald N. Rosenberg, *Courting Disaster* 54 Drake L. Rev. 812 (2006); Rosenberg, *Hollow Hope* at 343, 369–70 (cited in note 4). See Hirshman, *Victory* at 295 (cited in note 20); Pinello, *America's Struggle* at 44, 175 (cited in note 20).

23   Cole, *Engines of Liberty* at 51 (cited in note 7); Klarman, *From the Closet to the Altar* at 91–97 (cited in note 4); Pinello, *America's Struggle* at 59, 71 (cited in note 20).

24   See Klarman, *From the Closet to the Altar* at 119–20 (cited in note 4); *Kerrigan v. Commissioner of Public Health*, 957 A.2d 407 (Conn. 2008); *In re Marriage Cases*, 183 P.3d 384 (Cal. 2008); *Varnum v. Brien*, 763 N.W.2d 862, 904–5 (Iowa Sup. Ct. 2009).

25   See Klarman, *From the Closet to the Altar* at 128–29, 135–36, 156 (cited in note 4).

26   Geoffrey R. Stone, *Same-Sex Marriage and the Establishment Clause*, 54 Villanova L. Rev. 617, 620, 621 (2009). See Debra Bowen, *Statement of Vote, November 4, 2008, General Election* 7, 13 (2008), available at http://www.sos.ca.gov/elections/sov/2008_general/sov_complete.pdf; CNN, *California General Exit Poll* 6 (2008), available at http://media.sacbee.com/smedia/2008/11/05/18/prop8.source.prod_affiliate.4.pdf.

27   See Klarman, *From the Closet to the Altar* at 143–47, 151–54 (cited in note 4); A. G. Sulzberger, *Ouster of Iowa Judges Sends Signal to Bench*, New York Times (Nov. 4, 2010).

28   531 U.S. 98 (2000).

29   See Kaplan, *Then Comes Marriage* at 118 (cited in note 15); Hirshman, *Victory* at 310–11 (cited in note 20); Klarman, *From the Closet to the Altar* at 137–39 (cited in note 4); Jo Becker, *Forcing the Spring: Inside the Fight for Marriage Equality* 31, 40 (Penguin 2014); Cole, *Engines of Liberty* at 59–61 (cited in note 7).

30   See Maura Dolan, *California Supreme Court Reenters Proposition 8 Fray*, Los Angeles Times (Feb. 17, 2011); Klarman, *From the Closet to the Altar* at 139 (cited in note 4); Hirshman, *Victory* at 315–16 (cited in note 20); Becker, *Forcing the Spring* at 55 (cited in note 29).

31   *Perry v. Schwarzenegger*, 704 F. Supp. 2d 921, 991, 994, 996–97 (N.D. Cal. 2010).

32   See *Perry v. Brown*, 671 F.3d 1052 (9th Cir. 2012).

33   See *Hollingsworth v. Perry*, 133 S. Ct. 2652 (2013).

34 See Hirshman, *Victory* at 312–13, 317–21 (cited in note 20); Becker, *Forcing the Spring* at 249–50 (cited in note 29). *Gill v. Office of Personnel Management*, 699 F. Supp. 2d 374 (D. Mass. 2010); *Windsor v. United States*, 833 F. Supp. 2d 394 (S.D.N.Y. 2012).

35 699 F. Supp. 2d 374, 396–97 (D. Mass. 2010); Kaplan, *Then Comes Marriage* at 179 (cited in note 15).

36 See Becker, *Forcing the Spring* at 257–59 (cited in note 29); Cole, *Engines of Liberty* at 84–86 (cited in note 7); Solomon, *Winning Marriage* at 286–88 (cited in note 7); Press Release, Department of Justice, *Statement of the Attorney General on Litigation Involving the Defense of Marriage Act* (Feb. 23, 2011); Letter on Litigation Involving the Defense of Marriage Act from Eric H. Holder Jr., Attorney General, United States of America, to The Hon. John A. Boehner, Speaker, U.S. House of Representatives (Feb. 23, 2011).

37 See Michael D. Shear, *Law Firm Backs Out of Defending Marriage Act*, New York Times (Apr. 25, 2011); Hirshman, *Victory* at 336–39 (cited in note 20); Nate Silver, *Gay Marriage Opponents Now in Minority*, New York Times (Apr. 20, 2011); Klarman, *From the Closet to the Altar* at 161 (cited in note 4); *Gay and Lesbian Rights*, Gallup, available at http://www .gallup.com/poll/1651/gay-lesbian-rights.aspx.

38 See *Gill v. Office of Personnel Management*, 682 F.3d 1 (1st Cir. 2012).

39 See Kaplan, *Then Comes Marriage* at 86 (cited in note 15); Solomon, *Winning Marriage* at 285 (cited in note 7).

40 *Windsor v. United States*, 833 F. Supp. 2d 394 (S.D.N.Y. 2012). See Klarman, *From the Closet to the Altar* at 163–64 (cited in note 4).

41 See *Windsor v. United States*, 699 F.3d 169 (2d Cir. 2012).

42 Kaplan, *Then Comes Marriage* at 200–201 (cited in note 15).

43 133 S. Ct., 2675 (2013).

44 *Id.* at 2680–81, 2690–92.

45 *Id.* at 2692, quoting *Romer v. Evans*, 517 U.S. 633 (1996); *id.* at 2693–94, quoting the House Report 16.

46 *Id.* at 2694, 2693, 2695–96, quoting *Department of Agriculture v. Moreno*, 413 U.S. 528, 534–35 (1973).

47 *Id.* at 2705–9 (Scalia, J., dissenting).

48 *Id.* at 2709–11 (Scalia, J., dissenting).

49 Kaplan, *Then Comes Marriage* at 20, 295–99 (cited in note 15).

50 See *Gay and Lesbian Rights*, Gallup, available at http://www.gallup.com/poll/1651/ gay-lesbian-rights.aspx.

51 Tribe & Matz, *Uncertain Justice* at 49–50 (cited in note 2). See Michael J. Klarman, *Windsor and Brown: Marriage Equality and Racial Equality*, 127 Harv. L. Rev. 129 (2013); Carpenter, *Windsor Products* at 197–203 (cited in note 8). The animus rationale of *Windsor* has been much criticized. See Riva Siegel, *Foreword: Equality Divided*, 127 Harv. L. Rev. 1, 80, 88 (2013); Conkle, *Evolving Values* at 39–40 (cited in note 11); Carpenter, *Windsor Products* at 190–92 (cited in note 8). For a robust defense of the Court's analysis, see Carpenter, *Windsor Products* at 246–84 (cited in note 8).

52 760 F.3d 352 (4th Cir. 2014).

53 766 F.3d. 648 (7th Cir. 2014).

54   *Id.* at 654, 656, 658, 666. For Judge Posner's views on same-sex marriage twenty years earlier, see Richard A. Posner, *Sex and Reason* 311–14 (Harvard 1992).

55   See, e.g., *Garden State Equality v. Dow*, 216 N.J. 314 (Sup. Ct. N.J. 2013); *Griego v. Oliver*, 316 P.3d 865 (Sup. Ct. N.Mex. 2013); *Kitchen v. Herbert*, 961 F. Supp. 2d 1181 (D. Utah 2013); *Evans. v. Utah*, 21 F. Supp. 3d 1192 (D. Utah 2014); *Burns v. Hickenlooper*, 2014 WL 5312541 (D. Colo. 2014); *Obergefell v. Wymyslo*, 962 F. Supp. 2d 968 (S.D. Ohio 2013); *Bishop v. Holder*, 962 F. Supp. 2d 1252 (N.D. Okla. 2014); *Bourke v. Beshear*, 996 F. Supp. 2d 542 (W.D. Ky. 2014); *Bostic v. Rainey*, 970 F. Supp. 2d 456 (E.D. Va. 2014); *Lee v. Orr*, 2014 WL 683680 (N.D. Ill. 2014); *De Leon v. Perry*, 975 F. Supp. 2d 632 (W.D. Tex. 2014); *Tanco v. Haslam*, 7 F. Supp. 3d 759 (M.D. Tenn. 2014); *DeBoer v. Snyder*, 973 F. Supp. 2d 757 (E.D. Mich. 2014); *Henry v. Himes*, 14 F. Supp. 3d 1036 (S.D. Ohio 2014); *Latta v. Otter*, 19 F. Supp. 3d 1054 (D. Idaho 2014); *Geiger v. Kitzhaber*, 994 F. Supp. 2d 1128 (D. Ore. 2014); *Whitewood v. Wolf*, 992 F. Supp. 2d 410 (M.D. Pa. 2014); *Wolf v. Walker*, 986 F. Supp. 2d 982 (W.D. Wisc. 2014); *Baskin v. Bogan*, 12 F. Supp. 3d 1144 (S.D. Ind. 2014); *Brenner v. Scott*, 999 F. Supp. 2d 1278 (N.D. Fla. 2014); *Love v. Beshear*, 989 F. Supp. 2d 536 (W.D. Ky. 2014); *Lawson v. Kelly*, 58 F. Supp. 3d 923 (W.D. Mo. 2014); *Appling v. Walker*, 853 N.W.2d 888 (Sup. Ct. Wisc. 2014); *Pareto v. Ruvin*, 21 Fla. 889a (Fla. 11th Cir. Ct. 2014); *Huntsman v. Heavilin*, 21 Fla. 916a (Fla. 16th Cir. Ct. 2014); *Brinkman v. Long*, 2014 WL 3408024 (Colo. 17th Dist. Ct. 2014); *Wright v. Arkansas*, 2014 WL 1908815 (Sup. Ct. Ark. 2014); *Garden State Equality v. Dow*, 82 A.3d 336, 434 N.J. Super. 163 (N.J. Ct. Law Div. 2013).

56   135 S. Ct. 2584 (2015).

57   Cole, *Engines of Liberty* at 88–89 (cited in note 7).

58   135 S. Ct., 2599. See *Griswold v. Connecticut*, 381 U.S. 479 (1965) (contraception); *Loving v. Virginia*, 388 U.S. 1 (1967) (interracial marriage); *Zablocki v. Redhail*, 434 U.S. 374 (1978) (child support payments); *Turner v. Safley*, 482 U.S. 78 (1987) (prisoners).

59   135 S. Ct., 2602.

60   *Id.* at 2607.

61   *Id.*

62   *Id.* at 2626 (Roberts, C. J., dissenting).

63   *Id.* at 2628 (Scalia, J., dissenting).

64   *Id.* at 2639 (Thomas, J., dissenting).

65   *Id.* at 2629 (Scalia, J., dissenting).

66   *Id.* at 2642 (Alito, J., dissenting).

67   See, e.g., *Citizens United v. Federal Election Commission*, 558 U.S. 310 (2010) (campaign finance); *District of Columbia v. Heller*, 554 U.S. 570 (2008) (guns); *Shelby County v. Holder*, 133 S. Ct. 2612 (2013) (Voting Rights Act); *Parents Involved v. Seattle School District*, 551 U.S. 701 (2007) (racial integration); *Gratz v. Bollinger*, 539 U.S. 244 (2003) (affirmative action).

68   James Madison, *Speech to the House of Representatives, June 8, 1789*, in Jack N. Rakove, *Declaring Rights: A Brief History with Documents* 170, 174 (Bedford 1998).

69   See, e.g., *Meyer v. Nebraska*, 262 U.S. 390 (1923) (right to direct the education and upbringing of one's children); *Pierce v. Society of Sisters*, 268 U.S. 510 (1925) (right to direct the education and upbringing of one's children); *Skinner v. Oklahoma ex rel. Williamson*, 316

U.S. 535 (1942) (right to have children); *Rochin v. California*, 342 U.S. 165 (1952) (right to bodily integrity); *Griswold v. Connecticut*, 381 U.S. 479 (1965) (right to marital privacy); *Loving v. Virginia*, 388 U.S. 1 (1967) (right to marry); *Eisenstadt v. Baird*, 405 U.S. 438 (1972) (right to use contraception); *Roe v. Wade*, 410 U.S. 113 (1973) (right to abortion).

70 Cole, *Engines of Liberty* at 92 (cited in note 7).

71 Jennifer Calfas, Tyler Pager, & Erin A. Raftery, *Hundreds Celebrate Landmark Same-Sex Marriage Decision Outside Supreme Court*, USA Today (June 26, 2015); Jacob Koffler, *Crowds at Stonewall Inn Celebrate Gay Rights Victory Decades in the Making*, Time (June 26, 2015); Katharine Q. Seelye, *Praise for Ruling Jurist Who Wrote Massachusetts Gay Marriage Decision*, New York Times (June 26, 2015); Sheryl Gay Stolberg, *Gay Marriage Group Celebrates and Prepares to Shut Down*, New York Times (June 26, 2015); Democracy in Action, *Reactions to Supreme Court Ruling on Obergefell v. Hodges* (June 26, 2015).

72 Malia Wollan, *Crowds Gather in San Francisco to Celebrate Decision*, New York Times (June 26, 2015); Nick Corasaniti, *Companies Highlight Ruling on Corporate Websites*, New York Times (June 26, 2015); Laurie Goodstein, *Religious Leaders Who Support Gay Marriage Exult*, New York Times (June 26, 2015); Michael D. Shear, *President Obama Hails Decision in Emotional Statement*, New York Times (June 26, 2015); Democracy in Action, *Reactions* (cited in note 71); Justin McCarthy, *U.S. Support for Gay Marriage Stable After High Court Ruling*, Gallup (July 17, 2015); Gary J. Gates & Taylor N. T. Brown, *Marriage and Same-Sex Couples After Obergefell*, Williams Institute (Nov. 2015).

73 See Democracy in Action, *Reactions* (cited in note 71); Alan Rappeport, *Republican Candidates Disappointed by Decision*, New York Times (June 26, 2015); Alan Rappeport, *Scott Walker Calls for Amendment Allowing States to Define Marriage*, New York Times (June 26, 2015); Jonathan Topaz & Nick Gass, *Republican Presidential Candidates Condemn Gay-Marriage Ruling*, Politico (June 26, 2015).

74 See Democracy in Action, *Reactions* (cited in note 71).

75 Kevin Clarke, *Across the Nation, U.S. Bishops Deplore Supreme Court Call in Obergefell v. Hodges*, America: The National Catholic Review (June 26, 2015).

76 See Erik Eckholm & Manny Fernandez, *After Same-Sex Marriage Ruling, Southern States Fall in Line*, New York Times (June 29, 2015).

77 347 U.S. 483 (1954).

78 Laurie Goodstein, *Some Church Leaders Prepare for "Religious Freedom" Fight*, New York Times (June 26, 2015); Julie Turkewitz, *In Denver, Christian Groups Voice Concern Over Decision*, New York Times (June 26, 2015).

79 374 U.S. 398 (1963).

80 494 U.S. 872 (1990).

81 *Id.* at 878, 885.

INDEX

Page numbers in *italics* refer to illuistrations.

ABOUT THE AUTHOR

Geoffrey R. Stone is the Edward H. Levi Distinguished Service Professor of Law at the University of Chicago. He has served as both dean of the Law School and provost of the university, as well as chair of the Board of the American Constitution Society and as a member of the Advisory Board of the American Civil Liberties Union. He is an editor of the *Supreme Court Review*; editor of a twenty-volume series, *Inalienable Rights*; and author of numerous books on constitutional law, including *Perilous Times*, which won eight national book awards.